P9-AGX-392

AMERICAN
DREAMER

AMERICAN DREAMER

THE LIFE AND TIMES OF
HENRY A. WALLACE

JOHN C. CULVER
& JOHN HYDE

W · W · NORTON & COMPANY

NEW YORK   LONDON

Copyright © 2000 by John C. Culver and John Hyde

All rights reserved
Printed in the United States of America
FIRST EDITION

For information about permission to reproduce selections from this book,
write to Permissions, W. W. Norton & Company, Inc., 500 Fifth Avenue,
New York, NY 10110

The text of this book is composed in 11/13 Adobe Garamond
with the display set in Donatello Alternates
Composition by Matrix Publishing Services
Manufacturing by The Maple-Vail Book Manufacturing Group
Book design by Margaret M. Wagner

Library of Congress Cataloging-in-Publication Data
Culver, John C., 1932–
American Dreamer: the life and times of Henry A. Wallace / by John C.
Culver & John Hyde.
p. cm.
Includes bibliographical references and index.
ISBN 0-393-04645-1
1. Wallace, Henry Agard, 1888–1965. 2. Vice-Presidents—United States—
Biography. 3. United States—Politics and government—1933–1945.
4. United States—Politics and government—1945–1953.
I. Hyde, John. II. Title.
E748.W23 C85 2000
973.917'092—dc21
[B]   99-046444

W. W. Norton & Company, Inc.,
500 Fifth Avenue, New York, N.Y. 10110
www.wwnorton.com

W. W. Norton & Company Ltd.,
10 Coptic Street, London WC1A 1PU

1 2 3 4 5 6 7 8 9 0

FOR MARY JANE CHECCHI AND

LOUISE SWARTZWALDER

AND OUR CHILDREN AND

GRANDCHILDREN

CONTENTS

Illustrations follow pages 180 and 372.

AMERICAN
DREAMER

ACKNOWLEDGMENTS

John Culver's father and grandfather were staunch Republicans. The name Roosevelt was never mentioned favorably at family gatherings, and the name Wallace not at all. In 1948 he was in high school in Cedar Rapids, Iowa, when Henry A. Wallace ran for president on the Progressive Party ticket. He recalls picking up the newspaper in the front yard on the morning after the election and hurriedly taking it upstairs to his father. "Dad, Dad, Truman won!" he exclaimed. His father replied, "John, that's nothing to even joke about!"

Seventeen years later, having strayed from the Republican fold, Culver was a member of the U.S. House of Representatives when news came of Wallace's death. Newsmen asked each member of the Iowa congressional delegation to comment on the passing of the state's greatest son. In preparing his statement, Culver was reminded of what an exceptional life Wallace had lived but surprised by how little had been written about him. Despite Wallace's achievements—scientist, editor, economist, philosopher, secretary of agriculture, secretary of commerce, vice president, and presidential candidate—he was remarkably little known to most people in the United States.

Culver wanted to know why. It was then, thirty-four years ago, that he resolved to one day tell the story of Wallace's life. In 1988 he broached the idea of a biography to John Hyde, then a reporter in the Washington bureau of the *Des Moines Register,* who shared his interest in history, biography, Iowa, and Wallace. Together they set to work on a project that ultimately lasted a decade.

Wallace was an exceptionally complex and prolific man. He was a genuine expert in numerous fields and insatiably curious about everything else. He wrote more than a dozen books and thousands of letters, pamphlets, editorials, articles, and speeches, and he left behind a diary and an oral history of more than five thousand pages.

Comprehending this multifaceted man, with his idealistic temperament and elusive personality, is no easy task. The authors hope they have given the reader a fuller understanding of an extraordinary period in history and an appreciation for a man who played such a large role in it.

We are enormously grateful to the libraries and archives that helped guide us through this complex terrain. Our thanks go to staff members at the Franklin D. Roosevelt Library, the Library of Congress, the University of Iowa Library, the Iowa State University Library, the Boston Public Library, the Des Moines Register library, the Columbia University Library, the University of California at Davis Library, the National Archives and Records Administration, the Martin Luther King Library in Washington, D.C., and the National Agriculture Library in Beltsville, Maryland.

We wish to express our special gratitude to Earl Rogers, who until his recent retirement served as curator of the Henry A. Wallace collection at the University of Iowa. He was and continues to be an invaluable resource to all Wallace scholars.

Many people generously agreed to be interviewed for this project, and their help has been of inestimable value. These include Bob Arvidson, Saul Aronow, Calvin Baldwin, George Ball, Raymond Baker, David Belin, Foy A. Blackburn, William L. Brown, Agnes Carlson, Simon Cassady, Red and Lena Direktor, David Douglas, Leslie Douglas, Lee Fryer, Carl Hamilton, Charles Howard Jr., Esther Hughes, Lana Kausch, Penn Kimball, Karl Kueng, Paul McCollum, George McGovern, Norman Mailer, Harry Magdoff, Don Muhm, William G. Murray, Robert Nathan, Claude Pepper, Ruth Pinkston, Herb Plambeck, Joseph Rauh, Wayne Rassmussen, Mary Ellen Appleby Sarbaugh, Lawrence Shubow, Dorothy Stackpole, Lauren Soth, Fred Stover, Michael Straight, Robert Straus, Arod Taylor, Dora Taylor, Greg Taylor, Viola Scott Thomas, Art Thompson, James H. Weinman, and Harris Wofford.

We are particularly appreciative of the time and assistance given to us by members of Henry Wallace's immediate family. These include two siblings, James Wallace and Ruth Wijkman, and his three children, Henry Browne Wallace, Robert Browne Wallace, and Jean Wallace Douglas. Somewhere Henry and Ilo Wallace must be very proud of their children's productive and "worthwhile" lives. We are especially grateful to Jean Douglas for her many courtesies and for allowing us unrestricted access to family papers at Farvue farm.

Many others have helped us with their guidance and encouragement. We are thankful to each of them for their contribution to this book. These include Gar Alperovitz, Trevor Armbruster, Thomas Appleby, Bernard Aronson, John Morton Blum, Jacquelyn Blumenthal, Alan Brinkley, McGeorge Bundy, John Douglas, Philip A. Fleming, Dorothy Gilliam, Jerome Grossman, Morton Halprin, Harold Ickes Jr., Larry L. King, Richard Kirkendall, Philip Kopper, Norman Markowitz, David McKean, Charles J. Murphy, Vern Newton, Addison M. Parker, Gerald Piel, Evelyne Rominger, Arnold Sagalyn, Thomas J. Scanlon, August Schumacher, Ed Sidey, J. Samuel Walker, Harold H. Young Jr., I. Garth Youngberg, T. H. Watkins, James C. Wine, and Leonard Woodcock.

In addition we wish to express our appreciation for research assistance provided by Russian historians who reviewed Soviet and Communist Party archival materials but who for personal reasons prefer to remain anonymous.

We are profoundly grateful for the financial support of Richard J. Dennis and Thomas A. Dennis, whose assistance enabled us to undertake the project. We are also indebted to the Joyce Foundation and Susan Derrow for their kind support. Staff support came to us from Daniel David, Marcia Gilmore, Robert Herzog, Ann Pankow Davis, Karin Rutledge, and Emily Barrett Walters. We are appreciative of the efforts made on our behalf by our agent, Ron Goldfarb, the Mainstreet Media Foundation, the Arent Fox law firm, and, of course, our patient editor at W. W. Norton, Edwin Barber, who went the extra mile and then some.

John Culver wishes to extend a special note of gratitude to his wife, Mary Jane Checchi, whose steadfast love, encouragement, and support, as well as critical suggestions, were invaluable. His children, Chris, Becca, Cathy, Chet, and John, and many close friends (you know who you are) have politely and patiently tolerated his Wallace stories over the years. This has been the ultimate test of familial love and friendship. Thank you.

To the friends and family who have sustained John Hyde with good humor and wise counsel, he is forever in debt. Among those who have endured this project he sends thanks to Don Kaul, George Anthan, Margaret Engel, Myrna Sislen, Mark Noone, Ruth Logsdon, Herb H. Ottrudge, Chip and Susan Planck, John and Bea Swartzwalder, his sons, Kip Hyde and Ken Hyde, and his amigos at Takoma Kitchens. There are no words sufficient to thank his wife, Louise Swartzwalder, without whose love and perseverance there would be no book.

—John C. Culver
and John Hyde
March 1999

CHAPTER ONE

"GOOD FARMING, CLEAR THINKING, RIGHT LIVING"

Henry Agard Wallace was born October 7, 1888, in a modest frame house on an isolated farm in Iowa.

It was a golden autumn day, and farmers across the state could work outdoors without a coat. Harry and May Wallace, a young couple enjoying their first harvest season as husband and wife, occupied themselves with the routine of country life on their tenant farm in Adair County. May, barely twenty-one years old, picked flowers in the yard and fixed lunch for her husband. Harry, only a year older, fed the cattle and hogs and did his usual chores.

Shortly after sunset May gave birth to a boy.

About the birth there remained little lore. It was a quiet birth on a farm, the way Wallace women had borne babies for generations. No doctor or midwife was present. The nearest town, a tiny village called Orient, was five miles away by dirt road. Like most farm families, Harry and May Wallace saw no need to record the event beyond a notation in their Bible. Family members would learn of the birth in due course. Their firstborn child reached manhood and held high public office before he finally obtained a birth certificate.

This was the way of birth in Iowa, as normal as husking corn or rising at dawn.

Yet nothing about the Wallace family ever quite fit the norm. The Wallaces were different. They were part of, but apart from, the general husbandry of Iowa. They were smart and innovative and eager to take the lead. Unlike most farmers of the day, Harry had been to college and was a believer in "book farming," the application of scientific principles to agriculture. His young wife also had been to college and was trained in music and art. Like most Iowa farmhouses, Harry and May Wallace's home had no toilet, electricity, furnace, telephone, or running water. But it did have books and a piano, and it was brimming with ideas.

Nor was Harry a typical tenant farmer. The landlord in Harry's case was his own father, the Reverend Henry Wallace, and he was a man to be reckoned with. By 1888 Henry Wallace was a major landholder in Adair County, publisher of the largest local newspaper, and editor of the state's most influential farm journal. Governors sought his counsel; political parties wanted to put him in the U.S. Senate.

Henry Wallace was a sort of small-town leading citizen writ large. High-minded and strong-willed, he embodied virtues country people hold dear: honesty, duty, frugality, charity, simplicity. He even looked the part. He had sandy hair and twinkling blue eyes and full lips bent into a patient smile. The beard he wore throughout his adult life gave his long, narrow face a gentle and dignified appearance. Small wonder that by the end of his life he was almost universally beloved, known to thousands of midwestern readers as "Uncle Henry" Wallace, a member of the family.

Personal wealth and power did not interest Henry Wallace, although he gave his own family a measure of both. What consumed him was his mission, a belief that man must worship God through service to his fellow man. And the men Uncle Henry cared most about were farmers. Only by creating and sustaining a vibrant agricultural civilization, he thought, could the nation secure its future.

This belief—the cause of religion and duty and agriculture rolled into one— he stamped indelibly on the Wallace family name. This was Henry Agard Wallace's inheritance from the hour of his birth.*

"Remember," the boy was told as he grew up, "you are a Wallace and a gentleman."[1]

It was his glory and his burden.

***

*The Wallaces' practice of naming their first born sons Henry, together with an assortment of middle names, was and is a source of confusion to everyone outside the family.

The patriarch of the clan, Henry Wallace (1836–1916), had no middle name or initial.

His son Henry Cantwell Wallace (1866–1924) was known as Harry to friends and family and H. C. to business and political associates. Cantwell was his mother's maiden name.

Harry Wallace's son, Henry Agard Wallace (1888–1965), was called Young Henry throughout his youth. As an adult, he was usually called H. A. by associates and Henry by family members. His middle name was in honor of Horace Agard, a prominent Methodist minister related to his mother.

The Wallaces had been farmers in Scotland and Ireland for countless generations. The first of the clan to arrive in America was John Wallace, who left Kilrea, Ireland, in 1823 and landed in Philadelphia at age eighteen. From there he walked to western Pennsylvania and put down roots, which, to a Wallace, meant farming. Over time John Wallace made himself a figure of local importance, a man others in the area turned to for agricultural advice. In 1836 his first child, Henry, was born on the farm.

Henry Wallace would later write lovingly of his boyhood on the farm, of its fat pork sausages and cream as thick as pancake batter. But as a boy he dreamed of being elsewhere and doing otherwise. At eighteen Henry climbed aboard a railroad car, the first train he had ever ridden, and headed west. For the remainder of his life, Henry Wallace was an eloquent exponent of farm life, but he never again lived on a farm.

His ticket off the farm was the ministry. It was probably the only profession his religious parents would have found acceptable. After finishing his theological studies at Monmouth College in Illinois, he taught school for two years in a tough little town in northern Kentucky. In 1863 he married a petite, fine-boned young woman named Nancy Cantwell, daughter of an Ohio landowner and politician who had died while leading a cavalry charge in the second battle of Bull Run.

The first years after marriage were not easy ones. Parishioners in his small Presbyterian churches in Rock Island, Illinois, and Davenport, Iowa, were hidebound and difficult. Their strict orthodoxy did not appeal to him, and they found his "social gospel" altogether too broad-minded. The young minister and his wife tried to cut costs by living in a boardinghouse but still had a hard time making ends meet. In the final months of the Civil War, he accepted an appointment as a chaplain to northern troops, an experience that left him with a permanent horror of war. Shortly after the war's end, the couple's firstborn child, Mary, died in infancy.

By the end of the 1860s, Henry Wallace was emotionally spent and physically exhausted. "I would suffer the most excruciating pain after any severe exertion, generally on Sabbath night after preaching two sermons," he later wrote. "My limbs would become cold and it seemed impossible to get them warm."[2] A move to Morning Sun, Iowa, southwest of Davenport, improved his health for a time, but after six years his old ailments had returned in force.

His six-foot frame, which comfortably carried two hundred pounds during times of good health, became dangerously thin. He suspected he was dying of tuberculosis—consumption, he called it—a disease that had virtually destroyed his entire family. One by one over a period of twelve years, his seven brothers and sisters and his father had all died of "some sort of lung trouble." None of his siblings reached the age of thirty.

With a small inheritance left by his father, Wallace had begun buying land in Adair County, a couple of hundred miles to the west, and in early 1877 a doctor advised him to move there. "I will give you six months to live if you continue in that pulpit," the doctor said. "It's either out of the pulpit or into the boneyard."[3]

So, at age forty, with a wife and five small children, Henry Wallace left the pulpit and moved west.

The ancient struggle between prairie and forest, waged for centuries on the soil of Iowa, had not been fully resolved when pioneers came with their horses and plows. The state's location and climate gave neither grass nor trees an undisputed claim to the land. Iowa was neither east nor west, neither arid nor tropical. Iowa was midway and moderate. When the settlers arrived, grass was in the ascendancy but trees still covered about a quarter of the state.

Adair County, south and a little to the west of the state's center, was at the front line of the battle. When Henry Wallace began buying land there, much of Adair was still "raw prairie." Bluestem grass standing eight feet tall covered much of its twenty-four square miles. Trees, which easterners took to be a sign of good climate and fertile soil, were as scarce as people in the "State of Adair."

Madison County, adjoining to the east, was a different story. There the land was nicely forested. Farms and small towns had flourished in Madison for a generation. Henry Wallace inhabited both sides. He moved his family to Winterset, a prosperous small town that served as the seat of Madison County, and saw to his farms in Adair from a buggy. He thrived on being outdoors, and his health soon began to improve. Within five years he was fully recovered.

Farming land that had never been farmed was a tonic to Wallace. He introduced the first shorthorn bull, the first purebred hog, and the first Percheron horse to Adair County. Old-timers said it was impossible to grow clover in that part of the state, and Wallace took an almost spiritual satisfaction in proving them wrong.

But he also knew that intelligent farming practices alone were not enough to ensure the success of agriculture. Soon he was engaged in preaching of a different sort, trying to help farmers understand the political and economic forces that shaped their environment. A year after arriving in Winterset, Wallace was invited to give the town's Fourth of July address and proceeded to roast "machine" politics, excessive party loyalty, and mediocre schools. He finished up with a blistering attack on cheap money, a nostrum highly popular among farmers of the area.

"Among other things, I said that we had doctors—mostly politicians—who were doping the public under the pretense of curing evils, old grannies with their paregoric and catnip tea in the shape of greenbacks and fiat money intended to soothe the present discontent and to cause the people to forget the incipient growing pains of the country, etc. etc."[4]

The address set off a furious storm in Madison County and plunged Wallace into the county's vigorous newspaper war. For a time he contributed to the local Republican newspaper, the *Madisonian*, until falling out with the publisher over editorial control of his copy. Wallace responded by purchasing a half interest of the *Winterset Chronicle*, a forelorn little paper with only four hundred readers.

"I then started out, as an independent Republican or free lance, ready to meet all comers and goers in the journalistic field," he wrote. In ten months, the *Chronicle*'s circulation had increased to fourteen hundred, and Wallace bought the paper's remaining half interest. Within two years he took over his rival, the *Madisonian*. He relished controversy. "Nothing else is so harmful to the sale of a paper or a book as to have it absolutely ignored, and abuse is often much more effective than praise—so it was abuse I wanted."[5]

All but destroyed by disease before their move to Winterset, the Wallaces now were robust and flourishing. The newspaper quickly became a family enterprise. Freckled, redheaded Harry, a sunny and energetic boy of thirteen when his father bought the *Chronicle*, earned three dollars a week sticking type, cleaning presses, and delivering copies. Unlike his more dignified father, Harry reveled in the company of the rough-hewn men in the print shop. From them he learned the art of chewing tobacco, a practice he maintained for life.

Increasingly Henry Wallace's name and writings were cited around the state by friends who shared his views on agriculture and reform. Among his allies were James "Tama Jim" Wilson and Seaman Knapp, two men Wallace met at an agricultural meeting in 1879. Over the next quarter century Wallace, Wilson, and Knapp would leave a remarkable record as authors, educators, and public servants. Wallace became one of the nation's leading farm journalists. Wilson served sixteen years as secretary of agriculture. Knapp founded the extension service, which raised American agriculture from superstition to science.

Their first joint venture was an effort to break the barbed wire monopoly. Iowa was then in the process of being fenced off. So-called herd laws made farmers liable for damage their livestock did to neighbors' crops, and barbed wire was the cheapest and most effective type of fencing. But the manufacture of barbed wire was protected by patents that gave the Washburn-Moen Company of Worcester, Massachusetts, an effective monopoly.

Wallace, Wilson, and Knapp responded by forming their own organization, the Farmers Protective Association, to manufacture its own barbed wire and sell it at a price lower than Washburn-Moen's. Only farmers who paid one dollar a year in dues to the association were eligible to buy its wire. Thousands of farmers across the state recognized the bargain and joined up. When the Washburn-Moen Company challenged the association in court, claiming its patents were being violated, the association used the members' dues to fight back.

The court battle lasted five years, but in the meantime the association sold thousands of tons of barbed wire to Iowa farmers. Long before the disposition of the case, however, the barbed wire monopoly had lowered its price to meet the association's competitive challenge. The association, represented by the young Des Moines lawyer A. B. Cummins, later a prominent progressive Republican governor and U.S. senator, eventually prevailed in the U.S. Supreme Court. After winning its cause, the association disbanded.

By 1883 the three friends had become men of no small influence. Together they had created the Agricultural Editors' Association, to promote independent farm journalism, and the Iowa Improved Stock Breeders Association, to foster modern livestock practices. They had staged a coup of sorts at Iowa State Agricultural College, the state's lethargic land grant institution, and installed Knapp as "the professor of agriculture." Wilson had been elected to Congress. And Henry Wallace, small-town newspaper owner and gentleman farmer, had been named editor of the *Iowa Homestead*, the state's largest and most important farm publication.

Soon thereafter the owner of the *Iowa Homestead* found himself overwhelmed by debt and sold the paper to James Melville Pierce, a big-boned, hot-tempered small-town newspaper publisher. Wallace was retained as editor with an annual salary of $500 and a promise of complete editorial independence. The deal was sealed with a handshake.

Wallace plunged into his editorial duties with boyish enthusiasm, pressing the "mysterious power" of clover to enrich the soil while feeding animals, slashing the political and economic interests standing in the way of agriculture's success. "The paper of which I was then editor was not really so much of an agricultural paper as it was an anti-monopoly paper," he acknowledged. "The management soon found that anti-monopoly was the winning card."[6]

Wallace reserved his highest dudgeon for the railroads, the most potent monopoly of all. His biggest coup was an exposé of the railroads' discriminatory rate structure. The stories led to the electoral defeat of Iowa congressman William P. Hepburn, a powerful friend of the railroads in Congress, and the subsequent creation of the Interstate Commerce Commission to govern rail rates.

Henry Wallace moved to Des Moines in order to be closer to his duties at the *Iowa Homestead* but continued to maintain a home in Winterset. There Harry grew restless setting type. In 1885, at nineteen, Harry headed off to Iowa State Agricultural College in Ames. The experience was not invigorating. "The college was nominally an agricultural college, but very little agriculture was taught," Henry Wallace wrote. Harry, hardworking and quick-witted, soon figured he knew more than his teachers.

By the end of his second year, Harry had more or less had his fill of academia. During a visit home, he learned that one of his father's tenants planned to leave and saw a way out of Ames. "How would you like to have me for a tenant, on the same terms you have been renting for?" Harry asked his father. Henry Wallace assented, and Harry packed his bags for Adair County.[7]

The farm that Harry Wallace took over was large—some three hundred treeless acres—and lonesome. "Prairie wolves," as the farmers called coyotes, howled in the night, and rattlesnakes hid in the tall grass. The nearest town, Orient, was scarcely a town at all. Greenfield, the county seat, was ten miles to the north.

Farming under any circumstance was hard enough, but without the help of a spouse it was nearly impossible. In the summer of 1887, soon after moving to the farm, Harry proposed marriage to a handsome young woman he had met at Iowa State. May Brodhead was an easterner, born in New York City, but her parents died of tuberculosis before she was old enough to form a memory of them, and she was sent to live with a strict Methodist aunt in Muscatine, Iowa.

Harry Wallace, twenty-one years old and a sturdy five feet eight inches tall, arrived on a new trotting horse he had purchased for his courtship of May. She accepted his proposal forthwith. She had never lived on a farm and knew nothing of its labors, but she possessed an adventurous spirit. Harry "made farming seem most romantic," she said. May spent the remainder of the summer learning the arts of baking and homemaking.

On Thanksgiving Day, November 24, 1887, Harry Wallace and May Brodhead were married. Harry sold two pigs and bought a surrey to transport May and her trunk back to the farm. "The house wasn't much," May Wallace recalled. "A little story-and-a-half tenant house, nice enough, but with none of the conveniences, and not a tree near it—nothing but a windmill. But it was a good farm."[8]

May's introduction to farm life was harsh. Iowa had suffered three extremely cold winters in a row, and January 1888 was the worst time of all. Temperatures reached forty degrees below zero in parts of the state. More than a century later it remained the third-coldest month on record in Iowa. Wood for fuel was scarce, coal was expensive, and corncobs burned too hot and too fast.

By the time the ground had thawed and Harry was ready to begin planting, May was pregnant with their first child.

In the spring they set about to make the place a bit less forlorn. In an effort to break up the farm's treeless monotony, Harry planted a grove of catalpa trees along the property's edge. The big spreading trees, distinctive for their long seed pods, took hold, and the farm was known informally ever after as "the catalpa farm." They also planted mulberry bushes, maple trees, plum trees, and a small apple orchard.

The business end of the farm, that which aimed to make money, was livestock. Harry raised purebred shorthorn cattle, Poland China hogs, Percheron horses, and feeder cattle. The latter were full-grown steers, purchased at an age of two to three years and kept for six months or so, until they were "finished" or ready to market. If a farmer was lucky, he would earn enough by selling cattle to pay his costs. Hogs would eat the remainder of the grain and supply the margin of profit.

But Harry wasn't lucky. Corn, which sold for 32 cents a bushel in 1883, brought only 24 cents in 1888. A year later the price of corn dropped to 19 cents, its lowest value in more than a decade. The price of cattle and hogs suffered similar declines. The problem was the market—one of those cyclical downturns brought about by surplus commodities and broad economic conditions—which no farmer, not even one as industrious and intelligent as Harry Wallace, could surmount.

As Harry and May struggled to survive on the farm, Henry Wallace was in Des Moines with problems of his own. The progressive Republican cause— or "anti-monopoly Republican," as Uncle Henry called it—was suffering a series of setbacks. Wallace was especially disappointed when his friend and ally Governor William Larrabee refused to run for the U.S. Senate. (Wallace rejected an overture from Democrats that he stand for the Senate on their ticket.)

As progressive Republicans lost ground, cheap-money populists under the banner of the Farmers Alliance gained strength, much to Wallace's discomfort. In 1889, to the astonishment of everyone, farm unrest led to the election of a Democratic governor in Iowa for the first time since 1852.

And there was trouble of a more personal sort. James Pierce, the *Iowa Homestead*'s volatile publisher, began suggesting that the paper could do with less talk about monopolies and railroad rates and taxation. Wallace agreed to devote his attention mostly to agricultural subjects, but when he learned Pierce had accepted an offer from a Chicago firm to write favorable stories about its products in exchange for a lucrative advertising contract, he was livid. Wallace believed that his personal reputation was threatened.

But the Wallaces could do little more than bide their time. Uncle Henry now owned about a third of the *Iowa Homestead*'s stock and was in a poor position financially to walk away from it. Harry and May had committed all of their energy, plus a good part of May's modest inheritance, to making a go of it on the farm in Adair County. They wanted, indeed needed, to stay and succeed.

❦

The toddler running about the farm knew nothing of the family's troubles, of course. For Young Henry these were days of carefree adventure. His earliest recollection was of riding to town in a bobsled on a cold winter day, kept warm by snuggling under rugs spread across the laps of his elders. His playmates were his uncle Dan Wallace, Harry's younger brother by more than a decade, and a Scotch collie named Shep. From Dan he received his first pony ride; from Shep he learned the art of catching flies and burying bones. The biggest trauma in his life was finding himself lost in a cornfield, his socks full of sandburs, and yelling for help. "Where is mama's baby?" he cried.

"The old prairie flowers still bloom in my memory, and the smell of the penny-royal perfumed prairie hay still haunts my nostrils," Dan Wallace wrote forty years later. ". . . I can remember the cellar where we were wont to retire when the dark clouds rolled up at the close of a hot summer day. I think I could still pick out the beam in the hay mow where we killed the big rattler that was brought in from the field in a load of hay and mowed away one day. . . . Henry and I shared our first common misfortune when we laid away Shep, whose good judgment did not extend to a careful scrutiny of things such as sickle bars and rattle snakes that do their work under cover of the waving grass."[9]

Still, something was wrong on the farm. Dan could feel it when he visited during summers. Cholera broke out among the hogs. A purebred shorthorn herd had to be sold off to meet expenses. The cattle were sold for less than $100 a head, a third of what they had cost. Two handsome black gelding horses were sold at a sacrificial price to the fire department in town. May Wallace had used her small inheritance to buy Suffolk sheep and shorthorn cattle for the farm. Those were sold, too.

After five years of struggle Harry and May began to have second thoughts about the romance of farming. They had worked hard and had two healthy children—a daughter, Annabelle, was born in 1891—but not much else to show for their effort. Many years later Henry A. Wallace summed up their plight in a single sentence: "My father . . . had started to work farming when prices were higher than when he quit."[10]

Harry decided to return to Iowa State and finish his education. An invitation from Tama Jim Wilson had spurred the decision. By 1892 Wilson had retired from Congress and, at Uncle Henry Wallace's urging, accepted an appointment as Iowa State's "professor of agriculture." Looking for ways to strengthen the school's program, Wilson asked Harry to come back and finish his degree, after which he would be appointed to the faculty. Harry took the deal and in the fall of 1892 packed up his family of four and moved to Ames.

Henry A. Wallace arrived in Ames a shy boy, not yet four years old, who had almost never seen children his own age.

The move did not improve the Wallace family's fortunes. In Des Moines, Uncle Henry's running quarrel with James Pierce grew nastier by the day and his financial situation more perilous. The election of the Democrat Grover Cleveland to the presidency in 1892 was followed by a four-year recession that left Wallace temporarily unable to make ends meet. His land holdings, then about eight hundred acres, were mortgaged, and his name was on bank notes totaling some $30,000. The *Iowa Homestead* cut off dividends to pay for construction of a new building, and the salary Wallace received was not enough to pay his living expenses. "For many years thereafter," Henry A. Wallace later remarked, "I associated the word 'Democrat' with hard times."[11]

Harry Wallace scrimped along at Iowa State with just enough money for his family to survive. They lived in a tiny house by the Northwestern railroad tracks. In Young Henry's mind the new home was a place forever whipped by wind. Tumbleweeds and Russian thistles rolled across the yard and piled up against its walls. The sound of window panes shivering in a cold winter evening would always remind Henry A. Wallace of Ames.

Harry managed, during that first year of the panic, to complete two years of course work in a single year. The year left a terrible scar, however. Harry fell ill with typhoid fever and, without quite admitting to his family how sick he was, came close to death. The illness seemed to have affected his gall bladder. For the remainder of his life, his son believed, Harry Wallace "never was in first-class health."[12] In late 1893, while still bedridden with fever, Harry Wallace was awarded his bachelor's degree and appointed associate professor of dairying.

May Wallace was the family stalwart during those bleak days. She cooked and mended and gardened, nursed her husband, and cared for her children. It was May who taught her oldest son how to read and how to plant seeds and how to worship God. She was a religious woman, raised in the families of northern Protestant churchmen, and the strict habits associated with her stock were deeply ingrained in her.

May was abstemious and thrifty in the extreme. She did not drink alcohol, or even coffee, and greatly disapproved of tobacco. Salads she thought were "some new-fangled notion that was being foisted upon the American people by women's clubs." For women's clubs, with all of their good works and gossip, she had no use whatever, despite the frequent pleas of her mother-in-law to participate in them. Even if she had wanted to join them, she had no time. "What she couldn't have," her son observed, "she had no use for."[13]

Yet there was nothing dour about May Wallace. She was good-humored and had a spunky quality that greatly appealed to her father-in-law. May alone seemed able to put Uncle Henry in his place when he became particularly demanding. "I am not a Wallace," she would remind him cheerfully. "I only married one."[14] Relations with her socially conscious mother-in-law were, on the whole, less amicable.

For Young Henry these were agreeable, if somewhat isolated, years. His father was working hard at the college. His mother was busy with a growing family. A third child, John, was born in 1894. He knew few other children. He did, however, have a fondness for plants, and that led him to form the most unlikely of friendships. His pal was a tall, slender black man, thirty years of age, whose name was George Washington Carver.

Carver, the son of slaves, wandered through the Midwest for years after the Civil War before becoming Iowa State's first black student in 1891. There his gentle manner, enormous dedication, and religious devotion won him wide acceptance with students and faculty alike. Among Carver's friends was Harry Wallace. First as a student and then as a professor, Wallace spent hours with Carver and regularly invited him to his home for dinner. There Carver met Young Henry, the boy who loved plants.

Carver "took a fancy to me and took me with him on his botanizing expeditions and pointed out to me the flowers and the parts of flowers—the stamens and the pistil," H. A. Wallace recalled. "I remember him claiming to my father that I had greatly surprised him by recognizing the pistel and stamens of redtop, a kind of grass—grass *Agrostis alba*, to be precise. I also remember rather questioning his accuracy in believing that I recognized these parts, but anyhow he boasted about me, and the mere fact of his boasting, I think, incited me to learn more than if I had really done what he said I had done."[15]

More important, Carver had a sense that all living things possessed something divine, that God could speak from the parts of a flower or a blade of grass. Their walks continued for about a year, after which the Wallaces left Ames, but Young Henry had permanently absorbed the philosophy of his gentle friend.

Carver received a master's degree from Iowa State in 1896 and moved to the Tuskegee Institute in Alabama, taking with him only a few bulbs of the amaryllis plant he so loved. Young Henry and his friend did not see each other for almost forty years, by which time the boy had become secretary of agriculture and Carver was world famous as a chemist who developed hundreds of uses for the peanut and the sweet potato. Not until then did Wallace really understand how Carver had connected so strongly with him as a child, why Carver's philosophy of plants had so affected his own.

"Such botanists as Carver are exceedingly rare, but today they are increasingly important because the day fast approaches when the spirit of man must go out into understanding living things with as much fervor as it has gone forth into the understanding of steel, cement, machine tools, oil, gas, roads and airplanes," Wallace said many years later. "The ability to understand life in all its varied manifestations is the supreme criterion of man."[16]

By the time Young Henry was walking through the fields around Ames, his father had become a small-time publisher of sorts. Uncle Henry's son-in-law Newton Ashby had publicly supported Grover Cleveland during the 1892 campaign (alone among the Wallace clan) and been rewarded with appointment as U.S. counsel to Dublin. Ashby was thus obliged to rid himself of the *Iowa Farmer and Breeder*, a small livestock journal of little note and marginal profitability, of which he was the principal owner. Harry Wallace formed a partnership with Charles F. Curtiss, a fellow faculty member at Iowa State, and bought the semimonthly for a small amount of money. They moved it to Ames, renamed it *Farm and Dairy*, and began to concentrate mainly on dairying work being done at Iowa State and its extension station.

The paper's narrow focus and relative obscurity did nothing to discourage Harry Wallace's taste for controversy. In the spring of 1894 Wallace and Curtiss began to have questions about the integrity and scientific findings of an experiment station chemist and wrote a letter asking the college's board of trustees to investigate him. If the board refused, they added, they would publish their own report on him in *Farm and Dairy*.

The board weighed the matter, decided to take no action against the chemist, and added that any Iowa State professor who published criticism of a fellow staff member would be forced to resign. It was the wrong thing to say to a Wallace. *Farm and Dairy* promptly defied the board and published a scathing attack on the chemist.

A bitter brawl broke out on the Ames campus, roughly pitting the academic faculty against the extension staff, and eventually forced the resignation of Wallace, the chemist, and two other faculty members who had joined the fray. Curtiss was told to drop his interest in *Farm and Dairy* if he wished to remain on the faculty.

At the same time Uncle Henry's long feud with James Pierce was coming to a head. He was determined either to regain editorial control of the *Iowa Homestead* or be fired. His first move was to write a one-paragraph editorial, telling farmers it was time for the railroad commission to hear from them on the subject of the rate increase. Every farmer should send a postcard to the commission on the matter, Wallace suggested. The editorial did not appear. The next week he wrote a longer editorial on the issue and handed it to the print foreman with the instruction "This must go in."[17] Again the editorial failed to appear.

Wallace told Pierce to call a meeting of the paper's board. The issue of editorial control had to be settled. Pierce agreed, but for three weeks no meeting was called. Finally Wallace called his own meeting of the three-member board, presented it with a long editorial denouncing the rate increase, and moved that it be published. "This was promptly voted down—and then the battle was on."

Every day Wallace showed up at the *Homestead* expecting that his "head likely would be found in the basket," but Pierce bided his time until February. Then, on one hour's notice, Wallace was summoned to a board meeting, summarily fired, and told that his pay would end in three days. "I was then an editor without a paper," Wallace wrote later. Moreover, he was a major stockholder in a company over which he had no control. He had no way to sell his stock, and he could expect to derive no financial benefits, because the company had ceased to pay dividends.

The Wallaces had hit bottom. Henry Wallace, almost sixty years old, and his son Henry Cantwell Wallace, nearly thirty, were without jobs and without money. Their prospects looked as bleak as Iowa in February.

The Wallaces came to their own rescue.

A few days after his ouster from the *Homestead,* Uncle Henry traveled the thirty miles north to see his son in Ames. There Harry suggested to his father a plan: take over as editor of *Farm and Dairy* and turn it into a publication of general interest to farmers. Uncle Henry agreed on the spot. In early March, the little journal appeared with a new name, *Wallaces' Farm and Dairy,* and a new editor, Henry Wallace.

In later years Harry Wallace tended to sentimentalize the episode. He had made the suggestion, Harry wrote to a friend, because he knew "father would die if he could not have a platform to stand on and continue his work." He added, "It did not seem a very hopeful prospect, but on father's account it was the only thing to do."[18]

In fact, the Wallaces plainly had more to gain than to lose. The paper already existed, at least in embryonic form, so the cost of getting started was not large. Uncle Henry had a well-established following, which greatly eased the difficulty of defining their paper's identity. And the Wallaces had, in themselves, an energetic and inexpensive work force.

Their paper was a family affair from the outset. Uncle Henry was editor, Harry handled business matters, John sold advertising and subscriptions, and Dan helped in the print shop. In time even Uncle Henry's wife assumed the role of "Aunt Nancy" and offered a page of homemaking advice to farm wives. The name of their paper was *Wallaces' Farm and Dairy*; the apostrophe, quite deliberately, was placed after the *s*.

What they lacked was money. But there, too, the Wallaces found ways of making do. Tama Jim Wilson signed a bank note for $5,000 and renewed it each year for five years. Harry mortgaged the house he had purchased in Ames and used a life insurance policy to borrow another $5,000. Curtiss, who harbored academic ambitions and was eager to sever his ties with *Farm and Dairy*, took a note for his share of the paper.

From the start the Wallaces were extremely aggressive in both their business and their editorial dealings. An editorial penned by Uncle Henry in the first issue, entitled "A Word Personal," set the paper's moralistic tone. In it Wallace detailed the reasons why he had been fired from the *Iowa Homestead* and verbally declared war on Pierce. "No grief or loss of any kind has ever befallen me that has given me so many sleepless nights as the fact that I was suspected of being privy to deals of a corrupt character in connection with the *Homestead*," he wrote.[19]

Lest anyone miss the point, Wallace placed a boxed statement on page one declaring, "Mr. Wallace was for ten years, up to February 1895, the editor of the *Iowa Homestead*. His withdrawal from that paper was the culmination of trouble between him and the business manager as to its public editorial policy, Mr. Wallace wishing to maintain it in its old position as the leading western exponent of anti-monopoly principles. Failing in this he became the editor of the *Farm and Dairy*, over the editorial policy of which he has full control."[20] The statement continued to run on the front page of the Wallaces' journal for several years. Pierce, not one to turn the other cheek, published his own version of Wallace's departure, declaring that "the *Homestead* had felt obliged to rid itself of an incubus."

A bare-knuckle fight broke out. This was no squabble between businessmen; it was a struggle between good and evil. Uncle Henry Wallace, casting himself as the underdog, let no one doubt which man sat with the angels. Subscribers and advertisers were encouraged to choose sides, the result being that virtually every gain for Wallace was also a loss for Pierce. Scores of farmers formed "Wallace clubs" in support of him. Club members received a discount on the normal subscription price of fifty cents per year; more important, they became part of a moral crusade. Henry Wallace stumped tirelessly across the state, a fat pad of subscription forms always stuffed in his pocket.

The result was a huge outpouring of support for the Wallaces. The cloud that had hovered over the family for half a decade broke apart and scattered. Within weeks it was apparent to Wallace and his sons that *Wallaces' Farm and Dairy* would succeed. At the end of three months, the paper registered a small profit. "That year, 1895, is one of the most memorable of my life," Henry Wallace later wrote. "It brought me what seemed to be one of my greatest troubles, and witnessed the beginning of my greatest success. Above all, it made me understand more completely than ever before that people generally will stand by a man when they see that he is serving them faithfully."[21]

In the fall, after six months in operation, the Wallaces changed the name of their paper again, to *Wallaces' Farmer and Dairyman*, and began publishing weekly rather than semimonthly. And in January 1896 they moved the entire operation, Harry Wallace included, to Des Moines.

Young Henry was seven when he arrived in Des Moines. He had never been to school, although he could read well, and he still knew few children his age. His interest in plants far exceeded any other interest. "In my early life, I would say that I thought completely in terms of seeds, plants and farming," Wallace once remarked. "At that time, I had no thought of public life."[22]

Des Moines brought the boy a quick, sour taste of life as it existed above the level of plants. Harry Wallace moved his family to a house in a lower-middle-class area north of downtown Des Moines. His playmates had "great disdain" for those better off than themselves, and there was a certain roughness about the northsiders that jarred the quiet Wallace boy.

At the Oakland elementary school, where he entered the first grade, Young Henry excelled easily. His initial taste of success came when a teacher asked whether oak trees had flowers. The class unanimously, except for Young Henry, said they had not. With typical certitude Henry insisted that oak trees did indeed produce flowers. He knew because he had seen them. When the teacher "came out on my side, I was very much puffed up," Wallace recalled.

"The mere fact of having demonstrated a knowledge which the other children didn't have caused me to seek for more psychic returns along the same lines. I'm sure I must have made myself quite a nuisance to my companions, because they weren't in the slightest degree interested along those lines."[23]

The first year in Des Moines also marked Young Henry's first brush with partisan politics. The election of 1896 pitted William McKinley of Ohio, embodiment of Republican conservatism, against the Democrat William Jennings Bryan, the thirty-six-year-old firebrand agrarian from Nebraska. Bryan's candidacy terrified Iowa Republicans. He was handsome and charismatic, hailed from a neighboring state, and offered debt-ridden farmers an appealing solution to their problem—inflation.

No Republican presidential candidate had lost Iowa since the Civil War, but in 1896 it seemed possible. Both parties waged the most extensively organized campaigns in the state's history, and the Wallaces jumped in with vigor. Harry, in particular, was strong for McKinley. Young Henry's first political memory was of walking the streets of Des Moines with his father, counting yard signs and pictures placed in the windows of homes favoring McKinley or Bryan and concluding—to Harry's great relief—that the Republican would win.

Wallaces' Farmer and Dairyman was officially neutral. Editorially it endorsed neither candidate, but a series of stories written by Uncle Henry, purporting to analyze Bryan's "cheap money" plan in a nonpartisan manner, made it patently clear the Wallaces favored McKinley. James Pierce, Uncle Henry's bitter foe, greeted the articles with scorn. A cartoon in the *Iowa Homestead* portrayed the elder Wallace as a clown walking along the top of a fence. "An agricultural editor in his great non-partisan acrobatic act," said the caption. Wallace fired back with an editorial entitled "The Satanic Instinct," and accused those who attacked another's character of being cowardly instruments of the devil.

On election day McKinley carried Iowa by about 65,000 votes and won the presidency, but the outcome did nothing to quiet the feuding journalists. Pierce published a special eight-page edition outrightly accusing Wallace of having accepted a bribe to publish his anti-Bryan articles. "Shameful Political Venality!" said a large headline. "Henry Wallace Charged with Selling His Opinions and Changing Them to Make Them Salable." Wallace fired back with two stinging editorials and a $500,000 libel suit against Pierce.

"It was regarded as a very unusual thing, in fact, almost unheard of, for one publisher to secure judgment against another publisher for libel," Wallace wrote. "I would not have brought the suit but for the evident maliciousness of Mr. Pierce's article, and I thought it was time to put a stop to this sort of thing."[24] Wallace eventually won a $1,500 judgment against Pierce, which was sustained on appeal by the state supreme court.

The election of 1896 marked the full restoration of Uncle Henry's reputation. His influence among farmers was unparalleled, and within the Republican Party he was in high favor. Wallace was no reliable partisan—he would never be that—but his contribution to the Republican cause could hardly be overlooked. H. G. McMillan, the state Republican chairman, said Wallace was "without doubt the ablest and most forceful agricultural writer of his day."[25]

With the election settled, Iowa Republicans began quarreling over the spoils of victory. All Republicans thought Iowa had earned a seat in McKinley's cabinet, but they were split over whether to ask for the War Department or the Justice Department. It was Uncle Henry who offered the perfect answer. Iowa was "the outstanding agricultural state of the nation," Wallace told McMillan, and an Iowan should be secretary of agriculture. McMillan asked on the spot whether Wallace himself would be a candidate for the position. Wallace declined at once. Instead, he proposed his old friend Tama Jim Wilson.

In one stroke Wallace had redirected the state's political attention to its true economic interest—agriculture—and given Iowa an enduring claim upon the federal government's attention and support.

In March 1897 Wilson became secretary of agriculture. He remained in that position under three presidents until March 1913, the longest cabinet tenure in American history. With some good reason, Iowans often called him "Henry Wallace's secretary."

The decade that followed the founding of their farm journal brought the Wallaces little but good fortune. The great financial panic that had seized the country during the Cleveland administration eased, and farm prices at last began to increase. Corn that brought fourteen cents a bushel in Iowa in 1896 could be sold for fifty-two cents a bushel five years later. The threat of pitchfork populism, which so discomfited Uncle Henry, vanished with the financial panic. Progressive reformers, such as Robert La Follette in Wisconsin and Albert Baird Cummins in Iowa, began coming into their own.

As farmers began to prosper, so did the Wallaces' paper. In December 1898 they changed its name once again. Henceforth it was called simply *Wallaces' Farmer*. On the front page, below the paper's name, the Wallaces added a credo that summed up in six words what they and their paper stood for: "Good farming, clear thinking, right living."

The paper the Wallaces produced was compact, usually eighteen to twenty-four pages, and crammed with articles by, for, and about farmers: "The Model Draft Horse," "Potato Culture," "Scabby Sheep," "Trees on the Farm," "Facts about Hog Cholera." There was a page devoted to news about hogs, a page for dairy farmers, a horticulture page, a market page, and Aunt Nancy's "Hearts and Homes" page, sprinkled with inspirational poems, recipes, and homemaking tips.

Letters from readers were an important element of all farm journals, and *Wallaces' Farmer* contained dozens of them on every conceivable farm-related subject, from "How to Burn Dead Hogs" to "Baking Bread in Cold Weather."

Page two was Uncle Henry's domain. There he editorialized on the evil of monopolies, urged better farm tenancy laws, counseled farmers to refinance their debts, and preached the virtues of grass. During 1897 he wrote a series of gentle, eloquent "letters to the farm boy" that warmly sympathized with rural children's desire to see the world but urged them to hold fast to agrarian values. ("Don't go West, young man; don't go to the city; go to the agricultural college, and go to the agricultural end of that college.")[26] When it suited him, he was not above a bit of moralist outrage. News that the midway of the Pottawattamie County Fair was populated by mobs of "drunken, howling" men and "dirty, greasy, filthy, disreputable females" drew a heated rebuke.

In print and in person the Wallaces displayed a shrewd talent for promoting the welfare of agriculture and, not coincidentally, their farm journal. They sent "corn trains" and "dairy trains" and "good roads trains" around the state to lobby for better agriculture, marketing, and transportation. They formed clubs and sponsored competitions and imported experts to foster scientific farming practices. They helped organize the Corn Belt Meat Producers' Association and other groups to press the farmer's cause.

Nothing, however, so succeeded in cementing the bond between rural readers and *Wallaces' Farmer* as "Uncle Henry's Sabbath School Lessons." No feature was more popular or gave the paper greater credibility with religious-minded farm folk. Henry Wallace himself said the Sunday School lessons were the single greatest cause of *Wallaces' Farmers*'s success. They were, he wrote, "about the best work I have ever done."[27]

Readers across Iowa—and eventually far beyond—began to use the lessons in their home devotionals and to prepare for church meetings. Wallace's Bible lessons became an institution in Iowa, as much a part of rural life as pot-luck church suppers and the Saturday night bath. Mothers read the lessons to their children; farmers read them to their hired hands. Many farmers who claimed no faith whatever in scientific agriculture said they subscribed to *Wallaces' Farmer* only to read Uncle Henry's Bible lessons. Wallace continued to write these weekly lessons for the rest of his life. They provided him with a pulpit far grander than any he occupied as an active minister.* From it he could preach his liberal, loving theology to parishioners who came to regard him as a spiritual adviser and personal friend.

---

*At the time of his death in 1916, Wallace had a backlog of unpublished Sunday school lessons large enough to last two decades. *Wallaces' Farmer* continued to publish Uncle Henry's lessons until 1936.

Within two years of its founding, *Wallaces' Farmer* had around twenty thousand paying subscribers, several thousand more than the *Iowa Homestead* had when Wallace left it, and the family launched a vigorous campaign to double that number. After five years in business the Wallaces had retired their debts and were paying themselves regular salaries. Uncle Henry received an annual salary of $3,000; Harry and John, somewhat less. In under a decade the Wallaces had moved from small rented quarters to a four-story "modern, fireproof" building in downtown Des Moines they had built to house their plant.

The Wallaces' rising prosperity was reflected in Harry Wallace's rapidly improving circumstances. Young Henry could remember a day, not long after the family moved to Des Moines, when he took a walk with his father and looked longingly at the new wood-frame houses being put up in middle-class neighborhoods. "If we could get hold of $900, we could build a house like that of our own," Harry told his son.[28] Two years later Harry Wallace moved his family to another rented house on the west side of Des Moines.

The house was a large, ramshackle affair with sagging floors, but it had a sizable acreage, which greatly pleased Harry's garden-loving wife and son. By 1902 Harry had enough money to buy ten acres on the west side and construct a new home that cost more than $5,000. Finally, in 1912, Harry moved his family south of Grand Avenue to the city's wealthiest neighborhood. There he built a brick mansion that cost some $50,000.*

Indeed, the Wallaces' farm paper began to make so much money that it was referred to in journalism circles as "Wallaces' Gold Mine." Uncle Henry was almost embarrassed by the thought of it. Never comfortable with financial matters anyway, he established a trust to handle his personal funds and simply ceased to think about money. The trust provided Wallace and his wife with a small annuity sufficient to meet their needs and distributed the rest to charities and family members.

He enjoyed, thereafter, a life of comfortable gentility and great celebrity. He lectured, traveled abroad, preached, and corresponded with what seemed to be hundreds of friends. Preachers and poets, farmers and presidents sought his counsel. The broad front porch of Wallace's house on Sherman Hill, the quiet Victorian neighborhood where he had lived since coming to Des Moines, played host to the famous and the unknown.

---

*Three secretaries of agriculture have lived in the house Harry Wallace built at the corner of Thirty-seventh Street and John Lynde Road: H. C. Wallace, H. A. Wallace, and E. T. Meredith, who served in the position briefly during the final months of Woodrow Wilson's presidency. Numerous prominent people visited the home while it was owned by Harry Wallace, including Theodore Roosevelt and William Howard Taft. In 1917 John D. Rockefeller Jr. stayed there and observed "how nice this simple little country place is."

His sandy hair turned gray, his body thickened to 220 pounds, his health grew steadily better. One eye went blind, for reasons never understood, but his other eye retained perfect vision and allowed him to read widely. He still liked to argue—testing the wits of bright young men was a favorite pastime—but his prickly temperament grew smoother.

Those were the "happiest years," Wallace's youngest son, Daniel, once said, "with all the lawsuits settled, a paper of our own going, no business or political brawls to upset father's digestion or trouble the goodness of his spirit, and with money coming in regularly. The agrarian uproar had died with the Populist and Granger breakdown. Now everything was farmers' institutes, Chautauquas, Acres of Diamonds stuff—self-improvement. . . . Father went out and trooped for the New Day in Agriculture all over Iowa."[29]

CHAPTER TWO

"WHAT'S LOOKS TO A HOG?"

Seriousness was Henry A. Wallace's personal hallmark even as a boy in elementary school. Solemn, intent, determined, he would do all that was expected of him. Then he would do more.

The responsibilities he assumed as a boy, he once observed, were part of the stern fate of firstborn children. As the oldest son, it was his chore to shovel coal into the furnace and pump water to two upstairs tanks—one for drinking, one for washing. After the family moved to the western edge of Des Moines and gained a few acres of land, his job list expanded. "It was my duty to take care of the sow and her pigs, the cow and the horse."[1] He also took charge of the cows owned by his uncle John, who built a house next to Harry's. Young Henry received twenty-five cents a week from his uncle and came later to feel that an "injustice" had been committed when he discovered that the boy who took his place received three dollars a week.

Henry's only helper in his daily chores was his younger sister Annabelle, who would traipse along in the early morning darkness, lantern in hand, giving him light to slop the hogs or pry loose sorghum from the big rounded crocks in which it was stored. On particularly cold mornings Henry would lift her into the bran box, where she nestled while he milked a cow. Among his siblings only Annabelle, he remarked, seemed to share the sense of obligation that comes to children who have experienced hard times.

His other siblings came too late to know much about life's duties, in Henry's view. By the time they reached their formative years, the family's fortunes had greatly improved. John, born in 1894, was a carefree sort of child who inherited Harry Wallace's love of music. "Mother's sunshine boy," he was called in the family. James, born in 1896, was little attracted to work; his sport was tree climbing. His mother adored James and affectionately called him Wimpsie Wee, after a character in a children's magazine who loved to load his food with salt. Mary, with whom Henry eventually became very close, was born in 1898, and Ruth followed in 1901, when Henry was thirteen years old. All of May Wallace's six children were born at home. Henry did not learn until 1917, when his own first child was born, that some births took place in hospitals.

As his brothers and sisters grew, Henry tried without much success to impose his sense of discipline upon them. His two brothers particularly annoyed him. "Their main interest was having a good time in those days. . . . I never did accept the standards of the other boys in the neighborhood, but they did."[2] By the time Ruth arrived, Henry had more or less consigned them all to their fate. When Ruth "went on a tear" in one of her notorious temper tantrums, Henry's solution was to set her atop a bookcase and leave.

It was not a lonely childhood, as was sometimes later asserted. A child with so many siblings and cousins and school friends could hardly have been lonely. The house in which he grew to adulthood was big and noisy, filled with music from a player piano and the sound of children racing from room to room. Those were "very, very happy" years both at school and at home, he later said.

But if he was not lonely, he was a child of solitude. His great childhood passion was gardening, the quietest of pursuits. Often his friends would organize expeditions into the woods, and Henry would join them, but if no friends were around, he would go by himself. Being alone never troubled him.

As Henry grew toward adolescence, his father was less and less a part of his daily life. Henry A. Wallace once observed that he could barely remember a time during his youth when his father was not working. Harry Wallace worked with a steady intensity at everything he did. The business aspects of *Wallaces' Farmer*, which Harry controlled entirely, took large amounts of his time.

Harry was frequently away from home, going to meetings of agricultural organizations or lobbying on farmers' behalf. When he was not attending to business matters or civic affairs, Harry would plunge into chores about the house with an energy that astonished his oldest son. Even after five decades, Henry Wallace could describe with awe watching his father in a single afternoon pile up enough sorghum fodder to feed the cows and horses for two weeks.

If Henry saw less of his father, however, he saw much more of his renowned grandfather. Before moving to Des Moines, the boy had known his grandfather chiefly as a visitor on Thanksgiving and Christmas and special occasions. In Des Moines they would spend time together routinely. On summer days Uncle Henry and his grandson would take all-day buggy trips to a farm he owned in Warren County, south of Des Moines, talking of clover or hogs or God. Often they sat together in Uncle Henry's comfortable home on Sherman Hill, reading aloud letters the old man received from his vast network of friends.

Together the boy and his grandfather recited the short catechism of the Presbyterian Church. Henry A. Wallace could repeat it to the end of his days. "What is the chief end of man?" it began. "The chief end of man is to glorify God and enjoy him forever." As they recited the catechism, the boy could picture in his mind what God must look like. His grandfather was not a glamorous man, Henry A. once said, but he was a most substantial one. "That is, he was more like God."[3]

Young Henry did not fully appreciate, and come to share, his grandfather's broadly liberal religious views until he had reached manhood. As a child Henry A. felt closer to his mother's strict orthodoxy. And Uncle Henry's progressive social ideas could not have mattered much to his grandson. Young Henry showed little interest in public affairs until he was in college. Moreover, he found the stogies his grandfather perpetually smoked obnoxious.

But there was a part of Uncle Henry that affected the boy profoundly. There was a gravity about Uncle Henry, seriousness leavened by tolerance and goodwill, which imbedded itself in the boy's soul. Uncle Henry was a man who knew what was important—God and agriculture—and Young Henry made that vision his own.

Henry A. Wallace's other salient characteristic was his curiosity. He craved to know things. Usually he wanted to know them firsthand. A school chum told him about the usefulness of multiplication tables; Young Henry liked the concept but accepted it only after trying it out on a piece of chicken wire to determine the number of holes.

When he was a boy, his curiosity expressed itself mainly in the realm of plants. Everything about plants was a matter of intense interest. When his mother taught him how to crossbreed pansies, producing an offspring that was undistinguished but very much his own, he was fascinated.

When the family moved to a house on Des Moines's western edge, ten-year-old Henry's first act was to secure a portion of the property for his own use. There he established an elaborate garden and grew enough tomatoes, cabbages, and celery to feed the family. The animals he was obliged to care for were valuable, in Henry's view, chiefly because they supplied manure for his plants. He had particular disdain for horses and not much appreciation of hogs. Chickens were of more interest because his first business venture was to hatch and raise white wyandotte chickens for a man who supplied him with a hundred eggs.

In 1902 Henry came across a catalog from R. M. Kellogg in Three Rivers, Michigan, and began a lifelong love affair with strawberries. He ordered six types of strawberry plants—one called the Senator Dunlap—and set aside a portion of his garden for them. He tried without luck to assign two of the varieties to his brothers, Jim and John. "They didn't see why they should be compelled to take care of strawberries, just because I was interested in strawberries, although they did like to eat them."[4]

Soon it was corn that absorbed him. Starting about the time he entered West High School, at fourteen, and continuing for almost three decades, corn was the dominating aspect of Henry A. Wallace's life. Corn became his passion, his cause, the medium of his genius. He knew corn as well as he knew people, he said, and appreciated it as much.

His turn toward corn was natural. Corn was by far the most important crop produced by American farmers. If Uncle Henry's dream of a great agricultural civilization was to survive and flourish, corn had to be its backbone. Nowhere was that more true than in Iowa. "Corn is king," it was said there. The Wallaces understood this fact with great clarity.

Moreover, corn was an inherently fascinating plant to a budding botanist such as Young Henry. It offered unlimited opportunities for study and experimentation. Corn came in countless varieties, with endless shapes and sizes and weaknesses and strengths, and it could be easily manipulated by humans. Corn almost invited experimentation because it was a total captive of human beings. Without constant human cultivation—planting, fertilizing, harvesting, and replanting—corn would cease to exist. Freed from human intervention, Wallace guessed, corn as we know it would survive only a couple of years.

For centuries, beginning with the ancient Incas, corn farmers used a simple process of visual selection to perpetuate their crops. The farmer would decide which ears of corn looked best to him and set them aside as seed for the next year's crop. Over time this process obliterated "wild corn" and resulted, especially throughout the Midwest, in a certain uniformity of characteristics. Particularly popular around the turn of the century was a variety known as Reid yellow dent, which produced long, good-looking cylindrical ears covered from tip to butt with arrow-straight rows of kernels.

Reid yellow dent won a blue ribbon at the Chicago World's Fair in 1893 and quickly became the midwestern ideal. Agricultural organizations and institutions began sponsoring "corn shows," at which ears of corn were judged competitively according to their appearance.

Elaborate "show ring" standards were devised, and the judging of corn became a fine art. A perfect ear of corn was deemed to be 10^1/$_2$ inches long and 7^1/$_2$ inches in circumference. It should have twenty or twenty-two straight rows of plump, wide, keystone-shaped kernels that bore no evidence of shrinkage or blistering. The standards were based on bogus science, but they were no less important for that. The lucky farmer who won a corn show competition was rewarded amply with prestige and money. Hundreds of dollars were paid for winning ears.

At the edge of the corn show circus were a few nonbelievers: some skeptical old-fashioned dirt farmers, a handful of agricultural scientists who understood the great flaw in the visual selection process, and one shy high school boy in Des Moines named Henry A. Wallace.

That Young Henry would have doubts about corn shows was all the more remarkable because by 1902 his family was heavily engaged in promoting them. A corn contest organized by *Wallaces' Farmer*, open to any farm boy who could obtain three new subscriptions to the paper, drew entries from across the country. Hundreds gathered in the farm journal's lobby to witness the judging.

Moreover, the Wallaces had succeeded in attracting to Iowa one Perry G. Holden to help promote the corn shows. No more fabulous character ever strode across the Corn Belt than this slight, bearded man with steel-rimmed spectacles. Part teacher, part salesman, part businessman—and all showman— Holden was known as the Corn Professor, the Evangelist of Corn, and the nation's leading exponent of lovely looking Reid yellow dent. With Uncle Henry's help, Holden spread his message at corn shows, aboard special "corn trains" sponsored by *Wallaces' Farmer*, and through a professorship at Iowa State partly subsidized by the Wallace family. "No man ever engaged in more rapid and effective mass education of farmers than did P.G. Holden from 1902 to 1910 in Iowa," Henry A. Wallace later wrote.[5]

Young Henry rather liked the Corn Professor, at least the part of Holden that was more scientist than huckster. Holden first won the boy's heart by siding with him on a question of agricultural practice. Henry had been quarreling with his father over the proper way of fertilizing a tree. Put ashes in a ring around the tree's base of the tree, Harry insisted. No, the boy said, put ashes in a ring six feet from the tree's base so as to be closer to the tips of its roots. Holden sided with Young Henry, which pleased him greatly. It was the first time he had won an argument with his father.

In January 1904 Holden offered one of his short courses for farmers at Iowa State, and the fifteen-year-old Henry Wallace decided to attend. For two weeks he watched Holden preach the message of good farming and better living through beautifully shaped ears of Reid yellow dent. Hour after hour Holden expounded upon the proper aesthetic standards for the judgment of corn.

Most of Holden's students were completely persuaded by the professor's passion and sincerity. But to Young Henry the message didn't ring true. What did aesthetic standards have to do with yield? What did it matter that some variety of corn was said to be a "pure" breed or displayed "good constitution"?

At the end of a lecture, the boy decided to make his doubts known. "What's looks to a hog?" he asked.[6] A corn farmer's goal ought to be big yields. It was remarkable: a reserved teenager challenging an eminent expert on the very grounds of his expertise. It was also typical. From an early age, and for the remainder of his life, a central characteristic of Henry A. Wallace's personality was independence of mind. He was open to any idea, however silly sounding, until he could test its validity. He was prepared to reject any idea, no matter how broadly accepted, that would not stand the weight of inquiry.

And he was—this was another of those traits that frequently made people uncomfortable around Henry A. Wallace—altogether unsentimental in making intellectual judgments. That Holden was a well-meaning man who had done farmers great good was beside the point. That almost everyone who heard him accepted his teachings was irrelevant. That he was close to Uncle Henry and Harry Wallace and had befriended Young Henry mattered not. If Holden was wrong, he should be proven wrong.

Holden, of course, confidently reasserted his belief that good appearance reflected good quality. In any event, the professor said, Young Henry could easily test the theory for himself. Holden gave the boy several ears of corn on display and told him to use them for seed. The truth would reveal itself; the finest-looking corn would produce the biggest yield and the worst-looking corn the smallest.

Young Henry accepted the challenge on the spot. He returned to Des Moines with a bag of thirty-three ears of Reid yellow dent corn and prepared to put them to the test. In the spring he persuaded his father to let him use five acres of land behind their home. He numbered, labeled, and shelled each ear of corn. The seed from each ear he planted in two rows. All summer he walked through his sixty-six rows of corn, fertilizing and thinning, cultivating and weeding.

He did more. In order to eliminate the possibility of self-fertilization, which would reduce yields, he decided to detassel half his crop. That is, he cut off the corn plant's male sex element, the tassel, so it could not reproduce with itself. Cutting off the tassel is a simple task—a quick slice of a knife, and the tassel is gone—but detasseling a field of five acres was arduous work. For several weeks each row had to be constantly patrolled so that the detasseling could be done at precisely the right moment.

In the fall Young Henry harvested his crop, husked the ears, and stored them in thirty-three neatly numbered piles in his father's garage. He had only to wait for the corn to dry so that it could be shelled and weighed. He stared at the piles for days, aching to know their secret, and finally decided he could wait no longer. He calculated the percentage of an ear composed of cob and estimated the amount of weight lost through drying. This he could verify when the corn had actually dried. Ever a math buff, he devised a ratio of whole, fresh-picked ear to dried shelled corn.

In the evening, after his chores were done, this "too-solemn boy" sat in the garage, weighing and calculating, filling up sheet after sheet of paper with row upon row of numbers and contemplating the astounding results.[7]

He had ruined the Corn Professor. His experiment demonstrated beyond question that corn shows and show-ring standards and grand-champion corn auctions were a ridiculous waste of time and money. It was right there in his figures. The ears of fine yellow dent corn Holden had given him ranged in yield from thirty-three to seventy-nine bushels an acre. Some of the best-yielding ears were those Holden had judged to be the poorest. And the ear that Holden had singled out as the most beautiful of all was one of the ten worst in yield.

Holden continued to be a celebrity in Iowa, and corn shows remained popular for years. But the beginning of their decline was there in Harry Wallace's garage, in the hands of a teenage boy armed with a soft-lead wood pencil. Henry A. Wallace would become the most outspoken opponent of corn shows in the Midwest, relentlessly mocking the pseudo-science on which they were based. By the 1920s the corn shows were little more than a colorful relic of the past; in their place were scientifically conducted yield contests, devised by Wallace and his allies as a more appropriate means of judging agricultural excellence.

"Fortunately, a few farmers never 'took any stock' in Holden or Reid corn," Wallace wrote years later. "These mavericks went their own way, and a few, a very few, of their corns have been preserved. Holden rendered an enormous service, but we can also give thanks for the skeptics and the 'forgotten corns.' There is room for both 'forgotten corn' and 'forgotten men.' Neither corn nor men were meant to be completely uniform."[8]

"Probably no one got more out of a school or gave less to it than I did from September of 1902 until June of 1906," Henry Wallace later remarked of his career at West High School.*[9]

---

*West High, established in 1864, was Des Moines's first public high school. The school was closed in 1928, but the building continued in use for several decades as a facility for the mentally disabled, practical nurses, and persons studying for citizenship papers. Wallace was not its only famous student. The aviator Amelia Earhart attended West High from 1911 to 1913, when her family moved to St. Paul, Minnesota.

He took no part in the school's social and extracurricular activities. He did not date girls, although he said he admired several "from a distance because of their scholarship," and did not play football or join the glee club. West High was located just one block from his grandfather's house, but it was a two-mile walk from Young Henry's home, and he had neither the time nor the inclination to socialize. "You can't go out for football in the afternoon when you're walking four miles a day. You don't have enough time, you don't have enough vigor left over, especially when you have to milk a cow every night. It just didn't fit."[10]

There was another problem. He was strong but very scrawny. "Probably I didn't get quite enough of the right things to eat when I was younger and I had to work pretty hard and was simply delayed in developing."[11] Wallace finished his sophomore year at West High weighing just under a hundred pounds. During the next two years he gained forty-five pounds and reached his adult height of five feet, ten inches, but even then he was nobody's idea of a fullback. Wallace confined his physical energy, always considerable, to sandlot football. A brief stint as a high jumper ended when he broke a small bone in his left leg while gamboling down a mountainside near his family's vacation cabin at Green Mountain Falls, Colorado.

Instead of high jumping, Wallace developed an athletic passion that, by the standards of Iowa in the early 1900s, seemed downright exotic. He somehow acquired a Spalding rule book for tennis and set out to teach himself the sport. Neither Wallace nor anyone he knew had ever seen tennis played. In fact, he had never even seen a tennis court.

Wallace laid out a primitive dirt court on his family's property at Thirty-eighth Street and Cottage Grove and sent away for the necessary rackets, balls, and net. Soon he and his friends were facing each other across the net, batting a ball back and forth as many as sixty times, in what they thought was a good approximation of the game. Years later he could vividly recall the moment he first saw tennis played by someone schooled in it. "We were amazed when we found out that it was possible to hit the ball to create a top-spin," he said. "That had never occurred to us."[12]

For the remainder of his life, Wallace was a ferociously competitive tennis player but always without a trace of style or grace. His practice was to bound onto a court, often wearing long brown work pants and street shoes, and grind his opponents down through determination and force of energy. Left-handed in most respects, he was ambidextrous on the tennis court. Frequently he changed his racket from hand to hand between lobs. "I've never been able to develop proper tennis form simply because my habits were formed without any benefit of ever seeing a tennis player play," he said. "But our system did develop great pertinacity."[13]

Intellectually he was consumed with plants, and West High had little to say on the subject. In classes where he felt no relevance to real life—no "spark," as he put it—his interest flagged and his grades were indifferent. He barely escaped Latin with a passing grade and found little that appealed to him in literature classes. Even algebra, a subject he should have enjoyed, did not inspire him.

A German teacher managed to kindle in him a love of foreign languages, the study of which became a lifelong enthusiasm. And an American history teacher, N. H. Weeks, persuaded him that the study of the past had a bearing on the present. Weeks used the patterns of American history to demonstrate the importance of Senator Albert Baird Cummins's plan for progressive trade practices, the so-called Iowa Idea, and gave young Wallace "some glimmering of the fact that there is such a thing as policy in American history."[14]

There was about him the air of a farm boy, someone less worldly and sophisticated than his city-bred schoolmates. He showed up at times with manure on his shoes and, in his own words, was not "entirely respectable." He had a vague sense of being out of place. Yet there was a hint of intellectual arrogance about him, too. When he concluded that N. H. Weeks—the same history teacher whose lectures he admired—gave better grades to students who wrote longer papers, he set out to play the teacher for a fool. He began spelling out dates and inserting such irrelevant material as "I am now seated at my window looking out over the prairie of my native state, where far in the distance I see a skinny red cow peacefully chewing her cud." Then he moralized on the wrongness of judging a paper by its length. His marks improved, although he never learned whether or not Weeks actually read the papers.[15]

On the whole, Wallace recollected, he did "pretty well" in high school, but he remained critical of West High's social and academic pretentions. Its students came from Des Moines's wealthiest neighborhoods, and he found the school's "aristocratic" tone annoying. At the same time West High's course of study was far more limited than its boosters believed. Wallace was in college, he observed, before he found out about the Franco-Prussian War. "We learned certain fundamentals, but when we graduated we were a long distance from understanding the world which began to develop so fast after World War I."[16]

Within his head he was building something no less exotic than a tennis court in Des Moines. He was devising a philosophical system.

Philosophy and religion fascinated him, and his liberal grandfather encouraged speculation in such matters. In high school he began reading widely and thinking deeply about philosophy and tried whenever possible to engage his classmates in discussions. "I remember trying to create an appreciation for Emerson among my Sunday School class. One of the boys in the Sunday

School class was going to high school and having a great deal of trouble with American literature. I tried to open his eyes to Emerson, but it was no good. He couldn't do it."[17] Henry even tried his hand at writing about philosophical matters, but his efforts were "very primitive," he conceded as an adult.

Ralph Waldo Emerson, the great Transcendentalist writer and nonconformist thinker, provided the key to his exploration. This eventually led Wallace to read William James's *Varieties of Religious Experience*, which was to have a profound impact on him. Along the way he became much interested in the writings of an Emerson namesake, Ralph Waldo Trine, whose book *In Tune with the Infinite* was a highly popular work of spiritual inspiration during the first three decades of the twentieth century.

"Everything in the material universe about us, everything the universe has ever known, had its origin first in thought," Trine wrote. "From this it took its form. Every castle, every statue, every painting, every piece of mechanism— everything had its birth, its origin, first in the mind of the one who formed it before it received its material expression or embodiment. The very universe in which we live is the result of the thought energies of God, the Infinite Spirit that is back of all."[18]

As a public figure Wallace tried without any great success to use Trine's formulation in explaining his own reputed mysticism. In his oral history, acknowledging that he probably was a "practical mystic," Wallace explained, "I've always believed that if you envision something that hasn't been, that can be, and bring it into being, that is a tremendously worthwhile thing to do."

It was precisely the question of worthwhileness that so attracted Young Henry to Trine. "I suspect I'd turn up my nose at it today," he said as a man of sixty-two, "but then it seemed to perform that thing which is so essential in a young man—to center his rather diffuse energies and cause him to go through some rather strenuous thinking. 'What is worthwhile?' That was very important to me during those years. That was the all-important thing."[19]

And it was the matter of worthwhileness that formed the quiet, immutable bond between grandfather and grandson. There, in this realm of the infinite and man's relationship to God, they connected. It gave the boy a special quality in the old man's eyes. To his grandfather, Young Henry's affinity for spiritual matters made him a complete person. Completeness was a vital concept to the elder Wallace, a quality none of his own children quite possessed. Henry Wallace believed he had found it in his grandson.

By 1906 the humble agricultural college at Ames had begun to think of itself in grander terms. It was called the Iowa State College of Agricultural and Mechanical Arts, and its president declared it was "perhaps without peer in the country" in the field of agricultural education.

But the institution Henry A. Wallace entered that fall remained a backwoods "cow college" in many respects. Its buildings were ramshackle; it had no gymnasium or auditorium or even a permanent home for its library. Its walkways were unpaved and its sanitation system so poor that a sizable portion of its students were usually sick. It had a single dormitory, capable of housing half the school's two hundred female students. The rest of the women, and all fifteen hundred male students, had to fend for themselves.

Roughly one-third of the students were agricultural and veterinary majors. The agricultural students were required to select one of six courses of study, of which the most popular was animal husbandry. Plant life was Young Henry's passion, but he too chose to major in animal husbandry.

As in high school he found the course of studies not entirely fulfilling. "He was healthily skeptical of many things he was taught in class and was constantly challenging them," said Professor J. L. Lush. A roommate later recalled that Wallace "always wanted to know 'why' and could spend considerable time discussing some particular matter with a teacher. He was always a thinker. As I think of it now, he was half a jump ahead of the instructors in some classes."[20]

The teachers he most admired had about them a "quality of enthusiasm" that sparked in students a desire to learn, a characteristic, Wallace observed, that made them beloved by students and "nearly always distrusted by their fellow faculty members."[21] Others he considered merely intellectual hacks. He had already proven to himself the uselessness of corn shows, but his professors continued to prattle about the pedigrees and aesthetics of plants and animals. Wallace made little effort to conceal his disdain; the score of 87 he received in a livestock-judging class was his lowest ever in college.

Classmates remembered him as shy, considerate, studious, approachable, and, above all, serious. "He was always a good visitor, but the conversation was on a high level and if you wanted to discuss any particular subject you should be pretty well versed on it," said a roommate, M. W. Joiner.[22] He neither smoked nor drank, and even at a time when religion played a large role in college life, Wallace was regarded as deeply religious. He read widely, from William James's complex *Pluralistic Universe* to Sir Walter Scott's Waverley novels and Henri Bergson's *Creative Evolution*. James's essay entitled "The Moral Equivalent of War," which Wallace read during his senior year, greatly influenced his dedication to the cause of peace.

Wallace's idea of doing something useful with his spare time was to work in one of Professor Holden's experimental corn plots. The numerous extracurricular organizations on campus held little appeal. He was a member of the agricultural honorary fraternity, Alpha Zeta, and served as an editor of the

Iowa Agriculturist but devoted himself mainly to his intellectual and spiritual pursuits. "Henry was not what you would call a college leader," his roommate said dryly.[23]

Wallace would have agreed. "I didn't mature nearly as rapidly as the students do today," he said later. "I spent my time chiefly in studying."[24] His favorite pastime, when not studying, was walking. He liked to tramp through the woods near the campus. It was a way to keep fit and study nature at the same time. Occasionally he hiked the thirty miles from Ames home to Des Moines, although on most weekends he took the train. He had reached his full height, with broad shoulders and a deep muscular chest, but he still weighed barely 150 pounds.

Some of the students at the Hawkeye Club, a men's fraternal organization where he roomed for three years, nicknamed him Wally, but most knew him as H. A. His quiet, serious personality was reflected in his solid features. His face was long and rectangular, with heavy brows above his blue-gray eyes and a wide, sensitive mouth that seldom smiled. For a time he sported a mustache but concluded it was too much bother and shaved it off. His great shock of auburn hair seemed perpetually unruly, and his strong, rough hands gave proof that he was accustomed to farm work.

"He was not anti-social," said a fraternity brother, "nor was he pro-social." Often scruffy in appearance, with unshined shoes and a thirty-six-hour-old beard, he was hardly the picture of a ladies man. But he usually attended the Hawkeye Club's social functions and gamely brought a date when it was expected of him. On one occasion he entertained a female companion by giving her a tour of the campus poultry barn. His chief contribution to his fraternity's social life was the construction of another tennis court.

Even as an undergraduate Wallace liked to startle acquaintances with predictions that seemed almost bizarre. He foresaw a day when people would wear wristbands that would tell them the time and what was going on everywhere in the world. A single pill would be developed that would contain nutrition equivalent to an entire meal. China would become the most feared nation on earth. "Henry was always coming up with what the boys called a 'screwy' idea," said his roommate.

After reading F. H. King's *Farmers for Forty Centuries*, a classic study of Chinese agriculture, Wallace attempted to calculate "the most economical possible diet," based on the minimum amount of land necessary to grow enough food for one person. With that in mind he began eating only corn, soy beans, cottonseed meal, linseed meal, and rutabagas. "It didn't work very well," said Wallace. "It was obviously short in vitamins."[25] Another time he tried subsisting on nothing but strawberries and corn meal, until his mother ordered him to stop it.

With two fraternity brothers he tried to stay alive solely on oranges, to determine whether a light diet would improve their ability to study. And there was a diet consisting only of milk, based on a theory nobody ever understood. Once he gave up food altogether after reading a magazine article on fasting by Upton Sinclair. "I thought I'd try it out. I walked, I suppose, two or three miles a day and carried on my studies. It's amazing how much time you can pick up if you don't eat."[26] After a week, however, he noticed he had developed "rather an abnormal state of mind" and began eating again.

Sometimes these experiments crashed in small disaster, as when he appeared one day with splotches across his face. Did he have the measles or "barber's itch," a fraternity brother asked. Wallace hesitated but eventually admitted he had been trying to live on an experimental feed being given to the college's cattle.

In the early summer of 1909, at the conclusion of his junior year in college, Young Henry Wallace began his career as a journalist, a calling he would follow for most of the next quarter of a century. That summer, at the urging of his father and grandfather, he set off alone on a three-month tour of the American West, from the dusty plains of the Texas Panhandle to the great agricultural valleys of California and the breathtaking beauty of western Colorado's Grand Valley. He traveled by train, automobile, bicycle, horseback and on foot, at each stop filing dispatches on the state of western agriculture for *Wallaces' Farmer*. He was paid by the inch, at the same rate as all *Wallaces' Farmer* correspondents, and earned enough to pay his college expenses during his senior year.

His reports, written in the plain, unpoetic prose that was the hallmark of all his journalism, ranged from calf branding in Texas to irrigation projects in western Kansas. In California he was seized by the agricultural possibilities of the great valleys and predicted it would one day become the nation's leading farm state. What most impressed him, however, was not the grandeur of western scenery or the productivity of its farms but the difference in social attitude of western farmers who were willing to work together for their common good. The blessings of cooperation, preached fervently by Wallace's father and grandfather, had come to life in, of all places, the Wild West, he wrote.

> Co-operation goes hand in hand with irrigation. This is not because the irrigation farmer is a superior type to start with, believing in community interest and social confidence. On the contrary, he is very independent, but lack of capital and a crying need for water meant co-operation or leave the country. . . . All this soon develops in even the most independent of men a consideration for the rights of others and a realization of the benefits to be obtained by working together.[27]

Soon after he returned to campus in the fall of his senior year, Henry A. Wallace came of age. His family took unusual pains to express its pride in him. Harry Wallace chartered a railroad car to bring his son and all members of the Hawkeye Club and their dates to Des Moines, where the family marked Henry's twenty-first birthday with a formal dinner dance at a country club. Henry, a fraternity brother commented, was considered the "culmination of the Wallace intellect."[28]

From his grandfather, Henry received something both typical and remarkable. It was a letter. It gave Uncle Henry an opportunity to express joy in the way his grandson had grown to manhood and to charge him with the great responsibility of serving God and his fellow man. In a few short, prophetic paragraphs, the elder Wallace put into words the ethic that formed the family's core.

> We are proud of you, but "better is the end of a thing than the beginning thereof." The history of no man can be truly written until he is dead. There are few boys that have the opportunities that are coming to you. . . . The world is waiting for men who can do her work, and there is always a bigger job ahead of the man who performs faithfully the job that he is at now. . . .
>
> You must not expect to be a really big man unless you live a sincere, earnest, religious life. In other words, you want always to be on the side of the great Power that rules this world, and that we have learned to call "Our Father." In solving the questions that will come up from year to year and from day to day, the man who is on God's side is really on the side of the majority, although the world will not think so and he may for a time doubt it. Nevertheless, posterity will appreciate the man who does the right as he sees the right, and who has an eye single for righteousness.[29]

Eight months later Wallace graduated from Iowa State at the top of the college's agricultural division. His senior thesis, a forty-page treatise entitled "Relation between Live Stock Farming and the Fertility of the Soil," was both a technical analysis and a call for progressive reform. Soil conservation was a problem of national proportions, he argued, and the federal government should step in to protect that vital national resource if individuals failed to meet their obligations. "We have our choice," he said, "between that and ruin."[30]

He left college with a conviction, shared by his father and grandfather before him, that higher education had a great deal to offer agriculture, even if Iowa State did not.

Those were happy, heady days for the Wallaces. The family was prominent, its health good, its paper profitable. Starting in 1902, when the Wallaces retired the debt incurred in starting their journal, *Wallaces' Farmer* enjoyed almost two decades of rising growth and prosperity. By 1910, the year Young Henry graduated from college, his family's influence had reached new heights.

Uncle Henry had gained national recognition as a member of the Country Life Commission, a distinguished panel named by President Theodore Roosevelt to examine rural conditions and suggest progressive reforms. Shortly after the commission completed its work, the elder Wallace was elected president of the Conservative Congress, a nationwide group supporting sound environmental policies. Henry Wallace, said one of his admirers, was simply "the greatest agricultural editor of his day."

His son Harry Wallace involved himself heavily in the Young Men's Christian Association, the Masons, the United Presbyterian Church, an informal discussion group called the Prairie Club, and, increasingly, the Iowa Republican Party. An organization Harry Wallace founded and single-handedly ran, the Corn Belt Meat Producers' Association, had become one of the Midwest's most important farm groups, aggressively representing the interests of livestock shippers in their dealings with railroads and rate-setting commissions.

Even after Theodore Roosevelt was replaced in the White House by the more conservative William Howard Taft, the Wallaces continued to influence national agricultural and conservation policies through their ties to Agriculture Secretary James Wilson and his hard-charging, innovative bureau chiefs. They were particularly close to Gifford Pinchot, idealistic chief of the U.S. Forest Service, who led the fight for progressive conservation policies. When Pinchot's activities eventually led to his dismissal by Taft, the Wallaces backed the forester wholeheartedly. When Roosevelt attempted to reclaim the presidency from Taft in 1912, the Wallaces supported his third-party bid without hesitation.*

After leaving Ames, Young Henry did what came naturally for a Wallace. He joined *Wallaces' Farmer* as a full-time writer and editor and remained there as such for more than two decades. Only briefly did he entertain the idea of going to graduate school. Graduate school would only slow down the pace of his learning, especially his corn-breeding work, he told his father. It was an as-

---

*Pinchot was one of young Henry A. Wallace's heroes, along with his grandfather, Theodore Roosevelt, Tama Jim Wilson, and Liberty Hyde Bailey, dean of the Cornell University agricultural school. Wallace's sole political activity while a student at Iowa State was the organization of a club to support Pinchot for president. "A cultured person from the east, who at the same time was constructive, had a great influence in those days on young people of the west," Wallace later remarked. ". . . They had certain graces which we didn't have, and if they also had the 'goods,' in addition, why they became heroic figures to us."

tute observation. The international renown he was to gain in several fields—genetics, statistics, economics—was almost entirely the result of self-education.

His first summer on the paper was devoted to a walking tour of Iowa, and he returned with the conclusion that Iowa farmland was overpriced. His father and grandfather agreed and began a noisy campaign to warn farmers about the evils of land speculation.

Numbers fascinated him, and his articles were often brimming with statistical support. He had always been attracted to the abstract beauty of mathematics, but now he began to see its application to real life. A letter from a reader complaining about an article Wallace had written extolling the joys of raising hogs triggered his first serious effort to use math as a journalistic tool. Hadn't Wallace noticed, the reader asked, that hog prices were declining? Wallace hadn't noticed. To his chagrin he realized he had no idea why hog prices were going down, and he set out to discover the reason.

Wallace pored over page after page of figures—corn prices and supplies, transportation rates, weather statistics—but he had no mathematical means of relating these causal factors to the price of hogs. Soon he came across a book by the Columbia University professor Henry L. Moore entitled *Economic Cycles: Their Laws and Cause.* Wallace saw that Moore's use of curves could be applied to the problem of hog prices, but he had no idea how Moore had derived them. So he took the book to a mathematics professor at Drake University, in Des Moines, and asked how it was done. Wallace absorbed the professor's laborious explanation and set out to learn how to use calculus and a key-driven mechanical calculator to do the same thing with less effort. The course in calculus was self-taught, with the assistance of a textbook he found in the Des Moines Public Library. On the textbook's flyleaf was printed a simian saying that Wallace quoted with amusement for years to come: "What one fool can do, another can." The adage, said Wallace, became his motto.[31]

"So I learned how to calculate correlation coefficients and came to have a very great respect for quantitative methods of economic analysis," Wallace said. Just about anything that could be put into numbers was fair game to him. He analyzed the relationship between corn and hog prices and discovered a seven-year price cycle that allowed him to predict the market price of hogs with uncanny accuracy. He looked into the relation between economic development and population growth. He tried to find out whether the position of planets had an effect on the weather. He examined the economic impact of Britain's move toward free trade in the nineteenth century.

His more fanciful statistical musings, he acknowledged, were "simply what happens to the human mind when it is left alone with some figures in an office." The greater part of his work, however, was solid and substantial and lent to *Wallaces' Farmer* an air of authority enjoyed by few popular publications. His grandfather, in the autumn of his life but still an active editor, steadily turned Henry A. into the paper's most important scholarly resource. Often Uncle Henry scratched out a few lines on a topic that interested him and left his grandson to reason the matter to a conclusion.

Left to his own devices, Henry A. Wallace might have contentedly spent his days in his bare-bones office at *Wallaces' Farmer* and in the corn patch he kept behind his parents' fashionable home. But the Wallaces were believers in the value of travel and took care that Young Henry saw something of the world. In 1912 they sent their prodigy on his first trip to the East Coast and to Europe. The trip began with a visit to Washington, D.C., where he stayed in the apartment of Tama Jim Wilson and met several of the Agriculture Department's noted bureau chiefs.

Then he was off to France, Holland, Belgium, and Germany, first as part of a student tour group and then on his own, so that he could spend time at agricultural experiment stations. From the Continent he went to Dublin, where he met his grandfather's friend George W. Russell, a poet, mystic, and agrarian reformer known to the world as Æ. Their friendship, based upon mutual interest in spirituality, was to delight Wallace for the next quarter century.

In the spring of 1913 Young Henry's good fortune grew better still. He met Ilo Browne at an evening picnic in Des Moines. Ilo had a round, pretty face, sparkling brown eyes, wavy brown hair, and a radiant smile. Something in her calm, sweet demeanor attracted Henry from the moment they met. He returned from the party and told his sister, "That's the girl I'd like to marry."[32]

Ilo Browne was born in Madison County half a year before Henry A. Wallace's birth in adjoining Adair County. Her mother died when she was four. Her father, James L. Browne, remarried a year later and settled in Indianola, about ten miles south of Des Moines, enjoying the orderly life of a respectable small-town businessman. He died in 1911, leaving Ilo and her only brother with a substantial inheritance. Ilo studied voice at Simpson College in her hometown and then at Monmouth College in Illinois; like her father, though, she had only a limited interest in intellectual matters. After her father's death she traveled for a time in Europe and bought several "Paris gowns" that made her quite a striking figure in Iowa.

"Henry Wallace was on her trail every minute," said one of Ilo's friends. "He used to take Ilo driving in a dilapidated old car. Money never meant a thing to Henry, and his eccentricity didn't matter to Ilo."[33] His general obliviousness to customary courtship practices had an endearing quality of its own. On one of their dates Henry brought along his copy of *Farmers of Forty Centuries* so he and Ilo could discuss Chinese agricultural practices.

At times Henry's peculiarity was a bit much for Ilo's friends. They gossiped that he was existing on a diet of nothing but soybeans and cabbages, and grumbled about his unruly appearance. "Ilo, don't you think you could do something about Henry's ties," one of her friends asked. To Ilo, however, what mattered were the "splendid qualities" she saw in him. His quiet strength, his dedication to God and family, his serious demeanor—these were qualities she thought her late father would have admired. She felt with Henry a sense of comfort and security. It seemed, she remarked years later, as if she had always known him.

He proposed marriage in his usual low-key manner, with a gesture that seemed odd to her friends and thrilling to Ilo. Knowing nothing about diamonds, Henry borrowed a bag of them from a trusting Des Moines jeweler. "Here," he said to Ilo, "pick one out." She slept fitfully that night, with the bag of diamonds under her pillow.

They were married in Des Moines on May 20, 1914, in a ceremony performed by Uncle Henry. The bride was described as regal and the groom as appropriately dazed. When they departed the church, Henry climbed into the car and closed the door, not realizing he had left his bride standing on the sidewalk, until his friends started razzing him.

They gave no thought to enjoying their newlywed days in leisure. In a house they rented on Des Moines's western edge, Henry and Ilo immediately began to plan an ambitious commercial farming venture. Henry had saved about $2,000 during his four years at *Wallaces' Farmer*, but that was not enough to buy a farm, and Ilo's properties were too far away. So Ilo sold a Warren County farm and bought a forty-acre farm near Johnston, about six miles north of Des Moines. Harry Wallace purchased an adjoining forty-seven-acre tract and rented it to them. The farm they established combined two operations: seed corn production and dairying. Wallace's theory was that the dairy cows could eat fodder made from the corn they grew and at the same time supplement the modest wages he earned as a writer.

They nearly fell victim to their own energy. Within six months, Ilo was pregnant with their first child and trying to help run the dairying operation, while Henry was working the equivalent of two full-time jobs. Together they arose in Des Moines at four-thirty and drove Henry's battered Winston to the farm to do the morning milking. While Henry went off to work at *Wallaces' Farmer*, where he had been promoted to assistant editor, Ilo often drove the milk wagon along the route they established in the northern portions of Des Moines. In the late afternoon it was back to Johnston to do the evening milking, then back to Des Moines for a few hours' sleep.

Accustomed to hard work, Henry withstood the pace better than Ilo did, but the schedule began to take a toll on them both. Henry began losing weight, slowly going from 165 to 140 pounds, and often ran a low-grade fever in the afternoon. Ilo was exhausted, and eventually grew too sick to continue. A doctor diagnosed her illness as tuberculosis, the fear of which ran deep in the Wallaces. Ilo went to the Wallace family's vacation cabin, Maysmount, near Colorado Springs, Colorado, to recuperate.

A weary Henry carried on without her. She returned in a matter of weeks, rested but in delicate health. His own health showed no improvement, and while he basically ignored the fevers and chills that sometimes gripped him, there was no way to overlook the condition of his forty dairy cows. They were being attacked by bovine tuberculosis and contagious abortion. Many of those that did not die had to be isolated and slaughtered. Henry intently examined the remains, convinced there must be a link between tuberculosis in humans and drinking the milk of cows with bovine tuberculosis. But the connection to his own weakened condition eluded him.

It would be a decade before scientists established a link between contagious abortion in cows and undulant fever in humans. Long before that, Henry himself had been diagnosed with tuberculosis and had spent four months recovering at Maysmount, despite an inner conviction that he did not actually have the disease. He probably was right; in all likelihood he had contracted undulant fever, as he himself later concluded. But whatever the cause, the consequences were long lasting. His illness left him painfully thin. It would be fifteen years before he could obtain a standard life insurance policy. The episode greatly dampened his enthusiasm for the dairy business. Eventually the herd was destroyed, and Wallace turned his whole attention to something he truly understood—corn.

In the early days of May 1915, Wallace went for one of his frequent afternoon rides in the country with his grandfather. As they returned, they heard paperboys crying news of the sinking of the British passenger ship *Lusitania* by the German navy. Almost 1,200 passengers, including 114 Americans, died. "Grandfather was deeply upset," Wallace recalled. The elder Wallace was "profoundly disturbed for fear we would get into the war. . . . He had been through one reconstruction and he knew what it meant."[34]

Events were conspiring to draw America into the biggest war the world had ever known. President Woodrow Wilson gave repeated assurances of American neutrality throughout the summer of 1915, but the elder Wallace, having seen the carnage of civil war firsthand as a young minister, only grew more alarmed. He had concluded "there could never be world peace so long as any one nation or group controlled the great seas." The war in Europe, he said, was mainly a war for the "control of trade and traffic—Germany [felt] that she could have no certain outlet for her manufactures and commerce as long as England controlled the seas, and England realiz[ed] that she must control the seas in order to keep her trade with her widely scattered colonies."[35]

With increasing fervor the elder Wallace expounded on the need for a mechanism to control rampant nationalism. He was determined to make his case directly to the president. A meeting was arranged with the help of Supreme Court Justice James McReynolds, and at six o'clock one late October afternoon, the bearded old editor strode through the leaves on the White House lawn and was escorted to the Blue Room.

The war in Europe "must end sometime," Wallace began, and Wilson was the one man in all the world who would be in a position to suggest a plan for lasting peace. The basis of such a plan, he added, should be freedom of the seas enforced by an international fleet. Only then could all the nations on earth freely engage in trade without fear of molestation.[36]

Wilson listened intently. "Of course, you do not expect me to give you a definite answer on this point," he said.

"Certainly not," Wallace replied. "It is not a plan, simply a vision which may mature in time, and if it does mature will give us world peace for all time."[37]

The visit with Wilson was to be Henry Wallace's last great public mission. On the evening February 22, 1916, less than a month before his eightieth birthday, he went to the First Methodist Church in Des Moines, where he was to open a session of the Layman's Missionary Conference. Seated in the front pew, Uncle Henry pulled his watch from his pocket shortly before 7 P.M., when he was to speak. "It is almost time," he said.[38] In the next moment he suffered a massive cerebral hemorrhage and died.

The death of Iowa's most beloved figure was followed by a huge outpouring of grief from the great and the unknown alike. Condolence messages numbering in the thousands flooded in from every state in the nation, from virtually every township in the Corn Belt, and from around the world. "You do not need to be told how highly I thought of Henry Wallace, and how genuinely I mourn his taking away," Theodore Roosevelt wrote from his home in Oyster Bay, New York.[39]

It was the reaction of common folk, however, that most touched the Wallace family. "A steady line of sorrowing humanity filed past" his body as it lay in state in the church where he died, a local paper reported.[40] "Gray-haired men mingled with school children; mothers bent with age, high school girls, ministers, business men, students, clerks, workmen from factories and shops, newsboys with hushed voices, and persons from every walk of life—all friends of Uncle Henry—joined in paying this last token of respect and reverence."

Eighty schoolchildren from the Henry Wallace School filed past the casket, each leaving a pink Killarney rose in remembrance of their benefactor.

A short time before a large funeral service was held in Des Moines, Wallace's children and grandchildren gathered around his casket in his comfortable home on Sherman Hill to hold their own service. Teddy, Uncle Henry's canary, sang from his perch in the sitting room; the well-thumbed Bible remained open on its stand beside the old man's favorite chair. There they listened to a reading of a remarkable will.

"I desire to express to my children and grandchildren my mature conviction that life is worth while if it be lived worthily," Uncle Henry began. Bring balance to your spiritual lives, he advised, and allow neither emotion nor intellect to predominate. The Wallaces have prospered and been successful, he said, because "we have never thought of wealth or social position as ends in themselves, but merely as means of enlarging our possible usefulness to the community at large. Any serious departure from this policy will be fatal to the best interests of the family." The temptation, he added, will be to amass more wealth as you become more successful. "Avoid all this. Keep clean in speech, clear in mind, vigorous in body—and God will bless you."[41]

The assembled family members responded to his wishes by adopting a written pledge—the "Wallace Family Covenant"—declaring their solemn intention to lead lives worthy of their patriarch. Henry Cantwell Wallace, the firstborn son, presented the covenant and signed it first. One by one the family members stepped forward to sign the scroll. May Brodhead Wallace. Their children: Henry, Annabelle, John, James, Mary, and Ruth. Harry's sisters and brothers and their husbands and wives and children.

"We know that his great desire was that in his descendants should be multipled his power for good; that they should live worthily; that they should keep untarnished the family name which he so jealously guarded; that they should always and everywhere be men and women whom he could honor and respect; that they should carry on the work which he began."[42]

Having so declared, his sons and grandsons lifted up the casket and carried it to the public funeral.

CHAPTER THREE

"THE FIGHT . . . WILL GO ON."

Wallaces' Farmer mourned the passing of its guiding spirit in florid voice, and the family took every opportunity to remind Iowans of Uncle Henry's greatness. Tributes to the deceased editor were published in a booklet, followed by republication of his columns and folksy open letters to his great-grandchildren. Uncle Henry's Bible lessons, perhaps the most popular feature in *Wallaces' Farmer*, continued to appear every week until a two-decade backlog was depleted. For many Iowans it seemed as if Uncle Henry had never died. The paper's progressive views remained unchanged, its circulation continued to increase, its influence was undiminished. A slight rearrangement of the paper's masthead only hinted that anything had happened: Uncle Henry Wallace was bumped up a notch to the position of "founding editor," while Henry C. and Henry A. Wallace shared equal billing as the paper's "editors."

H. A., as most of his contemporaries now called the younger Wallace, did not have his father's interest in business or politics. But he was thoroughly a Wallace, sharing the family's religious devotion and sense of duty, its love of agriculture and liberal values. Moreover, H. A. gave to *Wallaces' Farmer* an intellectual shine unequaled by any farm journal in the nation. He could do amazing things with numbers—project the price of hogs a year distant, predict the fluctuations of land values—and there seemed to be nothing he did not know about plant disease or genetics or farm management.

"Our Henry," his father exclaimed, "has the best mind in the Wallace family for the past two hundred years."[1]

Along with the dress patterns and photographs of prize bulls, *Wallaces' Farmer* now routinely published complicated graphs exploring trends in commodity prices, sophisticated "market letters," and reports on the scientific work being carried out at experiment stations. In a typical statistical excursion, H. A. warned hog farmers in December 1916 they were not as well off as they believed. "As a matter of fact, [hog prices] are decidedly weak, when the price of corn is taken into consideration. No. 2 cash corn averaged around $1 per bushel for the month of November, 1916. The normal hog-corn ratio for November (ten-year average) is 11.2 bushels of corn to equal the value of 100 pounds of hog flesh. The corn price of hogs for November, 1916 was $11.20, whereas the actual price was around $9.55. In other words, hogs were $1.65 per cwt. less profitable than in the usual month of November."[2]

Increasingly the Wallaces argued that the war in Europe was lulling farmers into a state of false prosperity. "Ultimately the United States will have to bear its share of the burden of this war, but very likely for a year, and possibly for two or three years, after the war ends, we will continue on the high tide of prosperity, to be followed by a depression lasting for a number of years," they editorialized. With growing frequency they warned farmers, "Now would be a good time to reduce your debts."[3]

Nor were the Wallaces comfortable with war-driven profits from a moral viewpoint. In a long, somber Thanksgiving editorial, they asked, "Dare we assume that the great Ruler plunges half the world into war, that the other half may profit by the manufacture of war materials and the growing of foodstuffs? Who are we, and what have we done, that material blessings should be showered upon us so lavishly?"[4]

The clouds of war notwithstanding, the Wallaces were enjoying days of peace and satisfaction. Harry gained national recognition and respect as an editor and farm leader. He had the time, money, and good health to enjoy the commonplace pursuits of a prosperous businessman: an evening sipping whiskey with friends around a poker table, a round of golf with a pinch of chewing tobacco tucked under his lip. He developed a fondness for horses and in early mornings could often be seen riding through Des Moines's streets and parks—a "solid chunk of a man" with red hair and eyebrows to match.

Harry's eldest son shared none of his recreational interests. H. A. disliked horses, despised golf, and loathed the very idea of whiskey. He enjoyed a growing young family, the quiet of his experimental corn plots, the solitary challenge of abstract statistical analysis.

But different as they were, father and son remained the closest of allies, warriors side by side, with the utmost confidence in each other. H. A. admired his father's high principles and unbending determination. "He was not a hasty or a showy man," Gifford Pinchot said of Harry Wallace. ". . . But there was never any question where he stood. When it came to a matter of principle, you could count on him to stand up and fight with you to the last ditch. He stood up like a church."[5]

The hope for peace lingered into 1917, and to the very end the Wallaces prayed American blood would not be spilled in Europe. Only days before America entered the war, they editorialized, "We are hoping that our only need for an army will be to guard our defenses and patrol our munition plants and factories, our bridges and railway systems, and to suppress the activities of such enemies as may be within our gates. But we are beginning to understand that we are really getting into the trouble, and that once in, there will be no turning back."[6]

The end of hope came on April 2, when Wilson asked Congress to declare war on Germany. "The world must be made safe for democracy," he said. The Wallaces responded to the president's call, albeit with some reluctance. Their first editorial after war was declared, entitled "Putting Our Hand to the Plow," declared, "At the bottom, this whole business is a struggle to maintain the ideals upon which this great American republic was founded, and for which, when the pinch comes, we are always ready to fight. Emperors fight for commercial supremacy, for extension of their domain, for their right to rule. Democracies fight for human liberty, for the rights of man."[7]

If they were slow to accept America's participation in the fight, however, the Wallaces were quick to see the war's impact on farmers. "The people who are talking of price fixing don't seem to understand that the moment the government steps in and undertakes to fix prices on even the two articles of corn and wheat, it means a readjustment all along the line," they warned in mid-May. "It is like playing the old-fashioned game of jack straws."[8]

Sufficient food existed to feed American soldiers and European civilians, *Wallaces' Farmer* observed, if eating patterns could be changed. Specifically it recommended that people eat more corn. To prove the point, H. A. began another of his experimental diets, eating only corn, dairy products, and one egg per day, plus an occasional radish or bite of lettuce. His daily ration never cost more than thirty cents, H. C. Wallace noted in an editorial, and "he has maintained his weight, feels in perfect health, and has carried on his work both on the farm and in the office with entire comfort."[9]

By June the Wallaces' alarm had further escalated. The government was admonishing farmers to increase the production of hogs while at the same time discouraging them from feeding corn to livestock. The federal government's confusing, contradictory farm and food policies led the Wallaces to fear that mistakes were being made that could "bring about greatly increased suffering" to large numbers of people unless something was done.[10]

The Wilson administration did do something; in August it named Herbert Hoover, a forty-four-year-old engineering dynamo, to head the newly created Office of Food Administration. The stage was set for the Wallace family's longest and most bitter feud.

Hoover might have seemed an unlikely target of the Wallaces' wrath. Born in Iowa of Quaker stock, Hoover was honest, progressive, altruistic, intellectual. In 1912 Hoover, like the Wallaces, enthusiastically backed Theodore Roosevelt's presidential bid. At the start of the Great War, he organized a humanitarian food relief campaign in Europe that had saved the lives of millions. But Hoover had left Iowa at a young age to make a fortune in international mining and finance, and his sympathies lay with big business rather than with farmers. His vision was not that of a vibrant agricultural civilization but of a society made prosperous through greater efficiency, greater production, and greater standardization.

Hoover began his efforts with broad public support, thanks in no small part to the publicity talents of aides such as the muckraking journalist Ida Tarbell. "Food Will Win the War," said one of the Food Administration's many posters. "When in doubt, serve potatoes," said another. Hoover organized "meatless days" and "wheatless days" and made it an established truth that waste was unpatriotic. To "Hooverize" meant to economize for the greater purpose of winning the war.

The practicalities of controling food production "from soil to stomach" were infinitely complex, however. The law that created the Food Administration specifically controlled only the price of wheat. Hoover had to employ a variety of tactics both direct and indirect—licensing, purchasing authority, transportation, raw materials supply, industry cooperation, old-fashioned patriotism—to achieve his end. He wasn't shy. If bludgeoning was required, Hoover brought out the stick.

Almost immediately Hoover was forced to deal with the subject of corn and hogs.[11] The problem at hand was a shortage of fat in the European diet, which Hoover believed would lead to a nutritional disaster by 1919. The quickest way to get fat to Europeans was to supply it in the form of pork and lard, and Hoover set about to increase U.S. hog production by 15 percent. His first effort was to appeal to farmers' patriotism. A hog was as important to the war effort as a shell, one poster declared.

But the appeal to patriotism flew in the face of economic reality. Hog production in 1917 was in decline because of the high price of corn brought on by the war and an unusually poor crop. Corn sold on the Chicago market for

72 cents a bushel in September 1915; two years later the price of corn had been bid up to a record $2.10 a bushel. In order to achieve his goal of a 15 percent increase in hog production, H. A. Wallace argued in an editorial, hog farmers had to be assured a reasonable return on their investment.

Hoover read Wallace's editorial and concluded that it was correct. Exactly how to assure hog producers a profit, Hoover was not sure. So he turned to the Agriculture Department, which in turn looked to Harry Wallace's Corn Belt Meat Producers' Association for advice. Wallace suggested forming an advisory panel on hog production, and Hoover responded by creating the Swine Commission. The commission was headed by John M. Evvard, an animal husbandry professor at Iowa State and friend of the Wallaces. Harry Wallace was a member. Harry's son Henry signed on as the commission's statistician. For all practical purposes it was the Wallaces' Swine Commission.

H. A. Wallace quickly persuaded the commission that the best way to assure farmers a profit lay in linking the price of hogs to the raw commodity used to produce them—corn. He devised a complicated formula, establishing the historical ratio between the price of corn and the price of hogs, to give the government a "rough and ready" idea of the cost of producing hogs at any given time.

In late October the Swine Commission adopted the formula as its own and recommended that the government guarantee the price of hogs at a rate of return of at least 14.3 to 1—the price of 14.3 bushels of corn would equal 100 pounds of live hog—if it wanted to stimulated hog production.

Hoover was not enthusiastic. He didn't particularly like the ratio method, and he abhorred special-interest pleading. The idea of people profiting from the war effort—be they arms makers or hog farmers—revolted Hoover. Nevertheless, he needed fats and understood the logic of Henry A. Wallace's argument: patriotic or not, farmers eventually would respond to price in deciding how many hogs to produce. No profit, no hogs.

Hoover went partway. In early November he established the minimum price for hogs at 13 to 1 and announced the decision with a statement bound to raise suspicion:

> We will try to stabilize the price so that the farmer can count on getting for each 100 pounds of hog ready for market, thirteen times the average cost of corn fed into the hogs.
>
> Let there be no misunderstanding of this statement. It is not a guarantee backed by money. It is a statement of intention and policy of the Food Administration which means to do justice to the farmer.[12]

The Wallace family's great ambivalence toward war was never more apparent. The Wallaces were not philosophically pacifist, but the brutal combat in Europe—49,000 Americans killed in combat, another 230,000 wounded, and 57,000 dead of disease—sickened them. The war was rooted in European greed and nationalism, the Wallaces believed, and they detested that aspect of it. And war had an unfortunate tendency to bring out the deplorable tendencies in Americans. War profiteering was rampant; patriotic fervor often reached hateful levels. In Iowa, German-Americans were made to kiss the American flag in public and banned from speaking German in schools or even on the telephone. The only thing that made the war palatable to the Wallaces was Wilson's promise that it was a war to end war forever.

Moreover, the war posed a troubling personal problem for the Wallaces. The Selective Service Act, passed by Congress in May 1917, authorized the registration of all men between the ages of twenty-one and thirty (later expanded to forty-five). Henry A. Wallace registered for the draft on June 5, 1917, at age twenty-eight.

Clearly he was not eager to serve and could cite numerous reasons. He had a wife and young son who were dependent upon him.* He was still deeply involved in his farming operation. And his father, devoting increasing time to national YMCA activities, was relying heavily on H. A. to edit *Wallaces' Farmer*. On the last day of 1917, Henry A. Wallace filled out a Selective Serviced questionnaire asking to be exempted from the draft on three separate grounds, including his occupation and family status. He did not claim, as some critics later charged, to be a pacifist. Nor did he seek an exemption on grounds of health, as some family members later believed. He had been ill in 1915 with what he later thought was undulant fever, but at the end of 1917 he was to all appearances a vigorous 145-pound twenty-nine-year-old man.

In the end Des Moines Selective Service Local Board No. 1 placed Wallace in Class 3-J—necessary assistant, associate, or hired manager of a necessary agricultural enterprise—where he remained throughout the war. Henry Agard Wallace thus never wore the uniform of his country.

The Great War, which changed the lives of scores of millions, left him curiously untouched. He was not physically scarred or financially impaired; his views on politics, warfare, diplomacy, and democracy underwent no great change.

What was changing was all within him. He had begun to take the first steps of a long, intense, spiritual journey. What started him on this quest was known only to himself. The death of his grandfather may have had something

---

*The Wallace's first child, Henry Browne, was born September 8, 1915. A second son, Robert Browne, was born July 13, 1918. Their third and last child, Jean Browne, was born June 30, 1920.

to do with it. "Intellectually we cannot comprehend the Infinite," Uncle Henry warned in his will. "Religion is not a philosophy but a life, which ever tends toward harmony with the Divine."[13] Searching for such harmony, H. A. was no longer sure it was to be found in the Presbyterian Church of his youth. Intellectually he understood the church completely, but the "emotional experience" of a true religious life was missing.

The break came when H. A. began teaching William James's *Varieties of Religious Experiences* to his adult Sunday school class. It was, some of the church elders said, an inappropriate text for a Christian study group. Wallace did not argue, nor did he change his mind. He simply left the Presbyterian Church and never returned. He was on his own. For the next decade and a half, he explored the spiritual universe, sometimes to its outer reaches.

To anyone paying attention it was obvious by April 1918 that the government's corn-hog program was in trouble. The price of corn was sky-high in Chicago. With farmers acting in the mistaken belief that they were to be guaranteed a profit, hogs were being farrowed in record numbers. The actual price hogs brought on the Chicago market was $17.45 per hundredweight, which resulted in a loss to farmers of $5.73 per hundred pounds. Acutely aware of the situation, Harry Wallace insisted on action to increase hog prices and in reply got a curt letter saying there would be no change in the government's policy.

Wallace was livid. In increasingly fervent language the elder Wallace went to war with Hoover. He denounced the Food Administration's position as "illogical, unjust, and ridiculous." Hoover himself he derided as an "exceedingly big-brained business man" who should not make any more promises to farmers until he was prepared to carry them out. Hoover tried to make peace in a private letter to Harry Wallace, pleading that he had carried out his commitments "to the letter" under difficult circumstances. Harry replied bluntly that hog farmers needed profits, not carefully crafted words.[14]

Finally, in September 1918, Hoover abandoned the corn-hog ratio altogether and moved to establish hog prices at a flat $17.50 per hundredweight. This, he said, would be more fair to producers. The actual effect, H. A. Wallace rejoined, was to lower the ratio from 13 to 1 to 10.8 to 1, a level at which farmers were guaranteed a loss. Harry Wallace editorialized that farmers were the victims of "a straight confidence game."

Throughout 1919 and into 1920 Wallace continued to lambaste Hoover's effort "to bamboozle the farmers" and deny them a reasonable profit. "If we were asked to name one man who is more responsible than any other for starting the dissatisfaction which exists among the farmers of the country, we would instantly name Mr. Hoover," he wrote in February 1920.[15]

Hoover made more than one attempt to sue for peace with Wallace, but there was no peace. Hoover had inadvertently inflamed a fundamental character trait of the Wallace men: an uncompromising sense of righteousness. "Harry Wallace was a natural-born gamecock," said his friend Gifford Pinchot. "He was red-headed on his head and in his soul."[16]

The fight with Hoover led Harry Wallace to wage a bitter "anyone but Hoover" campaign to deny Hoover the 1920 Republican presidential nomination. "As a presidential candidate, no doubt he would be very satisfactory to the large business interests," Wallace wrote. "The farmers of the country, however, have already had enough experience with him to know that he is not the man they want in a position of power." The struggle over hog prices, H. A. Wallace wrote, illustrated "the extreme disadvantage under which farmers labor in bargaining with other classes of society."[17]

The response of the two Wallaces to this perceived disadvantage was in perfect character. Harry flew into action. His son wrote a book.

The elder Wallace launched a campaign to shake up the nation's "timid" land grant colleges and to establish a national agricultural research institution, funded by farmers themselves, that would provide unbiased scientific information to the grass roots. And he helped forge a new organization, the American Farm Bureau Federation, to put farmers on an equal footing with manufacturers and labor unions in dealing with other segments of the economy. The Farm Bureau quickly became one of the nation's most powerful agricultural voices.

H. A. Wallace's book *Agricultural Prices*, a 224-page study crammed with charts, graphs, and numbers, was a highly technical examination of farm commodity markets and pricing influences. Its seventh chapter was devoted to the fight with Hoover, although Hoover was never mentioned by name. Louis Bean, an outstanding statistician who worked for the Agriculture Department during the 1930s, called *Agricultural Prices* the first true econometric study published in the United States. At the time the book was written, Wallace later remarked, he thought "all economists dealt too much with economic theory" and believed that the truth ultimately was to be found in statistics.[18]

Wallace's central thesis was that farmers were ill served by the supply-and-demand system that determined the price they received for their products. Classical economists of the laissez-faire school defended the market system "as natural, as inevitable, and therefore desirable," but Wallace maintained that it put farmers at an inherent disadvantage.[19] Demand for food was inelastic, he observed, and farmers had no practical means of controlling supply.

"Of course," he added, "the law of supply and demand never has been repealed and never will be repealed. Instead of trying to repeal it, we should try to secure the best type of price-fixing machinery thru which this law may work. Man has not repealed the law of gravitation, but has devised such machines as automobiles, airplanes, etc., thru which he accomplishes his purposes notwithstanding."[20] Once farmers were disciplined enough to play their trump card—ultimate control of the food supply—other segments of society might "come to see the futility of sabotage as a price-sustaining force," Wallace wrote.

The profoundly radical nature of Wallace's argument owed something to the agrarian idealism of his grandfather, who harbored dark suspicions of businessmen and monied interests, and something to the writings of Thorstein Veblen, whose critique of unfettered capitalism formed the basis of the institutionalist school of economic thought. Wallace's first encounter with Veblen came in 1913, when he chanced upon *The Theory of the Leisure Class,* Veblen's scathing indictment of the idle rich. Once he had penetrated the heavy "protective coloration" of Veblen's prose—an almost indecipherable style devised "so he could hold on to his job," Wallace surmised—he was deeply impressed.[21]

The young editor met the economist twice and found him "a mousy kind of man . . . not a particularly attractive person." Nevertheless, he was dazzled by Veblen's brilliant mind. He was greatly influenced by Veblen's thinking on free trade, nationalism, and militarism. Veblen's books were among "the most powerful produced in the United States in this century," Wallace observed, adding that the economist was one of the few men of his time who truly "knew what was going on. [He] had a marked effect on my economic thinking."[22]

As the war staggered to a close in November 1918, most U.S. farmers were enjoying unprecedented prosperity. The Wallaces repeatedly insisted hard times lay ahead. H. A. made the case in historical and economic terms, arguing in prescient articles published in late 1918 and early 1919 that farmers were about to go over a cliff. A signed article entitled "Fundamental Land Values" examined the relation between commodity prices, land prices, and farmhand wages in Polk County, Iowa, over the preceding two decades and predicted that the speculative bubble was about to break. An unsigned article called "Farming Depression in England following the Napoleonic War" charted the rise in farm commodity prices in England from 1810 to 1813 and in America from 1915 to 1918 and foresaw disaster. Over and over, the Wallaces warned their readers to go slow, be careful, prepare for the worst. "Back down the ladder a rung at a time."

Most of their readers were not inclined to listen. There was no plan for agricultural reconversion to a peacetime economy, and hardly anyone seemed to care. Wilson was consumed by his campaign for the League of Nations, and after his near-fatal stroke in late September 1919 he was largely incapable of governing. Secretary of Agriculture David Houston, a man with strong ties to the Rockefellers and big business, dismissed the complaints of those who saw disaster on the horizon as "hysterical."

The 1920s began with America in the throes of a "Red scare" led by A. Mitchell Palmer, Wilson's ambitious attorney general. Even Harry Wallace was accused of harboring "Bolshevik" sympathies. The League of Nations lay crushed by the U.S. Senate, and the federal government was in confusion. As wartime economic controls lapsed, little thought was given to what would follow. Prohibition, which the Wallaces had always supported, began with the ratification of the Eighteenth Amendment, but its impact was hardly becalming.

The Wallaces were full of alarm. They took some comfort from the shift of David Houston to the Treasury Department and the appointment of the Des Moines publisher Edwin Meredith to head the Agriculture Department. Meredith, whose magazines included *Better Homes and Gardens* and *Successful Farming*, was a genuine Jeffersonian democrat and a personal friend of Harry Wallace.

Alas, Meredith's sad fate was to preside over one of the great calamities in the annals of agriculture. Farm income dropped from $16.9 billion in 1919 to $13 billion in 1920 and $8.9 billion in 1921. Farm exports during the same period slid from $4.1 billion to $1.8 billion. The price of corn, always a good indicator of midwestern prosperity, fell from $1.38 a bushel in 1919 to 67 cents in 1920 and 42 cents in 1921. The buying power of farmers, as measured by the parity index, fell by one-third.

As the farm crisis gained momentum, strident new voices arose offering rural voters rebottled populist remedies to cure their ills. The Wallaces—always progressive but never populist—were inexorably drawn to the political fray. Harry Wallace even entertained pleas that he run for governor of Iowa in 1920. Family tradition held him back, but when his friend Senator Albert B. Cummins faced a stiff primary challenge from a populist hellraiser named Smith Wildman Brookhart, the elder Wallace strode directly into the arena.

With Harry Wallace's help Cummins narrowly survived the challenge. Deeply grateful, Cummins and the state's junior senator, William S. Kenyon, recommended Wallace to the Republican presidential nominee, Warren G. Harding. "The best man I know of in the whole United States, with reference to [agriculture] is Mr. Henry Wallace," Kenyon wrote. "Wallace is a sturdy Scotchman, staunch, level-headed, and knows agricultural problems."[23] Harding took the advice. On July 26 Wallace accepted an invitation to meet with Harding at his home in Marion, Ohio.

Different as they were—and they were vastly different—Harding and Wallace developed a friendly rapport. For his part, Wallace regarded Harding as something of a blank slate upon which agricultural campaign policy could be written. In large measure he succeeded. He pressed hard for attention to agricultural issues during the campaign, suggested heavy reliance on the pro-agriculture plank in the Republican platform, and contributed the lion's share of Harding's major farm speech, delivered at the Minnesota State Fair in early September. Wallace personally wrote a flier called "Heart to Heart Talk to Farmers" and helped devise a newspaper advertisement attacking the Democrats' "unwise, unsympathetic agricultural policies."

In November, Harding and Calvin Coolidge smashed the Democratic ticket, the publisher James Cox and young Franklin D. Roosevelt, at the polls. The Republicans carried every state outside the Deep South. In the event of victory, Harding notified the farm editor three days before the election, "I shall very much want your assistance in making good the promises which we have made to the American people."[24]

Friends began congratulating Harry Wallace well before any cabinet appointments were announced. "I take it that you will be the next Secretary of Agriculture," Iowa State professor John Evvard wrote.[25] Virtually all of the major farm organizations backed him; only the Farmers' Union opposed him. Kenyon publicly declared that nothing would be so beneficial to the Republic as Wallace's selection. So certain did Wallace's appointment seem that Edwin Meredith wrote to offer his assistance in the transition. The *Des Moines Register* editorially commented that no one was more certain than Henry C. Wallace to sit in Harding's cabinet. It was all a bit embarrassing to Wallace. "The only thing I can do is grin a sickly grin and talk about something else," he wrote to his brother Dan.[26]

Few outside the Wallace family understood how truly reluctant he was to take the post. Harry still recalled the day he asked his own father why he had not pursued the chance to become secretary of agriculture. "No Wallace has ever held an office higher than Justice of the Peace, and I didn't want to mar the family record," Uncle Henry quipped. Deep within him, Harry felt his father was right. Gifford Pinchot, who was staying at the Wallaces' home when the formal offer to join the administration was received, said Harry nearly rejected it. "I urged him as strongly as I could to take the place, believing that in so doing lay the line of greatest usefulness," Pinchot recalled.[27]

Even Pinchot's entreaty might not have carried the day had Harry Wallace not had such confidence in his oldest son to carry on as editor of *Wallaces' Farmer*. Harry was far less sure of his brother John's ability to run the business end of the operation, but about his solemn, brilliant son, Harry had no doubts. He accepted Harding's offer.

A few days before his departure, the editorial page of *Wallaces' Farmer* again carried "A Word Personal" to its readers. It contained Henry C. Wallace's words of farewell. He explained his decision to accept the agriculture post, fretted about moving to a strange place, and praised the abilities of the new editor, his son.

"I will do the best I know," he promised.[28] With that Harry Wallace left his beloved Iowa, never to live there again.

Warren Harding's cabinet was a reflection of the Republican political landscape in the early 1920s. Big business ruled, but reformers in the tradition of Theodore Roosevelt were not insignificant. Such lions of the old order as Andrew Mellon and Charles Evans Hughes thus were seated beside progressives like Herbert Hoover and Henry Cantwell Wallace. Alongside these intelligent, principled men was an array of rogues and hacks the likes of which Washington had not seen in half a century. It was a recipe for disaster, especially since Harding, a man of modest intellect and a taste for earthly pleasures, had no particular views of his own.

The amiable president almost immediately was confronted with a dispute between Hoover and Wallace, who arrived in the cabinet spoiling for a fight. Hoover—the "Secretary of Commerce and the undersecretary of everything else," an observer joked—struck the first blow. In a letter to the head of a special congressional reorganization committee, Hoover suggested the Agriculture Department be stripped of all marketing functions, foreign and domestic. Wallace quickly retorted that Hoover's plan would reduce the department to a sort of glorified extension service, concerned only with helping farmers produce more crops so they could "sell them for what the buyer is willing to pay, and then go right back home and produce more as quickly as possible, taking no thought of the possible demand, nor of the price."[29]

Wallace saw Hoover's plan as a power grab. Hoover saw Wallace's reaction as turf protection. Wallace had gone the way of all bureaucratic flesh, Hoover complained.

Wallace had little trouble fending off Hoover's proposal. He had come to Washington with broad support from the agrarian establishment. It could be counted upon to back him in a fight. His power on Capitol Hill was greatly enhanced by the growing ranks of the American Farm Bureau Federation. By 1920, only a year after Harry Wallace had helped give it birth in Chicago, the Farm Bureau stood as the nation's largest farm organization. It had more than a million members, twice as many as the long-established National Grange, including 100,000 in Iowa alone.

The Farm Bureau's influence lay not only in numbers. Late in 1920 Wallace met with Senator William Kenyon and five Iowa congressmen in the Farm Bureau's Des Moines office and devised a tactic that greatly expanded the organization's clout in Washington. The congressmen agreed to address agricultural issues in a nonpartisan manner, voting whenever possible as a unit. So was born the "Farm Bloc." Within a year, some twenty senators were meeting regularly in the offices of Gray Silver ("the Silver Eel"), the organization's aggressive Washington lobbyist, to discuss strategy.

Hoover abhored the Farm Bloc as an expression of special interest. Harding distrusted it as insufficiently loyal to the Republican Party. The handmaidens of big business in Congress suggested it was illegal, or should be made so. But there was no denying the Farm Bloc's clout or the authority it implicitly provided to Wallace. What Harry Wallace did not have, yet, was a scheme to lift farmers out of the economic depression engulfing them.

In Des Moines his son offered a solution. "Less Corn, More Clover, More Money," was H. A. Wallace's slogan. Week after week he told farmers they should take 10 percent of their land out of corn production and cover it with a nitrogen-building legume such as clover. The resulting drop in supply would increase prices and enrich both farmers and their land, he said. "After everything has been taken into account, the fact remains that we have far more corn than we need," he wrote.[30] Few farmers took his words to heart, however. Farmers did what they thought was necessary to stay in business, and most of them thought that meant planting more corn.

H. A. tried another idea. If tariffs on imported goods were reduced or eliminated, he reasoned, manufacturers would be forced into real competition and the price of goods purchased by farmers would decline. He published figures showing that the cost of clothing, fuel, furniture, and other items was as much as 200 percent above 1913 levels, while the price of corn was 4 percent higher and the price of hogs 3 percent lower. He was no less critical of the price of labor. "The farmer's wage as measured by the prices of his crops are a third less than during the five-year period, 1911–1914," he wrote. "The working man's wages are from seventy-five to one hundred percent higher. . . ."[31]

Here the young editor ran headlong into political reality. The GOP was not about to forsake the high tariffs that protected big business, and organized labor certainly would not relinquish its payroll gains. The younger Wallace applauded the United States Steel Corporation for "courageously" bringing wages down to a level 50 percent above prewar levels, but few companies followed its lead.

As months went by with no improvement in the farm economy, Wallace explored other approaches. He suggested the Federal Reserve adopt a policy of mild inflation. He endorsed Charles Evans Hughes's disarmament plan, saying it would lower government expenditures and reduce the impulse of governments to make war in order to protect foreign investments. He called for construction of the St. Lawrence Waterway as a way to reduce freight rates. He asked for lower interest rates and strongly backed the Yale professor Irving Fisher's proposal for monetary reform.*

Another idea dear to H. A.'s heart was his plan for a government-operated storage system to smooth out the feast-or-famine cycle that had plagued farmers for centuries. He had first sketched out the idea in 1912, when he dubbed it the Joseph Plan. In the Book of Genesis, Joseph was said to have stored up the surplus crops of Egypt during seven good years and released them during seven years of drought. Farmers and consumers alike thus benefited. "Joseph was one of the earliest economic statesmen in history," Wallace remarked.[32]

Three years later Wallace discovered a book in the Des Moines Public Library entitled *Economic Principles of Confucius and His School,* by a Columbia University doctoral candidate named Chen Huan-chang. The book described a grain storage system established in China in 54 B.C. "When the price of grain was low, [the province] should buy it at the normal price, higher than the market price, in order to profit the farmers," Chan wrote. "When the price was high, they should sell it at the normal price, lower than the market price, in order to profit the consumers. Such a granary was called 'constantly normal granary.' "[33] The granary system survived in various forms for fourteen hundred years.

By the early 1920s Wallace had coined his own term for the grain storage plan. He called it "the ever-normal granary." "If any government shall ever do anything really worth while with our food problem," he wrote, "it will be by perfecting the plan tried by the Chinese [two thousand] years ago; that is, by building warehouses and storing food in years of abundance and holding it until the years of scarcity."[34]

Wallace's dream of an ever-normal granary would have to wait another fifteen years before being realized. None of the ideas bubbling out of the young Iowa editor caught hold. The harsh realities of farm life, meanwhile, only grew worse.

*Fisher advocated government manipulation of the gold content of the dollar so as to achieve a "dollar of constant purchasing power." His plan was similar to the "commodity dollar" proposed earlier by the Cornell University professor George F. Warren. In 1921 Wallace agreed to serve as vice president of the Stable Money League, an organization formed to promote Fisher's idea, and he remained heavily involved in the movement throughout the 1920s. The organization included many prominent economists and for several years was headed by Franklin Delano, uncle of Franklin Delano Roosevelt.

In the Mississippi River town of Moline, Illinois, a tall, intense plow manufacturer named George N. Peek had his own idea. At age forty-seven Peek had spent most of his adult life in the farm implement business; the only exception came during the war, when he worked for Bernard Baruch at the War Industries Board. There he met General Hugh Johnson, a brilliant, flamboyant man who would be Peek's on-and-off friend and enemy for two decades.

In 1921 they were friends. Together they had taken over the foundering Moline Plow Company, only to discover how devastating the crash of 1920 had been to agriculture. Peek put the problem baldly: "You can't sell a plow to a busted customer."[35]

Peek and Johnson decided if they wanted to save their company they had to save agriculture. Together they devised a plan and published it in a brief pamphlet entitled *Equality for Agriculture*. Their proposal became the heart of a monumental, decade-long fight to obtain a "fair exchange value" for farm products and profoundly affected the public careers of Harry Wallace and his son.

In essence Peek and Johnson proposed a scheme to dump agricultural surpluses on foreign markets. The idea was to establish a government-run export corporation, buy up farm commodities not needed for domestic consumption, and sell them overseas at a loss. High tariffs on agricultural imports would prevent foreign competitors from retaliating.

The idea of subsidizing exports, mercantilism, was not new, but Peek and Johnson also suggested a way to pay for it. They proposed an "equalization fee" to be paid by farmers participating in the program. The money raised by the fee would repay the export corporation for its losses. Therefore, they argued, the export plan would cost taxpayers nothing; farmers would recoup the cost of the equalization fee in the higher price of farm products. Consumers would have to pay more for food, of course, but the same was true of manufactured goods protected by high tariffs.

At the four-story brick-and-brownstone headquarters of *Wallaces' Farmer*, H. A. Wallace was quick to see the Peek-Johnson plan's benefits—and its flaw. Its most attractive feature was that farm income would go up. Tariff walls, which Wallace inherently disliked, would remain in place, but at least the Peek-Johnson plan would allow farmers to enjoy the spoils. But the flaw in the plan was real and troublesome to Wallace. The plan did nothing to curtail production. Already too much land was in production; too much soil was being destroyed to grow corn that nobody needed.

In his large second-floor office overlooking Independence Avenue in the nation's capital, Harry Wallace searched for a means to halt the farm economy's free fall. Farmland values had collapsed in half. By November 1921 farm purchasing power had slipped to 63 percent of its prewar level. Wallace was a doer, not a brooder, and he was itching to do something. Unfortunately, the Harding administration inclined to doing nothing.

Wallace concluded that his only hope was to enlist the aid of Harding himself. Harding was no activist; his approach was to let things be and hope for the best. He had the virtue of wanting to be everyone's friend, however, and Harry Wallace set out to be his friend. They played golf and bridge together and, Prohibition notwithstanding, enjoyed an occasional glass of bourbon. To Harding the secretary was plain old "Hank." There was nothing showy about Harry Wallace, none of Mellon's wealthy pretensions or Hoover's high-collar starchiness. Harry could tell a salty story at the expense of Scotchmen and make the president laugh out loud.

What was needed, Harry told the president, was an agricultural conference, a gathering of leaders from across the nation to discuss what was ailing the farmer. Of course, Harry Wallace knew what was ailing farmers: overproduction. The real purpose of a national conference, in his mind, was to put some much needed political pressure on the White House.

Harding was reluctant. Hoover and Mellon offered up visions of agrarian rabble-rousers hell-bent on vengeance against the Harding administration. But Harry Wallace eventually carried the day. "He sold Harding on his approach on many things just simply by playing Harding's own game, which was the game of being a good fellow," Henry A. Wallace observed years later. "Father could do that. I could never have done it, but Father did it. . . ."[36]

Wallace's six-day National Agriculture Conference opened in Washington on January 22, 1922, attended by 336 delegates from thirty-seven states. Twenty farm organizations were represented along with scholars, economists, editors, businessmen, and 80 actual farmers. Samuel Gompers personally represented labor. Peek and Johnson were there with their plan. So, too, was Henry A. Wallace.

The conference was a victory for principled progressivism. "The old-time correctives did not meet the situation," Henry A. Wallace wrote of the conference. "Bimetallism, trust-busting, railroad-baiting, were beside the point. [The key participants in the conference] wanted to do something about agriculture itself. They wanted—quite unwittingly—to modify the farmer's rugged individualism for his own good."[37]

As far as H. A. was concerned, the conference was a bit too controlled. He had wanted full-blown discussions of the tariff and monetary policy, but Harry Wallace rejected the idea. And he cashiered H. A.'s recommendation that Thorstein Veblen be invited to speak. Instead, the conference heard a soothing pep talk from Harding himself, in which the president acknowledged the "grim reality" of the farm crisis but said the only answer lay in giving "the farmer the chance to organize and help himself."[38]

The farm conference teemed with suggestions for government action, ranging from placement of a farmer representative on the Federal Reserve Board to federal regulation of the meatpacking industry. Tucked into one of the committee reports was the crux of the Peek-Johnson plan: a call for the federal government to "reestablish a fair exchange value for all farm products with that of other commodities."[39] The most intriguing plan, in Henry A. Wallace's view, was the University of Wisconsin professor Richard T. Ely's proposal for a national land use policy. A planned program of land utilization, Ely argued, would assure "prosperity for all economic groups," albeit at some cost to individual liberty.[40]

The time was not right for Ely's vision, however. There was too much that couldn't be done, too many things that couldn't be talked about in Warren Harding's world, H. A. thought as he went home. His father, his high-minded, hardworking father, was thwarted on too many fronts. H. A. returned to his little office in Des Moines and brooded. That chilly week in Washington, Wallace said years later, surely marked the beginning of his long, slow turn away from the Republican Party.

George Peek, on the other hand, settled into his quarters at the Shoreham Hotel and started peddling his farm plan to anyone who would listen. He cornered congressmen and badgered bureaucrats and pressed for a second conference devoted entirely to his fair-ratio plan. "I have known few men so determined and so little deterred by setbacks as George Peek in his long battle for the farmer," H. A. wrote.[41] One of Peek's first converts was Secretary of Agriculture Henry C. Wallace.

The problem lay in selling the farm plan to the president. Overburdened by the tasks of his office, perpetually anxious about the health of his wife, Florence, distracted by feuds and scandals within his administration, Harding was ill equipped to rise to a new challenge. Besides, the 1922 midterm elections were fast approaching, and Harding's main goal was to see the Republicans through them safely. Harry Wallace would have to bide his time.

Secretary Wallace knew as well as anyone how much trouble Republicans were in among farmers, but he loyally answered Harding's call for help. He appeared widely across the Farm Belt, defending the administration's record and pointing to such progressive advances as the Packers and Stockyard Act and the Grain Futures Act. At the same time Wallace missed no opportunity to warn farmers about the danger of overproduction.

The election proved bad news for Republicans, dramatically cutting GOP majorities in both the House and the Senate. Ironically Wallace's own hand was strengthened. Farm Belt conservatives were overwhelmed by progressives and populists of both parties. Even staid Iowa, less given to pitchfork politics than its neighbors, elected the firebrand Smith W. Brookhart to the U.S. Senate, a stern rebuke to the state's Republican regulars.

As far as Henry C. Wallace was concerned, the time had come to act.

By mid-1923 the industrial sector was booming—and wheat was selling for less than half its wartime price. Farm foreclosures were growing. The steady migration from farm to city continued unabated. Herbert Hoover and others maintained that the worst was over, that an expansion of credit was the only thing needed to tide farmers through the crisis, but Harry Wallace believed such policies only made matters worse. Farmers needed more than "an opportunity to go further into debt," he said.

Some form of government export corporation was needed to save the day, Wallace concluded, and he began pushing his closest lieutenants to gird for the fight. Henry C. Taylor, head of the department's newly created economics bureau, was dispatched to amass statistical support. Charles Brand, former chief of the department's marketing division was enlisted to draft legislation. Wallace's thirty-four-year-old son was pressed for editorial backing. H. A. Wallace's instincts favored internationalism—indeed, he was chairman of the League of Nations Society in Iowa—but slowly he came to accept his father's view.

Outside of his department, however, Wallace found few allies in the Harding administration. Hoover was again urging legislation to strip the Agriculture Department of its marketing functions, and the Interior Department continued its push for control of the Forest Service. The fight with Hoover turned intensely personal. Wallace referred, through tight lips, to "that man Hoover." The commerce secretary saw Wallace as "a dour Scotsman with a temperament inherited from some ancestor who had been touched by exposure to infant damnation and predestination."

Wallace was sustained by the belief that he would have Harding's support in the end. But the president—confused, demoralized, worried beyond measure by the scandals surrounding him—still was in no condition to think about the farm crisis. The president's weight had ballooned to 240 pounds, and his normally handsome face had a haunted, haggard look. He suffered insomnia, chest pains, periodic faintness.

Worried doctors prescribed rest, and Harding decided to take a leisurely train ride west, followed by a boat trip to Alaska. On June 20, 1923, the beleaguered president set off aboard a train dubbed the Superb, accompanied by a small army of aides, poker pals, reporters, and hangers-on. In Denver the party was joined, at Harding's request, by Harry and May Wallace.

Wallace spent hours with the president, playing bridge, joshing, counseling. The impact became apparent in Seattle, when Harding gave a speech on conservation siding with the agriculture secretary on virtually every issue. The party sailed northward, with Harding insisting on playing bridge almost nonstop. "There were only four other bridge players in the party, and we soon set up shifts so that one at a time we had some relief," Herbert Hoover remembered. "For some reason I developed a distaste for bridge on this journey and never played again."[42]

Harding's condition did not improve. In Vancouver, Harding delivered a faltering speech during which he dropped his text and gripped the podium. Dr. Charles Sawyer, the president's physician, announced he was suffering from tainted seafood, but a young naval surgeon, Dr. Joel Boone, was convinced the president had heart failure. A scheduled appearance in Portland was canceled. By August 2 Harding was in San Francisco, where, although bedridden, he was said to be improving. Early that evening, shortly after his wife finished reading to Harding a magazine article about himself entitled "A Calm View of a Calm Man," the president slumped silent.

Harry Wallace had just finished ordering dinner in his room when a Secret Service agent summoned him upstairs to the president's side. Hoover, Sawyer and several others were there, trying to revive the president while his wife sobbed "Wurr'n, Wurr'n." "We worked for a little time before giving up," Harry wrote his family.[43]

The nation genuinely mourned Harding's death. At the moment of his passing, he was one of America's most popular presidents. Harry and May rode the train bearing Harding's casket on the long trip back to Washington. "Day and night we pass through groups of people with heads uncovered as the train passes," Harry wrote his children in Des Moines. "There is a tremendous emotional appeal in the sight."[44]

Harry Wallace knew how much had been lost. Harding had begun the journey "not at all in sympathy with my views," Harry wrote. "He had been poisoned by a lot of misinformation. The further we went, the more clearly he saw that he had been fooled."[45] Now the presidency had passed to Calvin Coolidge, a tight-lipped New Englander with whom Wallace had no rapport. Whatever hope Wallace had of getting the Republican administration to back farm relief died in San Francisco.

With the odds stacked hopelessly against him, the secretary behaved in true Wallace fashion. He threw himself furiously into the fight. On September 25, 1923, he told the cabinet he intended to support the export-dumping plan and soon thereafter made his position public. Coolidge ignored Wallace; Hoover was furious. Wallace "was in truth a fascist, but did not know it, when he proposed his price- and distribution-fixing legislation," Hoover wrote.[46]

By November, Wallace had lined up Senator Charles McNary of Oregon and Representative Gilbert Haugen of Iowa to serve as the chief sponsors of the export corporation plan. The battle was on. Within days President Coolidge denounced the bill in biting terms. "No complicated scheme of relief, no plan for Government fixing of prices, no resort to the Public Treasury will be of any permanent value in establishing agriculture," he told the newly elected Congress.[47] Henry A. Wallace responded with an editorial campaign in support of the export plan and persuaded the Iowa Farm Bureau to endorse the measure at its state convention.

The Wallaces were in open warfare with the administration. Reports abounded that the secretary would resign or be fired. A popular rumor in Iowa had it that Harry Wallace would return to run for the governorship or the U.S. Senate. But Wallace didn't budge, and Coolidge was reluctant to fire a man so popular with farmers, at a time when the presidential election was less than a year away. The president contented himself with small humiliations, such as putting Hoover in charge of a one-day agriculture conference.

Introduction of the McNary-Haugen bill touched off a furious six-month battle. The National Chamber of Commerce, the bankers, and the grain processors and handlers lined up against it. The House Agriculture Committee received more than ten thousand endorsements of it. Harry Wallace personally testified in its favor. In the pages of *Wallaces' Farmer*, H. A. Wallace waged a relentless campaign to set off a "prairie fire" of enthusiasm for McNary-Haugen. It was not enough. After a month of spirited debate, the House voted 223 to 154 in June to defeat McNary-Haugen.

Keenly disappointed and knowing his days at the Agriculture Department were near an end, Harry Wallace decided to make his case in a book. Its thesis was stated in the title: *Our Debt and Duty to the Farmer.* No doubt thinking of Hoover, Wallace scathingly attacked men "willing to entertain a feeling of sympathy for farmers who are having a hard time, provided that sympathy costs them nothing and further provided that they are not asked to cease worshiping at the shrine of laissez-faire."[48] Half measures and voluntary cooperation would not solve the farm crisis, he said, any more than a man suffering from sciatica would find permanent relief in "hot fomentations and . . . medicines which stimulate the organs of elimination."[49]

Sciatica was much on Harry Wallace's mind. He had suffered periodic bouts of it for years. By late summer he was in agony. Accustomed to being in his office from 7 A.M. to 10 P.M., Wallace found it impossible to sit at his desk for more than two or three hours. Increasingly he remained in his apartment at the Mayflower Hotel, working on his book while propped up in bed. At night he could sleep no more than two hours at a time. Doctors pumped novocaine into the base of his spinal cord, which helped relieve the terrible pain in his legs, but his overall condition did not improve.

In early October, with nine of the book's eleven chapters complete, Wallace's doctors concluded that his problem stemmed from a severe typhoid attack he had suffered while in college and recommended removal of his gall bladder. "After four weeks of a good deal of misery," he wrote H. A. in October, "it seems that I have got to lose a part of my anatomy."[50]

The operation, conducted on October 15 at the naval hospital, was deemed a success. Wallace began recuperating. In a few days he was conducting bits of routine business and even instructed aides to deny a rumor he was about to resign. Suddenly on Friday, October 24 Wallace took a turn for the worse. Joel Boone, his surgeon, diagnosed the problem as toxemic poisoning but believed it could be treated.

By Saturday, October 25, 1924, Wallace's condition was truly grave. Shortly after whispering a few words indicating confidence in his doctors, Wallace fell unconscious. At noon Boone said the secretary's condition "could hardly be more unfavorable."[51] May Wallace wired her sons in Iowa. Henry, Jim, and their uncle John immediately boarded a train in Des Moines, but they had not reached the Mississippi River when word reached them of Harry's death. He died at 4 P.M. with May and his youngest child, Ruth, at his side. He was fifty-eight.

Late that afternoon Coolidge and his wife went to the Mayflower to offer condolences and assure May Wallace that the secretary was to have a big state funeral in the White House. It was not what May wanted. Her husband, she believed, was a martyr to the cause of agriculture. She longed only to return him to the soil of Iowa, but she knew Washington would have its way.

H. A. and Jim left the train at Columbus, Ohio, and flew to Washington on an army transport plane provided by Coolidge. Shocked and anguished, the family reacted bitterly to tributes being heaped upon Wallace by his foes. Coolidge praised the "splendid series of successes" achieved by Wallace in "the restoration and rehabilitation of this supremely important national interest." In Denver, Hoover declared the death "a great blow to the administration."[52] Privately Henry A. Wallace said Hoover was the main cause of his father's death.

The funeral service in the East Room was everything Henry C. Wallace would have disliked. Attended by members of the cabinet, the Congress, the Supreme Court, and the diplomatic corps, it was an ornately formal affair. A spit-and-polish military guard stood by the black casket, atop which was an elaborate wreath of carnations and roses from the Coolidges. Almost unnoticed was the little wreath of pansies, the flower May Wallace had used to teach her young son about crossbreeding, which May put at the foot of the bier.

Wallace's top aides were stunned and motionless. "As we sat in the East Room listening to the funeral service," said Henry Taylor, "there was little consolation in the thought that Wallace was again welcome in the White House." But, Taylor added, "consolation came two days later at Des Moines, when thousands of people from all over the state and beyond marched solemnly by the casket under the dome of the Iowa Capital, bearing silent testimony that the spirit of Henry C. Wallace yet lives and will continue to live in and through the lives of his followers."[53] At the time of his death, the *New York Times* commented, it was said that Harry Wallace could call more farmers by their first names than any other man in America.

From the Capitol the Wallace family brought the body home to Mayswood, to have the sort of quiet funeral they wanted. As the ceremony began at 2 P.M., the city of Des Moines paused for a moment of silence. He was buried near his father at Woodland Cemetery.

Henry A. Wallace returned to his office and gravely spoke into his Dictaphone the words that would appear in the next edition of *Wallaces' Farmer*. "The fight for agricultural equality will go on; so will the battle for a stable price level, for controlled production, for better rural schools and churches, for larger income and higher standards of living for the working farmers, for the checking of speculation in farm lands, for the thousand and one things that are needed to make the sort of rural civilization he labored for and hoped to see. He died with his armor on in the fight for the cause which he loved."[54]

CHAPTER FOUR

"A REVOLUTION . . . IS COMING."

Two decades had passed since Perry G. Holden, the great "Corn Professor," gave a high school junior named Henry A. Wallace several dozen ears of corn to plant and predicted with "an air of great finality" which would yield best. The boy needed only a year, a horse, and a Planet Junior cultivator to prove Holden wrong. The professor, as Wallace later remarked, "didn't really know anything about the relative yielding power of the different ears."[1]

Not much had changed for corn farmers in the intervening years, however. Seed was still hand-selected from the farmer's own crop. Great preference was still given to the uniform, cylindrical ears favored by corn show judges, and Reid yellow dent remained the most popular variety. Corn was still pollinated by the breeze, still harvested by hand. In the early 1920s corn farmers yielded an average of less than thirty bushels per acre, roughly the same as in the year of Wallace's birth.

But a new day was dawning. Within a matter of years corn farming would be transformed. Agriculture, guided for centuries by instinct and superstition, would henceforth be ruled by science. Corn yields would skyrocket, and huge machines would do the harvesting. The breathtaking change wrought in midwestern cornfields eventually would sweep across the world, encompassing not only corn but wheat and rice and soybeans and chickens.

Only a handful of men in 1924 understood what was about to happen. Foremost among them was Henry A. Wallace. He was the prophet and evangelist, the teacher and preacher of agricultural scientific advancement. "A revolution in corn breeding is coming which will affect every man, woman and child in the corn belt within 20 years," he wrote in the mid-1920s. "Our systems of farm management will be changed somewhat and it is even possible that both domestic policies and the foreign relations of the United States will be somewhat influenced."

In retrospect, Wallace looked upon this prediction and added, "How careful and over-conservative I was!"[2]

The revolution did not begin with Wallace or even in the Corn Belt. It began on the shores of Long Island Sound, where two men, quite unaware of each other, began conducting experiments with corn at about the same time Young Henry was putting Professor Holden's show corn theory to the test. One was George Harrison Shull, a quiet, bearded biologist at the Carnegie Institution Station for Experimental Evolution at Cold Spring Harbor, on Long Island. The other was Edward East, a chemist at the Connecticut Agricultural Station's experimental farm.

Both men sought to learn more about Charles Darwin's theory of evolution by finding out what happened when the process of cross-selection was thrown into reverse. By marrying the corn plant to itself, Shull and East demonstrated that inbred plants were markedly less vigorous. When the process of inbreeding was continued for a second and third generation, they noticed also that inbred plants displayed marked characteristics that remained constant from one generation to the next. Stunted inbred plants produced stunted offspring; starchy plants produced starchy offspring. Through inbreeding they had established "pure lines" of corn and, in the process, unwittingly rediscovered the genetic laws of Gregor Mendel.

When these inbred lines were in turn crossbred, the result was an explosion of hybrid vigor. But that was as far as Shull and East could go. The lush results of hybridization lasted only one generation. When the seeds from the hybrids were planted, yields began to drop dramatically. Henry Wallace, still a student at Iowa State, followed these experiments with rapt interest, but he could see no practical consequences. "I remember talking over their results with one of the men at Ames in 1910 and reaching the conclusion that the whole approach was probably impractical because of the difficulty of doing the hand-pollinating work," he said.[3]

Three years later Wallace tried his own hand at inbreeding. His tiny cornfield—"not more than ten by twenty"—was located in the backyard of Mayswood, the spacious Colonial brick house Harry Wallace built in 1912. Again he "reached the conclusion that the process was too laborious."[4]

Wallace fell back to crossing established varieties of corn. He corresponded with corn breeders across the United States, bought or begged their seed, crossed it, and crossed it again. "I still have a distinct recollection of Henry standing out in his corn patch before breakfast, reading the morning paper but also carefully looking over and communing with his corn," his brother Jim recalled.[5] When his enthusiasm outgrew the backyard garden, he obtained the use of five weed-infested acres of bottomland along nearby Walnut Creek. At one point he had some three hundred varieties of corn in the ground.

His experiments almost always ended in frustration. Two varieties might be crossed with spectacular result, but when the same plants were crossed the next year the offspring were often dismal. There was no consistency. "As a result of hard experience, my mind was forced to accept the conclusion that varieties might be uniform with respect to outward appearance and at the same time be tremendously variable with regard to genetic characteristics having to do with yield," Wallace said. In short, only pure lines gave predictable results. "By 1919, I had been driven completely into the arms of the East and Shull doctrines."[6]

At that moment Edward East appeared, quite literally, at Wallace's door. East had left the Connecticut experiment station for a professorship at Harvard, but he remained passionately interested in corn. He had come to Des Moines to persuade the talented young corn breeder to start a commercial seed company in eastern Illinois. Wallace wasn't attracted to the idea, but he was very interested in a paper the professor brought with him by Donald Jones, one of East's protégés at the Connecticut Agricultural Station.

Jones had carried inbreeding and crossbreeding one vital step further. He had inbred a line of Leaming corn, a popular midwestern variety, and produced a hybrid with good results. He also inbred a variety called Burr and produced another hybrid. Then he crossed the two hybrids. The resulting grandchild of this "double cross" was a hybrid of splendid vigor.

The scales fell from Wallace's eyes. He recognized at once the vast implications of Jones's experiment. With the double cross it would be possible to maintain pure lines and at the same time produce enough seed to make hybridization commercially feasible.

From the tiny universe of men who had experimented with inbreeding, Wallace began seeking what seed was available. His first pure-line cross was made in 1919 from inbreds supplied by the scientists in Nebraska and Connecticut. The result was a dwarfed ear of undistinguished appearance in which Wallace had total confidence.

Thereafter Wallace missed no opportunity to tout the glories of hybrid corn. Virtually every issue of *Wallaces' Farmer* had a reference to the importance of hybridization. He delighted in haunting the corn shows, showing up with one of his odd-looking nubbins, telling old-timers that his little ear would outproduce their beauteous monsters. Most of his readers had little idea what he was driving at, but Wallace was unfazed. "My grandfather used to tell me that you have to talk about a new idea to farmers for at least seven years before it begins to take hold," Wallace said. "So I kept it up year after year, issue after issue. . . ."[7]

To help establish the superior value of hybrid corn, Wallace and the Iowa State agronomist H. D. Hughes in 1920 established the Iowa Corn Yield Test, a statewide contest to determine which farmer had corn with the highest yield rather than the prettiest ears. The first such statewide contest ever held, it proved to be the death knell for corn shows. The contest, said Wallace, "did as much as any single force to demonstrate to Iowa farmers the worthwhileness of hybrid corn."[8]

Still trying to amass enough pure-line seed to serve as parent stock for his hybrids, Wallace didn't enter the 1920 corn yield contest. But he was literally planting the seeds of his future success. Early that year a scientist at the U.S. Department of Agriculture gave Wallace a few precious seeds of a corn plant from China called Bloody Butcher, distinctive for the reddish color of its pericarp Wallace promptly began inbreeding it.

Pressed for space as well as time, Wallace gradually shifted his breeding work to forty acres of sandy farmland his wife owned near Johnston, a few miles northwest of Des Moines, and some adjoining property purchased by his father. On Sunday afternoons it was his custom to drive with Ilo and their children to one of the farms where they would picnic and inspect the corn.

By 1921 Wallace had enough hybrid corn to enter the state corn yield contest. His yields were respectable but well back of the open-pollinated corn submitted by other farmers. Undeterred, he returned in 1922 with a new hybrid, an odd-looking reddish ear that was a single cross between Bloody Butcher and the Burr-Leaming inbreds he had obtained from Jones in Connecticut. He called it Copper Cross. Again Wallace finished behind the best of the open-pollinated varieties. But he was gaining, and he knew it. Other hybrids were starting to appear, too. For Wallace it was a supremely exciting period.

When the 1923 corn yield test was laid out under the big arched roof of the Iowa State armory, Wallace drove up to see it with George Kurtzweil, who worked for the Iowa Seed Company in Des Moines. As they wandered through the exhibit, with Wallace expounding happily on the virtues of hybrid corn, Kurtzweil suddenly interjected, "This is all very interesting, Henry, but what I want to know is when can we begin selling the seed?"

"Which one of the hybrids you see here would you like to sell?" Wallace asked without pause.[9]

Kurtzweil picked Copper Cross. Its distinctive color would tell farmers there was something different about it, Kurtzweil reasoned, even if they didn't know what. Copper Cross didn't win the 1923 test, but Kurtzweil was convinced he could sell it. That year Kurtzweil and Wallace signed a contract—the first contract for hybrid seed production ever drawn—giving Kurtzweil exclusive rights to grow and sell Copper Cross in exchange for a royalty paid to Wallace.

Kurtzweil produced the nation's first commercial hybrid seed corn crop on a single acre of his father's little farm east of Des Moines. When detassling time came, Kurtzweil's sister, Ruth, a schoolteacher home from her job in Puerto Rico, was pressed into service. In later years she delighted in telling her students that she had once single-handedly detassled all of the commercial hybrid corn grown in Iowa.

Meanwhile, Wallace and Earl N. Bressman, a graduate student at Iowa State, collaborated to write a popular textbook on corn. *Corn and Corn Growing*, a practical guide "written in the language of the farm," covered everything from botany and breeding to marketing and sales.[10] Widely used by colleges and extension services, the book went through five editions, the last appearing in 1949.

Somehow he also found time that year to be a part-time professor. Having told Iowa State professors for years that they needed to know something about statistics in order to evaluate their experiments, Wallace accepted an invitation to lecture on the subject. For ten Saturdays in the early spring, Wallace drove to Ames to teach a class of twenty professors and postgraduate students about the mysteries of independent variables, regression lines, and correlation coefficients. Often he lugged along a key-driven calculating machine borrowed from an insurance company in Des Moines.

The first problem he assigned had to do with the relation between height, weight, the girth of the waist, and the girth of the chest. The raw data came from his students' own bodies. "It's my observation that to hold the attention of post-graduates and professors you have to use more dramatic methods than you do with undergraduates," said Wallace. "Their intelligence is perhaps not quite as pliable as that of younger people. This did awaken their interest."[11]

Later he assigned the class a problem concerning the relation between farmland values and corn yield per acre in Iowa's ninety-nine counties. Subsequently he used the same problem as the basis for a short book entitled *Correlation and Machine Calculation*, co-authored with George Snedecor, a young mathematics professor at Iowa State. The volume was issued by Iowa State in 1925 and revised and reissued in 1931. "Both editions, but especially the first, were models of lucid writing and were widely influential," Iowa State professor Jay Lush wrote. Many researchers kept a copy of it on their desks for years as "an indispensable manual" on statistics.*[12]

In 1924 everything came together. Copper Cross demolished its competitors in the Iowa Corn Yield Test and was awarded a gold medal. It was the first hybrid to win the contest, and Kurtzweil was poised to make the most of it. "COPPER CROSS—An Astonishing Product—Produces Astonishing Results," said the Iowa Seed Company catalog. " . . . If you try it this year you will be among the first to experiment with this new departure, which will eventually increase the corn production of the U.S. by millions of bushels."[13] The excited copy, personally written by H. A. Wallace, worked as intended. Kurtzweil sold all fifteen bushels of Copper Cross he produced for the incredible price of $1.00 per pound. Kurtzweil's sale of Copper Cross seed brought in only $840, but the revolution had begun.

Two weeks after Harry Wallace's death, H. A. Wallace strode to the polls and cast a quiet protest against the political party of his father and grandfather. The Republican Party was consumed by big money and big business, in Wallace's view. President Calvin Coolidge was a man coldly indifferent to the agrarian cause. And the Democratic presidential candidate, the prominent lawyer John W. Davis, was no less a friend of Wall Street than Coolidge. H. A. opted for the third-party candidacy of Senator Robert La Follette, the "Little Giant of the West," who had spent a tempestuous lifetime battling for farmers and progressive causes.

It was a futile vote, and Wallace knew it. Coolidge won the election with 15.7 million votes, an outcome he attributed to "Divine Providence." Davis ran far back with 8.4 million votes. La Follette received 4.8 million votes and carried only his home state of Wisconsin.

Young Henry Wallace—thirty-six years old but still "Young Henry" to many Iowans—was now left to carry the family cause alone. The first order of business was to complete his father's unfinished book. In collaboration with Nils Olsen, a young Agriculture Department economist, H. A. wrote the final chapter of *Our Debt and Duty to the Farmer*. "The waste and distress resulting from the agricultural depression have forcibly shown the need for a sound long-term policy for the development of our agriculture," H. A. wrote

*As a result of Wallace's lectures, Snedecor began helping the college's researchers analyze data. In 1927 Snedecor established the Mathematics Statistical Service, later renamed the Statistical Laboratory, which over time gained national distinction as the leading biometric research facility in the land grant system.

in his father's name. "The welfare of millions of our people must not again be placed in jeopardy."[14]

H. A. wrote quickly, speaking in a rapid monotone into the glass mouthpiece of his dictation machine. When certain of his subject matter, he could produce as many as ten thousand words a day. And on this subject his grasp was complete. When he submitted the draft on December 1, H. A. assured the publishers that the final chapter might as well have come from Harry Wallace's own pen. "The ideas throughout are those of Henry C. Wallace," he wrote.[15]

He addressed Henry Cantwell Wallace's final words to farm leaders: "The men of vision must arise soon if the United States is to be saved from the fate of becoming a preponderantly industrial nation in which there is not a relation of equality between agriculture and industry. . . . They must set the minds of the farmers on fire with the desire for a rural civilization carrying sufficient economic satisfaction, beauty, and culture to offset completely the lure of the city."[16]

George Peek, for one, needed no prodding. Already the indomitable plow maker was pressing anew for passage of the McNary-Haugen farm relief bill. Peek built coalitions, founded lobbying organizations, sponsored conferences, formed commissions. And at his side, as propagandist and statistician and strategist, was Henry A. Wallace.

Wallace and his cohorts were among the few men in America who believed that the giddy self-confidence of the Jazz Age was misplaced. "It was a false prosperity," Wallace later wrote. "It concealed the fact that farmers were losing their farms by hundreds of thousands. Between 1920 and 1933, one farm in every four was sold for debts or taxes. The New Era glorified high prices but ignored higher and older debts. It blithely rejoiced in foreign loans to support our foreign trade, but made repayment of the loans next to impossible by ever higher tariffs. . . . Of the consequences of concentrated economic power it said nothing. Speculation was king. . . . there was no time for farm relief."[17]

Certainly not in 1925. Congressional agriculture committees passed versions of McNary-Haugen, but leaders in both houses blocked floor debate. In an effort to distract farmers, the administration offered toothless plans to improve cooperative marketing ventures. Those measures also failed.

But the issue would not die, and pressure in the farm states continued to rise. Wallace's personal sense of urgency over the farm situation was fueled by developments within the Department of Agriculture since his father's death. Henry C. Wallace had been replaced by the pliant William Jardine, president of Kansas State College. The inner circle of high-caliber aides and bureau chiefs that surrounded Wallace was decimated. At the Agriculture Department, as in most other government agencies, Herbert Hoover stood triumphant.

Faced with an agriculture secretary openly hostile to their plan, the McNary-Haugenites tenaciously pressed on. In May 1926 they succeeded in again bringing the measure to the House floor. Again they were defeated. In June the matter came before the Senate, where it was rejected on a vote of 45 to 39.

There was still no time for farm relief.

To his friends and neighbors in Iowa, Wallace was both known and unknown. Known best was his name. Three generations of Wallaces had succeeded in linking the family name to the cause of agriculture. Henry A. Wallace, last in this line of remarkable men, was a willing and able heir to the family tradition.

But H. A. was a different sort of Wallace. He had neither the avuncular persona of his saintly grandfather nor the outgoing civic-mindedness of his father. Politics repelled him except as a vehicle for improving rural life. Organizations such as the YMCA and the layman's Men and Religion Forward Movement, which deeply involved his father, held for him no attraction. His idea of a worthwhile activity was something like the Pow-Wow Club, a discussion group he helped organize. Each month the two dozen or so club members gathered over dinner to hear one of them deliver a paper, which was expected to be controversial.

He was indifferent to the pleasures of middle-class prosperity—he would have felt out of place in his father's handsome brick mansion and preferred to remain in the smaller house he and Ilo had built around the corner—and social niceties struck him as a waste of time. When a harried farm wife offered him a simple meal in a kitchen full of animals and children, Wallace expressed delight. His own wife would have been too embarrassed to serve such a meal, he said.

Around Des Moines, Wallace was accorded the respect his name and position commanded. Privately many thought he was a "queer bird." There was something vaguely suspect about Wallace's unconventional thought, and his progressive politics grated on Republican sensibilities. "Lots of people didn't like him because he wasn't a free and easy sort," one of his friends said. "At the same time, he was very modest and there was nothing cocky about him." High-minded and cerebral, reserved to the point of shyness, Wallace did not make conversation freely. When he spoke, it was with an even earnestness conveying little emotion. "He never argued with people or tried to convince them," a friend said. "He'd just dry up rather than argue."[18]

His circle of friends was small, close-knit, and eclectic. They came from no particular class or profession, and their personal habits and tastes varied widely. Short, witty Horace Spaulding, the city librarian, fed Wallace's voracious reading appetite. Simon Casady grew apples and raised chickens on a forty-acre farm south of Des Moines. There, on three isolated plots, Wallace produced some of his first corn inbreds. Bushy-browed Fred Lehmann was a lawyer, renowned for his baggy pants, uncombed black hair, and sarcastic sense of humor.* Addison Parker, another lawyer, was a man of impeccable dress and social grace. Don Murphy was Wallace's bright young assistant at *Wallaces' Farmer.*

Occasionally on Sunday afternoons the men gathered for a walk through Waterworks Park, near the Wallaces' home, or a game of tennis at Si Casady's farm (the loser had to hoe weeds) or a volleyball match on the court behind the *Wallaces' Farmer* building. Volleyball became something of a passion for Wallace. He joined the Des Moines YMCA team and became an expert "set-up" man. "He always plays hard and plays to win," said a friend. "I don't think he has a feeling it's very important to him to win, but when he sets his hand to a game, he wants to win it."[19]

Wallace approached fatherhood with the seriousness and sense of duty he brought to everything in life. He arrived home punctually for dinner every evening, and began every meal with the same grace: "Bless this food for our use and us for thy service, in Jesus' name, Amen." Conversation at the dinner table was expected to be intelligent and well mannered. Meals were usually prepared by a black housekeeper who lived with the family, but they were always served by Ilo. H. A. neither cooked nor carved.[20]

As a father his chosen role was that of an instructor. He devised a board game to teach his children the basic principles of money and markets. Directly and indirectly he encouraged them to be attentive and curious. On hikes through the woods he regularly stopped and asked them how to get back to the car. The two sons, in particular, were taught to share some of their father's intellectual interests. Henry B. was introduced to genetics through chicken breeding; Robert learned about statistics while helping his father punch data cards for a key-driven calculating machine. All of the children were expected to work in the half-acre garden behind the house, helping detassel, crossbreed, shell, and catalog their father's corn.

When H. B. was doing poorly in Latin because he saw no point in studying it, his father expressed his keen displeasure and took on the job of teacher.

---

*Lehmann and his wife shared the yard work at their home. He took care of the backyard; she tended the front. The backyard was a jumble of brambles, odd plants, and a large beehive; the front yard featured well-manicured grass and a flower garden. On one occasion the tall, rumpled lawyer was mowing the lawn for his wife when a new neighbor mistook him for a hired hand. "Would you mow my lawn when you get done with Mrs. Lehmann's?" she asked. "Oh, I might," Lehman replied. "How much does Mrs. Lehmann pay you?" asked the neighbor. "Sometimes she lets me sleep with her," Lehmann replied.

"The reason you're taking Latin is because you need mental discipline," H. A. told the boy. "So, I'm going to work with you every night from now until your next grades come out." H. B. recalled many years later, "Well, he had enough to do without working with me every night, but he did. . . . He followed that right through till the next grades came up. And I got a 1 [the highest grade]."[21]

At times, however, his efforts at instruction fell flat. One day he showed up with wooden swords and robes and told the puzzled children they were going to be Knights of the Roundtable. "Somehow it was supposed to bring alive a certain kind of view of society and whatnot," Bob recalled. "We were never quite clear on what it was all about, or why."[22]

Like his grandfather, H. A. was a quiet, tolerant, rather preoccupied figure within his home. He was, without any question, the authority figure. "If he said 'no,' you knew it was no," remembered Jean. When discipline was needed, he sometimes warmed his hand on a hot radiator in preparation for a spanking, but the spanking itself almost never took place. Only H. B. recalled ever being actually paddled, an incident that resulted in tension between them that silently lingered for life. "I never forgave him for that to the day he died," H. B. said long afterwards, "and don't today."[23]

By and large, however, the Wallace house was a contented one. H. A. and Ilo, while not "lovey dovey," appeared compatible and respectful. If no one saw them kiss, neither did anyone see them fight. There were sing-alongs around Ilo's piano on Sunday evenings and weekend jaunts in H. A.'s Winston touring car. There were numerous nearby woods to explore and plenty of animals with which to play. At various times the Wallaces had dogs, cats, chickens, a pig, rabbits, a fox, and a colony of white rats, which to the delight of the children escaped and produced a variety of spotted rodents by mating with wild rats. The children may not have understood Wallace's intellectual pursuits, but they knew he read avidly and remembered almost everything. When Bob came across a book of obscure facts entitled *Ask Me Another*, he was awed by his father's ability to answer every question.

They were much taken, also, by Wallace's great vigor. In contrast to Ilo, who seemed frail and insisted on a daily afternoon nap, H. A. was robust and tireless. He suffered from hayfever and allergies, as did his sons—Bob was almost asthmatic—but never complained and was seldom bedridden. On one of the family's annual Thanksgiving visits to Ilo's brother in Indianola, the Winston became stuck in mud behind a string of other cars. Although it was snowing and thirty degrees, H. A. got out, took off his shoes, and began pushing the cars in front. The result was a bad chill that sent H. A. to bed with a fever and tonsilitis. His oldest son remembered the episode vividly, because it was the first time he had ever seen his father in bed.*

Wallace's attitude toward children, in fact, was much like his attitude toward adults. If they had something serious to say, he would give them total attention. If they were frivolous, he could be short and blunt. When twelve-year-old Si Casady Jr. built an ingenious little engine out of discarded brass tubes and a rusty steel wheel, powered by steam from his mother's pressure cooker, he was thrilled when Wallace came into the kitchen to witness the contraption.

Many years later Casady remembered the encounter: "He watched it spit and sputter for a few moments, then looked at me and asked, 'What's it for?' " The boy was speechless. "It had never occurred to me that it was for anything."[24]

There was another part of Henry Wallace, no less important and certainly no less serious, that was known to few and fully understood by nobody. This was Wallace the mystic, the prophet, the ardent seeker of cosmic truth. Throughout the 1920s Wallace was engaged upon a fantastic spiritual voyage, a quest for religious understanding that took him from the pews of mainstream Protestantism to the esoteric fringes of Eastern occultism.

Although he later spoke and wrote extensively about his religious views—perhaps in greater detail than any American political figure of his day—he said relatively little about his personal search for truth. Even members of his family caught only glimpses of it. Yet the importance of religion to him can hardly be overstated. To understand Henry A. Wallace, his fellow cabinet member Frances Perkins once commented, one had to understand his religion.

Wallace would have agreed with the remark, but he probably would have said the same is true of all mankind. "Real religion," he said, has nothing to do with "church-going, or charity, or any of the other outward manifestations of what is popularly called religion." It is, rather, a broader and far more powerful force. "Religion is a method whereby man reaches out toward God in an effort to find the spiritual power to express here on earth in a practical way the divine potentialities in himself and his fellow beings," he said in a lecture given at the Pacific School of Religion in Berkeley, California.[25]

---

*Wallace seldom slept more than four or five hours a night. Usually he worked until midnight and arose before 5 A.M. His children believe Wallace had difficulty sleeping for long periods because of allergies and sinus trouble. The sinus problem may also have been the cause of his pronounced snoring. In any case, his restless sleeping patterns apparently made Wallace a difficult bedmate. H. A. and Ilo slept in separate bedrooms as far back as any of the children could remember.

His own reach toward God began at the side of his broad-minded grandfather and strict Calvinist mother. In college he had "imbibed the customary doctrines of laissez-faire economics and 'the survival of the fittest' evolution" and suffered a bout of religious skepticism. He found a remedy in the writings of Ralph Waldo Emerson and his disciples. A divine spiritual force—Emerson called it the Oversoul, Ralph Waldo Trine termed it the Spirit of Infinite Life and Power—flowed constantly through all living things, they taught. Through intuition one could come into contact with that divine force in a blade of grass, in an ear of corn, in oneself.

The search for "a God both immanent and transcendant" led him for a brief period to attend Roman Catholic services. He found the liturgy satisfying and was impressed by the devotional air of his fellow worshipers. "I had an instinctive feeling that I, also, would like to *genuflect*, to cross myself, and remain quietly kneeling after the conclusion of the mass, in silent adoration."[26]

When he explored the Aristotelian logic of Saint Thomas Aquinas and the Jesuit scholars, however, he found to his disappointment that "intellectual studies of this sort tended to destroy for me the spiritual beauty of the mass. For some reason the scholastic method of reasoning, as applied to religious matters, has the same effect on me as a closely reasoned Calvinistic sermon."[27] As in all things, Wallace did not want to be told what was true; he wanted to discover truth by himself.

After college he returned to the Presbyterian Church but remained an avid reader of works on religion and philosophy. In the writings of William James, particularly in *Varieties of Religious Experience* and *A Pluralistic Universe*, Wallace found an intellectual framework to support his view that not all truth was to be discovered rationally. Intuition, James wrote, gives all men their "first body of truth, and our philosophy is but its showy verbalized translation."

Thereafter his relationship with the Presbyterian Church was never more than uneasy. Increasingly he held the view that all organized religions have a powerful conservative streak that "forces them to hold to the past with utmost devotion." Change always threatens organized religion. "Thus it is that we have the historic conflict between the priest and prophet," Wallace wrote.[28]

What tied him to the Presbyterian church, despite his doubts, was his grandfather. Uncle Henry was a living example of a man who retained his progressive values and deeply spiritual nature while operating comfortably within the established church. Uncle Henry's death in 1916 cut the tie, and Wallace slowly drifted away. "After a time I felt that a critical attitude in the House of God . . . was not proper, and so I stopped going to church."[29]

The established Protestant churches in which Wallace had grown to manhood had come to seem infirm and extraneous, and he said so in blunt language. "The truly dismaying thing, of course, is the lukewarmness, the wishy-washy goody-goodiness, the infantile irrelevancy of the Church itself," he wrote in 1934.[30]

The immediate course of his religious journey after leaving the Presbyterian Church around 1919 cannot be charted with precision. No letters dealing with spiritual matters during the first half of the 1920s remain, and he did not keep a diary during the period. In the oral history he later gave to Columbia University, Wallace was limited and circumspect:

> I didn't join the Episcopal Church immediately after leaving the United Presbyterian Church—I didn't join the Episcopal Church until about 1930. I know that I'm often called a mystic, and in the years following my leaving the United Presbyterian Church, I would say I was probably a practical mystic. I've always believed that if you envision something that hasn't been, that can be, and bring it into being, that is a tremendously worthwhile thing to do. I'd go this far—I'd say I was a mystic in the same sense that George Carver was, who believed that God was in everything, and therefore, that if you went to God, you could find the answers.
>
> Maybe that belief is mysticism. I don't know.[31]

His comment was true as far as it went, but it fell well short of expressing the dedicated enthusiasm with which he plumbed the occult during the 1920s and 1930s. All manner of esoteric phenomena fascinated him: seances, symbols, secret societies, rituals, astrology, Native American religion, Oriental philosophy. In the realm of the mystical, little escaped his curiosity.

Wallace's interest in mysticism "was one that he did not conceal," said Paul Appleby, a young *Des Moines Register* reporter who was to become his top aide at the Agriculture Department. "It went in rather odd directions." At the Pow-Wow Club, to which Appleby also belonged, Wallace's papers consistently focused on mystical topics. Wallace's thoughts struck the club members as both highly intelligent and rather strange, Appleby said. "Very few would have said he was a screwball, but they would have said he was queer."[32]

Wallace entered the world of mysticism through the door of Theosophy. As early as 1919 he attended a meeting of the Theosophical Society at its Des Moines lodge, and his interest intensified over several years. It is unclear whether Wallace ever formally joined the Theosophical Society, but it is certain he regularly attended its meetings in Des Moines and elsewhere. In 1925 he helped organize a Des Moines parish of the Liberal Catholic Church, a group with close ties to the Theosophical Society, and performed minor clerical roles in it for several years. He remained actively interested in Theosophy at least until 1934 and embraced several of its key tenets for the remainder of his life.

One of Theosophy's most important teachings—the doctrine of pantheism—had been part of Wallace's thinking as early as his boyhood nature walks with George Washington Carver. The same concept of God as an infinite and universal presence that William James called More, was expressed by Theosophists as The Absolute. As one of Theosophy's founders explained it, "The Absolute does not think or exist, but is rather thought and existence."

Years later, as Wallace was preparing to run for president, he was asked directly whether he was a pantheist. "What do you mean by pantheism?" Wallace replied, smiling slyly. "The belief that nature, science and religion are as one," said the questioner. "If that's pantheism, I'm for it," said Wallace. "You can put in some economics, too."[33]

Theosophy had other attractions for Wallace as well. Its teachings were progressive by nature. There was no concept of hell or eternal damnation; indeed, since The Absolute was everywhere, all men shared a spark of the divine. The same philosophy led to a distaste for nationalism and strong appreciation of racial and religious tolerance.* In general, Theosophy took a limited interest in temporal affairs, but its view of "the brotherhood of man" was at one with the social gospel preached by Uncle Henry and no doubt appealed instinctively to his grandson.

Its liberal nature and its compatibility with modern science, in particular with the theory of evolution, made Theosophy popular for a time with artists and intellectuals. At its peak, in the mid-1920s, the Theosophical Society claimed to have more than seven thousand members in the United States, attending some 268 lodges. Many, but not all, of its members came from the ranks of vegetarians, antivivisectionists, Fabians, feminists, and other supporters of left-wing causes. The Irish poet William Butler Yeats was attracted to it, as were the Dutch painter Piet Mondrian and the French composer Erik Satie. Thomas Edison, inventor of the light bulb, and General Abner Doubleday, father of baseball, were members. So was Uncle Henry's friend George W. Russell, the Irish painter, poet, and agricultural journalist known as Æ.

---

*In his 1934 book *Statesmanship and Religion*, Wallace wrote, "No great religion, whether it be Christianity, Judaism, Buddhism, Hinduism or Mohammedanism, can recognize ideals which set up a particular race or class as an object of religious worship. While admittedly there has been but little true Christianity in the world during the past five hundred years, yet it would seem that a follower of Christ least of all should recognize nationalism as the commander of his spiritual self. From the standpoint of true religion, it is singularly unfortunate that so many faiths, churches and doctrines are confined by national boundaries and, therefore, take on national colorings. Any religion which recognizes above all the fatherhood of God and the brotherhood of man must of necessity have grave questionings concerning those national enterprises where the deepest spiritual fervor is evoked for purely nationalistic, race or class ends."

Theosophy did not regard itself as a religion, and the Theosophical Society most certainly rejected the notion that it was a church. It had no rituals or liturgy, nor any organizational hierarchy. It was called a secret sect, although it was not especially secretive. Meetings were open to anyone willing to sign a statement promising to study its teachings.

But Theosophy also was infused with supernaturalism, thanks in large part to its founder, Madame Helena Petrovna Blavatsky. The eccentric Blavatsky, or HPB as she preferred to be called, weighed 224 pounds and had close-cropped crinkly hair "like the fleece of a Cotswold ewe." She wore colorful blouses in the manner of Garibaldi's revolutionaries, could swear fluently in three languages, and was a lifelong devotee of hashish, which she smoked or ate with jam. One part philosopher and two parts fraud, Blavatsky claimed to be in contact with ancient goddesses and the souls of centuries-old spiritual teachers whom she called "Masters" or "Adepts."[34]

The core of HPB's work was an effort to meld the world's great religions and philosophies, Eastern and Western, all of which she believed sprang from the same ancient doctrine and expressed the same universal truth. Thus she combined elements of Hinduism, Buddhism, Jewish Cabalism, Spiritualism, Christianity, and Egyptian Hermeticism. The pantheistic God described by HPB was largely the Hindu concept of "the one Uncreate, Universal, Infinite and Everlasting Cause." And, like the Hindus, she believed in reincarnation (but in a progressive form that made the perfectibility of man inevitable) and karma, the spiritual law of sowing and reaping that serves as "an unfailing redresser of human injustice . . . a retributive law which rewards and punishes with equal impartiality."[35]

The Liberal Catholic Church was separate from the Theosophical Society but closely associated with its doctrines. It considered itself a Christian church—its liturgy and clerical structure were similar to that of the Anglican High Church—but it acknowledged that other religions offer divine truth. Its lay members were allowed "entire freedom in interpretation of creeds, scriptures and tradition, and of its liturgy and summary of doctrine." The church asked only that differences of interpretation be "courteously expressed."[36]

What the Liberal Catholic Church offered, and the Theosophical Society did not, was an opportunity for corporate worship. The number of people who found this option appealing was never large. Liberal Catholic Church membership in the United States probably never exceeded two thousand, even at its height in the mid-1920s.

Henry A. Wallace was one of those few. In mid-1925 he and several others established a Liberal Catholic church, or "mission," in Des Moines. Wallace, in his capacity as the mission's secretary, wrote letters to the church headquarters in Argyle, California, and to the Church of St. Francis in Chicago, saying the Des Moines church would celebrate "Prime service" at 10:30 on Sunday mornings. Ever the thrifty Scot, Wallace added, "Will you kindly forward to me six Liturgies of your cheapest binding which contain the Prime service?"[37]

By 1926 Wallace was in communication with Irving S. Cooper, the church's "Regionary Bishop for the United States," about the Des Moines mission's plan to purchase a house near Drake University for use as a church. Cooper responded with caution. "I have found by experience in other cities that sometimes people will not attend a service which is held in what looks like a private house," he said.[39] There was no further mention of the issue in Wallace's correspondence, and it is not certain how the Des Moines mission resolved its housing problem.

Wallace participated in the Liberal Catholic Church for several years. Often he wore vestments and performed clerical duties during the liturgy. Cooper, whom Wallace met personally at least once, even tried unsuccessfully to persuade him to become a priest.

Wallace made no effort to involve his family in Theosophy or the Liberal Catholic Church. Ilo and the children attended services at several Protestant churches—sometimes with H. A., sometimes without—before finally settling on the St. Paul Episcopal Church, where H. B. and Bob sang in the choir. Ilo told the children that H. A. attended services at a "high church" elsewhere.

The arrangement suited the boys fine. "I always felt like that was a worthwhile experience in my life, but not because of the church," H. B. remarked many years later. "It was the choir experience, adhering to the time schedule, doing everything right and doing it well. That was good." Besides, the church paid children in the choir $1.25 a month to cover the cost of travel, and since the Wallace boys also received streetcar money from their mother, H. B. and Bob turned a small profit.[39]

Two years after joining the Liberal Catholic Church, Wallace joined the Masons, another secret society rich with ritual but one with much closer ties to the American experience. George Washington, Benjamin Franklin, Theodore Roosevelt, and numerous other prominent men, including Wallace's own father, were active Masons. Wallace participated in both the Blue Lodge and the Scottish Rite branches of Masonry and received the Thirty-second Degree in November 1928. He stopped there—one step short of the Scottish Rite's highest rank—but maintained his affiliation with the Masons until the late 1940s, when he "demitted" from Masonic lodges in both Des Moines and Washington, D.C.

Clearly, however, Wallace's spiritual search had taken him outside the American religious mainstream. While his spiritual curiosity was benign, he was to pay a great price for it when he became a public figure. Had he understood the cost of his "spiritual window-shopping," as one of his fiercest critics called it, he undoubtedly would have been unfazed.

He was a serious man earnestly embarked upon the most serious of undertakings. His whole being was defined by his spiritual quest. "Fundamentally," he wrote to a friend, "I am neither a corn breeder nor an editor but a searcher for methods of bringing the 'inner light' to outward manifestation and raising outward manifestation to the inner light."[40]

In early May 1926, a few days after Admiral Richard Byrd became the first man to fly an airplane over the North Pole, nine men quietly gathered at Des Moines's Grant Club. There, in the obscurity of a basement room, they did something of vastly greater consequence than the admiral's dramatic flight. They created a company unlike any in history: the first firm ever devoted to the development, production, and sale of hybrid corn. They called their creation the Hi-Bred Corn Company. Later it would be known around the world as Pioneer Hi-Bred.*

They were hardly a picture of risk-taking venture capitalists. None had ever run a business. Only one of them—H. A. Wallace himself—had much money, and he was far from being rich. J. J. Newlin was a no-nonsense Quaker who managed the Wallaces' farm north of Des Moines. Si Casady was an apple grower and small-scale developer. Fred Lehmann Jr. was an abrasive lawyer who relished stepping on toes. Walter Welch was a salesman who shared some of Wallace's spiritual interests. George Kurtzweil sold seeds. Earl Houghton was a farmer. Jim Wallace, H. A.'s affable younger brother, worked in the production end of *Wallaces' Farmer.*

What they shared, these disparate men, was an enormous faith in Henry A. Wallace. The bankers, to whom Wallace had appealed for help in establishing the company, saw little commercial prospect in hybrid corn. Corn was corn, as the bankers viewed it, and it seemed unlikely that farmers would pay for seed they could have for free. To Wallace, however, corn was life itself. Corn was the bedrock of midwestern agriculture, and he knew how to improve it. He knew how to make it stronger and more abundant. And the men in the Grant Club basement believed him, even if they were a little shaky regarding the scientific theory underlying Wallace's vision.

---

*The firm's name was changed in 1935 to avoid confusion with the word "hybrid" and to distinguish it from competitors. Only after the name was changed did company officials learn that a small North Dakota seed company held a trademark on the word "Pioneer." Pioneer Hi-Bred did not obtain rights to the trademark until 1959. Nevertheless, the word "Pioneer" became synonymous with the company and today is indelibly linked to commercial hybrid seed. The company is now called Pioneer Hi-Bred International Inc.

For several years in the early 1920s, Wallace thought hybrid corn might be spread by some type of noncommercial mechanism, such as a nonprofit national institute. The enormous complexity of the task, however, finally persuaded Wallace it could be done only by well-trained specialists working in a carefully guided program. So he decided to form a company to produce and sell hybrid seed, and at the Grant Club he presented the incorporation papers and shareholder plan. There were to be seventy shares, and each share would cost $100. Wallace was to hold fifty shares. His friends committed to buy the other twenty shares. Almost $5,000 was raised on the spot, with the remainder to come as it was needed.

The person who really made Pioneer Hi-Bred possible was not in attendance. Ilo Browne Wallace was home with the children. It was Ilo who provided the funds for the Wallaces' fifty shares. To do that she used virtually all of the inheritance she received from her father's estate. The farmland near Johnston, which would become Pioneer's research and corporate headquarters, also had its roots in Ilo's family inheritance.

For years Ilo had patiently put up with H. A.'s enthusiasm for corn. She had battled rats in the basement where he stored corn over the winter, and endured his frequent absences to attend scientific meetings and corn shows. The endless research that engrossed him, and the genetic theory that lay below it, were matters she understood but faintly. But of her total confidence in her husband's genius there was no doubt.

For her faith in her husband, Ilo Wallace was to be amply rewarded. At the time of her death in 1981, at age ninety-three, Ilo Wallace was a wealthy woman. That year Pioneer Hi-Bred recorded sales of $478 million and earned a net profit of $63.5 million.*

In 1926, however, no one, including Henry and Ilo Wallace, foresaw the huge success that lay ahead. The company's early years were hardly auspicious. In its first year of operation, Pioneer harvested 1,000 bushels of seed corn and sold 650 of them, turning a profit of about $30. The founders were well pleased. "We were in business—the largest hybrid seed corn company in the world," said Jim Wallace.[41] H. A. was almost ecstatic. "I have watched and dreamed about this new method of corn breeding for so many years," he told the readers of *Wallaces' Farmer*, "that I am becoming quite excited now that I see the time of practical application drawing near."[42]

There was little else for Wallace to cheer about. The agricultural depression that had stubbornly lingered in the Midwest for more than half a decade

---

*In 1997 the Du Pont chemical corporation purchased a 20 percent share of Pioneer Hi-Bred International for $1.7 billion. In 1999, Du Pont purchased the remaining 80 percent of Pioneer for $7.7 billion. About one-quarter of Pioneer's shares were held by Wallace's three children at the time.

had begun spreading to other sections of the country, especially the South, where the price of cotton fell below fifteen cents a pound in 1926.

As prices fell, so did hope. There seemed to be no solution to the farm problem, at least none with any prospect of passage.

In Washington, Calvin Coolidge still rode tall in the saddle. The elections of 1926 gave Republicans more good news. Republican candidates easily triumphed throughout the Midwest, despite the troubled times. In Iowa, Republican candidates for governor, senator, and all eleven congressional seats won election. It was true that virtually every midwestern congressman of either party now supported some form of federal farm relief, but the men who controlled the Republican Party remained adamantly opposed.

Undeterred, the relentless McNary-Haugenites set out once again to battle for their cause. Their new slogan cleverly put the issue in terms of manufacturing versus agriculture, not Republicans versus Democrats: "Protection for all or protection for none." They tirelessly trolled the halls of Congress, while their legislative experts tinkered with the bill in an effort to win southern support. Wallace himself successfully wooed the powerful Alabama senator Lister Hill, whose brother Luther lived in Des Moines.

In February 1927, with the price of cotton sagging to 12.6 cents a pound, the strategy worked, McNary-Haugen passed the Senate by a vote of 51 to 43 and the House by a vote of 214 to 178. A few days later President Coolidge vetoed it with a prolix message that denounced the measure as unconstitutional, unworkable, expensive, coercive, and a bureaucratic nightmare. For good measure he chided farmers for seeking aid at the "expense of other farmers and of the community at large."[43]

Farm leaders were livid. Agricultural papers denounced the president in white-hot terms.

Wallace saw the hand of Herbert Hoover behind Coolidge's veto message. His alarm was heightened in early August, when Coolidge issued a cryptic statement saying he did not "choose to run" for reelection in 1928, leaving Hoover as the leading Republican presidential prospect. Hoover had betrayed farmers once before, Wallace told his readers, and if he could not be stopped, all chance of farm relief was dead.

Wallace and other McNary-Haugen leaders looked to the Republican governor of Illinois, Frank O. Lowden, a vocal supporter of export subsidy plans, as a possible savior. But Wallace also understood the lock that eastern manufacturers had on the party. Perhaps, Wallace told a group of farm leaders in St. Louis, they should begin looking for ways to "make over one of the old parties or failing that . . . start a new party" with roots in rural America.[44]

While Wallace pondered action at the ballot box, Peek pressed for yet another vote on McNary-Haugen. Peek was convinced the bill could be tailored to meet Coolidge's objections. Even if Coolidge couldn't be completely satisfied, he reasoned, the political demands of an election year would make it more difficult for the president to veto the measure again.

Even some of Peek's closest allies thought the effort was futile. "George, this is the last heat I trot," Chester Davis, the able Washington lobbyist for the McNary-Haugen bill, told Peek.[45] As usual Peek would not give up. The bill was modified to cover all types of farm products, and the Senate passed it by a wide margin in April 1928. The House followed suit in May. Once again, Coolidge issued a stinging veto. The Senate tried, but failed, to override it.

It was to be the last vote taken on McNary-Haugen. The long struggle for farm relief was in shambles. All hope that the Republican Party would one day come to the farmers' rescue was gone, as Wallace saw it. "The veto message has made it impossible for any farmer with self-respect to vote for Coolidge or for any candidate who, like Hoover, supports the Coolidge policy towards agriculture," he thundered in *Wallaces' Farmer*.[46]

His God-fearing readers well understood the righteousness of Wallace's call to leave the Republican Party, for he put it to them in the words of the Old Testament: "What portion have we in David? neither have we inheritance in the son of Jesse: to your tents, O Israel: now see to thine own house, David."[47]

CHAPTER FIVE

"A COMPLETE BREAK WITH ALL THAT I HAD BEEN"

A fortnight after Calvin Coolidge drove a stake through the heart of McNary-Haugen, Republicans gathered in Kansas City to pick his successor. It was no contest. Herbert Clark Hoover, tireless "boy wonder" of the Harding and Coolidge administrations, received 837 of the 1,089 votes cast on the first ballot.

The movement for farm relief seemed out of wind. Hotheaded supporters of McNary-Haugen had vowed to storm the Republican convention with 100,000 pitchfork-waving farmers; fewer than 1,000 showed up. Moreover, the farm leaders had no appealing alternative to Hoover. Governor Alfred E. Smith, of New York, the Democratic candidate, was a Catholic, an opponent of Prohibition, a friend of big-city machines. To the Protestant, tea-totaling, insular folk in rural America, Smith was like a visitor from a foreign land.

H. A. Wallace reacted cautiously to the unfolding campaign. He had long ago pronounced verdict on Hoover. As for the Democratic candidate, Wallace was skeptical. "It is quite commonly believed by well posted farm-minded people, that Smith would handle the farm problem in a fairer way than either Coolidge or Hoover," Wallace wrote. "However, he is so completely ignorant of everything connected with agriculture that much would depend on whom he selected for advice along this line."[1]

Longing for an alternative, Wallace drove to Illinois in an effort to persuade former Governor Frank O. Lowden to run as an independent candidate. Lowden was a hard-drinking, "horseback-riding, country squire type," Wallace recalled, who was sincerely angry over the Republican Party's betrayal of farmers. But Wallace's effort went nowhere. "I've had so many honors conferred on me by the Republican Party for so many years, that out of a sense of gratitude, I just can't do it," he said. The editor was unimpressed. "I didn't think it was a very good argument, but—that was his argument."[2]

In late September, Wallace went to Omaha to hear Smith speak on agriculture. Smith mouthed polite support for a farm relief program similar to McNary-Haugen. It wasn't much, but it was enough for Wallace. The following day Wallace appeared before a statewide meeting of the Farmers' Union and publicly cast aside his Republican heritage. "The farmer of the United States can best serve his own ends by throwing his influence to Smith," Wallace declared. He made similar remarks the next day at a convention of Methodist ministers. The men of God gave him a "very polite, very cold" reception, Wallace recalled.[3]

Soon he was riding around Iowa campaigning for Smith in a "very foxy big car" owned by Milo Reno, a wavy-haired hell-raising populist who headed the Iowa Farmers' Union. Reno was "an old-fashioned, radical American of the extreme sort," said Wallace.[4] They made an odd couple—an elderly rabble-rouser with a bullying air and a solemn young editor who loathed the gaudiness of political combat.

It was Wallace's first active participation in a campaign, and it was not a pleasant experience. Nor was there any solace in the outcome. Hoover won an overwhelming victory nationwide, and carried Iowa by almost two to one. Four years after Henry C. Wallace's death, his mortal enemy reigned supreme. For H. A. Wallace it was a bitter pill to swallow. Something profoundly personal colored his view of Hoover, he acknowledged. To an out-of-town visitor he had known for barely two hours, Wallace spoke quietly of the Harry Wallace's feud with Hoover and of the hatred that swept over him when his father died.

"Do you know, I hope I never again feel as intensely antagonistic toward any one as I did then," H. A. said. "I felt, for a while there, I felt, almost, as if Hoover had killed my father."[5]

A few months into Hoover's presidency, Wallace found relief, as his grandfather often had, in a trip abroad. His ticket out of town was provided, literally, by Leonard K. Elmhirst, a wealthy young Englishman who had become enamored of agricultural economics while studying at Cornell University. Elmhirst took it upon himself to host the First International Conference of Agricultural Economists, in September 1929 at Dartington Hall, his estate in southwestern England. He invited thirty-five of the world's top experts to attend.

Not everyone would have enjoyed the company of a group of quarrelsome academics, but Wallace found it invigorating. He delivered two papers. One was a highly technical study of "the 'graphic' versus the 'statistical' method of computing multiple curvilinear regression lines." The response disappointed him. "I put a lot of work into it," he remarked. "And the British didn't give a damn!"[6]

There was nothing technical about his second paper, however. It was a no-holds-barred critique of international trade policies, expressing Wallace's conviction that the world was headed toward a catastrophic economic "blowup" unless the United States lowered its protectionist tariffs. "When we demand that the European countries pay up the money they owe us and at the same time raise our tariff, it is just like our having hold of them back of the neck with one hand pulling them toward us, and using a pitchfork against their belly with the other hand poking them away from us." Wallace said. "This is bound to create a sense of frustration and desperation in foreign countries, and there's going to be trouble."[7]

From England, Wallace journeyed to the Continent, mixing sight-seeing with scientific inquiry at a relaxed pace. He viewed "the corn borer in its native habitat" in the Balkans, talked with agricultural scientists in Hungary, spent a nickel on a glass of beer in Germany (which he didn't like and was unable to finish).[8] He lingered for some time in Czechoslovakia, where his sister Mary, wife of the Swiss ambassador, was living.

From Prague, Wallace planned to head eastward across Russia and on to Japan. Shortly before his departure, however, a telegram arrived from Iowa that changed everything. *Wallaces' Farmer* had concluded a deal to purchase its longtime rival, the *Iowa Homestead*, it said. The deal would give *Wallaces' Farmer* control of the *Homestead*'s state-of-the-art printing plant, its roomy headquarters in Des Moines, and its large circulation base. The combined publication would have a quarter million paying subscribers. "I thought I had better go home," he said later.[9]

Wallace arrived back in October, full of misgivings. The two million dollars spent to purchase the *Homestead* would put *Wallaces' Farmer* deeply in debt, and he believed it was not an auspicious time to owe money. But there was nothing he could do about it. The publication was owned by his uncle John and his father's estate. H. A. was the editor but not a partner. The deal was done.

Wallaces' Farmer proudly announced its purchase of the *Iowa Homestead* in its October 26, 1929, edition. "In the future, as in the past, we will continue our efforts for 'Good Farming—Clear Thinking—Right Living.' "[10]

Three days later, with a cataclysmic crash on Wall Street, the nation began its descent toward economic collapse.

⬤

As the Wallaces moved into the gleaming white Homestead building on the western edge of Des Moines's business district, H. A. permitted himself a rare bit of nostalgic reflection. "It is rather sad to move from my dingy old office in the *Wallaces' Farmer* building to a well-lighted efficient office in *The Homestead* building," Wallace wrote. He recalled the moment five years earlier when he and his brother departed to visit their dying father: "Then I looked at the pictures on the wall which my grandfather had gathered together. There were autographed photos of [Theodore] Roosevelt, Gifford Pinchot, Liberty Hyde Bailey, et al. There was the old davenport upon which my grandfather used to lie and rest for half an hour after eating. There was the corner of the office where my father sat at his desk in late February, 1921, just before setting out for Washington." Now Henry A. Wallace found himself in a "larger room, with a terrazzo floor and a look of cleanliness" that he didn't particularly like. "There are no pictures to remind me of the past and I must set my face towards the future. . . ."[11]

The style and content of the combined publication—"A Weekly Journal for Thinking Farmers"—differed little from the old *Wallaces' Farmer*. Its pages, usually numbering about forty-four, contained an eclectic blend of sophisticated economic analysis, homemaking tips, agricultural news and science, rural humor, fictional tales, children's stories, and, of course, Uncle Henry's Sunday School lessons, still being drawn from the huge backlog he had left upon his death in 1916. Always there were plenty of letters from readers, in keeping with the long tradition of farm journals.

As an editor Wallace had perfect pitch. He knew his readers, knew what they wanted to read and what they needed to know. The editor's personal eccentricities—his vegetarianism, his exotic spiritual interests—were almost never displayed. The journal he edited was an unabashed promoter of hogs and Christianity and all things held dear by rural folk.* On occasion Wallace diverged from family tradition, notably in supporting Al Smith's candidacy, but always he did so within the context of the agricultural cause.

Tucked away among advertisements for cream separators and chicken feed, there was usually a small ad for the Hi-Bred Corn Company. "Our new sys-

---

*When Wallace's younger sister Ruth wrote a series of "barnyard stories" for children for *Wallaces' Farmer*, he insisted that she change only one line. She had written, "Wouldn't you hate to be a pig and live in some messy place?" H. A. instructed her that "you can't say 'hate to be a pig' in Iowa," Ruth recalled.

tem of picking seed ears only from detassled plants produces a vigorous, high yielding, high grade, early maturing corn."[12] Hybrid corn was Wallace's hope for the future, a symbol of his belief that science, properly employed, could liberate human civilization.

His company didn't amount to much. As late as 1929 it still had no full-time employees and no central office. Its research facilities were located in the basement of the Wallaces' home. Sales totaled merely a few hundred bushels and its profits a few hundred dollars. It could borrow money only on the basis of Wallace's personal signature. But the Hi-Bred Corn Company was his. It rested on his vision and moved at his direction.

One by one, Wallace began to assemble the team of men who would carry on his vision and lead Pioneer Hi-Bred to spectacular success. J. J. Newlin managed the farm. Nelson Urban, a recent graduate of Antioch College, in 1930 became the company's bookkeeper and head of its sales division. Raymond Baker, an Iowa State student fascinated by corn, was taken on as a hired hand. Later, as head of the company's research division, Baker was universally recognized as one of the world's leading corn breeders.

The most colorful member of the fledgling team was a gregarious young man from Coon Rapids, Iowa, named Roswell "Bob" Garst. Although no authority on genetics or anything else, Garst had hustle and a gift of gab. He had utter confidence in his ability to sell things, and one day a chance gust of wind convinced him he could sell Henry Wallace's high-priced corn.

Wallace had given Garst some hybrid corn seed and urged him to try it. Garst and a high school chum named Charley Rippey decided to attempt an experiment. They planted the hybrid corn in rows of two, alternating it with two rows of ordinary hand-selected corn from Rippey's farm. They were inspecting the field on a summer day, Rippey recalled, when "there came a wind and it blew all of mine down, but the hybrid corn was still standing . . . so there were two rows down and two rows standing up. That just amazed Bob."[13]

On the spot Garst became a true believer in hybrid corn, and he set out to cut a deal with Wallace. He proposed a franchise arrangement under which he would use Wallace's stock to grow seed corn; Garst would sell the corn in northern Iowa under the Hi-Bred Corn label and pay the company a royalty fee on each bushel sold. The fee would decrease as the number of bushels increased, up to 50,000 bushels. "Bob, I just love you," said Wallace. "You are such an optimist. There won't be 50,000 bushels of hybrid corn sold in your lifetime or mine."

Garst didn't blink. "I'll hit 50,000 bushels in five years," he told Wallace.[14] Amused by the young man's brashness, Wallace agreed. They sealed the deal on a handshake and operated amicably on that basis for the remainder of their lives. The handshake would make Garst a wealthy man. Within eight years, Garst alone was producing and selling double the number of bushels Wallace said would never be sold.

Moving from farm to farm across Iowa, Garst devised a brilliant method of marketing Hi-Bred's product. He would give a farmer enough hybrid seed to plant half a field and ask the farmer to plant it alongside the corn he was already growing. At harvest time, Garst would be entitled to one-half of the increased yield produced by the hybrid seed. If the farmer's seed yielded twenty-five bushels an acre and the hybrid seed yielded forty-five bushels, Garst would be entitled to ten bushels of corn.

Often it took three or four years to persuade a farmer that the large yields produced by hybrid seed were not a fluke. Once the farmer was convinced, however, the long-term benefits were enormous. Even in the depths of the Depression, newly converted farmers were singing the praises of hybrid seed, which cost an astronomical six dollars a bushel to purchase. "While the [sales method] didn't actually pay our bills at the moment, it did actually put us on the highway to success," recalled Wallace.*[15]

Wallace needed whatever optimism he could muster. Iowa, which had lived with hard times for almost a decade, skidded toward disaster. The price of wheat fell from $1.05 a bushel in 1929 to 68 cents in 1930. Corn dropped from 81 cents a bushel to 50 cents. Publicly Wallace held his fire on Hoover's farm program, but privately he told friends the president's economic ideas were "about 99% wrong."[16]

The heart of Hoover's agricultural program was the nonpartisan Farm Board, which was given a $500 million revolving fund and broad authority to stabilize commodity prices through cooperative marketing and other devices. By establishing government corporations that could buy and hold basic commodities, the Farm Board was, for a time, able to sustain U.S. farm

---

*Wallace began Pioneer Hi-Bred with no fixed idea of how the seed was to be marketed, and always gave full credit to Garst, Urban, and others who made the company a success. "In the corn business I've tried to outline certain broad policies which I thought would result in business success, but I have left to others the job of business itself," he said. The two principles Wallace insisted upon were, first, total honesty with customers and, second, high prices. If Pioneer told customers everything about a particular hybrid, its flaws as well as virtues, farmers would come to trust the company and repay its honesty. High prices, Wallace believed, were necessary to convince farmers they were buying something special, as well as to repay the company for the cost of its research.

prices somewhat above the world level. But the plan had no mechanism to restrict production. Wallace concluded it was doomed.

The mood at *Wallaces' Farmer* in its shiny new quarters on Grand Avenue was dark. Each day's mail brought heart-wrenching cries for help from farmers. There was little Wallace could say, nothing he could do. "I am afraid that the cup of iniquity of the Republican party is not yet full in spite of the very hard times from which so many people are suffering this year," he wrote to a friend.[17] Every month seemed worse than the last. The price of corn continued its dizzying downward spiral: 50 cents, 40 cents, 30 cents.

So many people bombarded Wallace with questions and theories about the economic disaster that Wallace finally wrote a prescient sixteen-page pamphlet entitled *Causes of the World Wide Depression of 1930* in order to respond to scores of letters. The tract laid out three central causes for the calamity sweeping the world. First, rapid technological changes, particularly the growing use of tractors, had resulted in a surplus of goods and lower prices. Second, huge war debts combined with high tariffs had unbalanced normal trade relations between nations. Third, the gold standard and the unwillingness of central banks to increase money supplies had resulted in long-term deflation, ruining millions of farmers who had contracted debts when prices were higher.

Wallace concluded the pamphlet with idealistic language that would echo through his speeches and writings for thirty years: "Finally the problem becomes a spiritual one. Do we believe in the abundant life or in the narrow contracted life? The forces pulling toward narrow, national selfishness are combating those working in the direction of international understanding."[18]

He was not speaking entirely in the abstract. His own circumstances were the least comfortable of his adult life. To a friend who asked him for money, he replied that he was unable to help. In at least one instance, he wrote a letter complaining about high property taxes on the Johnston farms. To those who requested him to speak, Wallace made plain that he would charge a traveling fee of eight cents per mile; when a University of Iowa professor sent him a check for $19.80 for an appearance in Iowa City, Wallace wrote back that he had been short-changed.

Hanging over everything was the financial condition of *Wallaces' Farmer*. Initially Wallace maintained a tone of cautious optimism about the merger, but after a few months it was clear that success was far from certain. Young applicants were turned away; a few members of the existing staff were laid off. In an effort to cut costs, *Wallaces' Farmer* dropped its weekly format and became a biweekly publication. Its agents were allowed to accept chickens instead of cash from farmers who could not afford the dollar-a-year subscription charge. Nothing helped.

In desperation, John Wallace asked H. A. to seek the help of the Wall Street financier Bernard Baruch, the friend and patron of George Peek. Wallace did, but to no avail. "He said what a shame it was to see young fellows be ruined, but he wasn't interested," Wallace recalled.

Without additional backing, John Wallace found it impossible to continue. "So, in 1932 we lost the paper," said H. A. Wallace.[19] The journal reverted to Dante Pierce, son of the founder of the *Iowa Homestead* and principal holder of the Wallace's debt. Pierce asked Wallace to remain as editor, and suggested that the publication continue to be known as *Wallaces' Farmer*. Wallace agreed.

An era had ended. The Wallace family no longer owned any part of *Wallaces' Farmer*. All that remained was H. A. and the family name.

The deepening economic crisis engendered a kind of paralysis in some men. In Wallace the calamity had an opposite effect. He seemed to be everywhere: speaking at farmers' picnics, meeting with farm organizations, writing for scholarly journals, pressing for "stable money," pleading for lower tariffs, seeking better corn, searching for the inner light.

One enormously ambitious project was an effort to determine whether there was a connection between weather and the positions of planets and the moon. With weekend help from his son Bob, Wallace laboriously entered a half century of data from the Des Moines weather bureau onto 18,262 punch cards, which could then be analyzed on an IBM card-sorting machine located in an office down the hall from his own.

The resulting correlations, while tentative, fascinated him. To a researcher at Yale he wrote with excitement, "There is some tendency when Mars has a heliocentric longitude of 220 to 240 degrees in the month of July, for the weather to be warmer than usual. This was the case, at any rate, in 1886, 1901 and 1916. . . . Some other things of this sort have come to light which seem to be four or five times the probable error."[20] The weather project eventually died out after Wallace was unable to persuade Iowa State to continue and expand upon his work.

All manner of things inflamed his curiosity. He was convinced that white leghorns could be used to produce superior egg-laying chickens, and he scoured the nation to locate the proper inbreeds. He decided he wanted to grow *Valeriana officinalis*, an herb used to produce sedatives and carminative drugs, and sought the help of Professor George Shull of Princeton to obtain some wild plants. He boosted the National Cornhusking Contest, a quasi-sporting event Wallace founded in 1922, which by the early 1930s was attracting tens of thousands of spectators to the annual championships. He grew interested in Gypsy music and wrote a Nebraska radio station to obtain more information about some songs he had heard. He touted the virtues of "a smart little Hungarian dog" called the puli.*

He corresponded widely on a vast array of topics. He mused about the raising of Khaki Campbell ducks, ruminated about wage-and-price cycles in Great Britain during the nineteenth century, scolded friends on the error of their ways. "If you will pardon my brutality, I would like to say that you have deliberately chosen to live in a dream world," he wrote an errant friend in Texas.[21] He analyzed the characteristics of various farm organizations, pressed for American participation in the World Court, expounded on proper monetary policy during a depression.

His letters were usually reasoned and courteous, but their content was unambiguous. Wallace left no doubt about his position and never shied away from disagreement. To a reader who disputed an editorial about corn prices, he wrote, "It will sooner or later be a very unfortunate thing for you if you fail to realize that there is such a thing as supply and demand. . . . I hope that when you step off your barn roof, gaily saying, 'There is no such thing as the law of gravitation' you will have a nice pile of hay ready to receive you."[22] On occasion he even seemed to solicit argument. To a young man who invited Wallace to attend his graduation from the Naval Academy, the editor replied with congratulations and a sly comment: "Personally I am quite a pacifist and I shall be interested in talking with you sometime about the fallacies of my position."[23]

On political matters Wallace frequently adopted a stance that put him at odds with both sides. "I am just as much disgusted with the Democrats as I am with the Republicans," he responded to a reader, "and would like to see the destruction of both of the old parties." (He added, in a prophetic comment on his own political demise, that starting a third party "is such a slow proposition that it is very difficult to get practical men interested.")[24] To a friend with socialist leanings, Wallace wrote, "[I] don't like the spirit of many of the socialists. It seems to me that they derive their strength too much by mere opposition to the existing order. I would like to see a sweeter spirit on the parts of the socialists."[25]

When he wasn't opining on religion or politics, Wallace was acting as a sort of one-man extension service for readers who sought his advice on everything from how to grow walnuts to ways of stopping hogs from killing chick-

---

*The puli, distinctive for its long coils of fur that reach to the ground and shimmer as it walks, was highly regarded as a shepherd dog in Hungary. It was said to have never attacked an animal it was guarding. As agriculture secretary, Wallace was instrumental in introducing the puli to the United States, with the intention of crossbreeding it to produce shepherd dogs of superior temperament.

ens. Typically his letters were one paragraph long and went straight to the point:

Mr. J.A. Record
Leon, Iowa

Dear Sir:

Every third year is a bad grub year. 1927 was a bad grub year and so was 1930. The next one will come in 1933. In 1931, however, you should be fairly safe in putting this land back to corn. In 1933, I think I would try to arrange to have this piece of ground in clover.

Very truly,
Henry A. Wallace[26]

And when he wasn't writing, it seemed to his family, he was reading. "He would almost always . . . bring home several books every night from the library," his son H. B. recalled. "They'd vary a lot in subject matter; he might be involved in psychology at one time and history at another time and physiology in another. . . . I don't know how fast he read, but he certainly must have done a certain amount of speed reading, because he'd have too much to read in the time he had. He had an extraordinary memory."[27]

It was not enough. The books, the letters, his family, his job, the punch cards and picnics, the corn-growing and -husking contests were never sufficient to satisfy Wallace's central need, which was spiritual. As *Wallaces' Farmer* edged toward insolvency and the economic-political crisis around him intensified, so did his quest for inner light. Beginning in 1931 and continuing for several years, Wallace was engaged in intertwining relationships with a composer who claimed to be an Indian medicine man, a prominent astrologer who believed he could predict the stock market, and a visionary medical doctor who founded a utopian commune in California.

In some measure this spiritual treasure hunt was related to his anxiety over the economic pressures mounting on him and the devastating plight of agriculture in general. Wallace himself made the association in letters suggesting the economic and political crisis could be solved only by a spiritual awakening. "This present civilization all over the world seems to be getting ready to take a nose dive without much struggle," he wrote. "It is extraordinary how people possessing such wonderful inventions for producing the good things of life can by common agreement get ready to throw it all overboard just because they are unwilling to have confidence in each other."[28]

Other factors may have been playing on him, too. Sometime in 1930 Wallace left the Liberal Catholic Church, which had become embroiled in a scandal involving its international leadership. He joined the Episcopal church where his sons sang in the choir. But family and the establishment church were insufficient to satisfy his needs. His continuing search led him eventually to Taylor Falls, Minnesota, a tiny town on the banks of the St. Croix River about fifty miles northeast of St. Paul, where he encountered the remarkable figure of Charles Roos.

Roos was a poet, composer of songs, and librettist of light operattas (*The Golden Pheasant, South in Sonora*) of no particular merit. Although of Finnish ancestry, he had adopted the persona of an Indian medicine man and was steeped in the lore and ritual of Native American religion. Indeed, he had been admitted to the Chippewa Nation and allowed to participate in ceremonies around the fires of medicine lodges. In a prior life, Roos believed, he and Wallace had been Seneca warriors.

High-strung and quarrelsome, Roos could be difficult and unpleasant to those around him. He shared none of Wallace's interest in science and mathematics, understood nothing about agriculture, and cared little about economics except for his own perpetually poor financial condition. He chewed tobacco and drank whiskey and found Wallace's aversion to meat downright laughable. He mocked Wallace as a member of the "Alfalfa Tribe" and addressed him as "Chief Noketchenbuffalomeatinbelly."[29]

But their differences hardly mattered. Within hours of their first meeting on a warm summer day in 1931, Roos and Wallace had formed a deep bond. "You are in truth a POSEYEMO (enlightened one)," Roos wrote a day after they met. ". . . I stand at your side facing the red West and hold your hand . . . and it is certain that sooner or later the 'Sioux' drums will throb to a new tempo for you and you will scalp-shave your head and heel-toe the magic ring."[30] Together they purchased a tract of land in a wooded valley near Taylor Falls and dubbed it the Hawks Nest. Roos proclaimed it "holy ground" where Wallace could "hold a lodge site in the Sioux Land."[31]

During the following eighteen months Roos and Wallace engaged in an intense exchange of letters, punctuated by occasional visits to the Hawks Nest. Roos's letters to "Poo-Yaw" (meaning "thirsty heart") or "Chief Cornplanter," as he called Wallace, were by turns witty, biting, and mysterious. Often he rambled on for three pages, recounting events of the day or railing against his foes or counseling Wallace, in a distinctive faux-Indian slang.

"Cornplanter: Noon. I am Lone Wolf. Squaw in East gathering Wampum. . . . I ache with foolish burdens on shoulders raw-hided thru a thousand foothills of Karma."

"He Goat: Beats Hell how HAW letters always come just as the squaw is parching the Antelope ribs. . . . I understand your case fully. And I am sticking right with you until you have come thru the Swamp of Doubt and have made safe passage over the quicksand bog. You are worth salvage!"[32]

Wallace had found a soul mate. It seemed to him that destiny had thrown the two of them together so that they could jointly "help work out the spiritual foundations for a true creative (religious, if you please) expression for the American people." The "most important" task facing them, Wallace wrote, was to seek "an opportunity to find the religious key note of the new age."[33]

Others around Wallace were less smitten. His uncle Dan, editor of a Minnesota farm paper, was introduced to Roos but only ended up drinking too much. Ilo visited the Hawks Nest but was quite unimpressed. "Mother thought the man was mad," said H. B. "She never thought he had any sense at all."[34] Besides, the sacred water that Roos gave Ilo to cure her "bowel trouble" had no impact whatever.

Through Roos, who spent his winters in Oceanside, California, Wallace next began actively corresponding with two of the West Coast's better-known seers: the astrologist L. Edward Johndro and the utopian physician William H. Dower. At Roos's suggestion Wallace wrote to Johndro in early 1932, hoping the astrologer's methods would help him analyze the weather data he had so painstakingly put on punch cards. Normal statistical methods were inadequate, Johndro told Wallace, because they "assume that all terrestial conditions can be accounted for by terrestrial causes within the mundane vicinity (in the world sense) of the event they are trying to explain."[35]

Dower, a disciple of Theosophy with a keen interest in Native American ritual, had established a cooperative farming colony and sanatorium, called the Temple of the People, near San Luis Obispo. He also ran a correspondence course on spiritual development and invited Wallace to subscribe. "Do you hear the inner call?" Dower asked. "The door of the Temple is open, and you are given the opportunity of entering and placing your feet on the Path that leads to Eternal Light and Life. If you would know the next step write now." Wallace returned the letter with a handwritten scrawl at the bottom of the page: "I would know the next step. H.A. Wallace, 19th & Grand, Des Moines, Ia. Personal."[36]

From Johndro, Wallace sought advice on all manner of things. Could Roos and he "best be of benefit to each other at Taylor's Falls or at some other place?" he asked. "Where in the corn belt can my seed corn breeding and seed corn selling be done best?" Should he consider a post he had been offered with the Iowa State extension service? Already he had turned down a professorship at Cornell University, he explained, and he had "karmic obligations to work out" to his wife and children in Des Moines. "Is my esoteric hookup best through [Roos, Dower, and Johndro] or through the Esoteric section of Besant Theosophical society at Ojai, California?"[37]

He even questioned Johndro about the benefit of astrology itself. "I wonder if I should pay much attention to astrology except from the standpoint of scientific curiosity. If the horoscope of St. Paul had been worked out it might have warned him . . . as follows: 'Beware of travelling east to Damascas. A psychic accident will befall you which will destroy your respectability, make you as wanderer on the face of the earth and eventually cause your imprisonment and death.' Should he have avoided the fatal trip?" Replied Johndro, "You seem to be against a hard proposition and to be in one of those Sun-conjunction-Uranus periods of 'difficult decisions.' . . ."[38]

Wallace's most urgent question, and the one to which Johndro gave the most study, was whether he should run for the U.S. Senate against the maverick Republican Smith Brookhart in 1932. Even as he raised the idea, Wallace expressed misgivings: "If I am forced out of the paper I may run for the Democratic nomination for Senator altho I am no more a Democrat than a Republican. This probably will result in my defeat because Iowa is still strongly Republican." Johndro studied Wallace's astrological wheel as well as Brookhart's and concluded, "There is probably no one the Democrats can pit against him in the state that will beat him this year. . . ."*[39]

Roos, on the other hand, eagerly encouraged Wallace to make the race and was convinced he would win. "It looks to me, as High Priest, that you should go to Washington on the Donkey, then come back and sit as Governor of Iowa. After that, when you are older, sadder, wiser, you may come and sit in Council with the Priests on the Windy Hill and we will make Sand Paintings to clear new trails waiting Chief Cornplanter." Wallace was wary and reluctant. "If I was successful, I fear the pressure of the new situation might make my peaceful exit to the Poseymo Council & the Inner Life under the Golden Maple more difficult. Chas., I would much rather talk with you about things of the next world than of this. But so it must be now for the time being. We of the esoteric tendencies must learn our lessons."[40]

---

*Johndro's predictive powers were no better than Wallace's. Brookhart was defeated in the Republican primary by Henry Field, a Shenandoah seed salesman who campaigned with a political Punch and Judy show mounted on the back of a truck. Amazingly, Field was defeated in November by Democrat Louis Murphy of Dubuque, a self-proclaimed "wet" on the issue of Prohibition.

Wallace didn't run for the Senate, didn't take the job at Iowa State, didn't leave *Wallaces' Farmer*, and didn't make a peaceful exit to his maple tree. By the fall of 1932, relationships between the four men were falling apart. Roos and Johndro were squabbling, in part over the issue of the Senate race. Dower was expressing reservations about Roos. Wallace was openly questioning whether astrology had any merit at all and had grown "doubtful about allowing ANYONE to have any occult (or other) leadership" over him. Johndro and Dower both assured Wallace they didn't really want to be anybody's leader. "No man is God's sole agent," Johndro wrote to Wallace; "each of us have something for someone, sometime; nothing necessary to all."[41]

His search had led Wallace back to himself. In that sense it held purpose and meaning. The "crystallization of thought which comes from prolonged observation and contemplation" of a subject had the power to "bring back a very real amount of truth," he said. To Wallace it didn't matter much whether the subject was science or astrology, business or the arts or the ancient scriptures. They were all "part of an even larger science," which could be comprehended only by continued search.[42]

❦

Misery and desperation had moved into the heartland like unwanted relatives who would never leave. The Wallace family's vision of a thriving rural society was in shambles; Iowa lay prostrate. Corn was so worthless that many farm families burned it to keep warm instead of lugging it to market. Total farm income fell by two-thirds between 1929 and 1932. Six of every ten farms in Iowa had been mortgaged to survive, and many of those did not. In the single, awful year of 1932, five of every one hundred farms in the state were foreclosed upon and sold at auction.

Most maddening of all was the presence of hunger and poverty in a land of plenty.* The "cure for hard times," Wallace told his readers, was well understood by the prophet Isaiah. "This cure is simply that a greater percentage of the income of the nation be turned back to the mass of the people." Yet the path to prosperity was blocked by "ignorance, prejudice, and hatred," he wrote. "It seems we must wander in the wilderness a while longer before our hearts are sufficiently purified and our minds sufficiently strengthened so that we can, on a worldwide basis, go in and take possession of the Promised Land."[43]

---

*When Arkansas was stricken with drought in 1931, Wallace organized a relief drive and collected three train car loads of corn and oats from Iowa farmers. Only after the cars were loaded did he learn that the Red Cross didn't have enough money to pay for transportation. The incident, Wallace thought, perfectly illustrated the insanity of an economic system that permitted want in the midst of plenty. He paid the $420 shipping cost himself.

Perhaps, he mused, a new prophet would rise up to show the way, a person who could do in America what Gandhi was doing in India. What was needed was a man of vision and imagination. The nation longed for leadership of the "Roosevelt-type."

The type of Roosevelt he had in mind was Teddy, the Wallaces' great political hero, who had been dead more than a dozen years. There was another Roosevelt, of course, who was very much available. Governor Franklin Roosevelt of New York was intent on following in his distant cousin's footsteps and was working hard to secure the Democratic presidential nomination. Like many farm leaders, Wallace was no more than lukewarm toward him.

Franklin Roosevelt appeared to be a child of privilege and the product of urban political intrigue. His views on farm policy, if he had any, were a mystery. "I thought he was just a typical easterner who didn't know too much about the west or about practical affairs—that is, the way ordinary people live," Wallace recalled. Still, Roosevelt was better than Newton Baker or John Nance Garner or other Democrats being touted by the business community, Wallace thought. Wallace's mood in the spring of 1932 was captured well in his own oral memoirs: "I was for Roosevelt, I think."[44]

There was no such indecision in the Roosevelt camp. Roosevelt wanted farm support and by early 1932 was actively pursuing it. So it was that on a sunny spring day in 1932, Henry T. Morgenthau Jr., Roosevelt's friend and Hudson Valley neighbor, chanced to appear at Henry A. Wallace's office door.

Morgenthau had an avid interest in his own farming operation, served as chairman of the New York State Agricultural Advisory Commission and as the state's commissioner of conservation, and was publisher of the *American Agriculturalist*, a small but influential New York farm journal. In this capacity, Morgenthau was active with the Standard Farm Paper Association, to which *Wallaces' Farmer* also belonged.

The match was less than perfect. Wallace had no interest in the business side of publishing, did not attend meetings of the Standard Farm Paper Association, and had never laid eyes on Morgenthau. The New Yorker struck Wallace as "a very nice fellow, rather bashful and diffident," but as a man who was "exceedingly weak and tender physically." Morgenthau, it seemed, was recovering from the bite of a black widow spider. Later Wallace concluded that Morgenthau was always recovering from something. "I've met very few people who impressed me as being so lacking in physical sturdiness."[45]

Morgenthau's case on behalf of Roosevelt didn't have much sturdiness either, as far as Wallace was concerned. Morgenthau "stated that Roosevelt was a very great man and, above everything, a very lucky man." He said it over and over. Roosevelt was a lucky man. Wallace was puzzled but "wanted to believe him."[46]

Far more influential than Morgenthau in drawing Wallace to Roosevelt was the unlikely person of M. L. Wilson, a little-known professor of agricultural economics at Montana State Agricultural College. Wilson had never played a role in Democratic Party politics; at the time Morgenthau was in Wallace's office touting his friend's luck, Wilson had not even met Roosevelt. But Wilson was afire with an idea, a genuinely radical idea that was to profoundly affect the course of American agriculture and the future of Henry A. Wallace. Wilson, a friend remarked, was "a mild man with wild ideas," and ideas were always the way to Wallace's heart.[47]

Wilson's idea was called the domestic allotment plan. Farmers who agreed to limit production would be rewarded with "allotment payments," which would supplement the income they received for crops on the open market. Its true purpose, however, was not to subsidize farmers but to control production. Wallace was attracted to the logic of it. If enough farmers participated, prices would rise and the need for allotment payments would be lessened.

Soon Wallace was serving on committees and attending conferences to push the domestic allotment plan. In actuality, it was only one of several farm relief proposals Wallace found plausible. "I was completely eclectic—there wasn't anything doctrinaire with me," Wallace recalled. "I was for anything that would work."[48]

As the 1932 presidential election approached, Wilson sought ways to push the domestic allotment plan onto the political playing field. Despite the fundamentally radical nature of the plan, Wilson found support for it in financial circles and even within the Hoover administration. Henry I. Harriman, president of the U.S. Chamber of Commerce, was persuaded by Wallace to see its merits. Insurance companies, which were ending up with vast amounts of foreclosed farmland, supported it. John Black, the distinguished Harvard economist who was serving as an adviser to the Farm Board, backed it and even persuaded the board's president, Alexander Legge, to endorse the concept of production controls.

The search for support among Democrats was more frustrating. Most farm organizations were unaware of or uninterested in the plan, and it certainly was of no concern to labor unions. Most of the party's top politicians had never heard of it. Then, in the spring of 1932, Wilson met a man who could open Democratic doors: Rexford Guy Tugwell. Handsome and urbane, Tugwell was a curly-haired Columbia University economics professor with a passion for "national planning" and an interest in Democratic politics. The son of a prosperous orchard farmer and canner, Tugwell maintained a lifelong interest in agricultural policy. By 1932 he was one of a small group of intellectuals advising Franklin Roosevelt.

Tugwell liked Wilson, with his professorial manner and precisely reasoned arguments, and he liked Wilson's plan. Moreover, he convinced Wilson that Roosevelt was the candidate who could make the domestic allotment plan a reality. A few weeks later, at a University of Chicago conference on agriculture, they added Wallace to the team. Shortly before Wallace was to deliver a paper arguing for an increase in the price of gold, Wilson casually introduced Tugwell to Wallace as "one of the Brain Trust."*

Wilson and Tugwell drew Wallace to Roosevelt, and in turn drew Roosevelt to Wallace. Days after the midsummer Democratic National Convention in Chicago, at which Roosevelt captured the nomination on the fourth ballot, a letter arrived at Wallace's office in Des Moines. It invited Henry A. Wallace, a registered Republican and son of a Republican cabinet officer, to lunch with the Democratic presidential candidate on August 13 at Hyde Park.

In Iowa the mood was ugly that miserable summer. Almost every day brought news of bank failures and farm foreclosures. "Penny auctions," where bands of intimidating farmers forced the sale of foreclosed property back to its owners for a few cents, became commonplace. Milo Reno, the aging agrarian demagogue with whom Wallace rode during the 1928 campaign, put on his old black Stetson and reemerged as head of a new organization called the Farmers Holiday Association. The idea was to withhold farm products from the market, by force if need be, until farmers were assured of receiving the "cost of production."

Like his forebears, Wallace was uncomfortable with populist insurrection. He thought Reno's notion of a farm strike was ill conceived at best, but he understood well the anger and frustration behind it. And he could not conceive of any solution so long as Hoover remained in the White House. For reasons rooted in the long agricultural farm depression and bitter personal experience, he longed intensely for Hoover's defeat. Wallace accepted Roosevelt's invitation with pleasure.

There was, however, another reason the invitation delighted him, and Roosevelt would have been flabbergasted by it. He saw the trip as an opportunity to explore American Indian religion and search for a past life in which he and Charles Roos roamed together as warriors.

Immediately after receiving the invitation, Wallace contacted Ruth Muskrat Bronson of the Department of Interior's Indian Bureau and Henry Roe Cloud

*"I liked Rex Tugwell very much," Wallace recalled in his oral memoirs. "I think he's fundamentally a very constructive person. He also is tender physically—not quite so tender as Morgenthau, but he constantly has hay fever or asthma or bronchial trouble which makes him very miserable. He's very fastidious physically."

of Yale University, seeking information about the Onondaga tribe and its spiritual leaders. "I am especially interested in having pointed out to me certain historic spots in the Hiawatha region. It happens that I am to be in Syracuse about August 12," he told them. He also arranged to lecture at Cornell University, which would defray his expenses.[49]

To Dr. Dower at the Temple of the People in California, Wallace wrote with urgency about his need to be with the Onondaga tribe. Dower, who had been initiated into the tribe thirty years before, replied, "You undoubtedly at some time lived with the Iroquois Indians as one of them, or you would not have this strong feeling of wanting to contact them; and this no doubt comes about because of some cycle in your life at the present time."[50]

Roos, too, was excited about Wallace's forthcoming journey, although he urged his friend not to forget about its real purpose. "Again I say you hit High Hills if you can land Sec. Agriculture under Roosevelt! Eight years at this post will give you great chance to give SERVICE to your country," Roos wrote. "Hop to it with vigor and belief and trust."[51]

The trip east was a success in every respect from Wallace's viewpoint. The lecture at Cornell was well received, and his visit to the Onondaga tribe proved deeply satisfying. Tribal elders confirmed his prior existence as an Iroquois warrior and invited him to participate in a "Fire Sacrifice" using "true Indian tobacco." The tribe's material existence weighed on Wallace, however. The Indian's poor living conditions and "a rather deplorable internal political situation" troubled him.[52]

If his visit with "some of the men who knew the old legends" fulfilled Wallace's expectations, the man he met in Hyde Park exceeded everything he had imagined. Wallace had expected to see a man born to "a background of wealth" and reared in the corruption of urban politics. Moreover, Wallace later told his readers, "I had heard that his legs were paralyzed, and I feared that he would be completely tired out." To Wallace's "great surprise" he found instead "a man with a fresh, eager, open mind, ready to pitch into the agricultural problem at once. . . . He knows that he doesn't know it all, and tries to find out all he can from people who are supposed to be authorities."[53]

Roosevelt's charm and uncanny ability to read personalities were in full play. As the lunch with Wallace stretched from its scheduled thirty minutes to almost two hours, Roosevelt happily speculated about the viability of a "shelter belt" of trees across the Great Plains, talked about plans for his own farmland in Georgia, and listened intently to the editor's discussion of the "tenancy problem" and the solutions that had been applied in England and Ireland. "Nothing—nothing at all—was said about his Cabinet appointments if he should be elected," Wallace later recalled. "We didn't discuss the election or the campaign at all. Not an iota. No politics, as such, came up at all that day."[54]

For the first time, Wallace had committed himself to the success of a politician rather than to a cause.

Wallace's first real opportunity to express his commitment came in September, when M. L. Wilson arrived in Des Moines and together they drafted a major agricultural address that would put Roosevelt on record in favor of the domestic allotment plan. Here at last was a chance to link the great cause of his life—the rescue of American agriculture—to politics at the highest level. Wallace was ecstatic. "It is heartwarming to work for appreciation such as yours," he telegrammed Roosevelt after completing a preliminary draft of the farm speech.[55] In the end the farm speech Roosevelt delivered in Topeka was a good deal more vague than the Wallace-Wilson draft, but it did include a carefully worded promise to raise farm prices without stimulating production. As far as Wallace was concerned, Roosevelt was for the domestic allotment plan, whether he said so or not.

Wallace returned to Iowa and threw himself headlong into the Roosevelt campaign. He lobbied farm leaders feverishly, editorialized at full throttle, and spoke to every political gathering that invited him, even serving as a Democratic counterpoint to the famed evangelist Billy Sunday in the campaign's closing days. On one occasion he denounced Hoover as the most dangerous man in America.

When Hoover gave his own farm speech to a sullen crowd in Des Moines on October 4, Wallace responded with sarcasm. The farmer "quietly sitting in his home must have been amazed to learn from Herbert Hoover that the depression was so completely conquered," Wallace wrote to Morgenthau. He added dryly, "New corn is selling for ten cents a bushel and hogs at three cents a pound on the farm."[56]

To the readers of *Wallaces' Farmer*, Wallace stated his case in the bluntest terms possible. "The only thing to vote for in this election is justice for agriculture," he wrote. "With Roosevelt, the farmers have a chance—with Hoover, none. I shall vote for Roosevelt."[57]

Roosevelt's careful courtship of the farm vote paid off. Nationally the election was a rout: Roosevelt received 22.8 million votes to 15.7 million for Hoover, but the truly stunning news came from the farm states. For only the second time since statehood, Iowa backed a Democratic candidate for president. For good measure Iowans sent a Democrat to the U.S. Senate, threw out the populist Republican governor, and elected Democrats in six of the nine congressional districts. Even the Republican Gilbert Haugen, venerable chairman of the House Agriculture Committee whose very name was synonymous with justice for agriculture, was defeated.

On the day after the election, Wallace sat in his office and quietly dictated a letter to Bernard Baruch. "I am writing you today to carry out a promise which I made to you as I was leaving your office . . . on Wednesday, March 23. At that time, you will remember that you made the statement that Iowa would never go Democratic, that the prejudice of the middlewestern farmer was so deep that nothing could ever be done to shake it." Wallace had promised to remind Baruch of these words on the day after the election.

"I don't think you realized last spring," Wallace said in closing, "and I doubt if you realize now how mightily our people in this section of the country are being shaken."[58]

which I made to you as I was leaving your office

"**W**ell, Heart of my Heart, it sure looks as tho Ioway went a bit against German Hoover!!" Charles Roos wrote his kindred spirit. "This fact alone makes you INTERNATIONAL, or at least National! Baby!!" Roos, of course, could not resist pointing out that Roosevelt's victory had been foretold. "Now I guess old HAW will cock an ear when the Sioux Drums throb! Roos might often be wrong, but the Red Gods are ALWAYS right!! Anyway, poor Cornplanter goes to Washington!"[59]

Roos had been saying for almost a year that Wallace would be named secretary of agriculture, and Wallace knew he was in contention. Support for him came pouring in from farm leaders, and speculation about his appointment was common in the press. But he also knew that many others were vying for the job, including Henry Morgenthau, farm editor William Hirth, Georgia congressman Cully Cobb, and even Rexford Guy Tugwell. Wallace said, rather disingenuously, that he was supporting the appointment of George Peek.

To those who wrote in support of him, Wallace maintained a stance of reluctance. "If the job were offered to me, I suppose I would take it although it would be with considerable misgivings," he wrote one well-wisher. "I know from my father's experience just what this job means in times like the present." Perhaps he could be of help to Roosevelt, he wrote another supporter, but added, "I sincerely trust that fate will not carry me into that hell down at Washington."[60]

Fate's intention was soon apparent. In late November, a few days after he sent Roosevelt a letter supporting the appointment of Peek, Wallace received a telephone call from Raymond Moley, the Columbia University professor who was first among equals in the Brain Trust. Moley said Roosevelt wanted to see Wallace in Warm Springs, Georgia, where he was vacationing after the campaign. Wallace understood the implication. Soon he was aboard a train headed for the red clay hills of western Georgia.

The sixty-eight-hour train ride was a trip into unknown territory for the young Iowa editor. He had never before been in the Deep South, and he was "utterly amazed and appalled at the red-gashed hillsides, at the unkept cabins, some of them without windows or doors. It was a situation, it seemed to me with an Iowa farm background, that was almost unbelievable."[61]

He was no better prepared for the sight that greeted him when he arrived at Roosevelt's shabby resort, on the morning of Monday, November 28. Something of a "carnival atmosphere" pervaded the place, Wallace thought. Knowing he was early, Wallace checked his suitcase at the ramshackle hotel and ambled along to Roosevelt's cottage. He arrived about nine and was greeted by a guard. "He told me that nobody was up yet," Wallace recalled, "which quite astounded me."[62]

When at last he was ushered into the cottage, Wallace discovered Roosevelt still engaged in his morning routine. For most of an hour the two men talked about agriculture while Roosevelt shaved himself with a straight-edged razor and consumed his breakfast. Then the Iowan was given over to Moley and Morgenthau for more hours of talk. With his high forehead and thin lips, Moley had a cerebral manner with which Wallace was comfortable. The professor's background was not in agriculture, but he seemed to grasp readily the political and economic implications of Wallace's thinking. By the end of the day, Wallace had concluded, perhaps unfairly, that Morgenthau's chief function in Warm Springs was "to get safe liquor for the evening cocktail."[63]

In the evening Wallace got another taste of Roosevelt's fabulous style. Over cocktails, of which Wallace did not partake, he watched in awe as Roosevelt "made himself utterly charming" to Senator Key Pittman, a Nevada Democrat whose mission in life was the promotion of silver. For an hour and a half, as Pittman tried in vain to turn the subject to his precious metal, Roosevelt spun out an incredible tale of buried treasure on Oak Island, off the coast of Nova Scotia. It was an exercise in deflection and distraction, conducted with gusto and élan, that Wallace would witness "a hundred times" over the next dozen years.[64]

As Morgenthau drove Wallace through the night to catch a train, the long day's events spun in his head. Something important had happened, but he was not entirely certain what it was. The trip to Warm Springs, Wallace said later, "was a complete break with all that I had been and all that I had known, and a new outlook on life."[65] He stood at a threshold but could see only dimly what lay beyond.

Wallace had not been asked to become secretary of agriculture, but he had somehow become part of Roosevelt's team. He had committed himself to go to Washington and work for passage of a farm relief program in the lame-duck Congress. It seemed to Wallace an "utterly fantastic and foolish" idea, but he would do it if Roosevelt wanted it done.[66] Roosevelt had not endorsed any particular plan of action, but he was committed to action. That was of

great importance. The president-elect was a "daring adventurer." Wallace was
ready to stand at his side.

An invitation to join the cabinet was not immediately forthcoming. Wallace
busied himself with meetings and bill-drafting sessions in Washington amid
a chaotic atmosphere that convinced him he was engaged in "utterly a wild
goose chase." No farm relief bill worthy of the name had a chance of becoming law. "How could you expect such legislation to be signed by Herbert
Hoover?" he wondered.[67] Wallace was slow to realize that Roosevelt's real purpose was not to overcome Hoover's resistance but to build support for an agricultural relief plan among farm leaders themselves. Any plan would suffice,
as far as Roosevelt was concerned, as long as the farm leaders were unified behind it.

While Roosevelt maintained a relaxed posture, staying mostly out of public view, Wallace found it difficult to wait out the Hoover presidency in silence. Farmers found the long interregnum almost intolerable. Many of them
wrote heart-wrenching letters to Wallace seeking help, or at least hope. Others took more direct action. Milo Reno's Farmers Holiday movement resumed
its militant activities. Sheriffs, insurance company lawyers, and even judges
were threatened with violence.

Roosevelt's formal offer of a cabinet position finally reached Wallace on
February 6, 1933. Wallace had just returned from speaking to mortgage bankers
in Omaha, fighting his way back to Des Moines through a blinding blizzard,
and he was exhausted. He fell into bed without opening the letter.

"Before I leave on a ten days' fishing trip I am going to ask you to assume
a task which is of the utmost importance to the whole Country," Roosevelt's
message said. "I want to have the privilege of having you as a member of my
official family in the post of Secretary of Agriculture." He asked Wallace to
reply by radio to the yacht *Nourmahal*, via the Navy Department's communications office.[68]

Wallace hesitated. For days he read and reread Roosevelt's letter, recalling
his grandfather's injunctions against politics and his father's travails in Washington. Six days passed. On February 12 a somewhat frustrated Raymond Moley telephoned Wallace to demand a reply. "There was a long pause, which I
vividly remember to this day," Moley later wrote. "Finally, after a verbal prod
from me, I got a hesitating and rather tremulous acceptance."[69]

"This may be true," Wallace later said of Moley's account. "I don't remember it." If he did hesitate, Wallace added, it was probably because he
"wanted to get word directly to Roosevelt and not through Moley to Roo-

sevelt." In any event, he had made the decision. He had cast his fate with Franklin Roosevelt. Shortly he penned a more formal response to his new chief, still fishing aboard Vincent Astor's yacht. "Your invitation can have but one reply," Wallace said. "I appreciate the honor and accept the responsibility. So far as it is in me I will carry my part of the 'family' burdens."[70]

CHAPTER SIX

"A QUARTER TURN OF THE HEART"

A day after accepting the cabinet post, Wallace quietly boarded a train bound for New York City. A sense of crisis stormed through the nation. As Wallace passed through Detroit for a brief visit with his sister Annabelle, the governor of Michigan was proclaiming an eight-day "bank holiday" to prevent a collapse of the state's financial institutions. But in New York, where Wallace met secretly with Roosevelt at his Sixty-fifth Street home, he found the president-elect full of sunny self-confidence. Roosevelt had just survived an assassination attempt in Miami but didn't even mention the incident to Wallace. He wanted to talk about ways of balancing the budget.

Wallace returned to Iowa with little to do but pack—and wait. Roosevelt did not reveal the appointment until February 26, a snowy Sunday in Hyde Park, when he invited reporters into his study after returning from church. There he announced the appointments of Wallace as agriculture secretary and James A. Farley as postmaster general.

Wallace was walking with friends in Waterworks Park, a spacious public park above the city's underground water galleries, when news of the appointment reached Des Moines. A young Western Union bicycle messenger somehow managed to find them and handed Wallace a telegram. Wallace read it and said nothing. The others were less restrained. "We were all delighted and of course said so," his friend Jim LeCron recalled, "but Henry was quite quiet about it. . . . Henry never got terrifically excited about things. He was very calm."[1]

Reaction to the appointment from others who knew him—farmers, mid-western dailies, the agricultural press—was almost universally favorable. Illinois farm editor Clifford Gregory called Wallace a "valiant battler" who would become "one of the big men of the cabinet." The *Des Moines Register* proclaimed the news with an eight-column banner headline: "WALLACE NAMED TO CABINET." A front-page cartoon by the *Register*'s famed cartoonist, J. N. "Ding" Darling, depicted a somewhat worried Roosevelt pointing to a stricken, bedridden patient named Agriculture. "He says he has shooting pains, a terrific headache, chills and fever and a queer feeling in his stomach!" says Roosevelt. Wallace, the confident family physician, replies, "Yes, I know! You see I'm rather familiar with the history of his case."[2]

"Nobody will come to him with an air of superior wisdom and try to tell him what he does not know about agriculture," said Harvey Ingham, the *Register*'s longtime editor. "Mr. Wallace will come as near to having both theory and practice as any man in the president's cabinet."[3]

Wallace's vast knowledge of his field and his intense sense of mission were certain to make him an unusual figure in Washington. Here was a man unswayed by avarice or personal ambition. Here was a man not given to compromise and niceties. It could be a little scary, really. Said one of his friends, "Henry would cut off his right hand for the sake of an idea—and yours too for that matter."[4]

Wallace's departure from Iowa was a melancholy task made more difficult by bank closings, which left him strapped for cash. Control of Pioneer Hi-Bred, his still-struggling hybrid seed company, was turned over to his friend Fred Lehmann. His farewell to the readers of *Wallaces' Farmer* eschewed the odd headline used by his grandfather and father on important occasions—"A Word Personal"—but his tone was much the same:

> This is the last time, for a while at least, that I shall be writing this column. I am going to Washington, March 4, to serve as Secretary of Agriculture in the Cabinet of President Roosevelt.
>
> I remember how my father left home twelve years ago to take a similar position under President Harding. He accepted a Cabinet place because he felt keenly the need of trying to restore the agricultural values smashed in the decline of 1920–21 and because he feared there would be a much more serious smash later on unless both the Government and the city people of the United States became aware of their debt and duty to the farmer. To this cause he gave his life. . . .
>
> While the situation of the world today is far more desperate today than it was then, I have an advantage he did not have—a chief who is definitely progressive, entirely sympathetic toward agriculture, and completely

determined to use every means at his command to restore farm buying power. . . .

I will try to do my part in Washington. No doubt I shall make many mistakes, but I hope it can always be said that I have done the best I knew.[5]

He would remain on the masthead of *Wallaces' Farmer* as "editor on leave" for another thirteen years, but he was never to return.*

***

His first steps into the national area were a bit wobbly. The day before the inauguration Wallace paid a courtesy call on outgoing agriculture secretary Arthur M. Hyde, which turned into a fiasco. First Hyde forgot the names of some of the career civil servants who headed the department's bureaus when he was introducing the men to Wallace. That was followed by a blunt declaration from Wallace that "drastic adjustments" in the department were coming. The bureau chiefs, some of whom had been with the department long enough to remember Wallace as "Harry's boy," listened in stunned silence. "He was virtually telling them they were going to have their heads cut off," said Nils Olsen, head of the economics bureau.[6]

Hyde volunteered no help to his successor, nor did Wallace think to ask. "We were very green," Ilo Wallace said later, "and knew nothing about the sort of arrangements that could be made, not even that we could ask for a limousine from the Department of Agriculture."[7] The result was a comedy of errors in which Wallace very nearly missed Roosevelt's inauguration altogether.

Inauguration Day, Saturday, March 4, began with a prayer service at St. John's Episcopal Church, across Lafayette Square from the White House. Only the Roosevelts, the cabinet members, their wives, and their grown children attended. Afterward, the new cabinet members milled about outside, some introducing themselves to others for the first time. The more experienced among them sped off in arranged transportation. Henry and Ilo Wallace found themselves alone on the street with Frances Perkins, the new secretary of labor, and her daughter Susanna. "I suppose we're all going to the same place," Perkins said to Wallace. "You're Miss Perkins, aren't you?" Wallace asked. "And you're the Wallaces, I'm sure," she replied.[8] They agreed to share a taxi to the Capitol.

---

*The Pierce family eventually sold *Wallaces' Farmer* to Capital Cities Communications as part of a package that included a radio station in Illinois. Ownership of the publication passed to the Walt Disney corporation with its purchase of Capital Cities. Disney subsequently sold the farm journal.

Wallaces Farmer—absent the apostrophe after the Wallace family name—continues to be published in a monthly magazine format.

Eventually they arrived on Capitol Hill, only to find themselves on the wrong side of the grounds. A policeman curtly rejected Wallace's plea that they be allowed to drive closer. "You should have gone some other way or come earlier. Look at the crowd!" They tried frantically to press their way through the assembled masses. "Will you let us through," Wallace begged. "Please. Kindly make way." It was slow going. Wallace concluded that their only hope of reaching the platform lay in blazing a new path.

"I hope you have your rubbers on," Wallace exclaimed to Perkins.[9] With that the two secretary designates began racing uphill across the open lawn. At the platform they found their seats already filled. Finally they found a place to stand at the far edge. It was hardly a moment of grandeur for Wallace and Perkins. They could see nothing of the ceremony and heard only fragments of Roosevelt's famous address. "The one thing I caught at the time was his reference to casting the money-changers out of the temple," Wallace recalled. He liked that.[10]

It was a cold and cheerless day, and Wallace watched the seemingly endless inaugural parade with "a feeling of imminent, dire crisis." There was no question of the new president's good intentions. "The question was, whether we could find the technical means to get out of it in a hurry, because people were so desperate," Wallace later commented.[11] As if to underscore his intention to begin acting immediately, Roosevelt gathered his new cabinet in the White House that evening and had Justice Benjamin Cardozo swear them in. Roosevelt jokingly said he was doing it to give them an extra day's pay.

Wallace didn't reach his new office until Monday. It was familiar territory. For more than two decades he had been in and out of the secretary's spacious second-floor quarters, located in the department's administrative offices at Fourteenth Street and Jefferson Drive. From its windows the secretary had an unobstructed view of the Washington Monument towering to the west and the serene beauty of the Mall to the north. In typical fashion Wallace simply arrived and went to work. The desk and office furniture were kept exactly as his predecessor had left them. The walls remained bare until Wallace had time to track down the department's official oil portrait of his father, which had been stashed from view during the Hoover years.

To the painting of his father, Wallace eventually added three artifacts to his office walls: a cartoon of Harry Wallace by Ding Darling, whose nationally famous work appeared daily on the front page of the *Des Moines Register*; an unsigned work by a Native American, depicting in bright colors a missionary holding a Bible; and a clay-colored work symbolizing the high place of corn in the Mayan civilization. Family, religion, agriculture. That was the extent of Wallace's taste in decoration.

More important than interior design was the plain table behind his desk. There, within easy reach, he kept a series of gray notebooks containing commodity prices and other agricultural data he had compiled over two decades. Around these one-of-a-kind notebooks were constantly changing piles of books and documents that constituted Wallace's reading of the moment. The work table, casual and unkempt, was the heart of his office. Utility came before appearance always.

The first hours and days in his new office were hectic and chaotic. A palpable sense of crisis—a feeling Wallace was determined not to let lapse into panic hung over the department like a fog. Action was demanded, but precisely what action was not clear. Although Wallace headed a department with 40,794 employees, he had virtually no personal staff and few top advisers as yet. The White House, not much better organized, was consumed by the banking crisis and not at all focused on the problems of agriculture. Given the circumstances, Wallace was forced to rely heavily on holdovers from the Hoover administration in whom he felt some confidence.

His first personnel action was to appoint Milton Eisenhower to head the department's information services. Eisenhower, the brother of Major Dwight D. Eisenhower, was a Republican, but Wallace quickly demonstrated a lack of concern for political pedigree. Wallace's only instruction was to make it clear "that it was essential to transform the department immediately into a vast action agency to restore parity of income to American farmers," Eisenhower later wrote.[12]

With few exceptions, it is doubtful Wallace even knew the political affiliation of his appointees. Certainly he never asked and didn't care. "There were two or three people who had been very active politically for the Republicans who came in and offered their resignations," Wallace recalled. "I didn't ask for them, but they came in and offered their resignations." He rebuffed several attempts by partisan New Dealers to have Eisenhower and other Republicans dismissed. Postmaster General Jim Farley, the administration's patronage chief, never interfered. "In the case of the higher positions, we never considered politics at all," said Wallace. "I don't think we ever fired anybody from the department for political reasons. . . . Farley never insisted on shoving off on us an incompetent person."[13]

Rexford Guy Tugwell left no doubt about wanting to be part of the New Deal. The surprise was which part. He could have opted for a White House advisory role, as his fellow Brain Trust member Raymond Moley had. But

Tugwell thirsted for action and sensed he would find it with Henry Wallace. He asked to be appointed assistant secretary of agriculture.

They presented a rather odd picture together—the dapper Columbia University professor and the tousled Iowa editor—but they made a good team. They were men of ideas and shared a vision of government that was activist and progressive. Wallace knew the practical aspects of American farming the way a sailor knew the stars. And Tugwell knew Franklin Roosevelt.

Their immediate problem was to make agriculture part of the action. The New Deal was less than a hundred hours old, but already Tugwell could see that "the ills of the farmers formed . . . only a rumbling in the Washington background; the monetary crisis was more dramatic and was monopolizing attention." Tugwell suggested he and Wallace take a walk and plot their next move. They had worked together only a few days, but Tugwell had seen enough to know that Wallace liked to walk and was not entirely comfortable in his new quarters. "He took shyly to his large office and sat uneasily sideways at the big desk in its center," Tugwell recalled. "He looked at first as though he had just strayed in from somewhere and wanted nothing so much as to find a way out."[14]

They sauntered west, toward the Washington Monument; by the time they returned, Tugwell and Wallace had come up with a plan that would change the face and future of American agriculture. Their scheme was simple and bold at once: give the secretary of agriculture sweeping executive authority, not tied to any particular plan, to rescue farmers. In concept, their idea was similar to the proposed "emergency" monetary legislation granting Roosevelt broad executive authority to deal with banking crises.

"It occurred to us that the protracted [congressional] wrangling we were dreading might be evaded by an omnibus emergency bill authorizing the proposals being pushed by competing lobbyists," Tugwell later wrote. "Decisions could thus be deferred and perhaps altogether removed from legislative bickering. Successful action, we thought, might smother arguments; and, best of all, we might get to work at once."[15]

Immediate action was essential. With each passing day, Wallace noted, "cotton was sprouting on an expanded acreage. Winter wheat was ripening. Spring wheat was going in. Hog and cattle numbers were reaching record numbers. . . ."[16]

That evening, March 8, 1933, Wallace and Tugwell met with Roosevelt in an effort to persuade him to expand the scope of the special congressional session to include the agricultural crisis as well as the banking emergency. Roosevelt approved their plan on the spot. He liked its flexibility and the possibility it held for avoiding a lengthy fight in Congress. Besides, he said, the farm legislation would give Congress something to do while he prepared bills on other fronts.

Wallace returned to the Agriculture Department and set immediately to work. The first step was to summon the nation's farm leaders to an "emergency conference" to be held in Washington only two days hence. Wallace personally phoned everyone who came to mind. By Friday, March 10, the heads of the American Farm Bureau, the National Grange, and some fifty others had gathered at the Department of Agriculture to discuss the crisis. The meeting was only three hours old when Wallace went on national radio to tell the country what was at stake. "Today, in this country, men are fighting to save their homes. That is not just a figure of speech. That is a brutal fact, a bitter commentary on agriculture's twelve years' struggle. What do we propose to do about it? . . . Emergency action is imperative."[17]

Wallace got what he wanted. At the close of the day, he was able to issue a statement saying, "The farm leaders were unanimous in their opinion that the agricultural emergency calls for prompt and drastic action. . . . The farm groups agree that farm production must be adjusted to consumption, and favor the principles of the so-called domestic allotment plan as a means of reducing production and restoring buying power. . . ."[18] The conference called for emergency legislation granting Wallace extraordinarily broad authority to act, including power to control production, buy up surplus commodities, regulate marketing and production, and levy excise taxes to pay for it all.

For the moment, at least, the notoriously fractious farm organizations had banded together in a single army and accepted Henry Wallace as their commanding general.

The sense of urgency was hardly theoretical. A true crisis was at hand. Across the Corn Belt, rebellion was being expressed in ever more violent terms. In the first two months of 1933, there were at least seventy-six instances in fifteen states of so-called penny auctions, in which mobs of farmers gathered at foreclosure sales and intimidated legitimate bidders into silence. One penny auction in Nebraska drew an astounding crowd of two thousand farmers. In Wisconsin farmers bent on stopping a farm sale were confronted by deputies armed with tear gas and machine guns. A lawyer representing the New York Life Insurance Company was dragged from the courthouse in Le Mars, Iowa, and the sheriff who tried to help him was roughed up by a mob.

Communist agitators such as the notorious Mother Bloor set up shop in hard-hit rural areas and began dispensing doughnuts and Marxist ideology. Farm state politicians responded to the radicalism with remedies that were themselves radical. In North Dakota, Governor William Langer used state troops to prevent local sheriffs from conducting foreclosure auctions. In Minnesota, Governor Floyd Olson imposed a moratorium on foreclosure sales by executive decree, an action later found unconstitutional. Seven other states took similar actions.

At the nexus of the farm protest was the indomitable Milo Reno, brash head of the Farmers Holiday Association, who by March 1933 had reached the height of his power and popularity. Reno's claim of ninety thousand dues-paying members was almost certainly an exaggeration, but his ability to create a ruckus was unquestionable. The day after Wallace's emergency farm conference concluded in Washington, Reno led some three thousand disgruntled farmers on a march to the state capitol in Des Moines, where he issued a sweeping list of demands and vowed to mount a nationwide farm strike if they were not met by May 3.

With time short and tensions high, Wallace and a handful of aides frantically set out to turn their plan into law. It was a daunting task. Wallace later wrote, "To make provision for flexibility in the bill; to give the Secretary of Agriculture power to make contracts to reduce acreage with millions of individuals, and power to make marketing agreements with processors and distributors; to transfer to the Secretary, even if temporarily, the power to levy processing taxes; to express in legislation the concept of parity—all these points, and a thousand others, were unorthodox and difficult to express even by men skilled in the law."[19]

The drafting was done primarily by Frederic Lee, former legislative counsel to the U.S. Senate then working for the Farm Bureau, and Jerome Frank, one of the brilliant young men dispatched to the New Deal by the Harvard law professor Felix Frankfurter. Hovering over their shoulders were Mordecai Ezekiel, a courtly southerner who had been one of Harry Wallace's bright young aides, Rex Tugwell, George Peek, and Chester Davis. "Occasionally I was suspected of having had something to do with it," Wallace commented wryly.[20] The draft was completed in four sleepless days.

Wallace walked it over to the White House and handed it to Roosevelt personally. The president in turn sent it off to Congress with a message to the nation: "I tell you frankly that it is a new and untrod path, but I tell you with equal frankness that an unprecedented condition calls for the trial of new means."[21] The New Deal was not yet two weeks old.

On March 16, H.R. 3835, entitled the "Agricultural Emergency Act to Increase Farm Purchasing Power," was introduced by Marvin Jones, the House Agriculture Committee chairman. "Seldom, if ever, has so sweeping a piece of legislation been introduced in the American Congress," said the *New York Herald Tribune*.[22] Wallace agreed, calling it "a contrivance as new in the field of social relations as the first gasoline engine was new in the field of mechanics."[23]

Nevertheless, Jones pushed the bill through the House with breathtaking speed. On March 22 the House approved the measure unamended, by a vote of 315 to 98. For a giddy moment it seemed to Wallace and his aides that their farm bill might become law in two weeks.

But reality soon confronted them in the Senate. The Farmers' Union president, John Simpson, if not the most powerful farm leader then certainly the most vocal, stated his opposition in blunt terms. An "army of bureaucrats" would be needed to enforce the measure, he told the Senate Agriculture Committee, and in the end they would not succeed. Far better would be a "cost of production" provision, Simpson said, which would guarantee farmers a fair return on their investment and labor.

For at least a dozen years, Wallace had argued that "cost of production" was a "will o' the wisp" price-fixing scheme that would, in effect, turn farming into a regulated public utility. Moreover, Simpson's scheme offered no means of controlling production and thus was incompatible with the very concept of the domestic allotment plan. Finally, Wallace maintained, the purchasing power of city dwellers was so low in 1933 that an effort to fix the price of food at a high level would result in an economic and political disaster.

The fact was, however, that "cost of production" was an easy concept to grasp and had wide appeal in farm states. Moreover, senators who favored addressing the farm crisis through inflation seized upon the farm bill as an opportunity to push cheap-money schemes. And the millers and processors, stunned by the rapidity with which Wallace's bill had been passed in the House, began to regroup and make their case against the excise tax provision.

The farm bill began to bog down. Slowly it began to dawn on Wallace and his team that they were in trouble. On April 13 their fears were confirmed when the Senate voted 47 to 41 in favor of an amendment incorporating cost of production into the bill. It was the New Deal's first legislative setback. A few days later the Senate narrowly rejected Montana senator Burton Wheeler's amendment mandating the free and unlimited coinage of silver. Inflationists treated the vote as a victory.

Roosevelt took the steam out of the inflationists by agreeing to accept several provisions, including reduction of the gold content of the dollar, as long as they were discretionary rather than mandatory. But the cost-of-production amendment remained in the bill, and Wallace began to prepare himself for compromise if not defeat.

Then, on April 27 in the tiny town of Le Mars, Iowa, the forces of radicalism went too far. A mob of six hundred militant farmers, returning from a nearby foreclosure sale, turned its attention on the courtroom of Judge Charles C. Bradley, who was hearing a case testing the constitutionality of Iowa's moratorium law. When the judge ordered the men to remove their hats and stop smoking, about a hundred of them surged forward, pulled bandanas over their faces, and dragged him from the courthouse.

Bradley was shoved onto the bed of a farm truck and taken to a crossroads outside of town, where his pants were removed and he was threatened with mutilation. A noose was pulled tight around his neck, and the mob demanded that the strangling judge promise no further foreclosures. "I will do the fair thing to all men to the best of my knowledge," he bravely gasped. A local newspaper editor who had followed the mob to the crossroads managed to persuade the men to stop short of murder. As a final indignity, the men filled a hubcap full of grease and put it on the sixty-year-old judge's head, filled his pants with gravel and threw them in a ditch. They left him dazed and alone by the road.[24]

The incident at Le Mars drew national attention; the *New York Times* gave it front-page coverage. Newspapers across Iowa denounced it as an act of cowardice and rebellion. Governor Clyde Herring declared martial law and dispatched troops. Reno tried to disavow the incident, claiming the men were not part of the Farmers Holiday movement, but his statement was widely disbelieved, especially after he sought the help of the famed criminal lawyer Clarence Darrow in defending the men.* Reno and his followers were subjected to a torrent of criticism, from which they never recovered.

The "Corn Belt rebellion" changed the dynamics of the farm debate. The Farmers' Union, which was closely associated with Reno and the Farmers Holiday movement, was greviously wounded. Wallace was seen as a moderate; the plan he espoused was "the middle course," in his own words, a course of action between the status quo and radicalism.[25] The Senate passed the farm bill with the cost-of-production provision, but the House stood firm against it in conference committee.

Time was not on the Senate's side. Cotton was sprouting, corn was being planted, hogs were propagating, and the nation's six million farmers wanted action. On May 10, recognizing that patience was wearing thin, the Senate voted 48 to 33 to abandon the cost-of-production amendment. The next day the Senate gave the measure final approval, and Roosevelt promptly signed it into law. In Des Moines, Milo Reno could see that the game was over. He called off his threatened farm strike indefinitely.

---

*Iowa military authorities arrested a total of eighty-six men, including the president of the Plymouth County Farmers Holiday Association, and kept them in carefully guarded stockades for more than two weeks. A plan to try the men in military courts under charges of criminal conspiracy and armed rebellion—Darrow's main point of interest in the case—never materialized. On May 1 the military raided the Communist Party headquarters in Sioux City, arrested several people, and seized a mimeograph machine, but Mother Bloor herself was not present and no charges were brought. Trials of the farmers, held in civil courts, resulted in light fines and jail terms ranging from one day to six months. Governor Herring revoked martial law on May 11, the same day the farm bill won final approval in Congress.

The twelve-year effort by farmers to "build a modern vessel with which to reach the new world" had at last succeeded, Wallace wrote in *New Frontiers*, published the following year. In less than two months Congress had fashioned a boat and the president had pronounced it seaworthy. "The craft was launched on May 12, 1933, and immediately set on a course toward social justice. At this writing we have not reached our destination, but our farming people are proceeding with confidence, and they have made remarkable progress, on the whole."[26]

Rarely has a public figure's talent so perfectly matched his opportunity. Henry A. Wallace, born to a family whose very mission was the preservation of agriculture, had become the mobilizing general of just such an effort. The prophet of reform had become the agent of change; the thinker had become the doer. Few men knew more about agriculture than Wallace, and no man anywhere burned with greater zeal to rescue farmers from their cruel misfortune. This was Henry Wallace's hour.

"It would have been impossible to have gotten these men [the leaders of various interest groups] to agree on anything if it had not been for the utter seriousness of the times," he remarked. "I've observed that whenever matters get completely serious in the United States, it is possible for these groups, which in ordinary times are continually fighting, to pull together to get out of the quagmire."[27]

Within days of taking office, Wallace and his aides had crafted a bill that was to effect the most dramatic change ever made in agricultural policy. President Roosevelt praised it as the most far-reaching farm bill ever proposed in peacetime. A Republican senator damned it as "the most revolutionary proposal that has ever been presented in the history of the government."[28] In less than two months this sweeping measure was law, and Wallace was constructing a huge new bureaucratic machine to administer its provisions. The law gave Wallace powers broader in scope than any cabinet officer had ever enjoyed, and he used them to put an imprint on agricultural policy that would endure for more than half a century.

Suddenly the young editor from Iowa seemed to be everywhere: pressing his cause in the committee rooms of Congress, explaining his policies to nationwide radio audiences, philosophizing before large audiences from Salina, Kansas, to Tuskegee, Alabama, to Chicago, Illinois. He mused about science before the Franklin Institute in Philadelphia and lectured on religion at the Chicago Theological Seminary, wrote an influential pamphlet on world trade and set out his policy views in *New Frontiers*, a 300-page book illuminated by his "dominating conviction that in the realm of economics social justice can be defined, that it can be measured and that it can eventually be realized if human beings will put their minds and hearts to the task."[29]

Bright young men from big-city law firms and rural universities, eager to be part of the New Deal, flocked to his department. The halls of the once sleepy agriculture building teemed with lawyers and lobbyists, left-wing farmers and right-wing businessmen, jaded newspapermen and jittery politicians. The place throbbed with activity: late-night meetings and long-distance calls, the clatter of typewriters and the bustle of aides. A wide-eyed visitor from Russia gazed upon a boiler-room operation brimming with keypunch operators and machines capable of cranking out eighty thousand checks a day and exclaimed, "Good Lord! This is a revolution!"[30]

The man at the heart of this revolution had not yet reached his forty-fifth birthday, and he struck many people as a walking paradox: a registered Republican in a Democratic administration, a vegetarian from a hog-producing state, a reserved and private soul in the most garrulous and public of professions. There was about him something unknowable, an odd coolness, a "baffling diffidence" that associates found hard to fathom.[31]

Yet there was a flip side to his personality that many people found fresh and appealing. He was utterly without pretense or guile. In a town where some politicians still wore high collars and frock coats, Wallace was rumpled and casual. Once, returning from a midday tennis match, he strode through the department's main lobby barefoot, absently carrying his street shoes in his hand. Cartoonists loved his wiry shock of unruly auburn hair and big toothy grin. Reporters delighted in his candid, freewheeling press conferences, the secretary stretched out sideways behind his desk with his feet propped up on a wastebasket.

"No swank," the author Sherwood Anderson wrote of him.[32]

It was all the more astounding, therefore, that this quiet, eccentric intellectual became a star. The youngest member of the cabinet, among its least-known and least-political members, he became one of the most-watched, most-talked-about people in Washington. The man who had known Roosevelt for less than a year became a valued adviser. He seemed in sync with the new administration's goals and had about him a sense of gravity and purpose. "Primarily he is a disinterested spirit, motivated by a sense of justice and scientific method," wrote the philosopher Ferner Nuhn. "There is little doubt that in Henry A. Wallace the Middle West contributes to national affairs an authentic figure."[33]

As Roosevelt had predicted, the emergency farm bill opened the floodgates. The very nature of the law, the vast and unprecedented authority it granted

to the secretary, made it inevitable the Agriculture Department would be subjected to intense, unrelenting pressure from everyone with an interest in growing, selling, or eating food—in other words, everyone. In *New Frontiers*
Wallace wrote,

> The corridors of the Administration Building were crowded with farm-
> ers, farm leaders, processors, and reporters, each with dozens of insistent
> questions, few of which could be answered then and there. From early morn
> until midnight and often later, delegations of dairymen, cotton growers,
> wheat growers, cling peach producers from California, and many others
> filed in and out of our offices seeking the way to make the new machin-
> ery whir into action in their behalf. Those were hectic days. Somehow
> we got through them though it was a rare day when an irresistible desire
> didn't crash into an immovable fact, with heavy damage to frayed nerves.[34]

Nothing like it had ever been attempted during peacetime, and every day
confronted Wallace and his aides with a thousand new questions. How could
a program be fair at the same time to the wheat grower, the miller, the grain
elevator owner, the baker, and the woman who buys a loaf of bread? What
was to be done with the huge store of surplus cotton already on hand? Who
would handle the enormous task of distributing, explaining, and processing
the millions of individual contracts necessary to implement crop reduction
agreements? The questions were complex and endless. Each answer seemed to
raise a maddening new set of questions.

An administrative nightmare confronted the new secretary. Virtually
overnight Wallace had to put in place a team of top administrators capable
of understanding agricultural realities, devising policy solutions, and manag-
ing the resulting programs. And each of these administrators had to be given
sufficient manpower to carry out his tasks. Scores of idealistic young people,
well meaning but ill trained, flocked to the cause. In short order the Department of Agriculture became the largest agency in the federal government and
was still growing at a rate of hundreds of people weekly.

Tales of confusion, inexperience, and, of course, bureaucratic warfare,
abounded. Talented young lawyers like Abe Fortas, later a Supreme Court
justice, showed up for work and found they had no desk or telephone. Adlai
Stevenson, who was to become governor of Illinois and twice the Democratic Party's candidate for president, recalled having to attend so many administrative hearings that he never had time to do the requisite paperwork. One
popular tale, gleefully circulated by old hands at the department, had a youthful city-bred administrator earnestly asking about a proposed growers code,
"But will it be fair to the macaroni growers?"[35]

Turmoil in the lower ranks was hardly Wallace's most vexing problem, however. A far more troublesome situation confronted him at the very top. George Peek had been named to head the Agricultural Adjustment Administration (AAA), the huge agency created to run the new farm program. His appointment, engineered by the Democratic power broker Bernard Baruch, for whom Peek had once worked, set the stage for "a virtual state of civil war" within the Department of Agriculture.[36]

Crusty and dogmatic, Peek still seethed with resentment over Wallace's appointment as secretary, a position he coveted. Moreover, Peek had no use for the domestic allotment plan, which was the heart of the AAA program. The old McNary-Haugen plan, with its reliance upon export dumping and a two-tiered price system, was Peek's "personal rock of ages," said one observer, and nothing could shake his faith in it.[37] The domestic allotment plan represented "the promotion of planned scarcity," Peek wrote in his autobiography, and he was "steadfastly against" it from the outset.[38]

The fighting began even before Peek came on the job. In a personal meeting with Roosevelt, Peek demanded that the AAA be made an independent agency, separate from the Agriculture Department and responsible only to the president. At Wallace's insistence Roosevelt rejected the idea but assured Peek he would have complete authority to run the agency.

Peek tested this power quickly and in unequivocal terms. On May 12, the day the farm bill was signed into law, he wrote to Wallace asking the secretary to transfer all authority given by the statute to him. Wallace replied at once, telling Peek, "Since I am the Secretary of Agriculture, the weight of responsibility and decision must rest largely on my shoulders."[39]

Furthermore, Wallace made it clear that Peek would not have total control over the agency's staff. The first indication of this was the appointment of Jerome Frank as the AAA's general counsel. Frank was liberal, brash, and Jewish. Peek loathed everything about him. In addition, Frank surrounded himself with idealistic left-wing lawyers like Lee Pressman and Alger Hiss—the "boys with their hair ablaze," as Peek put it—whom Peek also despised.[40] Unable to win Frank's dismissal, Peek finally used his own salary to hire Frederic Lee, a lawyer of more congenial views, as his "personal counsel" at the AAA.

The upper echelons of the Agriculture Department thus divided into three camps, and for six months they waged bureaucratic war in all its internecine glory. In one camp were Peek and his loyalists, whose goal was to raise agricultural prices through cooperation with processors and large agribusinesses. In a second camp were Frank and the idealists, who sought to promote social justice for small farmers and consumers. Somewhere in the middle were the "agrarian fundamentalists," led by Wallace, whose goal was to nurture back to life a vibrant agricultural civilization.

Given the Balkanized state of affairs, it was surprising the department was able to move at all. But piece by piece Wallace and his team began putting the machinery of agricultural recovery in place. They were keenly aware of the stakes. The AAA was the first and most visible New Deal recovery program. To have it fail would have been disastrous for the Roosevelt administration. And everyone, Peek included, understood that the farm crisis was real and had to be addressed.

The first and most painless program put in place by the AAA covered wheat. Wheat growers tended to be less divided than other commodity groups, and by mid-June half a million of them had signed up to participate in the domestic allotment plan. Participating farmers would receive government benefit payments in exchange for reducing the number of acres in production. It helped greatly that M. L. Wilson, the plan's foremost evangelist, was in charge of the AAA wheat program.

Also, many wheat-growing areas were affected by drought, which meant Wallace didn't have to worry about surpluses. "It would not be necessary to plow under growing wheat; nature had already done it—unequally, cruelly, to be sure, but decisively, and without provoking the resentment of consumers," Wallace wrote.[41] Many millers and bakers disliked the processing tax that went along with the wheat program, but when they realized they could raise the price of bread and blame it on the government, their resistance softened. The actual impact of the processing tax amounted to about one-half cent per loaf of bread, while bread prices increased by as much as two cents.

Cotton was another matter. Cotton had been selling during the winter of 1932–33 for five cents a pound, the nation had a carryover three times the normal size, exports had shrunk to nothing, and another big crop was on the way. The circumstances forced Wallace to accept a desperate solution: pay farmers to plow under a fourth of the national crop. Some 22,000 volunteers worked exhausting hours to sign up about a million cotton farmers for the program. In August more than ten million acres of growing cotton were plowed under, reducing the 1933 harvest from 17 million bales to 13 million. In return cotton farmers received government benefit payments of more than $100 million.

Wallace flew south during the plow-up and returned from an inspection flight over the Mississippi Delta with moist eyes and a sad heart. "Sooner or later, the question 'What is there in it for me?' will have to be translated into, 'What is there in it for all of us?' " he said. The cotton plow-up would succeed in its purpose, he predicted, but "to have to destroy a growing crop is a shocking commentary on our civilization."[42]

The dairy industry presented a different set of problems. There the AAA tried to raise prices through marketing agreements, which proved difficult to fashion and administer. "The attitude of the milkshed representatives was,

'For God's sake do something, and do it quick!' " Wallace wrote. What they really wanted, he added, was for the government to "set up a complete price schedule first . . . and examine the books later and at leisure."[43] Negotiations were long, arduous, and not entirely successful from any standpoint.

The most intractable problem facing the AAA, however, involved corn and hogs. "It was not from any lack of interest, but from an inability to see any way to help the Corn Belt, at least within a few months," Wallace said. ". . . Conferences by the score began and ended in my office, and as often as not many of us were ready to give up the problem as too tough."[44] The best they could come up with was a long-range program to reduce corn by ten million acres and hogs by seven million head. But the effect of the plan would not be felt by farmers until 1934, which would be too late for many of them.

A suggestion finally emerged from hog farmers themselves: begin slaughtering pigs weighing less than one hundred pounds instead of allowing them to reach their usual market weight of two hundred pounds. Pigs would eat less corn, the total number of pigs would be reduced by five or six million, prices would rise, and the edible portions of little pigs could be used to feed the hungry. Wallace fussed over details of the plan for a while, particularly over the necessity of following up the emergency slaughter with a long-term corn acreage reduction program, and then approved it. He announced it in mid-August at the Chicago fair.

No decision Wallace made as agriculture secretary proved more controversial than that to kill "six million baby pigs." Newspapers and politicians denounced it as "pig infanticide" and "pig birth control." Wallace was nonplussed. "Doubtless it is just as inhumane to kill a big hog as a little one, but few people would appreciate that," he wrote. "They contend that every little pig has the right to attain before slaughter the full pigginess of his pigness. To hear them talk, you would have thought that pigs are raised for pets. Nor would they realize that the slaughter of little pigs might make more tolerable the lives of a good many human beings dependent on hog prices."[45]

The little pigs did not die in vain. In October a special agency, the Federal Surplus Relief Corporation, was established; it distributed some one hundred million pounds of pork and pork by-products, such as lard and soap, to the needy. "Not many people realized how radical it was,—this idea of having the Government buy from those who had too much, in order to give to those who had too little," Wallace said. "So direct a method of resolving the paradox of want in the midst of plenty doubtless could never have got beyond the discussion stage before 1933."[46]

Six months after the AAA became law, Wallace could look back upon the "summer of unprecedented activity" with some satisfaction.[47] Tens of millions of dollars in government benefits had been paid out. Half the nation's six million farmers—representing more than three-quarters of its agricultural output—had signed up to participate in various AAA programs. Long-term programs to reduce production of several major commodities were in place. The price of cotton doubled. More than four thousand committees had been set up to administer the farm programs at the local level, making it the most decentralized and democratically participatory federal program in the nation's history. Best of all, from Wallace's standpoint, actual cash income of farmers rose 30 percent during the AAA's first year.

"The plowing under of 10 million acres of cotton in August, 1933, and the slaughter of 6 million little pigs in September, 1933, were not acts of idealism in any sane society," Wallace wrote. "They were emergency acts made necessary by the almost insane lack of world statesmanship during the period from 1920 to 1932."[48]

The AAA had made progress despite the best efforts of George Peek, and by the fall of 1933 it was widely understood that something must be done about him. Peek's outlook on the agency he administered had become almost paranoid. The place was crawling with "fanatic-like . . . socialists and internationalists" bent on the destruction of America, he declared. Jerome Frank and his "Lenin baby chicks" were out to destroy capitalism. Even Henry Wallace had succumbed to the collectivist spirit, in Peek's view. "There is no use mincing words," Peek later wrote. "The A.A.A. became a means of buying the farmer's birthright as a preliminary to breaking down the whole individualistic system of the country."[49]

Wallace tried for months to make the best of things. The secretary brushed aside the old agrarian's demands, pushed through production control programs in one commodity after another, and thwarted most of the blank checks Peek sought to grant to large agribusinesses. But each passing month made the situation more difficult to straddle.

Adding to Wallace's difficulties, the general climate of opinion in the farm states began to sour again. Farm purchasing power, as measured by the parity index, began to decline as the price of manufactured goods rebounded. Newspapers again carried stories about rural discontent and protest, and Milo Reno announced plans for a new "farm strike" to begin October 21. "While the farmer is losing his pants to his creditors," declared Senator Louis Murphy, a Democrat from Iowa, "[National Recovery Administration] prices are rolling up his shirt. We'll have a nudist colony of our own. . . ."[50]

Acutely aware of the turmoil, President Roosevelt authorized new steps to restore calm to the farm states. The Farm Credit Administration, under Henry

Morgenthau Jr., started the purchase of sixteen million bushels of wheat for "relief purposes" in order to bolster prices. A new cotton loan program was announced, raising prices a penny per pound. A new agency, the Commodity Credit Corporation, was established to get loan money into the hands of cash-strapped farmers. "Checks from the [AAA] were descending on the land in a gentle, pervasive rain, damping the prairie fire of farmers' anger," *Time* magazine reported.[51]

Perhaps most significant, Roosevelt finally yielded to the pleas of Wallace and others who urged a program of controlled inflation. On October 22, the day after Reno was to begin his latest strike, the president delivered his fourth "fireside chat" by radio, saying he was not satisfied with the rise in farm prices and promising to do better. "If we cannot do this one way we will do it another," Roosevelt said. "Do it, we will."[52]

The government immediately began a three-month purchase of gold in an attempt to increase commodity prices. The gold purchase, Roosevelt told advisers, was a direct effort to stem "an agrarian revolution in this country."

The administration's actions had the desired effect. Farm state legislators loudly backed each move, reflecting the mood of their constituents. Milo Reno retained his usual bluster—his supporters beat the stuffing out of a Wallace effigy after he delivered a raucous speech in Shenandoah, Iowa—but his threats proved hollow. Wallace, like the president, remained widely popular with rural folk.

In all of this, George Peek was no more than a bitter bystander. Frustrated by his inability to impose his will, increasingly isolated within the administration, Peek decided to bring matters to a head. On November 15 he wrote Wallace a memo accusing Jerome Frank of "sabotage" and demanding his ouster. "If you do not agree," he wrote, "may we not discuss the subject with the President?"[53] Wallace did not reply. On November 25 Peek repeated his demand. Wallace responded on December 1 with a suggestion that one of Peek's most loyal lieutenants be dismissed. Peek furiously refused.

A few days later Wallace left Washington to accompany Roosevelt on a visit to Warm Springs. Peek seized the opportunity to announce a half-million-dollar plan to subsidize the sale of butter in Europe. Peek's action was intended as a declaration of independence, but Rex Tugwell, acting secretary in Wallace's absence, took it as insubordination. Tugwell quashed the butter export and followed up with a cheeky letter to Peek saying he "assumed that you would agree that our agricultural trade cannot possibly be improved by selling abroad at a lower price than the market at home."[54]

Tugwell had forced a showdown. "It was becoming obvious that if we did not get rid of George Peek, he would get rid of us," Tugwell wrote.[55] If Peek thought the professor was an innocent in the arts of bureaucratic warfare, he was mistaken. In short order Tugwell made his case to several friendly reporters, secured Wallace's support, and took the matter directly to Roosevelt. Either Peek went or he would leave, Tugwell told Roosevelt. Probably Wallace would leave also, he added. Well, Roosevelt said with a smile, perhaps Peek would like to be ambassador to Czechoslovakia.

If Roosevelt really wanted to keep Peek in the administration, Tugwell said, a job should be found for him promoting foreign markets. Knowing Peek's views were entirely contrary to the free-trade internationalism espoused by Secretary of State Cordell Hull, Roosevelt laughed heartily. "Lordy, Lordy, how Cordell will love that!"[56]

Before Peek knew what was afoot, he found himself standing next to Wallace at a press conference where his entire tenure at the AAA was skillfully shredded. Wallace, "with all the fairness and restraint of a judge and without a single unkind reference to Peek," said the dairy program was a failure, that meatpackers would be forced to open their records before a marketing agreement was concluded, and that production controls, not export subsidies, were the solution to the farm problem. "That," said one reporter, "is the coolest political murder that has been committed since Roosevelt came into office."[57]

On December 11, confronted with a White House press release announcing his new job as special adviser on foreign trade, Peek resigned from the AAA.* For a giddy moment Tugwell and the progressives rode high in the saddle. "In this week's encounter of men and theories at the Department of Agriculture," Arthur Krock wrote in the *New York Times*, "the real 'winnah and new champion' . . . is Rexford Guy Tugwell." The *Des Moines Register* said Tugwell "had emerged as the strong man of the Administration."[58]

In time Tugwell would understand he had won a battle, not the war. "Not much later the opposing forces would feel strong enough to challenge us again," Tugwell later wrote, "and this time would win."[59]

Washington had never seen anything quite like Henry A. Wallace during the New Deal's first, frenetic year. There was, for one thing, his breathtaking energy level. Operating on four hours sleep, he regularly put in fourteen- to sixteen-hour days, working past midnight, arising at five, and briskly walking three miles through Rock Creek Park to the department from his apartment in the Wardman Park.

*Peek remained as a trade adviser until November 1935, after which he became an ardent New Deal critic and supporter of the isolationist America First movement. In 1940 he opposed the Roosevelt-Wallace ticket. Peek died in 1943.

There was also his extraordinary intellectual self-confidence. Longtime department employees had never seen a secretary deal with scientists and economists on their own terms, or rattle off facts and figures that almost always proved correct. "He carried pictures of statistical tables in his mind; he thought in exact quantities; and his mind moved outward to the enlarged consequences of small facts and occurrences with ease and rapidity," wrote Tugwell.[60]

Most striking of all, however, was his zeal and sense of purpose. He brought to his task the solemn dedication of a crusading reformer. It was this quality that let Wallace rise above his personal reticence. For all his quiet modesty, aides soon learned he could be blunt and unyielding.

Russell Lord, a young journalist brought into the department's communications division, recalled seeing Wallace meet late one afternoon with a well-dressed lobbyist for some special interest. Wallace listened patiently to the lobbyist's skillful argument, then stood up and softly said, "No." The lawyer was taken aback but continued to make his case until Wallace raised his hand in a quieting gesture. Wallace leaned forward and politely said, "Unless we learn to treat each other fairly this country is going to smash."[61]

Lord recounted the incident that evening to a fellow worker, Paul Porter, who later became head of the Federal Communications Commission. "Yes," said Porter. "I never saw anything like it. Don't it beat hell? He's a Christian."[62]

Wallace, it seemed to many of those around him, had begun to blossom in the climate of change that Roosevelt brought to the capital. Here was "a new type of public man, younger and intellectually more flexible," said Lord. "[It] seemed to most of us minor aides and beginners . . . that this Wallace, striking off daily new patterns of candid public address and behavior, and with an increasing unself-consciousness, grew visibly, daily and weekly, like one of his own Iowa corn plants, stretching in the sun."[63]

Nothing exemplified this growth as much as Wallace's willingness, even eagerness, to face the general public. He traveled widely and wrote prolifically in an effort to make the case for agriculture, for the administration, for social justice. In his first year as a cabinet officer, Wallace authored twenty-two major speeches and publications, setting out his vision of a "new frontier" of cooperation and the brotherhood of man.

"What we approach is not a new continent but a new state of heart and mind resulting in new standards of accomplishment," he wrote in *New Frontiers*. "We must invent, build and put to work new social machinery. This machinery will carry out the Sermon on the Mount as well as the present social machinery carries out and intensifies the law of the jungle."[64]

He became a sort of unofficial philosopher for the New Deal, preaching the social gospel as surely as his grandfather had preached it from rural pulpits. His message was never one of partisan politics—he distrusted both parties, and besides, he was still a registered Republican—but of morality and the common welfare.

"Religion comes first and from it springs the arts, the sciences, the inventions, the divisions of wealth, and the attitudes between classes and toward other nations," he said in a lecture at the World Fellowship of Faiths Conference in Chicago. "The millennium is not yet here although the makings of it are clearly in our hands."[65]

The "world is one world," he told the Federal Council of Churches, and men must learn to live for all mankind and not for themselves alone. "When cooperation becomes a living reality in the spiritual sense of the term, when we have defined certain broad objectives which we all want to attain, when we can feel the significance of the forces at work not merely in our own lives, not merely in our own class, not merely in our own nation, but in the world as a whole—then the vision of Isaiah and the insight of Christ will be on their way toward realization." What was necessary, he said elsewhere, was a "Declaration of Interdependence, a recognition of our essential unity and our absolute reliance upon one another."[66]

In late fall Wallace brought his message directly to the people on a speaking tour of the Midwest. It concluded with a broadcast address at the Des Moines Coliseum before several thousand farmers. He had come home, he said, to sum up what had been done and what lay ahead. He had come to find out whether his countrymen intended to return like dogs "to the vomit of capitalism" or move to a new age of cooperation and generosity.[67]

He finished slightly early, and recognizing he still had a few moments of broadcast time remaining, Wallace crumpled the speech into his pocket and gazed silently at the crowd.

"Only the merest quarter-turn of the heart separates us from a material abundance beyond the fondest dream of anyone present," he told them. "Selfishness has ceased to be the mainspring of progress. . . . There is something more. . . . There is a new social machinery in the making. . . . Let us maintain sweet and kindly hearts toward each other, however great the difficulties ahead."[68]

CHAPTER SEVEN

"FRAGRANCE FROM THAT OTHER WORLD"

Still there was the search.

The search for "inner light" that led Henry Wallace to Roos the medicine man, to Johndro the astrologer, to Æ the mystic poet—that search continued. Now it led to the most embarrassing chapter of his public life. By 1933 the search had led him to the guru.

The guru was Nicholas Konstantinovich Roerich. He was a man of many faces: an expatriate Russian of uncertain politics, a philosopher who dabbled in Oriental mysticism, a painter of international renown, a visionary activist for the cause of peace.

In some eyes Roerich was also a tax evader, a charlatan, a power-hungry egomaniac who betrayed the trust of his most fervent followers. At the end of the day, Wallace certainly would have agreed with all those accusations and more.

Exactly what happened proved difficult to untangle. The origins of the affair were secretive and mysterious, and it played across two continents over two decades. Over time it took on a life of its own. None of the key participants made an honest effort to explain what took place. Peripheral players, on the other hand, freely made use of whatever half facts and rumors were available to serve their purposes.

Many documents involving the Roerich case were privately written and held during Wallace's lifetime. Some of them were forgeries written specifically to damage him. Others were genuine but no less baffling. Wallace's own account of the episode was limited and disingenuous. The guru's version vanished when he fled U.S. tax collectors and took up residence in the Himalayas. Franklin Roosevelt, who was more than a casual bystander, left no written record of the matter from his perspective.

Whatever happened, it would cost Wallace both honor and standing during his lifetime and dog his reputation even in death—exasperating his admirers, delighting his detractors, confusing almost everyone.

Nicholas Roerich, or Nicolai Rerikh in his native land, was born into a prosperous St. Petersburg family in 1874. At the Imperial Academy of Arts he was regarded as a gentle, reserved, and singularly serious student. His graduation project, a painting entitled *The Messenger*, won praise from the composer Nikolay Rimsky-Korsakov and the writer Leo Tolstoy, two of Russia's greatest creative figures. Within a decade Roerich had married the beautiful Helena Ivanovna and gained appointment as administrator of an important museum. In 1912 he collaborated with Igor Stravinsky and Vaslav Nijinsky in producing *Le Sacre du Printemps* (The Rite of Spring), one of the century's most celebrated avant-garde ballets.

In 1918 the Roerichs left the fledgling Soviet Union and gradually made their way to the United States. Early in the 1920s they developed an interest in Theosophy. He abandoned the Slavic primitivism of his early days and began producing paintings suffused in hazy spiritual symbolism. She translated H. P. Blavatsky's major Theosophical tome, *The Secret Doctrine*, into Russian.

Slowly Roerich began to transform himself from an obscure émigré painter into a teacher of divine wisdom. He held himself out as a direct link to the supernatural "masters" who populated Madame Blavatsky's spiritual universe. With his domineering manner, piercing dark eyes, forked beard, and Tibetan robes, Roerich looked and played the part to perfection.

Roerich also displayed an extraordinary talent for separating wealthy Americans from their money. His chief benefactor was Louis Horch, a young New Yorker who had made a fortune as a foreign-exchange broker. Over the next decade and a half, before he turned against the guru in bitter rage, Horch put more than a million dollars into Roerich's pockets and projects. He purchased many paintings from Roerich's substantial cache, paid off the artist's old bills, and sent his son to Harvard.

He also helped Roerich establish the Master Institute of United Arts in New York City, housed in an apartment building Horch owned on Riverside Drive. The institute's credo grandly declared, "The gates of the 'sacred source' must be opened wide for everybody, and the light of art will ignite numerous hearts with a new love."[1] Important cultural figures, including George Bellows, Rockwell Kent, and Norman Bel Geddes, lectured at the institute.

The institute was replaced two years later by the Roerich Museum, the first in the United States devoted chiefly to the work of one artist. At its height in the early 1930s, the museum possessed more than a thousand paintings by Nicholas Roerich. These were more than works of art, Roerich told a select group of followers. They had been given special healing powers by Master Koot Hoomi and Master Morya, luminaries in the Theosophical universe.

In the mid-1920s the Roerich clan set off on an elaborate "expedition" to Central Asia. The painter proposed to meet the spiritual masters, purchase artworks, and paint the Himalayas. Horch financed the trip with several hundred thousand dollars, in return for which he obtained power of attorney over all of Roerich's financial affairs and the exclusive right to purchase all paintings produced during the journey. The journey lasted five years and included a mystery-shrouded two-month visit to Moscow, where he met with numerous political and cultural leaders, including Lenin's widow. The side trip to Russia aroused the lasting suspicion of the British secret service, which concluded that Roerich was a "worthless humbug" at best and a Soviet spy at worst.

By the time he returned to New York in the summer of 1929, Roerich was something of a phenomenon. Admirers hailed him as one of the world's greatest living artists. Theosophists called him "our magian star."[2] Horch had constructed a new, twenty-four-story art deco skyscraper in shades of purple and gray to house the Roerich Museum and its related enterprises. ("The Museum of Natural Mystery," quipped the *New York Times*.)[3] The dapper mayor of New York, James Walker, greeted him at city hall. The governor of the state, Franklin D. Roosevelt, met with him. The governor's wife, Eleanor, delivered a lecture on women's rights at the museum.

Perhaps most significantly, Roerich's proposal for an international treaty to protect cultural landmarks during wartime was winning applause from prominent figures at home and abroad. The idea was to fly a "banner of peace" above designated sites in order to protect them from attack. In response to the proposal, the University of Paris law faculty nominated Roerich for the Nobel Peace Prize.

<hr />

One of the visitors to the Roerich Museum in the summer of 1929 was a young farm editor on his way to Europe. There Henry A. Wallace met Nicholas Roerich for the first time.

Thereafter Wallace began a friendly, although rather formal, correspondence with Roerich and his associates. "Dear Mr. Wallace," wrote the Roerich Museum's vice president in October 1929,

It gave me great pleasure to receive your interesting letter. I regretted sincerely that you were unable to be with us the evening of the reopening of the Museum—an occasion which was most gratifying, and successful beyond our expectation. More than ten thousand people were present.

Very shortly I shall send you some new literature on our organizations, and should you have any suggestions, we should be delighted to know of them.

We will be happy to see you again whenever you are in New York.

Very cordially
Frances Grant[4]

Periodically, Wallace sent a brief comment or question about something he had read in the Roerich Museum's bulletin. Once he asked for more information about research on the medicinal uses of Himalayan plants that was being conducted by Roerich's associates. Another time he asked for "fifteen or twenty" kernels of corn grown in Asia by a friend of Roerich. From time to time Wallace sent unsolicited reports on his own labors. To Frances Grant he sent his pamphlet explaining the causes of the Depression. A "preliminary report" on his statistical study of the planets and their relation to Iowa weather was forwarded with a self-deprecating comment: "I thought perhaps Nicholas Roerich might be interested in glancing over this rapidly and then throwing it into the waste basket."[5]

In late 1931 Wallace paid a second visit to the Roerich Museum. Soon his letters became longer and more personal. In February 1932 he wrote Grant at some length about Roerich's recent statement "Souls on the Peoples" and the spiritual awakening Wallace believed lay ahead. "The great suffering now-a-days is undoubtedly harrowing the ground for the planting of seed," Wallace wrote. "But it does not yet fully appear as to just what kind of seeds will be planted."[6]

What had been straightforward—letters written on *Wallaces' Farmer* stationery, typed by Wallace's secretary—became furtive and far more complex. His messages now were often short, typed by Wallace personally on plain paper or handwritten in his distinctive left-handed scrawl, and were full of code words and shared references. "Dear M," he wrote, apparently to Frances Grant, ". . . You will remember the word I dreamed of and the two interpretations I placed on it and also that father paid a visit to the one interpreatation [sic]. . . . Give my high esteem and affection to the gentle one and his wife. May the radiant creativeness of S. of the chapple [sic] abide with and strengthen you continuously."[7]

When and in what order the letters were written cannot be known. Often they were undated, and references to contemporaneous events were gauzy. But at least by the time Wallace became a cabinet officer, he was involved with Roerich and his associates at a deeply personal level. On March 12, 1933, only eight days after taking office, Wallace wrote,

Dear Guru,

I have been thinking of you holding the casket—the sacred most precious casket. And I have thought of the New Country going forth to meet the seven stars under the sign of the three stars. And I have thought of the admonition "Await the Stone."

We await the Stone and we welcome you again to this glorious land of destiny, clouded though it may be with strange fumbling fears. Who shall hold up the compelling vision to those who wander in darkness? In answer to this question we again welcome you. To drive out depression. To drive out fear. . . .

And so I await your convenience prepared to do what I am to do.

May Peace, Joy and Fire attend you as always,

G

In the great haste of this strange
maelstrom which is Washington.[8]

At least some of these mysterious letters were of questionable authenticity. The typewritten letters, for example, contain spelling errors that would have been uncharacteristic of Wallace. Wallace himself did what he could to muddy the question of their authorship. When the letters almost became public during the campaign of 1940, Wallace prepared a statement (never released) flatly denying he wrote them. In 1948, when portions of the letters did become public, Wallace contemptuously refused to talk about them at all.

Several years later, in the oral history he gave to Columbia University, Wallace offered a carefully hedged explanation of the letters. The so-called guru letters, he said, consisted of "unsigned, undated notes, which I knew I had never sent to Nicholas Roerich, but there were a few letters addressed to Nicholas Roerich signed by me and dated which were written in rather high-flown language."[9]

This was Wallace's only recorded comment on the guru letters, and it was misleading at best. Many of the letters, as Wallace well knew, were not addressed to the guru but to others around him, including Roerich's wife and son and his chief assistant, Frances Grant. The authenticity of the handwritten letters, as Wallace in effect acknowledged, was indisputable. Even the typewritten letters comport, in tone and substance, with other letters of a spiritual nature written by Wallace during the 1920s and 1930s.

"Dear Prof. R," Wallace wrote Roerich in early 1934,

> . . . Long have I been aware of the occasional fragrance from that other world which is the real world. But now I must live in the outer world and at the same time make over my mind and body to serve as fit instruments for the Lord of Justice. The changes in awareness must come as a result of steady, earnest recollectedness. I shall strive to grow as rapidly as possible without undue violence. . . . Yes, the Chalice is filling.[10]

Wallace's private enthusiasm for Nicholas Roerich quickly began to color his activities as a public official. As soon as he arrived in the capital, Wallace became the leading champion of Roerich's Banner of Peace and pushed tirelessly for U.S. acceptance of the pact. "Your endeavor to furnish a symbol for the thought that beauty and knowledge should tie all of the nations together in appreciation of a common human purpose, however separate their apparent paths may be, has been of profound interest to enlightened people over the world for several years," Wallace wrote formally to Roerich in mid-1933.[11]

The State Department's attitude toward the treaty was cool, but Wallace hammered away. He raised the cause with Roosevelt personally, wrote letters of introduction for Frances Grant and Louis Horch, pestered Secretary of State Cordell Hull by memo and in person. At Wallace's insistence the three sphere symbol Roerich proposed for the Banner of Peace was printed on the title page of *New Frontiers*, the first book he wrote as a public official.* Slowly his lobbying had an impact. In the autumn of 1933 Hull grudgingly agreed to let Wallace represent the United States at a Banner of Peace conference held in Washington.

The Banner of Peace thus became a key topic in Wallace's private letters to Roerich and his associates. In reporting on developments, he adopted an elaborate code to refer to various parties. "Tigers" and "greater felines" referred to the Soviet Union. "Monkeys" meant Great Britain. "Land of Masters" was Mongolia. "Old House" was the State Department, and "Sour One" was Hull. The president was the "Flaming One" on good days and the "Waivering One" at other times. Wallace cast himself as "Galahad" or sometimes "Parsifal."[12]

---

*The symbol designed by Roerich for the Banner of Peace "suggests the maximum development of individual diversity within the limitations of the whole," Wallace wrote in *New Frontiers*. Perhaps so, but Reynal & Hitchcock, the book's New York publisher, was unfamiliar with the symbol and printed it upside down in the first edition, causing critics to say it to bore a resemblance to Mickey Mouse.

The coded language and furtive tone gave the letters an air of mystery that greatly enhanced their publicity value in the hands of Wallace's enemies. "In great haste," began one letter. "The tension is indeed very great," said another. "The tigers are going through various tricks but with respect to them the man now in charge at the Old House is excellent," said a note penned en route from Chicago to Washington in late 1933. "The Flaming One is soft-hearted toward the tigers and I fear has made commitments of some sort."*[13]

The Flaming One himself added considerably to the confusion. Roosevelt, perhaps influenced by his mother's enthusiasm for Eastern art and mysticism, took a personal interest in the Roerichs' causes.[†] Roosevelt met Roerich at least once, met with Roerich's associates on several occasions, and between 1934 and 1936 personally corresponded with Helena Roerich several times. "Mr. President," she wrote in a typical letter, "Your message was transmitted to me. I am happy that your great heart has so beautifully accepted the Message and Your lightbearing mind was free from prejudice."[14]

Indeed, it was Roosevelt who suggested to Wallace that he read an allegory by Arthur Hopkins called *The Glory Road*, which served as the basis for the coded language in the guru letters. Wallace thanked Roosevelt for his suggestion in a letter written October 28, 1933. Wrote Wallace, "Mr. President, you can be the 'flaming one,' the one with the ever-upward-surging spirit to lead us into the time when the children of men can sing again."[15]

Out of this peculiar mixture of politics and mysticism, of art and diplomacy, came an even more peculiar idea. In the waning days of 1933, it was proposed that Nicholas Roerich lead a government-sponsored expedition to collect drought-resistant grasses in Central Asia. Whether the idea originated with Wallace or with Roosevelt was unclear. Certainly Wallace was given and accepted blame for the misadventure while he was in public office.

---

*Roosevelt personally negotiated an agreement, announced in mid-November 1933, granting diplomatic recognition to the Soviet Union. In cabinet discussions Wallace expressed opposition to the agreement because of Soviet antipathy toward organized religion and because he suspected that the USSR planned to dump large amounts of wheat on the world market.

Wallace's attitude toward the Soviet Union was reflected in the guru letters, and his comments seemed to assume the Roerichs shared his views. Subsequent scholarship, however, has demonstrated the Roerichs were on friendly terms with the Soviet government and helped it raise cash by facilitating the sale of many artistic masterpieces to Western museums and collectors.

†In the oral history he gave to Columbia University, Wallace said about the president's interest in Roerich, "The link between Roosevelt and Nicholas Roerich was Roosevelt's mother, Sara, as well as his own intense interest in central Asia—all the way from Tibet to the Siberian border. The climate, the people, the history, the ecology, and the religion of this area fascinated him. He felt that this area was a breeding place for future wars and the relationship of this area to China, Russia, and Japan intrigued him. Because of his ancestors being linked with China he always attributed a greater importance to China than most people. . . . I'm sure, however, that the strongest bond between him and Nicholas Roerich was his mother."

In his oral memoirs, however, Wallace insisted the expedition was proposed by Roosevelt one day after a cabinet meeting. "[Roosevelt] had the idea that the Gobi desert had once grown trees and that when the trees were cut off, the climate had changed. . . . He felt the climate might be changed back by growing trees. I think Roerich had some idea along that line also. Roosevelt also thought that some of the plants of central Asia would be useful to the U.S. I told him that the U.S. Department of Agriculture had previously imported crested wheat grass (*Agropyron cristatum*) from this area and that this wheat grass was serving a useful purpose in our Great Plains area."[16]

At a minimum Roosevelt was aware of the planned expedition. When Budget Director Lewis Douglas, an affable conservative Arizona politician, initially balked at the cost of the mission, Roosevelt personally intervened. For three years U.S. farmers had been crippled by devastating droughts, and Roosevelt said the $75,000 cost of the proposed expedition was well justified if it returned with grasses that could withstand dry conditions.

Specialists at the Agriculture Department in fact were ecstatic when they first learned an expedition to Central Asia was in the works. They had sought money for an expedition to the Gobi Desert, one of the last unexplored regions of the world, since 1928. Knowles A. Ryerson, a forty-two-year-old scientist recently appointed by Wallace to head the Bureau of Plant Industry, enthusiastically appeared twice before the Senate Appropriations Committee to make a case for the expedition. Already he selected one of the department's most experienced explorers, Dr. Howard G. MacMillan, to lead it.

Ryerson's delight over the forthcoming expedition rapidly turned into a personal nightmare. On a wintry evening in early 1934, while he was hosting an informal dinner for a group of explorers at the Cosmos Club, Ryerson received an urgent call from Wallace. The secretary asked Ryerson to come immediately to his apartment at the Wardman Park. Ryerson arrived to find Wallace in the company of an intense, exotic-looking man, "bald as a billiard ball," with a Manchu mustache that drooped to his chest.[17] The man was Nicholas Roerich.

"Dr. Roerich's familiar with the Gobi Desert and can help us with the expedition," said Wallace. "Well, that's fine," Ryerson replied. "We'd be glad to talk to anyone who knows anything about it and will appreciate his help."[18]

Still confused about what was actually happening, Ryerson arrived at work the next morning and was called into Wallace's office. There he was informed that Roerich would not be an adviser to the mission but would lead it. "I felt almost shell-shocked and could hardly believe my ears," Ryerson later said. He turned to Wallace and blurted out, "He can't be. He's not an American citizen, and you've got to have regular employees on this. Manchuria is the hottest diplomatic area in the world at the moment."[19]

Nevertheless, said Wallace, Roerich would lead the expedition. Moreover the painter's son George, said to be an expert in Central Asian dialects, would be second in command.

Ryerson set out to subvert the plan. He found ready allies in the State Department, which already viewed Roerich with suspicion. At a meeting between Wallace and Stanley Hornbeck, the State Department official in charge of Far Eastern affairs, Ryerson watched with pleasure as Hornbeck set out the reasons why a U.S. expedition headed by a Russian painter could result in a diplomatic debacle. The secretary responded with an angelic smile. "I never saw a man so purple in the face and not keel over with apoplexy as Hornbeck was," Ryerson recalled later.[20]

Another man with long experience in Asian affairs, gravely warned Ryerson to avoid the Roerichs at all cost. "They're shysters! Don't have anything to do with them," the man exclaimed. "They're crooks! You can't trust them. They're unreliable. They're thought to be Russian agents, but they're out to get whatever they can for their own institution—that money-making racket in New York."[21]

Wallace eventually tired of Ryerson's warnings and ordered him to stop it. "Knowles," Wallace said in an angry voice, "I forbid you to discuss these people with anybody!"

"Well," Ryerson commented many years later, "the fat was in the fire."[22]

Ryerson seemed unable to please anybody. Wallace was mad at him for opposing the Roerichs. Wallace's chief assistant, former *Des Moines Register* reporter Paul Appleby, dressed him down for taking too much of the secretary's time. His own wife told him it was a lost cause. "You're foolish to send anyone with [the Roerichs]," Rex Tugwell told him. "You're headed for trouble." Ryerson sensed Tugwell was right but didn't see what he could do about it. "I was at the end of my rope," he said.[23]

So the Asian expedition chugged forward on parallel tracks that would never meet. On one track were Roerich and his son. On the other were Howard MacMillan and his assistant, a department botanist named James L. Stephens. They were supposedly part of a single expedition, but they sailed on different boats and landed at different ports.

By the time MacMillan and Stephens arrived in Yokohama on June 1, 1934, the Roerichs were ensconced in Tokyo, waving a letter from Wallace asking them to "lead and protect" the expedition and giving self-congratulatory interviews to the Japanese press. Each side cabled Washington that they were unable to contact the other. "This trip promises to be wholly an opportunist affair," MacMillan lamented to Ryerson.[24] Cordell Hull was livid and instructed the U.S. embassy in Tokyo not to assist the Roerichs in any way.

Within a few weeks the two teams had reached Harbin, in Japanese-controlled Manchuria. There some seventy thousand "white Russians" mixed together with Chinese and Japanese in a seething cauldron of intrigue. "It seems to me that it is like another Balkans," MacMillan wrote Ryerson. "It will always be the breeding place for wars." The Roerichs busied themselves handing out leaflets introducing Nicholas Roerich as "one of the greatest leaders of world culture" and proclaiming, "He has a marvelous equipment to be the leader of an international movement. He has power not only to plan but to act."[25]

MacMillan realized that the Roerichs' agenda included something other than plant life, but he also knew the situation was beyond his control. His "Dear Knowles" letters to Ryerson, describing events in increasingly exasperated terms—"Little by little our summer creeps along, and nothing seems to be accomplished"—took weeks to reach the United States, and even then Ryerson, distracted by the Dust Bowl and the duties of his new job, was unable to be of help.[26] The Roerichs, now protected by armed bodyguards, refused even to talk with MacMillan. At one point George Roerich sent a messenger to MacMillan's hotel with a phone number. Roerich was never there.

"I have yet to discover the most minute contribution which they have made to the expedition," wrote MacMillan, "except to hold us back for the better part of six weeks, perhaps to lose the season entirely, and to put us and the government to considerable expense and irritation." For their part, the Roerichs sent back word of their many scientific accomplishments and complaints about MacMillan and Stephens. "It seems that the two men have not a clear picture of the organization of the expedition . . . ," George Roerich wrote.[27]

By August the two teams had lumbered into Hailar, close to the Soviet border. The department botanists set about gathering grass seeds. The Roerichs, surrounded by eight guards in Cossack outfits, continued to foment trouble. At some point they announced their intention to travel to Jehol province, an area of active confrontation between the Chinese and Japanese, which they had been specifically told to avoid. Wallace suggested Ryerson send them a wire saying, "If that's the thing they think they ought to do . . . it's all right." "No," replied Ryerson, "you send that cable."[28]

In the end the Roerichs were literally driven out of Hailar, riding on a military half track with flags flying, headed for China. MacMillan managed a couple of times to catch up with George Roerich but never with "Papa," as he disdainfully called Nicholas Roerich. The painter cabled Wallace complaining that MacMillan and Stephens were uncooperative fellows who "did not think it necessary to visit the Leader of the Expedition." Ryerson suggested the botanists retreat to Shanghai for the winter, ending the fiction that they were in the same expedition as the Roerichs. "I didn't care what the Roerichs did," said Ryerson later. "They were doing what they wanted to do anyway, without any instructions excepting from Wallace."[29]

Wallace seemed to agree with Ryerson's plan but, after a weekend visit to Washington from Frances Grant, abruptly changed course. In Mid-September, Wallace summoned Ryerson to his office and showed him the draft of a cable reprimanding MacMillan and Stephens and recalling them to Washington immediately. "Will you send this or shall I?" Wallace asked. Ryerson tried to talk him out of it, but Wallace insisted. "That's my decision," said Wallace. "Then you send it," Ryerson replied. The cable, in Wallace's name, was sent September 20, 1934.[30]

Wallace wasn't finished. The following day he summoned the hapless Ryerson again, telling him he was being removed as chief of the Bureau of Plant Industry and dispatched to the newly created Office of Tropical and Subtropical Fruit in southern California unless he found another job within ten days. "I kept insisting on knowing why and he would give me no reason," said Ryerson. "The thing he finally hung it on was, 'I've come to the conclusion that you have given Mac instructions contrary to what I know about.' " Ryerson shot back, "In other words, you're saying that I double-crossed my chief. . . . I may be dumb on this job for I haven't had it a year, but I'm not that dumb."[31]

But Ryerson was finished in Washington. After reflecting on the matter for several days, he accepted transfer to the Office of Tropical and Subtropical Fruit and remained there for several years. He subsequently joined the faculty of the University of California at Davis and later became its chancellor.

The Roerichs were riding high. Their enemies within the Agriculture Department had been crushed. Others who harbored reservations lay low. Paul Appleby was in Rome with Rex Tugwell when he learned of Ryerson's demotion, and he refused to get out of bed. The State Department was paralyzed. The diplomats were at best uncertain about what the Roerichs were doing and, in any case, were powerless over the Agriculture Department.

And Wallace was more friendly to the Roerichs than ever. After recalling MacMillan and Stephens and destroying Ryerson's career, Wallace promptly issued apologies to the Roerichs. "I am writing to express to you once again my regret and indignation at the insubordination of these two members of the expedition. I feel that their actions, serious enough under normal circumstances, have placed in jeopardy the success of the expedition as well as the safety of its members. Please be assured that you have my complete confidence and approval in all your actions in regard to the expedition."[32]

The Roerichs responded with a request for more money. It was granted. To make sure everything went well, Wallace assigned a scientific adviser, Earl Bressman, an old friend from Iowa State with whom he had written *Corn and Corn Growing*, to serve as his liaison to the expedition.

The Roerichs' other, more covert ally also remained committed to their cause. President Roosevelt expressed delight over an article written by Nicholas Roerich, "The Deserts Shall Bloom Again," and suggested it be published in the United States. Moreover, he suggested, the time had come for action on the Roerich pact. Plans were set in motion for a formal signing ceremony.

On April 15, 1935, Pan American Day, representatives of twenty-one American countries gathered at the White House to sign the Treaty on the Protection of Artistic and Scientific Institutions and Historic Monuments, as the Roerich pact was officially called. Henry A. Wallace, designated the plenipotentiary of the United States, signed for his government while a beaming Roosevelt looked on. "Launched in the year 1935 at the beginning of the Holy Week before Easter, it can, and I believe will serve as the germinal essence for what eventually will be a New Deal among the nations," Wallace declared. "And in so saying, I am not talking about a New Deal characterized by emergency agencies but about the spiritual New Deal which places that which is fine in humanity above that which is low and sordid and mean and hateful and grabbing."[33]

The following day Wallace wrote several letters nominating Nicholas Roerich for the Nobel Peace Prize.

In Central Asia, however, the situation was hardly peaceful. Having obtained additional arms and ammunition from the American barracks in Tientsin, the Roerichs were riding through villages in Inner Mongolia surrounded by "followers of the bandit Semenoff," terrorizing residents and promising American assistance in the event of an uprising.[34] Chinese and Japanese authorities alike had come to regard the Roerichs with utmost suspicion. White Russians thought Nicholas Roerich was a Soviet spy, and the Soviets wondered why he was surrounded by White Russians.

Within the U.S. government there was a growing fear that the expedition was running amok. Officials at the Agriculture Department noted the Roerichs had forgotten about drought-resistant grasses and seemed to be seeking herbs to cure cancer. Diplomats in Asia sent back frantic reports of the Roerichs erratic actions.

Trouble was brewing among Roerichs' followers as well. Louis Horch, president of the Roerich Museum, began quietly moving to take total control of its operations, real estate, and collection. A lawsuit was filed. Stories about the Roerichs' activities began to appear in the press at home and abroad. In mid-June 1935 Wallace wrote Horch that in a few days he would be at the Newark airport for two hours on his way to Connecticut and would like to meet privately. Whatever was said during those two hours changed everything.

The warm tone of Wallace's letters to and about the Roerichs overnight became frosty. "I am exceedingly anxious," Wallace wrote formally to Horch, ". . . that [Nicholas Roerich] be engaged, both actually and apparently, in doing exactly what he is supposed to be doing as an employee of the United States Department of Agriculture engaged in searching for seeds valuable to the United States."[35]

On July 3, 1935, Wallace ordered Roerich "at the earliest possible safe moment" to move to "a safe region" in Suiyuan. Wallace's cable was followed a few days later with a letter from Bressman, saying, "The Secretary has asked me to inform you that plans should be made for drawing the Central Asian expedition to a close not later than January 1."[36]

Within days Bressman began a campaign of bureaucratic nickel-and-diming. "The Preaudit Difference Statement No. 22470 for $17.56 and for which you enclosed a receipt signed by Mr. N. Grammatchikoff requires a Reimbursement Voucher, Form 1012," Bressman wrote George Roerich on July 20. When George complained that the expedition had not received a check for the first half of February, Bressman sent along two copies of the government's "Budget and Finance Circular No. 13" and a curt note saying records indicated "the check was received by Mr. de Roerich, cashed by him and returned to the Treasury. . . ."[37]

The Roerichs seemed to have trouble seeing the big picture. They kept protesting that they were not really in any danger, and Wallace kept ordering them closer to civilization and urging them to finish up. By late August, however, it should have been clear to them that something was awry. The Treasury Department notified the Roerichs they owed the government $3,604 for expenses claimed without vouchers, the State Department declared the Roerichs were leading an armed party toward the Soviet Union "to rally former White elements and discontented Mongols," and Wallace personally warned them that "Department employees must not make statements reflecting on political situations in other nations."[38]

Two weeks later Wallace pulled the plug. In a succession of messages the Roerichs were told to turn over their guns, send in their seeds, and have no further dealings with Wallace or Bressman. Henceforth, they were told, all matters related to the expedition would be handled by F. D. Richey, new chief of the Bureau of Plant Industry. On September 21 Wallace ordered the expedition disbanded, followed by a press release announcing the decision, followed by a telegram warning the Roerichs that "there must no publicity whatever about recent expedition. There must be no quoting of correspondence or other violation of Department publicity regulations."[39]

In their sixteen-month journey through Asia, the Roerichs had produced a total of 20 plants—13 grasses and 7 leguminous plants. By contrast, the brief MacMillan mission had sent back 59 grasses and 41 other plants. Another two-man Agriculture Department expedition, operating in Asia at the same time, sent back more than 2,000 plants, including 726 soil-conserving grasses,

Although the expedition had ended, the fiasco was far from finished.

* * *

It had taken Wallace years to wise up. Aides had fought him openly and rolled their eyes in private. His personal secretary, Mary Huss, spoke in irritated tones about "those people in New York" and did what she could to prevent their access to him. Jim LeCron, a close aide and personal friend, repeatedly expressed misgivings about Frances Grant, whom he regarded as an "unpleasant, hatchet-faced woman" with sinister motives. Rex Tugwell, having at last concluded that Roosevelt was in some way involved, threw up his hands and maintained an attitude of amused indifference.[40]

Through it all Wallace stood by Nicholas Roerich with the steadfastness of Galahad. But having seen the light, Wallace turned against him in fury. In every way possible, Wallace set out to destroy the Roerichs and assuage his own embarrassment. Letters went out to American embassies, saying, "Much information has come to my attention which causes me to change my opinion [concerning the Roerichs]." The American consulate in India, where the Roerichs were headed, was advised that all official relations with the department had ended and asked that "any requests made to you by Professor Roerich" be forwarded immediately to Wallace personally.[41] At a press conference he suggested the Roerichs may in fact have been spies.

To Helena Roerich in Punjab, India, he issued what amounted to divorce papers:

Dear Madam:

I am writing this letter to you in my personal capacity to inform you precisely and definitely that I desire that there be no communication, direct or indirect, by letter or otherwise between the Roerichs (father, mother and sons) on the one side and myself on the other. Official business will be transacted with Frederick D. Richey, Chief, Bureau of Plant Industry, United States Department of Agriculture.

Very Truly
H.A. Wallace[42]

Louis Horch, whose own break with Roerich was complete, was reminded that all correspondence with the Roerichs and their associates should remain confidential—a reminder that was far too late. Joseph Grew, the American ambassador to Japan, received a personal explanation from Wallace about what had gone wrong. "Information which has come to my hands during the past year has caused me to be exceedingly disillusioned regarding [Roerich]," Wallace explained. "[It] appears . . . that he gave out unjustifiable statements on politics and other matters. It is said that he made unwarranted statements to Japanese officials, including His Excellency, The Minister of War, General Sonjuro Hayashi."[43]

On October 1 Wallace wrote to Internal Revenue Commissioner Guy Helvering, suggesting the IRS take a look at Nicholas Roerich's taxes. Enclosed was a memo, probably assembled with Horch's help, detailing several aspects of Roerich's finances. During 1931, for example, Roerich had a gross income of $10,623 and deductions of $3,761. On an adjusted income of more than $6,800, however, Roerich paid only $137.34 in income taxes. Wallace told the commissioner he would "appreciate your checking [these facts] at your earliest opportunity."[44]

The IRS did even more. It audited Roerich's taxes back to 1926 and concluded he owed $49,186. Then the State Department notified its consulate in India that, since Roerich had a huge unpaid tax bill, it wished to be notified immediately if he applied for an immigration visa.* For his part, Wallace volunteered to send any departmental monies still owed to the Roerichs to the U.S. Treasury instead. "Our experience with Nicholas Roerich has been quite unsatisfactory," Wallace said in a letter to Secretary of the Treasury Henry Morgenthau.[45]

Having spurred the tax collectors into action, Wallace began the arduous task of recanting his friendship with the Roerichs. He resigned his membership on the Permanent Committee for the Treaty for the Protection of Artistic and Scientific Institutions and Historic Monuments, of which he was

---

*Roerich and his family took up residence in India, never paid the tax bill, and never returned to the United States. He continued to paint and promote the Banner of Peace, and he was on friendly terms with many leaders of the Indian independence movement, including Jawaharlal Nehru, who visited Roerich's home in Kulu in 1942. Roerich died of heart disease in December 1947, leaving behind some seven thousand paintings, thirty books, a scaled-down version of the Roerich Museum in New York City, and the never implemented Roerich pact.

honorary chairman, and removed the Banner of Peace symbol from subsequent editions of *New Frontiers*.

When an anti–New Deal book called *Despotic Democracy* claimed that the Banner of Peace was the official symbol of the New Deal, Wallace drafted a letter to the publishers ridiculing the symbol he once held dear. "This is an injustice to the New Deal," Wallace said. "Aside from myself, I don't think I have ever heard a New Dealer say anything about this symbol. . . . The only comment I have ever heard a New Dealer make concerning the symbol was to the effect that the three balls reminded him of a pawnbroker's shop."[46]

In dozens of "personal and confidential" letters to political, business, cultural, and diplomatic figures—including every ambassador who had signed the Roerich pact in the 1935 White House ceremony—Wallace announced his break with Roerich. ". . . I am writing to let you know that I have decided reservations about him," Wallace said. "I also wish to let you know that I am not a friend of those who continue fanatically in their policy of aggrandizing a name rather than an ideal," he said, referring to Frances Grant and others who remained loyal to Roerich.[47]

The professor's dedicated followers, Wallace said in a letter to Governor Herbert Lehman of New York, "were worshipping Professor Roerich as a superman and were determined to stop at nothing in helping him to work out some extraordinary phantasy of Asiatic power."[48]

Perhaps most difficult to write, given his admiration for public servants, were letters to the three Agriculture Department officials Wallace had clearly wronged. "I wish to say," he told Knowles Ryerson, "that I have given considerable study to all aspects of the situation and have reached the conclusion that your motives were of the highest. Subsequent events have in considerable measure borne out your judgment." Ryerson responded breezily, "I am very happy . . . to learn that the situation you refer to has been satisfactorily cleared up."[49]

His apology to MacMillan, who had taken a position at the University of California at Los Angeles, was more muted. "In view of all developments, I can now see that your actions while on this expedition probably were guided by good motives," Wallace said. ". . . I nevertheless feel that you did not cooperate as fully as you might have with the leader of the expedition." In MacMillan's view it wasn't an apology at all. Perhaps Wallace agreed, because in late 1936 he tried again to make amends. "I thought you might like to know in writing that my observations of the past year have caused me to believe that your actions on the expedition of 1934 were prompted by the highest motives," Wallace said. "Furthermore, I now believe you behaved in an unusually difficult situation with courage, initiative and discretion."[50]

The apologies, the pursuit of back taxes, the recantations, and the resignations were not enough to make the Roerich affair go away, however. Too many people knew what had happened. Too many people thought something inappropriate or improper or simply weird had taken place. Their suspicions gradually seeped into the political atmosphere. That Wallace was a mystic, that something about him was strange, became a truism of politically cognizant people even if they didn't quite know why. Wallace could do nothing to change it. All he could do was live with it, expect the worst, and hope for the best.

And the worst was yet to come. In New York City an embittered Frances Grant still held high the flame of Professor Nicholas Roerich. And she had the letters.

CHAPTER EIGHT

"WHOSE CONSTITUTION?"

Quiet as a cornfield on a windless summer day, Henry Wallace's "revolution" had begun its spread across the fertile fields of the American Midwest. Farm by farm, township by township, the miracle of hybrid corn was taking root by the mid-1930s, and agriculture would never be the same.

Moving outward from their locus of operations at Johnston, Iowa, Wallace's small band of apostles made their conversions one by one. The irrepressible Roswell Garst trudged across every township in sixteen western Iowa counties, hauling with him eight-pound sample bags of seed, to convince skeptical and destitute farmers that Pioneer Hi-Bred seed could improve their lot. Nelson Urban, the part-time bookkeeper who had taken charge of the fledgling company's sales division, established a network of farmer salesmen across the state. If one farmer on every road could be persuaded to use hybrid seed, Urban reasoned, surely his neighbors would begin to see the benefits.

It was not an easy sell. At the depths of the Depression, corn sold in Iowa for ten cents a bushel. "It was cheaper to burn corn than it was to burn coal," Garst recalled.[1] Yet so superior were the results obtained by hybrid seed that Pioneer's salesmen were able to sell their product for the enormous price of $5.50 per bushel—and sell it all.

The men Wallace left behind to run Pioneer Hi-Bred were able, dedicated, and eclectic. At the helm was Fred Lehmann, a gruff Des Moines lawyer who served as the company's president after Wallace went to Washington. Lehmann was neither a farmer nor a scientist, but he shared two important principles with his friend Henry Wallace. First, both believed in research. Without a continuing, well-financed research program, the hybrid vision would quickly collapse of its own weight. In later years Wallace liked to tell audiences that his company alone spent more money annually on corn research than the U.S. Department of Agriculture and state experiment stations combined.

Second, Wallace and Lehmann insisted their customers should be treated with absolute candor. Pioneer salesmen were instructed to tell farmers everything—good and bad—about the hybrid strains they were selling and never to make exaggerated claims. "Lehmann realized people appreciated and paid for quality," said Raymond Baker, the young corn breeder who became head of Pioneer's research operations.[2]

Baker, once the company's all-purpose hired hand and corn-breeding assistant, began assembling a top-flight staff of botanists and geneticists. James Weatherspoon, a biological statistician, pushed the company to the edge of the computer age, making extensive use of IBM punch card–sorting machines and rotary calculators to track Pioneer's expanding research programs. Sam Goodsell designed a germination program that gave farmers accurate data about a hybrid strain's reliability.

With each passing year Pioneer became bigger and bolder. Experiment stations were established in Indiana, Illinois, and Minnesota in order to adapt Pioneer's products to other environments. A winter nursery was established in Argentina, and another station was built in Herndon, Virginia, close enough for Wallace to visit on weekends. State-of-the-art facilities replaced the converted chicken coop that had once served as Pioneer's drying and sorting plant.

Perry Collins, a young Guthrie County farmer who was one of Baker's first recruits, was to play a key role in the popularization of hybrid corn. Collins had only a high school diploma, in contrast to college-educated men who formed the bulk of Baker's team, but he had a dirt farmer's commonsense instincts. In the early 1930s Collins was dispatched to Pocahontas County in northern Iowa to develop hybrid strains suitable for colder regions with shorter growing seasons.

There Collins was confronted with the drought of 1934, one of a series of natural disasters that tormented American farmers during the Depression. Day after day, temperatures reached one hundred degrees, and desperate farmers watched the skies for rain that never came. Collins's little nursery of experimental corn plants mostly withered and died.

Collins was ready to scrap the entire crop when it occurred to him that the few plants that had survived the searing heat and prolonged drought were worth studying. "[We] decided that the best thing to do was to go ahead with whatever was able to withstand the conditions in 1934 and this decision proved very valuable when we found ourselves in another serious drought condition in the summer of 1936," he later said.[3] The result of his work was Pioneer's hybrid 307, a plant with strong roots, a dark green color, and an unusual ability to withstand the stress of drought. Almost overnight, demand for hybrid seed exploded.

In the twelve northern and central states of the nation's Corn Belt, stretching from Ohio to Kansas, only a fraction of 1 percent of all corn came from hybrid seed in 1933. A decade later, 78 percent of the region's corn came from hybrid seed. In Iowa, which led the way, the use of hybrid seed grew from less than 1 percent in 1933 to 99.5 percent ten years later. At least a third of it came in bags bearing the brand of Henry Wallace's company.

Wallace's victory was, of course, not without its financial rewards. After struggling to survive during its early years—Pioneer actually lost money in 1927 and again in 1932—the company began to show a steady profit beginning in 1933. Wallace's royalties that year amounted to $622.20, of which $500 was applied to new stock. In the following decade Pioneer's revenues grew by an astonishing 28 percent a year, from about $20,000 in 1933 to $2.5 million in 1942.

The increased use of hybrid seed was accompanied by a dramatic rise in corn yields. In 1931 the average corn yield in the United States was 24.1 bushels per acre, about the same as at the conclusion of the Civil War. A decade later, in 1941, corn yields had increased to 31 bushels per acre, and by 1981 they had grown to 109.8 bushels per acre. "In 1981, the United States produced more than three times as much corn on one-third fewer acres than in 1931," wrote Dr. William L. Brown, one of Baker's gifted young researchers who later became president of Pioneer Hi-Bred.[4] At least half of that growth was attributable to hybrid breeding.

The development and commercialization of hybrid corn in the United States was in actuality the first of the world's "green revolutions," Brown wrote. Its impact was at least as important and far-reaching as the famous "green revolutions" involving Mexican wheat and Philippine rice. In fact, the American experience with corn made those revolutions possible.

"The introduction of U.S. hybrid maize into Europe following World War II saved countless lives and transformed agriculture in that part of the world in an incredibly short period of time," Brown added. "The methodology of hybrid development quickly spread from the United States throughout the developed world, and U.S. genetic materials, where adapted, greatly enhanced the rapid development of commercial hybrids. Many persons deserve credit for this revolution, among the foremost of whom is H.A. Wallace."[5]

Yet this revolution, the central achievement of Wallace's life, was also its biggest paradox. Even as he was teaching Iowa farmers how to produce more corn, Wallace was in Washington wrestling with the problem of overproduction. And as he was bringing scientific advancement to the farm, he was setting in motion forces that would drive ever more farmers off the land.

He recognized the paradox. But he could never resolve it.

❧

"You have been doing one of the finest bits of public education that I have seen done by anybody in a very long time," the nation's preeminent journalist, Walter Lippmann, wrote privately to Wallace in May 1934. "More power to you."[6]

Wallace was in high gear. In 1934 alone Wallace traveled over forty thousand miles by car, train, boat, and plane. He made public appearances in all forty-eight states, delivered eighty-eight speeches, wrote twenty articles for magazines and journals, published two books and a lengthy pamphlet, received two honorary degrees, and met with reporters by the score.

He was everywhere: preaching the need for societal cooperation to the Federal Council of the Churches of Christ; denouncing unfettered individualism before a gathering of mortgage bankers; making the case for governmental activism before an association of economists; urging students at Cornell University to develop "fire and vigor" in their spiritual lives; arguing against the "tyranny of greed" in the pages of *Colliers'* magazine.

His book *Statesmanship and Religion*, based largely on a series of lectures he delivered at the Chicago Theological Seminary, won wide praise for its thoughtfulness and idealism. "Has any American cabinet officer since the days of 'The Federalist' written anything as significant and as politically potent and pregnant?" asked the columnist Lewis Gannett. Wallace's lengthy pamphlet making the case for free trade among nations, entitled *America Must Choose*, was warmly embraced by Secretary of State Cordell Hull and his predecessor in the Hoover administration, Henry Stimson.

Coincidentally, and without really trying, the once little-known farm editor was becoming an appealing national figure. Photos of him peering intently at a farm animal or inspecting a cornfield—often in shirtsleeves, his hair askew—were commonplace in newspapers and farm magazines. Reporters wrote glowing accounts of his "youth and energy," his lean frame and easy grin. "He does not look his age," wrote a *Washington Star* reporter. "He is a wiry young man with wiry reddish-brown hair that bristles in all directions from the part on the left side of his long head. In his gray-blue eyes a serious purpose seemed to have won only a slight victory over a quick understanding that is the mother of humor. Despite a pleasant, natural and infectious smile, seriousness was the order of his tanned face."[7]

"There is a deep pathos in his face, but he is strong, fond of simple living, fond of walking," said the journalist John Franklin Carter, writing anonymously as "The Unofficial Observer." "In Chicago recently he horrified his companion by insisting on walking from his hotel to the station, about half-a-mile distant. He carried his heavy suitcase and when his companion could no longer stagger under his, Wallace carried that, too."[8]

Wallace's eccentricities, at least the ones reporters could witness, were treated mostly with benign good humor. "He indulges in such unworldly hobbies as astronomy, higher mathematics and running up Pike's Peak," declared the writer Ray Tucker in *Colliers'* magazine. Newspapers carried accounts of his decision to give up "his latest dietary experiment," which consisted of drinking a glass of "soybean milk" every day at lunch in the Agriculture Department's cafeteria. "It was told . . . that he so disliked his big mahogany desk when he went to the Department of Agriculture that he worked on only one end of it," wrote *Time* magazine.[9]

Reporters were particularly fond of anecdotes about Wallace's lack of pretentiousness. They never tired of noting that he walked to work, enjoyed cheese sandwiches for lunch, and wore rumpled suits. "He cares so little for things of this world . . . that he refuses to ride in the luxurious limousine provided for him by the government," wrote Ray Tucker. "Its soft cushions bruise his humble skin and he bumps along in the cheap, rickety car of an assistant." Ilo Wallace's "simple meals" of nut bread and butterscotch pie were described on home and family pages.[10]

"Probably no other cabinet officer in this or any other administration would stop along a highway in the shade of a farmer's grove and revel in a choice lunch of cheese, watermelon, tomato juice, pop corn and crackers," wrote a reporter in the *Des Moines Register.* "Imagine the consternation of the grocery boy in Sac City. 'Give me two pounds of cheese,' said the mild mannered cabinet member, who personally supervised purchase of a picnic lunch. The lad reeled off eight or nine varieties of cheese. 'Nothing fancy; just give me some ordinary rat cheese,' the customer replied."[11]

If Wallace's simple lifestyle was easy for reporters to grasp, however, his elusive personality was not. So much of him was hidden from view—more than even his closest associates imagined—that gifted reporters struggled to capture him in words. They described him variously as "sincere and intellectually incorruptible," a man willing to compromise in order to further his cause, a "gloomy" economist, a "clean-toothed, smiling" optimist, a man of "scientific curiosity and exactitude of mind," "essentially a mystic and a moralist," a "fluent and easy speaker," a "man with no taste for speaking."[12]

The journalistic portraits of Wallace "seldom seemed to gibe," observed Wallace's friend and aide Russell Lord. "They wrote that he was simple, but exceedingly complex; that he wavered between ardor for the utmost advance of an interdependent civilization, with an abundance of material goods and gimcracks for everyone, and the simple desire to lie on green grass under trees and be let alone."[13]

"He is shy and modest by nature and he has been observed to resemble a schoolboy waiting for his turn 'to speak a piece,' " said one reporter. "He customarily either sits with his eyes half closed and stares into space or else fidgets and ruffles his tawny mane." Another saw him as a "self-confident man, in a quiet way," and still another said H. A., like all Wallaces, was "fierce and tribal in a quiet way."[14]

Whatever else they saw in Wallace, most of those who observed him glimpsed something out of the ordinary. He was cut from a different bolt of cloth than the politicians and celebrities they were accustomed to covering. Some found this quality strange and off-putting. "Henry's the sort that keeps you guessing as to whether he's going to deliver a sermon or wet the bed," said one politician.[15]

But others saw greatness in Wallace's mysterious personality. "He epitomizes American civilization in its most genuine native form," John Franklin Carter wrote in 1934, "the form which gave us an Andrew Jackson and an Abraham Lincoln. He is as earthy as the black loam of the corn belt, as gaunt and grim as a pioneer. With all of that, he has an insatiable curiosity and one of the keenest minds in Washington, well-disciplined and subtle, with interests and accomplishments which range from agrarian genetics to astronomy. . . . If the young men and women of this country look to the west for a liberal candidate for the Presidency—as they may in 1940—they will not be able to overlook Henry Wallace."[16]

While Wallace crisscrossed the country building support for the New Deal and its groundbreaking farm program, tensions within his department continued to smolder. George Peek's departure did nothing to halt the feud between old-line agrarians and young social reformers, for at bottom the fight was not over personalities or even policy specifics but over what, in the end, the New Deal really was.

The pragmatist agrarians believed their role was to restore the economic health of commercial agriculture. Not all of them were unfriendly to the notion of social change, but their overwhelming concern was to rescue farmers from the emergency at hand. If that meant playing ball with the agricultural establishment—the powerful southerners who controlled congressional committees, the big distributors, the packing houses, the Farm Bureau, the land grant colleges, and the extension agents—then play ball they would. There was, in their view, little to be gained, and much to be lost, by picking fights with the powers that be.

The social reformers—invariably called "urban reformers" by their critics, for most of them did not come from the farm—saw their task as the overhaul of a corrupt capitalist system. Big agribusiness, the Farm Bureau, and the agricultural colleges were part of that system, part of the problem, and had to undergo change if the promise of the New Deal was to be met.

Some of them undoubtedly were radicals who would have liked to see the old system crushed. But most of them would have agreed with Rex Tugwell, who argued for gradual experimentation in pursuit of liberal goals. "Liberals would like to rebuild the station while the trains are running; radicals prefer to blow up the station and forgo service until the new structure is built," Tugwell wrote.[17]

Both sides, with some justification, claimed Wallace as their own. His leadership in the crusade for farm relief, his solid credentials as farm editor and plant scientist, his family's long association with land grant colleges, and the farm establishment's top echelon stood him in good stead in the eyes of the Agriculture Adjustment Administration's agrarians.

The reformers, on the other hand, saw in Wallace a reflection of themselves: young, idealistic, open-minded, comfortable with intellectual give-and-take, and repulsed by the excesses of capitalism. Wallace himself knew he was part of both camps. "I more nearly understood both sides of this problem that any of these boys," he commented later.[18]

For extended periods of time Wallace managed to float above the fight and remain in the good graces of both camps. His low-key manner and frequent absences from the department allowed him to ignore most personality disputes. Increasingly he left day-to-day administrative details in the hands of his capable assistant Paul Appleby, a self-effacing man regarded by all factions as an honest broker.

But privately Wallace knew the struggle in his department was headed for a collision. "I am certain the situation will never be fully straightened out," he wrote in a diary he briefly maintained during the mid-1930s. Disputes such as the one confronting him, Wallace believed, were inherent in Roosevelt's leadership style. "In this administration, the objectives were experimental and not clearly stated. Therefore, there was certain to be, from the White House down, a certain amount of what seemed to be intrigue. I did not think that this situation would be remedied until the president abandoned to a considerable extent his experimental and somewhat concealed approach."[19]

The collision finally came in early 1935. The opposing forces were led by Chester Davis, the avuncular agrarian who replaced Peek as head of the AAA, and Jerome Frank, the hard-charging liberal who headed its legal division. Davis, born in Iowa a year before Wallace, had a long association with George Peek. Unlike Peek, however, Davis was fully committed to the domestic allotment program. And he had a self-deprecating wit and collegial style that enabled him to get along with Tugwell and other liberals with whom he did not always agree.

By early 1935, however, Davis had about had his fill of Frank and the young lawyers. The legal division's "sharp tricks"—its delays, its hidden agenda disguised in legalistic language, its leaks to reporters—were enough to make Davis talk about leaving government altogether. The liberals, in turn, saw Davis as little more than Peek with a smiling face. Davis, in their view, was all too ready to do business with the big corporations and plantation owners who stood on the necks of consumers and farm laborers.

The showdown came over cotton. Growers of cotton, unlike midwestern corn farmers, often were absentee landlords who depended on tenants to produce the crop. Some tenants were wage laborers, akin to the seasonal farmhands in the Midwest. But about 45 percent of the cotton tenants were "sharecroppers" who lived in shacks provided by the landlord, bought food at inflated prices in landlord-owned stores, and received a portion of the crop in lieu of wages.

In the eyes of its critics, the sharecropping system, laden with the politics of race and class, was nothing but a means of keeping tenants in a permanent state of debilitating poverty and social degradation. Socialist Party leader Norman Thomas called it "peonage—worse than peonage"—and crusaded noisily to expose its excesses.[20]

Not even the reformers believed that the Agriculture Department could dismantle anything as well entrenched as sharecropping in the South. But the liberals thought the AAA cotton program was making the plight of some sharecroppers even worse. The AAA contracts required cotton plantation owners to share government benefits with their tenants, but the provision was poorly enforced at best. Some landlords imposed harsh new conditions on their tenants; others simply chased sharecroppers off the land, leaving whole families destitute and homeless.

In June 1934, reacting to allegations that an absentee landlord had evicted some forty tenant families in Arkansas, sharecroppers formed the Southern Tenant Farmers Union. The biracial organization set out to fight for the economic and political rights of sharecroppers wherever it could: in courtrooms, in public opinion, in the gloomy gray corridors of the Agriculture Department. Landlords, recognizing the threat posed by the union, fought back with a fierce campaign of nighttime beatings, economic intimidation, and raw political power.

"There is a reign of terror in the cotton country of eastern Arkansas," Norman Thomas told a nationwide radio audience. "It will end either in the establishment of complete slavish submission to the vilest exploitation in America or in bloodshed, or in both."[21]

In an effort to ameliorate the situation, reformers in the AAA legal division sought to make use of an obscure section of the law that created the cotton program. It said cotton producers "shall insofar as possible, maintain on this farm the normal number of tenants" and "shall permit all tenants to continue the occupancy of their houses." The vagueness of the clause—it didn't say whether the planter's obligation was legal or only moral, and a huge loophole was created by the "insofar as possible" clause—made it useless as a legal weapon to the Southern Tenant Farmers Union.[22]

In January 1935 the AAA legal division set out to close the loophole. Late in the month the lawyers issued a new interpretation of the law, saying landlords were required by the contract to keep not only the "normal number" of tenants but the exact same tenants. The reinterpretation was drafted by Alger Hiss, a polished young lawyer who had worked extensively on legal matters involving the cotton program.

Knowing Davis would never approve the reinterpretation, Frank waited until the administrator was in Iowa to make his move. He persuaded Victor Chirstgau, a liberal former congressman from Minnesota who was second in command at the AAA, to announce the change in a telegram to local offices. Christgau, in turn, persuaded Appleby to send the telegram in the name of Henry Wallace.

The telegram caused an immediate explosion. Wallace was blindsided. Before he had even heard about the telegram, an Arkansas congressman and the head of the Arkansas Farm Bureau were in his office to complain about it. Davis girded for war and grimly headed back to Washington. "The new interpretations completely reversed the basis on which cotton contracts had been administered through the first year," Davis later said. "If the contract had been so construed, and if the Department of Agriculture had enforced it, Henry Wallace would have been forced out of the Cabinet within a month. The effects would have been revolutionary."[23]

On Saturday, February 2, a "very much disturbed" Davis told Wallace that either the legal department liberals would go or he would. Wallace did not act immediately, but his own response to the legal division's action was entirely clear and never changed. "I had no doubt that Frank and Hiss were animated by the highest motives, but their lack of agricultural background exposed them to the danger of going to absurd lengths," Wallace later said. "I was convinced that from a legal point of view they had nothing to stand on and that they allowed their social preconceptions to lead them to something which was not only indefensible from a practical, agricultural point of view, but also bad law."[24]

On Monday, emboldened by expressions of support he received from colleagues, Davis met again with Wallace and asked to be allowed to handle the situation. Wallace agreed. David named the men who would have to go, beginning with Jerome Frank. "It was under his general shelter that a cluster of trouble-makers had assembled," Davis said. ". . . He was the head and heart."[25]

The "purge of the liberals," as it came to be known, began the next day. Jerome Frank went first. "I've had a chance to watch you," Davis told Frank, "and I think you are an outright revolutionary, whether you realize it or not."[26] Frank's number two man, Lee Pressman, met a similar fate, as did Francis Shea, head of the legal division's opinions section. Gardner Jackson, number two man in the office of consumer affairs, was also dispatched. Victor Christgau was demoted but allowed to remain in the agency. Curiously Davis did not fire Alger Hiss, the lawyer who drafted the legal reinterpretation.

Late that day Frank and others who had been fired asked to meet with Wallace. The secretary said he would see two, but only two, of them. They chose to send Frank, their leader, and Hiss, the only one who hadn't been fired. It was one of the few times Wallace remembered meeting Hiss, and it was the last. Frank still harbored a notion that Davis must have acted on his own, as part of a planned coup against Wallace himself.

According to one account of the meeting, Wallace greeted them with tears in his eyes and his hand outstretched. "Jerome, you've been the best fighter I've had for my ideas, but I've had to fire you," Wallace was said to have exclaimed. "The farm people are just too strong." Wallace's own version, recorded in a diary, was considerably more dry-eyed. "I indicated that I believed Frank and Hiss had been loyal to me at all times, but it was necessary to clear up an administrative situation and that I agreed with Davis. They wanted to hear it direct from the horse's mouth."[27]

Wallace briefly mentioned the firings to Roosevelt at a White House meeting the following morning. Roosevelt made no comment. Then Wallace and Davis together faced reporters at a boiling, poisonous press conference. Wallace appeared "gray and haggard," an aide recalled, and his manner was "sad and uneasy." Finally Wallace settled on the analogy of a ship to explain his actions. "Well, you see we don't like to have a ship that lists stronger to the left or the right, but one that goes straight ahead."[28]

Wallace had set his course, but the purge of the liberals took a heavy toll. It was a sobering reminder of the limits imposed upon idealism by political reality. Young liberals began drifting away from the Agriculture Department, taking with them some of the energy and vision that had made it the New Deal's most vital agent for almost two years. Rex Tugwell, while acknowl-

edging that Wallace faced large obstacles from a Congress dominated by southern conservatives, was among the disillusioned. Within a few months he left
to head a new agency, the Resettlement Administration, created to help poor
and displaced farmers and tenants.

"He gave up his policy," Tugwell said of Wallace. "It was more failure of
leadership than anything else. It was letting himself be pushed around by what
I thought were pretty sinister forces." Perhaps even Wallace agreed in part.
Little more than a year after the liberal purge, Chester Davis was eased out
of the department and replaced by Howard Tolley, a California agricultural
professor with progressive views. "This rukus," as the aide Jim LeCron called
the purge, ". . . didn't do anybody any good. It didn't do Chester any good."[29]

Certainly it did Wallace no good. His reputation as a noble idealist took
a drubbing. The journalist Paul Ward dubbed him "the great hesitator," and
Raymond Gram Swing, in the *Nation* magazine, said Wallace had shown himself unwilling to stand up to big producers and agribusinesses and seize "economic power from the interests in agriculture who hold it and are increasing
it." Columnists hinted that Wallace had been bitten by the bug of presidential ambitions, or perhaps simply didn't know what he was doing. Some of
those who were fired, especially Gardner Means, a former newsman who had
cut his teeth on the Sacco and Vanzetti case, dogged Wallace for years with
unflattering stories and profiles.[30]

Wallace remained calm, convinced that he had no other choice than to fire
the liberals. "I was aware while all this was going on that it would probably
cause quite a storm of leftist wrath," he later commented. "It was a calculated
risk."[31]

The beleaguered AAA survived for another eleven months. Its demise came
precisely at noon Monday, January 6, 1936, when the Supreme Court declared
the Agricultural Adjustment Act unconstitutional by a six-to-three vote. Henry
Wallace's bold experiment—his "modern vessel . . . set on a course toward
social justice"—was brought to a standstill in a single stroke.[32]

The demise of the AAA was abrupt but hardly unexpected. For months the
Supreme Court had been signaling its hostility to the New Deal and all its
works. Conservative businessmen, seeking in courtrooms what they could not
achieve at the polls, began systematically challenging the administration's agencies and actions, and the strategy was succeeding. Their first major victory
came on May 27, 1935—Black Monday, as the New Dealers would call it—
when the Supreme Court unanimously struck down the National Industrial
Recovery Act (NIRA).

Knowing a Supreme Court challenge to the AAA would not be far behind—already some seventeen hundred lawsuits against the agency had piled up in lower courts—Wallace devoted many public appearances during the remaining months of 1935 to the case for New Deal activism. In books, magazine articles, and speeches such as the commencement address he delivered at Harvard in June 1935, Wallace argued repeatedly that the aim of the AAA was the fundamentally conservative goal of preserving constitutional democracy. "If we do not wish imperialism, or war, or communism, or fascism, or inflation, what is left?" he asked. "The question I would raise is whether a new unity can be built which is based on the principles of economic balance and an advancing culture. Is it possible to hope for an educated democracy, capable of making the necessary key economic decisions in a spirit which does not have its origins in hatred or greed or prejudice?"[33]

In certain respects Wallace believed that the AAA had a better chance of surviving a legal challenge than the National Recovery Administration (NRA). Unlike the highly centralized NRA, which eventually became unpopular with the business interests it was supposed to be saving, the AAA's county-by-county system of decision making and enforcement was widely viewed as fair and democratic. The nation's commercial farmers overwhelmingly supported the agency. Even city dwellers gave it general approval despite the slight rise in food prices and the constant complaints of many urban newspapers.

But the AAA had a powerful and determined foe in the food processors that paid the tax that generated revenue for the farm subsidies. Wallace could argue that the tax was actually an excise tax eventually passed along to consumers. He could make a case that the tax was a matter of fundamental fairness. "The processing tax is the farmer's tariff," he declared.[34] He could offer manufacturers a deal: agriculture would do without the processing tax if manufacturers would forgo the tariff. But no argument or appeal to good citizenship could make businessmen want to pay a tax they didn't want to pay.

The AAA case finally heard by the High Court grew out of a lawsuit brought on behalf of William M. Butler, a wealthy textile manufacturer who had served as Calvin Coolidge's campaign manager and chairman of the Republican National Committee. Butler challenged the government's right to collect the processing tax from his firm, Hoosac Mills, a once flourishing manufacturer of "stockings" used by Armour and Company to hold its sausages and hams. Funds for the legal battle came partly from Frederick H. Prince, a large shareholder in Armour, who was an implacable opponent of the New Deal. Prince was said to have spent a million dollars in legal challenges to Roosevelt's programs.

Prince's money was sufficient to buy the legal services of the former U.S. senator George Wharton Pepper, and it was money well spent. Pepper was the close friend and political patron of Justice Owen J. Roberts, at age sixty-four the youngest member of the Supreme Court and one not identified with the bloc of four arch-conservatives certain to vote against any New Deal program. It was Pepper who argued the Butler case before the Court and Roberts who wrote for the majority.

Agriculture, Roberts declared in a 7,000-word opinion, was "a purely local activity" not subject to regulation by the federal government. The processing tax was not intended to raise revenue but to serve a regulatory scheme, which took money from one segment of society to benefit another. If the AAA were allowed to stand, Roberts added, the rights of individual states would be "obliterated, and the United States converted into a central government exercising controlled police power in every state of the Union."[35]

Justice Harlan Fiske Stone offered a withering, almost contemptuous rebuttal, in his dissenting opinion. "Courts are not the only agency of government that must be assumed to have the capacity to govern," Stone declared. Congress "unhappily may falter or be mistaken" from time to time, but so too might the courts. The wisest course, he said, would be for the Court to admit that the Constitution "may mean what it says: that the power to tax and spend includes the power to relieve a nationwide economic maladjustment by conditional gifts of money."[36]

In less than a year the Supreme Court had struck down the NRA and the AAA, the two great "pillars" on which the New Deal stood. In the eyes of conservatives Roosevelt was ruined. His great plans and programs were nothing but shards scattered along the swampy banks of the Potomac. At the White House an aide put a piece of paper in front of Roosevelt reporting the Court's decision. He read it and said nothing. Then he smiled.

Roosevelt's smile was born of politics. The presidential election year was only one week old, and already his opponents had overplayed their hand. And, because they didn't recognize their error, Roosevelt was confident they would do it again and again.

There was no smile on Wallace's face, however. The political implications of the Court's decision didn't interest him, but the practical problems it posed for the department and farmers were stunning. "The farmers, like many of the rest of us, are a good bit like the man who has just had the breath knocked out of him," he said. "When he comes to he doesn't know whether to laugh, cry or cuss."[37]

Twenty-four hours after the Court acted, Wallace appeared on the NBC radio network to review the situation: "As an immediate consequence of the

Supreme Court's decision, processing tax collections have been stopped, benefit payments have been cut off, and the whole machinery of the Agricultural Adjustment Administration has necessarily come to a pause. Sign-up campaigns for the 1936 adjustment programs have, of course, been halted." Unless something was devised to take the place of the AAA, Wallace asserted, a "repetition of 1932" was in the works.[38]

Wallace was genuinely angered by the Supreme Court's decision. It was, in his view, poorly reasoned and philosophically bankrupt. He was particularly irked by the assertion in Roberts's opinion that agriculture was an entirely local activity. "In 1936, only the small farms tucked away in the hollows of the Appalachians and the Ozarks are producing chiefly for home use," he wrote, later adding, "Were agriculture truly a local matter in 1936, as the Supreme Court says it is, half of the people in the United States would quickly starve."[39]

His anger turned to outrage two weeks later when the Court ordered that $200 million of impounded processing taxes be returned to the manufacturers. "This is probably the greatest legalized steal in American history," Wallace fumed. The money had been collected from consumers and farmers by the processors and turned over to the government, he noted. "It now goes by Supreme Court order to enrich solely the processors. . . . I do not question the legality of this action, but I certainly do question the justice of it."[40]

Wallace promised "practical and immediate action" to remedy the situation. The course he took was thoroughly typical of him.[41] First he set out with furious determination to rebuild a mechanism for farm relief. Then he wrote a book.

Planning for a new farm program had, in fact, quietly been taking place for months. Anticipating that AAA might not survive the legal challenge, Wallace had put in place a team to devise a program that would meet constitutional objections. To head the team he turned to Howard Tolley, an economist who left the AAA in 1935 to become head of the Giannini Foundation at the University of California. By the time the Supreme Court acted, Tolley had produced plans for a new farm program, and Wallace sprang to action.

Only four days after the Court's decision, Wallace convened another meeting of farm leaders in Washington to outline a new program. The plan would empower the Agriculture Department to enter into rental agreements with farmers who would promise to replace certain soil-depleting crops—such as corn, wheat, cotton, and tobacco—with "green manure" such as grass and legumes. Money for the program would be appropriated by Congress. The plan would be administered at the local level by elected soil conservation district committees. The local committees, in turn, would be responsible to the department's Soil Conservation Service, which would determine conservation needs on a regional and national basis.

On February 27 Congress enacted the Soil Conservation and Domestic Allotment Act of 1936 almost exactly as Wallace had proposed. Roosevelt signed it into law two days later. It had taken only fifty-six days from the death of the New Deal farm program to its resurrection. Howard Tolley was named to administer the new program; Chester Davis resigned from government without comment. Wallace again addressed the nation by radio, explaining to farmers, almost in code, that a way to circumvent the Supreme Court decision had been found: "Its primary objective is wise land use. We hope, however, that as a result of the conservation of soil resources and the better use of land, supplies of the major farm commodities will be kept in approximate balance with demand, and we hope that the plan will have a favorable effect on farm prices and income. But any such benefits will be by-products."[42]

The Soil Conservation and Domestic Allotment Act of 1936 was a doubly sweet victory for Wallace. He had rescued the farm relief program and returned soil conservation services to the Agriculture Department all at once. The soil conservation program had been moved in 1933 to the Interior Department, where Wallace felt it suffered from neglect. "To see rich land eaten away by erosion, to stand by as continual cultivation on sloping fields wears away the best soil, is enough to make a good farmer sick at heart," Wallace had said in 1935. "My grandfather watching this process years ago used to speak of the voiceless land. In our time we have seen the process reach an acute stage, and we have at last begun to take to heart the meaning of soil exploitation."[43]

To fund the new farm program, Roosevelt proposed a combination of revenue-raising measures designed to pass constitutional muster. First he suggested an "unjust enrichment tax" intended to recoup the windfall given to processors by the Supreme Court. Second, he proposed a general excise tax on some agricultural processors intended only to raise general revenue. Finally, he proposed a new tax on the undistributed profits of corporations, which would generally replace the $500 million in revenue lost when the processing tax was struck down. After considerable debate and revision, Congress enacted all three proposals, which raised more than $750 million over the coming year.

Roosevelt clearly was impressed by the speed and suppleness with which Wallace had acted. Wallace had found a way to defuse a potentially explosive situation in the farm states, and he had done so in a way that almost certainly was constitutional. (The new law was eventually challenged and upheld by the High Court.) "Old Man Common Sense" the president called his agriculture secretary.

Wallace wasn't finished. Still appalled by the logic of the Court's opinion, he decided, without informing Roosevelt, to write a book attacking it. When he finally sent the finished manuscript to Roosevelt in May, it came back with only a brief notation in the presidential hand. "May you sell 100,000 copies."[44]

Whose Constitution: An Inquiry into the General Welfare was a 327-page review of constitutional history and analysis of the Court's role in American society. In a calm, straightforward tone, Wallace asked whether Americans had the right to act collectively, through their government, to improve themselves. "There always is, in economic matters, an appropriate time for change," he wrote. "Owners of concentrated wealth and economic power usually refuse to admit this. The Court has also frequently refused to admit it in time to effect the change smoothly and without grievous distress. When the Court in such situations refuses to budge, the average citizen rises up to inquire, 'Whose Constitution is it, anyway?' "[45]

Large portions of *Whose Constitution* were ghostwritten, but Wallace saved for himself the issue of soil conservation, because the whole farm program now rested upon a proper understanding of it. His chapter "Soil and the General Welfare" eloquently made the case for a national conservation ethic:

> Of all the circumstances which have combined to make this nation different from the nations of the Old World, rich soil and plenty of it, free or nearly so to all comers, stands first. Freeholders in a wide land of fabulous fertility, guarded by great oceans from foreign invasion, could erect separate strongholds of individual enterprise, free speech and free conscience. In no spread-eagle sense, but in plain truth, liberty and equality have been a natural outgrowth of our great gift of soil.
>
> But the dynamic quality which characterizes civilized man does not leave such a gift unmodified. If nature was prodigal with us, we have been ten times more prodigal with her. During the past 150 years, we white men have destroyed more soil, timber and wild-life than the Indians, left to themselves, would have destroyed in many thousands of years.[46]

Soil erosion and floods brought about by poor farming practices, and deforestation were national problems, he wrote. "Probably the most damaging indictment that can be made of the capitalistic system is the way in which its emphasis on unfettered individualism results in exploitation of natural resources in a manner to destroy the physical foundations of national longevity," he added. "Is there no way for the capitalistic system to develop a mechanism for taking thought and planning action in terms of the general welfare for the long run . . . ?"[47]

❊

Wallace had two assignments in the presidential campaign of 1936. One came from Roosevelt directly and went straight to the point. "Henry," the president said in February, "through July, August, September, October and up to the fifth of November, I want cotton to sell at twelve cents. I do not care how you do it. That is your problem. It can't go below twelve cents. Is that clear?" Wallace did as he was told.[48]

The second assignment was self-imposed and broad. Wallace wanted to help secure the reelection of Franklin Delano Roosevelt, thereby preserving the New Deal and its farm program.

A few of Wallace's associates thought he might have an additional motive. Rex Tugwell, Chester Davis, and Howard Tolley had all come independently to the conclusion that Wallace had his eye on the White House. More than one newspaper suggested Wallace would be Roosevelt's successor in 1940. "If he survives the political scalping parties . . . he will be only 52 years old by that time," said the *Washington Post.* "Also he is modest, moral and magnetic. Most of all he has a plan. As one scans the political horizon he is almost the only living man that does have a plan."[49] A couple of informal "Wallace for President" clubs sprang up in Texas and New York.

If Wallace himself had such ideas in 1936, however, he certainly kept them to himself. Nothing in his speeches, writings, or quoted remarks hinted, even obliquely, at presidential ambitions. To the contrary, he was notoriously averse to the sort of tasks associated with advancing oneself in politics. Louis Howe, the president's closest confidant, called from his deathbed asking Wallace to lead something called "Good Neighbor Clubs" in support of Roosevelt's re-election. The idea was to band together liberal intellectuals, feminists, churchmen, and other "nonpartisan" reformers in support of the Democratic ticket. Wallace agreed to Howe's request but after a brief, listless effort gave up and handed the job to Harold Ickes. "I just didn't see how to operate it," he said later. "It was just a coverup for political purposes to get folks who weren't Democrats. That method of approaching people never appealed to me. I thought it was a fraud and a fake."[50]

Wallace's general reluctance to involve the Agriculture Department in partisan politics became, if anything, even more pronounced. Alone among New Deal agency chiefs, he issued orders that patronage employees abide by the same restrictions as civil service employees, meaning they could play no active role in political campaigns. Members of local production control and soil conservation committees were required to resign if they wished to run for political office.

Indeed, far from showing any personal interest in Democratic politics, Wallace in early 1936 wasn't even a Democrat. Wallace didn't get around to changing parties until March 31, when he and Ilo showed up at the county courthouse in Des Moines to register as Democrats for the first time. He probably would have done it in 1934, Wallace casually told reporters, except on the last day of registration before the primary elections he was trapped in a snowstorm, and he had more or less forgotten about it afterwards.

But of Wallace's complete devotion to Roosevelt's cause there was no doubt. He was willing, even eager, to do battle. He pressed Roosevelt to make an issue of the Supreme Court decision and urged him to back new programs to protect farmers during years of bad harvest or natural disaster. Roosevelt, always intrigued by climate and its effect on society, embraced Wallace's farm proposals, but he was far more cautious about making direct use of the Court as an election issue. As a political issue, he had concluded, Court opinions were a tough sell. For the time being, he found it easier to make political use of the plutocrats—the "economic royalists"—in whose interest the Court was acting. He would leave Wallace and others to make a case against the Court itself.

The brief against the Court was summed up in the Democratic platform, written in the main by Wallace, Secretary of State Cordell Hull and Robert La Follette Jr., the progressive Republican senator from Wisconsin. "We know that drought, dust storms, floods, minimum wages, maximum hours, child labor and working conditions in industry, monopolistic and unfair business practices cannot be adequately handled by forty-eight separate state legislatures, forty-eight separate state administrations and forty-eight separate state courts," they wrote. "Transactions which inevitably overflow state boundaries call for both state and federal treatment."[51]

If that proved impossible, they added, the administration would seek a "clarifying amendment" to the Constitution, allowing the federal government to "regulate commerce, protect public health and safety, and safeguard economic security." That was as much as Roosevelt was willing to allow. He specifically rejected a provision, favored by Wallace, calling for a constitutional amendment to specify the exact meaning of the "general welfare" clause.[52]

In the platform's agricultural plank, Wallace offered a robust defense of the New Deal's farm program and its effectiveness in raising farm prices and income. The price of corn had doubled, wheat had increased thirty cents a bushel, cotton had gone up two and one-half cents a pound. Net farm income had nearly quadrupled, and farmers' purchasing power had been restored almost to prewar levels through the devaluation of the gold content of the dollar. All of this had been accomplished with democratic means, without resort to coercion or mercantilism.

At their national convention, which opened in Philadelphia on June 23, Democrats lost no time seizing the farm issue and tying it to the hidebound justices on the High Court. In a rousing keynote address, Senator Alben Barkley of Kentucky gleefully assailed the wealthy businessmen who brought down the AAA. "My friends, their bitter tears are not shed for the little pigs," said Barkley. "Their real grief comes from the fact of the slaughter of the fat hogs of Republican plunder which they had fed on the substance of the American people."[53]

In the galleries sat Henry Wallace, attending his first national political convention. Never a fan of high-flown oratory, and always repulsed by the coarser aspects of political life, he was not much impressed. In the oral history he later gave to Columbia University, Wallace summed up the five-day convention in four words: "It was very dull."[54] Of the convention's dramatic climax, when Roosevelt delivered his famous "rendezvous with destiny" speech before a roaring crowd of 100,000 people in Franklin Field, Wallace said nothing.

In fact, while most Democrats came away from the convention giddy with optimism, Wallace was more than a little worried. In the area of the country he truly understood, the Farm Belt, Wallace could imagine all sorts of difficulty ahead. Farmers could easily revert to their Republican roots. Small-town businessmen might turn away from the New Deal's unbalanced budgets and governmental activism. Isolationism and protectionism, bred deeply into the midwestern soul, could reemerge as potent weapons in the hands of the opposition.

Moreover, Republicans had picked a son of this region as their candidate. Governor Alfred M. Landon of Kansas, only a year older than Wallace and from a similar Bull Moose background, spoke the language of economy and efficiency that midwesterners understood. With his rimless eyeglasses and unpretentious personality—he liked to be called Alf and spoke in a voice as flat as Kansas—he seemed in some respects the perfect person to challenge an aristocratic easterner given to long cigarette holders and highfalutin speeches.

Landon's big problem was that few people in either party paid much attention to him. Roosevelt could hardly have cared less what Landon thought about anything; he was running against the "malefactors of great wealth" and Herbert Hoover's sorry legacy. Hoover didn't much care what Landon thought either. As far as Hoover was concerned, Landon was running a "holy crusade" to return the "Ark of the Covenant to the temple in Washington." Landon's running mate, the Chicago newspaper publisher Frank Knox, talked of little more than total destruction of the New Deal.

In concern, even alarm, Wallace wrote to Roosevelt after the conventions, urging him to focus on the politics of the farm states. "It is going to be necessary in that region to strip the hypocritical mask off the national Republican party and show up Landon as a weak and amiable tool," he warned Roosevelt. "We shall win, Mr. President, I am sure of it. But we shall have to work for it." To this and other similar admonitions, Roosevelt said nothing. He preferred to sail above the cacophonous political scene, cruising serenely off the northeast coast aboard the schooner *Sewanee*. Wallace gave up and went for a two-week stay at his mother's cabin in Colorado. It was his "first real vacation in seven years," he explained.[55]

Finally nature intervened. For the second time in three years, the Midwest was enduring a terrible drought. A great swath of the nation's midsection, stretching from North Dakota to Texas, suffered in searing heat beneath cloudless skies. In Kansas the temperature reached a hundred degrees for sixty consecutive days. Latest surveys put the national corn crop at barely 1.4 billion bushels, compared with almost 2.3 billion bushels in 1935. An estimated 350,000 farm families faced financial ruin.

In late August, Roosevelt set out to tour the region and hear suggestions for action. The tour was not political, or, as Wallace later put it, "theoretically it wasn't."[56] The train wound its way through Kansas, Nebraska, and the Dakotas and on to Salt Lake City before doubling back to Iowa. It was Wallace's first extensive look at Roosevelt on the campaign trail, and he was awed by the president's deft touch and the magical effect he had on crowds. "I want to thank you from my inmost being," Wallace wrote in a note to Roosevelt as the trip ended, "for the joy of seeing a great soul in action."[57]

The drought tour ended in Des Moines on a stroke of political genius. There Roosevelt convened a national conference on the drought and invited the participation of governors, senators, and other officials from eight drought-afflicted states. A huge crowd of 200,000 lined the streets to cheer the president. "He saved my farm," one man shouted as the president rolled past.[58]

Landon had little choice but to attend the conference, but his presence only served to heighten its political nature. The governor, looking natty in a light tan suit and sailor straw hat, conducted himself well but was no match for Roosevelt. The president, surrounded by Wallace and the top echelon of his administration, was in total command. Governors were invited to make presentations to Roosevelt in order of their state's admittance to the union, so Landon was reduced to speaking third, after the governors of Missouri and Iowa. Among other things, Landon suggested the need for more farm ponds in his state. The idea was acidly dismissed by Wallace, who observed that ponds were mainly useful for goldfish and young boys.

Thereafter Landon's hope of engaging Roosevelt in long-distance debate all but vanished. The elusive Roosevelt rolled through tremendous crowds in the major cities, offered soothing chats via radio, slashed the rich before massive rallies, but paid no attention to the Republican candidate. Instead, Landon was reduced to fending off attacks from the agriculture secretary, who was crisscrossing the Midwest warning farmers of the dangers in the Republican program. "It seems that the Republican leaders have learned nothing from the way in which they brought this nation to its knees in the disaster of 1931 and 1932," Wallace declared. "They propose to do the same thing over again."[59]

Where Roosevelt was funny and eloquent, Wallace was serious and straightforward. Unlike Roosevelt, who never mentioned his Republican opponent, Wallace attacked Landon by name and his program in detail. Wallace campaigned the way he played tennis, making up with energy and determination what he lacked in grace and skill. "Governor Landon's plan is a three-in-one proposition," said Wallace. "It is the Hoover Farm Board, the Hoover-Smoot-Hawley Tariff, and the Hoover Gold Standard, all bundled in the same old Hoover hack. And if farmers and businessmen ever climb into that vehicle again, it will drive them down the same old road to ruin."[60]

In mid-October Roosevelt made a final swing through the Midwest, giving a major speech at Omaha and, with apparent pride, showing off his popular secretary of agriculture. En route to Nebraska, Roosevelt stopped his train at Creston, Iowa, fifteen miles from Wallace's birthplace, to publicly praise him. "Down in Washington we have never had a Secretary of Agriculture, certainly not in our generation, who has understood farm problems so well as Henry Wallace, and who has tied them into the national economy as well as he has," said Roosevelt.[61]

A subtle but noticeable change took place as Wallace made his first steps onto the political stage. As Wallace became more political, his relationship to Roosevelt became easier and more personal. And as their personal relationship grew, Wallace's political stride became more confident. Richard Wilson, the *Des Moines Register* reporter sent to chronicle Wallace in Washington, could sense the change in Wallace's stature. "Of all the members of the New Deal cabinet, Wallace—originally a nonpartisan selection—now bears the most political responsibility and has been shoved forward as the No. 2 in the campaign," Wilson wrote.[62]

In November, Roosevelt carried the Farm Belt and almost everything else. He won every state but Maine and Vermont, scoring the biggest electoral college victory since James Monroe. In the popular vote Roosevelt buried Landon, 27,476,673 to 16,679,583. It was the largest plurality ever. "I knew I should have gone to Maine and Vermont," Roosevelt joked to reporters.[63]

Wallace soberly thought the president had made a more serious error. He believed that the president should have made the Supreme Court an issue and begun to build a mandate for reform. In this Wallace was prescient indeed.

CHAPTER NINE

"UP IN SMOKE"

A fortnight after the 1936 election, a small group of men gathered in a dusty town near the Arkansas-Texas border and embarked upon an incredible odyssey along back roads of the Mississippi Delta, across the Great Smoky Mountains and into the hollows of Appalachia. "What a trip!" exclaimed one of the men. "Two thousand miles of Tobacco Road."[1]

As they made their way across the region—sleeping in small country hotels, eating at humble roadhouses—they often stopped at tumbledown shacks where families slept on the floor and lived on corn bread and molasses, or by cotton fields where ragged children worked alongside men and women with haggard faces and diseased bodies.

One among them would climb out of the car to walk the fields and talk to local folk. How were the crops? he would ask. Who had suffered from malaria or pellagra or tuberculosis? What were the children learning in school? Did they have milk to drink, or oranges and green vegetables to eat? He listened in quiet sadness as they answered his questions with "perfect dignity." Then, without even mentioning his name, the lanky, long-faced stranger returned to the car and slumped into his seat.

"It's incredible," Henry Wallace mumbled over and over, "incredible."

"Wallace would slip off and walk out into the country alone, stopping people, talking with them, visiting them in their homes," recalled Felix Belair, a *New York Times* reporter who accompanied Wallace on the journey. "Not many people recognized him. And when I would tell some of them who they'd been talking to, not many believed it. They didn't figure it possible that a Cabinet member would be walking in on them, awaiting, just to see how they were getting along. . . . Along the road in the car he was watching everything, asking questions [or] just brooding, with those bushy eyebrows of his drawn down as if he was seeing more than he could bear."[2]

The experience appalled and unsettled Wallace. "I have never seen among the peasantry of Europe poverty so abject as that which exists in this favorable cotton year in the great cotton states," Wallace subsequently wrote in a *New York Times Magazine* article. "[The] city people of the United States should be thoroughly ashamed. . . ."[3]

He returned from the South with a willingness, heretofore resisted, to engage his department in the politics of rural poverty. Subsistence farmers scratching out a living on worn-out land, landless tenants, sharecroppers, and day laborers made up half of the nation's agricultural work force, yet they received only 12 percent of the national farm income. They obtained virtually no help from farm subsidies aimed at commercial farmers and landlords.

Within six months the Special Committee on Farm Tenancy, chaired by Wallace, had made recommendations to Congress and the Bankhead-Jones Farm Tenancy Act of 1937 had become law. The act allowed the government to make long-term loans to tenant farmers for the purchase of land and equipment. The Resettlement Administration was renamed the Farm Security Administration and established within the Department of Agriculture, where it would remain an aggressive and often controversial agency dedicated to combatting rural poverty.

Wallace's response to the trip was exactly what Rexford Tugwell had hoped it would be. Iconoclastic, articulate, and supremely self-confident, "Rex the Red" had become a lightning rod for conservative criticism of the New Deal. The Resettlement Administration, to which Tugwell devoted most of his energies after May 1935, had operated without congressional authorization throughout its brief history and had earned a reputation for scattershot policies and sloppy administration. The Resettlement Administration had mushroomed from twelve employees to more than sixteen thousand—making it the eighth-largest agency in the federal government—and had become, in Tugwell's words, a dumping ground for "everybody else's headaches."

Tugwell's dream of resettling subsistence farmers eeking out a living on marginal land was buried. Originally he had hoped to buy 500,000 subsistence farms, retire the land, and reestablish the occupants elsewhere; in the end the agency resettled only 4,441 families. Slowly Tugwell was drawn to do precisely what he did not want: provide meager loans and grants enabling subsistence farmers to buy a mule or a wood stove and continue living lives of grinding poverty.*

By late 1936 the besieged Tugwell had become convinced that the only way to save his agency was to transfer its programs to the Agriculture Department and then leave government. Wallace was initially noncommittal, but his eyewitness tour of "the Cotton South"—proposed by Tugwell and his chief assistant, Dr. Will Alexander—persuaded the secretary to take the agency under his wing. Alexander, a genial minister who devoted his adult life to racial harmony, was named to head the agency, renamed the Farm Security Administration, and Tugwell resigned from government at the end of 1936.

Wallace spoke by radio to explain why his department would henceforth involve itself with the rural poor. "I realize, of course, that there are many well-to-do people, both on the farms and in town, who raise the question as to why the federal government should do anything for these people," said Wallace. "My answer to this is that in proportion to the population, there are just as many farm people unemployed and just as many farm people in the relief category . . . as in the towns and cities. . . . Farmers comprising over 23 percent of the population have had to carry more than their share of the relief load."[4]

As Wallace moved unnoticed along southern back roads, Franklin Roosevelt was basking in cheers at the Inter-American Conference for the Maintenance of Peace in Argentina. In Buenos Aires two million people packed the streets and showered the president with flowers and shouts of "Viva la democracia! Viva Roosevelt!" Already heady from his huge reelection victory, Roosevelt returned from Latin America with a notion that his popularity had reached deific proportions.

Not until February 5, 1937—six days after celebrating his fifty-fifth birthday—did Roosevelt finally reveal what he had been contemplating during his travels. At a hastily assembled meeting of his cabinet, the vice president, and the Democratic congressional leadership, Roosevelt announced he would send to Congress, within the hour, a plan to reform the American judiciary. The core of the proposal would allow the president to appoint a new Supreme Court justice for each sitting justice who reached the age of seventy and did not retire within six months. Given the Court's existing makeup, the proposed law would entitle Roosevelt to name six additional justices immediately.

*Tugwell's agency did have one spectacular and totally unexpected success. Its innovative information division documented the trials of the rural poor with lucid writing and searing photographic images. Its writers and artists included Walker Evans, Dorothea Lange, Ben Shahn, Margaret Bourke-White, Gordon Parks, Russell Lee, Marion Post Wolcott, and Carl Mydans.

Roosevelt asked for no comments, took no questions, and wheeled out of the room. For the briefest moment, there was stunned silence. Then came one of the biggest explosions in the history of American politics.

Roosevelt adored the Court plan. He liked the simplicity of it. The plan could be enacted legislatively, without a constitutional amendment process, in a Congress overwhelmingly controlled by Democrats. He liked its cleverness. The plan he proposed was couched in terms of age and workload and avoided contentious debate over ideology and constitutional theory.

What Roosevelt could not, or would not, see was the extent to which the Court plan magnified lingering doubts about his slippery political style. Clearly this was no grand proposal to improve judicial efficiency but simply, as Herbert Hoover said within an hour of its introduction, a "court-packing scheme." Hatton Sumners, the scholarly chairman of the House Judiciary Committee, stomped out of the White House, with Wallace at his side, in a state of rage. "He was just everlastingly *furious*," Wallace recalled (supplying the emphasis himself). "I knew there was trouble ahead." Even Wallace had misgivings. "I thought it was a little too slick, if anything."*5

Roosevelt had counted heavily on overwhelming public support for his plan. He had misjudged the regard, almost reverence, many Americans held for the Supreme Court. When the Gallup poll showed the country to be deeply ambivalent about the Court plan, Roosevelt simply didn't believe it. Over and over he told associates, "The people are with me."6 Wallace, who had known George Gallup since the pollster was a journalism professor at Drake University in Des Moines and thought his methods were sound, believed Roosevelt was fooling himself.

Wallace was right. By the time hearings on the Court reform plan began in March, an effective bloc of opposition had formed in the Senate and no popular groundswell of support was apparent. Roosevelt was forced to abandon the transparent fiction that his bill was anything other than a plan to get his way in the Supreme Court and take his case to the public. "If we would keep faith with those who had faith in us," he thundered at a dinner of party faithful, "if we would make American democracy succeed, I say we must act— NOW!"7 Still, public sentiment was unmoved.

Wallace was not much more than an interested bystander to the fierce debate. He backed the Court plan "out of loyalty," but his support was halfhearted. The president's plan, Wallace said in a speech to the Farm Bureau

*Wallace had tried at least five times over the preceding year to win Roosevelt's support for a constitutional amendment. He argued for it in *Whose Constitution*, alluded to it in the Democratic platform, and twice spoke directly to Roosevelt about it during train rides in the fall campaign. Finally, during a cabinet meeting in early 1937 when Roosevelt reviewed his forthcoming State of the Union message to Congress, both Wallace and Ickes urged him to advocate a constitutional amendment.

in Richmond, Virginia, "simply proposed to add new blood to the Supreme Court; enough younger men who have been out in the hurly burly of a changing world . . . so that the attitude of the people as expressed in the election may be converted into action. That is all." He advanced the novel idea that the Court itself had an "unconstitutional attitude" because it had gone beyond matters of law into "the field of policy."[8]

He was more eloquent in constructing a theoretical case for governmental response to modern economic problems. In three lengthy, closely reasoned lectures called "Technology, Corporations and the General Welfare," delivered at the University of North Carolina in April, Wallace argued that the country could no longer afford the luxury of laissez-faire capitalism and an inactive government. "The impact of modern technology through the corporate form of organization, and the control by corporations over price and production, are such as to make the problem of the one-third of the population at the bottom of the heap practically hopeless unless the government steps in definitely and powerfully on behalf of the general welfare," he argued.[9]

Roosevelt and his political soldiers may have found the agriculture secretary's theorizing interesting, even profound, but they had precious little time for theory. They were fighting a war, and it was going badly. Senate opposition, led by the crusty Democratic senator Burton Wheeler of Montana with stealthy support from Vice President John Nance Garner, was proving sturdy and crafty. Chief Justice Charles Evans Hughes weighed in with a "bombshell" letter stating that the Court was suffering no overload at all. Moreover, the Court began handing the administration a series of legal victories, including a decision upholding the constitutionality of the Wagner Labor Relations Act. And in mid-May, the seventy-seven-year-old conservative justice Willis Van Devanter announced his plans to retire, giving Roosevelt an opportunity to appoint a liberal replacement.

Democratic congressional leaders were ready to sue for peace. Roosevelt could maintain he lost the battle but won the war, they observed, since the Supreme Court was behaving better. He could replace Van Devanter and be done with it. Or he could cut a deal. "If the president wants to compromise, I can get him a couple of extra judges tomorrow," Senate Majority Leader Joe Robinson declared.[10]

There were, however, complications. Roosevelt knew the Court could revert to its old ways as soon as the fight was over. And he knew also that two years earlier he had promised to appoint Joe Robinson to the next vacancy on the Court. The sixty-five-year-old majority leader had been loyal in pushing New Deal legislation through the Senate, but his own instincts were conservative. He had been Al Smith's running mate on the 1928 Democratic ticket, and he shared Smith's views on property rights. On racial issues Robinson stood with the Jim Crow South.

The day Van Devanter announced his retirement, as senators gathered around Robinson's desk calling him Mr. Justice, Roosevelt made another misjudgment. Instead of promptly naming Robinson to the Court and linking the appointment to the best deal he could get out of the Senate, Roosevelt only sent word that he wanted his original plan, all six new justices, period. Two weeks passed as Robinson fumed and a nasty battle broke out in the Senate over who would replace him as majority leader. Again Roosevelt erred. The president weighed in tacitly on behalf of Senator Alben Barkley, an obedient supporter of the Court plan, thus infuriating supporters of his amiable rival, conservative Mississippi senator Pat Harrison.

Vice President Garner, whose well-stocked liquor cabinet—the "bureau of education," he called it—had done so much to keep senators in line in the past, abandoned the fight altogether. With no attempt to disguise his contempt for Roosevelt or the Court-packing scheme, Garner boarded a train and headed home to Uvalde, Texas. Roosevelt pleaded for his return, but "Cactus Jack" would not budge.

As the situation in Congress degenerated, events at large also conspired against Roosevelt. Labor unions, invigorated by the Wagner Labor Relations Act, began massive organizing campaigns in the auto and steel industries. Led by John L. Lewis, the bombastic Iowa-born coal miner who had formed the aggressive Committee for Industrial Organization (CIO), workers shut down plants with an illegal but effective new weapon—the sit-down strike—and industrialists responded with injunctions and guns. The spiraling violence reached a horrible climax on Memorial Day when strikers bearing sticks and stones confronted armed policemen at the Republic Steel plant in South Chicago. In a few terrifying minutes, ten strikers were killed and scores of others were wounded or badly beaten.

Roosevelt watched the unfolding events with unease and alarm. He was appalled by the "excesses" of both sides, but he was in poor position to confront the situation. Industrialists despised him and everything he did. The CIO, which was the largest single contributor to Roosevelt's 1936 campaign, boisterously embraced the Court plan but made it clear it expected the president's support in return.

Roosevelt eventually settled on a response, which he first tried out privately in a conversation with Wallace and Cordell Hull. "A plague on both your houses," he said, quoting Shakespeare's *Romeo and Juliet.* Having received a good reaction from his cabinet officers, Roosevelt went public with the "plague" remark in a newspaper interview. It sent John L. Lewis, a man of Elizabethan eloquence, into a thunderous rage. "It ill behooves one who has supped at labor's table and who has been sheltered in labor's house to curse with equal fervor and fine impartiality both labor and its adversaries when they become locked in deadly embrace."[11]

At long last realizing that the original Court expansion plan was doomed, Roosevelt in early June called Robinson to his office, offered him the Supreme Court appointment, and asked him to salvage what he could from the Senate. The best Robinson could offer was a compromise that would give Roosevelt one additional appointment. Even that was not certain, but the majority leader promised to give it his all.

The art of politics now devolved to its rawest level: personality, maneuver, ingratiation, connivance. Roosevelt summoned members of his cabinet and staff to a retreat on Jefferson Island, in the Chesapeake Bay, owned by Bernard Baruch, and began three days of political stroking for members of Congress. "It was fixed up for duck hunting and poker playing and good sound drinking," Wallace recalled, "a glorious place of escape for those who were so-minded." Wallace himself was not of such a mind, but he was obliged to attend. Quietly disgusted, he contented himself playing baseball and discussing anthropology with an obscure New York congressman named William Sirovich.[12]

In early July, several days after the Jefferson Island affair, what was left of the Supreme Court expansion plan finally reached the Senate floor. Joe Robinson, his red face covered in sweat and his hands trembling in anger, struggled mightily to uphold his bargain with the president. The opposition responded with long, eloquent speeches that carried in them the hint of filibuster.

After several days of debate Robinson could hold out no longer. With stabbing pains in his chest, Robinson abruptly left the floor and went to his small apartment near the Capitol. His body, sprawled on the floor by his bed, was found there early on Wednesday, July 14. He had been reading the *Congressional Record* when he died.

Much of Congress boarded trains for Little Rock to attend Robinson's funeral. Curiously, Roosevelt did not. The administration was represented instead by Vice President Garner, at last coaxed out of his home in Uvalde. On the train back to Washington, Garner made it his business to assess the mood of the shattered Democratic Party, and reported the results to Roosevelt with brutal succinctness. "You're licked, Cap'n. You haven't got the votes."[13]

The end came swiftly. On July 22, four days after Robinson was lowered to his grave, the Senate voted 70 to 20 to kill the Court-packing bill. Roosevelt's humiliation came almost entirely at the hands of his own party; the entire Senate had only sixteen Republicans. Vacationing at his mother's cabin in Colorado, Wallace wired Roosevelt, "The defeat is not yours but is really that of the apparently triumphant ones. They have misread the signs of the future and have overlooked the claims of the nation. . . . History will be on your side."14

Roosevelt emerged from the episode with blood in his eye. His first opportunity for revenge came in mid-August when he announced the appointment of Alabama's Senator Hugo L. Black to fill the Supreme Court vacancy. Black was everything Roosevelt wanted at that moment in a justice. He was only fifty-one years old and looked even younger; he was a brass-bound liberal and had supported Roosevelt in the Court fight; he would certainly be confirmed by the Senate, which traditionally approved its own members by unanimous acclamation. And conservatives despised him. That suited Roosevelt fine.

The bitterness expressed by the appointment of Black to the Supreme Court would recur again and again as Roosevelt sought to punish those who had thwarted him. When the dust had settled, it became apparent how much had happened: Roosevelt had suffered his most humiliating defeat; the Democratic Party was engulfed by civil war; the "grand coalition" of labor, farmers, blacks, reformers, the rural South, and the urban North, engineered by Roosevelt during two presidential elections, lay badly fractured; the "Nine Old Men" on the Supreme Court had triumphed; and, in the words of Henry Wallace, the "whole New Deal really went up in smoke."15

"It was . . . the last time the New Deal really breathed defiance," Wallace said in his oral memoirs. "From then on, while many of us didn't realize it, it was a downhill slide—very much of a downhill slide."16

Congress had produced no major legislation during the long Court fight—the farm tenancy law was the best it could manage—nor would it pass anything important in the dreary remaining months of 1937. The business community, having tasted blood, seemed more determined than ever to spite Roosevelt. Labor unions became wary and defensive. And the need for action became more acute by the day.

Beginning in August with a break in the stock market, the economy showed signs of slipping backward. Industrial activity declined; steel production fell from 80 percent of capacity to 19 percent in only three months. Consumer spending declined sharply. Once again lines began appearing at soup kitchens in the major cities.

Farm prices dropped rapidly, reflecting the big surpluses that resulted from good weather that year. The 1936 farm legislation was simply inadequate to control production, and Wallace knew it would have to be rewritten. But neither Congress nor the president was of a mind to act. In mid-October a wave of selling sent the stock market tumbling, bringing back memories of 1929.

Roosevelt responded in a manner worthy of Herbert Hoover. "Everything will work out all right if we just sit tight and keep quiet," he told the cabinet.[17] Even though the federal budget showed a modest surplus, Roosevelt ordered the chief relief agencies to reduce spending and hinted that he wanted cuts at the Agriculture Department. Wallace considered the president's actions disastrous.

By late autumn the administration had split into three warring factions. On one side were Interior Secretary Harold Ickes, the presidential adviser Thomas Corcoran, the antitrust chief Robert Jackson, and others who counseled a renewed attack on wealthy industrialists and the idle rich. At the other extreme was Treasury Secretary Henry Morgenthau, who advised government to stand aside—"strip off the bandages, throw away the crutches"—and allow business to restore the country to economic vigor.[18]

Somewhere in the middle were Henry Wallace, Federal Reserve Chairman Marriner Eccles, WPA Administrator Harry Hopkins, and a subset of talented government economists who advised them. Although they differed somewhat in approach, they argued vehemently that a balanced budget was the wrong weapon for battling a recession. They maintained government should act as a "compensatory agent," spending heavily in times of deflation and taxing up surpluses during boom times.[19]

Wallace peppered the president with warnings and suggestions. "This recession need not go any further if we use the powers we have to prevent the repetition of the 1929–1932 downward economic spiral," he wrote to Roosevelt in November 1937. The obligation to act in an economic emergency had "prior claim" over the need to balance the budget. Federal spending under no circumstances should be less than seven billion dollars "unless private initiative shows a capacity for handling city relief, agricultural relief, conservation of natural resources, etc. to which private initiative has not thus far shown itself adapted," he wrote.[20]

He produced an econometric study on the ratio between government spending and national income, an early demonstration of what is now called the multiplier effect. The study "found that for each dollar which the government put in, the national income could be raised about four dollars." He proposed a cabinet-level committee to "bring forward proposals whereby a minimum of government money will put a maximum of private money to work" without inflation or unemployment. He pushed for what he called "incentive taxation," which would help release the "creative energy" of business.[21]

Over and over, Wallace stressed the importance of cooperation between business and government, between capital and labor. He even wrote a speech for Roosevelt in which he would have had the president say, "The all important thing at the present juncture is to increase the activity of city labor and city capital. These two great powers have at times acted as if they were trying to divorce each other. It cannot be done." The speech was never delivered.[22]

Wallace even tried in a cerebral way to make his case in political terms. Armed with a study by Agriculture Department statistician Louis Bean that analyzed every congressional election since 1854, Wallace told the president that "when business declines, the party which has hitherto been dominant loses in power and that the degree of loss in power is roughly proportionate to the loss in business." Thus, he said, "approaching the problem from a purely statistical point of view," the Democratic membership of the House would decline from 77 percent to 55 percent if nothing was done about the economy.[23]

Yet Roosevelt resisted action. Not until April 1938, when four million additional people had joined unemployment rolls and business activity staggered back to 1932 levels, was Roosevelt persuaded to authorize renewed spending for public works and relief programs, coupled with a new inquiry into monopolies and the concentration of wealth.

The general paralysis in Washington also greatly hampered Wallace's ability to refashion the basic farm program. Faced with an ill-tempered Congress, a deteriorating economy, and a fractured farm lobby—the Farm Bureau in particular had turned away from the New Deal—Wallace was able in 1937 only to obtain a congressional resolution saying the farm bill would have a high priority in 1938.

Holding Congress to its promise was not easy, but Wallace's nimble footwork and the onset of another growing season were finally enough to overcome inertia and confusion. In February 1938 Congress produced a complex, unwieldy bill full of compromise and gimmickry. Of the three major farm bills adopted during his tenure as agriculture secretary, it was the least shaped by Wallace, but it was a farm bill nonetheless, and he embraced it. "It tries in practical ways to bring balanced abundance to the people," he said.[24]

Whatever its shortcomings, the act contained one of Wallace's greatest successes. His long-held dream of an "ever-normal granary" finally was realized in law. He had written and spoken of it for most of his adult lifetime. He had documented its origins in Confucius, and found scriptual support for it in the biblical story of Joseph. He had preached its benefits to a generation of *Wallaces' Farmer* readers and had talked of it again and again during the two great droughts of the 1930s. Now at last Joseph's plan, Wallace's dream, was federal law.

Crops would be stored up in good years, used up in lean years. "We need a practical method to maintain balance, because that is the only way to have and to keep real abundance," he told his radio audience in 1938. "That way is to use our surpluses to balance our shortages. This is the purpose of the Ever-Normal Granary plan of the new act."[25]

The ever-normal granary, Wallace would later say, was the "action of which I was most proud as secretary of agriculture."[26]

And when war came, in the not distant future, the nation had good reason to be grateful. Jittery housewives could look at grocery store shelves and see adequate food at reasonable prices. The nation could face the uncertain situation abroad with assurance that its most basic need—food—was available in abundance. The ever-normal granary, said one observer, provided America with more national security than a flotilla of battleships.

***

"Henry Wallace gave more real strength to Franklin's administration at this time than it got from any other source," Rex Tugwell later wrote. "The Department of Agriculture was an idea factory; more imagination used in the public interest was evident there than anywhere else in Washington. . . . Moreover, as Franklin noted the signs of eroding loyalty everywhere around, it grew on him that Henry Wallace could be counted on to the limit. He might be maneuvering for the presidency—he undoubtedly was—but he was doing it within the accepted rules."[27]

Perhaps Wallace was eyeing the presidency, but his style was hardly orthodox. He never told anyone he wanted to run. He flatly refused to use the Agriculture Department's many patronage opportunities to advance his personal ambitions. Political well-wishers who offered their help were invariably advised to take it up with Paul Appleby, his top aide, but Appleby himself was operating without guidance of any kind from his boss. When Appleby raised the issue of a presidential campaign and suggested Wallace find an experienced politician to run it, the secretary merely replied, "Well, I suppose I'm one of those to whom it might happen."[28] No campaign manager was ever appointed.

Even his few overtly political appearances created doubts about his intentions. When Wallace delivered an address to some eleven hundred Iowa Democrats at their annual Jackson Day dinner in early 1938, he used it as an occasion to appeal for cooperation with business and Republicans. "Roosevelt Democracy needs a broader base if it is to last over the years," Wallace warned. "It must set about definitely winning the support of the small town business men of the north whose prosperity is so completely identified with farm prosperity. It must learn to cooperate with the managers of capital on a basis which will cause them to put labor to work productively year after year."[29]

"Iowa Politics Seethe after Wallace Talk," said a headline in the *Des Moines Register*. "Democrats welcome Wallace as a tremendous advantage as vote getter," wrote the paper's political reporter, C. C. Clifton, ". . . but he still may have to win his spurs as an organization, dyed-in-the-wool, name-blown-in-the-bottle Democrat."[30] He was a paradox—a nonpolitician in politics, a Republican-born agrarian in the party of labor—and a great many ordinary Democrats found him difficult to fathom.

Yet even without his active participation, there were signs of political activity on his behalf. Here and there, Wallace for President clubs popped up. Senator Clyde Herring, sometimes mentioned as a dark horse presidential possibility himself, publicly promised to lead a unified Iowa delegation for Wallace at the 1940 Democratic convention. Paul Appleby and Jim LeCron, his closest aides, began making "inspection trips" around the country to test the waters. One newspaper report said Appleby believed that Wallace could count on "as many as 200 delegates out of the 1,162 when the Democratic convention opens."[31]

"The foundation for this early preconvention campaign seems to be based largely upon mental telepathy," wrote Richard Wilson, the *Des Moines Register* Washington bureau chief, "for it is doubtful if the secretary of agriculture has specific knowledge of the representations that are being made on his behalf. And yet it cannot be doubted that he approves of the activity."[32]

The question before all others was the future of the man in the White House. Roosevelt told Jim Farley and others that the second term would be his last. But he was never one to limit his room for maneuver. He would not repeat Theodore Roosevelt's mistake of condemning himself to four years as a lame duck. When reporters raised the question of his plans in 1940, Roosevelt teased and parried but never quite answered the question.

For that matter it was not at all clear that Roosevelt would be able to win election to a third term. The Court fight and the recession had seriously weakened his position. The Democratic Party was in disarray. The New Deal was under challenge on every front. Polls showed two-thirds of the electorate opposed to a third term, their affection for the president notwithstanding. Wallace privately expected the president to retire at the end of his term. "I hadn't any idea at that time that Roosevelt would run again in 1940," he later said.[33]

Complicating the issue was the matter of who would run if Roosevelt did not. The leading possibilities according to the Gallup poll—John Nance Garner, James Farley, Cordell Hull—were unacceptable in Roosevelt's view. Garner was parochial and conservative. Farley was a Roman Catholic who had never been elected to anything. Hull was a man of fussy caution and in uncertain health.

Other prospects, too, carried liabilities in Roosevelt's seasoned eyes. Harold Ickes was "too didactic, too likely to blow up," he said. Governor George Earle of Pennsylvania, a confirmed liberal, was embroiled in a home state scandal. Former Governor Paul V. McNutt of Indiana, the current high

Henry A. Wallace's birthplace in Adair County, Iowa. *Courtesy of Jean Wallace Douglas.*

"Young Henry," shy and serious, as a boy growing up in Des Moines. *Courtesy of National Agricultural Library.*

Henry A. Wallace's home in Des Moines, around the corner from his father's mansion. *Courtesy of AP/Wide World Photos.*

Harry Wallace's family. *Back row, left to right:* Henry A., John, and Jim; *middle row:* May and Harry Wallace; *front row:* Ruth, Annabelle, and Mary. *Courtesy of Wallace House Foundation.*

Ilo Browne at the time
of her marriage to
Henry Wallace in 1914.
*Courtesy of Jean
Wallace Douglas.*

Young Henry Wallace
shows his grandfather
some hybrid corn in
1913. *Courtesy of
Wallace House
Foundation.*

Four generations of Henry Wallaces. *Clockwise from left:* Henry Agard Wallace; his father, Henry Cantwell Wallace; his grandfather Henry Wallace; and his son Henry Browne Wallace. *Courtesy of Jean Wallace Douglas.*

The Wallace family at home in the Wardman Park
apartments during his first year as secretary of
agriculture. *From left to right:* Robert, Ilo, Henry B.,
Henry A., and Jean. *Courtesy of Jean Wallace Douglas.*

"Never mind the political souveniers [*sic*], get a doctor!" Pulitzer Prize–winning cartoonist Ding Darling's comment on the Supreme Court decision to strike down the New Deal farm program. *Courtesy of the J. N. "Ding" Darling Foundation.*

Secretary of Agriculture Henry A. Wallace examines the official
portrait of his late father, Secretary of Agriculture Henry C. Wallace.
One of Wallace's first acts as secretary was to have his father's portrait
moved into his office. *Courtesy of Jean Wallace Douglas.*

The massive Department of Agriculture building on the Mall in Washington, D.C., pictured in 1938 at the height of Wallace's tenure. *Courtesy of National Agricultural Library.*

Henry A. Wallace and Rexford Guy Tugwell, the dapper professor who served as undersecretary of agriculture in the New Deal's early years. *Courtesy of National Agricultural Library.*

The War Production Board holds its first meeting in January 1942. Wallace, chairman of the Board of Economic Warfare, is seated third from the right. Donald M. Nelson, new chairman of the WPB and a key Wallace ally, is seated next to him in the center. Third from the left is Wallace's arch-rival, Secretary of Commerce Jesse Jones. *Courtesy of CORBIS/Bettmann.*

Notes on chicken
breeding in Wallace's
distinctive left-handed
scrawl. *Courtesy of
Wallace House
Foundation.*

Vice President Wallace in his "victory garden,"
a 50 x 100 foot plot on the grounds of the
Swiss delegation in Washington.
Courtesy of CORBIS/Bettmann.

Vice presidential candidate Wallace shows Attorney General (later Supreme Court Justice) Robert Jackson the art of boomerang throwing. *Courtesy of AP/Wide World Photos.*

Wallace was an avid, ambidextrous tennis player, but he was never very graceful. *Courtesy of Jean Wallace Douglas.*

Nicholas Roerich, mysterious painter and explorer who was at the center of the "guru letters" scandal. *Courtesy of Library of Congress* / New York World Telegram & Sun *Collection.*

President Franklin Roosevelt and his running mate in 1940. *Courtesy of Jean Wallace Douglas.*

Wallace takes the vice presidential oath of office
from John Nance Garner. President Franklin
Roosevelt and his son James watch from behind.
Courtesy of AP/Wide World Photos.

The vice president's effort to
interest senators in boxing ended
when he accidentally knocked out
Senator Allen Ellender of
Louisiana, *left*, in the Senate gym.
Courtesy of CORBIS/Bettmann.

commissioner to the Philippines, was a cypher on public policy issues. Henry Wallace was brilliant and solidly liberal, Roosevelt said privately, but he was "too aloof" and could never command support from the big-city bosses and other professionals. Wallace might be able to win a general election, Roosevelt said, but he could never capture the nomination.[34]

Through a process of elimination—too old, too conservative, too corrupt, too aloof—Roosevelt arrived in April at an astounding choice: WPA administrator, Harry L. Hopkins. He was young, only forty-seven, an energetic administrator, an ardent liberal, and a tough political infighter. Roosevelt was naturally attracted to Hopkins's cheerful blend of cynicism and idealism.

But Hopkins also had a staggering number of drawbacks. He had never run for office or shown any interest in doing so. He had no real geographical base of support, having grown up in Iowa and spent his adult life as a welfare administrator in New York. His first marriage ended in divorce. He had a taste for the fast life, in nightclubs and at racetracks, and a fondness for rather unsavory characters who could provide him the luxuries he enjoyed. And he had recently been operated upon for stomach cancer.

Roosevelt was unfazed. He had settled on Harry Hopkins. The first step toward the presidency would be to install Hopkins as secretary of commerce, from which vantage point he could mend fences with the business community and build an effective organization. Roosevelt told Hopkins he was the man.

Or perhaps he wasn't. Soon after telling Hopkins of his decision, Roosevelt met with Harold Ickes and discussed the long list of presidential possibilities. But at no point did he mention Harry Hopkins, and so implausible was the idea that it didn't even occur to Ickes. What did occur to Ickes, once all the names had been crossed off the list, was that only one name remained: Franklin Delano Roosevelt.

It was a tricky playing field onto which Wallace and his companions gingerly stepped in early 1938. One was never quite certain of the rules, or where the opposing players stood, or even who they were. All Wallace knew was where he stood. All else might change about him, but Wallace's sense of his own mission remained constant. Strange as it might seem, that was Wallace's most valuable political asset.

By the time cherry trees blossomed around the Tidal Basin that spring, some New Dealers were close to panic. The economy was mired in recession, Congress was in rebellion, events abroad were increasingly ominous. Roosevelt's hope of doing something for the "one-third of a nation" in poverty was still no more than a hope.

Key legislation, such as the wage-and-hour bill, was bottled up in congressional committees controlled by men who had lost all fear of Roosevelt. The long-awaited reorganization bill, modernizing the executive branch and creating a new department of welfare, was killed outright. On foreign affairs, too, the president seemed powerless. Nazi Germany overtook Austria on March 11, and there was little Roosevelt could do but watch in alarm.

At that juncture a small group of dedicated New Dealers set out to turn things around. Meeting in Harry Hopkins's home in Georgetown, they plotted a way out of the situation. At the meeting were Harold Ickes, Robert Jackson, the president's son James, the White House aides Tom Corcoran and Ben Cohen, and a handful of others. Not in attendance, because he hadn't been asked and wouldn't have gone anyway, was Henry A. Wallace.

At length the group seized upon a strategy that would make a bad situation much worse. Their idea was to purge from the Democratic Party those politicians who posed obstacles to Roosevelt and the New Deal. They nicknamed themselves the "execution committee" and began looking for upcoming primary elections where Roosevelt's personal popularity could be used to help liberal candidates. Roosevelt, still smarting from his defeat in the Supreme Court fight, loved the plan.[35]

And there were early indications it might work. In Alabama, the progressive senator Lister Hill survived a primary challenge from the reactionary Tom Heflin after Roosevelt campaigned with him. More dramatically, the liberal Democratic senator Claude Pepper won a hard-fought primary in Florida after receiving Roosevelt's blessing and "at least $10,000" in campaign funds delivered by Tom Corcoran.[36] In exchange for the help, Pepper agreed to make the wage-and-hour bill an important element in his campaign, and his victory brought almost instantaneous action on the legislation in Congress. Pepper's triumph was followed by another in Oregon, where the New Dealer Henry Hess defeated Governor Charles H. Martin in a primary. The executioners, now convinced of their power, looked for their next victim.

They found him in the unlikely person of Guy Gillette, a silver-haired, middle-of-the-road senator from Iowa. Gillette had on occasion opposed New Deal legislation, including the Court-packing plan and the wage-and-hour bill, but he was hardly a conservative ideologue. "He was always his own person, a completely independent man," Wallace later said. "We used to say that Guy would wrestle with his conscience and pray and always come out with the wrong answer. He was a completely sincere man."[37]

To oppose Gillette the executioners settled on a wavy-haired thirty-five-year-old congressman named Otha Wearin. He, like Gillette, had supported the New Deal by and large, though with occasional departures. But with encouragement from the executioners, Wearin quickly sought to portray the race as a test of loyalty to the New Deal and broadly implied that he was hand-picked by Roosevelt. Corcoran made a well-publicized secret visit to Iowa to express his support for Wearin. James Roosevelt, the president's son and secretary, accompanied Wearin to a Young Democrats rally in West Virginia. The administration withdrew its support for a new bridge over the Mississippi River at Dubuque, one of Gillette's pet projects.

What made the whole effort truly bizarre in the minds of many Iowa politicians was that Gillette was unbeatable. Governor Nelson Kraschel, a Democrat, the one liberal who might have made a serious challenge, had backed away from the race after discussing it with Roosevelt. Kraschel endorsed Gillette. So did most of the state's other top Democrats and newspapers. "Senator Gillette's opponents do not stand a ghost of a chance of defeating him in the primary," declared the state party chairman, K. E. Birmingham.

The campaign to beat Gillette did make sense, however, if its true goal was to derail Henry Wallace. At least three members of the execution committee had it in for Wallace. Corcoran felt he had not been sufficiently supportive during the Court fight. Wallace in turn thought Corcoran was shifty and manipulative. "I completely distrusted anything that Tommy Corcoran had anything to do with," Wallace later commented. Harold Ickes was engaged in a long-running turf war with the agriculture secretary over control of the Forest Service. In his diary Ickes grumbled that Wallace was "a selfish and not too forthright individual" who was "consumed with his political ambition."[38] And Hopkins, now harboring ambitions of his own, saw the Iowa primary as a chance to divide Wallace's base of support and establish his own reputation as a New Deal loyalist.

Wallace's stance from beginning to end was a position of neutrality in the Iowa primary. But since the executioners interpreted this as tacit support for Gillette, which it was, they set out to "smoke him out" through the use of friendly newspaper columnists. Throughout May, Wallace was pelted with suggestions by the columnist Drew Pearson and others that the Iowa primary had become a test of Wallace's loyalty to the New Deal. The columnist John Franklin Carter, at the time very close to Corcoran, wrote that Wallace could hardly afford sitting on the fence if he hoped to have any chance in 1940.

Wallace said nothing in public, but privately he fully shared the view of Iowa's top Democrats that the executioners' effort was futile and stupid. Three times he said as much to Roosevelt in person. "Some instinct told me that the thing wouldn't work, and I didn't want to be associated with something that seemed to me at the time not to be primarily a matter of principle," Wallace said in his oral history.[39]

Roosevelt himself was maintaining a stance of public neutrality, as a result of his personal pledge to Gillette, but his preferences were well known. Once, when Wallace was in Roosevelt's office discussing another matter, presidential secretary Missy LeHand appeared from an adjoining room and said, "Mr. President, this would be a good day for Henry Wallace to come out for Otha Wearin."[40]

Despite his direct refusal to support Wearin, Wallace later said, there was no change at all in Roosevelt's attitude toward him. "Roosevelt was not a dictator in any sense. . . . My refusal to go along didn't impair my relationship with Roosevelt at all. He was really, in those days, a lovely person to work with. You could be your own man. He understood."[41]

As Wearin's campaign began to sputter, Hopkins made a desperate effort to salvage the situation. He called *Des Moines Register* reporter Richard Wilson to his office and declared, "If I voted in the Iowa primary, I would vote for Otha Wearin on the basis of his record."[42] The statement sealed Wearin's fate. Iowa Democrats and newspapers exploded in indignation. Governor Kraschel sent a furious telegram to Roosevelt. Senator Burton Wheeler denounced Hopkins on the Senate floor. Gillette abandoned his above-it-all stance, returned to Iowa, and began campaigning in a tone of high dudgeon. While not attacking Roosevelt directly, Gillette denounced Hopkins and his fellow executioners as a "gang of political termites" boring from within to take control of the Democratic Party.

Recognizing that the primary was turning into a disaster for Roosevelt, Wallace and Senator Herring proposed a "peace pact" in which both candidates would pledge to support the winner. When Wearin refused to sign, Herring gave up all pretense of neutrality and endorsed Gillette. So did Kraschel. Wallace remained officially neutral, but his position was well and widely understood.

On June 6, primary day, Iowa Democrats turned out in record numbers to support what they perceived as their hometown boy. Gillette received twice as many votes as Wearin. On election night Wallace sent Gillette a warm telegram of support. "I hope all Democrats and all Republicans who favor the President's policies will now devote their earnest efforts toward re-electing you. . . . You may count on me for wholehearted support."[43]

If anyone was "smoked out" by the Iowa primary it was Franklin D. Roosevelt. Less than three weeks after Iowa Democrats soundly rejected the executioners' strategy, Roosevelt went on the air to embrace it. In a "fireside chat" written largely by Thomas Corcoran, Roosevelt laid down his challenge to congressional "copperheads," the Civil War–era Democrats who wanted peace at any price, and said he had every right to speak out on behalf of liberal candidates in Democratic primaries.

Soon Roosevelt was crisscrossing the nation aboard a ten-car train, telling voters who met his test of liberalism and who didn't. In Kentucky he smiled upon Senate Majority Leader Alben Barkley, who was fighting off a challenge from Governor A. B. "Happy" Chandler. In Texas he enraged the conservative Senator Tom Connally by awarding a federal judgeship to a man the senator had not recommended. He delivered similar snubs to senators in Colorado and Nevada.

In Georgia (his "second home") Roosevelt directly attacked the arch conservative Walter George as the senator sat stiffly behind him. The senator, said Roosevelt, was a "personal friend . . . a gentleman and a scholar," but on matters of public policy "he and I do not speak the same language." Working his way back to Washington, Roosevelt added Senator Ellison D. "Cotton Ed" Smith of South Carolina, Senator Millard Tydings of Maryland, and Congressman John O'Connor of New York, chairman of the House Rules Committee, to the hit list.[44]

An ugly cloud of discord and disarray, followed by defeat and humiliation, trailed Roosevelt as he moved through the primary states. One after another the conservatives used home state pride to turn the president's attacks to their advantage. Maryland voters, said Senator Tydings proudly, would never allow "her star in the flag to be 'purged.' " In the end only one of the conservative Democrats the president sought to purge, Congressman O'Connor, went down in defeat.

It remained for Wallace and others to pick up the pieces as best they could. "The Democratic Party is not going to break up," Wallace told Vermont Democrats. "But if it is to remain in national power, it must become both unified and liberal. In any national fight between reactionary Democrats and reactionary Republicans, the reactionary Republicans inevitably win."[45]

In late fall Wallace stumped across the Farm Belt, reminding audiences that corn was worth fifty-seven cents a bushel, electricity was humming through new lines in rural areas, farm income had doubled, and the nation's bounty was being stored up in the ever-normal granary. Did farmers want to keep the farm program going or "throw the whole thing over . . . try nothing at all and just trust to luck"? he asked.[46]

He campaigned hard in Iowa for Gillette and Kraschel, describing them as friends of the farmer who would prevent the "Old Deal crowd" from returning agriculture to serfdom. (The grateful Gillette responded effusively, calling Wallace "the greatest secretary of agriculture the nation ever had, not excepting his illustrious father.") But there was no turning back the tide. Gillette squeaked through with a 7,000-vote victory, precisely because Iowans thought he had stood up to the New Dealers. Kraschel was crushed in the guberna-torial race. Only two Iowa Democratic congressmen survived.[47]

Elsewhere the election was a disaster for Democrats generally and New Deal-ers in particular. Republican strength in the House almost doubled. In the Sen-ate, Republicans won eight new seats and lost none. The liberal bloc in Congress was cut in half. Of the thirty-three gubernatorial races, the Republicans won eighteen. Some of the nation's best-known progressive governors—Farmer-Laborite Elmer Benson in Minnesota, Progressive Phil La Follette in Wis-consin, Democrat Frank Murphy in Michigan, Democrat George Earle in Pennsylvania—went down in defeat.

Roosevelt's dizzying fall had taken just two years. Political observers put much of the blame on presidential hubris. Reporters took to quoting the Bible: "Pride goeth before destruction, and a haughty spirit before a fall."

Wallace's own assessment, offered after a dozen years of reflection, was broader, less personal, but no more comforting to the cause of liberalism. The United States, he said, is basically a right-of-center country and returns to form once a crisis has passed:

> Any political figure which sees clearly the nature of the reactionary forces which are more interested in holding onto the past by violence than mold-ing the future constructively can operate successfully politically in a democ-racy like the United States of America only during the brief period following the time when the reactionaries have demonstrated their ineptitude in terms of great unemployment and misery in the midst of plenty. This was the secret of the temporary power of the New Deal.[48]

That autumn Henry Wallace passed a milestone other men might have deemed important. On October 7, 1938, he turned fifty. Typically he took no notice. "He wouldn't have cared one iota," said his daughter, Jean. "I don't remember any birthday parties for my parents. Birthdays just weren't part of the Wallace tradition."[49]

He was no longer the youngest member of Roosevelt's cabinet. Secretary of the Treasury Henry Morganthau and Secretary of War Harry H. Woodring were both two years his junior. But he remained the cabinet's most vigorous figure, physically and intellectually, and had lost little of his youthful ap-pearance and energy. He had gained almost twenty pounds during his years in Washington but was still below average weight for a man of his height. His auburn hair was just beginning its turn toward steely gray. Despite the gen-tle prodding of his wife, he remained indifferent to appearance. He thought nothing of shedding his necktie and shoes for a quick game of badminton when one was at hand.

At fifty he still walked almost every day to his office. Often he was accompanied by Jim LeCron, a tall, loose-limbed man who was both friend and assistant to the secretary. When the schedule was tight, they strode briskly down Connecticut Avenue, causing a commotion as policemen abruptly stopped traffic to allow their passage through intersections. More frequently they took a circuitous three-mile route from the Wardman Park through Rock Creek Park to the Potomac River.

At one point LeCron and Wallace decided it would be a good idea to climb the Washington Monument every day as they passed by. After a few days of this, LeCron recalled, it grew "so monotonous walking up all those stairs with just a lot of stones around us that we didn't do it anymore."[50]

It was there along the Potomac that Wallace took an interest in boomerangs for which he gained much notoriety. LeCron and Wallace often crossed a portion of Potomac Park used by amateur golfers. When they found golf balls, they would compete to see who could throw them farther. One morning they were joined by Milo Perkins, co-administrator of the Farm Security Administration, who suggested they should try throwing boomerangs instead. The next day Perkins showed up with three boomerangs purchased at a sporting goods store. One worked and two did not, and immediately Wallace's curiosity was whetted.

Soon the three were throwing boomerangs every morning, checking out books to learn more about their aerodynamics, purchasing new ones, and whittling away at old ones to "get the right camber . . . and twist on the wings." Motorists stopped their cars, and passersby gathered to watch them. "It looked interesting to people," said LeCron. Photographers sought to take the secretary's picture. One hapless shutterbug knelt in front of Wallace to capture him as he threw and didn't think to look behind him for the return. The "boomerang came down and hit him in the head and skinned his scalp," LeCron recalled. "Scalp wounds always bleed a good deal so blood flowed freely. . . . Wallace was very apologetic about that one."[51]

Home life in the Wallace's spacious apartment at the Wardman Park was cheerful but unremarkable. His relationship with Ilo was neither effusive nor contentious. Theirs was a quiet love, built on an unspoken understanding of their roles in life. Ilo "never tried to give him advice," said LeCron. "I don't think he'd accept political or economic advice from her if she did give it." For his part, Henry confided almost nothing to his wife regarding public policy or political matters. Paul Appleby once invited Ilo to attend a political function in Pennsylvania, and she asked why it was important. To build support for Henry's candidacy, Appleby replied.[52]

"Candidacy for what?" Ilo asked.

"The presidency," Appleby responded.

"Oh, my, no!" she exclaimed.

Her nature was modest and unpretentious. Ilo was "a gentle sort of person who would have preferred to move back to Des Moines," said Appleby. She was also, he added, "very good looking." And because she had no special interest in political and policy matters, she was quite "indiscriminate" in her friendships. Ilo "tended to like everybody and she was an asset to [Henry]," said Appleby. "She was not self-seeking."[53]

Only one of their children, eighteen-year-old Jean, sunny and popular like her mother, remained at home. Their oldest child, twenty-three-year-old H. B., was in Iowa heavily engaged in chicken breeding at the Pioneer Hi-Bred facilities near Johnston. Twenty-year-old Robert was a student at Iowa State. His absence meant fewer birds and snakes around the Wardman Park, but there remained immense numbers of flowers, a by-product of the Agriculture Department's experimental greenhouses along the Mall.

It was a comfortable life but far from extravagant. Cabinet officers were paid $15,000 a year, and the Wallaces lived within their means. The Wallaces' total earnings from Pioneer Hi-Bred during his years in the cabinet amounted to no more than $10,000, Paul Appleby estimated. Even if they could have afforded more luxuries, Henry Wallace's stern frugality would not have allowed them. Aside from scientific research, on which he would spend freely, Wallace didn't like to part with money.

Washington was still a quiet village in many respects. The people who ran the federal government moved freely and socialized easily. Many prominent figures lived nearby. Robert Jackson and his family lived down the hall from the Wallaces. Colonel Dwight D. Eisenhower and his wife lived next door. Cabinet wives of that era were expected to hold occasional afternoon receptions, called "at homes," which anyone could attend. "Sometimes hundreds of people would show up," said Jean. "There were people you didn't even know, right off the street."[54] And when the socializing was done, Wallace invariably returned to work. Jean's lasting memory of her father during those years was of him sitting at his desk, feet propped up, speaking into a dictating machine. He loved to work. "Work For the Night Is Coming" was his favorite hymn.

At the Agriculture Department he presided over a yeasty environment that gloried in intellectual curiosity and playful eccentricity. When Wallace was in town, he almost always ate lunch in a room beside the main cafeteria where place settings and tablecloths were provided for an additional ten cents per plate. There Wallace and his aides would boisterously argue about everything from genetics to geography. Once a week a language tutor came and they spoke only in Spanish. Jokers called the noontime gatherings "Sec's Club."

The luncheons were rowdy, free-for-all affairs sometimes going far afield from agriculture. The unorthodox economist Marriner Eccles, famed defense attorney Clarence Darrow, poet and Theosophist George W. Russell, writer Sherwood Anderson, poet Robert Frost—all of them came to the secretary's table. Although Wallace himself was never ribald or profane, he clearly enjoyed the high-spirited company. "No matter how noble a man is, he needs to relax," said LeCron. "You can't go on turning the other cheek forever."[55]

Occasionally Wallace's insatiable curiosity would veer off in bizarre directions. Once he was found in his office stripped to the waist and hooked up to something called an "ultra-sensitive electric galvanometer," which its inventor claimed could detect the relative healthiness of one's body by picking up electrical currents. "What a sight," marveled LeCron.[56]

Wallace reveled in physical activity. Indian wrestling interested him, and more than one surprised reporter found himself on the floor after questioning Wallace's prowess. He still played tennis with graceless abandon, shifting his racquet from left hand to right as it suited him.

But it was his busy mind that most characterized him to associates. He was always wondering, always questioning, always pressing in unexpected directions. Wallace was as close to being a Renaissance man as anyone in American public life since Thomas Jefferson, Paul Appleby told his daughter. "He was an extremely curious individual, and I guess his curiosity got him into as much difficulty as anything," said the plant scientist William Brown. "He found it very difficult to disbelieve anything until it was proven wrong."[57]

Gove Hambidge, scholarly editor of the Agriculture Department's yearbook during the 1930s, spoke in his memoirs of Wallace's "deep interest in quite an extraordinary range of scientific problems." Wallace's approach to scientific questions, said Hambidge, is "usually fresh, bold, and unconventional. He rather enjoys making fun of the cautiousness of the average scientist and suggesting lines of research that sometimes sound haywire. Back of the suggestions, however, there is likely to be a great deal of quiet, sound thinking." Sometimes Wallace's hunches proved wrong, Hambidge wrote, and at other times they were "extraordinarily fruitful" and opened up new lines of scientific attack in fields ranging from nutrition to meteorology.[58]

On occasional Saturday afternoons Wallace would drop by Hambidge's home in the Maryland suburbs where members of the department's top staff gathered to play horseshoes. Wallace preferred a vigorous game of badminton. "To tell the truth, I guess I'm not old enough for horseshoes yet," he would joke. "I still prefer something with a bit of life in it."

Hambidge recalled an afternoon he and Wallace played five hard games. Then, with his hair mussed and his business trousers "smeared with a greenish-white mess" as the result of a fall, Wallace sat down for a rest. "We fell to talking about white rats," wrote Hambidge. Rats were fundamentally important to scientific research, Wallace mused, but what if the rats themselves were not standard? Wouldn't genetically unequal rats give unequal results? Perhaps there should be a "critical genetic study of the principal colonies used in our big laboratories," he said. And just as suddenly as he had turned to rats, Wallace bade Hambidge good-bye and left.

Badminton and white rats. Friendly and abrupt. Such was Wallace at age fifty.

"I think," wrote Hambidge, "Henry Wallace will live as one of the true galvanizers of scientific research in agriculture—and this in a period when major attention in the Department, as elsewhere throughout the government, has necessarily been given to economic and social questions. Sometimes I have thought that he should have been a scientist—that he would have done his best work in science. Or maybe it is best as it is. Scientific statesmen are much rarer than scientists. He is quite likely to become a mythological figure in the Department—one of those men of whom people say, 'There were giants in those days'—because of the elements of true greatness in his character, the breadth of his interests, and his way of going off at a tangent from convention."[59]

CHAPTER TEN

"DEMOCRACY IS ON TRIAL TODAY."

❦

As far back as the 1920s, Henry Wallace had been warning that restrictive trade and tariff policies would inevitably lead to an "explosion" ending in world war. In the earliest days of the New Deal, he counseled Americans to be watchful of events in Europe. "Beyond the seas, nations hurt by the terrible grind of ungoverned economic forces are in a warlike mood," Wallace wrote in a *New York Times* article. "Their men are arming. We want none of that, but the world is small."[1]

Now, as the decade drew to a close, his prophecy was proving terrifyingly accurate.

Wallace's thinking had been deeply influenced by the economist Thorstein Veblen, who argued that states such as Germany and Japan, which had developed a modern industrial economy without parallel democratic institutions, were bound to express their national identity in authoritarianism and warfare. Tariffs, Veblen held, were simply an economic expression of nationalism and as such were an invitation for trouble.

This line of thought made Wallace an uncommon figure among midwestern progressives of the era. Unlike William Borah of Idaho or George Norris of Nebraska or the La Follettes of Wisconsin, all firmly isolationist, Wallace tended toward internationalism. Fostering international trade was not only a means of helping American farmers, Wallace thought, but the surest path to world peace. In the cabinet he had been Secretary of State Cordell Hull's strongest ally in the effort to reduce trade barriers through negotiation of reciprocal agreements.

The rising tide of nationalism and militarism in Central Europe and Japan during the 1930s therefore came as no surprise to Wallace. But it alarmed him greatly, and he spoke with increasing frequency on the need for Americans to gird themselves with a strong faith in democratic values.

"Democracy is on trial today," he said in a 1938 lecture at the Pacific School of Religion in Berkeley, California. "It has been challenged in this country and in the whole world. . . . We Americans must not and will not let the rule of force replace the rule of law. But if we are going to succeed, our democracy must be efficient and it must have purpose."[2]

By the time this and five other of his 1938 lectures were published in a twenty-five-cent booklet entitled *Paths to Plenty*, Europe was well along the road to total war.* Hitler's Germany had enveloped the Austrian republic and would soon overtake Czechoslovakia with the craven assistance of Prime Minister Neville Chamberlain of Britain.

As the crisis built, President Roosevelt cast about for an effective response. He tried without success to persuade Chamberlain to participate in a conference with other democratic nations. He held a highly secret meeting with the British ambassador to outline a plan for getting U.S. aid to Britain and France. He privately laid plans for a huge increase in American air power and publicly called for an increase in military spending. He organized a Pan-American conference to encourage hemispheric solidarity.

For reasons partly of his own making but mostly beyond his control, Roosevelt's efforts mainly came to naught. Chamberlain, both imperious and timid, saw no need for U.S. interference. Germany and its allies viewed the president with contempt. And at home Roosevelt's ability to force his will on Congress had long since vanished. The troubling truth was that on foreign policy Congress was in tune with the mood of the American public.

What Roosevelt needed, and desperately so, was repeal of the Neutrality Act. Without the ability to supply Britain and France with airplanes and other weaponry, the United States could be little more than a cheerleader on the sidelines. But it was almost immediately apparent that repeal of the act, or even significant revision, would not be easily won.

As months passed with no congressional action, Roosevelt was reduced to sending personal messages to Adolf Hitler and Benito Mussolini asking them

---

*The booklet was reissued in 1940 as *The Price of Freedom*, with the addition of an eloquent introduction by David Cushman Coyle, a sometime aide to Harry Hopkins. "Henry Wallace, man of affairs, with knowledge of corn and cattle and forests, of markets and foreign commerce, manager of a billion-dollar enterprise, sets the living religion of America across the path of the heathen religion of the Conqueror of Europe," Coyle wrote. ". . . We had better understand the new heathen religion that hopes to conquer the world, and we had better understand our own and cultivate it, if we hope to survive. Henry Wallace is not playing with pretty pebbles, but deals here with the matters of life and death that are to be decided soon for our civilization."

to pledge no military action against thirty-three European and Middle Eastern nations for at least ten years. Wallace warned the president not to send it. "There is danger that people in foreign lands and even some in this country will look on your effort as being in the same category as delivering a sermon to a mad dog," Wallace said. And he was right; Hitler responded to Roosevelt's letter with open mockery.

By midyear Roosevelt was out of options. "I've fired my last shot," he pleaded to a group of senators. "I think I ought to have another round in my belt."[3]

"Mr. President," responded old Senator Borah, "there is not going to be any war in Europe."[4]

Some of those who had known Henry Wallace detected a change in him as the presidential election year approached. It was said he had become more cautious, more wary of political missteps.

But Wallace's early and total support of Roosevelt's drive for international collective security served in some measure to refute the charge. There was not much to be gained politically, and potentially much to be lost, by expressing support for Roosevelt's policy of engagement. Yet Wallace did so with strength and conviction, knowing it would pose a risk to his standing in Iowa and the Midwest, where isolationism was firmly rooted. "I spoke for this policy," he later said, "although I knew in the Middle West it would cost us votes."[5]

From the outset he had seen the Nazi challenge as a test of democratic institutions. "There are leaders in other lands who would like to see the forces of disunity conquer in this country," he told a Constitution Day audience in 1937. "They would like to see democracy fail, in order that their own nervous belief in dictatorship might be strengthened. . . . No man can say what the result will be beyond this: that democracy as never before, will have to prove itself by deed as well as word. Democracy in the United States must be made to work."[6]

He had once described the New Deal farm program as "a Declaration of Interdependence, a recognition of our essential unity and of our absolute reliance one upon another." The concept of collective security, he now argued, was the same thing on an international scale. "By amending our neutrality act we can avoid throwing our weight into the scales on the side of the aggressors."[7]

Opposing fascism, Wallace noted, was not the same as supporting Old World ways. "For 300 years we have breathed the free and open air of this North American continent. We have not yet become the slaves to national hates that smolder on and on for centuries. . . . [We] do not consider our-selves a part of the system of economic imperialism which dominates Europe and Africa and Asia. . . . To build up the wealth of Europe, both the people and the soil of the rest of the world have been exploited."[8]

Wallace was particularly effective in his biting critique of Nazi pseudo-science. "When we consider the almost insuperable difficulties placed in the way of the cattle breeder by such esthetic hurdles as color and indefinite points of conformation, we realize at once that the salvation of the human race can-not come through human genetics applied by a dictator," Wallace said in a lecture entitled "An Approach to Eugenics," delivered in 1938.[9]

"It is definitely a false eugenic idea to work toward some standardized pre-conception of the perfect man, such as the 'Aryan Race' of the Nazi mythol-ogy," Wallace continued. "No race has a monopoly on desirable genes and there are geniuses in every race. . . . Man does not live by bread alone, nor by genes alone.[10]

In February 1939 Wallace delivered an even more scathing attack on the "mumbo-jumbo of dangerous nonsense" that passed for Nazi science. Speak-ing to the Committee for Democracy and Intellectual Freedom, at the Wal-dorf-Astoria Hotel in New York City, he said the Nazi dictatorship "is teaching the German boys and girls to believe that their race and their nation are su-perior to all others, and by implication that nation and that race have a right to dominate all others." In fact, Europe is a great mixture of tribes and breeds, he added, and the dictators' assertions are "pure scientific faking."[11]

He told of his own boyhood acquaintance with George Washington Carver, the great black scientist, and said, "Superior ability is not the exclusive pos-session of any one race or any one class." He asked whether any scientist would care to claim that 100,000 babies taken from "poor white" families and raised in wealthy circumstances would turn out any differently from 100,000 well-to-do babies, or 100,000 German babies, or 100,000 Jewish babies.[12]

A master breeder who lived a thousand years might be able to "fix a stan-dard blue-eyed, long-headed, fair-haired type of the most approved Nordic specifications," Wallace observed. But a cow's color has nothing to do with its ability to produce milk, he said, nor does a man's hair have anything to do with his mental abilities. "And so it is quite possible that the master breeder, being concerned primarily with physical appearance, would find he had pro-duced a group of blonde morons—useful to him primarily as a superior type of cannon fodder."[13]

But he wasn't quite done. Turning to the largely scientific crowd before him, Wallace warned that devotion to true science is not enough. Scientists must also be committed to democracy and the general welfare.

The cause of liberty and the cause of true science must always be one and the same. For science cannot flourish except in an atmosphere of freedom, and freedom cannot survive unless there is an honest facing of facts. . . .

Democracy—and that term includes free science—must apply itself to meeting the material need of men for work, for income, for goods, for health, for security, and to meeting the spiritual need for dignity, for knowledge, for self-expression, for adventure and for reverence. And it must succeed. The danger that it will be overthrown in favor of some other system is in direct proportion to its failure to meet those needs. . . . In the long run, democracy or any other political system will be measured by its deeds, not its words.[14]

If Wallace was forthright in his support of Roosevelt, he was considerably more circumspect about his own political aspirations. Indeed, he continued long after the fact to deny that he had any presidential ambitions at all. He was never a candidate, he blandly asserted in the oral history he later gave to Columbia University, and never even heard talk of his running for president or vice president until mid-December 1939.

In fact, such talk had been in the air for years. Wallace might have chosen to ignore it for reasons of personal modesty, as Paul Appleby suggested, or because of his family's long distrust of political ambition. But he could hardly have been unaware of it.

As early as 1934 the columnist John Franklin Carter had suggested Wallace might be the great liberal hope in 1940. Eugene Meyer, publisher of the *Washington Post*, touted Wallace's prospects well before Roosevelt had even been elected to a second term. A Pennsylvania newsman made headlines in Iowa when he claimed Wallace was "the most likely candidate for vice president with Roosevelt in 1936." Throughout the 1936 campaign the *Des Moines Register* repeatedly suggested that Wallace's own presidential prospects were on the line.[15]

As Roosevelt's second term began, Richard Wilson wrote in the *Des Moines Register* that a "new Henry A. Wallace has been born out of the four years of the New Deal." The new Wallace is a bit less frank and a bit more genial, wrote Wilson. He "has begun to realize the importance of politics" and has "become a definite possibility for the presidential nomination in 1940."[16]

In July 1937 the *Saturday Evening Post*, the nation's largest-selling magazine, devoted nine pages to an article by sometime presidential speechwriter Stanley High entitled "Will It Be Wallace?" "It is an axiom of American politics that booms which bloom early are subject to frost," wrote High. "But if this boom withers; if, in 1940, Mr. Roosevelt's hands are laid on some other head, it will not be because Mr. Wallace has faltered in his understanding of the New Deal gospel or has failed, in his special field, to do a job of almost presidential proportions."[17]

A few months later *Look* magazine published a four-page spread called "Henry Agard Wallace: A Scientific Farmer and a White House Possibility." It included flattering photos of Wallace as a baby, a teenager, a corn grower, an ambidextrous volleyball player, and a cabinet secretary looking at a portrait of his father, as well as pictures of his house, his mother, his birthplace, his handsome family, and his "comely wife." At the end of 1938 Wallace's presidential prospects were the subject of a three-page analysis in *Time* magazine, which featured a handsome earth-toned portrait by the artist Grant Wood on the cover.[18]

By that time the *Des Moines Register* was regularly analyzing the strengths and weaknesses of Wallace's possible candidacy (he was deemed weak in the Northeast, but seven out of ten farmers thought he was doing a good job) and syndicated columnists such as Drew Pearson and Joseph Alsop frequently viewed his actions through the prism of presidential politics. Wallace might disavow an interest in the presidency, but journalists saw that as a time-honored strategy of presidential aspirants.

In fact, Wallace had no political strategy at all. He tended to think about politics in terms of policy, not tactics and certainly not personality. He was utterly incapable of pretense and guile. The art of political maneuver escaped him, or perhaps revolted him, and his lack of interest in other politicians' fortunes was legendary.

These qualities, combined with his "religious streak" and a certain intellectual arrogance, made him a highly unusual figure on the national political stage. Gerald W. Johnson, a political reporter for the *Baltimore Sun*, put it this way:

A politician who really does not care about making political "friends" is, in the opinion of political Washington, a flat contradiction of terms. Hence, in the case of Henry A. Wallace appearances must be deceptive. Behind the figure presented to the public gaze there must be another and very different man; yet no one, not even the most highly trained observers of the nation's press, has perceived that other man. Hence the frank bewilderment. Hence correspondents' confession that although they see him every day, and talk to him, and watch him, they don't know him.[19]

Nor did the public give much thought to Henry Wallace as a presidential candidate in the early months of 1939. The leading Democratic prospects according to first Gallup poll of 1939 were the same three men who led every poll in 1938: John Nance Garner, James Farley, and Cordell Hull. One had to look far down Gallup's list, to seventh place, to find the only New Deal liberal. And that liberal was Harry Hopkins. At the beginning of 1939 Wallace was not even an asterisk.

Wallace didn't show up on the Gallup poll until May, when he was reported to be tied for tenth place as the choice of Democratic voters. By that time Garner had rocketed from 20 percent, where he began the year, to 50 percent. Buoyed by his showing in the polls, Garner announced that he would not seek or accept another term as vice president. His statement was widely viewed as a declaration of his presidential intentions. Pundits began imagining a Garner-Farley ticket in 1940.

The Wallace noncampaign did achieve one important success during those months. Largely through Paul Appleby's determined effort, Wallace appeared by early spring to be assured of the Iowa delegation's support at the 1940 Democratic convention. Senator Guy Gillette and former Governor Nelson Kraschel gave Wallace their enthusiastic backing. Even Senator Clyde Herring, who nursed dark horse hopes of his own, offered a restrained endorsement. "If Henry Wallace is a candidate for president, and if he wants the Iowa delegation, I am in favor of his having it," Herring said. "We in Iowa owe it to him."[20]

That was the last straw for Harry Hopkins's lingering presidential hopes. Early in the year the commerce secretary announced that he would buy a home in Grinnell and reestablish residence in Iowa after twenty-seven years in New York and Washington. Hopkins, whose second wife had died, cast his decision as an effort to raise his young daughter in a more wholesome environment. But reporters seized upon its political implications and set the stage for a titanic battle of New Deal presidential hopefuls.

The battle was never fought. In late February, making his maiden appearance in Iowa before a black-tie dinner of Des Moines business executives, Hopkins became extremely ill. He retreated to Bernard Baruch's country estate in South Carolina and remained out of sight for weeks. Hopkins's friends continued political activities on his behalf, but they were no match for Wallace's supporters. Hopkins allowed the presidential effort to continue in a halfhearted way through May and then bowed to the inevitable.

He did not bow to Wallace, however. "First, last and all the time," Hopkins said, "my choice for President in 1940 is Franklin D. Roosevelt, and I believe that a great mass of the people agree with me."[21]

Hopkins thus joined Harold Ickes, Thomas Corcoran, and other members of the self-styled execution committee in calling on Roosevelt to seek a third term. And just as the intraparty purge of 1938 had fractured Democratic unity, the third-term issue now became a divisive new test of loyalty to Roosevelt and liberalism. Garner publicly declared his opposition to a third term. Farley made similar comments in private. Hull was silent as usual. Warfare broke out among Democrats.

Henry Wallace initially responded skeptically, almost negatively, to the third-term campaign. "I think it is altogether outside the province of any cabinet member to express an opinion on that subject," he said, somewhat oddly, to the *New York Times*.[22]

But with Hopkins out of the race, the Ickes-Corcoran clique—wags called them the "third termites"—began pressuring Wallace to prove his loyalty to the president by joining their cause. Wallace issued a carefully phrased promise to support any genuine New Dealer nominated by the Democratic Party, including, of course, Roosevelt. Clearly that was insufficient to the third-term supporters. For the remainder of the summer, they played a game of push-and-shove with the agriculture secretary, using favorite columnists and political allies to suggest varying degrees of apostasy. By late July they had succeeded in generating newspaper reports that Wallace was in danger of being ousted from the cabinet.

The idea of Wallace losing his job was ludicrous—Roosevelt himself described the stories as "tommy rot"—but attempts by the "palace guard" to undercut him were real indeed. Senator Herring, watching developments with growing disgust, offered a withering appraisal: "I know of no such attempt [to oust Wallace from the cabinet] but I wouldn't be surprised, for they have done things just as stupid and would be about as effective as in the past. If they try to get Henry's job they may find themselves out of a job, for I know how well the secretary of agriculture stands with the president."[23]

Wallace privately felt the Ickes-Corcoran crowd was doing active harm to the progressive cause, but he said nothing about it in public. In early August he sent Roosevelt a long, thoughtful letter warning of the dangers posed by demands for ideological purity.

To some extent, Wallace wrote, the administration had fallen victim to "the best organized and most irresponsible [Republican] opposition we have seen in many years." But he added, "it is worth while moralizing about the Democrats," too.

> It is still true that the Democrats in order to win must have a progressive candidate but it is also true that the 10 million progressives are not the only ones on the fence. There are many million other people who are very close to the farm, the small town and the small business men in the cities who were with us enthusiastically in 1932, to a somewhat lesser extent in 1936 and who are now raising many questions about government spending, la-

bor policies, etc. These people temperamentally are not progressives but they are fine people whose votes we must have. We must make some kind of suitable accommodation with these people. . . .

On a straight division of the electorate on a basis of the broadly liberal and the generally conservative, the definite majority is conservative. The Gallup poll shows that. So also does the way Garner runs in the Democratic polls. We have to have some means of getting basic, general support, and then covering that foundation with a liberal superstructure.[24]

Roosevelt never responded. A few days after Wallace sent his letter, the president departed for a long-awaited sailing vacation off the northeast coast; Wallace went to his rented summer home in Des Moines.

But events in Europe took no holiday. In late August, Roosevelt abruptly ended his vacation and returned to Washington. He arrived on August 24, the day Nazi Germany and the Soviet Union signed a ten-year nonaggression pact. A week later, at 2:50 A.M. on September 1, Roosevelt was asleep in the White House when the phone by his bed rang. It was William Bullitt, the ambassador to France, calling to inform the president that several divisions of Germany troops had invaded Poland. The second great war of the twentieth century had begun.

"Well, Bill, it's come at last," said Roosevelt. "God help us all."[25]

For a moment, an agonizing moment that stretched from days into weeks and weeks into months, everything was uncertain. A "fog of ambiguity" settled over events, in the historian Kenneth S. Davis's words. A confused, highly anxious American public watched as Britain declared war on Germany, and the United States proclaimed a "limited national emergency." Yet there was no combat between Britain and Germany, nor was there a crisis in the United States.[26]

In the hours after the war began, a wave of panic buying hit American grocery stores. But as Wallace said in a nationally broadcast address, there was no cause for alarm. "We are not in war and we have an abundance of practically all kinds of food," he said. "We have reason to rejoice in the strength of our position. . . . These housewives don't know it yet but they will soon find out that we have in agriculture a mechanism [the ever-normal granary] which in a measure does for agriculture what the government insurance of bank deposits does for banks."[27]

The panic subsided but not the uncertainty. America declared its absolute neutrality in the European conflict, but did what it could by word and deed to assist its democratic allies. Roosevelt simultaneously pledged total fealty to the spirit and letter of the Neutrality Act and redoubled his effort to repeal the arms embargo it imposed. On September 21 Congress was called into special session to again consider revision of the law.

By that time Roosevelt had enlisted an impressive array of Republican allies—including the 1936 Republican nominee, Alf Landon, his running mate, Frank Knox, Kansas editor William Allen White, and former secretary of state Henry Stimson—to push for repeal of the arms embargo. In order to win their support, Roosevelt imposed a sort of embargo of his own. All talk of a third term must cease, he told aides.

To say the least, American presidential politics had become exceedingly murky. Throughout the summer months, Roosevelt had begun setting out the criteria for an acceptable Democratic candidate in 1940. The candidate must be a liberal, must be able to get the nomination, and must be able to win the election. He had gone so far as to say he would bolt the party if the candidate did not meet his standards. "[I] am sufficiently honest to decline to support any conservative Democrat," he said.[28]

Who could meet Roosevelt's standards? Certainly not Garner or his ambitious protégé Jesse Jones, conservative head of the Reconstruction Finance Corporation. Farley could probably win the nomination, but his chances in the general election were doubtful. Harold Ickes was a Republican and had no hope of being nominated. Paul McNutt, Philippines high commissioner, wanted the job, but when Farley mentioned his name in a private conversation with Roosevelt, the president held his thumb up in the air and slowly turned it downward.

Then there was Henry Wallace. "What do you think of Henry?" the president asked Farley. Roosevelt quickly answered his own question: "I don't think he has It." Farley eagerly agreed. "I must confess I share the feeling around the country that he's a dreamer," Farley said.[29]

Several weeks later Roosevelt used precisely the same words in a meeting with Guy Gillette. The senator had gone to the White House seeking Roosevelt's blessing for a unified Iowa delegation supporting Wallace. Roosevelt said Wallace was a fine man but lacked "political It." The comment soon found its way into public print, although with some confusion as to whether Roosevelt said Wallace lacked "It" or "oomph."[30]

Whatever it was he lacked, Wallace thought he knew what Roosevelt meant. He believed the president was saying the Democratic Party would not nominate him, and he tended to agree. "Of course, anything is possible, but I didn't think it probable," he said later. ". . . I wasn't their kind of person—I was quite sure of that. It could only happen if Roosevelt demanded it. That was obvious to me."[31]

For all its murkiness, one thing about the political situation in the fall of 1939 had become quite clear to Wallace: "I was convinced Roosevelt wanted a third term." Not only did Roosevelt want to run again; events in Europe were rapidly making it mandatory that he do so, in Wallace's view. "Personally I felt that a third term for Roosevelt was inevitable. . . . I could see no other outcome."[32]

On October 25, three weeks after Roosevelt told Senator Gillette that the agriculture secretary lacked "political It," Wallace publicly joined the third-termites. "Mr. Roosevelt's background seems to equip him with exceptional qualifications as a helmsman to steer the country through both foreign and domestic troubles to a safe harbor," Wallace said at a press conference in San Francisco.[33]

His comment drew outcries from members of both parties in Congress, where the Neutrality Act revisions were still being debated, and a mild rebuke from the White House press secretary, Stephen Early. "It would have been kind and polite of the speaker to have consulted the victim before he spoke," said Early.[34]

But the "fog of ambiguity" surrounded this episode as everything else during that nebulous autumn. Wallace had consulted with "the victim" and told Roosevelt what he intended to say. After Early issued his apparent reprimand, Wallace repeated his call for a third term and added there was no need to apologize. Early's public rebuke, meanwhile, served its intended purpose of calming congressional waters. On November 3 Congress repealed the arms embargo.

Among those jockeying for position to succeed Roosevelt, there was a growing suspicion they were being had. Slowly the political professionals were learning what Wallace, the amateur, had already concluded. "The thing I was convinced of all during this period," he later said, "was that everything depended on Roosevelt, and that anyone who went out to be either president or vice president was sure to get it in the neck."[35]

The match had been struck, but the world was not yet afire. In the winter of 1939–40, the winter of the Phony War, the only real combat was in Finland, where brave Finnish troops were attempting to withstand an invasion by Russia. Henry Wallace watched the fighting with special concern. His sister Ruth, married to the Swedish diplomat Per Wijkman, was living in Finland when the war began. Wallace sent her a package of vitamins and a dose of brotherly advice: "If you can get some powdered brewers' yeast I would suggest that you mix it with the breakfast food each morning at a rate of one tablespoon each for yourself and Per and one teaspoon each for the children." Cod-liver oil and dried apricots were also recommended.[36]

There was still time during those uncertain months for a bit of lighthearted banter around the cabinet table over Wallace's request for $107,000 to fund something called the Bureau of Nematology. There was still time for dinner party gossip about a certain countess rumored to be changing the diplomatic face of Europe from a supine position. There was even time for Wallace to resume the diary he had briefly begun around the time of the departmental purge of 1935.*

Within the government the principal policy issue involving Wallace was a fierce interdepartmental battle over the U.S. Forest Service. Three generations of Wallaces had been participants in this great turf war. Uncle Henry Wallace had championed the cause of his close friend Gifford Pinchot, when the great progressive conservationist fought to place stewardship of the national forests in the Department of Agriculture.

Two decades later Secretary of Agriculture Henry Cantwell Wallace successfully fought off an attempt by the corrupt interior secretary Albert Fall to gain control of the Forest Service. And in the 1930s Henry Agard Wallace time and again beat back similar efforts by Secretary of the Interior Harold Ickes.

In early 1940 the Forest Service issue reared up once again, and this time Ickes seemed to have the upper hand. A governmental reorganization bill recently enacted by Congress had given the president broad latitude to move around federal agencies. Ickes and Louis Brownlow, father of the reorganization plan, were both pressuring Roosevelt to transfer the Forest Service to Interior. The death in late 1939 of Forest Service Chief F. A. Silcox and the need to name his replacement further complicated the issue.

By 1940 Ickes had made transfer of the Forest Service his personal cause célèbre. He was in open warfare with the "timber interests" backing the Forest Service and had gone so far as to assign aides to uncover unflattering information about Pinchot. Ickes accused the mustachioed old forester of fronting for "a motley crew of lumber barons" in an effort to win a cabinet appointment. Pinchot, never one to shrink from a fight, compared Ickes to

---

*Wallace continued to make regular entries in the diary during his remaining months as secretary of agriculture. After dropping the practice during the 1940 campaign, he resumed the diary in 1942 and continued it on a regular basis until leaving government in 1946. Although not as voluminous as Henry Morgenthau's diary or as pungent as Harold Ickes's journal, Wallace's diary offers a revealing portrait of himself as a public figure, a thoughtful, even-tempered man fully engaged in the great issues of his time and eager to make his mark. Like Wallace himself, his diary was frank but not mean-spirited, perceptive but seldom intimate. There are few references to his family, for example, and virtually none concerning his rich spiritual life.

Hitler and warned that "grabbing for power is not well regarded in the world of today."[37]

The fight became agonizingly personal for Wallace. Pinchot and others made clear they expected Wallace to stake his career on the outcome. Yale University forestry professor H. H. Chapman, president of the Society of American Foresters, reminded Wallace that his father had been prepared to resign from office over the issue. Wallace's top aides were spoiling for a public fight. To top it all off, Rexford Guy Tugwell, languishing in New York City as an aide to Mayor Fiorello La Guardia, began campaigning for the now vacant position of chief forester.

Wallace's handling of the issue once again served proof that his low-key persona was not to be taken for lack of skill as a bureaucratic infighter. Aides were told to prepare answers to Ickes on all substantive points, but under no circumstances to engage in name-calling with him, which they could not have won in any case. When Harry Slattery, head of the Rural Electrification Administration, approached Wallace with information he claimed could be personally damaging to Ickes, the secretary said he didn't want to hear it. He told Chapman to remain calm, fended off intense pressure from Pinchot to make a statement against transfer before the Senate Agriculture Committee, held back on the matter of a new Forest Service chief, and kept Tugwell at bay.

All the while Wallace was quietly building support for his position in Congress and earnestly trying to win the president's ear. Late in January, upon learning that Ickes had at last persuaded Roosevelt to issue the transfer order, Wallace made his case in direct, personal terms.

"This Forest Service move is highly controversial and I don't see where you will gain anything by raising it at this time," Wallace told the president. "You will gain a lot by avoiding it and by giving your attention to peace and foreign affairs."

"Yes, I agree with you heartily," Roosevelt replied. "The whole thing is a dammed headache but I am sort of hooked. Ain't it awful?"

"Well, I am sort of hooked, too, said Wallace. "I wish you would give me some light on it if you can."[38]

But there was no light. Another week passed, and more rumors reached Wallace that Roosevelt had agreed to a plan that would carve up the Forest Service and shift most of its responsibilities to Interior. At lunch with Roosevelt on February 13, Wallace again began discussing the matter. Suddenly Roosevelt looked up and said casually, "I wanted to tell you that that matter has been dropped."[39]

Only later did Wallace learn how close Ickes had come. Roosevelt had in fact signed an executive order transferring most of the Forest Service to Interior shortly before he told Wallace the "matter has been dropped." At that moment Wallace's careful spadework on Capitol Hill paid off. South Carolina's Senator James Byrnes, an ally of Wallace on the issue, went to the White House and bluntly reminded the president of his promise not to transfer the Forest Service without prior congressional approval. Roosevelt heard the senator out, smiled slightly, picked up the executive order he had signed, and tore it up.*

In this and other incidents there are hints of Roosevelt's fondness for his agriculture secretary. Loyal and earnest, liberal but tolerant, he appealed to Roosevelt's better nature, as Wallace himself put it. Roosevelt was the master politician, to be sure, but a part of him valued faith and simplicity. There was something satisfying about a man who could, without any self-consciousness, go on national radio and praise "the strength and quietness of grass."[40] There was something very genuine about a man who gave the president seed corn as an Easter gift, along with clear instructions about when and how it should be planted at Hyde Park.

Clearly, also, Roosevelt enjoyed Wallace's agile mind. Wallace's frequent memos on diverse subjects, his unerring mastery of fact, and his grasp of the big picture had become valuable to a president who enjoyed encounters with a keen intellect. Roosevelt reveled in give-and-take with associates. And he took an almost childlike delight in trying to catch Wallace in an error of fact.

At one cabinet meeting during these months, Roosevelt thought he finally had the agriculture secretary. Roosevelt had proposed selling off six million bales of government-owned cotton in an effort to help balance the budget. Wallace said the sale would not be legal until the price of cotton reached 11 cents a pound. Roosevelt said the price was already 11.5 cents a pound. "I told him that the price yesterday at the ten spot markets was 10.74 cents a pound," Wallace wrote in his diary. "He insisted my figures were wrong."[41]

The following evening, Roosevelt phoned Wallace in a state of exhilaration. He had noticed in the papers, Wallace recalled, that the "spot price of middling cotton was 11.07 cents, which was considerably different from the 10.74 cents figure which I had quoted the previous day. I asked him if the

---

*Ickes was by no means willing to let the matter rest. He continued to campaign for the Forest Service transfer in furious fashion. In May 1940 he began sending a series of highly vituperative letters to Wallace, Pinchot, and others, accusing them of disloyalty and foul play. The letter to Pinchot—"full of billingsgate," in Wallace's words—ran to twenty-eight pages and attacked not only the former forester but his wife in coarse terms. Wallace answered the first of these letters, but after consulting with Paul Appleby and others he decided to stop replying "in view of Ickes' mental state."

Ickes was still pounding on the Forest Service issue at the time of the Democratic National Convention in July 1940. Concerned that the fight would be seen as evidence of Democratic disunity, Wallace wrote Ickes a polite letter suggesting he "take back" his recent letters so they would not become part of the record. Ickes adamantly refused. "The vicious forces set in motion by Pinchot still exist in Agriculture," Ickes wrote. ". . . In the circumstances, it seems to me that your plea for 'party and national unity' comes a little too late."

11.07 cents price was not the spot price in New York and called his attention to the price I was quoting, which was the average of the ten spot markets. He said yes, his was the spot price New York, and backed away.[42]

"Then I said, 'Well, you pretty nearly had me, anyhow, Mr. President.' He then said, 'You may know about corn and hogs but I am a plantah from Geogah.'

"I said, 'Yessuh.' "[43]

The Phony War ended in the predawn darkness of April 9, 1940, when German troops attacked Norway and Denmark. The attack was terrifying in its swiftness and flawless in execution. By the end of the first day of battle, Denmark had collapsed entirely and most of Norway's major cities and ports were under Nazi control. The *Sitzkrieg* had ended and the blitzkrieg begun. Wallace learned of the attack while lying in bed at 2 A.M., when he heard newsboys crying "Extra!" outside the Wardman Park. "It seems to me undoubtedly we can expect the most extraordinary efforts on the part of the dictator nations," he wrote in his diary.[44]

Britain's attempt to confront Germany's hold on Norway quickly turned into a debacle. The policies of Neville Chamberlain, who confidently asserted only days before Germany's invasion of Denmark that Hitler had "missed the bus," stood in disgrace. On May 10, as members of his own party mocked him with his words, Chamberlain resigned as prime minister and was replaced by the pugnacious Winston Churchill. On the same day Hitler launched his march through the Low Countries, smashing through Luxembourg into Holland.

Within days German forces had torn open a fifty-mile gap in British and French defense forces, through which Nazi tanks and armored cars poured with breathtaking speed. On May 15, writing privately as one "former naval person" to another, Churchill issued a desperate plea for help to Roosevelt. He asked for the loan of forty or fifty old U.S. destroyers, several hundred aircraft, and antiaircraft equipment, the purchase of U.S. steel, and the deployment of U.S. ships to Irish ports. The president replied cautiously, promising to do what he could, and then went before Congress to ask for a $1.4 billion increase in military spending.

During those dark days Wallace paid a visit to Cordell Hull and found the old Tennessean in particularly gloomy spirits. "He visioned a world in which the Germans would be triumphant with the advantage of the British fleet," Wallace said in his diary. "He feels we shall be confronted with the necessity of deciding whether to trade with the Germans or to shape our economy without trade with Europe."[45]

Wallace tried repeatedly to force Hull into a more positive frame of mind. "When things are bad I like to do something about it," said Wallace. "Haven't you something to suggest?" But the secretary of state did not. "He steadfastly refused to do anything but paint a very bad situation."[46]

Wallace already had begun searching for positive responses and ways to bolster his beleaguered chief. As early as April 25 he had written Roosevelt a three-page, single-spaced letter about the international economic situation, impressing upon him the need for the continued large-scale purchase of gold as a means of bolstering the Allies' trading capacity. The letter was the first among many over the coming years on the need for postwar planning and the necessity for new international trade agreements.

Wallace took a particular interest in rubber and began pressing for increased production in the Western Hemisphere as a means of war preparation. Most U.S. rubber came from the Philippines and East Indies, which Wallace feared might soon come under Japanese control. When an Agriculture Department chemist told him about new methods of producing synthetic rubber secretly developed by Standard Oil, Wallace immediately relayed the information, and its importance, to Roosevelt.

Increasingly, he addressed foreign policy issues in his public speeches, trying to build support for the president's position. "This is an hour of trial for the entire world," he said in a speech to Department of Agriculture military veterans. ". . . For an entire continent, if not for the entire world, the sands of life as we have known it are running fast. . . . The ideas of the madmen run beyond all imagination. They respect force and force alone. We must be sufficiently armed therefore to command respect and fear from each and every aggressor. Only through such military preparedness can we be sure of peace. But military preparedness is not enough. Military preparedness has the same relation to agricultural and industrial preparedness as good arms and legs have to good vital organs."[47]

Above all, he pressed for new forms of hemispheric cooperation in the belief that Pan-Americanism offered an important source of strength to the United States. In particular, Wallace proposed the formation of an all-America selling corporation to bolster the trading position of Latin American countries and offset the economic muscle of the Germania purchasing corporation. He sent along portions of Thorstein Veblen's writings in an effort to broaden the president's view of the relation between the international situation and economics.*

---

*Privately Wallace had reason to believe that Roosevelt's views on the foreign situation were sometimes oddly shaped. There was, for example, Roosevelt's insistence that the Agriculture Department vacate its experimental farm in Arlington, across the Potomac River from Washington. The land was to be used to house part of an army batallion and a regiment of cavalry. "Apparently the president is very keen about having a lot of soldiers near Washington," Wallace wrote in his diary. ". . . The idea seems to be that the president has the War of 1812 in mind and doesn't want some foreign na-

Nor were all of Wallace's efforts of an extracurricular nature. Roosevelt assigned him to devise a report on how American agriculture might cope in the event that European trade was cut off. He placed Wallace on the newly formed National Advisory Defense Commission, an umbrella group coordinating the activities of business, labor, and agricultural leaders rapidly being brought into the war effort. And, in utmost secrecy, the president asked Wallace, his cabinet's only member with a scientific background, to serve as his personal liaison to Vannevar Bush.

Bush was an electrical engineer by training, a spare New England conservative by temperament. He had been a dean and vice president at the Massachusetts Institute of Technology before leaving academe to become president of the Carnegie Institute in Washington. Subsequently Roosevelt appointed Bush to head the National Defense Research Committee (an arm of the National Advisory Defense Commission), which was intended to coordinate the work of scientists on behalf of the war effort.

Bush was one of a handful of men on the planet who knew of the secret letter Albert Einstein had written to Franklin Roosevelt in August 1939 telling him "it may become possible" to build powerful new bombs based on nuclear chain reactions.[48] He knew also that German scientists were working on such a project at the Kaiser Wilhelm Institute in Berlin. Initially Roosevelt had assigned the top-secret matter to the Bureau of Standards, where it had languished for months. In June 1940 Roosevelt secretly transferred control of the atomic energy project to Bush's committee.

A fortnight later Bush spent a quiet evening with Henry Wallace. Only a few weeks had passed since Wallace told Hull, "When things are bad I like to do something about it." Now Wallace knew what could, undoubtedly must, be done. "It seems that if two or three pounds of Uranium 235 are assembled together in one spot," Wallace wrote in his diary, "a chain reaction would be set in motion and nobody knows what would happen. The result might be an explosion as great as that when the meteor hit Arizona many thousands of years ago. Or the result might be merely continuous heat. . . . In view of the German activity [Bush] absolutely must work on it, but at the same time it is one of the most dangerous jobs he has ever tackled."[49]

They were men of vastly different backgrounds, but they spoke the same language. The next afternoon, a Sunday, Wallace took Bush on an outing to the agricultural research station at Beltsville. "We had an enjoyable time in the open air," Wallace wrote. "His father was a Universalist minister. Bush himself has a farm in southeast New Hampshire, about sixty miles from

---

tion to come in and burn up Washington. Perhaps his ideas are sound, although responsible people seem to be inclined to pooh-pooh them."

Boston, where he raises turkeys. He would like to develop a machine to grub out the juniper in New England pastures."[50]

A juniper-grubbing machine—and the atomic bomb.

***

The German invasion of western Europe quickly crystallized the presidential race in the United States. Dozens of politicians and reporters collectively came to an understanding that Roosevelt would, indeed must, seek a third term. "The Democratic convention was held in Copenhagen this year," crowed a flippant Tommy Corcoran. Wallace said, in diary entry on April 24, that it was "quite certain" Roosevelt would run after Germany invaded Norway. Roosevelt probably reached the same conclusion about this time, yet he did not publicly state his intentions. He gave no one authority to manage his political affairs and appointed no convention manager. When Wallace visited an ailing Harry Hopkins at the White House in late May, Hopkins said he had not "heard the third term mentioned" since he moved there.[51]

His silence had a strategic purpose. The war made national unity imperative, and Roosevelt felt he must appear to be above politics. To that end he decided he had to be drafted by the Democratic convention. The call must be spontaneous and, if possible, unanimous. There would be no more tolerance for rivals or favorite sons. When a group of Iowans approached the president in May, asking permission to support Wallace on the first ballot, Roosevelt firmly told them no. An embarrassed Wallace hastily informed Roosevelt he had no part in their request. "I'll do whatever you want me to do," he said.[52]

There remained two other important political questions. First, whom would the Republicans nominate? Second, who would be Roosevelt's running mate?

The first question, on its face, was beyond Roosevelt's ability to control. The leading candidates were young New York prosecutor Thomas E. Dewey, Senator Robert Taft of Ohio, and Senator Arthur Vandenberg of Michigan. A dark horse possibility was Wendell Willkie, a Wall Street lawyer who was a native of Indiana. The three front-runners were conservative, although Dewey was said to have some progressive social views, and isolationist. Of Willkie not much was known, since he had never held public office and had no record.

As usual, Roosevelt's political skill was underestimated. Acting on the eve of the Republican National Convention in Philadelphia in mid-June, Roosevelt fired isolationist Secretary of War Harry Woodring (he had twice refused direct orders to ship airplanes to Britain on grounds that they were needed for American defense) and persuaded Secretary of the Navy Charles

Edison (the inventor Thomas Edison's son) to resign and run for governor of New Jersey.

In their stead he named two of the nation's best-known Republicans. Henry Stimson, who had been Herbert Hoover's secretary of state, was appointed to head the War Department. The Chicago publisher Frank Knox, a Bull Mooser who had been Alf Landon's running mate in 1936, was named navy secretary. The appointments neatly illustrated the deep internationalist-isolationist division within the Republican party and threw their convention into chaos.

As for the Democratic vice presidential nomination, mystery and intrigue prevailed. The Iowa Democratic Party chairman, Ed Birmingham, spoke for many when he burst into Wallace's office one day and exclaimed, "Now look here! What's going on?"[53] The same doubt and uncertainty that had surrounded the presidential nomination for the past year now enveloped the vice presidential nomination, compounded by the addition of a whole new group of second-tier figures who had designs on the job.

Senator James F. Byrnes of South Carolina, a jaunty Irishman who had emerged as a leading administration water carrier, was interested. So were House Speaker William Bankhead of Alabama, Senate Majority Leader Alben Barkley of Kentucky, Reconstruction Finance Corporation Chief Jesse Jones of Texas, Supreme Court Justice William O. Douglas of Washington State, Senator Clyde Herring of Iowa, and others. There was even the possibility, given Roosevelt's drive for national unity, of a fusion ticket with a vice presidential nominee drawn from the ranks of progressive Republicans. Senator Robert La Follette Jr. of Wisconsin, former Governor Alf Landon of Kansas, and New York City's mayor, Fiorello La Guardia, were considered possibilities.

Somewhere on this crowded field—nobody knew where, some didn't know he was even there—was Henry Agard Wallace of Iowa. He was fifty-one years old, a Democrat of only four years, a man more interested in the genetic properties of corn than in the precinct returns from Jersey City. He didn't drink alcohol or smoke cigarettes, and he cared far more about the ancient prophets than about the urban bosses.

Yet, by the same processes of thought with which Roosevelt had eliminated so many Democratic contenders over the previous months, one could see the emergence of Wallace. He was a genuine New Dealer, an internationalist, a loyalist on the Supreme Court and third-term issues. There was no hint of corruption about Wallace. He was a mainline Protestant. He had a strong geographic base and the support of an important constituency.

Moreover, Wallace was in vigorous good health, and anxiety over health had come to weigh increasingly on Roosevelt's mind. The presence of Harry Hopkins in the White House was now a daily reminder of the limitations imposed by illness. In a final preconvention chat with Farley on a humid evening in Hyde Park, Roosevelt indirectly said he would seek a third term and hinted he was considering Wallace as his running mate.

"Boss, I'm going to be very direct," replied Farley. "Henry Wallace won't add a bit of strength to the ticket. . . . He won't bring you the support you may expect in the farm belt and he will lose votes for you in the East. Beyond that . . . I think it would be a terrible thing to have him President. He has always been most cordial and cooperative with me, but I think you must know that the people look on him as a wild-eyed fellow."[54]

Roosevelt did not reply directly. Instead, he raised the issue of health. "The man running with me must be in good health because there is no telling how long I can hold out," he declared. "You know, Jim, a man with paralysis can have a breakup at any time. While my heart and lungs are good and the other organs are functioning along okay . . . nothing in this life is certain."[55]

It was "the first and last time in all the years I knew him," Farley later wrote, "that he ever discussed his physical condition with me."[56]

Wallace was aware his name was being mentioned. To visitors who said he should be the vice presidential nominee, he gave the same careful reply. The "man should be picked for vice president who would be most likely to contribute to victory in the fall."[57] He gave no indication he was such a man, nor did he deny it. He adopted no strategy and assembled no team on behalf of winning the nomination. Some Iowa Democrats wanted to commit the delegation to Wallace for vice president but he discouraged the plan, a stance that also avoided direct conflict with Clyde Herring's surging ambitions.

He was convinced Roosevelt wanted "total control" of the convention. Roosevelt alone would make the choice, Wallace believed. In that he was entirely correct.

He had received two hints of what the choice would be. They were hints only, but they came from sources so close to Roosevelt as to make them credible. The first came early from Sam Rosenman, the New York judge who served part-time as one of Roosevelt's speechwriters and closest confidants. At Appleby's urging, Wallace had spoken to a B'nai B'rith dinner co-chaired by Rosenman's wife. Afterwards Wallace and Rosenman chatted, and the secretary said he believed that Roosevelt should seek a third term. "In that case," Rosenman replied without hesitation, "you'll have to be the vice president."[58]

The second hint came late from Harry Hopkins. In a rambling discussion of the political scene, Hopkins reviewed the various vice presidential prospects. Hull was the obvious choice, said Hopkins, but he doubted whether the secretary of state would accept the job. Absent Hull, "the president might come as close to agreeing on me as anyone," Wallace said Hopkins told him.[59]

There was a sideshow aspect to all of this. The main event was in western Europe, where Germany was routing the forces of democracy. In the first days of June, British forces had retreated to the water's edge, where they were saved only by a makeshift evacuation from Dunkirk. On June 5 the German army moved into France and five days later reached Paris. On that day, June 10, 400,000 troops from Mussolini's Italy attacked the lightly held French Riviera. The "hand that held the dagger has struck it into the back of its neighbor," Roosevelt declared in a noted speech at the University of Virginia in Charlottesville.[60]

It took only twelve more days for France to collapse. Paris and half of metropolitan France became a German province. The remaining portions were to be governed by a puppet government friendly to Germany. The French fleet was neutralized.

Two days later the Republicans gathered in Philadelphia to pick their presidential candidate. The stage was set for two of the most extraordinary political conventions of the twentieth century.

CHAPTER ELEVEN

"THAT ONE MAN WAS ROOSEVELT."

No one quite like Wendell Willkie of Elwood, Indiana, ever strode into the political arena. He was a big, shaggy, bear of a man with a mussed-up mop of hair and an aw-shucks grin. For decades the Republican Party had been held in the tight grasp of conservative professionals in high starched collars. Now came Willkie the amateur, in his rumpled searsucker suit and casual straw boater, banging on the gates. There was something quintessentially American about him. He was so optimistic, so energetic, so breathtakingly candid.

He burst onto the scene from nowhere. He was a high-powered lawyer-businessman who had never run for office. He had voted for Roosevelt in 1932 and still called himself a Democrat as late as 1938. His domestic politics were distinctly progressive, and in foreign policy he was an outspoken internationalist. So unknown was Willkie within the Republican Party that as late as May 1940 he was the choice of only 3 percent of the party's voters in the Gallup poll, a distant fourth behind Thomas Dewey, Arthur Vandenberg, and Robert Taft.

Willkie's astonishing rise had been boosted immeasurably by two interrelated factors. One was the fluid state of American public opinion. (Wallace observed more than once during this period that public opinion was moving faster than Roosevelt.) The other was a huge buildup he received from some of the nation's most influential publications, including the *New York Herald Tribune, Time* and *Life* magazines, the Scripps-Howard chain, *Look* magazine, and the Cowles newspapers in Minneapolis and Des Moines.

At the end of the first ballot in Philadelphia, Willkie was in third place with 105 votes. Dewey had 360 votes; Taft was second with 189 votes. Then, as an enthralled nation followed the proceedings on radio, something remarkable happened. Thousands of supporters in the galleries chanted "We want Willkie! We want Willkie!" as the forty-eight-year-old utilities executive picked up strength on each successive ballot. On the sixth ballot Willkie surged over the top with 998 delegates. The effect on the nation of this robust exercise in democracy was electrifying. Here, it seemed, was a fresh-faced can-do sort of fellow come from America's heartland to do battle with "the Champ."

The reality of it was more complicated. Willkie was a sophisticated man with an unconventional lifestyle, more comfortable in the salons of New York intellectuals than in humble Hoosier homes. The galleries had been packed through chicanery, and the Republican Party was hardly of one mind about the policies, domestic and foreign, Willkie represented. The first indication of that reality was Willkie's choice of Senate Minority Leader Charles McNary of Oregon, an isolationist, as his running mate.

But all that hardly mattered. The public heard what it heard and believed what it wanted.

The effect of the Republican convention on Roosevelt and his men was sobering. Roosevelt's first impulse, he told his cabinet, was to run against Willkie as a mouthpiece of corporate America. Roosevelt "was convinced that Willkie at heart was a totalitarian," Wallace wrote in his diary. But the president also thought the Willkie-McNary ticket was the strongest the Republicans could have fielded. Wallace agreed. "[I] still think that Willkie is undoubtedly the most capable of the Republican candidates and that he has a more statesmanlike attitude on international relationships" than the other candidates.[1] Wallace also had high esteem for McNary, whose very name symbolized the long struggle for agricultural equity during the 1920s.

The Republican convention redoubled Roosevelt's determination that his own nomination be spontaneous. He had to be drafted by acclamation against his wishes. To that end he decided to write a letter, to be read by Speaker Will Bankhead at the opening session of the Democratic convention, telling delegates he did not desire to run again and releasing them from commitment to him.

So, with Roosevelt's risky strategy guiding them by stealth, Democrats began gathering in Chicago for their twenty-eighth national convention.

The political circumstances facing Franklin D. Roosevelt in the summer of 1940 could hardly have been more daunting. With the war in Europe threatening to become a catastrophe, with his countrymen deeply divided over American involvement, with the weight of tradition and much of the press against a president serving more than two terms, Roosevelt's fabled political skills were challenged on every front.

Forces over which Roosevelt had little or no control buffeted him daily from both the right and the left. Charles Lindbergh, the nation's most popular hero, denounced Roosevelt's war preparations in a national radio broadcast. German U-boats continued their deadly attacks on Allied ships. A group of thirty prominent Americans began agitating for compulsory military service. Congress moved uncertainly in many directions.

On the single momentous day of July 10—five days prior to the opening of the Democratic convention—portentous events filled the airwaves. On that day German warplanes began the Battle of Britain with their first direct attack on England. Roosevelt asked Congress for a massive, $4.8 billion increase in military spending. And Henry L. Stimson, having finally been confirmed by a divided Senate, became secretary of war.

The following day, Thursday, July 11, Henry A. Wallace boarded a train bound for Chicago.

On board with him were Harry Hopkins and a couple of his aides from the Commerce Department. In Hopkins's pocket was the one and only presidential directive he was to have for the next six days: Roosevelt's handwritten message to the convention stating he did not wish to run again.

Together Hopkins and Wallace constituted virtually the entire convention team for either Roosevelt or Wallace. Hopkins was acting alone, without Roosevelt's permission or prohibition. When Hopkins asked Wallace whether he planned to have anyone else in Chicago working on his behalf, the secretary said Undersecretary of Agriculture Claude Wickard might be coming out on Sunday. That was all. It was an amazing situation and, to Hopkins at least, an altogether scary one.

In Chicago, Hopkins set up a base of operations in suite 308–309 of the Blackstone Hotel, across the street from the convention hall. One of his rooms was already famous; it had served as the notorious "smoke-filled room" in which Republican bosses settled on Warren G. Harding as their candidate in 1920. The commerce secretary had no official power whatever. He wasn't even a delegate to the convention. His only authority derived from a telephone in the bathroom that was said to be a direct line to the White House. The phone was symbolic only. It never once rang until after Roosevelt had been nominated.

Wallace's headquarters, located in two small rooms on the third floor of the Stevens Hotel, was even less imposing. There was not so much as a plate of hors d'oeuvres, much less a bottle of bourbon, to entice passing delegates.

The unimposing Wickard, who had some experience in Indiana politics, took charge of operations. His wife, Louise, answered the phone. As political operations went, it was a forlorn and amateurish enterprise.

Wallace, typically, didn't care. He threw himself into the operations of the platform committee, where his task was to help fashion a foreign policy statement sufficiently broad to keep internationalists and isolationists from each other's throats. His only specific political instruction to Wickard was to refrain from seeking a vote binding the Iowa delegation to him for vice president.

The convention opened on Monday, July 15, with the eleven hundred delegates in a churlish state of mind. A huge gray picture of the president hanging behind the podium in the cavernous Chicago Stadium served as a constant reminder that their task was to renominate Roosevelt, but they approached the job with the enthusiasm of a chain gang, in the words of one reporter. Delegates felt confused and manipulated and showed it when Chicago's mayor, Ed Kelly, a big redheaded street-smart fellow, tried to stampede the convention for Roosevelt on opening night and received only tepid applause for his effort. Far warmer was the reception given to one of Roosevelt's opponents, the affable party chairman, Jim Farley. Even before House Speaker Will Bankhead rose to deliver a mind-numbing keynote address, Hopkins had concluded it would not be an auspicious moment to read Roosevelt's message.

Many New Dealers woke up the next morning in a state of panic. Harold Ickes fired off a highly alarmed telegram to Roosevelt. The "convention is bleeding to death and . . . your reputation and prestige may bleed to death with it," Ickes said. Secretary of Labor Frances Perkins was less hysterical but no less concerned. She called Roosevelt and urged him to come immediately to Chicago and address the surly delegates. "The situation is . . . just as sour as it can be," she said. Roosevelt declined the invitation and suggested she ask Eleanor Roosevelt to come instead. The conversation ended with a discussion of the vice presidential nomination. The president praised Wallace as a man who "thinks right" and "has the general ideas we have." He concluded by telling Perkins to go to Hopkins's room and tell him, "I have decided on Wallace."[2]

As Wallace devoted his entire attention to the arduous and contentious platform negotiations, his headquarters operation quickly fell into disarray. Wickard learned to his dismay that Luther Harr, chairman of the Pennsylvania Democratic Party, was waging his own, overt campaign on behalf of Wallace. Among other things Harr had ordered up political paraphernalia including balloons and twenty thousand matchbooks inscribed "Win with Winners—Roosevelt and Wallace." Wickard strongly believed balloons and matchbooks were not the path to Roosevelt's heart.

Paul Appleby had remained in Washington, considering it inappropriate for him to attend the convention, since he was a civil servant covered by the Hatch Act. But he kept in touch with events by phone and soon realized things were slipping out of Wickard's control. "Hold your horses," he told Harr in a telephone call. "Don't rent any more rooms. Don't let out a balloon and don't hand out a match. I'll be there in the morning." Within two hours Appleby had gone to a barber, cashed a check at a neighborhood store, dictated a letter of resignation from government, and boarded the Capital Limited headed west.[3]

That evening the pro-Roosevelt forces at the convention rebounded somewhat. Senate Majority Leader Alben Barkley, always a mighty orator, gave the delegates a hearty red-meat attack on Wendell Willkie, and the crowd loved it. But as he built to a powerful climax he drew from his pocket Roosevelt's letter saying he had not "any desire or purpose to continue" as president and brought the audience to stunned silence. Delegates looked searchingly at one another trying to discern what was happening.

Then from the ether a huge voice filled Chicago Stadium. "No! No! No! We want Roosevelt! We want Roosevelt! WE WANT ROOSEVELT!" As the relentless voice boomed over the public address system delegates picked up the chant, began waving state standards and marching around the hall. "The party wants Roosevelt! Everybody wants Roosevelt! The world wants Roosevelt!"[4]

It didn't take reporters long to find the source of the voice. Mayor Kelly, knowing the message Barkley planned to read, had left nothing to chance. In a tiny electrical room in the basement of the stadium, the major had installed one Thomas D. Garry and given him a microphone tied to the public address system. Garry, a small potbellied man with a powerful set of lungs, served as Chicago's superintendent of sewers. Newspapers called him "the voice from the sewers" and derided the demonstration as a shabby imitation of the thunderous gallery chant for Willkie at the Republican convention.

Shabby or not, however, the voice from the sewers had put the convention back on track. Hopkins was greatly relieved. When a reporter asked if the president's statement would cause any change in his plans, Hopkins blithely replied, "Not any, brother."[5]

Paul Appleby arrived in Chicago on Wednesday, July 17, and soon learned one reason for Hopkins's confidence. In an effort to build support for Roosevelt, Hopkins had let it be understood that the matter of his running mate was an open question to be settled by the convention. It seemed to Appleby that half of Chicago had an eye on the vice presidency.

To the list of well-established candidates—Paul McNutt, William Bankhead, Jesse Jones, James Byrnes, William O. Douglas—there were now added lesser contenders such as Senator Scott Lucas of Illinois, Congressman Sam Rayburn of Texas, Governor Lloyd C. Stark of Missouri, and Assistant Secretary of War Louis Johnson. Appleby put the number of would-be vice presidents at seventeen and rising.

Appleby was not totally dismayed. For one thing, he didn't believe for a minute that the vice presidential nomination would be left to the delegates. He agreed with Wallace that Roosevelt alone would make the choice. He also believed Wallace had a surprisingly strong and "very diversified" base of support that included Frances Perkins, the labor leaders Sidney Hillman and Phil Murray, Governor Culbert Olson of California, progressive southerners such as Senator Lister Hill of Alabama and Senator Claude Pepper of Florida, the Bronx political boss Ed Flynn, many delegates belonging to the League of Women Voters, the Iowa delegation, much of the Pennsylvania delegation, most of the Michigan delegation, and many delegates from agricultural areas.[6]

Appleby's strategy was to build on that base as best he could and repeatedly notify the White House, through whatever channels were available, that support for Wallace was solid. Actual political strength, he was convinced, would be more compelling to Roosevelt than matchbooks.

That evening the convention completed two major pieces of business. The platform was adopted, after Roosevelt bridged the gap between internationalists and isolationists by adding the words "except in case of attack" to a plank promising to keep America out of war. And, in an atmosphere that struck some observers as somber, the party picked Franklin Roosevelt as its presidential candidate. Perhaps because everybody knew who would win, or perhaps because Hopkins's strong-arm tactics had offended so many delegates, the mood in Chicago Stadium was something short of elation. The delegates gave Roosevelt $946\frac{1}{2}$ votes. Farley received $72\frac{1}{2}$ votes and John Nance Garner 61. Farley, ever the good party soldier, went to the podium and moved to make the nomination unanimous.

Roosevelt had his draft. He had won nomination to a third term, something unprecedented in American history, and he had done so without asking. And he had brought his party's conservatives to their knees, avenging the defeat and humiliation they had inflicted upon him during his second term.

But he was by no means finished.

⚜

Sometime during the evening Roosevelt had called the white-haired, courtly Cordell Hull and asked him to be his running mate. As Roosevelt fully anticipated, Hull refused. "I said 'No, by God!' and 'By God, No!' " Hull later recalled. With that, Roosevelt turned to Wallace. At last the phone in Hopkins's bathroom rang. The president identified his choice and told Hopkins to make it happen. Hopkins was not averse to Wallace, but he tried briefly to explain that it might be a tough sell. The mood in Chicago was sour, he said, and there was a widespread belief that the choice would be left to the convention. "It's Wallace," Roosevelt snapped.[7]

Wallace was notified by a 2 A.M. telephone call from Sam Rosenman. The judge congratulated the agriculture secretary and said he hoped Wallace would "play ball with the boss."[8] Wallace needed no encouragement. Although he was exhausted from the lengthy platform deliberations, Wallace immediately set to work drafting his acceptance speech. A few hours later he called Appleby and told him to come immediately to Hopkins's private room at the Ambassador Hotel.

When he arrived at about 7:30 A.M., Appleby found Hopkins sprawled on a couch in his pajamas and his bleary-eyed boss sitting nearby. "Shake hands with the vice president," Hopkins said in a chipper way. Appleby recalled feeling a little foolish. "In any ordinary case I would have slapped Henry on the shoulder or something rather than shaking hands," Appleby said later. But shake hands they did.[9]

They set out to map a strategy. The key, they concluded, was for Roosevelt to call the five or six men most likely to feel slighted by Wallace's nomination and soothe any bruised feelings. But when they informed Roosevelt of their plan he flatly rejected it. He would call one—and only one—of the disappointed contenders. The rest would have to be told by Wallace and Hopkins.

Roosevelt chose to call Farley, his longtime lieutenant and recent rival. In a voice as warm as it had ever been, Roosevelt informed his postmaster general, "Henry Wallace is the best man to nominate in this emergency." Farley said he planned to support Jesse Jones, arguing that the conservative Texan would be a bigger asset to the ticket. Roosevelt would have none of it. "I think Henry is perfect," the president said. "I like him. He's the kind of fellow I want around. He's honest. He thinks right. He's a digger." When Farley responded that many people considered Wallace a mystic, Roosevelt snapped, "He's not a mystic. He's a philosopher. He's got ideas. He thinks right. He'll help the people think."[10]

Even as they spoke, opposition to Wallace was mounting. Calls and telegrams poured into the White House protesting the choice. James Byrnes reached Roosevelt on the phone to express his personal disappointment. Roosevelt mollified the senator and persuaded him to work on Wallace's behalf. Speaker Bankhead was even more bitter when he reached Roosevelt, and he was not mollified at all. A group of eighty-five delegates backing Governor Culbert Olson fired off a cheeky round-robin telegram saying Wallace's nomination would be a "grave mistake" and declaring "that such dictatorial tactics should at least have been more subtly planned."[11]

Harold Ickes, seized by another bout of panic, sent Roosevelt a telegram saying Wallace would not do at all. Ickes suggested the University of Chicago's chancellor, Robert Maynard Hutchins, be named instead. If Hutchins was not acceptable, Ickes added, he would be proud to serve as the president's running mate himself. That at least drew a chuckle from Roosevelt. "Dear old Harold," he said, "he'd get fewer votes than Wallace in that convention."[12]

It fell to Wallace to deal with Paul McNutt. The former Indiana governor was summoned to Wallace's hotel room around noon in the hope that he could be persuaded to withdraw and give a speech seconding the agriculture secretary. McNutt arrived "an intensely disappointed man," in Wallace's words. For an interminable period of time, Wallace listened as McNutt listed all the reasons why he could have won the nomination "if the president kept his hands off." But at length McNutt agreed to second Wallace's nomination. They emerged and posed painfully for photographers.[13]

For Appleby the day was one long rush from brushfire to brushfire. Even the Iowa delegation was rumored not to be totally safe. Jesse Jones dutifully agreed to withdraw his name, but his real intentions remained open to question. The president's son Elliott, a former business associate of Jones, was telling delegates his father didn't care who was named and Jones would be quite acceptable. And there were disturbing reports that Farley was attempting to forge an alliance with McNutt.

The party's conservative wing was in open rebellion. Unable to stop Roosevelt, it was determined to stop Wallace. When Governor E. E. Rivers of Georgia raised the subject of the vice presidential nomination with Governor Leon Phillips of Oklahoma, he was surprised to hear Phillips exclaim, "Why, Henry's my second choice." Rivers asked Phillips who his first choice was. "Anyone—red, white, black or yellow—that can get the nomination," Phillips replied without a hint of a smile.[14]

In his headquarters at the Blackstone Hotel, Harry Hopkins smoked one cigarette after another. He was a beleaguered man. Party officials and discontented delegates, angry and frustrated over the whole convention, had found in the Wallace nomination a means to voice their rage. Clearly unsettled, Hopkins tried again to warn Roosevelt that Wallace's nomination was in jeopardy. Roosevelt had heard enough and laid down his marker. "Well, damn it to hell," he told Hopkins, "they will go for Wallace or I won't run, and you can jolly well tell them so."[15]

As the president was threatening to refuse the nomination, his wife was arriving in Chicago aboard a small charter plane. Farley went to the airport to pick her up. As she listened to Farley describe the deteriorating situation, the first lady grew appalled and alarmed. They decided she should speak with Roosevelt about it directly. Farley listened to Eleanor's end of the conversation as she spoke and later claimed in his autobiography that she said, "Henry Wallace won't do." She later claimed that Farley had misunderstood her—that she was merely passing along what she thought was the mood of the delegates.[16]

Whatever was said, Roosevelt was clearly irked. He asked to speak to Farley and impatiently told him, "I've given my word" to Wallace. "What do you do when you give your word?" he asked. Replied Farley, "I keep it. If you gave your word to Wallace you should keep it; but it was a mistake to give it."[17]

Mistake or not, the whole cast of characters—Wallace, McNutt, Farley, Appleby, Wickard, Bankhead, Mrs. Roosevelt—soon arrived at Chicago Stadium, where they took their places on the rostrum. Ilo Wallace, newly arrived from Des Moines, was seated next to the first lady. She had just survived her first ride on an airplane; now she was witnessing her first political convention. The evening began with a prayer from the Reverend Dr. Clyde McGee that "no bitterness or passion born of these troubled times" should cloud the convention's thinking.[18]

The first to be nominated, since Alabama was the first state in the roll call, was the native son William Bankhead. Bankhead, intoned the nominating speaker, was "cautious and constructive—prudent and progressive" and possessor of "a brilliant mind and knightly soul." Then Arizona, despite Appleby's effort to dissuade it, yielded to Maryland, which nominated Jesse Jones. Both nominations drew wild cheers.[19]

Appleby, meanwhile, had other problems. It had been agreed that Wallace's name would be placed in nomination by Frank O'Connor, a well-respected Dubuque Catholic who had attended every Democratic convention since 1912. But O'Connor was not a delegate and therefore technically ineligible to speak. Appleby frantically made arrangements for John Valentine, Democratic candidate for governor of Iowa, to deliver the speech if an objection was raised to O'Connor. In the event, no objection was raised. The next state called, Arkansas, yielded to Iowa and O'Connor began making his case.

Wallace, said O'Connor, was a "man of rare and unexcelled integrity of the very highest intelligence—a man who in his public and private life has never betrayed a friend or a principle; a man of ripe experience for these ominous times . . . a God-fearing, modest American of the highest character, worthy of and equipped to meet the responsibilities of any public trust." A chorus of boos and catcalls rained down upon O'Connor from the galleries. One delegate screamed into an open microphone, "Give us a Democrat. We don't want a Republican."[20]

A little seven-minute floor demonstration was staged for Wallace, less than half the time delegates had paraded for Bankhead. The situation could have been worse, Appleby thought. And he was right. The situation was about to become much worse.

While a speech nominating Senator Alva Adams of Colorado was being delivered, an apologetic McNutt approached Wallace with a copy of the speech he would give withdrawing himself from the race. "I'm sorry Henry," said McNutt, "this is the best I can do." McNutt would indeed withdraw, but he would not second Wallace's nomination as promised.[21]

As McNutt rose to speak, the galleries, packed with three thousand of his fervent supporters, threw the convention hall into bedlam. Barkley banged his gavel demanding order, while the white-haired McNutt basked in the ovation. "Stay in it, Paul," the galleries cried. His words were all but drowned in cheers. "America needs strong, logical, liberal and able leadership," said McNutt. ". . . We have such a leader in Franklin Delano Roosevelt. He is my commander-in-chief. I follow his wishes. . . ." McNutt never mentioned Wallace's name.[22]

Something close to mob mentality had taken over Chicago Stadium. Every mention of Wallace's name was greeted with boos and hisses, every mention of McNutt and Bankhead and Jones drew thunderous approval. Wallace's name was seconded by such popular figures as Governor Olson, the United Mine Workers chief Phillip Murray, and Congressman Sam Rayburn of Texas, but to no avail. Raucous jeers greeted them. On the platform Claude Wickard wondered briefly whether they were safe. Ilo Wallace was near tears. "You could see it," Frances Perkins later wrote. "Her brain was reeling inside her head. The antagonism was crushing." Eleanor Roosevelt gently reached over and took her hand.

"Why are they booing my Henry?" Ilo asked.[23]

Henry Wallace gazed into the middle distance, his mouth half open, expressionless. "It will come out all right," he said to Wickard, "it will come out all right." Behind the stillness of Wallace's face was "agony," Perkins thought. "He had a face of utter, blank suffering. . . . I have never lived through anything worse."[24]

At the White House, Franklin Roosevelt sat in the Oval Room playing solitaire, listening to the proceedings with growing disgust. It was difficult to tell from listening to the radio whether the pandemonium resulted from meaningless gallery rigging or reflected genuine delegate sentiment, but it no longer mattered. It was a hot, humid evening in Washington, and Roosevelt was out of patience. Suddenly he reached for a pad and began to scribble. Shortly he handed his notes to Sam Rosenman and told him to "clean it up" because he might have to "deliver it very quickly."[25]

In defiant prose Roosevelt proposed to tell the Democratic Party it had always failed when it thought "in terms of dollars instead of in terms of human values." The party "must go wholly one way or wholly the other," Roosevelt would say. "It cannot face both directions at the same time. By declining the honor of the nomination for the Presidency, I can restore that opportunity to the convention. I so do."[26]

Rosenman gulped in disbelief. Roosevelt calmly resumed playing solitaire.

The statement was never read. As the excruciating nominating process came to a close, Eleanor Roosevelt arose to save the day for Wallace and her husband. Her dignity, her utter sincerity, had a magical calming effect. The boisterous free-for-all suddenly ended. "We people in the United States have got to realize that we face now a grave and serious situation," she said. ". . . We cannot tell from day to day what may come. This is no ordinary time, no time for thinking about anything except what we can best do for the country as a whole, and that responsibility is on each and every one of us as individuals."[27]

The convention hall roared in approval. When business resumed, the galleries again chanted for McNutt and booed Wallace, but now they sounded petty and narrow. The idea of the nation without Roosevelt at the helm seemed unthinkable. The notion of denying him his chosen running mate had lost its appeal.

By the time balloting began, only Bankhead and Wallace remained in the race. In the early voting Bankhead appeared to be moving ahead, but his strength was confined mainly to the Deep South. Jimmy Byrnes and others moved around the floor to keep delegates in line. "Do you want a president or a vice president," Byrnes demanded.[28] The final tally was 626 11/30 votes for Wallace, 329 3/5 for Bankhead, and a scattering for others.

Speaker Bankhead, whether from disappointment or because of his advancing years, dispatched his brother, Senator John Bankhead of Alabama, to express loyalty to the ticket and move that Wallace's nomination be unanimous.

Wallace eagerly awaited his chance to speak. For all his gentleman-and-a-scholar demeanor, he looked forward to squarely confronting his foes. His acceptance speech, on which he had been working off and on since receiving Rosenman's early-morning call, was as clear as exposition of Wallace family idealism as he could muster. "Military defense—yes," his speech declared. "We cannot permit the wolf of ruthless totalitarianism inside our doors." But he added,

Complete preparedness is more than tanks and guns and aircraft. It is more than well-trained officers and adequate reserves. To repel the sneaking enemy that burrows from within, the all-important preparedness is moral preparedness and social preparedness. The best preparedness of all is every able-bodied person working whole-heartedly for our mutual security and defense in the belief that he or she is needed. You are needed. You are all needed to see that every child is properly fed and clothed, to see that every family has an opportunity to protect itself from hunger, cold and lack of shelter.[29]

The speech was never given. Byrnes pleaded, then insisted, that Wallace not read it. The nightmarish prospect of a Democratic convention booing the very man it had just nominated for vice president was too much to risk, Byrnes thought. With great reluctance Wallace agreed to stand down.

Instead, at twenty-five minutes past midnight, the delegates heard the voice of their leader speaking from the White House. Roosevelt spoke gravely of the "very full heart" and "mixed feelings" with which he confronted another four years in office. But he had concluded that as commander in chief he had no right to decline his service while asking others to serve their country. "To-day all private plans, all private lives have been, in a sense, repealed by an overriding public danger."

He thanked his friend Jim Farley and expressed gratitude to the convention for nominating Henry Wallace for vice president. Wallace's "practical idealism will be of great service to me individually and to the nation as a whole," Roosevelt declared.

"We face one of the great choices of history," Roosevelt concluded. "It is not alone a choice of government, government by the people versus dictatorship. It is not alone a choice of freedom versus slavery. It is not alone a choice between moving forward or falling back. It is all of these rolled in one."[30] He would accept the nomination.

Not every delegate heard the greatness of Roosevelt's eloquent speech. Some remained rankled by the week's events, by the tactics of his supporters, by his insistence that Henry A. Wallace be on the ticket. As delegates filed out of Chicago Stadium shortly after one on Friday morning, a die-hard delegate from Louisiana grabbed the party insider George Allen by the lapels of his coat and vented his rage. "No one wanted Wallace—absolutely no one. Name me just one man that did."

Allen looked at the delegate with a smile. "Brother, that I can do—and that one man was Roosevelt."[31]

❦

This was "no ordinary time," Eleanor Roosevelt told the Democratic convention. This would be no ordinary presidential campaign, Franklin Roosevelt added. Henry A. Wallace fit the theme. Here was no ordinary candidate.

Newspaper reporters struggled manfully to introduce the peculiar new vice presidential candidate to their readers. He was, virtually every reporter agreed, "shy" or "reticent" or even "extremely shy." In any case, he was unusual. "He doesn't like parties; he doesn't enjoy the rough and tumble of political campaigning; he doesn't drink; he doesn't swear; he doesn't smoke or chew, and he doesn't eat with gusto," wrote one reporter. "But he does like to hurl boomerangs on the Ellipse and walk around in the grass barefooted."[32]

The boomerangs were a godsend to reporters. They exemplified Wallace's intellectual curiosity and eccentricity. "He relaxes by learning something new," wrote one newsman. His dietary experiments offered more grist. The soybean milk experiment ended when he grew to dislike the taste, it was noted. More recently he had tried existing entirely on corn but stopped after losing twelve pounds. Even now, it was noted, Wallace's diet was largely vegetarian, although he sometimes ate bacon as a concession to his hog-producing constituents. "A cheese sandwich and a glass of milk is still his favorite repast."[33]

Ilo Wallace was described as a "quietly beautiful" wife, entirely devoted to her family's well-being and tolerant of her husband's ways. "It amuses her that her husband, who is so keenly interested in how foodstuffs grow, isn't the slightest bit intrigued by their preparation for the table. She relates that one time he had to get a meal 'on his own. I came home and found he had "cooked" a meal of milk, cheese and crackers.' "[34]

Wallace's unaffected manner, his very ordinariness, was also cause for remark. "While leaving his office for a Cabinet meeting or a committee meeting at the Capitol, Wallace resembles the proverbial absent-minded professor or a small businessman about to confront the income-tax collector. His hat sits on the back of his head, shock of bangs droop on his forehead, his clothes look like they come from a mail-order house and his arms bulge with documents."[35]

Wallace's family was painted in idyllic tones. His oldest son, H. B., was newly married and engaged in experimental chicken farming in Iowa. Robert was in graduate school. His "attractive daughter," Jean, had just completed her first year of college. A sort of "Scotch calm" pervaded the family, wrote the *Des Moines Register* columnist Harlan Miller. In the wake of Wallace's nomination in Chicago, one of Jean's friends asked whether she had phoned her father in excitement. "We didn't phone," she replied, "but we almost sent him a telegram."[36]

The candidate's seventy-three-year-old mother was similarly reserved. "I'm afraid I am proud of him," said May Wallace, although she added, "He could do more good if he stayed where he is." Henry, she said, "is a worthy son of a worthy father and a worthy grandfather." The fact that the son was a Democrat while the father and grandfather were Republicans was "just a happenstance."[37]

Most reporters observed that Wallace was a "deeply religious" man who could quote the Bible at will. Several observed, without amplification, that he was considered a "mystic." They were almost unanimous in praising his energy and intellect. "He can generate terrific energy in speech-making and writing, in battling for his agricultural policies, in his frequent 3-mile walks from hotel to office of mornings, or in tossing a boomerang, a hobby," a *Washington Post* reporter wrote. Norman Cousins, the young editor of the *Saturday Review*, rode with Wallace on a train back to Des Moines after the convention and came away in awe. "Wallace seems to have read every book I could think of," Cousins said.[38]

His restless mind was even cause for humor. A cartoon newspaper feature called "Private Lives"—a sort of "Believe It or Not" about celebrities and politicians—portrayed him seated at a desk playing with a slide rule and said, "Mr. Wallace tells us that the rumor is wrong about his working calculus problems for mental relaxation, but he has spent 'a great deal of time in the evening using methods of multiple and partial co-relation to determine the net regression lines defining the relationship of one variable to another.' "[39]

Nor was the serious commentary offered by columnists and editorial writers unkind to Wallace. The tumultuous final session of the Democratic convention was generally seen as a black mark not on Wallace but on the party itself. The *New York Times* columnist Arthur Krock, no friend of the Roosevelt administration, wrote, "Mr. Wallace deserved a better fate than the boos that greeted the mention of his name and the distaste of the delegates over nominating him. He is able, thoughtful, honorable—the best of the New Deal type."[40]

Wallace "is a man of intellectual integrity, honesty, tolerance and strong faith in the democratic system," the *Washington Daily News* editorialized. ". . . The boos didn't count. And they were not personalized to kindly, retiring and scholarly Mr. Wallace. Rather they were merely the futile expression of a long pent-up independence in a convention weary of being told."[41]

Wallace himself said more or less the same thing, albeit more modestly, at a short press conference the day after he was nominated. Asked what he thought about the boos and catcalls that greeted his name, he grinned and said with a little chuckle, "It was a Democratic convention."[42]

In the aftermath of the convention, while still enjoying favorable comment in much of the press, Wallace blundered. Asked whether he planned to resign from the cabinet in order to devote himself to the campaign, Wallace said he would not. "I believe Herbert Hoover remained in the cabinet when he was campaigning for the presidency, didn't he," Wallace said.[43]

The idea of using Hoover, of all people, as an excuse to remain in office was ludicrous, and newspaper editorialists wasted no time in saying so. Wallace's "inclination to follow in the footsteps of Mr. Hoover may sharpen the hostility of many Democrats toward his nomination," said the *Washington Post*. It was noted that Wallace was in charge of a "vast and complex" department with a billion-dollar budget that could easily be put to political ends.[44]

Wallace's stance rapidly became a fiasco. Hoover had actually resigned as commerce secretary shortly after winning the Republican nomination in 1928. Franklin Roosevelt had likewise resigned as assistant secretary of the navy after being nominated for the vice presidency in 1920.

Wallace quickly backtracked. In a statement issued on July 26, he said he would resign from the department or take a leave of absence without pay before he began campaigning. Even so, his statement had a certain grudging tone. The insinuation that the farm program could be used as a "sort of political machine" only showed the "amazing ignorance" of those making the allegation, he said.[45]

His decision to leave office grew out of a "sober second thought," said the *Post*. "But it is nonetheless commendable for that reason." Henry Wallace "is no professional pay roller or time-server," said the *Washington Daily News*. ". . . If elected he will be an honest vice president. If defeated, he doubtless will resume without bitterness the life of a public-spirited private citizen."[46]

So began Henry Wallace's departure from the Department of Agriculture after the seven and one-half most eventful years of its history.

Already Wallace had put in place a team of talented professionals to carry on his policies at the department. The matter of his replacement as secretary proved more nettlesome. Above all, Wallace wanted a person dedicated to continuation of the New Deal's farm programs. He also thought it was important for the new secretary to have some stature with farmers and their interest groups. The process of elimination finally narrowed the field to Undersecretary Claude Wickard, a "dirt farmer" and former Indiana state senator, who could be counted upon for reliable support of Roosevelt and his policies.

The choice of Wickard contributed substantially to a rift between Wallace and his senior aide, Paul Appleby. In Appleby's mind Wickard was unsophisticated and unqualified. Moreover, Appleby had been privately dreaming of a plan that would have revolutionized the workings of the executive branch. He envisioned the creation of a permanent assistant secretary, a nonpolitical civil servant, who would administer the department while the secretary established policy. Over time Appleby hoped the idea, modeled after the British system, would spread throughout the executive branch and professionalize its workings. Wallace himself was keenly interested in the plan.

Almost certainly Appleby saw himself in the role of the permanent assistant secretary. Just as certainly, he knew Wickard would never agree to such a plan. He pleaded with Wallace to take a leave of absence rather than resign, thus leaving Appleby in de facto charge of the department. The matter was finally settled by Roosevelt, who decided Wallace must leave government altogether before the campaign began. Disappointed if not embittered, Appleby was powerless to stop Wickard's elevation. Wallace submitted his resignation effective at the close of business on September 5, 1940.*

Wickard moved into the secretary's handsome second-floor office, with its taupe carpet and red leather chairs, in a state of bewildered excitement. He was acutely aware that he sat in "Henry Wallace's chair," administering "Henry Wallace's farm program" in "Henry Wallace's department." He knew full well the awe in which the department's employees held Wallace.[47]

Indeed, Wickard shared it. "He without doubt was the greatest Secretary of Agriculture the Department has ever had," Wickard wrote in his diary. "He was a great economist, scientist and humanitarian. I feel that everyone is measuring me by his standards."[48]

Wickard was right on all counts.

Under H. A. Wallace the Department of Agriculture had become a powerful engine for progressive action. The department had broken new ground on every front—economic, social, scientific—and permanently changed the relationship between government and agriculture, the nation's largest and most important enterprise. The size, the scope, and the energy of Wallace's department were without parallel in the history of peacetime government agencies.

When Wallace came to the department, it had some 40,000 employees. When he left, it had more than 146,000 workers, with field offices and representatives in every county in the nation. Its two huge buildings along the Mall in Washington contained ten and one-half miles of corridors; tipped on their ends and stacked atop each other, the buildings would tower over the Empire State Building, one writer noted, and far exceeded in size any other federal department's home. The department's expenditures more than quadrupled during Wallace's tenure, from less than $280 million in 1932 to $1.5 billion in 1940 (plus millions more for the relief of impoverished tenant farmers).

New organizations proliferated and flourished along its busy halls: the Agricultural Adjustment Administration, the Soil Conservation Service, the Federal Surplus Commodities Corporation, the Farm Security Administration,

*Appleby remained as undersecretary until January 31, 1944, although never on good terms with Wickard and increasingly estranged from Wallace. He later served as assistant director of the Bureau of the Budget and subsequently became dean of the Maxwell Graduate School of Citizenship and Public Affairs at Syracuse University. He also served as budget director of the State of New York.

the Federal Crop Insurance Corporation, the Rural Electrification Administration, the Farm Credit Administration, the Commodity Credit Corporation. These agencies were home to some of the New Deal's most innovative programs: production controls and land-use planning, direct income subsidies to farmers, erosion control and soil conservation programs, the ever-normal granary, food stamp and school lunch programs, assistance to sharecroppers and the rural poor, credit availability and crop insurance programs.

Under Wallace the department's research center at Beltsville, Maryland, became the largest and most varied scientific agricultural station in the world. Dozens of other laboratories and research stations were opened around the country. The department's scientists combatted plant and animal diseases and pests, from grasshoppers and chinch bugs to brucellosis and Dutch elm disease. They studied nutrition and, for the first time, attempted to popularize scientific approaches to good diet and food preparation. They sought new solutions to soil erosion and deforestation and water depletion.

Department scientists invented new uses for agricultural products and developed scores of new plant and animal varieties. Over fifty varieties of wheat were developed at the department during the 1930s. Thatcher wheat, which didn't exist when Wallace came into office, was growing on 14.5 million acres in the United States and Canada when he left. Hundreds of other plant and animal breeds—from drought-resistant grasses to the Hungarian puli sheepdog—were introduced in the United States by the department's explorers.

"Economic and political understanding is our duty," Wallace once said. But he added, "Scientific understanding is our joy." For Wallace there was no such thing as too much science, nor could there ever be an end to it.

Science, of course, is not like wheat or cotton or automobiles. It cannot be overproduced. It does not come under the law of diminishing utility, which makes each extra unit in the stock of a commodity of less use than the preceding unit. In fact, the latest knowledge is usually the best. Moreover, knowledge grows or dies. It cannot live in cold storage. It is perishable and must be constantly renewed. Static science would not be science long, but a mere junk heap of rotting fragments.[49]

Knowledge, for its own sake and for the general welfare, was the cornerstone of Wallace's department. Under him, the department's library became—and remains—the largest agricultural library in the world. The department's annual yearbooks were authoritative texts on topics ranging from nutrition to animal husbandry. Its economists produced solid, occasionally provocative books and pamphlets, sometimes straying far beyond the agricultural province.

National conferences considering agricultural problems from philosophical, historical, and sociological points of view were a standard feature.

The men who worked for Wallace looked upon "the Sec" with a combination of admiration and amazement. "I found that it was necessary always to be on the alert," said Dillon Myer, assistant chief of the Soil Conservation Service, "for you could never tell when the Secretary was going to ask for confirmation of a figure, or request detailed, specific information within the field that I was supposed to represent." E. N. Bressman, the plant scientist who had known and worked for Wallace for two decades, said, "His most outstanding quality is his ability to brush aside all superficialities that surround so much so-called scientific work and quickly get to the heart of the matter."[50]

The economist Mordecai Ezekiel said Wallace's great characteristic was "his intellectual honesty in using the facts as guides to action rather than excuses for action." The past eight years, he wrote on Wallace's departure, "have indeed been like a dream come true." Gove Hambidge, editor of the yearbook, remembered Wallace as the relentless pursuer of truth. "[There] is no escaping H. A. when he sets out to ask disconcerting questions, attack accepted fundamentals, formulate a bold new hypothesis, and suggest a campaign to turn up badly needed scientific facts," Hambidge wrote.[51]

Administratively, after a hectic beginning, Wallace's department became a model of effectiveness. The presidential aide James Rowe said it was the best-run department in the New Deal. Much of the credit belonged, as Wallace noted, to the disciplined, high-minded Paul Appleby. "He made a unique contribution to administrative techniques harnessed to the highest concept of the general welfare," Wallace said. Wallace's own idea of being a good executive was "to pick men of integrity who understand your policy objective" and let them do their jobs.[52]

Debate over the heart of Wallace's farm program—the stabilization of agriculture through production controls, marketing assistance, and income subsidies—lingered for decades. By some measures it failed. Total farm income in 1939, Wallace's last full year at the department, stood at $66 billion, well below the $79 billion earned by the farm population in 1929. Price levels for most farm commodities, as measured by the parity index, also were low in 1939. Corn prices were only 59 percent of parity; wheat prices were at 50 percent. Only the onset of World War II, it was argued, prevented Wallace's ever-normal granary from suffering the fate of Herbert Hoover's failed Farm Board.

Yet no one who remembered the devastated scene at the height of the Great Depression—ten-cent corn and penny auctions, falling land values and rising debt—could argue that the farmers' lot had not improved under Wallace. Total farm income in 1933 was only $39 billion. "In their futile efforts to keep up . . . farmers were forced to exploit unmercifully their lands," Wallace recalled in his departing message to the department's workers. "They mined their soil to produce more and more to sell for less and less."[53]

It was in establishing a mechanism to halt and reverse the downward spiral that Wallace achieved his greatest success. Wallace's farm program has been called the largest effort to achieve economic cooperation through democratic processes that the world had ever seen. Certainly it constituted a sea change in the relationship between farmers and their government, and it must be counted as one of the boldest social experiments ever undertaken in the United States. Its basic framework endured for half a century, during which time American farmers became the richest and most productive in the world.

That was Wallace's legacy.

Even those who disagreed with him did so with respect. "Sec. Wallace whose standards of conduct and taste are of the highest . . . might be called a fortunate man were not his good fortune the product of his character," the New York Times editorialized as he left office. "Whatever distrust of or opposition to his policies there may be, it is always accompanied with respect and esteem for the man . . . [H]is integrity, sincerity, disinterestedness and goodwill are manifest to all. He is an editor, author, economist, thinker and a farmer tinged with a little poetry and a little mysticism. In short, a gentleman and a scholar in the fullest sense of the phrase . . . a good man and a good fellow. . . ."[54]

Leaving the department he had known so long and done so much to change was a painful moment for Wallace. He permitted a rare bit of emotion to show through his Scotch-Irish reserve. "I confess to a wrench of the heart," he said at his final press conference as secretary, "at leaving this department where my father worked before me. This is not an easy parting for me."[55]

CHAPTER TWELVE

"A FUNNY WAY TO LIVE"

In late August, as German fighter planes continued their merciless assault on Britain and U-boats preyed at will on Allied ships in the Atlantic, Henry Wallace boarded a train in Washington and headed into the unknown terrain of a national campaign.

He was headed west, where, according to a general strategy mapped out with President Roosevelt, Wallace would concentrate his efforts. On board with him were Ed Flynn, the Bronx political boss who had replaced Jim Farley as chairman of the Democratic Party, and House Agriculture Committee Chairman Marvin Jones. They were to serve as a sort of traveling advisory committee for the fledgling politician. Their first destination was Des Moines, where Wallace would open the campaign with a speech formally accepting the nomination on August 29.

The plan called for Roosevelt to remain above the fray, playing the role of president and commander in chief. Wallace would be the slugger. For both the theme would be "peace through preparedness." Wallace would argue it in speeches; Roosevelt would stress it in a series of "nonpolitical" inspection tours of defense plants.

By the time the train was halfway to Iowa, the whole plan—including Wallace's candidacy—had nearly gone off the tracks. Wallace didn't know it, but the mysterious "guru letters" had come into Republican hands. The letters, which Wallace had written to Nicholas Roerich and his followers in 1933–34, had been whispered about for years. Now they had apparently come into the possession of Republican newspaper publisher Paul Block.

Democrats learned of the development through idle chatter at a cocktail party. Anna Rosenberg, regional director of Social Security in New York, overheard the gossip and rushed immediately to Washington to tell Harry Hopkins. "Oh God," said the alarmed Rosenberg, "out of a hundred million Americans we had to pick him for vice president!"[1]

Through an aide with ties to reporters, Hopkins managed to obtain photostatic copies of the letters. The originals were thought to be held by the Republican national treasurer in a Wall Street bank vault. As Wallace rolled westward, blissfully unaware of the situation, Hopkins frantically sifted through the letters, wondering what to do. He summoned Sam Rosenman to his room in the White House living quarters and plunked the letters on a card table without a word of greeting.

The two men rapidly concluded that the letters were political dynamite. If they became public, Wallace would appear mystical at best and irrational at worst. "Sam, is there any way we can get Wallace off the ticket now, or is it too late?" Hopkins asked. Rosenman believed it was too late.[2]

Late that evening, as they weighed the options and read the letters again and again, they called Paul Appleby at home and asked him to come to the White House immediately. Appleby had never seen the letters, but he instantly recognized Wallace's distinctive handwriting. He also knew of Wallace's erstwhile interest in the Roerichs and the fiasco of their expedition to Central Asia. At least some of the letters appeared to be genuine, Appleby said. With considerable misgivings he agreed to go that night to the Agriculture Department and search Wallace's files for further evidence.

The following morning Hopkins and Rosenman trooped down the hall to Roosevelt's bedroom. They found the president in a sunny mood as he was finishing breakfast and showed him the letters. Roosevelt glanced over five or six pages but went no further. Accounts of his reaction varied. Rosenman said the president's face darkened, and he gravely asked if they knew how the Republicans planned to use them. Another account had Roosevelt laughing heartily when he saw the letters.

Still another version, pieced together by the reporter Turner Catledge, quoted Roosevelt as asking whether Wallace's relationship with Frances Grant, the recipient of some of the letters, was physical or metaphysical. Told that their relationship was strictly spiritual, the president supposedly threw up his hands and exclaimed, "We can handle sex, but we can't handle religion."[3]

But by all accounts Roosevelt did not suggest or even contemplate replacing Wallace on the ticket. His only suggestion was that Appleby be sent immediately to Chicago, where Wallace would be spending the day, to get a grip on the situation. The fear was that Wallace, with customary candor, would be asked about the letters and blurt out, "Yeah, I wrote them—so what?" Appleby could at least rein in Wallace, even if he couldn't control the press.

Appleby reached Wallace by telephone, apprised him of developments, told him he was flying to Chicago, and urged him to avoid contact with reporters. He also described the general tone and content of the letters and asked whether Wallace had written them. "I guess that's right, Paul," Wallace replied.[4]

Appleby flew to Chicago accompanied by the New York lawyer Morris L. Ernst, who had assisted Wallace in writing *Whose Constitution?* They found Wallace huddled with Jones and Flynn in their train car, sidetracked at a station outside the city, all looking very "uneasy." The tension only increased when Appleby passed along rumors that reporters intended to confront Wallace in Chicago. Wallace said only that some of the letters might be forgeries. Jones offered a more practical strategy: avoid reporters but if confronted say that "thousands of letters reach your desk each week—they have been gone over with other people and you have no serious recollection of those particular letters.[5]

Ernst suggested another ploy. Dissemble, Ernst advised, and for good measure be indignant. Ernst's plan carried the day. Together the men drafted a statement that read in part, "The documents in question have been hawked around for many years at times to private individuals, at other times to publishers. . . . Your publisher must know the story of the disgruntled discharged employee [Roerich] . . . a tax evader, who dare not re-enter this land—from which all this stems."[6]

Wallace agreed to deliver the statement if necessary. Appleby was appalled but went along. He later referred to the episode as "a sore point on my conscience, because it was as nearly a dishonorable thing as I remember ever having been party to."[7]

As events unfolded, Wallace was never asked about the letters that day in Chicago. He slipped quietly into the city, attended a meeting at the University of Chicago, met privately with Chancellor Robert Maynard Hutchins, and reboarded his train unscathed. If any newsman tried that day to ask Wallace about the letters, there was no record of it. Wallace rolled on toward Iowa, and the guru letters sank back into the political underground, where they remained, submerged but hardly forgotten, for many weeks.

Roosevelt, the master political cardplayer, knew the game wasn't over. Wallace might have escaped from Chicago, but the Republicans still had the letters. They would find a way to use them if they could. With three-quarters of the nation's newspapers owned by Republicans—and many leading publishers openly assisting Wendell Willkie's campaign—it would not be difficult to find a venue for their publication.

But Roosevelt knew also that he had an ace in the hole. Her name was Irita Van Doren, a charming and beautiful woman who, as literary editor of the *New York Herald Tribune*, was a member of the nation's intellectual elite. Van Doren, as Roosevelt and all political insiders knew, was Wendell Willkie's mistress. Indeed, so open was their relationship that Willkie once held a press conference in the New York apartment they shared. Reporters didn't think to mention it.

Democrats had not made an issue of Willkie's private life, but faced with the explosive guru letters Roosevelt openly suggested the time for gossip might be at hand. If the Republicans used the letters, he told his aide Lowell Mellett, Democrats could spread rumors about Willkie "as a word-of-mouth thing" through speakers "way, way down the line." Roosevelt said he couldn't personally mention it, but "the Congress speakers, and state speakers, and so forth. They can use the raw material. . . . Now, now, if they want to play dirty politics in the end, we've got our own people. . . . Now, you'd be amazed at how this story about the gal is spreading around the country."*[8]

"It's out," Mellett replied. Roosevelt continued with specific reference to Van Doren: "Awful nice gal, writes for the magazine and so forth and so on, a book reviewer. But nevertheless, there is the fact." He suggested Willkie's wife, Edith, had "in effect . . . been hired to return to Wendell and smile and make this campaign with him."[9]

There things stood in uneasy truce. The mistress versus the guru. For the time being, both sides held their fire.

By the time he reached Des Moines, Wallace seemed to have put the unpleasantness in Chicago out of his mind. Friendly hometown crowds welcomed his arrival and movement around the city. Wallace lunched with the local chamber of commerce, met well-wishers at an afternoon reception and bantered with reporters. When newsmen persisted in asking agricultural question, Wallace joked that he was "running for vice president, not Secretary of Agriculture."[10] Ed Flynn, smartly dressed in a sky blue coat and tan shirt, reinforced the message. The president would stick close to Washington, Flynn said, and the brunt of the campaign would fall on Wallace.

---

*Roosevelt's comments about Willkie and Van Doren were recorded on a "continuous film recording machine," which had been secretly installed in a room beneath his office in the summer of 1940. Roosevelt wanted to experimentally record the biweekly press conferences held in his office. The recording device could be turned on and off with a switch inside Roosevelt's desk. Because he sometimes forgot to turn it off, fragments of Roosevelt's conversations with aides and politicians also were captured. Use of the machine was discontinued after the 1940 election.

The following day, August 29, a cheering crowd of ten thousand people packed into the Des Moines Memorial Coliseum to hear Wallace deliver his acceptance address. It was a hard-hitting speech, and Wallace delivered it better than anyone expected. Hitler and Roosevelt had come into power at almost the same time in 1933. "Adolf Hitler was the implacable enemy of all democracy," said Wallace. "Franklin Roosevelt was its eager servant and faithful defender before the whole world." Americans must support the champion of "freedom and democracy" in the fight against a "materialistic religion of darkness." "Against this dark and bloody faith we of the New World set the faith of Americanism, of Protestantism, of Catholocism, of Judaism. Our faith is based on the belief that the possibilities of an individual are not determined by race, social background or wealth."[11]

He finished with a stiff backhanded punch at the opposition. "Most Republicans may not realize it, but their party is the party of appeasement in the United States today," Wallace declared. "I do not wish to imply that the Republican leaders are willfully and consciously giving aid and comfort to Hitler. But I wish to emphasize that replacement of Roosevelt, even if it were by the most patriotic leadership that could be found, would cause Hitler to rejoice. I do not believe the American people will turn their backs on the man that Hitler wants to see defeated."[12]

The *Des Moines Register* summed up the vice presidential candidates's case with a glaring headline the following day: "Nazis Prefer GOP . . . Wallace." Republicans cried foul, and many newspapers called it a low blow. The *Minneapolis Star Journal* declared that its prediction that Willkie would run against Roosevelt and Roosevelt would run against Hitler was being borne out. The isolationist *Chicago Tribune* said, "Mr. Wallace made it clear that the New Deal Party is the war party. It bawls to arms and hunts the battlefield."[13]

Roosevelt expected the reaction, and he was delighted. "A grand speech and splendidly given before an apprehensive nation," he said in a telegram to Wallace. ". . . You have made a glorious start."[14]

Nor did Wallace have any doubts about the course he had set. "I determined to make the dominant issue in the campaign international affairs," he commented in his oral history. "I knew that it would cost us votes in the middle west because the people of the middle west were very strongly isolationist. There were also many German communities where I knew that we would lose utterly and completely. But . . . I was so certain that the welfare of the country demanded the emphasis on international affairs that I emphasized that at all times and started out in this particular speech emphasizing it."[15]

Following the Des Moines speech, Wallace set out on a campaign swing that would take him over the coming weeks to Chicago, through small towns in downstate Illinois, into Indiana and Missouri, back through Iowa, westward to Nebraska, and north to Minnesota. He traveled light, usually by car, with only his friend Jim LeCron, speechwriter David Coyle, and farm editor Clifford Gregory to assist him. Sometimes Ed Flynn or Marvin Jones or economist Leo Crowley, head of the Federal Deposit Insurance Corporation, would join them to offer advice.

Five or six times a day the little motorcade would stop and Wallace would speak extemporaneously to crowds of one or two thousand, sometimes as many as five thousand, gathered in fairgrounds or on courthouse lawns. It was, said an Associated Press story, "not unlike the campaign of the torchlight era—without the torchlights."[16]

Before farm audiences Wallace would sometimes jab at the Republican farm program—or lack of one, as he saw it—but always he spoke of "peace through preparedness" and the need to support Roosevelt's foreign policies. "It is strength only that Hitler respects," he said. "By preparedness we can win and hold our peace." Even before heavily German-American audiences, such as confronted him at Belleville, Illinois, he attacked Hitler as "the madman, who believes that the German race is superior to other races. We don't believe that in the U.S." When he was greeted with tepid applause, Wallace said he hoped all of German extraction in the audience had applauded. The crowd reacted with stony silence.[17]

His campaign began earning high marks precisely because it was so earnest, so lacking the customary hoopla, so very plain. "Those who want to be amused or to hear flamboyant platitudes were disappointed," an Illinois newspaper editorialized. "Those who want to hear a serious, common sense, straight-from-the-shoulder, extemporaneous discussion of domestic and international problems went away convinced that Wallace knows what he's talking about. . . ."[18]

Wallace grew emboldened and invigorated. The endless string of twelve-hour days left him "full of ginger and speaking better each new day," said one reporter. A *Des Moines Register* reporter following the trip said he had "found his niche . . . no more flashy than he ever was, he was making hay with his radiation of sincerity and warning audiences to beware of 'flannel-mouthed' political orators." Even Harold Ickes, who had predicted Wallace would prove disastrous as a campaigner, was impressed. "By the way," Ickes told his diary in mid-September, "Henry is doing extremely well on the stump. He is a new man. . . ."[19]

Seldom has a political campaign been conducted in the midst of greater crisis. In Britain hundreds died in the daily bombings; millions lived in terror amid the rubble. American families gathered anxiously around radios, listening to broadcasters describe the devastation, hearing Churchill solemnly declare that the fate of all civilization hung in the balance.

In Congress the first peacetime draft in American history was working its way toward passage. Even before it had finished the Selective Service debate, Roosevelt made an urgent new request for more money, asking $5.2 billion to build 7 battleships and 201 other ships of war. And even without asking Congress, the president by executive order sent 50 aging American destroyers to Britain in exchange for ninety-nine-year leases on British military bases in the Western Hemisphere.

Wendell Willkie's stance toward these events initially was supportive of the president and greatly helped relieve Roosevelt's political burden. Willkie backed the sale of arms to Britain and supported the Selective Service bill. He agreed (through the editor William Allen White, who acted as an intermediary) not to criticize the destroyers-for-bases deal once Roosevelt had acted. Indeed, Willkie's early disagreement with Roosevelt's foreign policy was that the president had done too little, not too much, to enhance military preparedness.

But Willkie's internationalist positions put him directly at odds with a large portion of his own party. He tried to finesse the problem by turning his attention to domestic affairs, but that posed difficulties, too. Willkie personally agreed with much of the New Deal; his quarrel was in details. As the Socialist Party candidate, Norman Thomas, put it after one of Willkie's speeches, "He agreed with Mr. Roosevelt's entire program of social reform and said it was leading to disaster."[20]

By mid-September, Willkie's dilemma was apparent to all. The Gallup poll showed Roosevelt leading 55 percent to 45 percent and gaining. Adding to Willkie's frustration was his inability to engage Roosevelt, who maintained a studied distance from the whole campaign. And increasingly he was nettled by the steady pummeling of Wallace and others.

Wallace in particular was hitting ever closer to the belt. "The Republican candidate is not an appeaser and not a friend of Hitler," Wallace said on a swing through rural Nebraska. ". . . But you can be sure that every Nazi, every Hiterlite and every appeaser is a Republican."[21]

Slowly Willkie began yielding to the temptation to strike back, to break with Roosevelt's foreign policy and make the war a political issue. The first indication of the shift came on September 9, a week after Roosevelt approved the destroyers-for-bases deal. Having promised not to criticize the trade, Willkie now attacked the president for circumventing Congress. "This trade is the most dictatorial action ever taken by any president," he said.[22]

A week later in Coffeyville, Kansas, Willkie pushed the attack further. "Mr. Roosevelt's oratory, as the defender of democracy, conceals the fact that by his own meddling in international politics, he encouraged the European conflagration. . . . And he was the godfather of that unhappy conference at Munich. . . . I warn you—and I say this in dead earnest—if, because of some fine speeches about humanity, you return this administration to office, you will be serving under an American totalitarian government before the long third term is finished." Three days later in Los Angeles, he warned an audience to "get ready to get on the transports" if Roosevelt was reelected.[23]

Willkie had found a new voice, even as he was losing his own. A throat condition had cost him most of his speaking ability. He was reduced to addressing crowds in a raspy whisper. Still, his new message touched a nerve. Almost immediately the Republican began gaining in the polls. Roosevelt had a real opponent.

As Willkie moved to change tactics, events forced the Roosevelt campaign to pause. On September 15, House Speaker William Bankhead died of a heart attack at age sixty-six. Three years earlier Roosevelt had declined to attend the funeral of Senate Majority Leader Joe Robinson on grounds that presidents attended only state funerals. But in the midst of a campaign in which he needed the support of old-line Democrats, Roosevelt had a change of heart.

Roosevelt ordered a special presidential train to transport Bankhead's body to a "state funeral" in Jasper, Alabama, where the president and virtually his entire cabinet would pay their respects. It was especially important that Wallace be present, since Bankhead was the last man standing in opposition to him at the Chicago convention. It was not the insufferably hot funeral in an Alabama church but the train ride back to Washington that was to prove eventful.

Amid much talk of politics, lubricated by liberal amounts of liquor, the teatotaling Wallace became uncomfortable and sought refuge in the dining car. There he became witness to Undersecretary of State Sumner Welles drinking heavily while lavishly expressing admiration for Mussolini. Wallace was scandalized, more by Welles's fondness for the Italian dictator than by his drinking, but the scandal was only beginning. After Wallace left the dining car, the stiffly proper Welles returned to his sleeping compartment and began soliciting homosexual sex from black railroad porters. Welles's behavior on the train would eventually lead to his forced resignation from government in 1942 and leave a lasting mark on U.S. foreign policy.*

---

*One of the porters was sufficiently offended by Welles's actions to file a complaint with the railroad company that employed him. The railroad company was partly owned by the former U.S. ambassador to France, William Bullitt, who wanted Welles's position for himself. Armed with the porter's allegation, Bullitt waged a long whispering campaign against the undersecretary. Bullitt was assisted in his efforts by Secretary of State Cordell Hull, who disliked Welles personally and distrusted his close relationship with Roosevelt.

Roosevelt resisted firing Welles until the rumor reached a congressional investigative committee. Faced with imminent public scandal, Roosevelt discharged Welles, but he bitterly resented the actions of Bullitt and Welles. Roosevelt flatly refused to give Bullitt another government post and virtually shunned his secretary of state during the war years.

And when Wallace reached Washington, there was a reminder that Republicans hadn't forgotten about him either. Henry Luce's *Time* magazine hit the stands with a cover story that repeatedly hinted at Wallace's strangeness. Although not entirely negative—the article described him as a "Will Rogers of the intellectuals" and said there "was no pose in the Wallace manner"— the story painted him as an "editor, savant, dreamer and mystic" who was given to vegetarian food experiments, "playing with astrology and numerology as a hobby," driving fast at night to "clear his mind," and rising at 5:30 A.M. to play tennis.*[24]

After a ten-day lull Wallace resumed campaigning in Indianapolis, where he attacked Willkie's record as head of a utility holding company before a cheering audience of ten thousand farmers. Then he began a month-long swing that would take him to St. Louis and Kansas City, into his native state, through the Southwest and on to Los Angeles, north to Oregon (where he went out of his way to praise his opponent, Senator McNary), across the northern tier of states to Minnesota and Wisconsin, and on to New York City, where he addressed seventeen thousand people at an American Labor Party rally in Madison Square Garden.

In speech after speech Wallace hammered away at "that same old hard-headed group, the powers that be of the G.O.P.," which would bring down Roosevelt on a promise of prosperity without sacrifice. "Against Hitler's total warfare we must quickly oppose a total defense," he declared. "This will involve sacrifices. . . . But if we really believe all we have said and done about the rights of man, and freedom and personal honor in this New World, I can see no other safe and decent course."[25]

As a political candidate he was refreshingly unconventional. In New Mexico he delighted his audience by suddenly switching languages, delivering part of his address in Spanish. (He was the first national candidate of either party to address a crowd in Spanish.) In the midst of the campaign, he penned a long article entitled "Judaism and Americanism" for the *Menorah Journal*, tracing the commitment of Old Testament prophets to "progressive religious, political and economic matters."[26] And to the discomfort of traditional Democrats, he steadfastly eschewed conventional partisanship, reminding au-

---

*Wallace replied to the "very friendly account" in a personal letter to Luce. Wallace acknowledged he had been interested in astrology, which he described as "simply Geocentric Astronomy," when he was studying weather but added that "astrology as a guide to life would lead to a fatalism that might cause many individuals to accept hard times as the force-ordination of the stars, instead of struggling to master their fates."

Wallace added that he never drove at night "or at any other time" to clear his head and did not play tennis before 7:30 A.M. "Oh well!—it is impossible to correct all the cockeyed stories. Moreover, it is obvious your slant is friendly, so I don't mind."

diences of his Republican heritage and of his father's service in the Harding and Coolidge cabinets.

He refused to attack the Republican vice presidential candidate, McNary, beyond arguing that the McNary-Haugen approach to farm aid was a thing of the past; twice he found himself on the same train as McNary, and the two candidates rode together and chatted amicably for hours. In Minnesota he even invited McNary to join him in a pheasant dinner provided by some local hunters. In Wisconsin, he went out of his way to praise the progressive Republican senator Robert La Follette Jr., causing several Democratic politicians to stomp off the platform in protest.

"I saw a lot of the country and met a lot of fine people," Wallace said later of the campaign. "But, you know, it's a funny way to live."[27]

In mid-October, Wallace stopped in Washington for several days to regroup. By every visible measure, the race was getting closer by the day. The chain-smoking peripatetic Willkie, tirelessly croaking out his case from the back of his twelve-car train, was drawing large and enthusiastic audiences. Despite his campaign's chronic disorganization, his uncertain message, and his undisciplined personal style, voters clearly were attracted by the kinetic energy he exuded. Opinion polls reflected the movement. The gallup poll reported Roosevelt's lead had been cut in half since Willkie began attacking his foreign policy.

Not only was the race getting closer; it was getting rougher. Both Democrats and Republicans indulged themselves with false rumors about the opposing candidates' personal lives and families. Reporters aboard the Willkie Special kept a running tally of the fruits and vegetables that had been thrown at the Republican candidate. Republicans attacked the president's son Elliott, who they said received special treatment when he entered the Army Air Corps as a captain. Nor had Republicans forgotten about Roosevelt's running mate.

Having passed through several hands, the guru letters were then in the possession of Paul Block, publisher of the *Pittsburgh Post-Gazette*. The rumor in Washington was that Block had paid Frances Grant, longtime Roerich disciple and herself the embittered recipient of some of the letters, a fee of $5,000 to obtain them. As Wallace stumped across the nation, Block rented a suite at the Waldorf-Astoria Hotel in New York and discussed the letters with other publishers and several Republican officials. Afterwards Block assigned his ace reporter, Ray Sprigle, who had won a Pulitzer Prize for exposing Justice Hugo Black's early membership in the Ku Klux Klan, to the "guru" story. By mid-October, Sprigle had drafted several installments.

Roosevelt's top aides were aware of the situation. Harry Hopkins even had copies of some of Sprigle's drafts. Charlie Michelson, the Democratic Party's feisty publicity chief, set out a defensive course of action, telling his aids to gather statements from church leaders attesting to Wallace's mainstream Christianity. Hopkins took the offensive. He showed the stories to Wallace and bluntly told him to avoid speaking to Sprigle under any circumstances. Wallace's traveling companions were told to keep Sprigle at bay with force if necessary.

So it was that Wallace began, on October 17, the last leg of his campaign for the vice presidency. Wallace stumped westward, first in West Virginia, then through Ohio and Indiana, with the intrepid Sprigle dogging his trail. Sprigle came close to his quarry in Bellafontaine, Ohio, and again in Indianapolis, only to be turned away. Finally, on October 19 in Chicago, Sprigle actually made it onto Wallace's train.

As Sprigle stood outside Wallace's compartment, the candidate suddenly popped out and asked the reporter how he spelled his name. Wallace wrote the name across the top of a two-page typewritten statement, handed it to him, and disappeared. "This material has been bandied about for so many years that it is clear that its use on the eve of an election spells nothing but the desperation of the supporters of Wendell Wilkie," Wallace's statement said in part. "The American public is of age. It will interpret as political bankruptcy any such publication by anyone." Even the "most psychopathic Roosevelt hater" would be revolted by the publication of such material, Wallace's statement added, particularly "since your first proposed article, as drafted, is not only libelous and outrageous in its departure from the truth but clearly is designed to raise in the midst of our citizenry minority religious suspicions and hatreds."[28]

The reference to "minority religious suspicions" was aimed at Block, who was Jewish. Whether the publisher was moved by the plea is unknown. It *is* known that Sprigle's stories were never published, and the general public did not learn of the guru letters in 1940.*

The decision to kill the stories probably was not Block's alone. In his memoir, *My First Fifty Years in Politics*, Representative Joe Martin, the Republican national chairman, said he made the decision. He was concerned that "voters might conclude that the Republican Party was resorting to a last-minute smear." Furthermore, Martin added oddly, "I didn't know anything about this fellow Guru. Maybe he had a great many more followers than any of realized. Why kick away their votes? Everything considered, therefore, I decided that the Republicans would not use the letters. That put an end to the matter."[29]

---

*Wallace was responding to Sprigle's stories. He did not see the actual letters until "quite a while after the campaign when Roosevelt laughingly showed me some photostats of material which had been offered for sale. . . . None of the material seemed to cause FDR the slightest concern."

Other accounts, however, said Willkie himself was consulted and decided the letters should not be published. Sam Rosenman said Willkie made the decision on the statesmanlike basis that campaigns should be about issues and not personalities. Still another version, published by *Newsweek* magazine and the *Des Moines Register* in 1948, said Hopkins personally reached Willkie by phone and threatened to begin talking about the candidate's mistress if the guru letters were published.

"That campaign," Wallace later remarked in his laconic way, "under cover, was exceedingly dirty."*30

❋

Wallace headed into the final stages of the campaign, still doing double duty for the Democratic ticket, amid circumstances as volatile as could be imagined. The Battle of Britain was at its height. On October 15 alone, 480 German planes dropped 380 tons of high-explosive bombs and 70,000 incendiary devices on London. The following day young American men were required to begin registering for the nation's first peacetime draft. Willkie was already ahead in several important midwestern states and gaining rapidly in the Northeast. To Roosevelt's intense irritation, Willkie was using a three-year-old comment by Winston Churchill in which he attacked New Deal economic policies as a "ruthless" war on private enterprise.

By October 18 Roosevelt had had enough. He issued a statement announcing he would give five political speeches before election day and summoned Sam Rosenman and Robert Sherwood to the White House. Five days later in Philadelphia, "the Champ" (as Willkie liked to call Roosevelt) came out swinging. "To Republicans and Democrats, to every man, woman and child in the nation, I say this: 'Your President and your Secretary of State are following the road to peace.' " But his political mood was anything but peaceful. "I am an old campaigner, and I love a good fight," he grandly declared.31

And a fight it was. The labor leader John L. Lewis weighed in with a nationally broadcast speech endorsing Willkie. Three days later Roosevelt struck back in Madison Square Garden, New York City's famed boxing arena, pounding the record of Republican isolationists. "There is the record on that;

*In the final days of the campaign, the *Chicago Tribune* attempted another personal attack on Wallace. It noted he had avoided service in World War I on the basis of classification as a "necessary associate, assistant or hired manager of a necessary enterprise." The *Tribune* said it was justified in bringing this to public attention because "Wallace has sought to impugn the patriotism of Wendell Willkie, who enlisted as a private at the outbreak of the war and rose by merit to a captain in the artillery."

the permanent crystal clear record. Until the present political campaign opened, Republican leaders, in and out of the Congress, shouted from the housetops that our defenses were fully adequate. Today they proclaim that this administration has starved our armed forces, that our Navy is anemic, our Army puny, our air forces piteously weak. . . . I wonder if the election has something to do with it."[32]

During the whole of the campaign, Willkie's name never passed from Roosevelt's lips in public. But at Madison Square Garden he personalized isolationist opposition to his preparedness program with three names that would achieve political immortality: Martin, Barton, and Fish. The rhythmical formulation of the three congressional isolationists' names delighted Roosevelt and had a magical effect on his audience. The crowd began chanting the names with him. They rapidly became catchwords across the nation; even schoolchildren who had no idea of their significance could recite the names Martin, Barton, and Fish. Willkie later said those three little words tied him more effectively to the isolationists than anything else spoken in the campaign.

The following day, against the advice of friends, Roosevelt personally participated in the first drawing of numbers for the draft. He watched solemnly as a blindfolded Secretary of War Henry Stimson drew the first cobalt blue capsule from a large glass bowl. "You who will enter this peacetime army will be the inheritors of a proud history and an honorable tradition," Roosevelt said. "You will be members of an army that first came together to achieve independence and to establish certain fundamental rights for all men."[33]

With attention focused on Roosevelt, the Wallace campaign labored on the side of the stage. In speeches delivered across the Midwest, he defended the administration's defense efforts, courted labor, tried to shore up farm support, and denounced the Republican record. In the closing days of the campaign, Wallace moved east once again and delivered a series of scathing speeches that sought to use Willkie's own words against him. "The Republican candidate has spoken of our national problems in a remarkably confused way," Wallace said in New York on October 31. "On no subject has he been more confused than on that of national defense, if the reports of his utterances in the press can be taken as correct." He continued,

Last April he spoke with apparent approval of our government's aid to England and France, and the moral embargo against Japan, saying: "No one of these things has involved us in a war."

In May he said: "The administration has done a pretty good job with reference to the foreign problem," and again: "I hope America can hand a set of brass knuckles to the democracies so they can take another sock at the dictatorships."

In August he said the President "has courted a war for which this country is hopelessly unprepared." He also said: "I promise . . . to outdistance Hitler in any contest he chooses in 1940 or after," and again: "I trust I have made it plain that in the defense of America . . . I should not hesitate to stand for war." But the billboards quote him as saying "I will not lead the country into war, vote Republican"—as if he had made up his mind not to stand for war on any terms. . . . Does he mean that he will outdistance Hitler and be the world conqueror? Just what does he mean? Or does he know what he means? Does anyone know what he means?[34]

In the final days both Democratic standard-bearers ended up in Ohio, considered a key electoral battleground. Roosevelt spoke in Cleveland, where he delivered an eloquent appeal for democracy. Wallace ended up in Steubenville, where he gave a speech entitled "Keeping Out of War." Willkie "has said that only the strong can be free, and that time he was correct," Wallace declared, But, he added, "the real defense against war, the real way to peace, cannot be found by anything so simple as turning the country over to the speculators and stock manipulators. Peace is a long dyke against the floods of danger, a dyke that has to be built with care and knowledge to stand firm at all points."[35]

The vigorously contested campaign had captured the American electorate's attention as no other in the nation's history. On election day, November 5, almost fifty million Americans, a record number, went to the polls. Both Roosevelt, the consummate professional, and Willkie, the brash amateur, harbored serious doubts about the outcome. Roosevelt was so worried that he ordered his bodyguard to prevent anyone, including his family, from entering his room while he listened to the early returns.

At Jim LeCron's spacious home in Washington, D.C., the scene was more relaxed. There Wallace's old friends from the Department of Agriculture gathered to track the returns. The new secretary, Claude Wickard, and his wife were there; so were the Applebys. Appleby brought along a state-by-state chart, which he undertook to keep current in his typically efficient way. There was bantering and talk of the war and periodic shushing as news came over the radio. It was very much like a thousand other election night parties, LeCron later remarked, except that one among them was a candidate for vice president.

By 11 P.M. the result was clear. Elmer Davis, the definitive radio voice of his day, declared that Roosevelt had carried the election. Roosevelt received about 27.2 million votes to 22.3 million for Willkie. The Democratic ticket carried thirty-eight states with 449 electoral votes; the Republicans won ten states—seven in the Midwest plus Maine, Vermont, and Colorado—with 82 electoral votes. Willkie had received 5 million more votes than the hapless Alf

Landon in 1936. He had received more votes, in fact, than any Republican candidate ever. But it was not enough.

Among the ten states carried by Willkie was Iowa, which he won by a vote of 632,370 to 578,000. The combination of isolationist sentiment, heavy German ancestry, and rural respect for Charles McNary's name was more than enough to offset home state pride in Henry A. Wallace. The result rankled Wallace, but Roosevelt viewed it philosophically. In all his presidential campaigns, Roosevelt noted to Wallace, he had never succeeded in winning Dutchess County or even his hometown of Hyde Park.

At the Roosevelt estate that evening, there was jubilation. At a midnight torchlight parade, Franklin Roosevelt delivered his customary greeting to neighbors. At the Commodore Hotel in New York City, Willkie sat for hours in a cloud of stale cigarette smoke refusing to concede. At the LeCron home, Wallace was his customary undemonstrative, quiet self. Having won the first— and only—election of his life, Wallace called Roosevelt, chatted for a few minutes, and handed the phone off to Claude Wickard.

Then he glanced at Ilo and said it was time to go home.

CHAPTER THIRTEEN

"CAN THE VICE PRESIDENT BE USEFUL?"

"My Dear Henry boy," May Wallace wrote the following morning. "And now Election Day is over and my son has been elected to be Vice President of our great U.S. Yes, I am proud of him! And I know you will give your very best efforts to help the people live comfortable lives in their own homes and educate their children.—Now, I want you to catch up on sleep, read something gay and interesting, and rest. Do you know how to rest?"*1

The answer was no. He wasn't very good at being idle. Henry Wallace's idea of a postelection vacation was "going to some Latin American country and soaking up the language." Language interested him. From a high school German teacher, he had absorbed the idea that "a language is the reflection of the heart, soul, mind and customs of a people." He had been studying Spanish for three years and wanted to go where it was spoken. He had more or less settled on Costa Rica or Guatemala.[2]

When he approached Roosevelt with the idea, the president immediately saw the trip as an opportunity to promote Pan-American unity. Undersecretary of State Sumner Welles

---

*Wallace replied a few days later:

> Dear Mother,
>
> You are right that the object of it all is to help as many people as possible live comfortable lives in their own homes and educate their children.
>
> A great many people have spoken to me of the deep wisdom of your comment "poor boy" when told I had to preside over the Senate.
>
> We are all well. . . .
>
> Much love

was consulted, and soon Wallace's little vacation was hardly a vacation at all. It was decided he should go to Mexico, as Roosevelt's personal representative, to attend the presidential inauguration of Manuel Avila Camacho.

Since Wallace had as yet no official rank—indeed, he was unemployed for the first time in his adult life—he was appointed "ambassador extraordinary" and put on the State Department payroll at fifty dollars a day plus five cents a mile for automobile expenses.

So, three weeks after being elected vice president, Wallace set out by car for Mexico. He rode in a humble green Plymouth, accompanied only by Ilo and a driver provided by the State Department. Following behind in their own car were Jim LeCron and his wife, Helen. LeCron had been Wallace's assistant at the Agriculture Department and was a fellow Spanish student.

At the outset there was little to suggest the remarkable consequences of their journey. Their trip would revolutionize world food production. Over time the daily lives of hundreds of millions of people would be affected.

The little two-car caravan wound its way into the South and headed westward to Texas. At one point its members were delayed by floods and, to the consternation of State Department officials, their whereabouts were unknown. They surfaced unobtrusively on a sunny afternoon in Laredo on November 25. By that time a large collection of U.S. and Mexican politicians, diplomats, and military officers had gathered to greet Wallace. Bands played, schoolchildren in native costumes danced, the mayor of Laredo gave a speech in praise of tourism, and Wallace greeted the crowd in Spanish.

The mission to Mexico came at a delicate moment in U.S.-Mexican relations. Both nations had important reasons to hope the visit would be a success. Roosevelt and Wallace viewed Pan-American unity as vitally important to U.S. security and were deeply concerned over pro-fascist movements active in several Latin American nations. They were keen to show support for Camacho, who was generally friendly to the United States and democracy.

Camacho, in turn, very much needed U.S. support. He had won his election over strong opposition from Juan Andreu Almazán, a conservative general whose followers included many Nazi sympathizers. Almazán had disputed the election results and gone into self-imposed exile in the United States. Rumors spread that he would return to Mexico with an armed force of ten thousand men to challenge Camacho's inauguration.

Under the circumstances the Mexican government was eager to show Wallace every courtesy. He would be the first official U.S. representative to attend a Mexican presidential inauguration, and his presence would be viewed as an endorsement of Camacho's legitimacy. The Mexicans proposed a grand entrance for Wallace and his newly expanded entourage. A special train, accompanied by a military guard with flags a-flying, was suggested.

The Mexicans were bemused when Wallace would have none of it. The vice president–elect insisted upon crossing over the Rio Grande by foot and thereafter traveling to Mexico City in his Plymouth, without U.S. security personnel or advance men. "That's the way Americans are coming into Mexico, and I want to see what they will see," Wallace declared. "Besides, I want to stop and get out and look at some corn if I feel like it."3

The Mexican people loved it. Tens of thousands waited in villages and along the Pan-American Highway for Wallace's car, trailed now by a caravan of fifteen more. He was cheered wildly as he passed. In Monterrey 150,000 people lined the streets and showered the "gran amigo" with confetti and flowers as church bells clanged and factory whistles blared. "I never flew the Atlantic or had a triumphal march down Wall Street, so this was my first paper rain," Wallace said with a grin.4

Along the way, Wallace often ordered the procession to stop so that he could visit rural markets or inspect cornfields or talk to schoolchildren in their native tongue. Marte Gómez, a scholarly man who had been named to be Camacho's agriculture secretary, accompanied Wallace, and they had a running dialogue about the state of Mexican agriculture and the rural economy. Wallace finally called a halt to the impromptu visits when he found out his hosts had been operating on a detailed schedule but were too polite to say anything when he wandered away. "I was just out to learn all I could," he later said. "I didn't realize that they were making a show of the whole thing."5

Wallace arrived in Mexico City on the evening of November 29. Already his visit was being called a success, and elements unfriendly to the United States were determined to damage it. A crowd of several hundred people stood sullenly outside the U.S. embassy awaiting the motorcade. Many held handbills, distributed by German agitators, falsely claiming that General Almazán had been captured and put in jail. The scene was tense but quiet. When the *Life* photographer Carl Mydans took a picture of the crowd, however, his flashbulb touched off a riot. Rocks and sticks filled the air as the demonstrators screamed "Viva Almazán" and "Death to the gringos."

A shower of rocks pelted the embassy building. Police arrived and began using tear gas. Mydans managed to take one more dramatic picture before being hit in the back of his neck with a club. The U.S. military attaché Gordon McCoy was struck on the shoulder with a blackjack and succeeded in knocking out his assailant with a single blow of his fist. Young CBS broadcaster Eric Sevareid found himself "caught for a moment between the tear gas pistols of the police and the crowd armed with stones. Only the most undignified ducking and running saved me."6

The rioters didn't know it, but Wallace was already inside the embassy compound. His motorcade had turned into an entrance to the ambassador's residence and had never passed by the chancery building. While police were subduing the crowd with clubs and gas, Henry and Ilo were being showered with confetti, and he was saying, without intended irony, "Your welcome and what I have seen in coming through Mexico toward your great capital has moved me profoundly."[7]

"I knew the mob was not representative of Mexico," said U.S. Ambassador Josephus Daniels. "The Mexican attitude was clearly seen in the great manifestations of popular affection for Wallace. . . ."[8] A day later, when Wallace entered the hall for the inauguration ceremony, the entire Mexican congress arose in a spontaneous ovation. The congress redoubled the honor a short time later by inviting Wallace to speak before it.

"[I] think I never heard the Good Neighbor doctrine . . . better stated than when he addressed the Mexican Congress," Daniels later wrote. Speaking in Spanish, Wallace said, "The most practical ideal for the people of this hemisphere is Pan-Americanism. Without hemispheric solidarity we can have no assurance of peace. Without peace, we cannot build in orderly fashion for that prosperity of agriculture, labor, and business which we so keenly desire."[9]

The Mexicans nearly smothered Wallace with affection. For days he attended an uninterrupted string of meetings, speeches, receptions, and banquets that left the embassy staff exhausted but only seemed to invigorate him.* "There cannot be too many meetings of men of good will," he said to Daniels. And each morning he was up early to play several sets of tennis. "Wallace never seemed to tire," Daniels wrote.[10]

Another politician, having completed a successful state visit, might have gone home in glory or headed for the beach. Wallace did neither. Instead, he lingered in Mexico for a month, conducting a personal inspection tour of Mexican agriculture. He traipsed up steep hillsides to see the corn grown in mountainous areas, talked about hybrid breeding with Indian farmers and eager students, visited the leading agricultural college at Chapingo, and studied the Mexican diet and farm implements and work patterns.

They traveled without U.S. aides or assistants, but the Mexican government insisted on sending three military attachés and a dozen or so secret servicemen with them. "They didn't bother us much but they were in the bushes around the hotel and everywhere else all the time," LeCron recalled. "And there was a cavalcade of motorcycle cops to lead us and all that, which was a nice gesture but somewhat of a nuisance in a way."[11]

---

*The prospect of the teetotaler Wallace on the diplomatic circuit was amusing even to Mexican journalists. One paper carried a photo of him clinking wine glasses with Josephus Daniels, like Wallace a total abstainer, and President Camacho, who rarely drank alcohol. The caption read "Los Tres Secos" (The Three Drys).

Wallace came away appalled. The very best corn farms he saw, in a low-land area near Zacapu, about two hundred miles northwest of Mexico City, produced only twenty bushels to the acre. A generation earlier it had produced twice that amount. Most Mexican farms yielded only ten bushels per acre, and the human labor needed to garner even that amount was heartsickening. The farmer planted corn with the aid of a pointed stick, weeded and harvested and husked it by hand, and hauled it to market "on his own back or his wife's back or the back of a burro."[12]

That year, in 1940, an Iowa farmer produced a bushel of corn with about ten hours labor. The farmers at Zacapu required two hundred hours to produce the same amount. The less fortunate farmers in hilly areas, where most Mexican corn was grown, worked five hundred hours to produce a single bushel of corn. Iowa, with one-eighth the population of Mexico, produced eight times as much corn in 1940. And for their efforts Mexican farmers earned—if the weather was good and the soil wasn't worn out—a total cash income of about $100 a year.

Wallace later wrote a lengthy account of his trip to Mexico for *Wallaces' Farmer*. It was the first time he had written anything for the publication, of which he was still "editor on leave," since he went to Washington. He said almost nothing about his diplomatic triumph but a great deal about Mexican agriculture.

"Eighty percent of Mexicans live on the land, and the poorer people depend for their sustenance very largely on corn, together with some beans," he wrote ". . . From the standpoint of the great bulk of people who live on the farms in Mexico, I can't help thinking that efficient corn growing is more important than almost anything else in Mexico. . . . [If] by 1955 hybrid corn should have increased the yield two bushels an acre, that small increase would be of tremendous significance to the Mexican people."[13]

The Wallace's remained in Mexico through New Year's Day. They had planned to drive back to Washington with the LeCrons, but Helen LeCron contracted malaria and was too ill to move. The LeCrons remained at the ambassador's residence in Mexico City, and the Wallaces returned to the United States by plane.

In Washington, Wallace immediately began trying to do something about the conditions he had seen. Even before he was sworn in as vice president, he met with an official of the Rockefeller Foundation and urged him to take an interest in Mexican agriculture. A few weeks later Wallace met with the foundation's president, Raymond Fosdick, and laid out his case.

"I said I thought it would be a fine thing if they went to Mexico but that they should not do much in the way of health work because I thought it would be a crime to make another Puerto Rico of Mexico with population crowding on the means of subsistence; that the all-important thing was to expand the means of subsistence; that the corn of Mexico was only yielding 10 bushels to the acre; that the principal source of food among the Mexican masses was corn. . . ."[14]

"The suggestion fell on fertile ground," the Harvard professor Paul Mangelsdorf later wrote. The Rockefeller Foundation "had begun to recognize that its world-wide public health programs, which had contributed effectively to controlling debilitating diseases such as hookworm, yellow fever, and malaria might be saving people from disease only to subject them to slow starvation resulting from inadequate diets."[15]

In short order Fosdick appointed a small "survey commission" to explore what might be done in Mexico. The result was the establishment of an agricultural experiment station in Mexico, the first in a worldwide series of research stations established by the Rockefeller and Ford foundations, that led to vast food production increases in Latin America, India, the Philippines, and other developing nations across the globe.

"By 1948," Mangelsdorf wrote, "Mexico, for the first time since the Revolution of 1910, had no need to import food. Twenty years after the beginning of the program corn production in Mexico had tripled and wheat production had increased five-fold. In spite of an unprecedented increase in population, the per capita food supply was greater in 1963 than it had been in 1943."[16]

One of the first scientists to join the Rockefeller station in Mexico, a young Iowa agronomist named Norman Borlaug, would win the Nobel Peace Prize in 1970 for his development of high-yielding wheat. The work of Borlaug and others in expanding yields of corn, wheat, and rice averted worldwide famine and saved an estimated one billion lives over the next half century.

Ever after, Borlaug would credit Wallace as the inspiration for the "green revolution." So also did the Rockefeller Foundation.

Shortly before noon on January 20, 1941, John Nance Garner stood on the ground floor of the Capitol waiting for an elevator that would take him to his last task as a public official: delivering the oath of office to his successor. Garner, seventy-two years old, had been on Capitol Hill since 1903, moving steadily from backbench Texas congressman to House minority leader to Speaker of the House to vice president of the United States. His unremarkable career, a journalist once wrote, was "based upon the obituary column and the power of inertia."[17]

At Garner's side was the abstemious man who would take the oath. Henry Agard Wallace was twenty years his junior, but that only began to describe their differences. Wallace was introverted and cerebral and idealistic and progressive; Garner was none of those things and proud of it.

As they waited for the elevator, Garner and Wallace found a small piece of common ground. Both men loathed the "plug hats" they were expected to wear at the inauguration ceremony. Wallace was always uncomfortable in formal clothing. Garner's hat, which he had borrowed from the journalist Bascom Timmons, didn't fit and kept falling off. Jointly they resolved to carry their hats rather than wear them. And so they waited, hats in hand, for the elevator. And waited. And waited.

At last Wallace became concerned that they would be late and suggested they dash up the two flights of stairs to the inauguration platform. Garner dourly refused. "While I'm vice president I'm going to ride up," he declared. They arrived seven minutes late.[18]

So it was that Henry A. Wallace, hatless on a cold winter day, became the thirty-third vice president at ten minutes past twelve noon. He made little of the moment. He gave no speech; he didn't even repeat the oath as Franklin Roosevelt had always done. Wallace's only public words were "I do," spoken in a strong clear voice. Then he quietly returned to the side of his wife, resplendent in a "svelte mink coat and purple orchid," to watch Chief Justice Charles Evans Hughes deliver the oath of office to Franklin Delano Roosevelt for the third time.[19]

A new day had dawned on Capitol Hill, symbolically marked by Wallace's first action as vice president. Before making use of his formal office in the Capitol, Wallace ordered the removal of the bar from which Garner poured copious amounts of whiskey to entertain his colleagues in the afternoon. Also taken out was a urinal in a corner of the office. The urinal, Wallace later said, "stunk to high heaven" and was no longer necessary since senators would not be imbibing there.[20] Henceforth the vice president's formal office would be just that—a formality. Wallace preferred to work in a book-lined suite of three rooms in the Senate Office Building.

The future of the bar in the vice president's office had become something of a running joke in the press. "It has been a standing inquiry for some weeks whether Wallace would continue the custom, which bound so many senators to Vice President Garner with the bottled-in-bond of friendship," said a report in the *Des Moines Register.* Wallace tried to respond in a good-natured manner. He said he hoped the senators would be satisfied with "good cigars" instead of liquor, although he didn't smoke, either.[21]

One senator's wife observed wryly that Wallace's idea of a mixed drink was iced tea and ginger ale. The senators were not amused. The vice president's formal office in the Capitol, Wallace later remarked in his oral history, "was exceedingly popular because of the whiskies available there. . . . I got rid of both the liquor and the urinal, and the senators no longer dropped around there except when I invited them in to eat with me. The attraction was gone."[22]

Ever the good scholar, Wallace sought to equip himself with as much information as possible about the powers and duties of the vice president before taking office. He turned to both the Library of Congress and the Senate librarian for research assistance. He learned that Americans regard the office as rather funny. The popular image of a vice president was Alexander Throttlebottom, hero of the 1931 George S. Kaufman–Morrie Ryskind musical comedy *Of Thee I Sing*. Throttlebottom was a politician so hapless that he got lost while on a sight-seeing tour of the White House, so unknown that he couldn't get two references to obtain a library card.

Even Wallace, as serious a public servant as ever drew breath, could see the humor in his new position. Speaking to a dinner of the electoral college, Wallace quoted with relish the observations of the newspaper columnist Finley Peter Dunne, writing in the voice of Irish barkeeper "Mr. Dooley": "All that his grateful countryman demands fr'm th' man that she has illivated to this proud position on th' toe iv her boot is that he shall keep his 'pinyons to himsilf."[23]

The Constitution gives the vice president only one duty: to serve as president of the U.S. Senate. Even there he can vote only to break a tie. Mainly a vice president's job, as Majority Leader Alben Barkley reminded Wallace in a speech welcoming him to the Senate, was to keep quiet.

Wallace took this bit of senatorial hazing in stride. He told reporters he had nothing more serious than tennis on his mind and vowed not to make any speeches for a good long while. If that was Wallace's intent, he was ill suited for the task. He had been engaged in serious public debate for most of his adult life. But for his interest in the issues of his time, he would not have been involved in politics at all.

His vow of silence lasted about a month. In late February, Wallace spoke to the National Farm Institute in Des Moines and delivered a passionate call for military preparedness to the fifteen hundred people present. "The price of democracy and peace in this hemisphere is based on our being more willing than the Nazis to sacrifice our goods, our time, and, if need be, our lives," he declared.*[24] The speech was aimed at building public support for President Roosevelt's plan to provide Britain with desperately needed military equipment through the lend-lease program.

The lend-lease proposal touched off one of the most closely followed congressional debates of the century. Hundreds of citizens pressed into hearing

---

*During a layover in Chicago en route to Iowa, Wallace walked alone to the Chicago Public Library and began browsing. A library worker recognized the vice president and introduced him to Herbert Hewitt, head of the reference room, who promptly supplied Wallace with two Spanish novels, two nonfiction works on South America, and a book called *The American Faith*, by Ernest Bates. "I liked the way he came in—as a citizen, without any show," Hewitt said later. "He was very easy to talk to and very kind."

rooms to hear the aviation hero Charles A. Lindbergh denounce the bill and Wendell Willkie express his support. The issue was of such importance that Wallace felt he should personally preside over debate.

It was not a happy introduction to the Senate. The debate was tedious and repetitive, in Wallace's view, lasting as long as seven hours per day. The Senate's vaunted tradition of limitless talk struck him as a waste of time. He was an outsider, not a member of the club, and he was content to remain that way. Senators sensed his attitude and responded in kind. It didn't help that Wallace often slumped in his chair and closed his eyes in apparent boredom.

Powerless to affect the proceedings, frustrated by the interminable legislative process, Wallace began looking for other means to make his mark. The speech in Des Moines was his first effort, and the response encouraging. Widely reported in newspapers around the country, the speech was denounced as "slander" by the government of Nazi Germany.

In the days that followed, supporters of lend-lease gained strength in the Senate. One crippling amendment after another was beaten back, and the bill eventually passed with a comfortable majority. Roosevelt signed the bill into law on March 11 and moved at once to begin the shipment of arms to beleaguered Britain. But the whole experience had not enhanced Wallace's respect for Congress and its customs.

"It seemed to me that they just didn't know what was going on in the world," he said later of the Senate's lend-lease debate. "I couldn't understand them."[25]

Thereafter Wallace displayed at best a modest interest in the workings of Congress. Usually he would preside over the Senate's opening hour of business, from noon to one, and leave to get something to eat. He seldom returned. The presiding officer's duties were left to whomever was handy. Wallace even missed his first opportunity to break a tie vote. He was dining on duck with friends when the Senate deadlocked on a bill allowing the navy to purchase beef from Argentina.

"One of the most futile occupations I know is presiding over the Senate," Wallace said later. The Senate's "totalitarian" committee structure and the abuses of its seniority system disgusted him.[26] Conservatives had a stranglehold on any piece of progressive legislation, and most members of the body seemed to respond to national concerns from a parochial perspective.

The vice president, Wallace later observed, "can influence action if he wants to, on the highly personal basis of having a drink with the boys and playing poker with the boys."[27] The operative words were "if he wants to," and Wallace didn't. He tried instead to interest senators in physical activity.

Only one senator, Allen Ellender, a Louisiana Democrat, accepted Wallace's invitation to spar with him in the boxing ring. Even Ellender lost interest after Wallace knocked him out. Newspapers noted that Wallace was the first boxing vice president since Theodore Roosevelt. He was also the last.

He had better luck persuading some senators to join him at paddleball. But that, too, waned quickly. Mainly senators went to their gymnasium for the steambath and free rubdowns they could receive, Wallace noted. After a few weeks he gave up and took his recreation in the House gymnasium, where younger members such as the Alabama Democrat John Sparkman and the South Dakota Republican Karl Mundt could be coaxed to play paddleball. The House gym, Wallace said, was his "equivalent of Garner's bar."[28]

For Wallace it was a period of decompression and adjustment. He had gone almost overnight from being the administrator of a massive and innovative government agency to being a man with frankly little to do. At the Agriculture Department he had a budget of a billion dollars and some 146,000 employees. Now he had a budget of $11,000 and a staff of four: secretaries Mildred Eaton and Mary Huss (the latter with him since his days as editor of *Wallaces' Farmer*), a young dictationist named Rafael De Haro (chosen because his native language was Spanish), and Harold Young, his personal assistant.

The most puzzling member of this tiny staff, in the eyes of Wallace's old associates, was Young. He was a huge, hearty man, weighing between 250 and 300 pounds during most of his adult life. He smoked cigars and drank "sufficiently," as Wallace put it, and he loved the gregarious, back-slapping, storytelling elements of political life. He was a liberal, but of the Texas populist variety. Young was far more at home in rough-and-tumble partisan politics than in the ascetic progressivism of the Wallace family.

Young, a Dallas lawyer, had come to Washington to run a small office set up by the Democratic Party to handle Wallace's affairs during the 1940 campaign. He was apparently hired at the suggestion of the Texas publisher Charles Marsh, a man who shared Wallace's liberal views and spiritual curiosity. Marsh had contributed heavily to the Democratic Party and privately gave at least $2,000 toward Wallace's living expenses during the campaign. Marsh was also Harold Young's brother-in-law.

Wallace had wanted his old Friend Jim LeCron, his personal assistant at the Agriculture Department, to continue with him. But the illness LeCron's wife had contracted during their visit to Mexico was enough to send him back to Des Moines. So Wallace turned to Young, a man he barely knew.

Strangely enough, they got along. Wallace enjoyed Young's good humor and regarded him as "an essentially honest, fine man." Wallace's family and friends in the Middle West were less generous in their opinion. They were "very dubious about Harold, because of these various habits he had," Wallace commented.[29] Young in turn admired Wallace's idealism and tolerated his eccentricities with genial patience. It was an odd alliance, but it lasted for seven years.

Wallace's only perquisites as vice president were the franking privilege and a big black Buick with a chauffeur on the Senate payroll. His salary remained $15,000 a year, exactly what it had been as a cabinet officer. Housing was not provided. The Wallaces stayed on in the Wardman Park but moved to a larger apartment. Ilo enjoyed the social status her husband's new job afforded and began winning high marks for her graciousness and beauty. One newspaper even placed her on its list of the ten best dressed women in America. She was frequently called upon to pinch-hit at the White House during Eleanor Roosevelt's absences. But Henry accepted his social responsibilities only with reluctance. Several weeks into the job he told a reporter he had decided to limit social engagements to Thursday and Sunday evenings—and not on Sunday if he could help it.

He played tennis more often than ever. He walked to his office, often striding alone down the Mall from the Lincoln Memorial to the Capitol. He tried out a dietary concoction devised by a professor at MIT that was supposed to contain all the nutrients needed for survival. (He concluded it worked but was monotonous.) He read South American newspapers and studied the latest developments in genetics. He persuaded CBS radio to begin a regular program of Spanish music and even helped pick out the songs. He hashed over the concept of a future United Nations organization with friends, discussed poetry with Robert Frost, talked to John Maynard Keynes about economics.

An article in the *Des Moines Register* described Wallace as "one of Washington's busiest men." A *New York Times* story carried the headline "Wallace Makes a Job of the Vice Presidency." In fact, however, Wallace was less busy than he had been for two decades, and the job he had made of the vice presidency still had no particular duties. Moreover, he was loath to involve himself in patronage matters, so his closeness to Franklin Roosevelt was of no political advantage to him.[30]

Perhaps, Wallace suggested to reporters, he could be a sort of roving goodwill ambassador with special concentration on Latin America. Or perhaps he could be a utility infielder for the president, performing whatever administrative tasks were needed at the moment. The latter idea was lifted from a magazine article, published in October 1920, entitled "Can the Vice President Be Useful?" written by Franklin D. Roosevelt.[31]

After five months of such dormancy, Roosevelt answered in the affirmative the question he had posed twenty years earlier. On July 9, 1941, he signed Executive Order No. 8839, establishing the Economic Defense Board (EDB), and appointed Wallace as its chairman. The board was to serve as a "policy and advisory agency" dealing with a wide range of international economic issues, including exports, imports, "preclusive buying" (the purchase of strategic materials in order to keep them out of enemy hands), foreign exchange transactions, international credit and transportation, the control of foreign-owned properties, and patents and all other matters related to foreign economics.

"I am sure that you know more about this field than anybody in town," Roosevelt told Wallace.[32]

Wallace's new job was described by Richard Wilson in the *Des Moines Register* as an "American minister of economic defense, and the chief planner of the new world order of the future when the war is over."[33] The latter task was deemed especially important by Wallace. Well before the United States entered the war, he began speaking publicly about the kind of world that should follow it.

"After the victory, what of the peace?" he asked in an April 1941 speech to the Foreign Policy Association. "The battle of the peace will be more difficult to win than the battle of the war. All Europe will be a mad swirl of chaotic forces. Unless we are prepared to help in the reorganization of a shattered world, these forces will leap from continent to continent and destroy even the United States."[34]

Wallace's role as EDB chairman was a historic first. "It is probably the first time in history that a Vice President has been given an administrative task," the syndicated columnist David Lawrence wrote. "Beginning in the Harding administration, the Vice President began to sit in the cabinet, but Mr. Roosevelt enjoys the distinction of putting a Vice President to work really as the No. 2 man in Government—a conception of the vice presidency popularly held but never realized."[35]

Henry Agard Wallace was back in business.

Roosevelt was not being merely charitable in giving Wallace a job. By mid-1941 he needed help. He had proclaimed it to be America's business to become the great "arsenal of democracy." He had announced a breathtaking goal of building fifty thousand airplanes a year. He had won passage of the innovative lend-lease plan to supply arms to America's allies. In late May he had declared an "unlimited national emergency" and called upon Americans to meet the crisis.

But words do not win wars, and the war mobilization effort had become an organizational and logistical nightmare. Army draftees were training with wooden guns. Airplane production during 1940 and 1941 combined was barely half the annual goal Roosevelt had established. Supplies of critical raw materials—rubber and aluminum, to name but two—were clearly insufficient for wartime needs. Stockpiles were slim to nonexistent. Estimates of the raw materials needed for full-scale war production were woefully inadequate. Large industries were reluctant to convert production to wartime needs, lest they lose civilian market share to competitors. Labor unions seized an opportunity to launch strikes in the auto, steel, and coal industries.

Roosevelt himself helped compound the general confusion. He resisted the necessity of telling Americans they must choose between guns and butter. And he continued to indulge his penchant for administrative untidiness. To Bernard Baruch and others who called for appointment of a "mobilization czar"—a single individual who could command the military buildup from one, all-powerful office—Roosevelt paid due respect but did nothing. He simply refused to give any one man, or even any group of men, authority sufficient to bring order to the situation.

The result was chaos, followed by failure, followed by more chaos.

For more than a year, beginning in May 1940, Roosevelt had brought into being one agency after another aimed at military preparedness. Thirty-five such agencies—from the Office for Coordination of National Defense Purchases, to the Office of Price Administration, to the Office of Facts and Figures—were scattered around Washington even before the United States had entered the war.

The first of these efforts, the National Defense Advisory Commission (NDAC), established the pattern of high hopes and failure that marked prewar mobilization. The commission had no executive authority and no chairman. Its seven members included distinguished men drawn from civilian ranks such as William S. Knudsen of General Motors, Edward R. Stettinius Jr. of U.S. Steel, and Sidney Hillman of the CIO. They were eager to serve but powerless to act. In theory they were responsible to a group of six cabinet officers, including Wallace, who made up the NDAC. In fact, they operated as independent agents and reported directly and individually to the president.

The NDAC staggered through the summer and fall of 1940 while Roosevelt and Wallace campaigned for election and paid it little heed. By November the commission "was punch-drunk" and close to collapse, Donald Nelson later wrote in his book on war mobilization, *Arsenal of Democracy*.[36] At the end of the year, as Nazi air raids on Britain reached their ferocious peak, Roosevelt abolished the commission and replaced it with the Office of Production Management (OPM). At its head he placed Knudsen and Hillman, symbolic of the need for cooperation of industry and labor in the war effort, as co-equals.

Knudsen and Hillman went to work with gusto and in short order were operating a burgeoning agency chock full of talented businessmen, labor leaders, economists, and statisticians. To head the important Division of Purchasing, they brought in Donald Nelson. As vice president and director of marketing for Sears, Roebuck, Nelson was accustomed to dealing with thousands of industrial suppliers. But the chronic problems that bedeviled the NDAC, the lack of central authority and interagency coordination, were still present at OPM. Turf wars abounded, the most important of which involved the relationship between the OPM and the War and Navy departments.

Nothing better illustrated the scope of the task facing OPM than its effort to establish "priorities and allocations" of raw materials. Someone had to decide, for example, whether steel would be used to build cars or combat planes or new production plants. These decisions were enormously intricate. It was all well and good to say all steel should be used for arms production, but without steel to build railroad cars and farm machinery there might be no way to transport arms or feed the troops.

To meet the problem, the OPM devised an elaborate system of priority ratings. Production facilities with an A-1 rating would have first access to necessary materials. Quickly, however, everyone had an A-1 rating, so the OPM devised an A-1-A rank, giving even higher priority to some projects. That was followed by AA-1 and AAA-1 ratings of even greater urgency.

By the summer of 1941 everyone knew that the OPM was "ready for the oxygen tent," as Nelson later put it. Production efforts were faltering, purchasing programs were wildly erratic (the army had 38 million pairs of socks stockpiled but zero combat boots), and the priorities system was lurching toward collapse. Businesses were confused at best and uncooperative at worst. And Germany's decision to invade the Soviet Union on June 22 faced the United States with the problem of helping a new ally in the struggle against fascism. "Nineteen hundred and forty-one," Nelson later observed, "will go down in history, I believe, as the year we almost lost the war before we ever got into it."[37]

Against this background, Wallace became chairman of the Economic Defense Board and assumed the role of a top aide in the president's mobilization efforts. His first step was to seek a director to manage the new board's vast array of responsibilities. Here he did something out of character: he chose a friend. It was sometimes said of Henry Wallace during his years at the Department of Agriculture that friendship with him was a career liability, because he went out of his way to avoid any show of favoritism. In this instance, however, Wallace sought the assistance of Milo Perkins, probably then his closest personal friend aside from Jim LeCron.

Perkins had made a small fortune manufacturing burlap bags in Texas before joining the Agriculture Department in 1935. He came to Washington because he wanted to help his fellow man, and he had concluded that the best way of doing this was to work for Henry Wallace. He proved to be an industrious, innovative manager in a variety of agriculture programs. Regardless of his role, Perkins once said, his job always was to take "H.A.'s ideas and put them into action."[38]

By mid-1941, when he was serving as the department's director of marketing, president of Federal Surplus Commodities Corporation, and administrator of the school lunch and food stamp programs, the forty-one-year-old Perkins was close to exhaustion. He was working eighteen-hour days, smoking one cigarette after another, and daily gulping down twenty cups of coffee in an effort to stay alert.

Suddenly Perkins found himself flat on his back in Johns Hopkins Hospital with a stomach ailment that puzzled doctors concluded was probably fatal. Doctors removed a portion of Perkins's intestines but were still uncertain of his long-term prospects. Perkins was characteristically direct about his predicament. "Why didn't somebody tell me how sick I was?" he bellowed.[39]

Perkins was still in his hospital bed when Wallace came to talk to him about the EDB position. Wallace, who was not completely aware how sick Perkins had been, asked whether he felt up to the job. Perkins immediately arose from his bed and pronounced himself ready to work. Wallace announced Perkins's appointment as director the following day and named the Princeton economist Winfield William Riefler as assistant director.

One of the board's first tasks was enforcement of an executive order issued by Roosevelt to impose a blacklist of some eighteen hundred Latin American companies that were purchasing goods in the United States and funneling them to Axis countries. To help assure that the U.S. government was speaking with one voice regarding Latin American economic relations, Nelson A. Rockefeller, the State Department's coordinator of inter-American affairs, was added to the EDB as a permanent member.

Wallace and Rockefeller developed a cordial relationship based on their mutual fondness for Latin American culture and for tennis. They often had dinner together on Sunday night, where they would study Spanish and listen to Latin American folk songs.

Wallace had barely settled into his role as chairman of the EDB before Roosevelt assigned him a new and even more complicated task. In mid-August, shortly after returning from the secret shipboard meetings with Winston Churchill that produced the Atlantic Charter, Roosevelt asked Wallace to head a new superagency to coordinate all aspects of defense mobilization. A running feud between Knudsen and Hillman had created an intolerable situation at OPM.

On August 28 Roosevelt issued Executive Order No. 8875 creating the Supply Priorities and Allocations Board (SPAB) and designating Wallace as chairman. The agency was Roosevelt's response to Churchill's call for more arms delivered more quickly. As usual, however, Roosevelt's solution to the problem only added more confusion.

The SPAB was superior to the OPM but also thoroughly interrelated with it. Knudsen and Hillman served on the SPAB while they remained codirectors of the OPM. Bureaucrats moved easily between the two agencies. The administrative situation was symbolized by the role of Donald Nelson, who was named executive director of the SPAB but continued to serve as director of priorities at the OPM. Thus Nelson was William Knudsen's subordinate and superior at the same time. The SPAB, said Nelson, was "certainly an administrative anomaly."[40]

Only six months after taking office, Wallace had become the most powerful vice president in the nation's history. No vice president had ever wielded such administrative authority, much less a policy voice of consequence. Roosevelt "used me in a way which made the office for a time a very great office," Wallace later observed.[41]

Yet, as Wallace was quick to note, his authority derived entirely from the president. With "the will and desire of the president," Wallace was the second most powerful man in Washington. Without it he was Alexander Throttlebottom. "Of course," Wallace observed, "nobody has less power than a vice president. There's no power there—none."[42]

And nobody had any idea how far he could or would take the new role he played. "My position was to some extent weak because there was no historical precedent for what Roosevelt did in precipitating me into key positions in the war effort," he remarked.[43] His strength, on the other hand, lay precisely in the fact that Roosevelt had placed trust in him. Wallace was Roosevelt's man, and it was widely assumed he was doing what Roosevelt wanted done.

Wallace wasted no time doing exactly that. At its first meeting, held in the boardroom of the Social Security building, at the foot of Capitol Hill, the SPAB set out its goals and issued a plainly worded statement to the public. "Our general policy is simple," said the statement. "Production shall be stimulated and organized to the limit of the nation's resources. Every available man and machine must be employed either on direct defense requirements or at work essential to the civilian economy. Along this road lies protection of our freedom and of the basic economy necessary to the maintenance of that freedom."[44]

The statement marked a turning point in the long struggle between the "all-outers," who sought to put the nation's great economic engine completely into the fight against Nazism, and the "part-outers," who maintained that defense needs could be met with little disruption to the civilian economy. With the arrival of Wallace and the SPAB, the all-outers were in control.

The major loser was William Knudsen, an able man, an acknowledged authority in the field of industrial production, but always reluctant to disrupt the civilian economy. "I never had any question whatsoever of Knudsen's complete patriotism," Wallace commented later. "I did have a feeling that he wanted too much to maintain business as usual and that his judgment couldn't be trusted on that account." As for Knudsen's codirector at the OPM, Wallace said bluntly, "I never completely trusted Sidney Hillman."[45]

The only man on the scene with "an intellectual comprehension of the job to be done" was Executive Director Donald Nelson, and Wallace "went straight down the line" with him: "I trusted his liberal instincts and the breadth of his intellectual understanding."[46] Nelson, a business executive unusually sympathetic to the New Deal, had a mutual respect for Wallace.

"They made a good team, even if the team did not actually last very long," wrote historian Bruce Catton in his book on defense mobilization, *The War Lords of Washington*. Catton, then the young publicity director at the SPAB, was fascinated by the contrast between Nelson, the "hale and hearty" extrovert, and Wallace, the introverted intellectual with the zeal of a prophet. "Wallace was a harder man to get acquainted with than Nelson," Catton wrote, "but much easier to understand."[47]

Their partnership in the fall of 1941, Catton concluded, was "the best thing that happened to America all year." Together they fought to "get the unthinkable questions asked and answered," and the result was a vast unleashing of national resources in the mobilization effort. In the first month of the SPAB's existence, military production increased 15 percent, followed by a 26 percent growth in the second month. Even the *Wall Street Journal,* no particular friend of Henry Wallace, acknowledged that the SPAB was the "youngest, toughest, smartest, and—so far—most successful defense agency."[48]

The key to the SPAB's success was its emphasis on allocations, as opposed to priorities, and its willingness to use legal authority to back up its decisions. It issued orders requiring an increase in steel production by ten million tons a year, placed tough restrictions on civilian construction projects, banned the civilian use of copper, and required equipment to be repaired rather than replaced whenever possible.

Underlying its actions was Wallace's broad view of the American economy as an interrelated instrument. One of the SPAB's first actions was an order encouraging full-scale agricultural production. Adequate nutrition was vital to the civilian infrastructure and military might, Wallace believed. The idea that America could be mobilized for war merely by placing large equipment orders with big business—an attitude most prevalent in the Army and Navy departments—struck him as dangerously shortsighted.

"I have sometimes felt that one of the great services Henry Wallace rendered the country was his insistence, at the first meeting of SPAB, on talking of production as 'more essential' and 'less essential,' rather than as 'essential' and 'non-essential,' " Nelson later wrote. ". . . Broadly speaking there is no such thing as 'non-essential' production in the United States. Our economy is vast and complex; its parts fit together with infinite intricacy. . . ."[49]

Wallace involved himself heavily with the workings of both the EDB and the SPAB. The original idea was that he need not be much more than a figurehead chairman who could straighten things out by the superiority of his official position. "It's a very nice thought," Wallace later commented, "but you don't really accomplish things by sitting on high. You've really got to grapple with the hard, day by day problems."[50]

Nor did he confine himself to the EDB and the SPAB. Suddenly Wallace was all around Washington, with the notable exception of the U.S. Senate chamber. He involved himself in policy debates, met with leading journalists, pushed for preparedness in speeches and social engagements. He pressed Roosevelt to be strong in dealing with the Japanese. ("I do hope, Mr. President, you will go the absolute limit in your firmness in dealing with Japan.")[51] He strolled through the National Gallery of Art with the French statesman Jean Monnet, played tennis with the broadcaster H. V. Kaltenborn, argued about extending lend-lease to the Soviet Union at a stag dinner with foreign policy leaders.

By late autumn Wallace was heavily engaged in winning a war that had not yet begun and for which the United States was ill prepared. Already the issues that would dominate his life for the coming decade had begun to emerge: the danger to democracy posed by unbridled capitalism and nationalism; the necessity for international trade and cooperation as a guarantor of peace; the responsibility of wealthy democracies to extend political and economic freedom to poor peoples around the world.

And already Wallace had begun to inform the war with a moral purpose—something Roosevelt steadfastly avoided—and to envision the sort of world that would emerge from military conflict. "The wisdom of our actions in the first three years of peace will determine the course of world history for half a century," he declared.[52]

In early November, Wallace proposed that he begin giving one major speech every month about the war and what would follow it, and Roosevelt enthusiastically agreed. The war gave America a "second opportunity to make the world safe for democracy," which it must not squander. Young Americans must understand that "the essence of democracy is belief in the fatherhood of God, the brotherhood of man and the dignity of the individual soul," he said.[53]

In early December, Wallace set forth his vision of a postwar world in an article entitled "Foundations of the Peace," published in the *Atlantic Monthly*. "The overthrow of Hitler is only half the battle; we must build a world in which our human and material resources are used to the utmost if we are to win complete victory," he wrote. "This principle should be fundamental as the world moves to reorganize its affairs. Ways must be found by which the potential abundance of the world can be translated into real wealth and a higher standard of living. Certain minimum standards of food, clothing and shelter ought to be established, and arrangements ought to be made to guarantee that no one should fall below those standards."[54]

A few days after the *Atlantic Monthly* article appeared, Wallace went to New York City with Secretary of Labor Frances Perkins to meet with Latin American officials. They were there to discuss the need for Pan-American unity and his vision of a world in which democracy and abundance would become reality.

The date was Sunday, December 7, 1941.

Shortly after lunch that day (1:25 P.M. on the East Coast; 7:55 A.M. in Hawaii) Japan launched an air attack on the U.S. fleet stationed at Pearl Harbor. Wallace learned of the attack from someone who heard a news flash on the radio. A few minutes later a White House operator reached him on the phone and said a plane was waiting at the airport to return him to Washington immediately.

Wallace went directly to the White House, where he learned the grim facts: 2,403 American lives lost, hundreds more wounded, the battleship *Arizona* and 18 other ships ruined, hundreds of planes destroyed or damaged. Roosevelt had cabled the words "Fight Back" when he learned of the attack, but the United States had managed to inflict merely a glancing blow. The Japanese lost only 29 planes and 55 men.

Wallace stayed at the White House through the long evening, discussing the situation with Roosevelt personally, then sitting through somber meetings with the cabinet and congressional leaders, remaining until almost midnight to talk again with Roosevelt and Sumner Welles. The president was "really very gravely concerned," Wallace later said. "We all were drawn very close together by the emergency. Americans are very good when they really get up against it."[55]

The following day Wallace and virtually all top officials in the federal government assembled in the House of Representatives chamber to hear Roosevelt call for a declaration of war. "Yesterday, December 7, 1941—a date which will live in infamy—the United States of America was suddenly and deliberately attacked by naval and air forces of the Empire of Japan."

That afternoon, as both houses of Congress were acting on the war resolution, Wallace gathered members of the Supply Allocations and Priorities Board in his office to consider the next step. At 2:30 P.M. the SPAB issued a statement in fighting words.

"A united people will harness the unparalleled might of the United States to one slogan—victory. From this moment we are engaged in a victory program. We can talk and act no longer in terms of a defense program. Victory is our one and only objective, and everything else is subordinate to it."[56]

CHAPTER FOURTEEN

"THE CENTURY OF THE COMMON MAN"

❦

Twenty-eight months had passed since the day Albert Einstein in his famous letter to Franklin Roosevelt had suggested the possibility of building an atomic bomb. Much had happened: a war in Europe, Winston Churchill, the third term, the draft, the Battle of Britain, lend-lease, a war in Asia, mobilization, Pearl Harbor.

One thing had not changed, however. The atomic bomb remained only a distant possibility.

The few men who grasped the theory of nuclear fission and understood its awesome destructive potential had become frustrated and alarmed. Many of them were foreign born—Leo Szilard, Eugene Wigner, and Edward Teller of Hungary, Enrico Fermi of Italy, Victor Weisskopf of Austria—and had good reason to fear a world in which Adolf Hitler had an atomic weapon. Every passing month brought fresh evidence that a nuclear bomb could be built, and that scientists in Nazi Germany were aiming to do it.

Pressure on the U.S. government to make a decision with respect to atomic energy was developing on several fronts by the fall of 1941. Scientists working separately at Princeton, Columbia, the University of Chicago, and the University of California at Berkeley were more certain than ever of the practicality of building an atomic weapon. A secret panel of scientists in Britain known as the MAUD committee reached a similar conclusion.

Another committee, established by the National Academy of Sciences (NAS) and led by Arthur Compton, a Nobelist in physics at the University of Chicago, had produced two reports favorable to the project and was at work on a third. And the youthful Harvard president, James Bryant Conant, head of the National Defense Research Council and an early skeptic, had at last come to support the project's feasibility.

By October, Vannevar Bush, head of the Office of Scientific Research and Development, decided things had ripened sufficiently to warrent the president's personal involvement. Bush contacted Henry Wallace, his liaison with the president, who agreed the hour had arrived.

The fateful meeting was held on a Thursday afternoon, October 9, 1941, with only Roosevelt, Bush, and Wallace present. Bush relayed the conclusions of the MAUD committee's report and the recent thinking of American scientists. He tried to describe what such a weapon would mean. A bomb with an explosive core of only twenty-five pounds would be the equivalent of 1,800 tons of TNT, he noted, and could pose dangers yet unknown. Moreover, it would be enormously costly to build.

The three men talked extensively about the long-term consequences of such a weapon. By its very nature it would change the face of warfare and international diplomacy. "We discussed at some length after-war control," Bush wrote in a memo about the meeting to Conant.[1]

The meeting did not lead to an immediate decision to build the bomb. There were too many unknowns. But the meeting had a singularly important outcome. Instinctively, but very emphatically, Roosevelt concluded that nuclear policy would be determined by the president and no one else. Scientists would build it only at his direction. The military would use it only upon his order. Congress would not be consulted and the citizenry not informed.

Soon after their meeting Roosevelt appointed a small secret committee to advise him on atomic policy. The members of this group, named the Top Policy Group, were Secretary of War Henry L. Stimson, Army Chief of Staff George C. Marshall, Bush, Conant, and Wallace. The committee would report to Roosevelt alone, and he alone would make decisions.

Events at last began to move swiftly. Only a few weeks after Roosevelt appointed the Top Policy Group, Compton's NAS panel completed its third and final report on the feasibility of building a nuclear weapon. In six succinct double-spaced pages, the committee outlined the scientific challenge and concluded it could be met.

Before transmitting the report to Roosevelt, Compton began to lay groundwork for its acceptance. The physicist sought out Wallace for a friendly game of tennis; as they finished, Compton turned gravely to the great issue at hand. "Please give this report your most careful attention," he told Wallace. "It is possible that how we act on this matter may make all the difference between winning and losing the war."[2]

The report was given to Roosevelt on November 27, but already Wallace had advised him of its contents. As Bush handed the NAS report to Roosevelt, the president gave verbal approval for an accelerated research program and promised the necessary funds would be forthcoming. Within ten days Bush, Conant, and Compton had devised a plan of action—the so-called S-1 program—and contacted Wallace to press for its immediate approval.

On December 16 Wallace summoned members of the Top Policy Group to discuss the S-1 program. Only Wallace, Bush, and Henry Stimson could attend. (Marshall was out of the city; Conant was ill.) On that day the Top Policy Group gave its blessing to the S-1 program, including the basic research needed to develop a pilot plant, and sent its recommendation to Roosevelt.[1]

Two days later Vannevar Bush met again with the S-1 scientists to report on developments and map the next steps. The "atmosphere was charged with excitement—the country had been at war nine days, an expansion of the S-1 program was now an accomplished matter," Conant wrote. "Enthusiasm and optimism reigned."[3]

The December meeting of the Top Policy Group marked Wallace's last official involvement with the atomic bomb project. In mid-1942, after months of confusion about who was really in charge, the project was put under military control. Brigadier General Leslie Groves, a hard-charging Army Corps of Engineers officer who specialized in getting things done at whatever cost, was placed in command.

Wallace continued to serve, however, as an informal link between Vannevar Bush and the president. Bush met periodically with Wallace throughout the war and briefed him on the progress of what came to be called the Manhattan Project. On at least one occasion, in April 1944, Wallace was also briefed on the project by Groves personally. (Wallace judged Groves to be "slightly pathological" as well as antisemitic and a "Roosevelt hater.")[4]

By his own choosing, Wallace did not immerse himself in the project's scientific and engineering details. But he was aware of its existence and keenly interested in its progress. Years before his successor, Harry S. Truman, knew of the bomb's existence, Wallace had given much thought to its diplomatic and military implications. He understood that control of the bomb—civilian versus military; nationalistic monopoly versus international regulation—was of critical importance.

---

*Roosevelt did not reply directly, nor did he ever put his approval of the atomic bomb project into writing. The closest thing to it was a cryptic handwritten note from Roosevelt to Bush on January 19, 1942. The note said the third and last NAS report was being returned and gave a veiled indication to proceed. The text of Roosevelt's letter reads: "Jan 19 / V.B. / OK—returned—I think you had best keep this in your own safe / FDR."

The secret of the bomb colored much of his thinking about postwar planning and security arrangements. He supported building it, believing it might well mean the survival of the United States. He early understood that once it existed it might be used. The nuclear genie could not be returned to its bottle. But he knew also that nuclear science was not the province of any one nation. It could not be the exclusive weapon of capitalism and colonialism, and it need not be the tool by which mankind eradicated itself.

If any one day marked the zenith of Henry A. Wallace's influence and authority as a public official, it would be January 15, 1942.

On that gray wintry day, Wallace was not only the nation's number two elected official—vice president of the United States and president of the U.S. Senate—but a force to be reckoned with on many fronts. As a member of the Top Policy Group, he was one of a handful of men advising the president on the nation's most secret military project. He was chairman of the Supply Priorities and Allocations Board (SPAB), the chief agency responsible for parceling out vital resources and spurring wartime production. He was chairman also of the Board of Economic Warfare (BEW), the principal agency responsible for wartime foreign economic concerns.*

"Henry Wallace," wrote James Reston in the *New York Times*, "is now the administration's head man on Capitol Hill, its defense chief, economic boss and No. 1 postwar planner. He is not only Vice President, but 'Assistant President.' "5 And even beyond his official roles, Wallace had become a formidable figure in ways more difficult to categorize. His ties to Roosevelt had grown stronger since the election—at least Wallace thought so, as did many other politicians and journalists—and he freely offered the president advice on a wide variety of subjects via frequent memoranda and private conversations. Wallace had the president's ear, it was believed, and his impact on policy was substantial.

Beyond Washington, too, Wallace had become a figure in his own right. As a writer, speaker, thinker, and man of public affairs, he had much to say about war and peace, democracy and God, and millions of Americans were listening.

On that chilly January afternoon Wallace was attending a grim SPAB meeting when word came that he and Executive Director Donald Nelson were to go immediately to the White House. They rode together and were waved through

*The agency, formed in mid-1941, was originally called the Economic Defense Board. After Pearl Harbor it was renamed the Board of Economic Warfare and its duties broadened.

the White House's heavy security immediately. Inside, the president's genial gate-keeper, Edwin "Pa" Watson, took them directly into the Oval Office.

Thirty-seven days had passed since Pearl Harbor, and the president's face "had lines of strain and fatigue," Nelson later wrote. Roosevelt was obviously a very tired, very serious man. He launched directly into an assessment of the war, of the desperate struggle for survival into which the nation had been plunged, of the monumental production task that lay ahead, and of his faith in democracy to meet the test. He talked for almost an hour as Nelson and Wallace sat in silence.[6]

At length he came to the point. Roosevelt had at last decided to place war production under control of a single agency, and place that agency under control of a single man. This man would serve as both chairman and chief executive of the new agency. His job would be to provide ships, planes, and weapons to defeat the enemy, and at the same time provide for a stable civilian economy. Roosevelt saved the big news until last. The name of the war production chief would be Donald M. Nelson.

"I looked at him and blinked," Nelson recalled. ". . . I was not only shocked, I was thunderstruck, and not only thunderstruck, but speechless—utterly speechless, I think, for the first time since I learned to talk." There is no record, in Nelson's book or in Wallace's account of the meeting in his oral history, that the vice president had anything to say, either.[7]

As Nelson left the Oval Office, Wallace lingered behind and asked whether the president wanted him to remain on the War Production Board as a member, although not as chairman. Roosevelt did.

If Wallace was disappointed that he would not head the new agency, he gave no sign of it. Robert Sherwood, in his book *Roosevelt and Hopkins,* said Wallace was one of several candidates for the post, and Wallace speculated that he probably could have had the post had he wanted it. He said he did not.

Nevertheless, the January 15 meeting in the Oval Office marked a kind of milestone in Wallace's public career and in his private relationship with Roosevelt. "Henry A. Wallace, still the most active vice president in history, has served in this capacity for more than a year, but is not yet quite the 'assistant president' that some observers thought President Roosevelt would make him," the *Des Moines Register* said two months later. ". . . As matters stand now, Wallace is one of a dozen top men in the administration who hold positions within the 'executive office of the president.' "[8]

Nor, Wallace began to learn, was his relationship with Roosevelt quite what he imagined it to be. "I always thought I had a very friendly personal contact with the president," Wallace remarked in his oral history. "It was not until later that I found out how many very friendly personal contacts he had with many people, and I realized that what seemed to me to be an altogether unique experience was perhaps not as unique as I thought at the time. . . . He did have a great capacity for communicating warmth. I later on reached the conclusion that he more or less turned this on automatically."[9]

Slowly there would build in Wallace a "sense of distrust" toward the president.[10] He would develop a feeling that Roosevelt was not as genuine, as supportive, as much a champion of principled liberalism as Wallace had wanted to believe. He could not pinpoint exactly when this vague, uneasy feeling began. But it would quietly gnaw and grow inside him until the day, two and a half years later, when Roosevelt betrayed him utterly.

But for the moment a job had to be done, a war won, and Wallace forged ahead with his usual dedication. As chairman of the Board of Economic Warfare he continued to have important executive responsibilities. The agency's chief tasks were to provide the U.S. military and industry with natural resources vital to prosecute the war, and to keep those resources out of enemy hands. With the hyperenergetic, idealistic Milo Perkins at his side, and with a staff of some three thousand economists, planners, and administrators to back him up, Wallace pushed the agency onto a highly aggressive and innovative path.

As Wallace saw it, the job at hand was not only to win the war but to win the peace. The outcome of the war had to be more than restoration of the status quo. He sought a postwar world in which New Deal liberalism thrived in America and would spread throughout the world. Most of all he wanted to end the deadly cycle of economic warfare followed by military combat followed by isolationism and more economic warfare and more conflict.

Wallace's solution to the problem was an amalgam of the institutional economics of Thorstein Veblen and the social gospel espoused by his grandfather. His vision of the postwar world featured international economic cooperation, an end to imperialism, the abolition of poverty and illiteracy, and a global federation with sufficient power to maintain world peace. "Now at last the nations of the world have a second chance to erect a lasting structure of peace . . . such as that which Woodrow Wilson sought to build but which crumbled away because the world was not yet ready," Wallace declared.[11]

That path soon led Wallace and Perkins into the muck of bureaucratic swamp water.

The State Department was jealously guarding its export- and import-licensing prerogatives. The Lend-Lease Administration was making its own arrangements for shipping vital materials to America's allies. The Reconstruction Finance Corporation (RFC) and related federal lending agencies under the control of Secretary of Commerce Jesse Jones were determined to dictate terms for import purchasing. Nelson Rockefeller, coordinator of hemi-spheric affairs at the State Department, was setting up various development corporations in Latin America more or less on his own account. The Department of Agriculture had its own procurement authority for foreign pur-chases. Certain administrators in the War Production Board viewed them-selves as "courts of last resort" on foreign purchases.

If this bewildering situation continued, Wallace argued in a strongly worded memo to Roosevelt on March 18, "THERE CANNOT BE ANYTHING BUT FRUSTRATION AND CONFUSION." He supplied the capital letters him-self. Wallace demanded "clear-cut authority" for the BEW to do its job, the power to hire and fire its own personnel, and enough money to carry out its responsibilities. His main goal was to circumvent Jones and the RFC, whose "banker mentality" prevented the BEW from obtaining the necessary funds for purchasing and development loans.[12]

Confusion surrounding the economic situation mirrored the general un-tidiness of Roosevelt's management style. "With regard to matters of that sort, the president was a very bad administrator," Wallace later said. "He contin-ually allowed messes to develop between individuals. . . . It may be that he had a very good policy mind but a very poor administrative mind. He didn't seem to see through this kind of difficulty, or if he did see through it he wanted to have this kind of difficulty emerge."[13]

Perhaps for that reason, Wallace speculated, Roosevelt seemed to want his vice president to stay free of "the hurly-burly of administrative detail" in or-der to protect him from the inevitable scars. If that was Roosevelt's desire, Wallace added, it was a pipe dream. "[You] cannot be responsible and at the same time not be responsible."[14]

Wallace backed up his private memo with public remarks, delivered to a farm audience in Omaha, in which he praised American farmers for their all-out production and contrasted their effort to the meager stockpiling and plan-ning carried out by certain government agencies and their industrial allies.

For a moment Wallace seemed to gain the upper hand. After a further ex-change of memos ("Time is short. . . . Let's go!" Wallace declared) and sev-eral meetings, Roosevelt issued a new executive order on April 13 detailing the BEW's authority.[15] The order appeared to give the BEW power to make all decisions with regard to exports and imports. The RFC was left to write checks and keep the books.

As the *St. Louis Post-Dispatch* described the order the next day, "The crum-bling empire of Jesse H. Jones has lost another great province through Pres-ident Roosevelt's executive order transferring to the Board of Economic Warfare authority not only for the procurement, but the financing and pur-chasing of raw materials from abroad."[16]

The president's order also skewered the State Department by allowing the BEW to send its own personnel abroad to negotiate purchases. In addition the order gave the BEW a role in postwar planning, which the State Department considered its special province.

Wallace's victory was more apparent than real, however. The State Department, with Cordell Hull and Sumner Welles acting in rare accord, insisted that Roosevelt revisit the order.* After a series of meetings intended to calm the waters, Roosevelt issued another order in May, which restored some of the State Department's authority. Privately he told Wallace and Perkins to proceed with postwar planning but "not to do enough of it so we would get caught by the State Department."[17]

Wallace agreed to the modification in the interest of wartime harmony. In atypical language he instructed Perkins to tell Roosevelt "that anytime it would help lighten the president's load and promote the general welfare, the president could hang Milo's ass and my ass on the Lincoln Memorial Bridge and paddle them every morning."[18]

As for Jesse Jones, the fight had only begun. The commerce secretary was an experienced bureaucratic warrior. The stall was his weapon of choice. Jones later explained the tactic with winking candor to a congressional committee: "When we thought the [BEW] orders were proper, we complied promptly. When we thought the orders were not . . . we tried with great patience to reason with them."[19]

Soon it became obvious that issuing an executive order was one thing; carrying it out was another. Employees scheduled for transfer from the RFC to the BEW could not be moved, because Jones's agency didn't have time to supply the names. Loan payments demanded by the BEW were indefinitely delayed while Jones's bankers went over the details. Field officers for the BEW and Jones's government-owned corporations found themselves in competition and at cross-purposes.

In addition Jones's strong ties to Capitol Hill, assiduously courted for more than a decade, enabled him to launch flank attacks to keep his enemies off balance. The first strike at Wallace came through arch-conservative Texas con-

---

*Hull suffered a "nervous collapse" in the wake of Pearl Harbor and had just returned to work when Roosevelt signed the BEW order. According to Wallace's diary, Hull's initial objection to the order stemmed from the authority it gave to Morris Rosenthal, head of the BEW office of imports. When Hull discovered that Rosenthal would have control of this area "he went straight up in the air at the thought of the Department of State being dictated to by a Jew," Wallace wrote.

By this time Wallace had also developed a "profound distrust" of Sumner Welles. He had concluded that Welles's "deep-seated admiration for Mussolini" and the pope would have disastrous consequences in Latin America. Wallace told Hull directly that he "did not care to work with [Welles] on matters having to do with the Board of Economic Warfare."

gressman Martin Dies, chairman of the House "Special Committee on Un-American Activities" and close ally of Jones. In a "letter" to Wallace dated Saturday, March 28, 1942, and given to reporters the following day, Dies charged that "at least thirty-five high government officials employed by the Board of Economic Warfare have public records which show affiliation with front organizations of the Communist Party."[20]

Dies's juiciest charge was aimed at one Maurice Parmelee, a $5,600-a-year economist on the BEW payroll. In 1931, Dies noted, Parmelee had written a book called *Nudism in Modern Life*. Dies alleged the book contained 35 pages of "obscene" photographs and 300 pages of text advocating nudity in homes, schools, and the workplace. "Surely, Mr. vice-president," Dies declared, "there is no place in a post-war planning agency for a person who advocates such a crackpot and immoral plan."[21]

Wallace hit back smartly. Even before newspapers had a chance to print Dies's original smear, Wallace issued a stinging four-page rebuttal that accused the congressman of seeking "to inflame the public mind by a malicious distortion of facts." The nation was at war, Wallace noted pointedly, and "the doubts and anger which this and similar statements of Mr. Dies tend to arouse in the public mind might as well come from [the Nazi propagandist Joseph] Goebbels himself as far as their practical effect is concerned."[22]

Public reaction to Dies-Wallace exchange generally fell in favor of the vice president. Newspapers viewed it as only the latest example of Dies's unquenchable thirst for publicity. Congressional leaders were miffed that Dies had implied the charges grew out of a committee investigation. In fact, other members of the committee had never heard of them. Roosevelt brushed off the incident with a quip. "You know that the vice president is employing a nudist," Roosevelt said at the outset of a meeting with congressional leaders. Then, shaking his finger at Speaker Sam Rayburn, he added, "But in the House of Representatives we have, Sam, something much worse. They have an exhibitionist!"*[23]

---

*Maurice Parmelee's book on nudism was published in 1931 by respected publisher Alfred Knopf. A libel suit, filed in connection with an English edition, resulted in a lower-court opinion that photographs in the book were obscene. Dies quoted from this opinion in his attack on the BEW employees but did not note that the decision had been overturned on appeal.

Wallace noted the appellate court decision and added, "Not one person in a hundred thousand in this country is interested in nudism. Mr. Dies has twisted a few isolated facts in an effort to create an impression that the Board of Economic Warfare is planning a nudist post-war world for the United States. In calmer times this would make him the laughing stock of the country."

The episode had a curious denouement. Two weeks after Wallace issued his ringing defense of Parmelee, whom Wallace had never met, the economist was abruptly fired by the BEW without explanation. Parmelee tried to meet with Wallace and publicly appealed to have his job back but was rejected on both counts. Instead, he was given a position at the Railroad Retirement Board.

If the attack on Wallace had backfired, Jones was unconcerned. The commerce secretary had one big ace in the hole. At the very moment Wallace was fending off Dies's attack and attempting to consolidate power at the BEW, Jones was quietly helping the president's son Elliott resolve a "serious financial problem" resulting from an attempt to start a radio network in Texas.[24]

Jones, by far the wealthiest member of Roosevelt's administration, arranged the buyout of a $200,000 loan Elliott had received from the Great Atlantic & Pacific Tea Company's president, John A. Hartford, for $4,000, and personally advanced the money needed to complete the deal. The president expressed his profound gratitude to Jones for the "special favor" to his family. Five years passed before Elliott repaid Jones, in a letter that began, "Dear Uncle Jesse."[25]

About the "special favor" Jones had provided, Henry Wallace knew exactly nothing.

⊗

This was no ordinary turf war. In Wallace's mind the success of the war effort, at home and abroad, hung in the balance. "[We] are writing the postwar world as we go along," he said in a memo to Roosevelt. The end of the war would give America a "second chance," he said, to help establish a world "where security, stability, efficiency and abundance would prevail." The errors that followed World War I could be avoided if the American people and their government acted wisely, and the time to begin was at hand.[26]

Wallace recognized that success would not come finally through memos and executive orders but through broad public understanding of the issues he was addressing. Once again, as he had in November 1941, Wallace set out to inform the war with moral purpose.

The press of events had cut short his intention to deliver one major address a month. He had spoken publicly to a couple of farm audiences and delivered brief remarks to a class of new army officers at the Aberdeen Proving Ground, in Maryland, where his son Bob was among the graduates.

His period of relative public silence ended with a thunderclap on Friday, May 8, when Wallace spoke before a dinner of the Free World Association in New York City. The thirty-minute speech was entitled "The Price of Free World Victory," but it came to be identified around the world with its most famous phrase: "The Century of the Common Man."

The speech was as pure an expression of progressive idealism as Wallace could muster. Delivered at a moment of maximum national peril—the Battle of Coral Sea had just ended, and American forces had succumbed to the Japanese onslaught on Corregidor—it became Wallace's most famous wartime address. For millions of Americans it defined America's mission in the war and the vision of a peaceful world to follow.

He began quietly, almost tremulously. "This is a fight between a slave world and a free world," he said. "Just as the United States in 1862 could not remain half slave and half free, so in 1942 the world must make its decision for a complete victory one way or the other."[27]

The concept of freedom, he explained, was rooted in the Bible, with its "extraordinary emphasis on the dignity of the individual," but only recently had it become a reality for large numbers of people. "Democracy is the only true political expression of Christianity," he declared, adding that with freedom must come abundance. "Men and women cannot be really free until they have plenty to eat, and time and ability to read and think and talk things over."

Others had joined Americans in the march to freedom, Wallace noted, including those, such as the Russians and Chinese, with little experience in democracy. "Everywhere the common people are on the march," Wallace declared.

When the freedom-loving people march—when the farmers have an opportunity to buy land at reasonable prices and to sell the produce of their land through their own organizations, when workers have the opportunity to form unions and bargain through them collectively, and when the children of all the people have an opportunity to attend schools which teach them truths of the real world in which they live—when these opportunities are open to everyone, then the world moves straight ahead.

There had been setbacks, he noted. At times the "people's revolution" had turned bloody and excessive. Demagogues had diverted the march to progress. "But the significant thing is that the people groped their way to the light," he added. And having seen the light, the people would fight with "the ferocity of a she-bear who has lost a cub" to maintain their freedoms. "The truth is that when the rights of the American people are transgressed, as those rights have been transgressed, the American people will fight with a relentless fury which will drive ancient Teutonic gods back cowering into their caves. The Götterdämmerung has come for Oden and his crew."

Modern science, Wallace continued, "has made it technologically possible to see that all of the people of the world get enough to eat. Half in fun and half seriously, I said the other day to Madame Litvinov [wife of the Soviet ambassador to the United States]: 'The object of this war is to make sure that everybody in the world has the privilege of drinking a quart of milk a day.' She replied: 'Yes, even half a pint.' The peace must mean a better standard of living for the common man, not merely in the United States and England, but also in India, Russia, China, and Latin America—not merely in the United Nations, but also in Germany and Italy and Japan."

The "century of the common man" was Wallace's answer to Henry Luce's call for an "American century" at the end of the war. In a lengthy editorial published in early 1941, the publisher of *Time* and *Life* had advocated U.S. intervention in the war precisely because it would leave America in a position of unparalleled power. "It now becomes our time," Luce wrote, "to be the powerhouse. . . . [We must] accept whole-heartedly our duty and our opportunity as the most powerful and vital nation in the world and in consequence to exert upon the world the full impact of our influence, for such purposes as we see fit and by such means as we see fit."[28]

Wallace never mentioned Luce by name, but his rebuttal was clear. Said Wallace,

> Some have spoken of the "American Century." I say that the century on which we are entering—the century which will come out of this war—can be and must be the century of the common man. Everywhere the common man must learn to build his own industries with his own hands in a practical fashion. Everywhere the common man must learn to increase his productivity so that he and his children can eventually pay to the world community all that they have received. No nation will have the God-given right to exploit other nations. Older nations will have the privilege to help younger nations get started on the path to industrialization, but there must be neither military nor economic imperialism. The methods of the nineteenth century will not work in the people's century which is now about to begin.[29]

Economic slavery and colonialism must be abolished, he said. International cartels serving "American greed and the German will to power" must be subjected to international control. The Axis war machine, and the culture from which it grew, must be dismantled forever. Racism must not be tolerated. "[When] the time of peace comes, the citizen will again have a duty, the supreme duty of sacrificing the lesser interest for the greater interest of the general welfare. Those who write the peace must think of the whole world. There can be no privileged peoples. We ourselves in the U.S. are no more a master race than the Nazis."

Wallace concluded in terms that vibrated with religious passion:

> There can be no half measures. . . . No compromise with Satan is possible. We shall not rest until all the victims under the Nazi yoke are freed. We shall fight for a complete peace as well as a complete victory.

The people's revolution is on the march, and the devil and all his angels cannot prevail against it. They cannot prevail, for on the side of the people is the Lord.

⊗

Henry Wallace had thrown down his gauntlet by nationwide broadcast, but response to his speech was initially slim. His friend Addison M. Parker, a Des Moines lawyer, wrote to say it gave "the spiritual as well as the realistic note that we have needed." Another friend, Donald R. Murphy, editor of *Wallaces' Farmer*, said it was "the strongest, the most emotionally mature speech that has been made on our side since the war started." For the most part, however, as Wallace later observed, "very little attention was paid to it during the first two or three days."[30]

The first real notice of it came when *PM*, a liberal afternoon newspaper published in New York City, twice reprinted the text in its entirety. The printed version drew public praise from the nationally syndicated columnists Raymond Clapper—he likened the speech to Lincoln's Gettysburg Address—and Dorothy Thompson. And it drew the attention of A. N. Spanel, president of the International Latex Corporation, who paid to have it reprinted in the *Washington Post* and *Women's Wear Daily*. Both publications were quickly inundated with requests for copies.

In response to this demand the L. B. Fisher Company on May 28 published the speech in pamphlet form and within six weeks sold more than twenty thousand copies. At the same time the federal government's Office of Facts and Figures began distributing hundreds of thousands of copies of it. Elmer Davis, a popular broadcaster who had become head of the government's wartime propaganda agency, told Wallace "the one thing he wanted to do in the Office of War Information was to carry out" the policies laid down in the speech.[31]

Eventually "The Price of Free World Victory" was translated into twenty languages, and millions of copies were distributed around the world. Reynal & Hitchcock, longtime publishers of Wallace's writings, coupled it with several of his other speeches and articles and issued it in book form in 1943 as *The Century of the Common Man*. And that book, in turn, was folded into a larger book entitled *Prefaces to Peace*, which also contained *One World*, by Wendell L. Willkie, *The Problems of Lasting Peace*, by Herbert Hoover and Hugh Gibson, and a collection of essays by Sumner Welles called *Blue-print for Peace*. In sum, Wallace later said, "The Price of Free World Victory" probably "had more impact than any other speech I have ever given," with the possible exception of the speech that led to his dismissal from government in September 1946.

Of course, not everyone liked the speech, least of all the State Department, ever wary of intrusion by outsiders into foreign policy. Wallace's first taste of the department's view came two days after he delivered the speech, when he attended a luncheon for the president of Peru at the home of Assistant Secretary of State Adolf Berle. "When we arrived at the Berles' place, we found about eight policemen on the street outside, four or five in the front yard, and two or three in the backyard," Wallace wrote in his diary. "Berle said in his heavy choppy way, 'I suppose there are so many policemen here because of your talk about revolutions.' "[32]

State Department officials, claiming to be acting at the behest of local advisory committees, moved in several countries to block distribution of a pamphlet containing the speech, on grounds that illustrations depicting labor strikes and the French Revolution would disrupt local order. The first instance of this came in Cuba, less than a month after the speech was delivered.

Press reaction to Wallace's speech also was not altogether approving. The *New York Times*, which tended to reflect the State Department's positions, took a dim view of it. The *Wall Street Journal* said it promised more than America could ever hope to deliver and therefore was deceiving to people in underdeveloped countries.

And Henry Luce, who had great pride in his "American Century" editorial, took personal umbrage. There followed a semicordial exchange of letters between them, in which Luce argued that an "American century" would improve the lot of poor people and Wallace responded that the phrase rubbed "the citizens of a number of our sister United Nations the wrong way." The letters did nothing to improve relations between them. Wallace later observed, "From that time on, Henry Luce seemed to be on the other side of the fence, as far as I was concerned."[33]

Conservatives, at home and abroad, disliked the speech, as Wallace had anticipated. Republican businessmen, Roosevelt's constant antagonists during his first two terms, correctly saw Wallace's speech as part of an effort to spread the New Deal around the world. British Tories—Winston Churchill first among them—intensely resented Wallace's attack on colonialism. Conservative elements of the Catholic Church objected to his revolutionary rhetoric and his call for universal literacy. Old-fashioned racists derided it as a call for "a quart of milk for every Hottentot."*

*The "quart of milk for every Hottentot" phrase was coined by William Witherow, chairman of the National Association of American Manufacturers. So widely was it quoted that millions of people, including Franklin Roosevelt, came to believe it was part of Wallace's speech. Witherow later expressed regret over the words.

Whether praised or damned, however, "The Price of Free World Victory" framed a great debate. The speech offered liberals a reason for fighting and hope for a better world to come. It challenged conservatives to articulate an acceptable alternative. And it bestowed upon its author the status of a prophet, whom some would follow and others would destroy, as America plunged into a brave new world.

It was said of Henry A. Wallace that he loved mankind but was not particu-larly interested in individuals. He struck some people as cold and aloof. His reserved manner, his famous disdain for chitchat, his disapproval of strong drink and salty talk carried with it a whiff of intellectual arrogance and moral superiority.

Yet those who saw Wallace as strange viewed him mainly through the prism of politics. There was another Wallace, modest and genuine, who was entirely comfortable with the common men and women who passed through his life. Occasionally he and Ilo would escape from Washington on a Sunday after-noon and drive about the Maryland countryside, sometimes stopping to chat with a farmer about crops and bugs and weather. His high public office was never mentioned.

One day as he passed more or less unnoticed through the crowded lobby of the Mayflower Hotel, he came across a photographer struggling to carry his gear. Wallace mumbled a shy hello, hoisted up a heavy black box full of equipment, carried it to the street, and went on his way.

What might have appeared an ordinary human gesture to many rural mid-westerners seemed out of place in official Washington. Said the historian Scott Hart, in a book on the capital in wartime, "An official of his rank, according to the manual of Washington amenities, was not obliged to reach for a tele-phone directory, much less to lift it. The action suggested a man who, though having reached the heights, was unable to abandon the manners of the farm, where if one man carries two buckets of chicken feed an unencumbered per-son by his side takes hold of one."[34]

His most treasured pastime was gardening, the most humble and solitary of pursuits. Throughout the war years he arose early morning to work alone in his "victory garden," located on the grounds of the Swiss legation, a short distance from the Wardman Park. His sister Mary Bruggmann, wife of the chief of the Swiss legation in Washington, arranged for his use of the land.

In this garden Wallace met Juan Ramón Jiménez, a poet who had fled Spain during the civil war and was working in wartime Washington as a literature professor. The capital city knew nothing of Jiménez, nor he of it. He was an obscure and lonely man, until one day he chanced upon a man working in a garden—a man "timid yet firm at the same time"—and struck up a conversation.

"Of all my acquaintances in this country," Jiménez recalled, "none have I come to understand better nor more quickly." The two men spoke the same language—the language of God and agriculture, democracy and idealism—and often they spoke in Spanish. Later Jimenéz wrote of his new friend in a Mexican literary journal:

> There can be no doubt that this man is a mystic, made of the same stuff as the greatest of the Spanish mystics, St. Teresa de Jesus, St. John of the Cross, Louis de Leon. He is militant in his faith as they were. . . . St. Teresa's "God Can Be Found in a Well Watched Kettle" means to Henry Wallace, "God can be found in a dairyman's milk-pail and in a farmer's corncrib. . . . He is convinced of an enduring and just principle of ancestry—every man is the son of his own words and deeds.[35]

Months after making Wallace's acquaintance, after reading Spanish poetry with him and sharing their deepest spiritual convictions, Jiménez mentioned his new friend to some colleagues. From them the professor learned for the first time that his friend was vice president of the United States. "Was it possible?" Jiménez rushed to the garden and found Wallace working alone.

"I said, 'Señor Wallace, tell me the truth, are you the vice-president of the United States?'" Wallace laughed and answered, "Si, Juan Ramón, lo soy" ("Yes, John, I am"). Then without stopping he added, "Look, aren't my tomatoes magnificent? Take some along with you for lunch."

Juan Ramón Jiménez later gained worldwide acclaim as one of the century's greatest poets and was awarded the Nobel Prize in literature in 1956. He knew Wallace only briefly—and entirely outside the realm of politics—but he believed he had seen greatness. Unwittingly, Jiménez had also captured part of Wallace's problem as a political figure. The mystical quality, which Jiménez so admired, totally bewildered the secular political culture of Washington. American politicians were expected to declare their belief in the Almighty and perhaps attend a mainstream church occasionally; they were not expected to find God in a dairyman's milk pail.

Even those who admired Wallace were sometimes taken aback by his humility. Jo Davidson, the prominent sculptor whose likeness of Franklin Roosevelt appears on the dime, twice did busts of Wallace and found him "shy, almost gauche." In the beginning Wallace "did not give of himself easily," Davidson wrote. "But he looked up at me from time to time. He gave you the feeling of wide open spaces, a clean beauty, and of strong healthy optimism. He didn't seem to waste his energies in useless words or gestures."*[36]

When Davidson was commissioned to execute a second bust, Wallace traveled to the artist's farm in Pennsylvania to spend the weekend. Davidson went to the train station to pick him up. "I looked for him in the Pullman cars but he was not there," Davidson wrote in his memoir, *Between Sittings*. "Then I spotted him with bag in hand, walking rapidly from one of the coaches. As he walked down the platform, nobody seemed to recognize him. He had the faculty of not being seen."

After a long day posing in the artist's studio, the two men went into Davidson's home for tea. They had been talking about methods for growing mushrooms. Suddenly Wallace excused himself, went to his room and returned in shirtsleeves. "I am going to find Sam," he said, referring to Davidson's gardener.

"We had no idea what he was up to," Davidson wrote. "He often stepped out for a bit of fresh air. It began to get dark and we went out to look for him. There, behind the studio, I saw Sam shyly holding a lantern while the Vice-President of the United States was digging a trench for my mushroom pit."

---

*Jo Davidson's first bust of Wallace, completed in 1940, a magnificent work executed in only two sittings, is now part of the permanent collection of the National Portrait Gallery in Washington. Davidson peered deeply into his subject and produced a work of "fire and soul," the *Christian Advocate* wrote. "The features came alive with character, and into the expression of the eyes there crept the characteristic Wallace look—the lifted look of a man with his face toward the storm but with his eyes seeing beyond. The sculptor called his work 'The Seer.' "

The second bust was commissioned during Wallace's vice presidency. As Davidson noted wryly in his memoirs, "The American tradition is that Presidents of the United States are painted and Vice-Presidents are 'busted.' The Vice-President's bust should be a head and shoulders, executed in marble." The second bust, a more conventional likeness, sits in a niche in the U.S. Capitol.

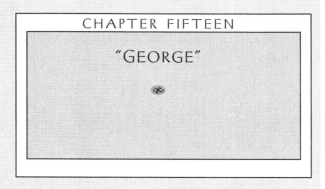

CHAPTER FIFTEEN

"GEORGE"

In Washington, newspaper columnist Harlan Miller once wrote, "when you ask a tableful of journalists or officials the question, 'Who has the best mind in the cabinet or other topnotch federal posts?' the answer is likely to be 'Henry Wallace, of course.' " To those who knew him, Miller said, Wallace was "an earnest, consecrated, simple, pious, shy, reserved, studious, scientific idealist with a warm curiosity about every realm of knowledge."[1]

Miller obviously had not invited Jesse Jones to his tableful of journalists and officials. As far as Jones was concerned, Henry Wallace was a crackpot, a misty-eyed dreamer, a messianic do-gooder out to force a glass of milk down the throat of everyone on earth whether that person wanted it or not.

Jones was a formidable foe. Tall and amiable, the sixty-eight-year-old Jones came from the rough-and-tumble world of Texas real estate and banking. Like his mentor John Nance Garner, he was a fiscal and social conservative with no interest in politics as a vehicle for change. In Washington, Jones had amassed enormous power, first as a member of the Reconstruction Finance Corporation board under Herbert Hoover, then as its chairman under Franklin Roosevelt. By 1942 his vast empire stretched from the Department of Commerce to the Federal Loan Agency, the RFC, the Export-Import Bank, the Federal Housing Agency, and several other government corporations formed to finance the war effort.

"Jesse Jones wielded greater power for a longer period than any human being in the history of the United States," Wallace later remarked.[2] Public money controlled by Jones gave him huge clout both in Congress and among businessmen, and he was not shy about rewarding his friends and punishing his enemies. Even those who did not especially like him, Franklin Roosevelt included, often found themselves in his debt.

The fight between Wallace and Jones grew into the most celebrated intragovernmental squabble of the era. As the feud intensified, it became, in the words of one historian, "a war within a war."[3]

Broad and complex, the fight involved a wide range of commodities, from cobalt to palm oil, from zirconium to quinine. But nothing symbolized the battle better than rubber. "I backed rubber when I was Secretary of Agriculture," Wallace later told a Senate committee. "I backed rubber when Congress tried to take the appropriations away entirely. Rubber is a hobby of mine."[4]

Indeed, as early as April 1939, it was Wallace who acted unilaterally to shore up the nation's rubber reserve. Convinced war with Japan had become increasingly likely, Wallace worked out, with the assistance of Ambassador Joseph Kennedy, a direct commodity trade of 600,000 bales of surplus U.S. cotton for 90,500 long tons of rubber owned by England. Although small when measured against the nation's actual requirements, the trade nevertheless accounted for almost all of U.S. rubber stockpiles at the end of 1939.

The man officially charged with stockpiling rubber, however, was Jesse Jones. In June 1940 Congress created four large companies under the purview of the RFC, including the Rubber Reserve Company, assigned to build up stockpiles of vital materials. Jones, sure that a war with Japan would be short, saw no urgency to act. Even in February 1942, when Japanese successes in the South Pacific had cut off 90 percent of the world's natural rubber supplies, Jones was assuring Congress that the United States "would be getting all the rubber we need from the Dutch East Indies" by the end of 1943.[5]

The situation was dire. Total U.S. rubber stockpiles in 1941, in government and private possession, amounted to only 540,000 tons. The U.S. Army and Navy would need all of it and more to fight the war. Tapping every available source of natural rubber, including Latin America and Africa, would add another 175,000 tons and still leave the United States 224,000 tons short of meeting lend-lease and vital civilian needs.

Amid mounting alarm and confusion, wartime administrators set out to overcome the crisis. At the War Production Board, Donald Nelson focused on mass production of synthetic rubber. With strong backing from Wallace, Nelson in early 1942 established a goal of producing at least 300,000 tons of synthetic rubber in 1943 and doubling that amount by 1944. He later revised the goal for 1944 to 800,000 tons, an incredible amount, which, even more incredibly, was met.

At the BEW, Wallace and Milo Perkins concentrated on the development and procurement of natural rubber. Their approach grew out of the board's mission, which involved preclusive purchasing and the importation of strategic materials, as well as Wallace's keen interest in agriculture and foreign economic development.

They keyed on the Amazon River basin. At the start of the war, the United States negotiated an agreement to purchase all the natural rubber Brazil could produce through 1947. In return, the Rubber Reserve was supposed to commit as much as $5 million to develop the Amazon basin.

There were problems on both sides of the bargain. Crude rubber production in the Amazon had been in decline for decades. By 1942 rubber production in the basin was less than half its level in 1910. The United States might buy all of Brazil's rubber, but it fell well short of enough.

On the other hand, the Rubber Reserve was slow and parsimonious—deliberately so in Wallace's view—in both its purchasing and development activities. Jones thought like a banker: all loans had to be fully secured by property, all purchases had to be made as economically as possible. "The Reconstruction Finance Corporation does not pay $2 for something it can buy for $1," Jones told Congress. The philosophy of the BEW, by contrast, Jones asserted, was "Damn the expense!"*[6]

In the field Jones's attitude displayed delay and neglect. As late as April 1942 the Rubber Reserve had only a single staff member assigned to rubber development in the Amazon basin. The BEW responded by sending dozens, eventually hundreds, of its own personnel to South America. Jones finally expanded the number of Rubber Reserve officials in South America to eighty-six, touching off a bureaucratic rivalry in the field that Jones saw as wasteful and duplicative.

For Wallace and Perkins it only meant continued friction and frustration. The BEW men could issue as many orders as they wished, but without money, which Jones controlled, they were powerless to make anything happen. Jones did whatever he wanted to do, as Wallace saw it, and kept a paper trail to cover his tracks.

A central point of conflict concerned the health and safety standards of South American workers. The BEW had developed estimates that, even with

*The BEW's efforts to develop natural rubber had its failures. A plan to form corporations to develop and procure rubber in the Belgium Congo and the Cameroons came to naught. Another plan, to develop a 100,000-acre rubber plantation in Haiti using the cryptostegia plant, was stalled for months by Jones on economic grounds and eventually succumbed to disease and poor management. The Haitian cryptostegia project, as Jones's allies were pleased to note, produced only five and a half tons of rubber at a cost of $6.7 million—or $546 per pound of rubber. Even Morris Rosenthal, head of the BEW imports office, acknowledged that the Haiti project "was a complete failure."

a healthy work force, some forty thousand men would be needed to extract twenty thousand tons of rubber a year from the Amazon basin. But conditions in South America were anything but healthy. Many workers were afflicted with malaria, malnutrition, venereal disease, or the effects of bad water. In any given year one-third of the rubber workers in the Amazon basin died and another third were too sick to work.

Perkins argued, with Wallace's full support, that production of rubber and other commodities could be increased only with a healthier, more stable work force. They sought to accomplish this both by direct assistance, such as the shipment of 350,000 tons of staple foodstuffs to improve the diet of South American workers, and by imposing health and safety standards in contracts signed with companies and governments producing commodities purchased by the United States.

The "labor clauses" inserted in BEW contracts required producers to "maintain such conditions of labor as will maximize production," to comply with the labor laws of the country of origin, to furnish "adequate shelter, water, safety appliances, etc.," and to consult with the buyer regarding wage scales. The contracts required sellers to "cooperate in a plan to improve conditions of health and sanitation" of workers, with the seller and the U.S. government sharing costs equally.[7]

To Wallace the "labor clauses" were not only morally just but economically sensible. "The BEW thought we could get more products if somewhat greater stimulus was offered to the working men in foreign countries in the form of salaries reflecting to some degree the advance in price, and in the form of food made available to them." Or, as Milo Perkins put it more bluntly, "It isn't radical to believe that you can get as much of a return by increasing the food to a human being as by increasing the food to a mule."[8]

To Wallace's foes the "labor clauses" were folly. The conservative Republican senator Robert A. Taft of Ohio accused the BEW of "setting up an international W.P.A."[9] The State Department was wary, fearing the labor clauses would be seen as interfering in the domestic affairs of other nations. South American business interests objected to their cost and said they would lead to unionization. Jesse Jones opposed anything that changed the customary relationship between capital and labor.

Douglas H. Allen, the head of Jones's rubber procurement program, summed up the loan agencies' attitude in a showdown argument with Wallace: "Mr. Vice-President, the people in the Amazon basin are no different from other peoples. Their greatest incentive to work is their desire to eat. Give a primitive people like that all the food they want and they will do no work. We will get no rubber."[10]

Perkins responded in a voice dripping with sarcasm. "Henry, I guess we just can't give away food in the Amazon and still get rubber; maybe we had better forget about it."[11]

⁂

Jesse Jones later called the fight over rubber one between those who favored synthetic rubber, namely himself, and those who favored natural rubber, especially Wallace. That was revisionist fiction.

Wallace was fully apprised of various scientific methods used to produce synthetic rubber. On several occasions he had detailed discussions about the matter with Dr. Chaim Weizmann, the noted chemist and Zionist leader. Jones, on the other hand, was initially reluctant to back any rubber program at all. Only after the oil industry came to understand the enormous financial benefits it could reap from the development of synthetic rubber did he become enthusiastic.

Wallace was concerned, however, that a huge new industry established by the synthetic-rubber program might lead to a push for protection and isolationism after the war. "How to get enough rubber in a hurry—this is the question of the hour," Wallace wrote in the *New York Times Magazine.* "But just over the hill is another question we shall have to face. That is: Will the rubber policies we adopt now lead to World War No. 3 later on?" A renewal of isolationism and protectionism "would tear down our chance to cement the firm and friendly ties that can give us national safety," Wallace added.[12]

The solution in his view was for the federal government to assume ownership of synthetic-rubber plants after the war. The emergency of war, Wallace wrote, "should not be used to build up vested interests which, after the war, would be sitting on the doorstep of Congress clamoring for a tariff." Once again Wallace quarreled with Jones, who opposed government ownership of the industry and intimated that his friends in Congress "would have something to say about the matter" at the conclusion of the war.[13]

Jones's comment reflected a stark reality: the synthetic-rubber issue had become intensely political, centering on the interests of the oil industry, which was deeply entangled in Democratic Party politics. It was a fact Wallace understood and lamented. The petroleum industry's leading political broker was Edwin W. Pauley, a California oil executive and lobbyist who also served as the Democratic Party's national secretary-treasurer. In terms of ethics Wallace regarded Pauley as "probably one of the least pleasant smelling" people he had met in public life.[14]

"His approach to the national economy would be totally different from mine," Wallace said of Pauley in his oral history. "His approach, essentially, was that of a hunter at work in the forest of national economics, trying to bring down what game he could. He felt that was what all genuine, red-blooded Americans should engage in. I wasn't interested in his hunting activities. Naturally he distrusted me." Wallace's misgivings about Pauley led him to warn Roosevelt to keep a distance. The president ignored the advice.[15]

Partly in an effort to prevent oil industry domination of the rubber issue, Wallace urged development of synthetic rubber from grains such as corn, wheat, or molasses. But that further politicized the issue. Farm state congressmen seized on synthetic-rubber production as a means of promoting their own interests. "It is obvious to me," Wallace remarked sourly in his diary, "that oil and alcohol people between them, with agricultural support sucked in from the alcohol end, are going to form a block to gouge the American consumer. . . . Jesse's plea is that of the isolationists and his slant is purely political."[16]

Only one thing was clear about rubber in mid-1942—there wasn't enough of it. The more Wallace pressed for decisive action, the more Roosevelt seemed uncertain. Finally he appointed a small commission, headed by financier Bernard Baruch, to investigate and make recommendations. In September the commission delivered its report, concluding that the United States would "face both a military and a civilian collapse" unless the rubber shortage was addressed immediately.[17]

The commission's report included stinging criticism of the Rubber Reserve and Jones's ineffective efforts to stockpile rubber before the war. Its recommendations included centralizing the government's rubber activities under a single administrator, which Roosevelt did almost immediately, and implementing nationwide gas rationing, which he did after the midterm elections in 1942.

Roosevelt designated the War Production Board as the agency responsible for rubber, and in mid-September its chief, Donald Nelson, named William Jeffers, president of the Union Pacific Railroad, to be rubber administrator. As recommended by the Baruch commission, Jeffers concentrated largely on synthetic rubber, while leaving procurement and development of natural rubber in the hands of Jones's Rubber Reserve and Wallace's Board of Economic Warfare. Tension between Wallace and Jones continued to simmer without quite reaching the boiling point.

Jones's hand was strengthened by the 1942 elections. Democrats lost forty-four seats in the House of Representatives and nine in the Senate. For the remainder of the war, Congress would be effectively dominated by a coalition of southern Democrats and conservative Republicans. Wallace, who took no active part in the elections, as a gesture to wartime unity, now saw clearly that liberals were on the run.

He said as much to Roosevelt personally. After the president's annual Thanksgiving church service, Wallace told him that Washington was rife with rumors that "men in uniform were going to run the country for the next ten years" in league with big corporations involved in the defense industry. It was apparent, Wallace added, that new assaults on the BEW were coming.[18]

Logically the BEW probably should be split up and its functions turned over to the Commerce and State Departments, Wallace said, but that would be "unfortunate from the liberal point of view." He proposed instead to get even more involved in the BEW's daily affairs and fight it out. "Much to my surprise," Wallace wrote in his diary, "the President said, 'Fine. Go ahead.' "[19]

The fight resumed at once. On December 2 Jones appeared before the Senate Committee on Banking and Currency, meeting in executive session, and complained that the BEW was busily negotiating wasteful, costly, socially radical contracts overseas that he was powerless to stop. Wallace demanded the right to respond, and on December 8 he and Perkins appeared jointly before the committee to refute Jones's testimony point by point. The BEW had indeed fought the RFC on occasion, Wallace acknowledged, but only in the interest of winning the war. "In the future," he said, "let's have more fights and fewer shortages."[20]

His testimony was regarded as effective, but it hardly ended the feud. As the liberal journalist I. F. Stone put it to the readers of *PM*,

It would be a mistake to believe that the attempt to hamstring the BEW is over. It would also be a mistake to believe that this is merely a conflict between Jones and the BEW. Behind Jones is the State Department, and behind the State Department are those forces, clerical and capitalist, which have no intention of letting this era become, in Wallace's phrase, the Century of the Common Man. . . . The BEW must be got out of the war before peace comes, lest the old order for which the State Department stands be endangered. The Metternichs are ganging up on the BEW because the BEW is Wallace, and Wallace is the champion of the common man.[21]

Stone's prediction came true in short order. Two weeks later Rubber Administrator Jeffers gave Jones's Rubber Reserve sole responsibility for the procurement and development of natural rubber. The action astounded Wallace, who protested to Roosevelt that the decision was remarkable in light of the Rubber Reserve's poor record.

His protest went for naught.

The second half of 1942 marked the war's turning point. Beginning with the great sea battle off Midway Island in early June, Allied forces began to take the offensive. By November, General Dwight D. Eisenhower had invaded North Africa with an Allied force of 400,000, U.S. ships had inflicted heavy losses on the Japanese fleet at Guadalcanal, and Russian forces had survived Germany's grueling siege at Stalingrad. "Victory" was the word of the hour.

But whose victory? And for what? For progressives, Henry A. Wallace first among them, these were months of doubt and discouragement. From abroad came sounds of the old order reasserting itself. Winston Churchill announced that the Atlantic Charter's call for democratic self-determination did not apply to colonies in the British Empire. In India, which Wallace regarded as the key to British intentions, Gandhi's crusade for independence was met at 10 Downing Street with scorn and resistance.

In Washington wealthy businessmen—the "dollar-a-year men" Roosevelt had once promised to resist—ruled virtually every wartime agency. Great symbols of the New Deal, such as the Civilian Conservation Corps and the Works Progress Administration, fell victim to the budget ax. "War is the great killer of liberalism," Wallace lamented privately.[22]

Wallace forged ahead, attempting in speeches and articles to impose upon the war a vision of liberal mission and tolerance. "America, the heir of the religious concepts of Palestine and the culture of Rome and England, is building in the full sun of a new day for a peace which is not based on imperialistic intervention," he said in a speech entitled "Why Did God Make America?"[23]

Wallace did have his articulate critics. Walter Lippmann, the most renowned newspaper columnist of the era, said Wallace's idealism was unrealistic and unattainable. "National ideals should express the serious purposes of the nation," Lippman wrote, "and the vice of the pacifist ideal is that it conceals the true end of foreign policy. The true end is to provide for the security of the nation in peace *and* in war."[24]

But Wallace had supporters, too, and not all of them liberal Democrats. "Victory is too much looked upon merely as something that will bring relief from peril," wrote John Foster Dulles, then chairman of a committee on postwar goals for the Federal Council of Churches and later secretary of state under President Eisenhower. ". . . The addresses by Mr. Wallace and the final chartering of our courses by Mr. Hull are beginning to create the content for the dynamic faith we need."[25]

The big question, for Wallace as for all New Dealers, was where Roosevelt stood. Roosevelt's need for wartime unity was paramount, and publicly he could do nothing to rile conservatives. But privately there were hints he agreed with Wallace's postwar views.

On several occasions, for example, Roosevelt indicated to Wallace his own reservations about Churchill and the British Tories. He thought England was a second-rate "tired old power" well behind the United States, China, and Russia in importance. He was "profoundly concerned" about Britain's handling of India. The president told Wallace he thought the U.S. military should be relatively small after the war, and that peace should be enforced through international collective security.

Roosevelt also told Wallace it was "highly essential that the United States and Russia understand each other better." When Wallace responded that "the conservatives in both England and in the United States are working together and that their objective will be to create a situation which will eventually lead to war with Russia," Roosevelt seemed to agree.[26]

On the other hand, Roosevelt continued to deny the BEW control over its own spending and was reluctant to give it a free hand in postwar planning. Wallace constantly stressed the importance of free international airways and airports—a kind of down payment on the concept of collective security—but Roosevelt never backed the idea. Concerned as Roosevelt may have been about India, he declined a request to send U.S. troops there, because of Churchill's objections. The fact was, the president told Wallace, the shape of the postwar world would be determined by Stalin, Churchill, and himself, so the plans being laid by various parts of his administration did not mean all that much.

At times during this period Wallace clearly was speaking for Roosevelt. One such occasion was Wallace's "Tribute to Russia" before the Congress of American-Soviet Friendship in November 1942. The speech was delivered at Roosevelt's urging, and its content had his specific approval. A fear had risen that Russia would accept a separate peace, and the goal of Wallace and Roosevelt was to persuade the Soviets to fight on.

"This meeting demonstrates just one thing—the desire and the determination of the American people to help Russia and help her now," Wallace declared.[27]

Americans and Russians had much in common, said Wallace. "Both peoples were molded by the vast sweep of a rich continent. Both peoples know that their future is greater than their past. Both hate sham." Then, in words destined to haunt him over the coming decade, Wallace launched into a discussion of "the new democracy," which he said must include not only political democracy but economic, educational, ethnic, and gender democracy as well.

Some in the United States believe that we have over-emphasized what we might call political or bill-of-rights democracy. Carried to its extreme form, it leads to rugged individualism, exploitation, impractical emphasis on states' rights, and even to anarchy.

Russia, perceiving some of the abuses of excessive political democracy, has placed strong emphasis on economic democracy. This, carried to an extreme, demands that all power be centered in one man and his bureaucratic helpers.

Somewhere there is a practical balance between economic and political democracy. Russia and the United States both have been working toward this practical middle ground.

And finally: "The new democracy by definition abhors imperialism."[28]

❋

In the closing weeks of 1942, as Wallace paddled steadily to the left, an undertow of conservatism grew ever more powerful. It might not be visible, but Wallace could feel the strength of its pull. Wallace told Roosevelt it was "common gossip in Wall Street that the President had gotten over his foolishness now, that he had settled down and that we were now headed toward the kind of world in which Wall Street felt comfortable and at home. I said the Tories in England were also now feeling very much more comfortable." He warned of a State Department clique called the Riga group, which "felt that Russia was the real enemy" and aimed eventually to provoke a war against the Soviet Union.[29]

There were alarming reports of U.S. collaboration with profascist French forces in North Africa, of Allied differences over self-determination in India, of troubling fascist strength in Latin America. In his diary Wallace observed darkly that it was "increasingly clear" the State Department intended "to save American boys lives by handing the world over to the Catholic Church and thus saving it from communism."[30]

There was a rumor that the army's G-2 intelligence unit routinely asked the stock question "Do you know . . . the Vice President?" as a means of discovering whether an applicant "has ideas which are too progressive for the Army organization."[31]

Wallace's misgivings about Britain were deepened when he learned, in a private meeting with Vannevar Bush, that England was pressing the United States to share "certain technical information having to do with the atomic bomb." Bush opposed such sharing, and so did Wallace. Years later Wallace observed to his friend Donald Murphy, "Of course I wanted to have peacetime utilization of atomic energy made available, but I distrusted Britain— Tory Britain—as much as I did Russia."[32]

As the year came to an end, Wallace again expressed his concerns to Roosevelt. Administrative chaos continued in Washington, Wallace said. The fight with Jesse Jones raged on. Congressional conservatives were eagerly probing for "weak spots." Certain "bigoted Catholics" were scheming to gain control of the Democratic Party.

"I told the President that there were people in the United States at the present time who were moving definitely toward producing a post-war situation which would eventually bring us into war with Russia," Wallace wrote in his diary, "and another group moving into a situation that would eventually bring us into war with England. The time had come, I said, when we must begin to organize skillfully and aggressively for peace."[33]

A few hours later Wallace delivered a speech called "World Organization" at a banquet marking the eighty-sixth anniversary of Woodrow Wilson's birth. It was the fullest expression to date of his vision for the postwar world—and it marked a milestone at which Wallace's views no longer jibed with the times, with several powerful institutions of national life, and with Roosevelt himself.

"The task of our generation—the generation which President Roosevelt once said has a 'rendezvous with destiny'—is to organize human affairs that no Adolf Hitler, no power-hungry war mongers whatever their nationality, can ever again plunge the whole world into war and bloodshed," Wallace began. ". . . Soon the nations will have to face this question: Shall the world's affairs be so organized as to prevent a repetition of these twin disasters—the bitter woe of depression and the holocaust of war?"

The "worldwide new democracy" to emerge from the war must be built upon the enduring American principles of "Liberty and Unity," Wallace said, which was to say "home rule and centralized authority." No longer could Americans be like the "strong, well-armed pioneers" who thought they could defend themselves without the "expense and bother" of joining their neighbors in establishing a police force.

The United Nations, like the United States one hundred and fifty-five years ago, are groping for a formula which will give the greatest possible liberty without producing anarchy and at the same time will not give so many rights to each member nation as to jeopardize the security of all.

Obviously the United Nations must first have machinery which can disarm and keep disarmed those parts of the world which would break the peace. Also there must be machinery for preventing economic warfare and enhancing economic peace between nations. Probably there will have to be an international court to make decisions in cases of dispute. And an international court presupposes some kind of world council, so that whatever world system evolves will have enough flexibility to meet changing circumstances as they arise.

. . . We in the United States must remember this: If we are to expect guarantees against military or economic aggression from other nations, we must be willing to give guarantees that we will not be guilty of such aggression ourselves.[34]

❦

Milo Perkins looked like any of the myriad middle-aged businessmen who took on tasks in wartime Washington. A man of medium height and build, with slicked-back brown hair and sleepy gray eyes, he cut an ordinary figure. He had an easygoing smile, wore slouchy suits, was slangy and personal in speech. "O.K., guy," was a favorite expression.[35]

But no one who crossed Milo Perkins's path thought he was just another government chair warmer. Perkins was intense, able, tireless, and innovative. "That guy talks our language," a food distributor once said when Perkins was establishing the food stamp program in the late 1930s. "If the government were filled with Milos we wouldn't have so many administrative messes to clean up. He goes at a thing hammer and tongs."[36] Sometimes Perkins became so absorbed in his work that his wife, Tharon, would drive him to and from work, instruct him on what to wear and eat, and put spending money in his wallet.

He had built a reputation as a man who could get things done, specifically things Henry A. Wallace wanted done. He had come to Washington, one journalist wrote, with a "rarish blend, a knowledge of what it was to meet a payroll and a consuming desire to do good on a vast and lofty scale." And he had succeeded time and again. Even Dean Acheson, a State Department official not always friendly to Wallace, called Perkins the best administrator in the capital.* On the flip side, Perkins was aggressive, even ruthless, full of "zip and ginger," more likely to employ a stiff shove than sweet reason.[37]

And in January 1943, the month he turned forty-three, someone was definitely in Milo Perkins's way. Jesse Jones had placed one roadblock after another in the BEW's path. Jones had undercut the BEW in Congress, frustrated

---

*The Board of Economic Warfare was at its high point in early 1943. It had some 3,600 employees with a payroll of about $8 million. Some 350 of its employees were stationed abroad.

More than 100 of its employees were businessmen with expertise in the import-export trade. These men, who had earned between $15,000 to $75,000 in private enterprise, worked for government salaries of $5,600 to $9,000. Perkins was proud that the BEW employed no "dollar-a-year" men. Employees were required to sever former business relationships before going on the BEW payroll. "[Perkins] thought the practice of employing dollar-a-year men in other organizations had resulted in those men having an allegiance, from time to time, to something else than the general welfare," Wallace wrote in his diary.

There were about 120 professors on the BEW payroll, but Wallace noted that the bulk of its work force was drawn from private enterprise and other government agencies. He added, "Perkins and I were both known as liberals, but the vast majority of people in BEW were rather on the conservative side."

its efforts to acquire strategic materials, and hamstrung its attempt to improve social conditions in underdeveloped countries. Perkins had had enough. It was time to shove Jones aside.

Perkins's initial plan was to effect a transfer of Jones's lending agencies to the BEW in their entirety. The plan, required the approval of the budget bureau, however, and it balked. So Perkins reworked the idea. The new plan called for the BEW to issue its own executive order, giving it complete operational control over the importation of strategic materials. An RFC agency would do no more than write the checks it was asked to write. Wallace approved the plan, and on January 20, 1943, BEW Order No. 5 was published in the *Federal Register*. It would become effective on February 25.

Order No. 5 was published while Roosevelt was holding secret strategic discussions with Churchill in Casablanca, and the president was not informed in advance. Wallace wrote Jones a bland letter saying the order was an attempt to clarify responsibilities and eliminate duplication.

A furious Jones held his fire. Weeks passed with no response from the RFC. In mid-February the BEW requested a list of lending-agency employees who could be transferred, but the RFC gave no answer. Finally Jones's top assistant, Will Clayton, replied that the loan agencies would "need substantially all" of their present employees.[38] Wallace protested. Jones repeated Clayton's stance in stronger terms.

In the meantime Jones brought his complaint directly to Roosevelt. He argued that Order No. 5 was a "strained and extra-legal construction" of its original powers. He proposed a sixty-day hiatus during which the situation would be studied. Roosevelt said he had no time for study and handed the matter to James F. Byrnes, his newly appointed coordinator of wartime economy.* Byrnes first tried to persuade Wallace to accept the sixty-day cooling-off period. Wallace, seeing nothing to be gained by further delay, refused. Instead, he suggested both sides back away: the BEW would rescind Order No. 5, Jones would return rubber procurement to the BEW. This time Jones refused.

Under pressure, however, Jones offered a compromise. "If the president approves," he wrote Wallace, "we will turn over to you the U.S. Commercial Company which you can use for the purpose of development and procurement of strategic materials abroad as well as for preclusive buying in which it is now engaged."[39]

---

*A courtly politician and skilled conciliator, Byrnes had served as a representative and senator from South Carolina and gained a reputation as a Roosevelt loyalist. He resigned from the Senate in 1941 to accept appointment as an associate justice of the Supreme Court. A year later Roosevelt appointed Byrnes to be his "number one inflation-stopper" as head of the Office of Economic Stabilization. A few months later, in May 1943, Byrnes became the "czar of czars," as head of the Office of War Mobilization.

Wallace accepted the offer. Brynes was elated. "The prospect for peace seems bright," he wrote the president.[40]

❦

Shortly before reaching his temporary truce with Jones, Wallace asked the president whether he ought to visit Latin America. There were several reasons. Invitations from Central and South American countries had been piling up, and Wallace was eager to make the trip. He was profoundly concerned about the state of inter-American relations. Several Latin American countries still maintained diplomatic and trading relationships with the Axis powers. At least one country, Argentina, was openly sympathetic to fascism. Moreover, Latin America was the base of many BEW operations, and Wallace was eager to inspect them.

Roosevelt approved, although he also very much wanted the vice president to visit Russia. Wallace insisted Latin America should come first and within days announced plans for a forty-day, seven-nation goodwill tour to begin in mid-March. The trip would take him to Costa Rica, Panama, Chile, Bolivia, Peru, Ecuador, and Colombia.

Before departing, Wallace gave two more provocative speeches on national and international affairs. Both were delivered on March 8 in Ohio.

The first address, entitled "The New Isolationism," was delivered to an audience of farm leaders gathered to mark the tenth anniversary of the New Deal agricultural program. It posed a series of prophetic questions:

> Will farmers and city workers both be taken for a joyride on the roller coaster of boomtime prosperity, only to end up in the ditch of a worse depression than before? As soon as the war is won, will shortsighted policymakers again shut us off from the rest of the world? Will our country fail to grasp this second opportunity to build a world of peace and cooperation? Will our leaders engage instead in a mad nationalistic race for supremacy on land and water and in the air? . . . Will our leaders foolishly and selfishly deny that hunger and want and suffering in the rest of the world are of any concern to us? Will a spineless policy of drift once more lead us straight for the falls?[41]

Later in the day Wallace addressed the Conference on Christian Bases of World Order, at Ohio Wesleyan University. His speech, entitled "Three Philosophies," explored the differences between Nazism, Marxism, and what he called the "democratic Christian philosophy" of the United States.

"Those who think most about individualism preach freedom," Wallace said.

Those who think most about unity, whether it be the unity of a nation or of the entire world, preach the sacred obligation of duty. There is a seeming conflict between freedom and duty, and it takes the spirit of democracy to resolve it. Only through religion and education can the freedom-loving individual realize that his greatest private pleasure comes from serving the highest unity, the general welfare of all. This truth, the essence of democracy, must capture the hearts of men over the entire world if human civilization is not to be torn to pieces in a series of wars and revolutions far more terrible than anything that has yet been endured. Democracy is the hope of civilization.[42]

The most controversial portion of the speech, however, was a stark section warning of the dangers ahead:

We shall decide sometime in 1943 or 1944 whether to plant the seeds for World War III. That war will be certain if we allow Prussia to rearm either materially or psychologically. That war will be probable in case we double-cross Russia. That war will be probable if we fail to demonstrate that we can furnish full employment after this war comes to an end and if fascist interests motivated largely by anti-Russian bias get control of our government. Unless the Western democracies and Russia come to a satisfactory understanding before the war ends, I very much fear that World War III will be inevitable.[43]

The "double-cross" remark drew headlines around the country and caused a furor on editorial pages and in Congress. "It is difficult for me to understand why an American should believe that the United States might double-cross Russia and not believe that Soviet Russia might double-cross the United States," the columnist George E. Sokolsky wrote in the *New York Sun.* Senator Arthur Vandenberg, a Michigan Republican, professed to find it "amazing" for a vice president "to suggest that America is capable of double-crossing Russia, double-crossing anyone. . . . I do not think there is any possibility of having such a thing happen."[44]

❦

One week later Wallace flew out of Miami to Latin America. Over the next five weeks he traveled 11,833 miles. His planes landed and took off twenty-four times. He used regularly scheduled commercial flights and insisted on no special treatment. He traveled light and, as always, wanted as little ceremony as possible. He expressed a preference for simple food and said he would be happy with recordings of Spanish folk music if anyone wanted to give him something. The entire party consisted only of Wallace; Laurence Duggan, a State Department expert on South America; Hector Lazo, the Guatamalan-born number two man at the BEW; and a couple of Secret Service agents.

Wallace wrote his own speeches—short but frequent—and delivered them in Spanish. The popular Mexican actress Margo joked that Wallace spoke Spanish about as well as the popular band leader Xavier Cugat spoke English. But he spoke well enough to be understood, and that drew the admiration of Hispanic audiences. They adored him.

A crowd of 65,000 people—15 percent of the country's population—greeted Wallace at his first official stop, in Costa Rica. So many pressed to see him as his motorcade made the three-mile trip from the airport into San José that it several times came to a halt. Wallace amazed the crowd by climbing out of his car and walking ahead. "The reception accorded Mr. Wallace was the greatest in the history of Costa Rica," wrote a *New York Times* reporter.[45]

In his first address, to the Costa Rican congress, Wallace spoke of "freedom from want" and called for an equitable worldwide distribution of goods after the war. "In order to attain freedom from want, the theory of sustained yield and of the free interchange of products between nations must be accepted and followed without artificial boundaries," Wallace declared. ". . . In such an economic system, health, strength and happiness have a common denominator in adequate diet."[46]

From San José he traveled forty miles by car to lay the cornerstone of a building to house the Inter-American Institute of Agricultural Sciences, a facility he had first proposed in 1935. The institute was established to promote better food crops, but the war had turned its attention to rubber development. Wallace praised its work as a symbol of "effective Pan Americanism." From there he pressed farther inward to inspect rubber research projects and a plantation where cinchona seeds had been planted to produce quinine.

The next stop was Panama, where he attended an agricultural fair, inspected the Canal Zone, and spoke to the National Assembly. Again he was received warmly. But nothing could have prepared him for the thunderous welcome in Chile. There a crowd of 300,000 greeted his plane, and more than a million people waving banners and torches and cheering wildly watched as he walked arm in arm with the Chilean president, Juan Antonio Ríos, through the streets of Santiago. "I am deeply moved," Wallace said from the veranda of his guest house.[47]

Wallace's stay in Chile, the centerpiece of his Latin American tour, was full of extraordinary moments. The German-trained Chilean army goose-stepped in salute to the apostle of democracy. At a reception in his honor, the country's Roman Catholic archbishop was seen happily chatting with the leader of Chile's Communist Party. A crowd of 40,000 appeared from nowhere when he showed up in a remote mining village on a golden autumn afternoon, and Wallace gave a rare display of emotion when a twelve-year-old girl, holding the hand of her two-year-old brother, presented the vice president with a bouquet of flowers she had grown herself. "In the name of Chile," she said proudly.[48]

In Santiago 100,000 people pressed into a stadium built to hold 80,000 in order to hear the "gringo simpático." So impatient were they that Chile's foreign minister was booed off the stage when his introduction grew too windy. "We are of the New World, we North and South Americans," Wallace told them. "The responsibilities that rest upon us are tremendous. We are the repositories of the worth of Western civilization."[49]

Even officials of the State Department were awed by Wallace's reception. "Never in Chilean history has any foreigner been received with such extravagance and evidently sincere enthusiasm," Ambassador Claude Bowers reported to the State Department. ". . . His simplicity of manner, his mingling with all sorts of people, his visit to the workers quarters without notice . . . and his inspection of the housing projects absolutely amazed the masses who responded almost hysterically."[50]

Not everyone loved him, of course. Right-wing newspapers in Argentina called his failure to visit a slap to the country's honor. Leftist agitators portrayed him as an ambassador of Yankee imperialism. Some clerics, for whom anticommunism was quasi-religious dogma, were riled by his repeated calls for good relations with Russia. In Peru the totalitarian regime greeted his arrival with the widespread arrest of dissidents. In Colombia he was peppered with protests about the low level of U.S. assistance since the war began.

Nor were the State Department and the Federal Bureau of Investigation, altogether sanguine about Wallace's activities. They kept a watchful eye on the background of political and labor leaders who came in contact with Wallace. And shortly after his return from South America, an agent in New York reported to the FBI chief, J. Edgar Hoover, that he "had information which indicated strongly that Vice President Wallace was being influenced by Bolivian Communists."[51]

Wallace's appeal to the vast majority of common people, however, no one could deny. In La Paz, Bolivia, more than two miles above sea level, he astounded local residents by playing two brisk sets of tennis soon after his arrival. In Ecuador he pumped out of a jungle on a handcar when his train broke down.* In Peru and Colombia he wandered far into the interior to visit missions operated by Catholic and Protestant church groups. Once his Secret Service men were horrified to find him missing when they awoke; they later found him talking amiably with a group of peasant farmers near a large lake.

Wallace's interest in the lives of common people sometimes embarrassed his hosts, but there was little they could do to stop him. The *Telégrafo*, an Ecuadoran newspaper, offered a graphic account of his visit to Guayaquil:

> Mr. Wallace covered the whole city. And he examined us with eagle eye, and saw everything, much to the horror and disgust of the Governor of the Province. At the foot of the hill he alighted from the car. He entered one of the miserable houses there. "Let's see how the common people live," he said, and he went right in through the back door. It was worse than a mule stable. On the dirt floor, naked children, skinny, filthy. He asked permission and he entered a room where the women were. A coal stove, bunches of dirty rags, filth, misery. That's what Mr. Wallace saw.[52]

Wallace's visit was widely heralded as a triumph of personal diplomacy. By the end of the trip, a dozen Latin American countries had declared war on Germany, and twenty countries had severed diplomatic relations with it. Even the *Baltimore Sun*, normally a vociferous critic, praised Wallace's effort. "Whatever his shortcomings in other respects, he was an admirable ambassador of the good-neighbor policy," the paper editorialized. ". . . By personal example he sought to prove that Americans are simply people, everyday, homely, neighborly folk."[53]

❈

Nothing had changed for the better while Wallace was away. Order No. 5 was still in limbo. Transfer of the U.S. Commercial Company had not taken place. The feud between the RFC and the BEW, simmering during Wallace's absence, again neared the boiling point.

Events came hard and fast in May. A threatened nationwide coal strike; Allied victories in North Africa; U.S. possessions in the northern Pacific regained. In the middle of the month, Winston Churchill paid his third visit

---

*On the same day Wallace's train broke down, April 20, Roosevelt made a brief visit to Mexico. It marked the first time in U.S. history that a president and vice president were out of the country on the same day. Some newspapers editorially questioned who was in charge of the country, but White House aides observed that constitutionally Roosevelt was still president no matter where he happened to be.

to wartime Washington and brought into focus many of the crucial issues facing the Allies. Never reluctant to give his opinion, the British prime minister remained as opposed as ever to the "second front" in Europe that Stalin devoutly wanted. The best way to aid the Soviet Union, he maintained, was to invade Europe through Sicily and Italy, drawing German land forces away from the Russian front.

Churchill was equally blunt and confident about the postwar world. At lengthy luncheons with top U.S. officials in the British embassy and the White House, both attended by Wallace, he outlined his vision. Wallace summed it up succinctly in his diary: "He would have . . . England and the United States really run the world."[54]

Churchill's world would be divided into three spheres of influence—an American region, a European region, and a Pacific region—each with its own regional organization. Atop these would be "one supreme organization" dominated by England, the United States, and Russia. Each nation would have its own armed forces and provide troops for the supreme power. He was "very vague" about the internationalization of airpower and airports, Wallace said.

The United States and England should have a "special non-written understanding" of alliance, Churchill maintained. "He said the United States and England could pull out of any mess together," Wallace wrote. "The bait was attractive and most of those present swallowed it. . . . [Churchill] was spending all his energy on building an atmosphere of 'We Anglo-Saxons are the only ones who really know how to run the show.' " One of his pet ideas, in fact, was a proposal for joint British-American citizenship.

"I said bluntly that I thought the notion of Anglo-Saxon superiority inherent in Churchill's approach would be offensive to many nations of the world, as well as to a number of people in the United States," Wallace wrote in his diary. Churchill replied, with a candor born of "quite a bit of whiskey," that Anglo-Saxons were superior and "should not be apologetic about it."

Perhaps all American citizens, including those of Latin America, should be included in the joint citizenship plan, Wallace responded. Churchill answered, "If we took all the colors on the painter's palette and mixed them up together we'd get just a smudgy grayish brown." Wallace interjected, "And so you believe in the pure Anglo-Saxon race, or Anglo-Saxondom Ueberalles."[55]

Wallace came away from the luncheons charmed by Churchill socially and appalled by his philosophy. "As far as the war is concerned, we owe him a great debt of gratitude," Wallace later remarked. "As far as the peace is concerned, he's one of the architects of World War III."[56]

At the height of his visit, on May 20, Churchill addressed a joint session of Congress and delivered a stirring call for total victory over the forces of totalitarianism.

One day later George Perkins was killed during a Marine flight-training exercise in Florida. He was eighteen years old, the only remaining son of Milo and Tharon Perkins. The son's last words to his father had been "Stay in and slug."[57]

What might have depressed or defeated another father had the opposite effect on Milo Perkins. In mourning, Perkins redoubled his effort. He was more convinced than ever that the lives of men and women in uniform depended on the success of America's wartime agencies in providing necessary support. The sorrow he felt over his son's death was transferred into anger at those who, through delay or neglect, were impeding victory. The walking embodiment of delay and neglect, in Perkins's mind, was Jesse Jones.

Jones did his part to fuel the fire. Appearing before the Joint Committee on Reduction of Nonessential Federal Expenditures, chaired by arch-conservative Senator Harry Byrd of Virginia, Jones painted a picture of the BEW as a bloated, wasteful agency that duplicated and delayed the RFC's own efficient work. The following day another Jones supporter, Senator Kenneth McKellar of Tennessee, carried the attack to the Senate floor. McKellar charged, incorrectly, that the BEW was operating illegally since a "congressional appropriation has never been made for the payment of a single person employed in the BEW."[58]

Perkins was enraged. "Jesse didn't wait a week after my boy was killed before he went to Congress and told his goddamned lies." He demanded an opportunity to appear before Byrd's committee. Appearing calm but inwardly seething, Perkins forcefully rebutted McKellar's charges and defended the BEW's "extremely aggressive policy" of purchasing strategic materials.[59]

Perkins' testimony did not end the matter, however. Soon Jones's top lieutenant, Assistant Secretary of Commerce Will Clayton, was appearing before the Byrd committee to reiterate the attack on the BEW. Asked directly whether Order No. 5 had aided the procurement program, Clayton responded, "No, I do not think it has."[60] Meanwhile, Wallace and Jones were exchanging increasingly rude letters over the ongoing failure to transfer the U.S. Commercial Company to the BEW.

Then came an interlude that, curiously, made the dispute even more personal. On June 6, 1943, Wallace delivered a commencement address at his daughter's graduation from the Connecticut College for Women. The speech was a moving tribute to Milo Perkins's fallen son and all that he represented. It was entitled simply "George."

He began by remembering George Perkins as a fine, strong athletic young man with high hopes and ideals. "He was a pacifist, almost of the Quaker type, and the dignity of the individual, regardless of race, creed or color meant everything to him," said Wallace. When the war began in Europe, George was opposed to getting involved, but Wallace told him that "before we could start to work on the kind of world he wanted it would be necessary to use force to destroy the power of the aggressor nations—to destroy their power so completely as to make it impossible for them to break the peace again." Wallace continued,

> George had supreme confidence in his generation, but less in my generation. He looked on many of the public men of our time as incipient appeasers. He considered them smallminded and shortsighted . . . and that they were unlikely to rise to the challenge of the fundamental verities when brought face to face with the job of rebuilding a shattered world.
>
> In a letter written shortly before he was killed, George said: "It's after the war that the real fights will start. . . . That's the time when we who are doing the fighting will need some real leadership. This war is our job and we are going to win it on the battle fronts, come hell or high water. The really tough job is going to begin after the war when the forces that got us into this one will be pitted against the men who've got the guts to fight for a world in which everybody can have a chance to do useful work."
>
> . . . Through George's meteoric life and symbolic death, I was forced into a more complete appreciation of the meaning of the death of Christ to his disciples. Something bright and shining and full of hope had passed from the world. It just couldn't be. Death couldn't end all. Christ must live. He must live in the world forever. Somewhere there must be a perpetual song of resurrection, ringing forth continuously the message of peace and good will. And now I conclude this vivid personal experience by saying: May it so be that my George, your George, and all those who have sacrificed their lives will inspire us to effective action that they will not have died in vain.[61]

The stage was set for the final showdown with Jesse Jones.

CHAPTER SIXTEEN

"THOUGH HE SLAY ME"

Henry Wallace's tributes to his son were still ringing in his ears when Milo Perkins once again went to Capitol Hill to defend his agency. This time it was an appearance before a Senate appropriations subcommittee chaired by Kenneth McKellar. The senator bore in upon another example of the BEW's supposed extravagance: a project to plant cinchona plants in Central America to produce quinine.

McKellar said the war would be over by the time any quinine was produced. Perkins said the quinine could be extracted quickly in an emergency. Besides, he added, the delay in planting cinchona was the fault of the RFC. American boys, he said hotly, were dying because of bureaucratic bungling in Washington.

Perkins realized immediately he may have stated his case too strongly. He called Wallace and said "[the testimony] doesn't read as gently as . . . [I] thought it would."[1] He feared it would only perpetuate the fight with Jesse Jones, and his fears were well founded. Jones promptly sent Will Clayton to Capitol Hill to rebut Perkins's testimony. If there had been delays, Clayton said, they were caused by the necessity of renegotiating the BEW's meddlesome contracts.

Wallace and Perkins decided to bring the situation to a head, and they did so spectacularly. On June 29, 1943, Wallace released a blistering twenty-eight-page report analyzing Jones's failure to stockpile strategic materials prior to April 1942. "There are times when the sense of public duty outweighs the natural, personal reluctance to present facts of this nature," Wallace said in an accompanying statement. "This is such a time."[2]

Wallace's sense of public duty outweighed his tact. Even some of his allies were shaken by the document's scathing language and personal tone. Jones was accused of making "harmful misrepresentations" and employing "obstructionist tactics" with regard to the BEW. "On April 13, 1942, the President vested in the Board of Economic Warfare complete control of all public purchase import operations. Mr. Jones has never been willing to accept that fact. He has instead done much to harass the administrative employees of the Board in their single-minded effort to help shorten this war by securing adequate stocks of strategic materials," Wallace asserted.[3]

The heart of the report was a fact-filled commodity-by-commodity analysis of Jones's stockpiling record. The liberal journalist I. F. Stone summed up the bill of particulars with devastating precision:

The [Office of Production Management] had asked for 3,000 tons of beryl ore, which is used as an alloy with copper. Jones had made one contract for 300 tons, none had been delivered. The OPM had recommended the purchase of 178,571 tons of castor seeds, which provide a hydraulic fluid for war machines and a protective coating for plane motors. None had been purchased. The OPM asked for 2,500 tons of cobalt, which strengthens high-speed cutting tools. By April 13, 1942, Jones had contracted for the purchase of 159 tons. The OPM wanted 6,000 tons of corundum from South Africa with which to grind glass and lenses for military purposes. No purchases were made.[4]

So it went, in category after category. No palm oil for making tinplate. No flax fiber for making parachute webbing. Less than one-tenth the necessary amount of sisal, used to make binder twine. No tantalite to manufacture radio tubes. No zirconium for making ammunition flares and blasting caps. "The Board of Economic Warfare is a war agency; it is not a part of the permanent machinery of government," Wallace concluded. ". . . For the duration, however, I feel [the BEW's employees] should be free from this hamstringing bureaucracy and backdoor complaining of Mr. Jones and his employees."[5]

Jones hit back furiously the same day. He called Wallace's charges "hysterical" and "filled with malice and misstatements." He flatly claimed, "There has been no serious delay by us of any vital program."[6] He called for a thorough congressional investigation and promised he would have more to say later.

The Wallace-Jones exchange caused a furor in the press and within the White House. "This was undoubtedly the worst of all the public brawls that marred the record of the Roosevelt Administration and it gave to the American people—not to mention the people of other United Nations—an alarming sense of disunity and blundering incompetence in very high places," the speechwriter Robert Sherwood observed in *Roosevelt and Hopkins.* "Roosevelt was extremely angry at Wallace for this outburst and at Jones for the manner in which he snapped back."[7]

On June 30 Roosevelt again ordered James Byrnes to resolve the dispute. Byrnes acted immediately, sending identical letters to Wallace and Byrnes summoning them to a meeting at 4 P.M. in his White House office. Some two hundred reporters and others, alerted to the confrontation, pressed around the east gate hoping to capture the participants.

Wallace arrived first and promptly handed Brynes's letter back to him, saying a phone call would have sufficed. Then he questioned whether Byrnes had any authority to deal with the dispute, since it involved foreign and not domestic policy. Byrnes insisted the matter was within his scope. If that was so, Wallace told Byrnes, "he should have gotten into the problem long before this." Byrnes bristled.[8]

About this time Jones came in "glowering and glum," saying that "Henry Wallace had called him a traitor." He refused to shake Wallace's outstretched hand and took a seat. Wallace responded with a taunt: "I see by the *New York News,* which has a circulation of two million, that they think you are going to hit me the next time you see me. Is that true, Jesse? Are you going to hit me?" Jones scowled and repeated that he had been called a traitor.[9]

Briefly it crossed Byrnes's mind that he might be the referee of something more than a verbal shouting match. "Wallace was cool but Jones was hot, and I feared he might physically attack the V.P.," Byrnes wrote in his memoir, *All in One Lifetime.*

"You don't think Jesse is a traitor, do you?" Byrnes asked Wallace.

"No, I haven't called him a traitor and I don't think he is," Wallace replied.

"Will you make a statement to that effect?"

"I am sure there is no statement which I can make that would be satisfactory to Jesse," said Wallace.[10]

Wallace was probably correct, but Byrnes doggedly pursued a cease-fire. The meeting lasted more than two hours, at the end of which a plan of sorts emerged. Wallace would apologize to Jones and agree not to press Order No. 5 for the time being. The BEW would go to Congress and seek its own appropriation. Jones would promise not to work against the BEW on the Hill. Jones left the meeting without supporting the plan. Nor did he object to it.

Byrnes pressed Wallace hard to make a public statement. Wallace suggested Byrnes write out what he had in mind. Byrnes did so in longhand, and they negotiated on the wording. Byrnes insisted on only one change. Wallace had proposed saying, "Mr. Jones agreed to this policy decision." Byrnes preferred, "Mr. Jones did not object to this policy decision."[11]

Wallace did not expressly promise to deliver the statement, but an hour after leaving Byrnes's office he gave it to White House reporters in exactly the form Byrnes had proposed. The statement, only three paragraphs long, said the BEW and the RFC would continue under their "present arrangement" until the BEW could arrange its own funding and that Jones "did not object" to this policy. Wallace added,

> I advised Mr. Jones that . . . I had no intention to reflect upon his patriotism or his interest in the war effort. I intended to assert that the delays in RFC in acting upon projects had delayed the war effort. I did not state or intend to create the impression that his personal motive was deliberately or intentionally to delay the war effort.
>
> Our difficulties have had to do with strong differences of opinion with regard to the quantities of various products to be obtained at a given time and place. That there should be these differences of opinion may reflect upon the judgment of the individuals involved but such differences do not reflect upon the desire of the individuals to serve their country.[12]

If there was an apology in Wallace's statement, Jones couldn't find it. A couple of hours after Wallace issued his statement, Jones put forth a one-paragraph rebuttal. "Mr. Wallace . . . repeats that delays of the RFC have retarded the war effort. This dastardly charge is as untrue as when he first made it. As for the rest of his statement, Mr. Wallace was not authorized to speak for me. I will continue to speak for myself and as previously stated I shall insist upon a Congressional investigation."[13]

Byrnes remained discreetly silent about his own role in drafting the vice president's statement and let Wallace take the heat.

Roosevelt seemed to take events in stride. This was hardly the first fight to break out in his administrative family, after all. When reporters asked about the Wallace-Jones strife at his biweekly press conference, he shrugged it off with little more than a groaning reference to quarreling children.

To Wallace personally the president gave no hint of displeasure. Their first conversation after the meeting in Byrnes's office was friendly. Wallace said he thought the president let him off "very lightly" at his press conference and expressed appreciation. Roosevelt replied to him "in quite an apologetic way," Wallace wrote in his diary.[14]

Over the Fourth of July holiday, Roosevelt relaxed at Hyde Park and showed little concern over the Wallace-Jones feud. His only mention of it was a rather droll criticism of Byrnes's inability to handle it. "Byrnes will not inherit the earth if his inheritance is conditioned on the success of his job," Roosevelt said to his aide William Hassett.[15] The subtext of his remark displayed an understanding of Byrnes's own presidential ambitions.

For at least a couple of days, there was a sense that the worst might be over. Jones's demand for a congressional investigation was irksome to the White House, but when a Republican congressman filed a resolution calling for a formal inquiry, Byrnes adroitly maneuvered to have it quashed. Indeed, some observers concluded Wallace had not only survived but gained the upper hand. "Let no one call Henry Wallace an ineffectual dreamer," wrote I. F. Stone. "He has just won his second victory in six months over Jesse Jones. In this town, which worships 'toughness' but usually mistakes the loud-mouthed for the strong, this is an achievement."[16]

Stone spoke too soon. At the end of the first week of July, Jones issued a thirty-page rebuttal of Wallace's charges and again called for a congressional investigation to exonerate him. "Squandering the people's money even in wartime is no proof of patriotism," Jones declared. Perkins, without consulting Wallace, responded in strong language. "Mr. Jones has thrown up a smoke screen but he has not proved and cannot prove that he bought what the Vice-President charged him with not buying," Perkins said.[17]

Wallace stood by his man. "I told him I thought it was a fine thing he had made the statement and that I was glad he could not get in touch with me prior to releasing it," Wallace wrote in his diary.[18]

The president was genuinely dismayed. Once again he ordered Byrnes to end the public shouting match. Byrnes fired off nearly identical letters to the combatants. "Public recrimination by the head of one war agency against another is bound to hurt the war effort and lessen the confidence of the people in their government," he wrote. He warned both men to make no further statements except in response to a congressional inquiry.[19]

But Wallace was in no mood to give Jones the last word. On July 12 he wrote Roosevelt a stern letter that included new figures showing his original charges against Jones were if anything understated. The letter was a virtual ultimatum. The president should appoint a commission, perhaps headed by Bernard Baruch, to investigate the charges and either remove Wallace from his position or given him the power he needed. Even Milo Perkins was startled by its tone. "That was a pretty strong letter you sent to the Boss," he said.[20]

Wallace's letter plunged the "palace guard," as he called the inner circle of Roosevelt's advisers, into cold panic. They feared Wallace intended to publish it, facing Roosevelt with a painful choice of siding with his idealistic vice president or a powerful conservative cabinet member. Byrnes and others urged

Roosevelt to immediately reorganize foreign economic operations. Whatever Roosevelt may have thought of their plea, events of the following day sealed the fate of Wallace and the BEW.

Hundreds of BEW employees gathered on July 15 to pay tribute to George Perkins. They had contributed money to purchase an ambulance in his memory, and Milo Perkins spoke to them in gratitude. Lean and haggard, Perkins soon moved beyond the cause for which George died and launched into a stunning personal attack on Jones. Perkins said Wallace had only done what "any red-blooded American" would do when he kicked over a rock and saw "slimy things crawling" underneath.[21]

Perkins later insisted his talk was off-the-record, but a *Washington Times-Herald* reporter was present and provided a vivid account of the remarks in the next day's paper. That was the last straw, as Wallace suspected the moment he saw the paper. On July 15 Roosevelt sent identical letters to Wallace and Jones (written by Byrnes) abolishing the BEW and transferring its powers, together with several RFC subsidiaries, to the newly created Office of Economic Warfare.

"I have come to the conclusion that the unfortunate controversy and acrimonious public debate which has been carried on between you in public concerning the administration of foreign economic matters make it necessary, in the public interest, to transfer these matters to other hands," the president said. "There is not sufficient time to investigate and determine where the truth lies. . . . My action today is not intended to decide that question."[22]

To make the lesson clear Roosevelt also sent a letter to the heads of all government agencies. If they felt it necessary to publicly disagree with another agency, he said, they should submit their resignation at the same time.

To head the new Office of Economic Warfare, Roosevelt tapped Leo T. Crowley, a Wisconsin Democrat who served as chairman of the Federal Deposit Insurance Corporation and, since 1942, as alien property custodian. Crowley was more noted for his interest in Democratic Party politics than for foreign economic concerns, but he was on friendly terms with Byrnes and was acceptable to Roosevelt. That was enough.

Reaction to Wallace's firing and the abolition of the BEW followed predictable lines. Milo Perkins reacted with furious bitterness toward Roosevelt, although he later came to recognize the part his own emotional condition played in events. "Ninety percent of the scum inside me has boiled to the surface," he said.[23]

Jesse Jones savored the moment with a public statement making it clear he was the winner. "I concur most heartily," he said of Roosevelt's action. Years later he was still crowing. In a chapter of his autobiography dealing with the RFC-BEW feud, entitled "How Henry Wallace Missed the Presidency," Jones summed up his view: "Mr. Wallace was out of a war job. He was once more just the Vice President with little to do but wait for the president to die, which fortunately did not occur while Henry was Vice President."[24]

Roosevelt's inner circle viewed the president's decision as an indication of Wallace's political demise. Robert Sherwood, no doubt reflecting Harry Hopkins's viewpoint, said Wallace's firing ended all possibility of his remaining on the Democratic ticket in 1944. Harold Ickes gloomily told Wallace his ouster meant "we have already lost the peace."[25]

Press reaction was similar. The *New York Times* commented with satisfaction that Wallace's fortunes were at an all-time low and still sinking. The columnist I. F. Stone concurred, but with dissatisfaction. "Franklin D. Roosevelt has again run out on his friends," Stone wrote. "The letters to Wallace and Jones are a repetition of the 'plague o' both your houses.' . . . Now, smugly even-handed, [Roosevelt] equally rebukes the loyal and the disloyal, the lieutenant who risked his political future for the war effort and the lieutenant who sabotaged it. Justice itself could not be more blind."[26]

Most typical of all was Wallace's own response. His only comment to reporters was restrained and respectful: "In wartime no one should question the overall wisdom of the Commander in Chief."[27] When asked for more, Wallace smiled and left to work in his garden.

In private he was hurt but undaunted. Meeting with a group of angry BEW executives the day after his firing, Wallace spoke from the heart and counseled loyalty to their leader. As was often the case in such moments, he quoted from the Bible: "Though He slay me, yet will I trust Him."

A few days later Wallace wrote a note to Roosevelt about a speech he was scheduled to deliver at a labor rally in Detroit on July 25. Wallace knew the speech would now be seen in a new light. "The first question of people about the Detroit speech," he wrote to Roosevelt, "will be, 'What does Mr. Wallace think now about the president?' I am going to settle that in the first two minutes."*[28]

And so he did. The speech combined a tribute to the president with a slashing attack on the enemies of liberalism. He began,

> Three months ago in South America I found the lowliest peon looked on President Roosevelt as a symbol of his dearest aspirations in the peace to come. So it is also in China and occupied Europe. I have known the President intimately for ten years and in the final showdown he always puts

---

*Roosevelt later replied, "It was good of you to write me as you did. . . . I was forced to conclude that under all the circumstances there was no other course for me to pursue. It is needless for me to tell you that the incident has not lessened my personal affection for you."

human rights first. There are powerful groups who hope to take advantage of the President's concentration on the war effort, to destroy everything he has accomplished on the domestic front for the past ten years. . . . Sooner or later the machinations of these small but powerful groups which put money and power first and people last will inevitably be exposed to the public eye.[29]

With an eye toward the racial conflict that had recently occurred in Detroit, Wallace added, "Our choice is between democracy for everybody or for the few—between the spreading of social safeguards and economic opportunity to all the people—or the concentration of abundant resources in the hands of selfishness and greed. . . . We cannot fight to crush Nazi brutality abroad and condone race riots at home. . . . We cannot plead for equality of opportunity for peoples everywhere and overlook the denial of the right to vote for millions of our own people."

The world, Wallace concluded, "is one family with one future." And in that future he still intended to play a part.[30]

As he had before, Henry Wallace found solace in the rich black soil of Iowa. For several weeks after his Detroit appearance, Wallace drove around his native state inspecting crops and talking to farmers in the coffee shops of rural communities. The vice president slipped in and out of town without advance notice or fanfare, usually accompanied only by the Democratic Party state chairman, Jake More, who doubled as his chauffeur.

After a meeting with farmers and civic officials in Greenfield, Wallace permitted himself a moment of nostalgia and paid a brief visit—his first since 1910—to the Adair County farmhouse where he was born. He chatted on the porch for a minute with its current residents, Clarence Bowen and his wife, and drove off.

Farmers, who had been in a surly frame of mind a year earlier, were feeling better. Crops were good and prices high. The manpower shortage that had bedeviled farmers since the outbreak of war had been relieved with the help of high school students and businessmen who worked in the fields after hours. Wallace did some calculating and concluded that farmers were working about ten more hours per week since the war began but added that the same was true of factory workers.

Topic number one of course was the war. Allied troops were pressing the invasion of Sicily to its bloody, successful conclusion. Mussolini had resigned and fled Rome. Near the end of Wallace's Iowa vacation, U.S. planes delivered a stunning blow to the Japanese air base at Wewak, New Guinea.

But of the "War in Washington," as columnists sometimes called the BEW-RFC dispute, there was not much talk in Iowa. Speculation about Roosevelt's action still rippled through the nation's editorial pages and journals of opinion. Elsewhere in the world Henry A. Wallace had become a figure of polarizing controversy. In Iowa, though, he was still a mild-mannered, slightly graying fellow who knew more about corn than anyone else.

The years in Washington had done nothing to still his interest in every imaginable subject. He obtained some elderberry seeds from a scientist at the University of Maryland and passed them on to Raymond Baker, Pioneer Hi-Bred's chief plant breeder, with advice about their cultivation. He talked to a reporter about his "victory garden" and ruminated on the beetles that had attacked his bush beans.

He wrote to Henry Ford and suggested the Ferguson tractor would be more popular if its cultivator shovel were mounted on the front end. To the bedridden teenage son of a friend, he delivered a lecture on the cycle of birth-to-maturity-to-decay that marked all civilizations and advised the boy to use his idle time to read world history. He studied Portuguese, gossiped with a diplomat about Mussolini's mistresses, introduced Milo Perkins to azalea plants.*

Regardless of how he diverted himself, however, what was really on Henry Wallace's mind was Henry Wallace. His diary and letters portray a man groping for answers about what had happened to him and why. He was trying to figure out whether he was still in the game and, if not, how he could get back in.

Perhaps, as he had suggested to Harold Ickes, he was the casualty of a trend toward "bipartisan American fascism." Perhaps his firing was the inevitable outcome of Roosevelt's penchant for assigning responsibilities without accompanying authority. Perhaps he had been unwise to back Milo Perkins so completely. "From my own personal point of view," Wallace later commented in his oral history, "I suspect that [Perkins] made a great many enemies for me, as a result of his aggressiveness."[31]

Or maybe he had been the victim of Jesse Jones's talent for political survival. Wallace had suggested as much in a letter to Roosevelt shortly before

---

*Concerned about Perkins's intense work habits at the BEW, Wallace virtually dragged him from his office one day and took him to his home in Bethesda, Maryland. There he produced some tomato plants and insisted Perkins learn to do something with his hands. Over time Perkins and his wife, Tharon, became enthusiastic gardeners.

After the BEW was abolished, Wallace suggested they begin an azalea garden in memory of their two sons. Perkins took on the project with customary energy and over a nine-year period established one of the largest azalea gardens in the country. The garden is now owned by Landon School, a private institution attended by both Perkins children, and is the site of an annual azalea festival attended by hundreds of visitors.

he was fired. He mentioned that a Chicago newspaperman had told him Jones was always careful to get the president's initials on "questionable" documents. The intimation that Jones had a secret power over the president, Wallace now learned through a friend in the White House, apparently "touched a very tender spot" with Roosevelt and caused him to be "very much alarmed."[32]

Or possibly he was done in by the increasingly insular group of men close to Roosevelt. Wallace made careful note of the people who were with Roosevelt when the decision to fire him was made—Jimmie Byrnes, Harry Hopkins, Sam Rosenman—and pondered their influence. He noted in his diary that Perkins now referred to Hopkins as "the Rasputin in the White House." And Wallace recorded the complete text of a Raymond Clapper column written after he was fired, observing that "a smell of decadence" and a "stifling miasma of court intrigue" now hung over Roosevelt's White House.[33]

Perhaps the Democratic Party had been the culprit. A letter of encouragement to Wallace from William Allen White, the progressive Republican editor, warned him not to expect too much from his adopted party. "You shinny on your side, and I'll shinny on my side," White wrote. "God knows there is plenty for us to do in both parties. And the conservatives are about as plentiful and mean on one side as the other—little fools led by big scoundrels!" Wallace replied with a modest defense of the Democrats. "Frankly, I think it is much easier to get rid of a certain type of reactionary influence in the Democratic Party than it is to get rid of it in the Republican Party," Wallace wrote. "The tragedy of my father was that he tried to fight the reactionary influence in the Republican Party."[34]

Perhaps. Maybe. Possibly. In fact, no one could say for certain what had triggered Wallace's fall or what the future held. By the end of August, however, Wallace had returned to Washington and reached several conclusions.

First, Roosevelt would seek a fourth term. The president might not know it himself, Wallace told several people, but he would run again. Wallace's friend Charles Marsh, the Texas newspaper publisher, recounted a conversation in which the president's son Elliott said, "Pop has tried for twenty-five years to become President and he is going to keep on being President as long as he can."[35] It struck Wallace as true. Also, Roosevelt was almost honor bound to run again if the war had not ended.

Second, Roosevelt's chief concern at the moment, aside from winning the war, was to maintain his influence with Congress and the Democratic Party. If the postwar goals of international cooperation and disarmament became a reality, as Wallace believed the president desired, Roosevelt had to retain the confidence of the urban bosses and conservative southerners who were key elements of his coalition. When Roosevelt abolished the BEW, Wallace told *Des Moines Register* reporter Richard Wilson, he "was merely thinking about getting votes in the Senate so we could win the peace as well as the war." It was "quite appropriate that [Roosevelt] should be conservative at the moment," Wallace added, and equally appropriate "that I should be in the position of leading the progressive forces. I said I thought the President was happy to have it this way."[36]

Third, Wallace had reason to believe he still enjoyed Roosevelt's personal confidence. The chatter of newspaper columnists notwithstanding, Wallace wrote in his diary, Roosevelt "is really very fond of me except when stimulated by the 'palace guard' to move in other directions."[37]

There were even indications of regret on Roosevelt's part. When a compilation of Wallace's wartime speeches was published under the title *The Century of the Common Man,* Roosevelt penned a warm note of appreciation, saying he particularly liked the commencement address about "George." Roosevelt's note came "as close as a man of this sort ever comes to making an apology," Wallace wrote in his diary. Either that or the president "was playing a very shrewd political game."[38]

Finally, Wallace concluded that his future as a public figure rested with the people, not with the nexus of political-bureaucratic-journalistic power brokers in Washington. If he was to marshal the forces of progressivism in the cause of a just and lasting peace, he would have to do it in public view. His own future would take care of itself.

A Chicago politician sympathetic to Wallace offered practical advice on winning the 1944 vice presidential nomination: secure a list of all Democratic National Committeemen and potential convention delegates, line up professional insiders, start some sort of front organization with a name like United Nations for Peace to work on his behalf. No, Wallace responded abruptly. "Practical politics of this kind simply did not appeal to me."[39]

If the events of summer had left Wallace's status uncertain, they also liberated him in a sense. Short of criticizing Roosevelt directly, he was free to say almost anything he wanted. He had the time and inclination to do so, and no one could prevent it. Wallace made his independence crystal clear at the beginning of September when he agreed to speak in support of a congressional resolution supporting the establishment of a permanent United Nations with the "power to carry on the war, occupy territory liberated from the Axis, administer relief and economic rehabilitation, and provide machinery for the peaceful settlement of disputes."

Wallace knew the resolution lacked Roosevelt's support, and he flatly refused the president's request that the speech be submitted to Secretary of State Cordell Hull in advance. "I said I was through having speeches cleared by Cordell Hull," Wallace wrote in his diary. ". . . I said I had done everything I could to cooperate with Cordell, and that I had gotten no thanks for it and I was through." Wallace was privately irked that Hull had said at a diplomatic party that he was against three things: "isolationism, internationalism and Wallaceism." The remark was passed along to Wallace by his sister Mary Bruggmann, who attended the party.[40]

The speech, entitled "What We Fight For," was delivered on September 11 to a massive rally in Chicago Stadium sponsored by the Chicago United Nations Committee to Win the Peace. It was a thumb in the eye to conservatives, isolationists, protectionists, nationalists, and anyone else who might have thought Henry Wallace had been silenced. He opened with white-hot rhetoric that was deliberately insulting to Chicago's leading newspaper and its isolationist publisher:

> Those of you who must read the McCormick press know the inevitable conflict is here. Now—not tomorrow. We shall soon know whether the Common Man shall have "democracy first" or whether under the smooth phrase "America first" the Common Man shall be robbed. Beautiful advertisements and slick editorials say "Let our soldiers come home to America as it used to be." What they are really saying is "Let us go back to normalcy, depressions, cartels and a war every twenty-five years."

The peace that followed World War I failed, Wallace declared, because political democracy was not combined with economic democracy. The mistake must not be repeated. The "America first" slogan was an invitation to war, he asserted, because "under it envious, hungry peoples, the have-not nations with per capita resources less than one-fifth our own, will inevitably rise up to tear us down."

His support for the United Nations resolution was qualified, Wallace said, only because he thought it did not go far enough in addressing the problem of international business cartels. "Let us not be deceived into thinking that attacks on cartels are attacks on American business," Wallace added. "On the contrary, cartels are the greatest menace to the American business principles of free private enterprise and equal opportunity."

He concluded with an urgent call for a fair and enduring peace. "Time will not wait. The breath of the future is on us as it has never been before. We cannot escape. The day about which the prophets and seers of many nations have dreamed for 3,000 years is rapidly approaching. May wisdom and understanding guide our president and the ninety-six senators as they try to make the dream of universal peace a reality."[41]

In late October, Wallace delivered two more broadsides against greed. In a speech on transportation he accused the railroads of plotting to "seize control" of newer forms of transportation such as airways and waterways.*[42] A few days later he leveled a broader attack on monopolies in a long article entitled "We Must Save Free Enterprise," published in the *Saturday Evening Post.* Wallace argued the time was at hand to think about "demobilizing our war production" in ways to protect "the little man with the big idea." Small businessmen were worried that "the large government [wartime] plants may be taken over by monopoly groups or operated by the government itself," Wallace wrote. "The small businessman especially fears that, in the stampede for raw materials, he will be elbowed and choked out of the market as he was elbowed and choked out of the major branches of war production. . . . It must be our resolve that small business shall not be the No. 1 economic casualty of this war."[43]

Wallace recommended revamping the tax structure to give economic incentives to businessmen willing to "expand production and create new industry." He proposed federalizing incorporation law to prevent "charter mongering" by states with weak statutes such as Delaware. And he suggested reform of the patent system so it would not "be used as a weapon of oppression by large aggregates of wealth." Capitalism itself need not be scraped, Wallace said, but the "perversion of its instruments" must be remedied. There "are other ways to cure a headache than by decapitation," he wrote.[44]

His sharp rhetoric attracted notice. Even some of Wallace's friends thought his tone—with jarring references to "midget Hitlers" and "demagogues" who would "cut the throat of progress and . . . despoil labor"—too strident. "Steady, Mr. Wallace," counseled the liberal *Christian Century* magazine. For many others, however, his tough speeches were red meat to the hungry. "There is not a man in the country, or anywhere in the world, who is saying the things Wallace is saying," wrote the columnist Max Lerner.[45]

Conservatives saw in his speeches a revival of anti–Wall Street "Bryanesque populism" threatening not only big business but Roosevelt's wartime coalition. "What we really have then is a Left-wing New Deal whose spokesman

---

*The transportation speech was delivered to a meeting of civic and labor organizations in Dallas, Texas, hometown of Wallace's chief political aide, Harold Young. Young was eager for Wallace to raise the progressive banner in Texas and tried to arrange for him to appear before the Salesmanship Club of Dallas, a group composed mainly of conservative businessmen. To Young's amazement, the club rejected the offer and instead invited Young himself to speak.

Young replied with a puckish letter saying this "is the first time anybody has said, 'We do not want Mr. Wallace to make a speech. We would like for you to address us.' I shall frame your letter in a fine gold frame. I shall do more than that. I am accepting your invitation. . . ."

is Mr. Wallace, attacking what many in the inner-circle of Washington regard as the appeasement of business by the President," the former Brain Truster Raymond Moley wrote in the *Washington Evening Star.* "The object of this rebellion is either to drive the New Deal toward a position very far to the Left in 1944, or to break away and create a radical party. . . ."[46]

A line in the political sand had been drawn. On one side stood Wallace and the progressive cause; on the other were conservatives, corporations, portions of the Roman Catholic hierarchy, British imperialists, native isolationists, and southern segregationists. The labor leader Sidney Hillman now came calling on Wallace offering money and organizational strength. Liberals eager to support Wallace, such as the film director Orson Welles, were in turn sent to Hillman.

Eleanor Roosevelt stood on Wallace's side of the line. At a private dinner with Wallace in the White House, the first lady said she hoped her husband would not run again. To Wallace's amazement she told him if he were nominated he would win. "She went on to say that the difficulty would be to get me nominated—that, of course, she and the President would be for me as the logical one to carry out the policies of the President," Wallace wrote in his diary. To a friendly journalist she observed, "Henry Wallace has come out in the last year. He is showing signs of definite leadership . . . but I wish my husband would carry some of the burden and not let us get bogged down."[47]

From the other side of the line came reports of anti-Wallace activity. A Vermont Democrat warned that Harry Hopkins was pushing for a fourth term for Roosevelt while being silent on the question of his running mate. Raymond Gram Swing, a journalist with close ties to Hopkins, was spreading word that Wallace "would not do for vice president," because he was "too controversial."[48]

Jimmie Byrnes was said to be covertly seeking support from southern senators in his own quest for the vice presidency. Supreme Court Justice Robert Jackson complained to Wallace that his fellow justice William O. Douglas was spending virtually all his time running for the vice presidency. A reporter for *Time* magazine said his organization was promoting Speaker of the House Sam Rayburn, with the expectation that Rayburn would eventually throw his support to Douglas.

Jack Bell of the Associated Press summed up the political situation in a story published in late November:

> Henry Wallace is carrying on a unique campaign for renomination as Vice President on the personal assumption that President Roosevelt will be a candidate for a fourth term.
> Although he reputedly has been scratched from the race by Administration insiders who feel he would be of little vote-getting value in 1944, Wallace has no intention of accepting their verdict. He is out to prove to the President

that he represents labor and liberal elements in the Demo-cratic Party that must be reckoned with at the next National Convention. . . .

The Vice President knows from experience that if President Roosevelt is a candidate he will pick his own running-mate. His friends say that if he is able to demonstrate that he speaks for the liberals and labor it will be difficult for Mr. Roosevelt to cast him aside.[49]

The war years had drained Roosevelt physically, but left intact his talent for mystery. No one could be certain whether he would run again, or who his running mate might be. Roosevelt relished the uncertainty. Mystery enhanced his flexibility and power.

By the time Jack Bell's speculative story was appearing in newspapers, Roosevelt had again disappeared from sight. The president was secretly making his way to Cairo for a series of high-level meetings with Winston Churchill and the Chinese leader Chiang Kai-shek. As his plane approached Cairo along the Nile River valley from the south, Roosevelt caught a glimpse of the great pyramids and "my old friend the Sphinx." It made him smile.[50]

The Cairo conference was an exercise in frustration and stalemate. Churchill was annoyed by the attention given to China and, to the great irritation of the American team, once again evidenced a reluctance to open a second front by invading Europe across the English Channel. Churchill, anti-Bolshevik to the core, saw no reason to hurry while Russians and Germans were killing each other with great efficiency. The conference ended with nothing settled.

From Cairo the two leaders traveled to Teheran for their first joint meeting with Joseph Stalin. The possibilities for discord, even disaster, seemed all too real. But in Teheran, Roosevelt's legendary political cunning came into full play. Churchill quickly found himself on the defensive as Stalin pressed relentlessly for the invasion of western Europe and Roosevelt, while seeming to play the middleman, skillfully backed him up.

At the Teheran conference issues of monumental importance—the sort of issues Henry Wallace had been reflecting upon in his speeches on the postwar world—at last were on the table. The Allies committed themselves to a doctrine of "unconditional surrender" by Germany and Japan.

There would be no Allied invasion of the Balkans. Russia would declare war on Japan once Germany had been defeated. Germany would be demilitarized and rendered weak for a generation to come. The United States would not go to war to preserve the independence of the Baltic republics—Lithuania, Latvia, Estonia. The map of Poland would be redrawn, with Russia gaining territory and Germany losing some. The shape of the United Nations organization began to emerge, with a pledge that the United States, Britain, Russia, and China would act as the "four policemen" to assure peace.

Of greatest importance, Operation Overlord, code name for a cross-Channel invasion of France, would begin by mid-May 1944. Churchill left the meetings in a black mood. "Stupendous issues are unfolding before our eyes," he told his British colleagues, "and we are only specks of dust that have settled in the night on the map of the world."[51]

Yet there was an irony in Roosevelt's position. He was commander of the forces of freedom, champion of the democratic cause, probably the most revered man in the world. But in the United States he was more sorely tested than ever. Roosevelt returned to a capital awash in partisanship and intrigue. Bureaucratic disputes, the signature of Roosevelt's administrative style, were more prevalent than ever. Congress was cranky and conservative. The press seized every opportunity to predict his demise.

Japanese-Americans, apparently ungrateful for their imprisonment in concentration camps, were in revolt. In November several hundred of the prisoners, armed with knives and clubs, captured the administrators of a camp at Tule Lake, California. Roosevelt was livid. The mutiny should be put down harshly, Roosevelt said at a December 17 cabinet meeting, "and it did not make any difference what the Japs in Japan thought about it." It was Wallace who talked him down. "Wait a minute, Mr. President," Wallace responded. "It makes a lot of difference to the Americans whom the Japs have in camps in the Philippine Islands."[52]

Even the U.S. military, theoretically under Roosevelt's direct command, was at times defiant. At some point during 1943, Roosevelt learned that the army's counterintelligence corps, called G-2, had extended its Communist-hunting zeal to investigations of his vice president and even his own wife. Roosevelt responded by disbanding G-2, merging its functions with a new unit called the Security and Intelligence Corps.

Another "spy story" involving Wallace landed on Roosevelt's desk in early 1944. The American spy Allen Dulles, located in Switzerland, had been handed what seemed to be an astonishing document. It purported to be a communiqué from Dr. Charles Bruggmann, the Swiss minister in Washington, informing his government of information given to him "in strictest confidence" by Vice President Henry Wallace. According to the document, the vice president said the U.S. government was deeply pessimistic about a recent conference of foreign ministers in Moscow. It quoted Wallace as saying the United States and Britain might have to fight the war "alone" or "even against the Russians."[53]

Dulles, who later served as head of the Central Intelligence Agency, knew two facts that gave the document some plausibility. First, he knew that the Abwehr, Germany's military intelligence agency, routinely monitored Bruggmann's dispatches. Second, he knew Bruggmann was Wallace's brother-in-law and that the two men were said to be on close personal terms. Dulles forwarded the document to his boss, Major General William J. "Wild Bill" Donovan, head of the Office of Strategic Services (OSS), the U.S. wartime spy agency. Donovan took the document to Admiral William D. Leahy, the president's top military aide, who gave it to Roosevelt.

Whether the document reflected wishful thinking in the German foreign ministry or was a deliberate effort to embarrass the United States with its Russian allies may never be known. It is known that Roosevelt never believed it for a minute. He immediately forwarded the document to Wallace, together with a handwritten note about its origins. "Obviously, of course, the story told in it is so utterly untrue that I am sure it could not have originated from your brother-in-law," the president wrote Wallace. He suggested not even mentioning the matter to Bruggmann, who "is a fine fellow and wholly with us."[54]

Three days later, on January 17, 1944, Wallace responded to the president's letter. The document, Wallace said, "indicates to me very clearly that the keystone of the German foreign policy is to drive a wedge between Russia on the one hand, and the British and the Americans on the other. Such a wedge, successfully driven, represents the only hope the Germans have (barring a secret weapon of unexpected power which I don't think they have). The hope of an enduring peace depends in very large measure on closer relationships between the United States and Russia. The Germans are willing to go to any lengths to prevent that from coming to pass."[*55]

---

*The exchange of letters between Roosevelt and Wallace settled the matter as far as they were concerned, but the story did not end there. In 1950 the Iowa-born Leahy published a volume of personal diaries, entitled *I Was There*, containing an account of the incident but with no reference to Roosevelt's letter dismissing its truthfulness. Leahy quoted from the OSS document at some length and said its content "did not seem to surprise Roosevelt."

Leahy continued with a paragraph noting that the night before he received the OSS document he had attended a dinner for Wallace given by Ambassador Andrei Gromyko at the Russian embassy during which the vice president "made a short address that was said to be in the Russian language."

In his oral history Wallace said Leahy "had no business printing this material he knew to be false" but added that the incident was "such a small thing that it really isn't too important." Wallace noted the Swiss official "who faked the document" was later jailed.

In 1971 author Ladislas Farago resurrected the OSS incident in a book on German espionage during World War II, *The Game of the Foxes*. Farago's account roughly mirrored Leahy's, except to add that "it is not impossible that the Vice President's gross indiscretion had something to do with F.D.R.'s decision to replace him with Senator Harry S. Truman, who had no Swiss brother-in-law, during Roosevelt's upcoming term."

Farago's speculation went unchallenged. Wallace had been dead for several years when the book was published, but his diaries and oral history, both of which contained copies of Roosevelt's letter, were still sealed.

Wallace privately appreciated Roosevelt's support, but in public he gave no quarter. The president's men had been seeding rumors that Roosevelt might look to Speaker of the House Sam Rayburn as his 1944 running mate. Rayburn was a Texas, popular in Congress and with the party's southern faction. Wallace viewed the rumors as no more than an attempt to curry favor with Congress. Rayburn, Wallace wrote in his diary, was an honest and competent legislator with no more potential as a national figure than John Nance Garner.

Nevertheless, Wallace moved to challenge the Rayburn rumor at the earliest opportunity. And he did it in a way that seemed also to challenge Roosevelt himself.

At his last press conference in 1943, Roosevelt had told a lingering reporter of weariness with the term "New Deal." In Bunyanesque terms, he said "Dr. New Deal" was the man who had helped the country recover from internal illness. But on December 7, 1941, the country had "a very bad accident," and "an orthopedic surgeon, Dr. Win-the-War," had been called in to replace the previous physician. *Time* magazine carried the comment one step further, announcing the "death" of the New Deal in its obituary column.

On January 22, 1944, Wallace rose to differ. At a Jackson Day dinner where Sam Rayburn was the featured speaker, he defended the New Deal as the ongoing effort to put human rights before property rights. "The New Deal is not dead," Wallace declared. "If it were dead the Democratic party would be dead, and well dead. But the Democratic party is not dead, and the New Deal has yet to attain its full strength." He continued,

> The New Deal is as old as the wants of man. The New Deal is Amos proclaiming the needs of the poor in the land of Israel. The New Deal is New England citizens dumping tea in Boston Harbor. The New Deal is Andrew Jackson marching in the twentieth century. The New Deal is Abraham Lincoln preaching freedom for the oppressed. The New Deal is the New Freedom of Woodrow Wilson fighting the cartels as they try to establish national and international fascism. The New Deal is Franklin D. Roosevelt.[56]

Party regulars in the audience, who had paid $100 a plate to honor one of their own in Rayburn, glowered. Even Eleanor Roosevelt, sitting to Wallace's side, looked annoyed. "Roosevelt, himself, had tried to bury the New Deal and Mrs. Roosevelt, I think, thought that I should have thrown in a few extra shovelsfull," Wallace commented in his oral history. ". . . As a part of this theme he had cultivated a great many people whom he had formerly looked on as being very much against him. I didn't go along on that approach."[57]

Mistake or not, Wallace was unapologetic. At stake was the future of the Democratic Party—not to mention his own—and Wallace intended to make a fight of it. The *Washington Post*, for one, got the point. "[He] left out one name. In point of fact, the New Deal today is Henry Wallace. . . . It may be that his speech of Saturday evening will prove to be his political swan song. But it was a doughty speech, one which should command the respect of even those who disagree with his ideas. The New Deal banner in his hands is not yet furled."[58]

Within days Wallace was on the West Coast, banner in hand, delivering a series of hard-hitting speeches on the future of American society. It was a distinctly personal effort. The Democratic National Committee was neither consulted nor asked for help. Speaking arrangements were made through local liberal and labor organizations. Expenses were paid personally. Harold Young, his political aide, said the trip cost Wallace about $1,000 and Young about $750. He added forlornly that his boss insisted they pay for everything, including breakfast, out of their own pockets.

In Los Angeles he spoke on the theme "What America Wants" and delivered a progressive laundry list of social needs: full employment, responsible health and old-age insurance, low freight rates and improved roads, free enterprise and opportunity for small businesses, good schools and cultural resources.

In San Francisco he talked on the topic "What America Can Have": prosperity and abundance, good food and wise public health programs, affordable housing and electrification, soil conservation and flood control. America could even have a balanced budget, he said, if it was willing to provide full employment. "The greatest economic sin is the waste of human labor. . . . The greatest threat to a balanced budget is unemployment."[59]

He summed up his vision of a nation at peace and at work with a speech entitled "America Can Get It," delivered in Seattle on February 9. The country must have the spiritual will to work for the "general welfare," Wallace said. It must recognize that individual prosperity rests upon societal prosperity. "Time is pressing," he added. "Victory will bring problems on us so thick and fast that we must be prepared to make instant and correct decisions."[60]

The next stop was Springfield, Illinois, where he spoke on Lincoln, a man of faith who led his nation through a great war despite the "swarms of little men" who misrepresented and maligned him. "So long as there is human need in the United States it is criminal for men to be idle," said Wallace. ". . . The people of America are our most precious possession. The poorest people of America are our most valuable untapped market. Men are more important than dollars. Abraham Lincoln believed this."[61]

Soon he was back in Washington, speaking about justice for Jews and blacks. To the American Palestine Committee he gave tribute to Jewish bravery and spiritual tradition—"No people have suffered so continuously in order to obtain freedom of religion and freedom of expression as the Jews"—and offered a prayer for toleration and cooperation in the Jordan River Valley. To a group of minority newspapermen, he offered frank acknowledgment that the plight of blacks "is a particularly unhappy commentary upon the practice of democracy" in America. He pledged to work for a "double victory" against dictatorship abroad and bigotry at home.

"Those who fight for us in this war belong to many parties, many creeds and many races. This is a people's war. The peace must be a people's peace—for all the peoples and races of mankind."[62]

By the time Wallace finished touring, he had tossed about the word "fascist" so widely and provocatively that the *New York Times* decided the time had come for him to explain himself. Wallace responded in a lengthy, if not altogether convincing, article in the *Times Magazine.* "A Fascist is one whose lust for money or power is combined with such an intensity of intolerance toward those of other races, parties, classes, religions, cultures, regions or nations as to make him ruthless in his use of deceit or violence to attain his ends," Wallace wrote.

Every Jew baiter and Catholic hater and anti-black demagogue was a fascist at heart, Wallace said. Loosely defined, there were probably "several million" such fascists in the United States. More narrowly viewed as those who seek money or power through violence and deceit, there were "several hundred thousand" American fascists. He added,

The American Fascists are most easily recognized by their deliberate perversion of truth and fact. . . . They cultivate hate and distrust of both Britain and Russia. They claim to be super-patriots, but they would destroy every liberty guaranteed by the Constitution. They demand free enterprise, but are the spokesmen for monopoly and vested interest. Their final objective, toward which all their deceit is directed, is to capture political power, so that using the power of the State and the power of the market simultaneously they may keep the common man in eternal subjection.[63]

Wallace named no names, and his detractors saw an element of demagoguery in Wallace's rhetoric. He had made his case so broadly that virtually anyone opposed to his ideas could be termed a fascist. That included a hefty chunk of the Seventy-eighth Congress, roiling with partisanship, parochialism, sectionalism, racism, and old-fashioned ambition. Nothing about Wallace's tough idealism endeared him to men whose main concern was the next election.

Congress was in an ornery mood in early 1944. It ignored or smothered most of Roosevelt's initiatives, giving the president his biggest drubbing since the Supreme Court–packing fight. Even his bill to give soldiers the right to vote by federal absentee ballot was squashed by southern concerns over states' rights and the poll tax. His veto of a revenue measure prompted an enraged Alben Barkley to deliver a scathing speech on the Senate floor in which he resigned as majority leader and urged his colleagues to override the veto. The Senate promptly did so, and then reelected Barkley as majority leader.

For Wallace, Barkley's theatrical gesture was easily the most dramatic Senate session over which he had presided. But he could do little except watch. By inclination and conviction Wallace had set himself apart from a significant portion of Congress. The president might try to flatter Sam Rayburn by encouraging speculation about the vice presidency; Wallace would tell black newspapermen that segregation was a stain upon democracy. His remarks could be interpreted as a slap at Rayburn and all those who backed him; Wallace knew full well that no black person had ever cast a vote for Sam Rayburn, since blacks were systematically excluded from voting in Rayburn's district.

Wallace was in the awkward position of wanting very much to help Roosevelt, particularly on postwar peace plans, but having no real way of doing so. For it was on Capitol Hill that Roosevelt was most in need of help, and there Wallace was least effective. His discomfort in the halls of Congress seemed almost physical. Allen Drury, a young United Press reporter assigned to the Senate Press Gallery, caught his first glimpse of Wallace during this period and tried to put his impression into words:

> The man's integrity and his idealism and his sainted other-worldliness are never in question: it's just the problem of translating them into everyday language and making them jibe with his shy, embarrassed, uncomfortable good-fellowship that is so difficult. Henry Wallace is a man foredoomed by fate. No matter what he does, it is always going to seem faintly ridiculous, and no matter how he acts, it is always going to seem faintly pathetic—at least to the cold-eyed judgements of the Hill. It is something indefinable but omnipresent.[64]

There was an irony here, too. Despite the "cold-eyed judgements of the Hill," and notwithstanding the strident liberalism that grated on congressional nerves, Wallace had never been politically stronger. He had taken his case to the people, and there at least he had received a fair hearing. A Gallup poll published March 5, 1944, showed Wallace with a "commanding lead" among rank-and-file Democrats over his most likely opponents for the vice presidential nomination.

Nationwide Wallace's support equaled the next three candidates' combined: Wallace, 46 percent; Cordell Hull, 21 percent; Jim Farley, 13 percent; Sam Rayburn, 12 percent. They were distantly followed by James Byrnes, with 5 percent, and Senator Harry Byrd of Virginia, with 3 percent. Wallace held a big lead in every region of the country, including, surprisingly, the southern states.

Another poll, taken after Alben Barkley's dramatic resignation and reinstatement as majority leader, showed Wallace with a two-to-one lead over the Kentucky senator. And a survey of fifty Washington reporters conducted by the *New York Herald Tribune* revealed another big lead for Wallace: twenty-four writers predicted Wallace would be renominated; fourteen picked Rayburn.

Practical politicians on Capitol Hill might find Henry Wallace an enigma, but poll figures were something they could understand. Some who had written him off as politically dead began to hedge their bets. Senator Harry Truman of Missouri, widely admired within Congress as a level-headed, straight-shooting party regular was among those who dropped by Wallace's office to express his support.

Wallace took it with a grain of salt. The favorable polls, the comments of politicians, meant but little. He knew that in 1944, as in 1940, only one vote mattered—Roosevelt's.

Trying to guess what Franklin Roosevelt was thinking was Washington's favorite parlor game. "The President is certainly a water-man," Henry Wallace wrote in his diary. "He looks in one direction and rows the other with the utmost skill."[1] What, for example, was one to make of Roosevelt's comment to a man who called on him just after the Gallup poll showed Wallace far ahead of his rivals? "It looks pretty black for Henry, doesn't it," the president offhandedly remarked. Was he trying to throw Wallace's foes off the trail? Was he signaling that Wallace would not be on the ticket? Wallace didn't know; no one knew.

The president, Wallace later observed, had a "feminine mind" that did not "always produce the same answers." He elaborated, "By feminine I mean proceeding by a process of intuition and indirection. I'd say he had a golden heart, but I wouldn't want to be in business with him. . . . He was a truly great man, there's no doubt about that—but very unpredictable."[2]

Another factor mattered, too. Roosevelt's closest associates could see, but not fully gauge, it: the president was sick; his face was thin and haggard. His tan complexion had turned gray, and dark circles appeared under his eyes. His hands trembled, and he coughed, soft and low, almost constantly. Even his buoyant temperament was affected. He sometimes seemed disengaged, at other times uncharacteristically snappish. He slept as much as twelve hours a day but was still exhausted.

Roosevelt had returned from Teheran with "a touch of the flu," he told Wallace, and would be back to normal soon, but weeks of bed rest brought no improvement.[3] His annual State of the Union message to Congress was submitted in writing because he was too weak to deliver it in person. By March his daughter, Anna, had become so alarmed over his appearance that she privately demanded information from his physician, Rear Admiral Ross T. McIntire. The doctor said Roosevelt was suffering from nothing more than bronchitis.

McIntire, an ear, nose, and throat specialist, knew enough to suspect the problem was deeper than a bronchial infection. In late March the doctor took his sixty-two-year-old patient to the naval hospital in suburban Bethesda, Maryland, where he arranged for Roosevelt to be examined by Commander Howard Bruenn, a young heart specialist. Bruenn was shocked by the gravity of the president's condition. The president had severe "hypertension, hypertensive heart disease, cardiac failure (left ventricular) and acute bronchitis," all indicative of advanced arteriosclerosis.[4]

In layman's terms the president was suffering from high blood pressure and hardening of the arteries and was a prime candidate for a stroke or heart attack that could leave him paralyzed or dead at any moment.

Bruenn recommended prolonged bed rest, dietary restrictions, treatment with medications, and immediate cessation of Roosevelt's two-pack-a-day cigarette habit. McIntire accepted Bruenn's diagnosis only with reluctance. He had been Roosevelt's doctor from the start of his presidency and had seen him regularly bounce back from illnesses. A war raged, it was an election year, and McIntire believed there was no chance Roosevelt would accept Bruenn's plan.

But McIntire also remembered the stroke that brought Woodrow Wilson's presidency to a tragic end. As a young navy doctor he had assisted Wilson's physician, Rear Admiral Cary Grayson, and he understood the historic consequences at stake.

McIntire settled on a middle course. Roosevelt would not be informed of his condition. He would be treated with digitalis and other drugs without his knowledge and coaxed into cutting back on salt and cigarettes. Bruenn would be shifted to the White House to treat the president, reporting to McIntire and not to Roosevelt. The press would be casually informed that Roosevelt showed signs of arteriosclerosis but "no more than normal in a man of his age."[5] And Roosevelt would be persuaded to take a vacation, someplace where he could rest in seclusion and without interruption.

Roosevelt agreed to go. He never asked why the vacation was prescribed, nor did he question why Commander Bruenn, a cardiologist, went along.

Under those almost surreal circumstances, the president of the United States, commander in chief of the greatest armed force the nation had ever assembled, vanished. On April 8 Roosevelt boarded a train for South Carolina, where he was to rest at Hobcaw Barony, a 23,000-acre estate owned by Bernard

Baruch. He remained there for a full month, his whereabouts unknown to all but to his family, doctors, and closest aides. Reporters, accustomed to wartime secrecy requirements, accepted his absence without question.

Wallace's last contact with Roosevelt in the early spring of 1944 came the day before he departed, and it was unsettling. After a cabinet meeting Wallace lingered to talk with Roosevelt privately. Wallace was alarmed by a rumor that Churchill once again was maneuvering to postpone the long-awaited cross-Channel invasion of Europe. He asked Roosevelt point-blank whether Stalin knew the invasion might be delayed for a month. Stalin did not know, Roosevelt said. "Stalin should know," Wallace replied bluntly.

Wallace made his case in the strongest possible terms. At length Roosevelt wearily promised to tell Stalin what was happening. "Stalin will take it better from me than he will from Churchill," he said. At the close of their conversation, Roosevelt told his vice president he "was going away for awhile so he could be in a house where no telephone could reach him." He looked worn and shaky, Wallace observed.[6]

"His spirits were excellent," Wallace wrote in his diary, "but it seems to me that his appearance was worse than I have ever seen it."[7]

No word was more commonly attached to Henry Wallace's name than "dreamer."

The word almost became part of his résumé. "It has come to be the accepted thing to ridicule Wallace and speak of him as an idealist and a starry-eyed dreamer," Ralph McGill wrote in the *Atlanta Constitution*. Sometimes he was more than just a dreamer. He was a sort of dreamer archetype, the king of all dreamers. An editorial entitled "The Dreamer's Peace," in the *Grand Rapids Herald*, began, "With Vice President Henry Wallace perhaps the leader, the dreamers of this country are conjuring up every sort of Utopian peace imaginable."[8]

His critics intended the word to be pejorative, meant to portray Wallace as an impractical and otherworldly man. "Mr. Wallace's calling is that of a prophet," wrote the columnist Walter Lippmann. "There is a wide difference between prophecy and government. . . . [He] is a mystic and isolated man to whom the shape of the real world is not clear, in which he is not at home and at ease."[9]

Wallace's defenders countered the "dreamer" charge mainly by arguing it was untrue. Franklin Roosevelt used to call him "Old Man Common Sense," a man grounded in fact and science. The *Atlanta Constitution* editor McGill compared Wallace to Woodrow Wilson, another statesman derided as a dreamer. "Well, we see now that Woodrow Wilson wasn't walking around in the clouds," wrote McGill. "It was [Senator Henry Cabot] Lodge and all the practical realists who followed Lodge who were the real screwballs and the real dreamers and crackpots."[10]

Here was a man, said Wallace's friends, as comfortable in statistics or genetics or economics as he was in pulling weeds from his garden. "Wallace is among the most genuinely learned men in American public life since Benjamin Franklin and Thomas Jefferson," wrote the author Paul Sifton, and like those eminently practical men both a scientist and a philosopher. "Wallace is the first great man of the coming American Renaissance."[11]

Wallace did not protest the term. He saw "dreamer" as a term of praise, one who knew what was not—and envisioned what could be. All great ideas, all great inventions and accomplishments, began with a dream of what could be. "The real question," Wallace later mused in his oral history, "is, 'Can your dreams for the welfare of man be brought into action here on earth?' "[12]

In the spring of 1944, Wallace had been pondering the "dreamer" issue when the snippet of a poem came to mind.

> I am tired of planning and toiling
> In the crowded hives of men,
> Heart-weary of building and spoiling
> And spoiling and building again.
> And I long for the dear old river,
> Where I dreamed my youth away,
> For the dreamer lives forever,
> But the toiler dies in a day.[13]

The poem was called "The Dreamer." Wallace had heard it many years before from an old friend, Des Moines lawyer Addison Parker. In a spare moment Wallace wrote a note to Parker asking whether he still remembered it. Parker sent back a copy of the poem, written by John Boyle O'Reilly, along with a letter recalling how he'd heard it. As a young man Parker had gone to hear William Jennings Bryan when the famed populist spoke in Des Moines in 1909. Bryan observed that he had been called a dreamer and quoted from the poem in response. Parker continued,

Bryan then went on to say something to the charge of being a dreamer like this: "However, I am not willing to rest my defense on what might be termed poetic license, so I have turned to the Book to which I always turn to confound my enemies and confuse my critics—The Bible, and I find there was more than three thousand years ago a man by the name of Joseph of whom his brethren said, 'Let us kill him for he is a dreamer of dreams.'

But fortunately for them and their people they did not succeed in their murderous designs and seven years later they went down to Egypt and bought corn of the Dreamer to feed their starving people!"[14]

"Don't be disturbed if you are a voice crying in the wilderness," Parker told Wallace, "because you may recall that the first voice that cried in the wilderness is still echoing through the ages and until it is heeded there will be no peace, I fear, in this troubled world."[15]

If Wallace was disturbed, he gave no sign of it. He dreamed on.

❧

At the moment Wallace was dreaming about Siberia. He saw in its vast snowy expanse the possibilities for peace and progress. He envisioned a great highway stretching northward from Buenos Aires through South and Central America, into Mexico, across the United States and Canada, into Alaska and across the Bering Strait to Asia. Along this mighty ribbon of concrete would develop scientific, commercial, and cultural links that over time would bond the peoples of three great landmasses in lasting peace. Siberia was a new frontier, a kind of "Wild East" as Wallace saw it, with limitless opportunities.[16]

In Wallace's view, if "the century of the common man" were to become a reality, attention must be paid to the economic and social conditions of Asia's millions. "Eighty percent of them live on the land," he noted to a group of conservationists. "Not more than twenty percent of them can read or write. Their average family income is considerably less than one hundred dollars a year. They are scourged by disease and bitter hardships. It is our privilege and responsibility to help them to a better way of living for the sake of ourselves as well as for them."[17]

Eager to see the area for himself, and longing to be of use, Wallace pressed Roosevelt to let him make a tour of Asia. At the outset Wallace sought a broader mission, starting in Moscow and continuing across the Asian continent to Siberia, then south to China, the South Pacific, Australia, and Ceylon. Roosevelt rejected the Moscow stop because he thought it would be politically fatal for Wallace, already viewed as leaning far to the left. And he believed visiting the South Pacific would be too risky.

In the end Roosevelt approved an abbreviated mission across the northern Pacific to Siberia—a goodwill gesture with no real diplomatic purpose—and a briefer visit to China, where Wallace could assess Chiang Kai-shek's faltering situation and make recommendations. Roosevelt specifically insisted upon the China visit and overruled Secretary of State Cordell Hull's protest that Wallace was not suited for the mission, because he was unschooled in diplomacy.

In the retelling of events leading up to the 1944 Democratic National Convention, the Soviet Asia–China trip took on a sinister coloration. It became a symbol of Roosevelt's political cunning that he would dispatch his vice president, a supposed liability, to exile in Siberia and Outer Mongolia just before the convention. In fact, the trip was Wallace's idea and initially resisted by Roosevelt.

Wallace left for Asia on May 20, 1944, and returned to Washington fifty-one days later, on July 10, nine days before the Democratic convention opened in Chicago. He traveled 27,132 miles and logged more than 135 hours of flight time in the 26-ton C-54 Skymaster cargo plane that ferried him around. The bulk of his trip, almost four weeks, was spent in Siberia. There he visited twenty-two cities—from Velkal to Irkutsk to Alma-Ata—by air, car, train, and river boat before crossing into China, where he spent only sixteen days. His visit to Chungking, where Wallace carried out his sole diplomatic assignment, lasted four days.

It was a momentous time. The long-awaited invasion of Normandy was launched. Allied forces at last broke out of Anzio and began pursuing German troops northward. Germany launched its first rocket bombs at London. Allied troops captured Saipan in the Pacific, and Cherbourg on the coast of France. American B-29s for the first time attacked a Japanese main island from the Chinese mainland. U.S. ships and planes delivered a crushing blow to the Japanese in the Battle of the Philippine Sea.

At home the president signed an act that became universally known as the GI Bill of Rights. The Republican Party nominated Governor Thomas E. Dewey of New York and Governor John Bricker of Ohio as its candidates for president and vice president. Delegates from forty-four nations began a conference in Bretton Woods, New Hampshire, that would reshape the world's monetary structure.

Throughout it all the vice president of the United States was almost completely out of touch. He received few communiqués from his government, and his contacts with U.S. officials were fleeting. On D-day, while Allied forces were struggling to secure their hold on Omaha Beach, in Normandy, Wallace was attending a banquet in his honor in Krasnoyarsk Territory, a vast, sparsely populated region midway between the Ural Mountains and the Pacific Ocean. He learned of the invasion when the territory's governing official arose to propose a solemn toast to the long-promised Second Front.

If war reports were scarce, news of any other sort hardly existed. "I didn't receive any news on the political front—none whatsoever," Wallace later said.

In fact, the only news he received from home was given to him by Madame Chiang Kai-shek, who told him of the birth of his first grandchild.[18]

As always Wallace preferred to travel light.* No personal staff, security agents, political advisers, or reporters accompanied him. His traveling party consisted of John Hazard, chief liaison officer of the Foreign Economic Administration's Division for Soviet Supply, who served as Wallace's guide and translator while in the Soviet Union; John Carter Vincent, head of the Division of Chinese Affairs in the Department of State; and Owen Lattimore of the Office of War Information, an expert on Mongolia added to the trip on Roosevelt's recommendation.

The trip had a kind of cat-and-mouse quality. Wallace's Soviet hosts were determined to impress their prominent guest with displays of industrial accomplishment. Wallace wanted to learn as much as he could about the region's agriculture and science. The Soviet's offered cultural diversions, while Wallace wanted to play volleyball. The Soviets gave him lavish banquets; Wallace preferred a cheese sandwich.†

Whenever possible Wallace strayed from the official schedule and tried to visit working farmers and agricultural researchers. The rural folk of Central Asia impressed him as "people of plain living and robust minds, not unlike our farming people in the United States," Wallace later wrote. "Much that is misinterpreted here as 'Russian distrust' can be written off as the natural cautiousness of farm-bred people."[19] Soviet officials, narrow-minded and oafish, impressed him far less.

---

*He did bring along some distinctly Wallace-like gifts for his hosts. They included fifty baby chicks, which Wallace arranged for his brother Jim to ship to Minneapolis so he could pick them up en route to Siberia; some melon seeds, which took root in China and still grow there; and a portrait of Stalin done in radioactive paint. Wallace later tried unsuccessfully to find out whether Stalin actually received the portrait, and whether the Soviet leader was amused that it glowed in the dark.

†In their memoirs Rachel and Israel Rachlin wrote of Wallace's visit to their small Siberian village. Word came that a "high-ranking foreign politician" would pay a visit. With the honor of the village at stake, frantic efforts were made to clean, paint, whitewash, and wallpaper the place to perfection.

At last the big day arrived. After touring a research station, Wallace attended a great banquet. "According to the Russian custom, all of the food had been put on the table beforehand," the Rachlins wrote. "The table groaned under the weight of sliced meat and all kinds of delicacies fetched from far and near. There was herring, caviar, various kinds of smoked fish, various meat dishes, several kinds of piroshki, and, of course, a wide selection of drinks—wine, vodka, cognac and champagne. It was an impressive sight, especially in view of the fact that the war was still going on and the country was subject to a strict rationing system.

"After Wallace had sat down, he searched around for something on the well-provided table. Everybody at Selektsionnaya held his breath, wondering terror-struck what might be missing. Wallace approached his interpreter, who, to everybody's relief, explained that the vice president would like to have a glass of milk. The danger had passed. Nobody had imagined that an American vice president would drink milk. Fortunately, Selektsionnaya did not lack milk. . . ."

At one point Wallace strayed so far that he disappeared altogether, vanishing up a mountainside while on a hike. A distraught John Hazard anxiously awaited his return while envisioning a *New York Times* headline reading, "Vice-President Lost."[20]

Wallace had prepared for the trip by studying Russian, and managed to make a few short speeches in the native tongue while in Central Asia. Usually they were little homilies about friendship between the Russian and American peoples and the need for cooperation after the war. Wallace's Russian was slow and halting, but his audiences responded with enthusiasm.

The Wallace party reached its westernmost point at Tashkent, an "oasis" city of more than one million people in Uzbekistan. There he was met by U.S. Ambassador W. Averell Harriman and a delegation of U.S. and Soviet officials. Over three days they conferred about U.S.-Soviet relations and Wallace's observations on Central Asia. Wallace passed along a personal letter to Stalin, expressing a desire for amicable postwar relations. Harriman told Wallace his trip "had done an amazing amount of good."[21]

Harriman returned to Moscow and dispatched an approving report to the State Department. Wallace had been met with "great cordiality and respect" by officials and agricultural experts and "with enthusiasm on the part of the Russian audiences," Harriman said. Then he invited Western reporters to a catty off-the-record session where he portrayed the vice president as a collectivist.

"All his life Wallace has been trying to get farmers to accept science," Harriman declared. "Here he sees that scientific methods are forced on the farmer, and it is heaven for him. . . . There is a question whether the increased efficiency is worth giving up freedom. I don't think Wallace fully appreciates the value of freedom. . . . Wallace believes in none of the things he did as Secretary of Agriculture. He believes in a collective society."[22]

Even in Moscow, Harriman could feel which way the wind was blowing in the United States, and he was prepared to sail with it.

❦

Wallace crossed into China on June 18 at Tihwa, in the western province of Sinkiang. He had passed into a different world, one of corruption and decay. To Wallace the state of Chinese civilization was symbolized by its agriculture. Sharecropper families, forever in debt to wealthy landowners, used water buffaloes and hoes to scratch a meager living from tiny plots of land. Pigs were taken to market belly-up on wheelbarrows pushed by hand along dirt paths. Monks used "lottery sticks" to give farmers planting advice.

Perhaps Averell Harriman would have admired the "freedom" of Chinese agriculture; to Wallace it was a system of superstition and subsistence. It begged for scientific and political reform.

The Wallace party reached Chungking, seat of the Nationalist Chinese government, on June 20. Clearly, substantial reform of any sort was unlikely in China. The Kuomintang, Nationalist China's ruling party, was concerned largely with personal power and fortune. Wallace referred to them in his diary as "thugs" and "stooges."

Generalissimo Chiang Kai-shek, while nominally leading his country in war against Japan, spent his time nursing passionate hatreds of the Soviet Union and the Chinese Communists, who controlled much of northern China. The Gimo's clique, centering on his Wellesley College–educated wife, was riven by strife and intrigue. Popular support for the Nationalist government, outside of Chungking, hardly existed.

Further complicating matters, Chiang waged open warfare with General Joseph "Vinegar Joe" Stilwell, the no-nonsense U.S. commander of Allied forces in Southeast Asia. Chiang regarded the acerbic general as rude and arrogant and repeatedly called for his replacement. Stilwell in turn believed the United States had been "forced into partnership with a gang of fascists under a one-party government similar in many respects to our German enemy."[23]

And Stilwell had battles of his own to fight—with General Claire Chennault, a strongly pro-Chiang American who headed the Chinese air force, and with the British, more concerned about preserving their empire than about helping China.

Small wonder that Wallace, admittedly a novice in Chinese affairs, was doomed in his mission before he began.

Roosevelt had set out five objectives for Wallace's talks with the Kuomintang leaders. He wanted China to bring its ruinous hyperinflation under control; to become actively involved in the war against Japan; to unify its military operations with the Communist Chinese in the north; to allow U.S. military observers into Communist-held territory, with the aim of establishing Allied air bases in the north; and finally, to resolve its differences with the Soviet Union before the war ended.

The last point was vitally important, since Roosevelt saw China—with the United States, Britain, and the Soviet Union—as one of the four "great powers" that would enforce peace through the United Nations after the war.

Wallace quickly abandoned the first objective; Chiang's government, given its tenuous condition, could not exert the discipline necessary to control inflation. Wallace pressed the other points, but four days of discussion with Chiang and other Chinese and U.S. officials left him frustrated and dispirited. Typical of his reaction was a June 22 entry in his diary: "We get to the Gimo's about

6 and plunge into Conversation II. This time [John Carter] Vincent was present and we listen to the Gimo's case against the Communists. It was full of bitter feeling and poor logic. . . . I was very sad after the second conversation."[24]

Wallace had no way of forcing Chiang to comply with Roosevelt's requests, but he did have two pieces of bait. One was an offer from Roosevelt to serve personally as an arbiter between the Chinese Nationalists and Communists. Chiang seemed unimpressed. He said such a role would only result in embarrassment to Roosevelt, since Communists could never be trusted.

The other was a peaceful overture from Stalin. In a recent conversation with Averell Harriman, which was passed along to Wallace at Tashkent, Stalin said Chiang's government had its share of crooks and traitors but was nevertheless the best vehicle available to fight the Japanese. Far from being in league with the Chinese Communists, Stalin referred to them as "margarine" Communists committed more to agrarian reform than to ideological purity. Chiang simply rejected Stalin's observation. The Chinese Communists were "more communistic than the Russian communists," he insisted.[25]

Over and over, Wallace pressed Roosevelt's central point: "There must not be left pending any situation which will lead to conflict with Russia." The warning had no effect as far as Wallace could tell. Wallace left Chungking a discouraged man. Chiang, he said, was a man of "almost feminine charm" whose grasp on reality was less than firm. "I like [Chiang] but I do not give him one chance in five to save himself," he observed in his diary.[26]

Wallace won from Chiang only one significant concession: a promise to allow U.S. military observers into Communist territory. In return, Chiang asked Roosevelt to send a personal representative to Chungking who could short-circuit the power of Stilwell and U.S. Ambassador Clarence Gauss.

From Chungking, Wallace flew to Kunming, where he spent three days as the houseguest of General Chennault. There Wallace blundered badly.

Because of scheduling constraints and the possibility of bad weather, Wallace had rejected an invitation to visit Stilwell in Burma. Now, in Kunming, he came under the spell of Chennault, a "swell fellow" whose "amazing" military feats could eventually spell victory for Nationalist China. He visited Chennault's frontline airfield at Kweilin (soon to be overrun by the Japanese) and met the optimistic generals who believed that China and Chiang could be saved by airpower.

And he listened for hours as Chennault and his top aide, newspaper columnist Joseph Alsop, pressed their case against Stilwell. In their view, Stilwell's ground campaign in Burma was a flop, his relations with Chiang had deteriorated disastrously, and his attitude toward the Chinese Communists was too soft. Stilwell should be recalled, they said, and to their surprise Wallace expressed agreement.

When Alsop suggested Wallace send a cable to Roosevelt urging Stilwell's replacement, Wallace consented. Alsop dragged a typewriter into Chennault's living room and hammered out the proposed message. John Carter Vincent, sitting nearby, made no objection. Wallace even proposed that he recommend Chennault as Stilwell's replacement. Alsop was realistic enough to know this would cause a "maximum row" at the Pentagon and would never be accepted by General Marshall. Instead, Alsop proposed that Wallace suggest General Albert Wedemeyer—a smooth, ambitious, thoroughly anti-Communist officer whom Wallace had never met—and the vice president agreed.*

Wallace signed his name and sent the cable to Washington, where it was added to a pile of other complaints against Stilwell and forgotten.†

With that Wallace reboarded his plane and worked his way out of China via Outer Mongolia. From there he returned to Siberia, where his determined Soviet hosts gave him one last toast-filled banquet, and then departed for Alaska.

Critics of Wallace's trip to Asia deemed it a fiasco. Wallace was derided as amateurish and unproductive, even counterproductive, and he drew complaint from every quarter.

The British wanted to throttle him. The very idea of a woolly-minded American standing on Asian soil denouncing imperialism inspired rage at the British Foreign Office. To the astonishment of the British, he did it not once but twice. At a banquet speech in Chungking, Wallace said, "In Asia there are political and racial entities now in a state of colonial dependency, whose aspirations to self-government should receive prompt and positive attention after victory."[27] A joint communiqué issued by Wallace and Chiang Kai-shek expressed the same sentiment. Lord Halifax, the arch-conservative British ambassador to the United States, cried foul to anyone who would listen, Wallace included.

---

*Future accounts of Wallace's cable from Kunming invariably characterized it as recommending Stilwell's "recall" to the United States. The cable itself did not do so. It suggested China be "separated" from Stilwell's command, which included India and Burma, and turned over to someone enjoying Chiang Kai-shek's "full confidence." The endorsement of Wedemeyer was similarly indirect. It read, "While I do not feel competent to propose an officer for the job, the name of General Wedemeyer has been recommended to me, and I am told that during his visit here he made himself persona grata to Chiang."

†General Stilwell was recalled in October 1944 under pressure from Chiang Kai-shek. The command of U.S. forces in China was given to General Wedemeyer. At about the same time, U.S. Ambassador Clarence Gauss, whom Wallace came to hold in high regard during the China trip, resigned and was replaced by Brigadier General Patrick Hurley. Stilwell died of cancer in October 1946, more than two years before Chiang's government succumbed.

John Paton Davies Jr., an aide to Stilwell who attended the conference in Chungking, wrote off the vice president's pronouncements as nothing more than "political flatulence" and expressed scorn for Wallace's "ostentatiously rustic approach to diplomacy." Stilwell himself regarded Wallace as "another junketing, big-noise Mr. Fixit from Washington." Joseph Alsop described the visit as "less than deft" and said it helped convince him that Wallace "was a man whose judgment could never be trusted when he strayed more than six feet from a manure pile." Owen Lattimore mocked Wallace's "topics of conversation with highly-placed Chinese" as being little more than "soybeans, strawberries, fruits, rainfall, and irrigation."[28]

Wallace personally felt good about the Siberian leg of his journey. He believed he had helped engender a "broad basis of mutual understanding" that could lead to "expanded postwar world trade" and the exchange of agricultural and scientific information between the Soviet Union and the United States.[29] His critics called it a waste of time.

But even Wallace had to admit his conferences in Chungking yielded little. He had stressed the "need for reform in China, particularly agrarian reform, to which Chiang agreed without much indication of personal interest," Wallace wrote in a lengthy report on the trip to Roosevelt. "Economic hardship and uninspiring leadership have induced something akin to physical and spiritual anemia" in China, Wallace said, adding that "Chiang, at best, is a short-term investment."[30]

It was high irony, therefore, that Wallace ended his China trip by supporting the foes of General Stilwell. The salty general was the walking embodiment of the very views Wallace professed: a realist who saw the urgent need for basic reform, a democrat who viewed British colonialism with disdain, a patriot who nevertheless understood the necessity of military coordination with the Chinese Communists. Moreover, Wallace made his recommendation without seeing Stilwell or, at Roosevelt's direction, any member of the Chinese Communist leadership. "So his ill-advised counsel to the president regarding American representation in China was a piece of airy irresponsibility," wrote Davies.[31]

These harsh judgments were only the beginning, however. Over time the trip turned into a nightmare.

In the winter of 1948–49, when Communists won total control of mainland China and Chiang Kai-shek retreated to the outpost of Formosa, Wallace's trip to Asia assumed almost legendary status in the "Who lost China?" debate that gripped America. Fueled by the well-financed "China lobby" and its allies in the Republican Party, sinister speculation arose about the true motivation and purpose of Wallace's visit. Rumors abounded that he tried to force the Nationalists into an unholy alliance with the Communists, or that he had written a secret report to Roosevelt advocating Chiang's overthrow.

Virtually everybody associated with the trip saw his career damaged or destroyed. Louis Budenz, a Fordham University assistant professor of economics who frequently testified before Communist-hunting congressional committees, charged in 1951 that Wallace had been under "Communist guidance" from alleged party members John Carter Vincent and Owen Lattimore during the trip. Budenz based his allegations on unspecified "official reports."[32]

Vincent, by then ambassador to Switzerland, survived an internal State Department "loyalty trial" only to be fired when John Foster Dulles became secretary of state in the Eisenhower administration. Lattimore, by then a professor at Johns Hopkins University, narrowly escaped prison after a judge dismissed perjury charges against him in 1955.

John Paton Davies Jr. struggled through eight loyalty board reviews in as many years and then was fired by Dulles because of "bad judgment" in predicting Chiang Kai-shek's fall. Even Wallace was hauled before the Senate Internal Security Subcommittee and asked to explain himself.

Wallace did his best. He released the complete texts of his report to Roosevelt and the cable from Kunming, observing, correctly, that his recommendations were "the opposite of pro-communist." He wrote a long letter to President Harry Truman precisely detailing the roles of Vincent and Lattimore and accepting full responsibility for all actions and messages coming out of China. Vincent, he explained, served as a reporter and interpreter and assisted with preparation of the Kunming cable recommending Stilwell's ouster from China; Lattimore played no policy role at all.*[33]

He gamely defended his observations and recommendations, noting they were similar to those made by many others, including Ambassador Clarence Gauss, a Republican. "In short I urged President Roosevelt to help the Generalissimo's government to help itself, by bringing back to power the better men in the Chinese Nationalist ranks. . . . History suggests that if my recommendations had been followed when made, the Generalissimo would have avoided the disasters resulting from the Japanese offensive in East China later that summer. And if Chiang's government had thus been spared the terrible enfeeblement resulting from these disasters, the chances are good the Generalissimo would have been ruling China today."[34]

---

*To his credit, and at considerable risk to his professional standing, "journalist Joseph Alsop defended Wallace's account. Alsop demanded to testify before the Senate Internal Security Subcommittee, where he corroborated Wallace's version in every detail, including the key role he played in drafting the cable to Roosevelt.

Wallace's words went for naught, drowned out by the wave of anti-Communist hysteria sweeping through America in the early 1950s.

His credibility was not helped by revelations that he had been deliberately deceived by the Soviets during his tour of Siberia. Most notorious was his visit to the northern port city of Magadan, a gold-mining center, which Wallace described glowingly in *Soviet Asia Mission* as a bustling "combination TVA and Hudson's Bay Company." Subsequent accounts from escaped prisoners indicated Magadan was in fact a slave labor camp, which Soviet officials elaborately transformed into a "Potemkin village" prior to his visit. Watchtowers were dismantled, wire fences removed, prisoners herded out of sight.[35]

Wallace was obliged to issue a sort of public confession of his sins. In an article entitled "Where I Was Wrong," published by *This Week Magazine* in September 1952, Wallace wrote, "I had not the slightest idea when I visited Magadan that this . . . was also the center for administering the labor of both criminals and those suspected of political disloyalty. . . . As I look back on my trip across Soviet Asia to China, I can see after reading accounts by former slave laborers who escaped from Siberia that I was altogether too much impressed by the show put on by high Russian officials. . . ."[36]

But the humiliation of Senate hearings and journalistic mea culpas lay far ahead. As Wallace flew through the clouds back to American soil, he could not have foreseen them. Nor did he have cause to feel his mission had failed. Indeed, when he reached Seattle on July 9, he sounded well pleased by what he had observed and done. In a Sunday evening report to the American people, broadcast nationwide via radio, Wallace declared, "I have faith that American economic leadership will confer on the Pacific region a great material benefit and on the world a great blessing. . . . Here are vast resources of minerals and manpower to be developed by democratic, peaceful methods—not the methods of exploitation but, on the contrary, the more profitable method of creating higher living standards for hundreds of millions of people. It was a wonderful trip. . . . With victory, we can continue to work together in peace. . . . We are on our way.[37]

By the time Wallace spoke those words, the campaign to dump him from the Democratic ticket in 1944 was at full steam. The anti-Wallace movement had many players with many motivations. Sometimes unaware of each other's actions, they shared a consuming passion to stop Henry A. Wallace from becoming the next president of the United States. Those were the stakes, the Democratic Party insider George Allen later said, that united them in conspiracy. Their campaign was, in Allen's wry phrase, "the conspiracy of the pure in heart."[38]

At the heart of the conspiracy—the "Sir Galahad of the righteous band," in Allen's words—was Ed Pauley. "He was the knight with the shiniest armor and the sharpest spear. . . . He was the original anti-Wallace man in the Democratic-party camp," wrote Allen.[39] As the party's treasurer and chief fund-raiser, Pauley had a large influence among party regulars and working politicians.

A big, hulking man with a fedora on his head and a cigarette in hand, Pauley was not a deep thinker. "He's a typical go-getting businessman," Wallace observed in his oral history. "I don't know whether he played football or not, but he would be of the ex–football player type."[40] But Pauley knew what he wanted: he wanted Wallace out. Beginning in 1943, about the time of Wallace's ouster from the Board of Economic Warfare, Pauley made it his business on endless fund-raising trips around the country to recruit allies in the campaign against Wallace.

Pauley's most important early recruit was General Edwin M. "Pa" Watson. " 'Pa' was a genial soul, who had taken an indefinite number of years to get out of West Point," Wallace commented. "I guess they finally let him graduate out of sheer pity. He had a very broad face—universally beloved—not knowing what the whole thing was all about, really."[41]

But Watson was an influential man. The steady thinning of Roosevelt's inner circle through illness and death had made Watson the presidential appointments secretary. Watson determined whether or not people saw Roosevelt and, if so, for how long. By early 1944 Pauley had persuaded Watson to give easy entrance to "convention delegates, national committeemen, state chairmen and governors" with a brief against Wallace. For Wallace's supporters the gate was closed.[42]

Another key recruit was Robert Hannegan, a handsome dark-haired lawyer and former semiprofessional baseball player, who had come through the ranks of Democratic politics in St. Louis. With the help of U.S. Senator Harry S. Truman, Hannegan became collector of internal revenue in St. Louis in 1942. In short order, again on Truman's recommendation, he was named commissioner of internal revenue and, finally, chairman of the Democratic National Committee in 1944.

Like all practical politicians, Hannegan expressed friendship easily. At the start of his climb to national prominence, he wrote the vice president an effusive note requesting a photograph and declaring himself "a Wallace man." His true loyalty, however, was never in doubt. He was a Truman man first, last, always. One of his first acts as party chairman was to organize, with Pauley, a series of "George Washington dinners" for influential party supporters around the country. The dinners usually featured an intimate talk by House Speaker Sam Rayburn or Senator Truman. Wallace "was seldom sought as a speaker, and, when he was, we discouraged it," Pauley explained. "He was no good at raising money, and beyond this, he usually provoked an argument within the party ranks."[43]

With Hannegan's entrance into the anti-Wallace movement came a contingent of other party officials and power brokers. Among these were Oscar R. "Jack" Ewing, the party's vice chairman; Charles Michelson, the party's crafty longtime publicity director; George Allen, a witty conservative who was the party's national secretary; Edward Kelly, mayor and political boss of Chicago; and Hannegan's two immediate predecessors as national chairman, the Bronx boss Ed Flynn and Postmaster General Frank C. Walker. The more odoriferous big-city bosses, such as Frank Hague of Jersey City and Ed Crump of Memphis, were less visible but squarely in the anti-Wallace camp.

Their opposition to Wallace was stated in various ways, but at bottom it came down to an assessment that Wallace was not one of them. They were undoubtedly correct. Flynn, who had supported Wallace for vice president going into the 1940 convention, had by 1944 concluded that Wallace "seemed to have become the candidate of the radicals of the country." Walker, a modest man with cordial manners and a benign Irish face, simply could not fathom the "Protestant saint" from Iowa. "To me he just did not seem to be part of this world," Walker wrote in his autobiography.[44]

George Allen offered the baldest account of his antipathy toward Wallace. In his pre-dawn dreams, Allen wrote,

I see President Henry A. Wallace sitting in front of a microphone in the Oval Room of the White House, reading a message to the peoples of the world. His forelock droops appealingly over his right eye. His flat Iowa voice proclaims that the United States of America shall henceforth be called the Soviet States of America, that all Democrats from Mississippi weighing more than two hundred pounds shall be rendered in order that unwashed comrades in Greater Russia can be assured an adequate soap supply, and that scientific socialism shall bring to the Western Hemisphere that same conditions that prevail through the glorious territories of mother Russia.[45]

Outside the small orbit of party officials, the anti-Wallace campaign included congressmen, cabinet members, local officials, political appointees, and elements of the Catholic Church—fueled by a mixture of ideology, personal rivalry, and old-fashioned ambition. Several wanted Wallace's job, including Senate Majority Leader Alben Barkley, Supreme Court Justice William O. Douglas, "Assistant President" James Byrnes, and House Speaker Sam Rayburn.

If none of those would do, there were plenty of other names in the air. There was talk of the industrialist Henry Kaiser, federal appellate judge Sherman Minton, ambassador to Britain, John Winant. On Capitol Hill reporter Allen Drury wrote in his journal, "Fond hopes are blossoming in a dozen Senatorial breasts."[46]

Each had his supporters. Barkley had the hearts of many Senate Democrats. Douglas was backed by former White House aide Thomas Corcoran, Mayor Ed Kelly of Chicago, former Ambassador Joseph Kennedy, and, to some extent, Interior Secretary Harold Ickes. Rayburn had the support of many House members, the oil industry, Commerce Secretary Jesse Jones, and Ed Pauley. Byrnes was liked by many southern conservatives and party regulars, including Harry Truman, who agreed to nominate the South Carolinian at the convention.

A steady stream of anti-Wallace messages from nonpoliticians also passed through Pa Watson's open gate. Walter Lippmann, Wallace's sometime tennis partner, opined that the vice president was emotionally unsuited to be president. "We can't take the risk," said Lippmann. "This man may go crazy. We know that Roosevelt is not immortal." Aubrey Williams, former head of the National Youth Administration, canvassed the South and declared that the region demanded two things. "First, that some other person besides Wallace be selected for vice president. Second, that no plank be put in the platform regarding racial discrimination." FBI Director J. Edgar Hoover weighed in with a report claiming a Wallace aide had used improper means to gather information about two Polish-Americans with strong anti-Soviet views.[47]

Then there were the British, alarmed by a pamphlet Wallace had written, *Our Job in the Pacific*, expressing in summary form many of his standard postwar goals. Among these were international control of airways, economic aid for Asian industrial development, the demilitarization of Japan, and self-determination for people living in colonial areas, including India. The pamphlet, written with the help of John Carter Vincent and Owen Lattimore, was published by the reputable, but left-leaning, Institute of Pacific Relations.

Before the pamphlet was even in print, however, a British secret service agent had obtained a manuscript copy and sent it to his superiors. The agent, Roald Dahl, was a dashing young Royal Air Force fighter pilot who had been shot down and severely burned while on a mission over Greece in 1941. Subsequently Dahl became an agent of British Security Coordination assigned to Washington, where he befriended Wallace, Eleanor Roosevelt, and other influential figures.* Wallace and Dahl played tennis and walked together; Dahl

*Roald Dahl later gained wide recognition as an author of children's books, including *Gremlins* and *Willie Wonka and the Chocolate Factory*.

seemed to have genuine affection for Wallace, if not for his views. "He was a lovely man, but too innocent and idealistic for this world," Dahl later wrote.

Sometime before Wallace departed for Asia, Dahl attended a social gathering at the Washington home of the Texas newspaper publisher Charles Marsh. There he saw Marsh and Wallace reviewing the manuscript of *Our Job in the Pacific.* After Wallace left, Marsh showed the manuscript to Dahl. The agent took the manuscript downstairs, where he said he could read it in privacy. Instead, he called a contact at British Security Coordination and told him to come quickly to Marsh's house. "I handed the draft through the car window and told him he must be back with it in fifteen minutes," Dahl recalled. "The man buzzed off to the BSC Washington offices and duly returned the manuscript to me on the dot."[48]

Dahl immediately saw the importance of the manuscript in British eyes. "This is very serious," he said to Marsh. "You know Churchill is likely to ask the president to get a new vice president." Marsh responded with customary self-confidence, "Don't be a child. Grow up. Don't you know that the most certain way to be sure that Wallace will continue to be vice president is for the word to get around that Churchill is against him?"[49]

From Washington the manuscript was routed to New York, where Sir William Stephenson ran Britain's secret service operations in the United States. Then it crossed the Atlantic and was given to "C"—code name for Sir Stewart Graham Menzies, Britain's wartime spymaster. Menzies took it to Winston Churchill. The document's call for liberation of colonial peoples in Asia "stirred Winston to cataclysms of wrath," according to one observer.[50] Soon British agents were busily gathering information on the Institute of Pacific Relations, the background of Vincent and Lattimore, even the activities of Nicholas Roerich on the ill-fated Agriculture Department mission to Asia in the 1930s.

If the British feared that their interference in American politics would create a backlash in Wallace's favor, they hid it well. Lord Halifax, Britain's ambassador to the United States, personally protested Wallace's "regretable" statements to Secretary of State Cordell Hull. Sir William Stephenson went even further. "I came to regard Wallace as a menace and I took action to ensure that the White House was aware that the British government would view with concern Wallace's appearance on the ticket at the 1944 presidential elections," he later commented.[51] His messenger was Ernest Cuneo, an American lawyer married to a member of Stephenson's staff, who sometimes served as a go-between for the British secret services and the U.S. government.

One person not active in the anti-Wallace movement, although Wallace suspected otherwise, was Harry Hopkins. On New Year's Day 1944 Hopkins had once again fallen gravely ill. He remained in various hospitals until July

4. Adding to his burden was the death of his eighteen-year-old son, Stephen, killed in combat in February.

With Hopkins ill, Wallace away in Asia, and Eleanor Roosevelt constantly traveling around the world, the voice of liberalism within the White House had been reduced to a whisper. As the convention approached, Franklin Roosevelt was isolated and ailing. He had returned from his long rest at Bernard Baruch's estate with a jaunty declaration that he was fit and ready for battle, but all who saw him knew otherwise. "He had aged considerably and was not anywhere near the man physically or mentally that he was in 1932," wrote Ed Flynn. " . . . He was more inclined not to argue than to argue."[52]

The state of Roosevelt's health redoubled the determination of the anti Wallace conspirators and allowed them to flourish without much countervailing influence. The president himself had not yet joined the conspiracy—indeed, he had given all the mixed signals and evasive replies that marked his personal style—but neither was he in control of the situation. Plots were hatching, rumors rife. Half a dozen ambitious men aggressively maneuvered for the vice presidency. And the president, in the words of his son James, simply did not "give a damn."[53]

Such was the lay of the land when Henry Wallace arrived back in Washington on July 10.

CHAPTER EIGHTEEN

"THE SAME OLD TEAM"

In Washington the conspirators waited for their prey to return, eager to make Henry Wallace quit without a fight.

Wallace was still on the West Coast when events went into motion. Judge Sam Rosenman, the president's confidant and speechwriter, called to say it was urgent that he and Harold Ickes meet with Wallace as soon as possible. Wallace agreed to have lunch with them on Monday, July 10, the day of his return to Washington. He could guess what they wanted.

The Skymaster cargo plane touched down in Washington about 9:30 A.M. Wallace had been traveling for fifty-one days, logging enough miles to circle the globe at the equator, and the trip had been physically demanding. He was tired, gaunt, and a bit out of sorts.

Thirty minutes after his arrival Wallace attempted to phone Roosevelt, only to have Pa Watson tell him the president wanted him to see Rosenman and Ickes first. Wallace was to come to the White House for an "on-the-record" conference at 4:30 P.M. Wallace arranged for the lunch to be moved from Ickes's office, where he would be certain to encounter reporters, to his apartment at the Wardman Park.

The lunch began on a cordial, if disingenuous, note. Rosenman and Ickes spent half an hour making "polite inquiry" about Wallace's trip. Then they got to the point. "Ickes said how much I had grown in his esteem," Wallace later recalled. "He said I was a true liberal and that he and I were the only two liberals left in the government. . . . Ickes then went on to make it clear that I had made many enemies, that I was a bone of contention in the convention, and that I ought not to let my name be presented."[1]

The words were hardly out of Ickes's mouth before Rosenman added that Roosevelt wanted Wallace as his running mate. As Wallace interpreted the conversation, they were trying to convey the impression that Roosevelt preferred Wallace but did not think he could win in Chicago.

The lunch with Rosenman and Ickes established one thing: Wallace would be no willing victim. Wallace abruptly ended the conversation by telling them, "I am seeing the president at four-thirty. I have a report to make on a mission to China. I do not want to talk politics." Rosenman and Ickes "beat a hasty retreat," Wallace said.[2]

Ickes clearly thought he was doing Roosevelt's bidding. Over a two-hour lunch on the White House porch the day before, Roosevelt had said Wallace was "first on the list" but added that he would not insist on Wallace, as he had in 1940, and confided that Ed Flynn had told him Wallace would cost the Democratic ticket between one and three million votes.[3]

As was often the case, however, Ickes knew less than he thought he did. Roosevelt had said he would be departing on a military trip Thursday, and Ickes got the idea the president would not even see Wallace before he left. "He is leaving the dirty work to Sam Rosenman and me," Ickes wrote in his diary.[4]

The dirty work, however, was just beginning.

At four-thirty on Monday afternoon, Wallace gave his report on China to Roosevelt, and they talked cordially for more than two hours. Then Roosevelt opened a conversation on politics by advising Wallace to tell reporters they had not discussed politics at all. "I am now talking to the ceiling about political matters," Roosevelt proclaimed.

The president said Wallace was his choice for the vice presidential nomination and he would be willing to make a statement to that effect. Wallace asked whether Roosevelt would be willing to say, "If I were a delegate to the convention I would vote for Henry Wallace."

"Yes, I would," Roosevelt replied.

But, Roosevelt added, a "great many people" had told him Wallace could not be nominated unless the president insisted, and even then the outcome was doubtful. "I at once broke in and said I would not want him to do what he did in 1940, that if I had known about it in advance I would not have advised him to do it in 1940," Wallace later recalled. "I said I did not want to be pushed down anybody's throat, but that I did want to know definitely whether he really wanted me and was willing to say so. He was very ready with his assurance."

Having given his assurance, Roosevelt once again became evasive. He said he "could not bear the thought" of Wallace's being rejected by the convention. He told Wallace to think of his family and "the cat-calls and jeers" and the humiliation of defeat. "I am not worried about my family," Wallace replied. He added in his oral history, "At this stage of the conversation I was thinking, 'I am much more worried about the Democratic Party and you than I am about myself and my family.' "[5]

Roosevelt asked Wallace to return for lunch the following day and again on Thursday. On that inconclusive note the conversation ended.

Tuesday, July 11, dawned hot and heavy in Washington, presaging an eventful day. Franklin Roosevelt at last announced he would run for a fourth term in office. Wallace met again with Roosevelt to refine the strategy for their renomination. And, on that day, Roosevelt finally joined the conspiracy to dump Henry Wallace.

It began at a morning press conference in the Oval Office. With almost two hundred reporters crowded around his cluttered desk, Roosevelt casually mentioned he had sent a letter to Bob Hannegan. Then he read the letter. "All that is within me cries to go back to my home on the Hudson River, to avoid public responsibilities. . . . Such would be my choice," Roosevelt wrote. But there was a war to win, a peace to secure, an economy to be put on solid ground. "Therefore, reluctantly, but as a good soldier, I repeat that I will accept and serve in the office, if I am so ordered by the Commander in Chief of us all—the sovereign people of the United States."[6]

The Democratic presidential nomination was settled. All eyes turned to the second spot on the ticket.

At noon Wallace returned to the White House for lunch. He entered through a back gate to avoid reporters and brought with him a glorious Uzbek robe, a present from Tashkent officials to the president, plus some stamps and coins he had purchased for Roosevelt in Outer Mongolia.

Again they talked politics. Wallace gave Roosevelt the draft of a statement, worked out by Senator Joe Guffey of Pennsylvania, intended to seal the vice president's victory on the first ballot. "It appears the convention will name me," the statement would read. "I trust the name with me will be Henry A. Wallace. He is equipped for the future. We have made a team which pulls together, thinks alike and plans alike." Roosevelt said he had worked out different wording but wanted to incorporate Guffey's language in his statement.[7]

And again the president became evasive. He mentioned that many people looked on Wallace "as a Communist—or worse," quickly adding that "as a matter of fact, there was no one more American than myself, no one more of the American soil." Roosevelt raised the common accusation that Wallace "wants to give a quart of milk to every Hottentot." Wallace retorted that he had never made such a statement. "That was said for me by Mr. Witherow, President of the National Association of Manufacturers." The president seemed surprised.[8]

They parted as cordially as ever, Wallace certain he would have a written endorsement from Roosevelt.

That evening Roosevelt met the conspirators. They came for dinner and afterwards gathered in the president's second-floor study. Roosevelt sat in his armless wheelchair—so weak he could barely turn its wheels—tapping his cigarette holder in his teeth. Around the room sat Ed Pauley, Frank Walker, Ed Kelly, Ed Flynn, Bob Hannegan, George Allen, and the president's daughter and son-in-law, Anna and John Boettiger.

Together they sifted through the list of possible candidates, chewing over their strengths and weaknesses, narrowing the field one by one. Wallace went first. His name, in fact, was barely mentioned. None of the bosses wanted him, and Roosevelt offered him no defense. Sam Rayburn and Alben Barkley were dismissed as baggage-laden southerners. Besides, the president observed, Barkley was two years older than he was.

Jimmie Byrnes was popular with the party leaders, but blacks and labor would not tolerate him, Roosevelt said. And Byrnes, born a Catholic, had converted to Episcopalianism when he married. Such a conversion had the potential to alienate Catholics and Protestants alike, the president said.

Roosevelt talked up Supreme Court Justice William O. Douglas. He was a vigorous liberal and, at age forty-five, "looked and acted on occasions like a Boy Scout." He played an "interesting" game of poker, and he was bright. Roosevelt savored the thought that Douglas graduated at the top of a Columbia University law school class that included Thomas E. Dewey. The bosses squirmed but said little; Douglas was no more a party regular than Wallace.[9]

At length Roosevelt looked to Hannegan and said, "All right Bob—start talking." Hannegan seized his chance. Harry Truman had been a good senator and a loyal supporter of the president, Hanengan said. Truman was politically astute and popular among rank-and-file Democrats and, coming from a border state, would strengthen the ticket in the South. Roosevelt gave no commitment. He closed the session by saying both Truman and Douglas looked like strong candidates.*[10]

As they filed out of the White House, most of the men believed they had accomplished their mission. Frank Walker wasn't so sure. The postmaster general well knew Roosevelt's celebrated ability to cover his tracks. "Go back and get it in writing," he whispered to Hannegan. The party chairman dashed back

---

*Accounts conflict on this point. Frank Walker, in a posthumously published autobiography, recalled Roosevelt saying roughly, "Boys, I guess it's Truman."

Paul A. Porter, then the party's publicity chairman, said Hannegan told him soon after the meeting that Roosevelt's tone was pro-Truman. Then, according to Porter's secondhand account, the president grabbed Hannegan's wrist as he was leaving and said "something like this: 'Okay, Bob, we'll make it Truman.' "

Roosevelt left no written account of the meeting.

upstairs, claiming he had forgotten his coat, and asked Roosevelt to put his opinion on paper. Roosevelt grabbed an envelope and scratched out a brief message on the back. He would be happy to run with either Douglas or Truman.[11]

Hannegan went back downstairs to the waiting Walker. "I've got it," he said.[12]

⁂

Only later did Hannegan read what was on the envelope and discover, to his amazement, that he did not have exactly what he thought he had. He had wanted Roosevelt to express approval of Truman or Douglas. Roosevelt had reversed the order of the names, leaving the impression Douglas might be his first choice.

Nevertheless, Hannegan had more than Wallace did. Hannegan could not actually use the letter, since showing it would reveal the actual order in which Roosevelt had put the names, but he could imply he had an ace in the hole. The bosses fanned out across Washington to spread word of the fateful White House meeting. Wallace was out, they confidently told reporters. So were most of the other would-be candidates. They had it from the top.

Frank Walker had the unenviable task of telling Byrnes he was finished. Hannegan assigned himself to tell Wallace.

Byrnes reacted furiously to the news. He told Walker he would drop out only if Roosevelt personally ordered him to withdraw. This Roosevelt declined to do, as Byrnes anticipated. Brynes next sought a firm commitment from Harry Truman to place his name in nomination. Truman promised he would.*

Hannegan had no better luck with Wallace. Meeting with the vice president at the Wardman Park, Hannegan told him he did not have a chance and should pull out. Wallace flatly refused. Hannegan "said he had been with the president last night and he thought the president was going to indicate me as first choice—and someone else as second choice—and by so doing this would automatically result in the second choice person getting all of the dissident votes and, therefore winning," Wallace later said.[13]

Wallace responded bluntly. "We might as well understand each other," he said. "I will not withdraw as long as the president prefers me." Hannegan emerged from the Wardman Park in a foul temper, telling a waiting reporter that Wallace was a "terrible person" and should have the good grace to withdraw. At a cocktail party later in the day, Hannegan boasted, "I told the son-of-a-bitch just where to get off."[14]

---

*Truman later told associates Byrnes had deceived him. When he asked Truman to make the speech, Byrnes implied he had a "Go" from Roosevelt. Truman replied, "Why sure, Jimmie, if that's what the president wants I'll not only nominate you but I'll work for you." When Truman's account of the conversation became public in the 1950s, Byrnes expressed shock and issued a lawyerly denial.

Not only had he failed to bluff Wallace out of the race, but the vice president had reason to believe his position was by no means hopeless. If anything, Wallace seemed to be gaining strength. Reports from Harold Young, the convivial Texan who looked after Wallace's political affairs, indicated a solid core of two hundred delegates would back the vice president on the first ballot. Many more would join if not prevented by the "unit rule," which required some state delegations to vote as a bloc for one candidate.

Sidney Hillman, head of the CIO's Political Action Committee, said labor stood squarely in Wallace's corner. A small but determined cadre of progressive senators, led by Joe Guffey of Pennsylvania and Claude Pepper of Florida, had joined the Wallace team and promised to serve as his floor managers in Chicago.

The press had given Wallace widely favorable coverage in the wake of his Asian tour. In Washington movie audiences erupted in cheers when newsreels showed footage of Wallace in China. And perhaps most significantly a new Gallup poll, leaked to Wallace in advance of publication, showed him with a large and growing lead among Democratic voters. The poll had him leading in all regions of the country, including the South. Nationwide, Gallup reported the following preferences among Democratic voters: Wallace, 65 percent; Barkley, 17 percent; Rayburn, 5 percent; Senator Harry Byrd of Virginia, 4 percent; Brynes, 3 percent; Douglas, 2 percent; Truman, 2 percent; and Undersecretary of State Edward Stettinius, 2 percent.

"The old American love of the underdog is beginning to work," Allen Drury wrote in his journal. "At the moment his fate is hanging entirely in the balance, Henry Wallace for the first time has become popular with his countrymen."[15]

The following day Wallace made his third and last attempt to be certain Roosevelt supported him—and nobody else.

He arrived at 1 P.M. and sat some forty minutes while the president finished a meeting. As he was finally entering the Oval Office, he saw, out of the corner of his eye, Hillman's back. "It was obvious that Sidney Hillman had been conferring with the president for more than an hour," Wallace wrote in his diary. Precisely what was said in their meeting, he never knew.*

The president began with small talk, but Wallace cut in with a request. "I would like to have the privilege of putting your name in nomination," Wal-

*Matthew Josephson, in *Sidney Hillman: Statesman of American Labor,* said Roosevelt showed the labor leader a copy of his note to Hannegan and tried to persuade Hillman not to oppose Truman if Wallace did not succeed on the first ballot. The assertion is undocumented, however.

What is certain is that Hillman and Phillip Murray held a news conference the same day, July 13, during which they gave Wallace the CIO's unqualified endorsement. Murray, president of the United Steel Workers of America and the CIO, later told Wallace it appeared Hillman was about to mention another candidate who would be acceptable to organized labor, but Murray cut him off. "The CIO is definitely committed to Wallace. . . . We are not going to trade," Murray declared in his deep Scottish burr.

lace said. Roosevelt demurred. The job had already been offered to Alben Barkley. Wallace could deliver a seconding speech.

The vice presidential matter, Roosevelt explained, would be handled in a letter to Senator Samuel D. Jackson, the convention chairman. Roosevelt would send it from Hyde Park the next day. It would say that if he were a delegate, he would vote for Wallace, but that he did not wish to dictate to the convention. "He wanted to get the wording just right so it would not seem in any way like a dictation—but so that it would be just me," Wallace noted in his diary.

Roosevelt talked about the meeting with the professionals on Tuesday evening. They all thought Wallace would hurt the ticket, Roosevelt said. "If you think so, I will withdraw at once," Wallace replied. "I have no basis for a judgment of my own," said Roosevelt. "The only way I could find out would be to drive among the farmers in Dutchess County." But there was no time for that. It was "mighty sweet" of Wallace to offer his withdrawal Roosevelt added, but he could not think of accepting it.

So it went. Roosevelt skated one way and another; Wallace stood his ground. Wallace finally asked point-blank whether Roosevelt was planning to do as Hannegan asked and submit an alternative name to the convention. The president answered in one word: "No." He did not mention that he had already done as much.

They talked about convention logistics. Roosevelt would not be in Chicago. He would be traveling by train to San Diego, where he would depart by ship for a meeting with General MacArthur in Hawaii. Wallace could get in touch with him in California by calling an aide in the White House.

As he readied to leave, Wallace said, "Well, I am looking forward with pleasure to the results of next week—no matter what the outcome." He reached out his hand to the president. Roosevelt grasped it heartily and drew Wallace close. "While I cannot put it just that way in public, I hope it will be the same old team," Roosevelt said. The president flashed his full smile.

Wallace moved to the door, and Roosevelt offered a final thought. "Even though they do beat you out at Chicago, we will have a job for you in world economic affairs."[16]

Roosevelt's letter to Senator Jackson went out as promised on July 14 but was not made public until July 17, the day before the convention opened. The letter constituted "perhaps the coolest and cruelest brush-off in all the long Roosevelt career," Allen Drury wrote in his journal.[17] The letter said in part,

> The easiest way of putting it is this: I have been associated with Henry Wallace during his past four years as Vice President, for eight years earlier while he was Secretary of Agriculture, and well before that. I like him and

I respect him, and he is my personal friend. For these reasons, I personally would vote for his renomination if I were a delegate to the Convention.

At the same time, I do not wish to appear in any way as dictating to the Convention. Obviously the Convention must do the deciding. And it should—and I am sure it will—give great consideration to the pros and cons of its choice.[18]

In other words, Drury observed, "If you want him, well, OK. If you don't, well, OK. Suit yourself. And so long, Henry."[19]

More than Roosevelt's usual obliqueness was at work, Wallace concluded. The president's "mind was a sick mind," he said. His brain may not have had a sufficient supply of blood to function properly, Wallace guessed. Maybe Roosevelt had forgotten his conversation with the bosses, or he had convinced himself his answers to Wallace were accurate in some technical sense. In any case, "a well man could not have handled the situation when I was with him on Thursday as he did," Wallace commented. "I mean he would have told me clean and straight."[20]

It made no sense to Wallace—it never would—for Roosevelt to deceive him elaborately. Roosevelt had only to tell him to pull out. Wallace had offered to withdraw. He made the offer three times, in fact, and Roosevelt rejected it each time.

Roosevelt's milk-and-water endorsement letter satisfied only himself. Certainly the Wallace camp had hoped for more. Nor was it the final coupe de grâce the party bosses wanted. Less than a week remained before the convention opened; several candidates were still in the running, and Wallace's sizable bloc of supporters stood fast. The professionals had only their control of the convention machinery and a little note from Roosevelt on the back of an envelope.

Hannegan desperately set out to remedy the situation. His chance came on the afternoon of Saturday, July 15, in Chicago's Rock Island Railroad yards, where the president's railroad car was briefly sidetracked while en route from Hyde Park to San Diego. Hannegan, in the company of Mayor Ed Kelly, went to talk with Roosevelt one more time about the vice presidential nomination.

The fifty-two-minute meeting, Hannegan later told his family, was heated and difficult. Hannegan wanted the president to endorse no one at all, but Roosevelt had already written his letter to Senator Jackson and would not withdraw it. Hannegan returned to the note written on the envelope. By naming Douglas first, he argued, its impact was weakened. Douglas had gone hiking in the Oregon mountains and wasn't even campaigning for the post, Hannegan said. Truman was the man for the job. Eventually Roosevelt wearily relented.

"When a man who meant business, as Hannegan meant business, was talking that way to the president, the feminine side of the president would succumb to the dominant Hannegan and say, 'All right,'" Wallace later commented.[21]

Roosevelt wrote a longhand letter putting Truman's name first. Hannegan took the letter to an adjoining compartment, where Grace Tully typed it on White House stationery. Roosevelt signed it, and Hannegan tucked it into a copy of *National Geographic* magazine and departed.

"Dear Bob," it said. "You have written me about Harry Truman and Bill Douglas. I should, of course, be very glad to run with either of them and believe that either one of them would bring real strength to the ticket. Always Sincerely, FDR." The letter was postdated July 19.*[22]

❦

Six astonishing days followed, days of sweat and hard liquor, melodrama and intrigue, that would mark a turning point for the Democratic Party and the nation. The stakes could not have been higher. Hannegan and his cohorts knew the Democrats were selecting not one president but two: Roosevelt and the man who would succeed him. The bosses meant to use every means at their disposal to prevent Henry A. Wallace from being that man. And they nearly lost to a bunch of amateurs.

First Jimmie Byrnes had to be gotten out of the race—and Harry Truman in. Neither task proved easy. Byrnes still eagerly sought the nomination and was gaining strength among southerners. Truman, committed to Byrnes, in-

---

*The various permutations of Roosevelt's notes to Hannegan, and the postdating of the final version, subsequently caused much confusion. No copy of the first note, scribbled on an envelope on July 11, was ever found. Some think Hannegan destroyed it. At least one historian has argued that Hannegan obtained a signed, typewritten version of the note the following day. If so, it too has been lost.

The July 15 (dated July 19) letter reversing the names—both the longhand and typewritten versions—remained in the possession of Hannegan's widow until 1960, when Harry Truman persuaded her to donate them to his presidential library. By that time, many historians had accepted the account of Grace Tully, claiming she placed Truman's name first, at Hannegan's request, when she typed the letter.

Tully's account was inaccurate. The longhand and typewritten versions of the July 15 letter were identical. Both put Truman's name first.

Wallace did not learn of the July 11 note, placing Douglas's name first, until 1950 when George Allen published a memoir, *Presidents Who Have Known Me*. Even then he remained uncertain about the exact sequence of events. "I would very much like to know whether Roosevelt had determined on the second name thing with Hannegan before he told me that there would not be a second name on July 13th," Wallace said in the oral history he gave to Columbia University in 1951. "I would like to know that."

Adding to Wallace's puzzlement was a July 17 letter from Roosevelt to George Norris. The former senator had written from his deathbed to express alarm over rumors the Democrats might nominate Wendell Willkie for vice president. There was not much chance of that, Roosevelt replied, although "feelers were put out about a week ago." Roosevelt said he was "honestly trying to keep out of the Vice-Presidential contest" and had done nothing other than give his personal endorsement to Wallace.

"This is rather extraordinary in view of the fact the president had given this letter on behalf of Truman and Douglas just two days previously," Wallace said in his oral history. "That Monday he wrote the letter to Norris he must either have forgotten that he'd given the letter to Hannegan, or he must have felt that Hannegan would never use the letter in public."

tended to keep his word. Some doubted Harry Truman even wanted to be vice president. He was happy in the Senate, and he knew a national campaign would resurrect stories about his association with the corrupt Pendergast machine in Kansas City. Perhaps his wife would suffer embarrassment when the nation learned she was on his Senate payroll at $4,500 a year. Loaded with anxiety, Hannegan greeted Frank Walker when he arrived in Chicago. "We haven't got a candidate," he exclaimed.[23]

But Roosevelt had given the bosses a valuable tool. He told Hannegan and Kelly the vice presidential nominee must have the approval of the labor leader Sidney Hillman. "Clear it with Sidney" became the most famous, or infamous, four words of the 1944 campaign.

The dictum gave Hannegan and his cohorts a wedge that they used with great dexterity. Their strategy was to establish Byrnes as the front-runner in the "Stop Wallace" field, knowing he would never suit the liberal Hillman. At the same time Hillman might be persuaded to support someone other than Wallace if that would stop Byrnes.

So it was that Byrnes was assured his nomination was "in the bag," and the jaunty South Carolinian arrived in Chicago brimming with confidence. He would have seven hundred votes on the first ballot, he declared, more than enough to win the nomination.

That was Sunday, July 16. The next two days brought a bewildering kaleidoscope of confusion, rumor, threats, plots, and counterplots. Everyone knew something, and no one knew anything. There were hotel room schemes and barroom deals, whispered confidences and tumultuous conferences—a constant "shifting of events and violent interplay of forces," as one observer put it. Byrnes dined with Kelly. Truman had breakfast with Murray. Hannegan talked with Hillman. The bosses huddled in a secret Lake Shore apartment.[24]

A constant stream of delegates and politicians moved through Hannegan's seventh-floor suite in the Blackstone. Outside his rooms a small army of reporters kept watch in the red-carpeted corridor, scrounging for gossip. All Chicago spoke of "the letter" Hannegan supposedly had from Roosevelt. But no one saw the letter. "Do you want to see it," Boss Kelly teasingly asked. "I don't have it here. I'll show it to you tomorrow."[25]

There was indeed a letter for all to see, but not the one under Mrs. Hannegan's mattress. On Monday morning, July 17, Roosevelt's letter to Sam Jackson regarding Wallace ("If I were a delegate . . .") was released to the public. It was a weak endorsement to be sure, but it was the only one in public view. And it unequivocally said the vice presidential choice was up to the delegates. The president would not dictate.

Harold Young put a brave face on it: "I think it is a swell recommendation," Young told reporters, "and any man could get a job on it."[26]

Roosevelt's letter only added to the convention's Byzantine atmosphere. Within hours a dozen "favorite son" candidacies had popped up, mainly in southern states, further muddying the waters.

For Jimmie Byrnes, Monday marked a dawning realization that all was not as it seemed. From Hannegan he learned of the president's "clear it with Sidney" order and throughout the day sought support from Murray and Hillman. He got nowhere. Murray even threatened a boycott of the Democratic ticket if Byrnes was on it.

That evening the bosses gathered again and decided to call Roosevelt for guidance. They reached him on his train somewhere near El Paso. They spoke to him one by one—Hannegan, Kelly, Flynn, Walker—and received the same message. Byrnes would be a "political liability." Truman was the man. "The president settled the matter beyond all doubt," Walker later wrote. "He spoke to me last. 'Frank,' he said, 'go all out for Truman.' "[27]

The bosses moved accordingly. In short order Hannegan had dinner with Hillman and Murray and played his trump card. If the labor leaders withdraw Wallace, the party chairman said, "we will withdraw Byrnes." The labor leaders gave no promise.[28]

On Tuesday morning, July 18, Truman went to Hillman's room in the Ambassador East Hotel for a breakfast of croissants and café au lait. They made quite a pair: the Lithuanian-born labor leader, trained to be a rabbi, and the plain-spoken bow-tied Missouri politician. Truman had come to tout Byrnes's candidacy. "No," said Hillman. "We are for Wallace." Then Hillman crossed the line that Murray had said would never be crossed. "But we would have two choices after Wallace. The second of those would be Douglas. I'm looking at our first choice now."[29]

Wallace later said he never understood this act of Hillman's. Perhaps Hillman deemed Wallace not far enough to the left. Or perhaps he just felt the fix was in and made his accommodations. "Suffice it to say that Sidney Hillman was a very skilled and a very suspicious operator who had his eye firmly glued on the main chance," said Wallace.[30]

Meanwhile Byrnes sank fast. He reached Roosevelt by phone but received no satisfactory explanation of the letter that purportedly mentioned Truman and Douglas but not Byrnes. Later in the day Truman came to Byrnes's suite and asked to be released from his commitment to nominate him. The Missouri delegation had voted to nominate Truman himself, he explained. Byrnes assented. The final blow came in a late-afternoon meeting with Hannegan. The party chairman confirmed that Roosevelt had called Byrnes a "political liability." Hannegan heard it personally, and so had three others.

It was over. In four frantic days Brynes had gone from shoo-in to has-been. That evening he wrote a letter withdrawing his candidacy "in deference to the wishes of the president" and began packing his bags. He left Chicago without ever seeing the inside of the convention hall.[31]

Wallace played no role in the pre-convention frenzy. Backroom deals were not his style. He wanted to be renominated, Wallace observed in his oral history, but he "wasn't going to do anything about it." His attitude conveyed the impression that "he had resigned himself to the convention's decision without so much as lifting a finger," wrote the *Des Moines Register* reporter Marr McGaffin. Wallace was nominal chairman of the Iowa delegation, but he had not even planned to attend the convention.[32]

Such diffidence chilled his backers. "He is wholly unprepared for the devious type of warfare which is being waged around him, and is almost unaware of it," wrote Assistant Attorney General Norman M. Littell, an ardent Wallace supporter, in his diary. ". . . One has flashes of amazement and anxiety, too, as if a child were walking into a sawmill among a lot of flying buzz-saws."[33]

So while Harold Young and "the CIO boys" set up shop in Chicago, Wallace remained in virtual seclusion in Washington. "Since Wallace returned from his trip to China and held a lengthy press conference, confined exclusively to that tour, he has locked the doors, pulled down the blinds and disappeared almost completely from public view," wrote McGaffin. He avoided reporters and became suddenly camera shy. When a photographer surprised him in the lobby of the Wardman Park, Wallace suddenly tackled him and tried to wrestle away his camera.* He had few contacts with his supporters in Chicago and no advice for them when he did.[34]

---

*The photographer, Robert Woodsum of Acme newspictures, had waited five hours in the Wardman Park lobby for Wallace to pass through. As the vice president was talking to a clerk at the mail desk, Woodsum approached and asked to take a picture. "No, no, no," Wallace replied. Wallace trotted out of the building with the photographer in pursuit.

Wallace was on a landing at the foot of the building's front steps, in a crouching position with a briefcase in one hand, when Woodsum snapped his picture. "Give me that plate—I want that plate," Wallace shouted. "I backed away from him, honestly startled," Woodsum later told a reporter for United Press. "I hadn't expected any trouble."

Then, according to Woodsum, Wallace emerged from his crouch "like a professional wrestler [and] sailed through the air and grabbed me around the neck with his free arm. I was bent over trying to protect my camera and his tackle caught me off balance. We went to the floor, with him on top of me and his arms still around my neck. . . . We threshed around for several seconds."

With Wallace still sitting on Woodsum's chest, they negotiated over the plate. Wallace finally agreed to go outside and pose for a picture if Woodsum would destroy the plate, and the photographer agreed. As they were going outside, Wallace explained that he had once fallen asleep in a barber chair and a photographer had taken his picture. "That made me very angry," Wallace said.

"We parted on amiable terms," Woodsum said.

The "Wallace organization" in Chicago was in fact more of a disorganization. On Sunday, when its headquarters opened in a reception room at the Stevens Hotel, it had neither floor managers nor placards ready for the convention hall. Harold Young and C. B. "Beanie" Baldwin, a former Agriculture Department official and current aide to Sidney Hillman, took over the Wallace operation more or less by default. The floor campaign was assigned to a committee of four: Senators Joe Guffey and Claude Pepper, Governor Ellis Arnall of Georgia, and Assistant Interior Secretary Oscar Chapman.

Delegate counts were difficult to obtain, given the swift-moving political currents, but early guesses gave Wallace only 200 votes on the first ballot (589 votes were needed to win). The convention machinery was firmly in the bosses' hands. Only one man could make a difference—Franklin Roosevelt—and he was far away, his whereabouts a military secret.

Under the circumstances, Baldwin and Young concluded, "if we were to have any chance of winning the nomination it would be necessary for Wallace to come to Chicago." Wallace resisted. Jake More, Iowa party chairman, sent him a long, almost desperate telegram pleading for his appearance. There "is much confusion in this convention," More said. "Your opinions have been attacked. . . . I think you should come out here and shake hands with the folks."[35]

Wallace finally relented. He and Ilo departed by train from Washington on the evening of Tuesday, July 18. Even then he was quiet about it, choosing to board the Baltimore and Ohio at a little-used terminal in Silver Spring, Maryland, instead of Washington's Union Station.

His wariness was understandable. His experience in the same cavernous hall four years earlier had been lonely and humiliating. This convention had the earmarks of a similar bruiser.

Yet, from the moment of his arrival in Chicago on the morning of Wednesday, July 19, Wallace could sense the difference four years had made. This time crowds were friendly, and flashbulbs popped wherever he went. People in restaurants asked for his autograph. Passersby on sidewalks stopped to offer him encouragement. Scores of eager, earnest delegates filled meeting rooms to hear him say a few words and pledge their support.

His first stop was a press conference at the Stevens Hotel, where 150 reporters crowded around to hear him. Wallace perched on a table, his legs dangling over the side, and gave it to them straight. Would he withdraw, as Hannegan hinted so often? "I am in this fight to the finish." What were his chances? "I really haven't the slightest idea." What about the president's letter leaving the choice to the convention? "The letter did what I suggested." Did he have a strategy? "Right here," he said, patting a briefcase that held the speech he would give on Thursday.[36]

Inside Chicago Stadium delegates gathered for the first convention session Wednesday afternoon. It was a routine affair, but there was a sense of excitement in the crowd. A fight raged for the soul of the party, and Democrats loved a fight. In the midst of the session, delegates learned that in Japan the cabinet of Premier Hideki Tojo had resigned following the fall of Saipan. History was being made before their eyes.

At the Stevens Hotel the Wallace headquarters was a blur of activity. Reports came in from this delegation and that, vote tallies were revised and strategies mapped out. The news seemed generally better, if not good enough. Wallace still fell short of a first-ballot majority. His team decided to have Hillman call Roosevelt, but he never made contact. Overtures went out to Senate Majority Leader Alben Barkley, still in the running as a favorite son from Kentucky. A friendly Barkley made no commitment. From the North Carolina delegation old Josephus Daniels, the former ambassador to Mexico, indicated with a wink and a nod that he would do what he could for Wallace, although he was not in a position to say so publicly.

Wallace embodied calm. While hardly indifferent, he was content to let events run their course. Roosevelt still held the key to everything. Wallace knew only that the president would get what he wanted.

In the early evening Wallace joined his friend Norman Littell for dinner at the Chicago Athletic Club. At a quiet table for two, they settled in for a leisurely chat. It was almost unbelievable to Littell. Here was the vice president of the United States at the most crucial moment of his political life, talking about methods of growing cotton in the Soviet Union and the plight of poor farmers in China. At length Littell could stand it no more. What about the business at hand? "I am perfectly happy about the outcome," Wallace said blandly. Littell demanded an explanation.

"I mean this: There is only one issue in my nomination and that is the existence of liberal government in the United States. I happen to be the symbol of that issue. . . . It is the cause of liberalism which is at issue and not my own fortunes."[37]

With that they went to Chicago Stadium, where Wallace made his first appearance on the convention floor. When he entered the huge crowd burst into a spontaneous ovation. The cheering lasted for a quarter hour.

In the long and gaudy history of American political conventions, few days were as extraordinary as Thursday, July 20, 1944.

For the handful of professionals who ran the convention—or thought they did—the day began at low tide. Alben Barkley, mightily disgusted by the president's hidden-hand machinations, was threatening to back out of delivering Roosevelt's nominating speech. Hannegan was being goaded about "the letter" by Claude Pepper and others who broadly hinted no such document existed. From Washington, Eleanor Roosevelt suggested Pepper take the convention floor and call Hannegan a liar. Harold Ickes had at last become wise to the bosses' game and strenuously endorsed Henry Wallace.

Worse still for the bosses, Harry Truman remained balky. Byrnes was out, but Truman not yet in.

Once again Hannegan turned to Roosevelt for help, and the president readily gave it. Hannegan set up a hotel room meeting with Truman and several of the bosses. As they were talking, Roosevelt called, and Hannegan held the phone out from his ear. Truman could clearly hear the president's booming voice.

"Bob, have you got that fellow lined up yet," Roosevelt asked. "No, Mr. President," said Hannegan, "he is the contrariest Missouri mule I've ever dealt with."

"Well, you tell him that if he wants to break up the Democratic Party in the middle of a war, that's his responsibility," Roosevelt responded.

Hannegan hung up the phone and looked at Truman. "Now what do you say?"

"Oh shit," Truman replied. "Well, if that's the situation I'll have to say yes, but why the hell didn't he tell me in the first place?"[38]

Meanwhile, Barkley, swallowing his anger, had placed Roosevelt's name before the convention. It was a sturdy, workmanlike speech, but reporters thought it lacked his usual zing. The cheers were more for Roosevelt's name than for anything Barkley said.

The orchestrated demonstration ran its course. Then came Henry Wallace's moment. Dressed in a gray double-breasted suit, his hair for once neatly trimmed, Wallace looked ever bit the mild-mannered intellectual. Only sixteen years had passed since he gave his first, awkward political speeches on behalf of Al Smith before small knots of Iowa farmers. Now he stood in Chicago Stadium before a crowd of thirty thousand, and he briefly savored their cheers.

Then he let fly.

"The strength of the Democratic Party has always been the people—plain people like so many of those here in this convention—ordinary folks, farmers, workers, and business men along Main Street," Wallace began.

Jefferson, Jackson and Woodrow Wilson knew the power of the plain people. All three laid down the thesis that the Democratic Party can win only if and when it is the liberal party.

Now we have come to the most extraordinary election in the history of our country. Three times the Democratic Party has been led to victory by the greatest liberal in the history of the United States. The name Roosevelt is revered in the remotest corners of this earth. The name Roosevelt is cursed only by Germans and Japs and certain American Troglodytes.

The first order of business was to win the war quickly, Wallace continued. Next must come the winning of the peace. "The Voice of New World liberalism must carry on." He added,

> The future belongs to those who go down the line unswervingly for the liberal principles of both political democracy and economic democracy regardless of race, color or religion. In a political, educational and economic sense there must be no inferior races. The poll tax must go. Equal educational opportunities must come. The future must bring equal wages for equal work regardless of sex or race.
>
> Roosevelt stands for all this. That is why certain people hate him so. That also is one of the outstanding reasons why Roosevelt will be elected for a fourth time.

The Democratic Party could never succeed in being better conservatives than the Republicans, he declared. Likewise, Republicans who try to pursue progressive policies are doomed to failure. "I know because my own father tried it," said Wallace. "Perhaps Wendell Willkie may have learned in 1944 a little of that which my own father learned in 1924. The Old Elephant never changes and never forgives." Then he said,

> By nominating Franklin Roosevelt the Democratic Party is again declaring its faith in liberalism. Roosevelt is a greater liberal today than he has ever been. His soul is pure. The high quality of Roosevelt liberalism will become more apparent as the war emergency passes. The only question ever in Roosevelt's mind is how best to serve the cause of liberalism in the long run. He thinks big. He sees far.
>
> There is no question about the renomination of President Roosevelt by this convention. The only question is whether the convention and the party workers believe wholeheartedly in the liberal policies for which Roosevelt has always stood. Our problem is not to sell Roosevelt to the Democratic convention but to sell the Democratic Party and the Democratic convention to the people of the United States. . . .
>
> Issues that will be with us for a generation—perhaps even for a hundred years—will take form at this convention and at the November election. . . .
>
> As head of the Iowa delegation, in the cause of liberalism, and with a prayer for prompt victory in this war, permanent peace, and full employment, I give you Franklin D. Roosevelt.[39]

The speech was electrifying. Chicago Stadium roared back its approval with the most genuine ovation given any speaker at the convention. In the press box at Chicago Stadium, the columnist Thomas L. Stokes leaped from his seat in tears and said it was a magnificent speech. "But goddam it, it isn't smart politics," Stokes exclaimed.[40] In fifteen crisp paragraphs—during which he used the words "liberal" and "liberalism" eleven times—Wallace had flung down his gauntlet.

He had stood stiff-necked before the convention delegates and told them forthrightly what was at stake. "Whether conservatives squirmed or Southerners saw red or New Dealers cheered, Henry Wallace's speech was the first that riveted the delegates' attention," wrote *Time* magazine. "It was blunt, grave, tactless. It easily explained why Henry Wallace was the best loved and the best hated man in the stadium."[41]

In McCook, Nebraska, a dying George Norris listened to the speech and reached for his pen. "I do not suppose it would be considered a proper speech for that occasion by the politicians," the former senator wrote to Wallace. "If you had been trying to appease somebody you made a mistake, but you were talking straight into the faces of your enemies who were trying to defeat you, and no matter what they may think or what effect it may have on them, the effect on the country and all those who will read that speech is that it was one of the most courageous exhibitions ever seen at a political convention in this country."[42]

At the close of the afternoon session, the bosses were near panic. Roosevelt had been easily (although not unanimously) renominated, and Wallace's speech had turned it into a victory for liberalism. All hope that Wallace would walk meekly off the stage was gone. Their most significant argument on behalf of Truman—that Wallace could not win in Chicago, because he was so unpopular—was visibly untrue. To stop Wallace they would have to beat him outright.

At eight o'clock, as delegates gathered for the evening session, Hannegan played his biggest card. Meeting with reporters outside the convention hall, he produced the long-rumored letter from Roosevelt saying he would be pleased to run on a ticket with Truman or Douglas.

The effect was not exactly what Hannegan intended. The letter did not clearly endorse Truman, as Hannegan had intimated, but rather expressed a willingness to run with Truman or Douglas. And what did the opening line ("Dear Bob, You have written me about Harry Truman and Bill Douglas") mean, reporters asked? Hannegan had been caught in a half-truth, which reporters thought was as good as a lie. As word of the letter spread like wildfire through Chicago Stadium, many delegates viewed it less as a blow to Wallace than as proof that something underhanded was taking place. To Wallace's supporters the letter was only confirmation that Harry Truman was the "bosses' candidate."

The main order of business that evening was Roosevelt's acceptance speech. A massive crowd, numbering close to forty thousand, packed into the sweltering hall to hear his words. Spotlights lit up a huge portrait of the president, as the familiar voice boomed from loudspeakers on the convention stage.

He was speaking, Roosevelt explained, from "a Pacific Coast naval base" where he was conducting his duties as commander in chief.*43

Once again Roosevelt said he longed to retire but would accept the nomination out of duty. He would not campaign "in the usual sense," because that would not be fitting. Besides, there wasn't time. "What is the job before us in 1944? First, to win the war—to win the war fast, to win it overpoweringly. Second, to form worldwide international organizations, and to arrange to use the armed forces of the sovereign nations of the world to make another war impossible within the foreseeable future. And third, to build an economy for our returning veterans and for all Americans—which will provide employment and decent standards of living."44

The hall gave the disembodied voice a rousing cheer. The organ played and delegates waved placards saying, "Roosevelt and Victory" and "Roosevelt and a Lasting Peace." The demonstration was long, loud, and in accord with the script. As it wound down, however, something unexpected happened. The galleries erupted with a demand for Henry Wallace.45

Suddenly Chicago Stadium was rocked by deafening chants of "We want Wallace! We want Wallace!" On the podium Sam Jackson banged his gavel and called for order. He had no effect. "WE WANT WALLACE! WE WANT WALLACE!" The convention organist, a loyal employee of Boss Kelly, inexplicably joined the stampede and began playing the "Iowa Corn Song." The hall reverberated with its rollicking chorus: "We are from I-o-way, I-o-way. . . . That's where the tall corn grows." All was bedlam. The "Madhouse on Madison Street" had never been more insane.†46

---

*Roosevelt delivered the address from his railroad car, stationed at the San Diego naval base. He sounded solemn but otherwise hale and hearty. It was all the more shocking, therefore, when newspapers published a photograph the next day showing him haggard and thin, with dark rings under his eyes and his jaw slack. "It was at this point that the people, rather than the politicians, began to think of their President as a sick man," wrote Jim Bishop.

†Party professionals later complained that the CIO had packed the galleries with Wallace supporters, a contention supported by the *Chicago Tribune* and passed along as fact by some historians. Beanie Baldwin and Wallace vehemently denied the assertion. Baldwin said the CIO wanted to pack the galleries, but was unable to do so, because Mayor Kelly controlled ticket distribution. "Actually, in spite of our best efforts, we were unable to obtain more than 125 gallery tickets for our supporters," Baldwin later wrote.

In fact, Baldwin maintained, Kelly gave out—in some cases sold—some 15,000 tickets to "loyal Democrats" presumed opposed to Wallace. Many spectators entering the hall also were given a flier quoting Wallace (out of context) as having said, "The Catholic Church is the Whore of Babylon." Once inside the hall, however, the spectators joined the Wallace demonstration.

The idea that Kelly's constituents would support Wallace struck party pros as ludicrous, but it didn't surprise Wallace. He noted he had attracted some 25,000 Chicagoans to the stadium the previous year with no help from Kelly's machine. "The Chicago Stadium was in the 24th Ward, and I was enormously popular in the 24th Ward," Wallace commented in his oral history. "It's a Jewish ward and . . . the situation was such that it was practically 100% Wallace."

On the podium Hannegan, red-faced and sweaty, could see his worst nightmare coming true. The convention was bolting out of control. Above the din he shouted to Kelly for help. "We have fire laws," said the mayor. Kelly moved to the entrance and began to fling open doors, allowing hundreds more into the already overcrowded arena. Meanwhile, a city worker was dispatched with an ax, with orders to silence the organ by cutting its cables if necessary. At the back of the hall, Norman Littell watched the pandemonium with tears in his eyes. "There was nothing synthetic or simulated about [this] demonstration," he wrote. "It was the real thing."[47]

In the Florida delegation Senator Pepper reached the same conclusion. "I stood on my chair and observed the number of state standards visible in the Wallace parade," Pepper wrote. "It appeared that most states were represented. This could mean only one thing—broad support for Wallace—because chairmen would not allow their delegates to parade for a candidate they objected to strongly. Emotions ran high. I was convinced that if a vote could be taken that evening, Wallace could be nominated."[48]

Pepper began jumping up and down on his chair, the Florida standard in hand, demanding recognition. Chairman Jackson would not give it. "I shouted at the top of my lungs and waved my standard violently, to no avail," Pepper said. With no way of addressing the chair, because Florida's microphone was dead, Pepper took his standard and began elbowing his way through the crowd toward the podium. At the edge of the platform was the bosses' last line of defense: a little gate that guarded the entrance to the podium itself. A railroad labor union man whom Pepper knew tended the gate, and he readily allowed the senator to pass through.

Pepper began climbing the steps toward the podium. The bosses could see him coming. So could reporters and hundreds of others. Hannegan screamed at Jackson to adjourn the session, but the balding senator hesitated. "This crowd is too hot," said Jackson. "I can't."

"You're taking orders from me," Hannegan yelled back, "and I'm taking orders from the president."[49]

Pepper was one step away from reaching the podium when Jackson relented. Jackson gave him a little glance and banged his gavel, calling for yeas and nays on a motion to adjourn. The crowd roared, "No, no, no, no." The ayes have it, said Jackson. The session was adjourned. The organ fell silent, the lights dimmed, and Mayor Kelly's police began clearing the aisles.

It was over. Pepper had led the Pickett's Charge of the Wallace movement.

***

The next morning Jackson approached Pepper in his hotel lobby and offered an apology of sorts. "Claude, I hated to do what I had to do last night, but

I saw you coming up those steps and I knew if you made the motion the convention would nominate Henry Wallace. I had strict instructions from Hannegan not to let the convention nominate the vice-president last night. So I had to adjourn the convention in your face. I hope you understand."

Pepper understood perfectly. In his autobiography he wrote, "What I understood was that, for better or worse, history was turned topsy-turvy that night in Chicago."

And indeed it was. The Wallace movement would advance no further. Overnight the bosses worked feverishly to secure Truman's nomination. Ambassadorships were offered. Postmaster positions were handed out. Cold cash changed hands. Frank Walker was said to have called every state chairman that night, assuring each one that Roosevelt wanted the Missouri senator as his running mate.

There would be no more explosions in the convention hall. The organist forgot how to play the "Iowa Corn Song," and Chicago policemen strictly limited admission to the stadium. Thousands of Wallace supporters were denied entrance, and those who made it in were scattered hither and yon. "Some of them were so far apart they had to signal each other with flashlights," said a radio newsman. Large portions of the galleries were altogether empty.[50]

The convention session of Friday, July 21, lasted nine grueling hours. Even the self-styled "amateurs" running the Wallace effort were savvy enough to see the change inside the stadium. Beanie Baldwin could smell defeat. "The machine was simply too powerful," he said. Inside Room H, an air-conditioned inner sanctum below the podium, an endless parade of delegates passed through to enjoy some liquid refreshment and shake hands with "the new vice president"—Harry S. Truman.[51]

Still, the Wallace forces never gave up. Wallace had said he was in the fight to the finish, and he meant what he said. Iowa judge Richard Mitchell placed him in nomination with a spirited speech that was enthusiastically applauded. Even stronger was Claude Pepper's seconding speech, a little gem of "brevity, clarity and force," one delegate observed. Shame would fall upon the delegates if they rejected a man because he was "too democratic for the Democratic National Convention," Pepper said.[52] Governor Arnall of Georgia followed with a call for delegates to repudiate the tactics of the urban bosses.

Truman was nominated by his Missouri colleague, Senator Bennett Clark, who delivered a listless speech emphasizing his war record and pedigree as a "Democrat by inheritance as well as by conviction."[53] A demonstration followed, lively enough to offset Clark's poor performance.

Then came a nearly interminable succession of favorite son nominations. Paul McNutt, whose flame briefly burned bright at the 1940 convention, was nominated again. Senator John Bankhead, brother of Wallace's chief opponent at the 1940 convention, was nominated. In all, seventeen names were placed before the convention.

The bosses had calculated the large number of favorite son candidacies would make it impossible for anyone to win on the first ballot. With Wallace stopped short of victory, momentum would shift to Truman—the "Missouri compromise," as reporters called him—as the favorite sons threw their support to him. Their strategy worked to perfection.

Even so, Wallace's showing on the first ballot surprised many observers. Wallace led throughout the vote, carrying many midwestern states unanimously and racking up majorities in such large states as Pennsylvania, California, and Michigan. The vote at the end of the first ballot was $429^1/_2$ for Wallace and $319^1/_2$ for Truman, with the remainder scattered among favorite sons and protest candidates.

At this point Chairman Jackson announced the convention would proceed directly to the second ballot. There would be no dinner break, no time for the Wallace forces to make mischief.

In anticipation of the bosses' strategy, the Wallace forces deliberately held back about seventy votes on the first ballot so as to indicate some momentum of their own in the second round. Their hope was then to draw upon some hidden reserves—old Josephus Daniels in North Carolina, progressive Alben Barkley in Kentucky, an antimachine element in Illinois led by Harold Ickes—to put them over the top. The hidden reserves remained hidden, however. Wallace's "poll tax must go" speech made it all but impossible for Daniels and Barkley to gather support for him in the South. In Illinois, Ickes could do no more than fight Mayor Kelly to a draw.

As the second roll call of states began, Wallace did show additional strength. He peaked at 489 votes, 100 short of the goal. Then, as Beanie Baldwin later put it, "the dam broke."[54] The first to go was Maryland, where Governor Herbert O'Conor withdrew in favor of Truman. Senator Bankhead of Alabama was next. The rout was on. At the gallery box where Harry Truman had joined his wife and daughter to watch the voting, photographers pressed around to take pictures. Boss Kelly held the senator's hand aloft in the manner of a prize fighter in a victory.

"I could see Hannegan at the front edge of the platform motioning excitedly to this delegation and then to that," wrote Norman Littell. "For all the world, he was like an organ player pulling great stops on a giant organ. First to the left, then to the right and then in the center, as one delegation after another, through its speaker, rose to the microphone standing by the aisle and announced its vote."[55]

It was Bob Hannegan's proudest hour. On his tombstone, Hannegan later said, he would like to have inscribed, "Here lies the man who stopped Henry Wallace from becoming President of the United States."[56]

Bowing to the inevitable, the Iowa state Chairman, Jake More, moved to make the vote unanimous for Truman. But the bosses were not in a mood to be friendly. Jackson ruled the motion out of order. The voting continued. At the end the vote was 1,031 for Truman, 105 for Wallace, 4 for William O. Douglas.

The convention closed with a distinctly humble little acceptance speech by the vice presidential nominee. He appreciated the honor and would do his best, Truman said. "He might have been accepting the nomination for presidency of the Kiwanis Club," one Wallace delegate grumbled.[57]

Wallace had long since left the hall and was relaxing in his room at the Stevens by the time Truman spoke. Around 10 P.M. he asked a few close associates whether they wanted something to eat, and they ordered a meal of scrambled eggs and fruit from room service. A constant stream of supporters moved through the room expressing rage and sorrow and bitterness over the outcome. Joe McLeod, city editor of the *Washington Post*, stared glumly at his food and cried like a baby.

Through it all Wallace was "undoubtedly the most cheerful person in the room," one of his colleagues recalled. He was proud of his stand and sanguine in defeat. He took satisfaction in the fact that the "Democratic leaders had to work many times as hard to stop me in 1944 as they had to put me over in 1940. . . . It was a fine fight, and everything is all right."[58]

CHAPTER NINETEEN

"POETIC JUSTICE"

On the evening of defeat, the vanquished sent a telegram to the victor. The wire to Harry Truman was straightforward, if not exceedingly warm. "Congratulations upon your enlarged opportunity to help the President and the people. Both of us will do our maximum for Roosevelt and what Roosevelt stands for. Sincerely, Henry A. Wallace."*[1]

While Wallace's telegram was going out, another came in from the architect of his defeat. It was quite warm and anything but straightforward. "You made a grand fight and I am very proud of you. Tell Ilo not to plan to leave Washington next January. Franklin D. Roosevelt."[2]

Wallace could only shake his head in puzzlement.

What could the telegram mean? Its tone was friendly, as friendly as Roosevelt's voice when he drew Wallace close and said he hoped it would be the "same old team." Then the president had been "absolutely and utterly convincing," Wallace said. Now Wallace was convinced of only one thing: "If Roosevelt had kept hands off I could have been named."[3]

He did not know, either, what Roosevelt meant by his cryptic reference to not leaving Washington. A part of him didn't care. Stoic in defeat, at heart he was disappointed and disgusted. "I don't know if I wanted to stay or not—it just depended," Wallace later remarked. Nor did he know how

*Western Union was barred by wartime restrictions from delivering messages of congratulations, and in confusion it delayed Wallace's message. Two days later from Quincy, Illinois, Truman sent a wire thanking Wallace. "I tried to call on you but you had left the hotel," Truman said.

Ilo felt about it. "I never asked her," Wallace said. "I didn't talk to her about things of this sort."[4]

The next morning the Wallaces left Chicago for Des Moines. Ilo rode to the LaSalle Street station in a car with friends, but Henry preferred to walk. He wore a sporty Panama straw hat and passed through the crowded train station almost unnoticed. He had declined to announce his travel plans in advance because that "would be seeking publicity." He chatted briefly with a reporter who spotted him, then climbed aboard the Rock Island line for Iowa.[5]

Rolling through the midwestern countryside, Wallace reflected on what he had done, what might have been, what he would be. He was fifty-five years old, about the same age his grandfather had been when he set out to edit the fledgling *Wallaces' Farmer*. The following years had been Uncle Henry's most productive. Perhaps the Democratic convention marked such a beginning in his own life.

❖

Wallace pondered his fall but never reached an explanation that satisfied him. While still in Des Moines, he wrote a long memo to himself setting out the chronology of events leading to his defeat. He saved journalistic accounts of the convention and attempted to judge their accuracy. For years he followed the careers and memoirs of the various players, trying to fit the pieces.

He collected rumors avidly: Tommy Corcoran was the link between the British Tories and the American Catholic hierarchy. Ed Flynn had told Roosevelt the Democratic ticket could have all the money it needed if Wallace was dumped. Ed Pauley fanned the conservative flame by telling businessmen Wallace would mean higher taxes. Bernard Baruch had offered Roosevelt a million dollars if he ran on a ticket without Wallace. Sidney Hillman had betrayed the labor cause in order to gain personal influence.

The Chicago convention thus became a lens through which Wallace viewed the Democratic Party and its politicians. When the Democratic convention chairman, Senator Jackson, died at age fifty-six in 1951, for example, Wallace categorized him simply as "the man who got the vice presidential nomination for Harry Truman." The United States was run by a "government of city bosses" and would be as long as the Democratic Party was in control. "The internal foulness of the Democratic Party had not yet reached the point of lancing the boil."[6]

Bitterness suffused this, a feeling the nomination had been stolen from him by unscrupulous men using underhanded means. He flatly rejected suggestions that his own lack of political skill had much to do with it. "It has been said that I was politically naive, and I don't think I ever played the game from a political point of view. . . . I was using different standards. My method of action was different, that's all."[7] He was interested solely in ends; his opponents cared only about means.

In the end, Wallace's thoughts always came down to one unanswerable question: Why had Roosevelt done it? Perhaps he was maneuvering for congressional support of his postwar goals, or was securing party unity through selection of a compromise candidate acceptable to both liberals and conservatives, or had he simply lost confidence in Wallace?*

No theory, however, explained Roosevelt's duplicity in Wallace's view. It was "an awful lot of trouble to go to when all he needed to do was call me in and say, 'I don't want you to run.' " Wallace commented. "That's all he needed to do."[8]

Roosevelt may have miscalculated the effect of his actions. If he had hoped to convince the public that the convention dumped Wallace of its own accord, he failed totally. Politicians and the press alike put the decision squarely in Roosevelt's lap. Said *Time* magazine, "The Wallace wing lost because Franklin Roosevelt had weighted the scales against it. For Franklin Roosevelt, absent only physically from this convention, as in 1940, was still undisputed master of the Democratic Party. With his support Henry Wallace might again have won the Vice Presidential nomination. But the President chose to buy party unity instead."[9]

And therein lay another miscalculation. Dumping Wallace brought no peace to the Democratic Party. On the contrary, when Wallace returned to Washington in mid-August, he found a huge stack of letters, telegrams, and editorials on his desk denouncing the convention and Roosevelt in vehement terms. Some two thousand letters were received in a single week, including messages from such notable Americans as Archibald MacLeish, Sumner Welles, Paul de Kruif, Felix Frankfurter, Frances Perkins, Nelson Rockefeller, Walter Reuther, Upton Sinclair, Abe Fortas, and David Lilienthal.

"That convention did the President no good, and for that I am truly sorry," wrote Harold Ickes. "A little more of Hannegan and the President may find himself in a shambles in November." Mark Etheridge, editor of the *Louisville Courier Journal*, spoke for many liberals in a stinging letter to Roosevelt, accusing him of playing a "shell game" at the convention. "Truman may have

---

*A report on the Democratic convention from the Soviet ambassador, Andrei Gromyko, to Foreign Minister Vyacheslav Molotov offered its own explanations for Wallace's defeat, including his radicalism and the strength of the "party apparat" in controlling conventions. "But the most important reason for Wallace's defeat and Senator Truman's nomination has been a desire of the Democratic majority to gain support from southern Democrats," Gromyko added. "This is precisely the Democratic group that Senator Truman . . . represents. . . . To prevent a disarray in the Democratic ranks on the election's eve is extremely important for Roosevelt.

improved the ticket had he not become, unfairly, I believe, the symbol of duplicity and the fair-haired child of the Southern racists and Northern city bosses," Etheridge wrote.[10]

Conservatives gleefully joined the president's liberal critics. The "facts cannot be disputed," wrote the *Baltimore Sun* columnist Frank Kent. "What they add up to is a plain doublecross. Beyond a doubt Mr. Wallace would have been renominated but for the active opposition of Mr. Roosevelt. . . . At any rate, no man in politics has been given shabbier treatment, with less reason, in a long time."[11]

Even members of Roosevelt's family rallied behind Wallace, although they avoided direct criticism of the president. "There is no question in my mind but that Henry Wallace would rather be defeated in a fight which he has undertaken than trim his sails or disavow a belief which he held," Eleanor Roosevelt wrote in her newspaper column.[12]

Anna Boettiger, the president's daughter, was deeply disturbed by goings on at the convention. Through a friend she went word to Paul Porter, then an official at the Democratic National Committee, that she regarded him as "a son-of-a-bitch" because of the way he treated Wallace in Chicago.

Retorted Porter, "You go tell Anna Boettiger, 'So's your old man.' "[13]

❖

A steady stream of callers moved through Wallace's office bearing messages of complaint and congratulation and conciliation. Alben Barkley, thoroughly disgruntled with Roosevelt, said, "It makes you awfully depressed when you know a fellow will do things like that." The CIO chief, Phillip Murray, told the vice president that Harry Hopkins had suddenly become liberal again and was blaming Wallace's defeat on everyone but himself. Federal Reserve Board Chairman Marriner Eccles dourly declared Roosevelt was "not a liberal anymore" and would, probably should, be defeated by Thomas Dewey. Iowa Catholic priest Maurice Sheehy came in "mad as a wet hen" saying Hannegan, Flynn, Hague, and Kelly were "crooks who ought to be in jail—and probably would be eventually."[14]

To all of them Wallace had more or less the same response: "There was only one thing to do, and that was to go down the line for the president on November 7." Indeed, there was a certain "serenity" about Wallace after the Chicago convention, the columnist Marquis Childs observed, born perhaps of the knowledge that "for the first time in his political career he has independent stature. Henry Wallace today is not walking in anyone else's shoes."[15]

Among those who came to see Wallace was a "very doleful" Harry Truman, who began by saying the week in Chicago was the most unhappy of his life. "You know this whole matter is not of my choosing," Truman said. "I went to Chicago to get out of being vice president, not to become vice president." He worried the campaign would be hard on his family and predicted Republicans would "dig up all the dead horses which I thought I had safely buried." He expressed concern, frankly, that he wasn't quite up to the task. "I am not a deep thinker as you are," he told Wallace. He asked for the vice president's continued friendship.

Wallace smiled sweetly and said, "Harry, we are both Masons."[16]

Wallace did not believe that Truman was as reluctant as he proclaimed. Truman, he suspected, actually had waged a clever campaign for it. "His method was to hold the basket for every anti-Roosevelt and every anti-Wallace apple that fell from the tree," Wallace wrote in his diary. "He did this without ever stealing a liberal apple."[17]

Truman left the interview appearing much relieved. Wallace had promised to work for the Democratic ticket and had said "nothing, in any way," that could be "interpreted as anything less than friendly." Privately, however, Wallace had formed a judgment of Truman that would vary little over the years: "He is a small man of limited background who wants to do the right thing . . . a small, opportunistic man, a man of good instincts, but therefore probably all the more dangerous. As he moves out in the public eye, he will get caught in the webs of his own making."[18]

Frank Walker also came to make amends. The postmaster general said he had been for Truman and made no apologies for it, but he wanted Wallace to know he had said nothing against the vice president personally. As he was leaving, Wallace said, "Frank, I want you to know I have nothing whatever against you." He underlined the "you" with his voice. Two days later, August 16, Wallace received a note from Bob Hannegan. "Without any attempt at meaningless flattery, I want you to know that I have a genuine feeling of admiration and regard for you . . . ," Hannegan began.[19]

The flattery, not "meaningless" at all, had a purpose. Hannegan's note and the visits of Truman and Walker reflected political reality. Underestimating Wallace's strength going into the convention, they had done nothing to endear themselves to progressives while there. They would need the support of Wallace and the liberals in order to win in November.

As Harold Ickes put it (belatedly but with apparent sincerity) in his letter to Wallace, "There isn't any doubt, and I have so written the president, that you came out of the convention stronger than the man who was nominated in your place. . . . Neither is there any doubt, as I have also tried to make clear, that next only to the President you are the strongest man in the Democratic Party."[20]

What would Wallace do with his strength? He repeatedly pledged to support Roosevelt in the general election and promised to campaign personally.

But he would be his own man. He would not speak at the bidding of the Democratic National Committee, Wallace told friends. He would pay his own expenses. And he would say little until he had a chance to see Roosevelt and determine the president's postwar plans.

His opportunity came on August 29.

Wallace went that sunny day to the White House for lunch. Roosevelt looked well, his spirits high. They ate beneath a big magnolia tree on the White House lawn, as Anna and her two children, Buzzie and Sistie, darted in and out of the conversation. The talk was cordial, with a bantering undertone that reflected some tension between the two men.

Roosevelt began by asking Wallace whether he had shown his telegram to Ilo. ("Tell Ilo not to plan to leave Washington next January.") Wallace responded with dry humor. "Yes, but Mrs. Wallace didn't know whether she could earn enough money on the strength of that wire to support me in the style to which I was accustomed."

They talked of the forthcoming election and how Wallace might help. They gossiped about Bill Bullitt's adventures as a major in the French army and his "perfectly terrible" campaign of rumor against Sumner Welles. They discussed the Dumbarton Oaks conference on establishment of a permanent United Nations and mulled over plans for the settlement of Alaska.

And they talked about Chicago.

As soon as Chicago came up, Wallace recorded in his diary, Roosevelt began "to skate over thin ice . . . as fast as he could." Roosevelt told Wallace he was "four or six years" ahead of his time and that what he stood for would "inevitably come." Wallace said he was pleased by the convention and its aftermath because it demonstrated "the people were for me."

Wallace's problem at the convention, Roosevelt allowed, was insufficient reserve strength. At the 1932 Democratic convention, Roosevelt explained gaily, he had faced just such a problem himself. That was when he made a deal with John Nance Garner, giving the Texan the vice presidency and Roosevelt his victory. He explained at some length how the deal was crafted.

It was more than Wallace could stomach. In one searing moment the "extreme Christian attitude" he had always maintained toward Roosevelt gave way to naked bluntness.

"Mr. President, I could have made a deal, too, but I did not care to do it."

Wallace added that he knew "exactly what happened" in Chicago but chose to support Roosevelt because his name was a symbol of liberalism at home and around the world.

With the cards on the table, Roosevelt moved to assuage the feelings of his vice president. He wanted Wallace to remain a part of his administration. Wallace could pick any job in government other than that of secretary of state. The State

The vice president speaks with crewmen of his plane during a
stop on his Soviet Central Asia–China tour in May 1944.
Courtesy of Jean Wallace Douglas.

Helen Keller, famed blind-deaf humanitarian, places
her fingers on Wallace's mouth at a Madison Square
Garden rally in fall 1944. Behind them, partially
obscured from view, is actor-director Orson Welles.
Courtesy of CORBIS/Bettmann.

British Prime Minister Winston Churchill
addresses Congress in May 1943, as Vice
President Wallace and Speaker of the House
Sam Rayburn watch from behind.
Courtesy of CORBIS/Bettmann.

Wallace, chairman of the Iowa delegation, stands amid supporters at the 1944 Democratic National Convention. Speaking to him is Judge Richard Mitchell, Democratic candidate for governor of Iowa. *Courtesy of CORBIS/Bettmann.*

Seated casually on a desktop, Wallace chats with reporters after arriving at the Democratic National Convention in July 1944. "I am in this fight to the finish," he told them. *Courtesy of CORBIS/Bettmann.*

Vice President Wallace and his successors:
Harry S. Truman, *right*, and Alben
Barkley. *Courtesy of CORBIS/Bettmann.*

Wallace packs his belongings as
he prepares to leave the vice
presidency in January 1945.
Courtesy of CORBIS/Bettmann.

Wallace delivers a short address from his
apartment in the Wardman Park on the
evening of his forced resignation from the
cabinet. With him are his wife, Ilo, his
daughter, Jean, and his poodle, Brutus.
Courtesy of CORBIS/Bettmann.

Wallace waves to the crowd in Shibe Park as
he accepts the presidential nomination at the
Progressive Party's founding convention in
July 1948. *Courtesy of AP/Wide World Photos.*

A sound truck in New York City's Garment
District spreads the word of a Wallace rally
in 1948. *Courtesy of University of Iowa
Library,* © *Julius Lazarus.*

Wallace with his
Progressive Party running
mate, Senator Glen Taylor,
and Taylor's son Gregory.
Courtesy of the Wallace family.

Singer-actor Paul Robeson and Wallace during the 1948 campaign. *Courtesy of University of Iowa Library,* © *Julius Lazarus.*

Surrounded by the children of Progressive Party campaign workers, Wallace is entertained by folksinger Pete Seeger. *Courtesy of University of Iowa Library,* © *Julius Lazarus.*

Wallace speaks to a crowd of 15,000 on
a street in Berkeley, California, after
being denied permission to appear on
the University of California campus
during the 1948 campaign.
Courtesy of AP/Wide World Photos.

OPPOSITE. Wallace speaks in Pittsburgh
during the 1948 campaign. Note the
numerous eggs splattered at his feet.
Courtesy of AP/Wide World Photos.

The house at Farvue, Wallace's farm
in Westchester County, New York.
Courtesy of Jean Wallace Douglas.

Henry Wallace, his days in politics
happily behind him, stands near
the barn at Farvue. *Courtesy of Jean
Wallace Douglas.*

"The Seer," Jo Davidson's bust of Henry A. Wallace. *Courtesy of Smithsonian Institution / National Portrait Gallery.*

Pulitzer Prize–winning cartoonist Frank Miller's tribute to Henry Wallace, which appeared on the *Des Moines Register*'s front page after his death in 1965. *Courtesy of* Des Moines Register.

Department certainly would have been Wallace's first choice. Roosevelt assumed as much, but Cordell Hull was "an old dear and he could not bear to break his heart." He wanted Wallace to have a hand in foreign economic affairs and to sit in on "some international conferences" dealing with postwar organization.*

Roosevelt has been telling Wallace for months that he intended to turn to the left once the election was over and the war won. Early on he would sit down with Wallace and make a list of people to give the boot. The first name on Roosevelt's list was "Jesus H. Jones," Roosevelt's nickname for the arrogant commerce secretary.

"Well, if you are going to get rid of Jesse, why not let me have Secretary of Commerce, with RFC and FEA thrown in?" Wallace asked. "There would be poetic justice in that."

"Yes, that's right," Roosevelt replied.

It sounded like sweet revenge, a concept Roosevelt understood well. Wallace denied it. "I took the [Commerce Department job] because I didn't think I could take less than a cabinet post and I didn't want to cut the throat of anyone that the president wanted to keep in," Wallace commented in his oral history. "The only one that he'd indicated he was going to get out was Jesse Jones." Besides, Wallace added, feeling vindictive toward anybody "gives that person a power over you."[21]

Whatever was at play—vindictiveness or poetic justice—the result suited both men seated beneath Andrew Jackson's old magnolia tree. Roosevelt had made a deal.

The fate of Jesse H. Jones was sealed.

Wallace kept his promise. He campaigned hard for the Democratic ticket throughout the fall, swinging early through New England and the South. In October he embarked on a nine-state tour through the Midwest, stumping for several days in his native Iowa, jabbing at the "colossal" ignorance of the Republican candidates on farm issues. "Farmers: Think long and seriously before you put into power those who will destroy the farm program as an effective agency for agricultural readjustment."[22]

---

*The British secret service agent Roald Dahl later told Wallace the British government feared that Roosevelt might offer the State Department to Wallace and weighed in strongly against it. Aside from the State Department position, Dahl said, the British government did not care what job he was given.

Wallace also learned through his friend Frank McDougall that the British were suggesting Wallace be appointed head of the Food and Agriculture Committee of the United Nations, thereby removing him from politics for several years.

Twice he spoke before large audiences in New York's Madison Square Garden. The first rally, organized by the sculptor Jo Davidson and the Independent Committee of the Arts and Sciences for Roosevelt, drew 21,000 people who paid from 60 cents to $2.40 to hear Wallace. The future, he declared, has "one essential—the continuous rebirth of liberalism." He continued, "You may well ask what I mean by a liberal person. A liberal is a person who in all his actions is continuously asking, 'What is best for all the people—not merely what is best for me personally?' Abraham Lincoln was a liberal when he said he was both for the man and the dollar, but in case of conflict he was for the man before the dollar. Christ was the greatest liberal of all when he put life before things."[23]

His second speech at Madison Square Garden, a few days before the election, was Wallace's only campaign appearance with Truman. Aides to Truman were nervous, fearing the largely liberal audience might boo him, but Wallace solved the problem by entering the hall arm-in-arm with the vice presidential nominee. Wallace's speech directly addressed the disappointment of his followers. "Some people tell me that here and there you can find someone sulking in his tent because he doesn't like something a reactionary Democrat has done. Well, neither Truman nor Roosevelt is a reactionary Democrat. Moreover, I say to you that if any reactionary Democrat has offended you, he has probably offended me a thousand times as much."

He added, with words he underlined in the text, "This has been and is a people's war. The peace must be a people's peace. The way to get it is to re-elect Roosevelt and then make the Democratic Party into a truly liberal party."[24]

Wallace remained his own man throughout. He paid his own expenses and traveled with little or no staff. On one leg of his midwestern trip, he stood in a crowded coach car from six in the evening until two in the morning, unrecognized by his fellow passengers.

His independence gave him freedom to address matters the party professionals preferred to stifle. Most strikingly, Wallace began speaking on behalf of civil rights for blacks and minorities. He appeared in Harlem with the New York City councilman Adam Clayton Powell Jr. and in a black neighborhood of Chicago with Congressman William L. Dawson. He went out of his way to attended an integrated cocktail party in still-segregated Washington, D.C. All Americans must share in postwar prosperity, he declared. "I want specifically to include the Negro and every other minority group."[25]

Franklin Roosevelt and Harry Truman, each for his own reason, found the 1944 campaign irritating. Roosevelt called it the strangest campaign of his life. Thomas Dewey, grim and self-righteous, acted as if he were prosecuting Roosevelt for a crime. Truman called it the dirtiest campaign of his career. He was smeared by accusations that he was Jewish, that he had been a member of the Ku Klux Klan, that he had benefited financially from the Pendergast machine in Kansas City. None of it was true. Moreover, he was left to fend entirely for himself. Roosevelt gave him no direction, offered no defense, and sought no advice.

Wallace, meanwhile, had a fine time. Crowds loved him, and, since he wasn't on the ballot, no one bothered to attack him. He could defend Roosevelt on his own terms and ignore Truman. Best of all, Roosevelt, finally roused, began to sound like the liberal warrior of old. He spoke eloquently on behalf of a permanent postwar peacekeeping organization, defended the record of the New Deal, offered up a renewed version of his "economic bill of rights," attacked the reactionaries and isolationists who ran the Republic Party.

Roosevelt hit Chicago on October 28 in full form. Before 100,000 people in Soldier Field—another 125,000 listened via loudspeakers outside its walls—he called for a peacetime economy of sixty million jobs, incentive taxation, new conservation and crop insurance programs, free collective bargaining, decent health care and housing. Wallace heard it on a car radio as he traveled through western Michigan and was exhilarated.

The goal of sixty million jobs "is perhaps high," Wallace wired Roosevelt, "but I glory in your daring and, as you say, America can do the seemingly impossible." He added, with reference to a statistical study produced by his friend Louis Bean, "We are predicting you will carry 36 states, have a three million popular majority and one hundred electoral college majority."[26]

Roosevelt wired back, "Glad you liked the Chicago show. I promise to make good on the sixty million jobs if you will do the same on your predictions regarding 36 states, the popular and electoral college majorities. . . . Hope to see you soon."[27]

Wallace's electoral prediction fell only slightly short of the mark. Roosevelt carried thirty-six states, but his popular majority was more than 3.5 million. In the electoral college Roosevelt won with 432 votes to 99 for Dewey.

Again Wallace wired Roosevelt. "Forgive me for having been conservative [in my prediction]," he said. "You will now have sufficient majority to put through full employment legislation." Over radio Wallace declared, "Bipartisan isolationism has been destroyed. Full steam ahead for a people's peace and jobs for all has been ordered. It is now a job for a people's Congress to support Roosevelt."[28]

Roosevelt wired back, "My affectionate thanks to you for your magnificent contribution to the campaign. I will see you soon in Washington. Roosevelt."[29]

Rain seemed to be Franklin Roosevelt's lot during the closing days of the 1944 campaign. In New York City he had been soaked to the skin as he rode for four hours through the streets in the back of an open-top Packard. It was a heroic answer to Republican whispers that he was too sick to govern.

Still more rain poured down upon him when he returned to Washington on November 10. Roosevelt again seemed vital. He insisted on riding from Union Station to the White House with the top down, so he could wave to the thousands of people gathered along Pennsylvania Avenue. With him in the back seat were the men who symbolized the shifting political tide: Henry A. Wallace and Harry S. Truman.

Once they had dried off, however, it became obvious that Roosevelt's show of strength was a façade hiding a man in physical decline at sixty-two years of age—two years older than Truman, six years older than Wallace. Equally alarming to Wallace was the deterioration of Roosevelt's mental powers. After an afternoon cabinet meeting, Wallace wrote in his diary that judging from "the character and quality of his remarks . . . his intellect—but not his prejudices—will now begin to fade pretty rapidly."[30]

Wallace was correct. The final weeks of Roosevelt's twelfth year in office were marked by vacillation and indecision. Sometimes he leaned in Wallace's direction, sometimes not. Eleanor Roosevelt pled for Wallace to leave government and lead the liberal movement at the helm of a greatly expanded political action committee. Friends asked him to reconsider becoming head of the UN Food and Agriculture Committee. Others suggested he would be happier as labor secretary or back at the Agriculture Department.

Cordell Hull entered a hospital and told Roosevelt he would resign, opening the way for Wallace at the State Department. But Roosevelt never spoke of it. To the contrary, Roosevelt was reorganizing the State Department without consulting Wallace at all. Early on he appointed Will Clayton, right-hand man to Jesse Jones, assistant secretary for foreign economic affairs.

At the end of November, after a visit to Hull at the Bethesda Naval Hospital, Roosevelt appointed Undersecretary of State Edward Stettinius Jr., former chairman of U.S. Steel, the new secretary.

Three days later the *New York Times* published a report, based on a leak, that Wallace would be appointed secretary of commerce. Wallace guessed the leak was an attempt to galvanize his enemies. He sent Roosevelt a terse reminder of their conversation under the magnolia tree. "MY INTEREST IN POETIC JUSTICE IS STRONGER NOW THAN EVER STOP SIXTY MILLION JOBS WILL REQUIRE YOU PLUS PERFECT COORDINATION BETWEEN AGRICULTURE LABOR AND COMMERCE STOP MY JOB SEEMS TO BE COMMERCE STOP ORGANIZATION PLANS SHOULD FOLLOW NOT PRECEDE THESE APPOINTMENTS STOP THANKS IF I MAY SERVE."[31]

A few days before Christmas, Roosevelt met privately with Wallace and seemed to redeem his promise. "I got your wire," Roosevelt said. "It is all right. You can have commerce." Wallace said he didn't want the job unless the president was "really enthusiastic" about him taking it. The president said he very much wanted Wallace to be commerce secretary and would give him the Reconstruction Finance Corporation as well. Wallace had drafted a memo outlining his plans for reorganizing the Commerce Department, which Roosevelt read and approved.[32]

The conversation was dismayingly unfocused. Wallace talked about legislation to promote full employment and international trade agreements. Roosevelt wandered into a discussion of astrologists' predictions the war would not end until 1947. Wallace detailed the need for incentive business taxation and new policies regarding capital formation. Roosevelt gave a strange lecture on his theory that native workers in the tropics are more healthy when they are naked.

"His mind isn't very clear anymore," Wallace wrote in his diary. "His hand trembles a great deal more than it used to. . . . His extraordinary discursiveness may have served a purpose as president, but as he gets older it makes him less and less capable as an administrator and more and more irritating to administrators."[33]

As he was leaving, Wallace asked what he should say to the press. Tell them "we focused particular attention on reforestation in Iran," Roosevelt replied.[34]

Wallace had the job, yet he didn't quite have it. Roosevelt made no public announcement of Wallace's appointment and couldn't seem to find time to write the letter he had promised to send Jesse Jones. Word of Roosevelt's decision seeped through the political community, and various people began stopping by to congratulate Wallace on receiving a job he could not admit he had. The Texas newspaper publisher Charles Marsh, always an avid collector of gossip, passed along a report that Jesse Jones was spoiling for a fight. "According to Charles, Jesse said the president would have to dynamite him out," Wallace wrote in his diary. "Obviously Jesse is doing his best to put on a warlike appearance."[35]

On Friday, January 19, 1945, the last full day of his vice presidency, Wallace made another attempt to clarify his status. There would be no other opportunities. In three days Roosevelt said he would be leaving for many weeks. His destination was unstated.

Roosevelt still had done nothing to formalize Wallace's appointment, nor had he informed Jesse Jones of the decision. He would do so at 2 P.M. the following day, Roosevelt said. He mentioned that a couple of senators had seen him to protest removing Jones as federal loan administrator. There should be no problem, Roosevelt said. The Senate would act promptly on the nomination when it resumed business on Monday.

Once again Roosevelt said how pleased he was that Henry and Ilo Wallace would remain in Washington, and how "heartbroken" he was when Wallace was not renominated in Chicago. "I would have won if your Postmaster General had stayed out of it," Wallace retorted. The president said Frank Walker had acted without his knowledge or consent. In his diary Wallace wrote in uncharacteristically earthy language, "I did not even think the word 'bullshit' because I was interested in another matter which I wanted to call to his attention."[36]

The "other matter" was a plea for Roosevelt to be his own man both at home and abroad. Domestically he needed to control the reactionary forces at work within the Democratic Party. In foreign affairs he needed to check the imperialist designs of the British. And, Wallace told the president, he needed to start taking better care of himself. He owed it to the American people who had just reelected him. Roosevelt wasted too much time talking to people, Wallace told him. The current conversation was scheduled for five minutes and already had lasted forty-five.

"He took it like a small boy listening to his mother," Wallace wrote in his diary. "I knew, also, that he was just as unpredictable as a small boy."

Wallace spoke of the pleasure he had received in serving Roosevelt as agriculture secretary and vice president. Roosevelt in turn indicated how much happiness he derived from seeing Wallace.

"It was all so hearty that it seemed like he meant it," Wallace wrote.[37]

At noon on Saturday, January 20, Franklin Roosevelt was sworn into office for the fourth time, and Harry Truman became the thirty-fourth vice president of the United States. Henry Wallace was out of a job.

The ceremony, a short, solemn affair, took place on the south portico of the White House in deference to Roosevelt's weakened condition. The weather was cold and gray; a crowd of about five thousand watched from the snow-packed ground below. Henry Wallace, smiling, held the Bible on which his successor took the oath. Roosevelt received his oath from Chief Justice Harlan Stone and delivered a brief address. "We have learned that we cannot live alone, at peace; that our well-being is dependent on the well-being of other nations far away," the president said.[38]

Roosevelt's entire body shook violently as he grasped his reading stand to steady himself. Flashes of pain surged through his chest. Woodrow Wilson's widow, watching nearby, was seized by the image of her own incapacitated husband at the end of the last world war. Wallace, seeing the president upright for the first time in months, realized he had lost at least twenty pounds and had not long to live. "He was a gallant figure—but also pitiable—as he summoned up his precious strength," Wallace said in his diary.[39]

Jesse Jones was in his office a few hours later when a phone call came from the White House. The president would like to see him at noon on Sunday. Minutes afterward a second message came from the White House. This one was in writing, and it was signed by Roosevelt. "Dear Jesse," it began. "This is a difficult letter to write . . ." Roosevelt added some words of flattery and got to the point:

> Henry Wallace deserves almost any service which he believes he can satisfactorily perform. I told him this at the end of the campaign, in which he displayed the utmost devotion to our cause, traveling almost incessantly and working for the success of the ticket in a great many parts of the country. Though not on the ticket himself, he gave his utmost toward the victory which ensued.
>
> He has told me that he thought he could do the greatest good in the Department of Commerce, for which he is fully suited, and I feel, therefore, that the Vice-President should have this post in the new Administration.

There were a number of ambassadorships vacant, Roosevelt added. Jones should "see Ed Stettinius" if he wanted one. "Always Sincerely, Franklin D. Roosevelt."[40]

Jones was livid. Wallace could be secretary of commerce if he wanted, but the thought of his arch-rival running his beloved Reconstruction Finance Corporation was more than he could bear.

At their meeting the following day, according to Jones, Roosevelt offered him the ambassadorship to France, Italy, or England as well as the chairmanship of the Federal Reserve. Jones declined each offer. The president asked him to remain on the job until Wallace was confirmed. Jones bade him goodbye. "It is not good-bye," Roosevelt said. "I'll see you when I get back."

"Mr. President, I think it is good-bye," Jones replied.[41]

Jones returned to his office and penned a stinging message of reply to Roosevelt's letter. "You state that Henry Wallace thinks he could do the greatest amount of good in the Department of Commerce and that you consider him fully suited for the post," Jones wrote. "With all due respect, Mr. President, while I must accede to your decision, I cannot agree with either of you."[42]

With that he dispatched the letter to the White House and resigned as secretary of commerce and chairman of the RFC. He retained only the title of federal loan administrator. Then he released to reporters both Roosevelt's letter—edited to remove a reference to the president's forthcoming trip—and his own reply.

Thus did Jesse Jones, not Roosevelt or Wallace, announce his ouster to the world.

There would be no time to savor poetic justice, however. News of Wallace's appointment and Jones's demise hit Congress like a V-2 rocket. Old antagonisms toward Roosevelt and the New Deal reared up anew. The intensity of the fight over Wallace reminded some reporters of the great struggle that consumed the Senate in 1937, when Roosevelt proposed to pack the Supreme Court. As Allen Drury put it in his journal, "The President has found something for Henry and all hell has broken loose."[43]

Newspaper editorialists eagerly joined the fray. "The fourth term was scarcely twenty-four hours old before it thus became known that into the hands of the most radical, impractical and idealistic dreamer in his entourage, Mr. Franklin D. Roosevelt had placed a large measure of responsibility for the ultimate liquidation of billions of dollars' worth of industrial property now under the control of the Federal government," the *New York Sun* opined. "The man once responsible for plowing under cotton and corn and for the slaughter of little pigs will be in an excellent position, when reconversion comes, to plow under a substantial portion of private enterprise."[44]

From London, *The Times* declared the debate over Wallace's nomination could "rank in American history . . . as pregnant with significance in the future. It involves all those mighty issues which agitate men's minds when they look forward to the world after the war—the true function of Government in a democratic state; the yearning to be rid of the scourge of unemployment; the conflict between the social conscience and the nostalgia for the old ways. . . . Mr. Wallace's conception of a world set free from hunger, want, and fear through a deliberately fostered policy of expansion is one that commends itself to the sympathies of many people. . . ."[45]

Wallace's opponents wanted to defeat him outright if possible; if not, they intended to remove from his control the RFC and all the wartime lending agencies that had been under Jones's authority. On Monday, January 22, the same day Wallace's nomination arrived in the Senate, Georgia Democrat Walter George submitted legislation to separate the Federal Loan Agency from the Commerce Department and reestablish its independent status.

That evening Roosevelt slipped quietly out of Washington bound for Yalta and fateful meetings with Churchill and Stalin. Roosevelt and most of his top aides would be gone for weeks, their whereabouts unknown to reporters and all but a few politicians. Roosevelt still had said nothing publicly in defense of his Commerce Department nominee. Wallace would make the fight alone.

The front line of the Wallace-versus-Jones battle was the Senate Commerce Committee, chaired by the gentlemanly, erudite, conservative Josiah Bailey of

North Carolina. The committee would pass judgment on both the George bill and Wallace's nomination, in that order, Bailey declared. The first witness to testify concerning the George bill would be Bailey's friend Jesse Jones.

Jones came into the committee room like a conquering hero, casually chewing gum and waving to photographers, and plumped cockily into the witness chair. He surveyed the capacity crowd and asked the chairman whether he might say something off the record. "I suppose you may," said Bailey. "I'm just wondering who gets the gate receipts," said Jones. The room exploded in laughter. This was his kind of crowd.[46]

Jones read a prepared statement saying the vast lending authority of the RFC and its sister agencies should never be given to someone "willing to jeopardize the country's future with untried ideas and idealistic schemes."[47]

Then he turned himself over to questions from the committee members, who seemed almost in awe. Just how big was the RFC? It was "bigger than General Motors and General Electric and Montgomery Ward and everything else put together," said Jones. How did he conduct his business? By the seat of his pants, Jones replied. Just what were the limits of his lending powers? "We can lend anything that we think we should. Any amount, any length of time, or any rate of interest . . . to anybody that we feel is entitled to the loan."[48]

It was all chummy and offhanded—a bit too offhanded, in the view of Allen Drury. Gradually "a rather appalling picture emerged," he wrote in his journal. Congress had authorized $32 billion in wartime loans; Jones had disbursed only $18 billion and had recovered only $9 billion of that. Jones could not recall any restriction placed on his lending authority by law, or even what the length of his term as head of RFC was supposed to be. "No, I don't know. I'm not sure," he said. Then he swung to the audience and asked, "Does anybody know?" Once again there was laughter.[49]

Only Claude Pepper was hostile. If Jones could serve both as commerce secretary and as loan administrator, why couldn't someone else do the same thing, Pepper asked. "If you are trying to ask me if Henry Wallace is qualified for both jobs, I will say, 'No,'" Jones replied. There was not "another fellow in the world" who could do both jobs, Jones said.[50]

"Never has the fallacy of tailoring government to individuals been more forcefully proven," Drury observed. "In a way, this whole situation serves the Congress right."[51]

The weight of sympathy on Capitol Hill seemed clearly on Jones's side after his appearance. A reporter spotted Wallace's political aide Harold Young walking across the grounds and suggested Jones was being made a scapegoat.

"Jesse!" Young drawled. "What about Aygard [sic]?"[52]

Wallace's turn came one day later, Thursday, January 24. It was a moment of high drama. When he entered the packed committee room, the crowd gave him a three-minute ovation. Chairman Bailey insisted on decorum. Wallace appeared tense but eager. Any thought that Wallace might craft his testimony to appease the committee, or that he might withdraw altogether, vanished quickly as he launched into a twenty-nine-page take-no-prisoners attack on his opponents.

The allegation that he lacked the experience necessary to run the RFC "does not fool either me or the American public," he said at the outset. "You know and I know that it is not a question of my 'lack of experience.' Rather it is a case of not liking the experience I have."

> The real motive underlying these suggestions for stripping the Department of Commerce of its vast financial powers has, of course, nothing to do with my competence to administer these powers. The real issue is whether or not the powers of the Reconstruction Finance Corporation and its giant subsidiaries are to be used only to help big business or whether these powers are also to be used to help little business and to help carry out the president's commitment to sixty million jobs. . . .
>
> This is not any petty question of personalities. This is a question of fundamental policy. It is the question of the path which America will follow in the future.[53]

The path Henry Wallace had in mind included full employment, assistance to small businessmen, federal housing and health insurance, a guaranteed annual wage, strengthened old-age benefits, control of monopolies, and other progressive measures. If Congress did not approve, Wallace said bluntly, it should strip the RFC from the Commerce Department. "For I can tell you here and now that if the RFC is left in the Commerce Department, I will use its power in the interests of all the American people."

He had decided "to present the most provocative document" he could, "instead of following the tactic of being very cautious," Wallace commented later.[54]

Under questioning from the committee, Wallace defended his own administrative and business experience. The Department of Agriculture, he noted, gave out more loans with a higher rate of recovery than the RFC enjoyed. Senator Pepper led Wallace through an account of his role in founding Pioneer Hi-Bred. The man said to be an impractical dreamer acknowledged that his company had sales of more than four million dollars in 1944.

Wallace testified for some five hours. He spoke, wrote Allen Drury, with the "really rather magnificent candor and courage which are his two best qualities. He spoke of a dreamer's America, but it was the same kind of dreaming that America was originally and that America someday yet may be—an America of peace and prosperity and good will and humanity. . . . There was something obscene about the fact that a man as essentially good as he is had to be subjected to such an ordeal."[55]

The committee did not wait long to render its opinion. The next day it voted 15 to 4 for the George bill to remove all lending agencies from the Commerce Department. Then the committee, controlled by Democrats, voted 14 to 5 against the nomination of a former Democratic vice president to be secretary of commerce.

Roosevelt had departed with instructions that he was not to be bothered with messages about domestic matters except in case of emergency. By week's end Sam Rosenman had concluded an emergency was at hand. After consulting with Wallace and Alben Barkley, the judge radioed a long memo to Roosevelt. Wallace's nomination was doomed, Rosenman said, unless the president indicated he would sign the George bill or took immediate action to transfer the lending agencies out of the Commerce Department by executive action. Even this might not be enough to save Wallace, Rosenman warned, but it was the only chance he had.

There was no immediate response from Roosevelt. Admiral Leahy, Roosevelt's military aide, later wrote that he personally felt the nomination was a mistake and thought the president was too busy to be bothered.

Action moved to the Senate floor. The strategy of Wallace's opponents was to bring his nomination to a vote before the George bill was considered. This, as Barkley informed Roosevelt in a separate message, would mean certain defeat for Wallace. Senator Bailey said he would move at the first opportunity for the Senate to go into executive session, which would automatically make Wallace's nomination the first order of business.

Bailey's first opportunity came on February 1, a week after Wallace testified before the committee. Shortly after noon Bailey moved the Senate go into executive session, and the tension-filled roll call began. The running tally swung one way and the other, ending in a dramatic 42-to-42 tie vote. Senator Robert Taft of Ohio, leading the Republican opposition, immediately jumped up to change his vote to nay. This would put Taft on the winning side and thus in a position to move for reconsideration.

In a split second Majority Leader Barkley sought recognition and gained control of the floor. Taft protested vigorously. Vice President Truman, who was presiding, recognized Barkley and told Taft he could move to reconsider "at any later time." Thus, with some quick thinking by Barkley and timely support from Truman, was Henry Wallace's nomination rescued.

The tie vote was the high-water mark of opposition to Wallace. Barkley pressed for an immediate vote on the George bill, which passed on a vote of 74 to 12 after two hours of debate. The majority leader then won a delay on

Wallace's nomination until March 1, allowing time for the House to pass the George bill and for the president to sign it.

In the House a coalition of Republicans and southern Democrats, led by the Mississippi congressman John Rankin, did its best to defeat the George bill. The policy question was clearly not the issue. Everyone understood it was actually a vote on Wallace. The New York Republican congressman Leonard Hall accused Wallace of acting as if he had "received a call to change the New Deal to the New Communism."[56]

Off Capitol Hill, Wallace's supporters rallied to his defense with testimonial dinners and a cascade of letters and telegrams. For a time the measure was bottled up in the Rules Committee, but the Democratic leadership muscled it free. A motion by Wallace's opponents to send the George bill back to committee narrowly failed, on a vote of 204 to 196. Thereafter the George bill passed the house, on a vote of 400 to 2.

While the bitter wrangle over his nomination continued in Congress, Wallace relaxed quietly in the Wardman Park doing what might be expected of him. He wrote a book. Its title was *Sixty Million Jobs*. In it he outlined the path to a full-employment economy, a just society for the common man, an America actively engaged in the peaceful endeavors of international trade and cooperation.

We can attain the goal of sixty million jobs and a national income of two hundred billion dollars "without a Planned Economy, without disastrous inflation, and without an unbalanced budget that will endanger our national credit," he wrote. But this can be accomplished only with an eye toward the general welfare of all people.[57]

The battle over the Wallace's nomination began with a thunderclap as Roosevelt departed for Yalta. It ended in a soft drizzle as he returned at the close of February and signed the George bill.

The following day, March 1, Roosevelt reported on the Yalta conference to a joint session of Congress. It was a long, lifeless speech that told congressmen little more than they had already learned from the newspapers. Roosevelt appeared gray and exhausted, and he began by apologizing for delivering the speech while seated. "I know you will realize that it makes it a lot easier for me not to have to carry about ten pounds of steel around on the bottom of my legs."[58]

Two hours after Roosevelt finished speaking, the Senate approved Henry Wallace's nomination to be secretary of commerce. The vote was 56 to 32.

Wallace accepted his partial victory with dispassion. "It's really rather surprising that they finally confirmed me, in view of the very strong presentation I made before them."[59]

CHAPTER TWENTY

"THIS MUST NOT BE."

A quiet rain fell on Washington the afternoon of Thursday, April 12, 1945. The Senate whiled away several hours debating a water treaty. The House ground through routine business and adjourned early. The president rested at his cottage in Warm Springs. The vice president, presiding over the Senate, occupied himself writing a letter to his mother and sister. Then he walked across the Capitol for an afternoon drink in Sam Rayburn's hideaway office.

Secretary of Commerce Henry A. Wallace spent most of the day in his office, an elaborate tennis court–sized room bequeathed to future secretaries by Herbert Hoover, holding meetings and taking calls. But Wallace, too, left work early, for a late-afternoon dental appointment.

Secretary of commerce for only forty-two days, Wallace had made a fruitful beginning, he thought. His plan to reorganize the department had breathed life into its moribund bureaucracy, already improving morale. Plans were afoot for an activist legislative agenda. Surveys of postwar housing and manufacturing needs had been launched and key appointments made. Alfred Schindler, an experienced administrator with the Federal Loan Administration, became undersecretary and Harold Young solicitor general.

Events abroad during those forty-two days also inspired satisfaction. Everywhere Allied troops routed the enemy. The U.S. Army had crossed the Rhine and stood only fifty-seven miles from Berlin. From the east the Red Army continued its relentless offensive. Poland, Bulgaria, Romania, and East Prussia fell under Russian military control. In the Pacific,

U.S. troops had secured Manila and Iwo Jima. U.S. Marine and Army divisions had invaded Okinawa. U.S. planes daringly bombed Tokyo by daylight.

Yet an ominous undertone haunted the events of March and early April. Small fissures in the grand alliance of antifascist nations, differences Roosevelt had tried to paper over at Yalta, began to appear. Stalin had promised free elections in Poland, but clearly Russia's own security came first. The Poles were "free" only to elect a government friendly to the Soviet Union. Stalin and Roosevelt exchanged testy notes.

In Asia, Roosevelt's hope for a strong and friendly government in China was being swamped by an internal political situation hurtling toward civil war. Chiang Kai-shek would neither negotiate with the Communists nor make the reforms necessary to hold them in check. Roosevelt's long-standing desire for self-determination in Indochina had run head-on into British intransigence and French aspirations. Wallace followed the Asian situation closely and with growing concern.

Those weeks sorely tested Roosevelt's vaunted political skill. Soon diplomats would gather in San Francisco to craft a permanent United Nations organization, which Roosevelt hoped would usher in a generation of peace. To accomplish his aims, however, Roosevelt had to persuade a skeptical Congress, dampen British colonial ambitions, calm Russian chauvinism. Nor was the nation done with war. Roosevelt would need Allied help, that of the Soviet Union in particular, to defeat the defiant Japanese.

As Roosevelt faced those monumental challenges, his body was failing him. A cloud of sickness and death hovered over the White House. Pa Watson had died at sea returning from Yalta. Harry Hopkins went straight to the Mayo Clinic for care.

At times during those weeks Roosevelt displayed his old buoyancy. More often he seemed an invalid. On March 22, the last time Wallace saw him, Roosevelt had displayed both conditions in a single evening. The occasion was a dinner of the White House Correspondents Association at the Statler Hotel. As he was wheeled into the room, trumpets blaring "Hail to the Chief," Roosevelt seemed not to know where he was. He neither waved nor acknowledged the crowd's cheers. But a short while later he seemed lively, enjoying himself as Danny Kaye and Fanny Brice entertained the diners.

A somber Wallace watched from the head table, sitting "silent and earnestly intent, even in the midst of the most uproarious laughter," as a reporter put it.[1] His heart longed for the vibrant, liberal Roosevelt of old, the only man who could usher in the century of the common man. Wallace now had a recurring dream, in which he and Roosevelt walked across a grassy field. Roosevelt moved freely, without crutches or braces. It was a joyous dream, but only a dream.

Three weeks later, as Wallace sat in the dental chair on that rainy afternoon of April 12, he learned that Franklin Delano Roosevelt was dead, felled by a massive cerebral hemorrhage. He was sixty-three years and two months old.

In Minneapolis, Hubert Humphrey, a young public-relations man planning his first run for mayor, had just written Wallace a letter expressing hope that Wallace would be the Democratic candidate for president in 1948. As he signed it, Humphrey heard news of Roosevelt's death. He added a postscript in his own hand that spoke for millions of liberals at that moment:

> I've just heard of the death of our great President. May God bless this nation and world.
>
> I scarcely know what to say. It is as if one of my own family has passed away.
>
> If ever we needed men of courage—stout-hearted men, it is now. I simply can't conceal my emotions. How I wish you were at the helm. I know Mr. Truman will rise to the heights of statesmanship so all important in this hour. But we need you as you have never been needed before.[2]

One by one the members of Franklin Roosevelt's team came to the White House. Some—Harold Ickes, Frances Perkins, Henry Morgenthau, and Henry Wallace—had served with him from the beginning, through the country's greatest depression and history's bloodiest war. Now, on the eve of victory, he was gone. Wallace thought of Moses, who led his people to the Promised Land but was denied entrance himself.

Roosevelt had been president so long—more than twelve years—that many Americans could not imagine the presidency without him. No one could guess what sort of president the unknown and untested Harry S. Truman might be. Even those who knew Truman could only speculate about his views on foreign policy, his administrative talents, his leadership potential. He was a middle-aged man from Middle America, as ordinary as a two-door Ford. The century of the common man, if one were coming, would be led by one of its own.

By 7 P.M. the cabinet secretaries, the chief justice, the Speaker of the House, and Truman's wife and daughter had all assembled in the Cabinet Room. At 7:09 P.M. Truman, wearing a double-breasted gray suit and polka-dot bow tie, received the oath of office from Chief Justice Harlan Stone. Truman seemed dazed. At the side of the room, Henry Wallace watched the brief ceremony with a doleful expression. He never spoke of his thoughts.

A brief cabinet meeting followed; Truman requested everyone to remain on the job for the time being. Someone asked whether the United Nations conference in San Francisco would still open on April 25. Yes, Truman replied. Afterwards Henry Stimson drew the new president aside and informed him that a "new explosive of almost unbelievable power" was being built by the United States. It was Truman's introduction to the secret of the atomic bomb. Then, having had a long day, Truman returned to his five-room apartment on Connecticut Avenue, downed a turkey sandwich and a glass of milk, and went to sleep.[3]

Truman's very commonness, his plainness of speech and simplicity of habit, had an appealing quality. And he was not without political skills, which he displayed on Saturday, April 14, when he asked Henry Wallace and James Byrnes, his rivals for the vice presidential nomination, to accompany him to Union Station to meet the train bearing Roosevelt's body. It was a gesture both generous and appropriate. Eleanor Roosevelt, who had flown to Georgia in order to accompany her husband on his final journal, seemed especially pleased by Wallace's presence.

As the solemn procession made its way back to the White House, some 350,000 people lined Pennsylvania Avenue, watching Roosevelt's flag-draped coffin pass on a caisson drawn by six white horses. At the White House the casket was placed in the East Room, where a simple funeral service was held at 4 P.M. Only two hundred people, the capacity of the room, were in attendance.

That evening the casket was reloaded onto the interment train, accompanied by Roosevelt's personal and official families, for a final trip to Hyde Park. Wallace kept a journal aboard the train that captured, in brief and clear-eyed terms, the end of an era. It began,

> We left Washington a little after ten o'clock on Saturday evening. The Cabinet members were all together in Car Six. Morgenthau was completely tired out and had almost nothing to say. Ickes was bent over and aged— and had plenty to say, most of it uncomplimentary to the new President and his friends. Stettinius was obviously ill at ease and uncertain, as Henry Morgenthau put it "nervous as a witch." Harold Ickes was picking on Mrs. Ickes with the querulous, semi-humorous remarks of an ageing man. The cord which had bound the Cabinet had snapped.[4]

Wallace had his first meeting with the new president on April 27, 1945. "I told him I was prepared to serve him as loyally as I had Roosevelt—provided he wanted me to do so," Wallace wrote in his diary. "He was very emphatic in saying that he did." In fact, Truman asked Wallace to take on the additional job of surplus property disposal.[5]

They spoke of the war—Truman confided that he believed Hitler was dead—and the importance of international airways in postwar policy. Jointly they groused about the "connivers" around Roosevelt. The conversation moved to foreign affairs. Wallace spoke of certain elements in China and Poland that would like to see the United States get into a war with Russia. "That must not be," said Truman.[6]

The meeting was friendly, direct, professional. Wallace came away with an impression of Truman that would vary little over the coming months. "Truman was exceedingly eager to agree with everything I said," Wallace commented in his diary. "He also seemed eager to make decisions of every kind with the greatest promptness. Everything he said was decisive. It almost seemed that he was eager to decide in advance of thinking."[7]

To reporters outside the White House, Wallace said that he and Truman had "understood each other perfectly."[8] So they had. At the heart of their understanding was a desire to carry on the policies of Franklin D. Roosevelt. But they approached this understanding from vastly different perspectives— Truman that of a politician, Wallace that of a philosopher. From their vantage points both men could claim the Roosevelt legacy. Their eventual clash was inevitable.

Truman unquestionably did want Wallace to remain in the cabinet. Wallace commanded the loyalty of a sizable portion of the Democratic Party, its labor and liberal elements, and Truman, the good politician, recognized his value to party unity. Wallace was equally sincere in his pledge to serve his new chief loyally. From the first day of Truman's presidency, Wallace unequivocally rejected any suggestion that he seek the presidency for himself in 1948.

"I know that you have spent your money unselfishly and have given generously of your time in your efforts to aid me," Wallace wrote one supporter. "Nevertheless, I believe that the work you are doing in my behalf is harmful. All of us should be devoting our time and energies to winning the war and securing lasting peace and full employment. . . . I strongly urge you, therefore, to immediately discontinue your efforts in behalf of 'Wallace in '48.' . . ."[9]

Whatever the basis of Truman's respect for Wallace, it certainly did not extend to the other "professional liberals" he had inherited from Roosevelt. Truman rapidly thinned the New Deal ranks—"the lowest form of politician," he called them—from his cabinet and staff. Matthew Connelly and Harry Vaughan, trusted factotums from Truman's Senate office, took over key White House positions. Charles Ross, a high school classmate who had won a Pulitzer Prize as a reporter for the *St. Louis Post-Dispatch*, became press secretary.

Postmaster General Frank Walker was replaced by Democratic National Chairman Robert Hannegan. Paris-born, Harvard-educated attorney general

Francis Biddle was dispatched to the War Crimes Court, replaced by the conservative assistant attorney general Tom Clark. Lewis Schwellenbach, a low-energy former U.S. senator from Washington State, succeeded Frances Perkins at Labor. Secretary of Agriculture Claude Wickard was bumped to the Rural Electrification Administration and replaced by New Mexico congressman Clinton Anderson.

Other cabinet changes followed swiftly. Secretary of the Treasury Henry Morgenthau ("a block head nut," in Truman's words) was succeeded by Judge Fred M. Vinson, a former Kentucky congressman. Most significantly, James F. Byrnes, the conservative South Carolinian who was Roosevelt's self-styled "assistant president," became secretary of state and, thus, next in line to the presidency.

Within six months only three of Roosevelt's cabinet members remained. And only two of those—Wallace and Ickes—could be regarded as New Dealers. The third was Secretary of the Navy James V. Forrestal, an intense former Wall Street investment banker whose views were hardly progressive.

More troubling to Wallace, however, was the drift of Truman's foreign policy. From the outset Truman inclined to heed those who counseled him to "get tough with Russia." At his first meeting with Foreign Minister V. M. Molotov, on April 23, Truman was blunt and undiplomatic. Friendship between the United States and Russia must be based on "the mutual observation of agreements and not on the basis of a one-way street," Truman said.

"I have never been talked to like that in my life," Molotov replied, according to Truman's diary. "I told him, 'Carry out your agreements and you won't get talked to like that.' "[10]

Truman's rough handling of Molotov was fueled largely by reports from Ambassador Averell Harriman in Moscow. In Eastern Europe, Russia was quickly transferring power solely to Communist partisans. Harriman reported a particularly grave situation in Poland.

By the beginning of May, at the United Nations conference in San Francisco, Harriman had sharpened his views. "I have come to the conclusion," he told an off-the-record gathering of leading journalists, "that on long-range policies there is an irreconcilable difference . . . between the United States and Great Britain on the one hand, and Russia on the other. The difference is this: Russia apparently intends to pursue a policy of Marxian penetration wherever she can build up her own security system to protect her socialist conception—and we want a world of free nations and peoples."[11]

A reporter promptly forwarded Harriman's remarks to Wallace, who was puzzled by their bristling tone. Less than a year earlier in Tashkent, Harriman had been "quite pro-Russian" in attitude. Now he even opposed Russia's request for a $6 billion loan to help rehabilitate its war-ravaged economy.[12]

Harriman "is perhaps more nearly the father of our present [Cold War] Russian policy than any other single person," Wallace said later, in his oral history. ". . . He arrived at a certain approach long before Truman knew what he was going to do."*[13]

Even more disturbing, in Wallace's view, were the efforts of U.S. representatives to win admission of Argentina into the UN. Argentina had been friendly to the Axis powers throughout the war, and its presence in the UN, Wallace believed, would be seen by the Russians as indicative of American intentions to build a solid anti-Communist bloc consisting of the United States, Latin America, Great Britain, and its colonial states.

Nelson Rockefeller, the State Department's top man on Latin American affairs, had "placed the unity of the hemisphere above the unity of the world," Adlai Stevenson, a U.S. delegate to San Francisco, remarked to Wallace. "The only conclusion I could reach from Stevenson's statement was that we had definitely entered on an era of power politics—with the United States on one side and Russia on the other. . . . Stevenson said that under such circumstances the Russians necessarily would play their own game, not trusting the world organization. They would see themselves out-voted again and again in the Assembly.

"I must confess," Wallace added, "that Stevenson's analysis of San Francisco made me feel very much depressed concerning a constructive outcome on behalf of world peace."[14]

Wallace's personal representative in San Francisco, Commerce Department aide Frank Waring, did little to brighten his mood. One dispatch recounted efforts by the U.S. delegation to defeat language making "the right to work and the right to education" part of the UN's goals. Waring said the U.S. delegates "in some strange way" imagined that universal education "would permit communist propaganda in the United States."[15]

By May 6, two days before Germany's surrender, Wallace's diary was full of gloom. "More and more it begins to look like the psychology is favorable toward our getting into war with Russia," he wrote. "This must not be. It seems incredible that our people should drift toward this whirlpool which will inevitably end in world communism."[16]

A discomfiting *New York Times* story during this period shed light on Truman's attitude toward the Soviet Union. In June 1941, the *Times* reported, the

---

*Wallace had known Averell Harriman since 1932, when the Iowa editor gave an address on international trade policies to a group of Wall Street financiers. They had a generally cordial relationship, in part because of Wallace's regard for Harriman's sister, Mary Rumsey.

Averell Harriman "gives the superficial appearance of being dumb and hesitating," Wallace commented later. "That impression is an incorrect one in my opinion. He may find it very difficult to express himself but he has a very strong will and when he eventually makes up his mind, he pursues his course relentlessly."

then senator Harry Truman had said the United States should help Russia if Germany seemed to be winning the war, and help Germany if Russia was winning. "And that way let them kill as many as possible" of each other, Truman stated. This "instinctive attitude" toward Russia might prevent it from entering the war against Japan on a timely basis, Wallace observed in his diary. Russia "may reach the conclusion that it is desirable to see as many Americans and Japanese killed as possible."[17]

Now and then good news did break through the clouds. In Europe the U.S. military behaved in strict accordance with decisions made at Teheran and Yalta and cooperated fully with Soviet forces on matters of strategy and occupation. Winston Churchill's call for U.S. and British soldiers to shake hands with their Russian counterparts "as far to the east as possible" was ignored. The military, in a way, was in alliance with Wallace at the moment. General George Marshall and his colleagues still believed that Soviet assistance would be vital in the war against Japan. They saw nothing to be gained by alienating Stalin at the moment of victory in Europe.

Public opinion in United States was with Wallace too. Except for some ethnic communities, notably Polish-Americans, the taste for further fighting in Europe had waned. Americans saw Russia as a valued wartime ally that could be a peacetime friend. America had never fought a war with Russia, and there was no broadly held belief that it should.

There was hope, too, when Truman sent Roosevelt's closest adviser, Harry Hopkins, on a last mission to Moscow. Hopkins returned full of optimism that Stalin would compromise with his American allies. Donald Nelson, the former war production chief, told Wallace he had visited with Truman and the president had "the right slant on the Russian problem." In his diary Wallace said he hoped "Truman's attitude meant that Stettinius, Harriman and Rockefeller would not continue to run the same kind of dangerous anti-Russian show as they have been running."[18]

Wallace's own contacts with Truman also were heartening. True, in Truman's view, the Russians could be annoying, "like people from across the tracks whose manners were very bad." But every time Wallace counseled friendly relations with the Soviet Union, Truman agreed. He even asked Wallace for an autographed copy of *Sixty Million Jobs*, which argued that good trade relations with the Soviet Union were essential to postwar peace.[19]

Late in May, Wallace met with Truman again to review a speech he planned to give at a banquet honoring him with the Churchman of the Year Award. It was a short speech, devoted almost entirely to the cause of international cooperation and tolerance. Truman read it line by line, making his own observations as he went through the text.

"No president has done so much to promote good will as President Roosevelt," Wallace proposed to say.

"And that is right," said Truman.

"I am satisfied this is the policy of President Truman," Wallace's speech added.

"It is," Truman interjected.

"President Truman is following the Roosevelt policy."

"I certainly am," Truman declared.[20]

The heart of Wallace's tribute to his fallen chief was this:

> More than any other man he knew that those who write the peace must think of the whole world or else condemn their children to nationalism, regionalism, imperialism, confusion, and finally to World War III.
>
> . . . If Roosevelt were with us here tonight he would rejoice in the victory in Europe, but he would be looking on victory only as a prerequisite of enduring peace. . . . He would not underestimate the strength of the enemies of peace. These enemies of peace are those who are deliberately trying to stir up trouble between the United States and Russia.
>
> . . . Before the blood of our boys is dry on the field of battle these enemies of peace try to lay the foundation for World War III. They proclaim that because the ideologies of the United States and Russia are different, war between the two is inevitable. They seize upon every minor discord to fan the flames of hatred.
>
> Those people must not succeed in their foul enterprise. . . . I know this is the policy of President Truman. I am also satisfied that it is the policy of the vast bulk of the American people.[21]

Truman read it all and said he agreed with every word of it—agreed so heartily he wanted to make the reference to his own policies even stronger. "I know this is the policy of President Truman." Yes, said Harry Truman, that was good.[22]

The Department of Commerce building, completed in 1932 at a cost of $17 million, was a monument to Herbert Hoover. One block wide, three blocks long and seven stories high, the granite and limestone building had fifteen entrances, six inner courtyards, sixteen stairways, and eight miles of corridors. Its thirty-seven acres of floor space, as big as a fair-sized vegetable farm, were enough in 1945 to house 10,000 department workers, numerous wartime emergency agencies, the Patent Office Search Room with its eight million U.S. patents, an aquarium with forty-eight tanks and 2,000 fish, and a departmental library of 200,000 publications on commercial and industrial subjects.*

Its very location bespoke importance. It occupied the entire west end of the Federal Triangle, from Constitution Avenue on the south to Pennsylvania Avenue on the north, looming like a fortress above the adjacent White House grounds. When he walked to work, Wallace liked to enter through a Fifteenth Street doorway, under the inscription "Commerce defies every wind, outrides every tempest, and invades every zone."

"That's what my father used to say about Mr. Hoover and his Department of Commerce," Wallace observed dryly.[23]

Obviously Henry Wallace would not have Hoover's power. Hoover had all but run the country from that building. Nor would he have the clout of his predecessor, Jesse Jones, who controlled a gaggle of federal lending agencies. The Commerce Department per se has very little authority, Wallace liked to note.

"The Department of Commerce is in some respects a unique government department in that it has practically no functions of a regulatory or control character," Wallace observed before a congressional committee. "Its operations can be described almost entirely in terms of various services: scientific, technological, aeronautical, statistical and economic, which it provides for the business community in the public interest."[24]

But that left plenty for a man of Wallace's dedication and imagination to do. His goal was a "people's peace" and a "peace of abundance," and he saw a large role for a strong, activist federal government. "My interpretation of the responsibility of government is that in the early postwar years, action should be taken to check the decline in employment . . . and government should be authorized to initiate its own supplementary programs if such stimulation fails to do the job," he wrote in *Sixty Million Jobs.*[25]

The problem facing the country was this: America in 1945 produced $200 billion in goods and services, almost double its production in any year before the war. It had 52 million domestic workers and 12 million people in uniform. The nation would very soon have to find work for millions of men and women in war-related service and find an outlet for its enormous productive capacity to avoid another cycle of unemployment and depression.

The key, Wallace said, lay in recognizing that "the future of the American worker lies in the well-being of American private enterprise, and the future

---

*The Department of Commerce had 32,339 employees when Wallace became secretary, roughly one-fifth the number who worked for him in his final year at the Department of Agriculture. Of these, 10,102 people worked at the Commerce Department's Washington headquarters.

of private enterprise lies in the well-being of the American worker. . . . [To-gether] as one team, there are no limits on what America can accomplish."

In other words, a nation that can produce the ships, planes, and tanks needed to fight a great war could produce the "houses, cars, clothing, education, recre-ation," and other necessities "on a scale that staggers the imagination." Ameri-cans should think not only of pent-up demand for consumer items but of the "people's backlog of unfinished national business" when the fighting ended.

> The items on this list include our need for more houses than ever be-fore, more hospitals, more schools, more rural developments, more and bet-ter transportation facilities, more industrialization in the South and other regions where people normally are under-employed and don't produce enough—and, finally, more international cooperation to build up the un-developed human and natural resources of other lands. These are some of the people's unfilled orders that must go onto the books of the nation. They represent millions of jobs and work to be done everywhere that needs only a touch of government encouragement and stimulation to release the driving power of private enterprise.[26]

To meet these goals would require a degree of national planning that, Wal-lace acknowledged, many businessmen still regarded as the devil's work. But he argued for a middle course, something between the "planned economy" of socialist states and the traditional laissez-faire of capitalist economies. The cen-terpiece of Wallace's plan was a "national budget," or a "full employment bud-get," which would take into account not only government receipts and expenditures but all economic activity, public and private, everywhere in the country. This would allow the government to act responsibly to promote growth or reduce unemployment or combat inflation as necessary.

The concept found legislative expression in the full-employment bill, largely the work of Wallace and a team of prominent industrialists and economists. "Under this measure, the Federal Government would, for the first time, rec-ognize its overall responsibility for assuring opportunity of employment to all who are able and willing to work," Wallace said in testimony before the Sen-ate Banking Committee. President Truman gave the bill strong backing.[27]

Old-guard Republicans and southern Democrats, who disliked its civil rights implications, doggedly fought the measure and managed to remove most of its mandatory features. But when it finally passed, as the Employment Act of 1946, the bill was clearly a progressive victory and a step toward Keynesian economics. Among other things, it established the Council of Economic Ad-visors to offer the president ongoing economic counsel, and the Joint Com-mittee on the Economic Report, doing the same for Congress.

On other fronts, too, Wallace pressed his vision of "economic democracy" for America. He appointed a high-powered committee to study the patent system, long geared to favor monopolies and international cartels. He took a keen interest in government research, seeking to make such information equally available to all businesses.

He created the Office of Science and Technology within the department and envisioned something akin to the agricultural extension service to assist small businesses in using new scientific developments. And he placed particular emphasis on envigorating the department's foreign trade offices, which he believed would be crucial in postwar international development.

As usual Wallace found time to indulge his insatiable curiosity. He took flying lessons and became the first cabinet secretary to pilot his own plane. He led in introducing red sinde cattle from India into the United States. He studied chicken breeding and persuaded his sons, H. B. and Bob, to take an interest in the commercial possibilities of poultry hybridization.

All of this, however, was done in the long shadow of world affairs, always on Wallace's mind. Events, tumbling pell-mell, were thrusting the planet into a new and terrifying era.

The first of these events took place at 5:30 on the morning of July 16, 1945, in a blinding flash of light over the New Mexico desert. In the days following the atomic blast, the Big Three wartime allies opened a conference in Potsdam, Germany; the allies issued a joint demand for the unconditional surrender of Japan; British voters stunned the world by throwing Winston Churchill out of power; the U.S. Senate approved the United Nations Charter; and on August 6, U.S. planes dropped an atomic bomb on Hiroshima, Japan, killing eighty thousand people instantly and thousands more over time.

On August 8, exactly three months after V-E day, as promised, Russia entered the war against Japan. A million Russian soldiers immediately crossed into Manchuria. The following day U.S. planes dropped a second atomic bomb on the Japanese city of Nagasaki. On Tuesday, August 14, 1945, Japan surrendered.

The war was over. The atomic age had begun.

"I just don't remember how I felt at the time," Wallace later commented. "Perhaps these massive events maybe numbed me—I just don't know what it is." He was "terrifically interested" in the atomic bomb project, he said, but his primary concern was "that the darn thing went off."[28]

To his credit, Wallace did not criticize—either then or later, publicly or privately—Truman's decision. Present at the inception of the project, Wallace had helped persuade Roosevelt "it was something to put money into." To have second-guessed Truman when the weapon was actually used would have been intellectually dishonest.*[29]

Nevertheless, the explosions weighed heavily on Wallace's mind. For millions of Americans the bomb meant an end to a long and bloody conflict. For Wallace it marked a new era with the potential for unlimited abundance or unimaginable destruction. Who would control this powerful force? For what purpose?

These questions had to be answered at a time when much of the world roiled in political chaos and economic devastation. Good U.S. relations with the Soviet Union, a centerpiece of Wallace's thinking throughout the war, struck him as more important and less certain than ever. "There is altogether too much irresponsible defeatist talk about the possibility of war with Russia," Wallace declared soon after the war ended. He added, "In my opinion, such talk, at a time when the blood of our boys shed on the fields of Europe has scarcely dried, is criminal. There are certain people—and they are the rankest kind of un-Americans—who are anxious to see the United States and Russia come to blows. . . . [30]

Within the U.S. government, however, Wallace's approach never stood a chance in the face of issues that steadily raised tensions between America and the Soviet Union: the future of Germany, the postwar governments of East-

---

*Perhaps Wallace knew of moral objections to the bomb raised earlier in 1945 by Leo Szilard and other atomic physicists. Szilard's mounting concern about the consequences of using the bomb led him to persuade Albert Einstein to write Roosevelt about the matter. The letter, which asked that Szilard be given an opportunity to make his case to the president in person, was sent in late March. Einstein's message was in Roosevelt's cottage at Warm Springs—perhaps unread and definitely unanswered—the day he died.

Einstein's letter reached Truman during the first weeks of his presidency. The new president referred the scientists to James Byrnes, who held no public office at the time but served as Truman's personal representative on the "Interim Committee." This committee was a highly secret panel charged with advising Truman about matters related to the atomic bomb. In May, Szilard and two others met with Byrnes in Spartansburg, South Carolina, but their case proved unpersuasive.

Wallace learned of Byrnes's involvement of July 6, 1945, when he went to pay his respects to the new secretary of state. Byrnes referred "at some little length" to the nation's top military secret and said the weapon should and would be used. Wallace thought it was "rather astounding" that Byrnes even mentioned the bomb.

Byrnes was "deeply concerned that all this vast amount of money that had been invested in the Manhattan project [$2 billion] should not prove to have been wasted," Wallace said in his oral history. ". . . He, therefore, wanted the bomb to be dropped so as to prove the money had not been wasted. That's a rather natural reaction for a congressman."

Wallace also came away from the conversation feeling that Byrnes thought "the atomic bomb would come in handy vis-a-vis Russia in her handling of countries immediately on her western border." In his memoirs, Byrnes denied ever having used the atomic bomb as an instrument of diplomacy.

ern Europe (especially Poland), administration of the UN, reparations and economic assistance, access to a warm-water port through China, postwar governance of Japan. In all these matters Russian stubbornness and suspicion was met by displays of American military and economic might.

"It is obvious to me," Wallace wrote in his diary after a cabinet meeting in August, "that the cornerstone of the peace of the future consists in strengthening our ties of friendship with Russia. It is also obvious that the attitude of Truman, Byrnes, and both the war and navy departments is not moving in this direction. Their attitude will make for war eventually."*[31]

Within days of the war's end, Wallace was lobbying Truman for a seat at the atomic discussion table. The future development of atomic power "would have very great influence on the expansion of commerce," Wallace told the president, and the secretary of commerce should be involved. Wallace added that if the world situation was so serious as to require continued universal military training, it would be "wise to decentralize our industry and our population" so as to make the United States less vulnerable to atomic attack. "Truman seemed to agree," Wallace said.[32]

A few days later the military commander of the atomic bomb project, General Leslie Groves, addressed business leaders at Wallace's request and bluntly illustrated the uncertainty of atomic policy. Nuclear fission was a military matter then and for the foreseeable future, Groves told the businessmen. Atomic energy would "not be practical for peacetime purposes for many years, probably after all of us at the meeting were dead," Wallace recorded Groves as saying.[33]

Obviously the bomb called for sober talk. But Wallace did not start it. Rather the bomb landed on the cabinet table via Secretary of War Henry L. Stimson, then in the final days of a long and grand career in public service.

Serious and scholarly, Stimson epitomized New York establishment Republicanism. He first held public office under Theodore Roosevelt. He was William Howard Taft's secretary of war when Henry Wallace was still in college. Under Calvin Coolidge, Stimson was governor-general of the Philippines, and for all of Herbert Hoover's administration he was secretary of state.

---

*Wallace liked the attitude of the supreme allied commander in Europe far better than that of the president. On August 14 Wallace wrote a note to General Dwight D. Eisenhower, praising him for some friendly remarks about Russia quoted in an Associated Press dispatch. "I have no fear about our being able to get along with Britain, but with regard to Russia there is danger of our taking an attitude which will cause trouble in the future."

Eisenhower replied in part, "So far as a soldier should have opinions about such things, I am convinced that friendship—which means an honest desire on both sides to strive for mutual understanding—between Russia and the United States, is absolutely essential to world tranquility. Moreover, I believe that most of the Russians I have met share this conviction."

Austere and erect, with his close-cropped hair parted in the middle and a gold watch chain across his vest, Stimson was a model of old-fashioned conservative rectitude. There was nothing of the "dreamer" about Henry Stimson.

Yet it was Stimson who now made a radical proposal—to share the bomb with the Soviet Union. He made his case in a long memorandum to President Truman on September 12, which warned against wearing the bomb "rather ostentatiously on our hip" as a weapon of U.S. diplomacy.

> I still recognize the difficulty and am still convinced of the ultimate importance of a change in Russian attitude toward individual liberty, but I have come to the conclusion that it would not be possible to use our possession of the atomic bomb as a direct lever to produce change. I have become convinced that any demand by us for an internal change in Russia as a condition of sharing in the atomic weapon would be so resented that it would make the objective we have in view less probable. . . . Accordingly, unless the Soviets are voluntarily invited into the partnership upon a basis of cooperation and trust, we are going to maintain the Anglo-American bloc over against the Soviet in the possession of this weapon. Such a condition will almost certainly stimulate feverish activity on the part of the Soviet toward the development of this bomb in what will in effect be a secret armament race of a rather desperate character. There is evidence to indicate that such activity may have already commenced. . . .

Stimson concluded by arguing for a direct approach to the Soviet Union, not as part of a "general international scheme." Of course, there were risks, but they were far outweighed by benefits of permanent peace. "The chief lesson I have learned in a long life," Stimson added, "is that the only way you can make a man trustworthy is to trust him."[34]

The issue of atomic energy arose in the cabinet a week later, on Stimson's seventy-eighth birthday and his final day as secretary of war. Stimson's memo was not at issue—Truman never gave it to other cabinet members—but rather a more moderate proposal to share basic scientific information about atomic energy with other nations.

According to Wallace, Stimson began by saying "there was no possible way of holding the scientific secret of the atomic bomb," and therefore "there should be free interchange of scientific information between the different members of the United Nations." This would strengthen America's relationship with Russia. There was nothing belonging to either country that the other coveted, Stimson added.

Dean Acheson, representing the State Department in Byrnes's absence, sided with Stimson. Abe Fortas, representing Interior Secretary Harold Ickes, did too. Others, such as Treasury Secretary Fred Vinson, Attorney General Tom Clark, and Navy Secretary James Forrestal strongly disagreed.

When Wallace finally spoke, it was to ask a question: What specifically was under discussion? "Whether or not the scientific information regarding atomic energy should be shared with other members of the United Nations," Truman replied. They were not discussing the sharing of "factory techniques or 'know-how,' " the president added.

"I then went at some length into the whole scientific background," Wallace wrote,

> describing how foreign Jewish scientists had, in the first place, sold the president in the fall of 1939. I indicated the degree to which the whole approach had originated in Europe, and that it was impossible to bottle the thing up no matter how much we tried. I . . . spoke of the danger of developing a "Maginot Line" attitude of mind. I said there was the gravest danger that by putting the screws on our scientists and trying to maintain what we thought was a secret, other nations would go far beyond us in their discoveries. I advocated strongly the interchange of scientific information but not the interchange of techniques or "know-hows." I also advocated that in case scientific information were made freely available to Russia, that we should have as a quid pro quo proviso that there be as much freedom for American scientific workers to work in Russian laboratories as for Russians to work in American laboratories.

Several others pitched in, on both sides. Some argued for delay. On that note the meeting ended, and Henry Stimson was taken to the White House Rose Garden, where he was awarded the Distinguished Service Medal by President Truman. Henry Wallace left for a meeting with scientists at the University of Chicago, unaware that he was about to suffer a reprehensible smear on his public reputation.[35]

The next day's editions of the *New York Times* carried a story saying, "President Truman's Cabinet debated a proposal made by Secretary Wallace to give the secret of the atomic bomb to Russia." Wallace, of course, made no such proposal, nor had he addressed it. In fact, he had specifically opposed the sharing of weapons technology.[36]

Wallace denied the accuracy of the story, and several others, including Truman, denounced the leak and supported his denial. Truman told reporters Wallace had no greater role in the discussion than other cabinet members and had made no proposal of his own. But as Wallace understood all too well, "Denials of things of this sort just serve to intensify the impression, rather than lessen it. . . ." A lie, Wallace said, is almost impossible to straighten out once it has "a good head start."[37]

Wallace was intensely interested in the source of the leak. Reporters told him it had come from the White House press office, but Wallace believed Press Secretary Charlie Ross was a man of the "very highest standards" and tended to doubt the rumor. Nor did he believe that Truman personally was involved. Truman thought it had come from Leo Crowley, the lend-lease administrator, whom he thereafter banned from cabinet meetings.

Dean Acheson suspected Forrestal. Wallace doubted that, too, although he thought the navy secretary "was to some extent unbalanced." The later publication of Forrestal's diaries confirmed Acheson's suspicion.

But of one thing Wallace was certain: the leak was designed to harm him. It "served certain purposes so well" that it could hardly have been an accident.

"At that time, I had quite a strong hold on the affections of a large segment of the American population," he remarked in his oral history. "I was getting along very well with various leaders in Congress; building up a strong Department of Commerce; and I think certain interests were very eager to destroy my political influence. This was just too bright and shining a mark."

The atomic bomb leak was the beginning of a "rolling snowball," Wallace said. "I could see what was coming."[38]

CHAPTER TWENTY-ONE

"ONE WORLD OR NO WORLD"

By mid-1945 Henry Wallace had begun to ponder his future. After a dozen crowded years in Washington, he approached his fifty-seventh birthday not as "tired old man," as was said of many New Dealers, but certainly as one entitled to take stock and look ahead.

Not surprisingly he decided to buy a farm. With his wife, Ilo, and a sister, Mary Bruggmann, serving as scouts, he narrowed the choice to several properties in New York State. The idea of living in New York came originally from Franklin Roosevelt, who liked to picture himself living in neighborly proximity with Wallace after their public careers had ended. Wallace apparently gave no thought of returning to his native Iowa, where he was still listed as "editor on leave" of *Wallaces' Farmer.*

By early summer the Wallaces had settled on a gently rolling 115-acre tract in Westchester County, near the Connecticut border, and on June 6, 1945, they bought it for about $51,000.* Located near the tiny village of South Salem, about fifty miles north of New York City, the farm suited a man of Wallace's public and private interests.

The farm had once been owned by the family of John Winant, New Hampshire's progressive former governor and wartime U.S. ambassador to England. Its most recent owner, Marshall Pask, used it for a dairy operation run by a tenant farmer. The dairy herd came with the farm, but the Wallaces

*Mary Bruggmann put her name on the deed because Wallace did not wish to give the impression he was about to quit the administration. Henry and Ilo Wallace bought the farm from her the following year.

did not wait long to sell the livestock. They had had quite enough of dairying early in their marriage, when Henry would arise before dawn to tend cows before going to work at the farm paper. That experiment ended in exhaustion and undulant fever.

The Wallaces did not mean to move to New York right away. Indeed, the property's spacious two-story home had neither central heat nor hot water. But the farm was rich with possibilities, and Wallace savored the prospect of a life on the soil. He called it Farvue, after a farm once owned by his grandfather, and began to stock it with chickens and strawberries.

The sudden end of the war left little time to dream of farming, however. A vast array of problems all but overwhelmed Harry Truman and his neophyte administration.

At home the problem was "reconversion," the wrenching adjustment from wartime mobilization to peacetime production. Everybody wanted something—now. Business wanted increased profits. Labor unions wanted higher wages. Farmers wanted more money for their crops. Mothers and fathers wanted the return of their children in uniform. The public wanted an end to rationing and controls. Wartime restrictions had left Americans flush with almost $240 billion in savings, and they were itching to spend it. But each of these demands, no matter how politically compelling, held risks: inflation, unemployment, monopoly, shortages.

Abroad the United States faced complexity and danger. Much of Europe was economically prostrate. Tens of millions of people teetered near starvation. Other millions clamored for self-determination or seized opportunities to avenge ancient claims and rivalries. Britain wanted to keep its empire; France wanted its colonies returned. Russia demanded security in the form of compliant neighbors. China neared civil war. Latin America seethed with discord and intrigue. The fate of Germany and Japan had to be settled. Peace treaties awaited negotiation, and the United Nations had to be set on a sound footing.

Not to mention the atomic bomb. In Wallace's mind the bomb outweighed everything. "Atomic power means 'one world or no world,'" Wallace wrote Truman. ". . . We must move with speed, determination and faith. The stakes are the human race. We cannot fail. We cannot delay. . . . If we fail there will be a senseless armament race and chaos.' "[1]

The "atomic bomb problem" was in fact three interrelated problems, in Wallace's view. He set these out in a long memo to Truman.

First, there was the effect of the bomb on America's relations with other nations. "As long as the United States makes atomic bombs she will be looked upon as the world's outstanding aggressor nation," Wallace wrote. This would be "a very dangerous position" for a democracy, he said. A democracy could never launch a nuclear attack "without warning," whereas a non-democratic nation could. "Therefore, ten years hence a non-democratic nation, with only one-third as many bombs as the United States, could destroy American industry in half a day." Steps should be taken immediately to place atomic weaponry under international control with the aim of destroying "all weapons of offensive warfare. . . . An atomic bomb race between nations means the end of humanity."

Second, the United States should recognize and promote the unlimited civilian benefits offered by atomic energy. "The civilian application of atomic power must not be held back by the Military," he told Truman. If America allowed "vested interests," whether civilian or military, to block the peaceful development of atomic power, other nations would "out-strip us as they step into the new age." Useless military secrecy regulations must be discarded. "Science must be unbound again and scientists must be allowed to talk again to their fellow American citizens." It was as if God were saying to America, "I expect you to live according to the social rules of abundance," and if you fail, "I shall turn this power of light and peace into a power of darkness and war— and the final state of Man will be ten times as miserable as it has ever been."

Third, the control of U.S. atomic energy should rest with a civilian atomic power commission, its director appointed by the president and confirmed by the Senate. The commission should deal with the practical engineering development and use of atomic power, together with "appropriate safeguards" for the benefit of business, labor, agriculture, consumers, researchers, and the military. "The expenditures destined for the war program should be largely turned over to scientific research," Wallace said. "God has given us, through this tremendous discovery of atomic energy, the unique opportunity to build one single human community on the highest spiritual level, accompanied by unlimited material facilities."[2]

Wallace presented his memo to Truman at a one-on-one meeting on October 15, 1945. Truman read it sentence by sentence. "He said he agreed with it throughout," Wallace noted in his diary. "He said this was what he had been trying to say right along in the statements which he had made." For good measure, Truman added that "Stalin was a fine man who wanted to do the right thing." Wallace responded that "apparently the purpose of Britain was to promote an irreparable break between us and Russia." Again Truman agreed.

"I said Britain's game in international affairs has always been intrigue," Wallace added. "The president said he agreed. I said Britain may have plenty of excuse for playing the game the way she does; it may fit into her geographical position, but we must not play her game. The president said he agreed."[3]

After six months with Harry Truman, Wallace had learned to take his constant expressions of agreement with a grain of salt. "He does so like to agree with whoever is with him at the moment," Wallace commented in his diary. The president's actions and public pronouncements were another matter. There his course appeared far less certain. A foreign policy speech in late October left Wallace wondering whether the president had any policy at all. Perhaps "like the famous water-man he was looking one way and rowing another," Wallace observed in his diary. "But nobody seems to know which way he was looking or which way he was rowing."[4]

Still, Wallace's stand on civilian control and application of atomic energy seemed to sway the president. Truman had earlier supported an atomic energy bill sponsored by Senator Edwin Johnson of Colorado and Representative Andrew May of Kentucky, both Democrats, which would have left nuclear policy largely in military hands. Now, under pressure from Wallace and others, Truman began to back away.

The May-Johnson bill, actually drafted in the Department of War, emphasized the military uses of atomic energy, restricted research and the sharing of scientific information, and established a control board dominated by military and government officials. The board would have vast authority to impose severe penalties for security violations.

"I am confident that with the May-Johnson bill as it now stands, it would be easily possible for certain groups that definitely do not stand for what you and I stand for to gain an astonishing amount of control in an amazingly short time," Wallace wrote in a follow-up letter to Truman. It was "all-important" for the person in charge of atomic energy to be "brought immediately under the control of the president," he said.[5]

Wallace had important allies in the atomic scientists themselves. By late fall the scientists were in a state of great alarm over the drift of the administration's policy. Their concerns were brought personally to Wallace by Dr. J. Robert Oppenheimer, the brilliant theoretical physicist who was the scientific head of the project to build the bomb.

Oppenheimer and Wallace walked together to the Commerce Department one morning discussing the scientist's concerns. Oppenheimer told Wallace that Stimson had proposed sharing the bomb with the Russians but that Secretary of State James Byrnes felt "we can use the bomb as a pistol to get what we wanted." Oppenheimer added that Russia would surely be able to build its own bomb within a few years.

The present mishandling of the bomb, Oppenheimer thought, would lead to the "eventual slaughter of tens of millions—or perhaps hundreds of millions—of innocent people," Wallace recorded in his diary. He added, "The guilt-consciousness of atomic scientists is one of the most astounding things I have ever seen."[6]

By December, Truman had withdrawn support for the May-Johnson bill, and Congress buried it without a vote. In its place came legislation sponsored by Senator Brien McMahon, a Connecticut Democrat, to create a five-member atomic energy commission appointed by and responsible to the president. The McMahon bill, written with the help of Dr. Edward U. Condon, the eminent physicist whom Wallace named to head the National Bureau of Standards, encouraged civilian application of atomic energy, permitted the international exchange of scientific information, and supported the concept of UN control.

With strong support from Truman and Wallace, the McMahon bill was passed. The commerce secretary, testifying before the Senate Special Committee on Atomic Energy, said the legislation could help point the way to "a new and undreamed-of mastery of the secrets of the universe in the interest of a better life for all." Civilian control of atomic energy, he said, would help "prevent undesirable forms of authoritarianism" from gaining control of the nation.[7]

Conversely Truman and his foreign policy advisers seemed headed arm-in-arm with the British toward a confrontation with the Soviet Union. In a speech before a joint session of Congress, Truman called for universal military training, which struck Wallace as a "prelude to World War III."[8] Britain had asked for a $4 billion loan to aid reconstruction; such a loan should be matched by equal assistance to Russia, Wallace believed, but when he suggested it to Assistant Secretary of State Will Clayton, he was told Russia didn't need it.

In November, Truman met with the leaders of Britain and Canada to discuss international control of atomic energy. Four days of negotiation produced a proposal for international control and inspection, the elimination of nuclear weapons, and the free exchange of scientific information. But the plan would be implemented in phases, each step awaiting the "successful completion" of the preceding step. In Wallace's view, the step-by-step approach was simply a scheme to keep atomic weapons in the hands of the Americans and the British.

At the next cabinet meeting Wallace openly disagreed with the phased-in approach to international control. "I said this . . . suggested that Russia would have to pass the first grade in moral aptitude before she would be allowed to enter the second grade of moral aptitude." Truman said he thought it was the best approach to dealing with Russians.[9]

In his diary Wallace wrote that Russia's participation in the plan probably would "depend on just how far along her scientists are in atomic energy investigations. If they have made a really great advance, they may not care to accept England, the United States and Canada as their teachers in international morality."[10]

Most frightening to Wallace was the casual, almost flippant, White House attitude regarding control. He raised the matter at a cabinet meeting in early December, and Secretary of War Robert Patterson replied that there were no atomic bombs. Patterson admitted, however, that material to fashion atomic bombs was available and that they could be assembled in less than a day. General Leslie Groves controlled the material, Patterson said.

"No one man should be in charge," Wallace replied.[11]

The following week Wallace told Truman in a private meeting he was "seriously disturbed" at Groves's dominant role. Groves was a man of fascist tendencies, a Roosevelt hater who had once called the president a son of a bitch and was not above telling off-color stories about Eleanor Roosevelt, Wallace said. People in a "certain group" in the army "had their own ideas as to what constituted national security," and one couldn't tell what they might do with such a weapon.[12]

The issue arose again at a cabinet meeting on December 14. Patterson noted with some annoyance that General Groves had been asked how many bombs existed when he was testifying before Senator McMahon's committee. The senators probably didn't really want to know, Patterson said. "The president at this moment chimed in to say that he didn't really want to know either," Wallace noted in his diary.

"I promptly intervened to say with the greatest earnestness, 'Mr. President, you should know; also the Secretary of War should know, and the Secretary of the Navy,'" Wallace continued. "[I] hammered with all the energy I could—to the effect that the president himself must have this information."

At that point Truman "retreated in some confusion" and said he should know, and in fact did know "in a general way."

Wallace was aghast. "I thought it was utterly incredible that Patterson and the president should be willing to trust full information and responsibility on this to a man like Groves and his underlings without knowing what was going on themselves."

At the conclusion of the meeting, Dean Acheson, who had represented the State Department, approached Patterson and flatly declared, "I don't think we ought to continue making atomic bombs." Patterson again said "we don't have any atomic bombs" but could make them quickly. Acheson shook his head and told Wallace, "It was the old hen and egg proposition. We would not trust other nations until they trusted us—and until they trusted us we would not stop making atomic bombs. On the other hand, the other nations could not start trusting us until we stopped making atomic bombs."[13]

Wallace added sadly in his diary, "Arguments of this kind have absolutely no effect on an opaque mind like Bob Patterson's. It is a shame that Secretary Stimson could not have continued as Secretary of War."[14]

⁂

As Wallace walked into the White House one day in late 1945, he found himself surrounded by reporters asking when he planned to resign as commerce secretary. A nameless "self-starter" on the White House staff had apparently planted the rumor. Wallace replied that Truman had given him "one hundred percent cooperation" on all matters. Then he walked straight into Truman's office and recounted the question and his answer.

"I don't want you to resign," Truman replied, "and that comes from the heart."[15]

Wallace believed him. Harry Truman indeed had every reason to mean what he said. Americans were in an impatient frame of mind, eager to be rid of wartime sacrifices, wanting more of everything except perhaps of government itself. After an initial honeymoon in which the public rallied behind the untested president, his popularity had begun to decline. Journalists spoke critically of the "little men" surrounding Truman. "To err is Truman" was a widely popular pun.

More than a few people had concluded Truman was a small-bore politician in a job too big for him. Even Truman indicated some uncertainty. He should have been "a piano player in a whorehouse," he said in the presence of Wallace and several others. At least houses of ill repute posted a sign saying, "Don't shoot the piano player—he's doing the best he can."[16]

Truman could handle the shots being fired by congressional Republicans and their allies in the press. Partisan sniping went with the territory. More troubling were elements of his own party—organized labor, farmers, and liberal intellectuals—with whom his bond was weak. These were "Wallace people," and Truman knew it. The two people absolutely essential to his "political team," Truman remarked to an associate, were Henry Wallace and Eleanor Roosevelt.

Truman's sincerity was reflected by a stunning change of attitude in Postmaster General Robert Hannegan. In 1944 Hannegan had done as much as any man to deny Wallace the Democratic vice presidential nomination. By late 1945 Hannegan was Wallace's strongest supporter in the cabinet. In every instance, whether debating control of the atomic bomb or the need for full-employment legislation, Hanengan adopted a progressive position arm-in-arm with Wallace. And the party chairman often urged Wallace to speak before liberal audiences and as a liaison to organized labor and agriculture.

The need for Wallace's help was painfully clear. Labor was in a state of open rebellion. Steelworkers demanded a wage increase of two dollars per day. Mine workers called for a strike over the issue of organizing foremen. Other unions asked for a 30 percent increase in pay. Truman used national security grounds to seize twenty-six petroleum plants in order to keep them running. A much touted labor-management conference opened in November and immediately dissolved into a shouting match. By December 1945 half a million workers were on strike nationwide, and the administration's price control program was in disarray. Phil Murray, the CIO chief, told Wallace bluntly he had lost all confidence in Truman.

The agricultural sector was slipping into a full-blown crisis. Farmers bridled at the continuation of rationing and price controls, while business and labor sought a bigger share of the pie. By December food rationing (except sugar) had been ended, but this increased domestic demand and threatened massive inflation. Then U.S. officials finally recognized that war-ravaged Europe was on the brink of starvation. A distraught Harry Truman told the nation only a "superhuman effort" could prevent the death of tens of millions and announced new restrictions on grain inventories and marketing. This only angered farmers and consumers, without alleviating the European food crisis.

Europe's hunger was shameful in Wallace's view, and only underscored the need for immediate large-scale American loans and aid. What made sense from a moral and economic standpoint, however, ran counter to the get-tough instincts of Truman's foreign policy advisers. Even the loan to Britain was being questioned on grounds that it would inevitably force the United States to offer similar assistance to Russia. And Truman, for all his agreement with Wallace in private, had grown less open to persuasion. In December, when Secretary of State Byrnes returned from a foreign ministers conference in Moscow optimistic that the Russians had shown some flexibility, Truman berated him for being insufficiently tough. "I'm tired of babying the Soviets," said the president.[17]

Wallace found himself in an ironic position. His views on governmental policy—his whole reason for being in public life—grew ever less influential. Yet precisely because of those views and the deep affection he commanded within the Democratic Party's liberal wing, Wallace was all but untouchable politically.

Events in early 1946 highlighted Wallace's uneasy relationship with Truman.

One source of alarm was the ever-louder tom-toms of war. During a spectacularly contentious dinner party at the columnist Joe Alsop's home, Wallace exchanged verbal blows with almost everyone present over the issue of Russia. William Gaud, executive assistant to James Forrestal, said the United States should "kick the Russians in the balls" and denounced Wallace's call for free Russian access through the Dardanelles as "crap." Alsop noted approvingly the army's insistence upon "complete encirclement" of Russia with U.S. bases in Iceland, Greenland, the Aleutians, and Okinawa.

"There is only one logical action that can be taken if the Alsop point of view is adhered to, and that is to provoke a war with Russia as soon as possible," Wallace wrote in his diary.[18]

Wallace also fretted over the mounting strife between labor and management and Truman's strident anti-union stance. By February two million workers were off the job, the largest wave of strikes in the nation's history. At the president's request Wallace jumped into the steelworkers' strike and persuaded the CIO chief Murray to accept a proposed wage increase of 18.5 cents an hour. But steel companies refused the offer unless the government allowed large increases in steel prices, which Wallace thought unwarranted. Truman caved in, offering the companies a price increase of five dollars per ton, which settled the strike but opened the door to further business attacks on price controls.

Finally, Wallace disliked the pattern of cronyism that permeated the White House. In quick succession during the first weeks of 1946, Truman named George Allen, Democratic politico and professed member of the anti-Wallace conspiracy, to head the Reconstruction Finance Corporation and sent his imperious naval aide, Jake Vardaman, to join the Federal Reserve System's board of governors.

Then, in late January, Truman nominated Edwin Pauley to be undersecretary of the navy, an apparent stepping stone to secretary in a few months.

Nothing had changed Wallace's mind about Pauley. His activities in Russia as head of the U.S. delegation on war reparations reeked with anecdotes of petty self-dealing. To contemplate making Pauley the number two man in a department that controlled vast oil reserves was staggering.

Wallace squirmed, saying nothing in public about Pauley, but Secretary of the Interior Harold Ickes would not stand by. The combative seventy-one-year-old Ickes volunteered for questioning by the Senate committee considering Pauley. He made sure the senators knew what question to ask.

"Did Mr. Pauley ever tell you the filing of the government suit to claim the [oil reserves in California's offshore] tidelands was bad politics, that it might cost several hundred thousand dollars in campaign contributions?"

Ickes savored the moment with a long silence and then replied, "Yes." Specifically, Pauley had told Ickes at Roosevelt's funeral that he could raise $300,000 from oil interests if the government did not press its offshore claim.[19]

Pauley denied the charge, and Truman stood behind him. "Honest Harold" wasn't the only honest man in Washington, Truman said. But Ickes, an inveterate diarist, promptly produced notes to back up his charge. As he did so, Ickes also sent Truman a stinging letter of resignation implying the president had asked him to commit "perjury for the sake of the party" on behalf of Pauley.[20]

Wallace was certainly not displeased by Pauley's rough treatment, or much surprised by Ickes's flamboyant departure. "All I can say about Ickes is that he had a real passion for public service and self-aggrandizement, and he couldn't tell where one left off and the other began," Wallace said in his oral history.[21] Several of Ickes's cabinet colleagues, including Jimmie Byrnes, called him to commiserate on the evening of his departure. Wallace did not.

Two days later Truman spoke to Wallace "with some feeling." He hoped that if Wallace ever disagreed with him, they could "sit down and talk things over." Truman declared himself "an honest man" and said he thought Wallace believed that also.

"Yes," Wallace replied. His mind raced backward to the two occasions, six months before the Chicago convention, when Truman said he supported Wallace's renomination. "The way in which the phrase ['an honest man'] was used in Washington always amused me," Wallace observed later. "It's a propaganda device, that's all." Still, Wallace thought Truman probably honest in the Washington sense. "The trouble is that he has no solid background of information and therefore is too much influenced by friends whose motives are not always good."[22]

Franklin Roosevelt had been dead less than a year. Of the ten people in Roosevelt's last cabinet, only one remained: Henry Agard Wallace.

The Cold War could be said to have started on March 5, 1946.

Tension between the United States and the Soviet Union had been evident since early 1945. International conferences ended in frustration and suspicion. Decisions on control of the atomic bomb fostered discord. A report on world conditions prepared by the War Department brimmed with fear of Russia.

By early 1946 relations between the United States and its wartime ally the Soviet Union festered. Russia had brutally positioned a string of compliant buffer states between itself and Western Europe. Communist forces fomented civil war in Greece and China. The Soviets were plundering the industrial resources of eastern Germany and Manchuria.

Soviet pressure on Iran plunged the infant UN General Assembly into its first important debate. U.S. officials responded with a plan to encircle the

Soviet Union with a permanent string of military bases. In late January, Truman proposed a $3.75 billion low-interest loan to Britain without any mention of Russia's request for $6 billion in aid.

Almost everything went from bad to worse in February. Stalin gave a militant speech announcing a Soviet increase in military production. Wallace thought Stalin's speech was essentially a response to the U.S. "encirclement" plan. Whatever the motivation, Stalin's speech triggered an 8,000-word analysis of Russia by George F. Kennan, the American chargé d'affaires in Moscow. This "long telegram" would become the central text of American foreign policy for a generation. "[We] have here a political force committed fanatically to the belief that with the U.S. there can be no permanent modus vivendi, that it is desirable and necessary that the internal harmony of our society be disrupted, our traditional way of life be destroyed, the international authority of our state be broken, if Soviet power is to be secure," Kennan wrote.[23]

He proposed a policy of "containment," which would meet and rebuff Soviet advances on every front. Secretary of the Navy James Forrestal seized on Kennan's telegram and promptly made it required reading for hundreds of military offices.

Kennan's message was followed by one from General Lucius D. Clay, military commander of the U.S. occupation zone in Germany, warning of Soviet intentions to unify the country under its auspices. Then came news that a Communist spy ring had been exposed in Ottawa. Late in the month Senator Arthur Vandenberg, the Republican foreign affairs spokesman, delivered an inflammatory speech asking, "What is Russia up to now?" Not to be outdone, Secretary of State James Byrnes delivered an anti-Russia speech of his own the next day, saying the United States could not "allow aggression to be accomplished by coercion or pressure or by subterfuge such as political infiltration."[24]

Thus was the stage set on March 5. On that day Winston Churchill spoke at Westminster College in Fulton, Missouri. He was introduced by President Harry S. Truman, who said, "I know he will have something constructive to say to the world."

What Churchill had to say was essentially a call for an Anglo-American military alliance—a "fraternal association of the English-speaking peoples"— to stand foursquare against the Soviet Union. "From Stettin in the Baltic to Trieste in the Adriatic an Iron Curtain has descended across the Continent," Churchill rumbled. What the Soviets desired, he said, was "all the fruits of war and the indefinite expansion of their power and doctrines." Russia posed a "growing challenge and peril to Christian civilization." Only British and American military strength could meet it.[25]

Truman sat behind him applauding.

Churchill's words hit the United States like a thunderclap. "Iron Curtain" immediately entered the political vocabulary. Public opinion of the Soviet Union, waning for months, plummeted rapidly. Concurrently, fear of Communist underground activity in the United States increased, neatly dovetailing with public apprehension over labor's industrial strikes. Churchill had announced the birth of the Cold War and its sibling, the Red Scare, all at once.

Churchill's speech sent a shudder through Wallace, who learned of it at a dinner party given by Dean Acheson. The Australian ambassador to the United States, Dick Casey, and his wife reviewed the speech in glowing terms. "I promptly interjected that the United States was not going to enter into any military alliance with England against Russia; that it was not a primary objective of the United States to save the British Empire," Wallace noted in his diary.

Mrs. Casey put her hands on her hips and "went almost into a frenzy," Wallace continued. "She proclaimed that the purpose was to save the world—not the British Empire. . . . I said instead of talking about military alliances it was high time to talk about an effective method of disarmament. I said it would destroy the United Nations to have two of the chief members of the United Nations ganging up on a third member."[26]

Time would prove Wallace wrong. NATO did align itself against Russia. But much of what Wallace said at that contentious dinner party proved prophetic.

I said I didn't see how these war-like words of Churchill now could have any more real influence on the Russians than his war-like attitude toward the Bolsheviks had in 1919. I said the American people were not willing to send American boys to fight anybody now; that certainly the Russians did not want to fight anybody now; that in all probability the situation would finally work out on a basis that would cause the Russians completely and utterly to distrust us; that it would cause the Russians to engage in a race with us in the making of atomic bombs; that while they might be a long way behind us at the present time, they would have enough bombs to destroy us fifteen years hence; . . . that they would have no hesitation in continuing their fifth-column activities in all the nations of the world; that they could use these fifth-columnists effectively to destroy our form of government."[27]

Acheson, Casey, and Charles Bohlen, head of the State Department's Russia section, vehemently disagreed with Wallace. Columnist Walter Lippman sat through the conversation in silence. On the way home, Ilo Wallace told her husband that Mrs. Lippmann had whispered that she and her husband agreed with Wallace.

⚉

Churchill's dramatic speech produced no immediate change in U.S. policy. Nor did it seem to alter Wallace's relationship with Truman. In fact, Truman seemed unmoved by the speech. He told reporters—and Wallace personally—that he had not known in advance what Churchill was going to say.* He offered a crisp "no comment" when reporters asked what he thought of it. Reaction to Churchill's address in many prominent newspapers, including Eleanor Roosevelt's and Walter Lippmann's influential columns, was roundly negative and reflected Wallace's point of view.

Wallace soon challenged Churchill's remarks in public. The occasion, ironically, was a testimonial dinner for Averell Harriman given by the American Society for Russian Relief on March 19. "The United States owes Russia an undying debt of gratitude," Wallace declared. "The citizens of the Soviet Union paid a heavier price for our joint victory over fascism than any other people." He added,

> [Just] as some military men profess that the only road to peace is atomic bombs, bases, huge appropriations for armaments and arctic expeditions, so the Soviets may feel that the only road to peace is for them to give the capitalist nations tit for every tat. . . .
>
> The only way to defeat communism in the world is to do a better and smoother job of maximum production and optimum distribution. . . . Let's out-compete Russia in the most friendly spirit possible, for we must realize that, militarily speaking, there could be no final victor in any armed conflict between our two great nations.[28]

As usual, Wallace showed his speech to Truman before it was delivered. Once again Truman said he agreed with it. Don't hesitate to repudiate it if

---

*Truman was lying. He knew of its content from Byrnes and Churchill several days earlier. On the evening before it was delivered, Truman read the actual text of the speech while traveling by train with Churchill to Missouri.

In a private conversation with Wallace on March 12, Truman said again (as he had at a press conference) that he had not seen the speech in advance. The president "went into the details of how he had been sucked in and how Churchill had put him on the spot," Wallace noted in his diary. "I said I thought Churchill had insulted him by coming out with a proposal of this sort in the United States with him on the platform. I said that the peace of the world hinged on the United States—not on a military alliance between Britain and the United States. Truman said he agreed."

it causes embarrassment, Wallace told the president. "Don't worry about that," Truman replied. "What you are saying here is good sense."[29]

The day following, Wallace handed Truman a long memo detailing his criticism of Churchill's proposal. "The American people do not want an English-speaking alliance," Wallace wrote. "They will not support a policy of ganging up with Russia against Britain, or with Britain against Russia. In an age of atomic energy they see clearly that this is the road to utter tragedy."

The United States, Wallace suggested, should reassert its faith in the United Nations and launch a "positive and constructive" diplomatic offensive to resolve disputes between Britain and Russia. It should propose plans to settle the Iranian dispute, to allow the "joint sharing and control" of Middle Eastern oil reserves, to prevent the splitting of Europe into hostile blocs, and to hasten international control of atomic energy. Truman warmly thanked him for the memo.[30]

Perhaps Truman was not being entirely disingenuous. In hard reality other matters in the spring of 1946 were occupying him. The Russians and the British would have to wait their turn.

By April 1946 tens of millions neared starvation in Europe. In the United States confusion over price and production controls had led to widespread discontent among farmers and a thriving black market in meat and other commodities. A new wave of strikes threatened to close coal mines and railroads. Truman's response was unnerving. In May he seized bituminous coal mines, and shortly thereafter he took control of the railroads.

On May 25 Truman made a dramatic appearance before Congress, proposing to draft striking railroad workers into the army and to force them to work. The action was averted only by a last-minute settlement of the dispute announced while the president was still speaking, but the seeds of governmental antistrike injunctive powers—later embodied in the Taft-Hartley Act—were planted.

Truman's popularity went into a free fall. His approval rating fell from 82 percent in January to 52 percent in June. Democratic Party chairman Hannegan, facing crucial midterm elections, desperately sought Wallace's help with labor, farmers, blacks, and liberals. For a Jackson Day political speech to be broadcast nationwide by radio, Hannegan wanted only two speakers: Truman and Wallace. In May, Wallace toured several states and, with Hannegan's encouragement, spoke before left-wing audiences in New York City.*

---

*Harold Young, still Wallace's political adviser, was especially opposed to an appearance before a rally organized by the American Labor Party, which he said was dominated by Communists.

Wallace made the speech. "The word 'Communist' is used so loosely nowadays that no one can say what the truth is," Wallace observed in his diary. "Anyone who is further to the Left than you are—and whom you don't like—is a Communist."

But as Wallace pleased liberal audiences, he drifted further from the administration's center.

Longtime liberal allies, such as Beanie Baldwin and Henry Morgenthau, urged him to resign and prepare to challenge Truman in 1948. Harold Ickes, now head of the Independent Citizens Committee of the Arts, Sciences, and Professions, could barely contain his scorn that Wallace remained in Truman's cabinet.

At the same time the foreign policy and economic views that endeared Wallace to liberals maddened conservatives. In a *Life* magazine article Joe Alsop attacked Wallace's "irresponsible intervention" and "plainly indefensible" meddling in foreign affairs and said he was a "symbol of the terrible confusion which now afflicts American liberalism." The *Washington Times-Herald*, in a lead editorial on Truman's labor policies, urged the president to dismiss Wallace. "He stays on in Truman's cabinet, hostile to Truman's policies, and Truman has not got up the nerve to fire him. Yet."[31]

As the spring of 1946 slid into summer, the Truman administration bounced from crisis to crisis. No sooner had the railroad strike been resolved than a raucous fight broke out over price controls

With price controls set to expire at the end of June, the administration sought legislation to extend its essential features for another year. Businessmen and congressional conservatives fought the proposal vigorously. Some large manufacturers began withholding goods from the market to await a lapse of controls. This created shortages and consumer unrest. Chester Bowles, the competent but beleaguered administrator of the control program, resigned in frustration in June.

Shortly before the price control program was due to expire, Congress enacted new legislation riddled with loopholes favorable to business. Many of Truman's conservative advisers, especially new secretary of the treasury, John W. Snyder, urged him to sign it. But the bill was too much for Truman to swallow. He took a calculated risk and vetoed it. He assumed Congress would come up with something better.

The veto, cheered by liberals, was but a Pyrrhic victory. Absent any controls, prices rose fast. Inflation, held to 3 percent since the war ended, climbed 5.5 percent in July alone. Food prices grew by 13.8 percent. Amid the public uproar Congress passed new price control legislation in much the same form as the bill adopted in June. This time Truman signed it.

Wallace did what he could to build support for Truman among liberals, but it was an uphill fight. At a conference of young progressives during the summer, Wallace pleaded for continued faith in the Democratic Party. Democrats had their flaws, Wallace said, but they were "ten times" more progressive than Republicans. As for the possibility of organizing a third party in 1948, Wallace added, that would "insure beyond all doubt the election of a reactionary Republican."

Beanie Baldwin, vice chairman of the National Citizens Political Action Committee, bluntly rebutted Wallace to his face. If Truman did not improve, Baldwin said, a third party would be formed whether or not Wallace approved. Wallace ruefully admitted in private that Baldwin was right.[32]

Once again Wallace set out to change Truman's course, at least on the issue that mattered most. On July 23 he handed Truman a twelve-page, single-spaced letter, intended only as a private communication, setting out his views on Russia and proposing avenues to "achieve a permanent peace." For a thousand years, Wallace said, Russian history had been a struggle to "resist invasion and conquest." With good reason, he said, the Russians "see themselves as fighting for their existence in a hostile world." Wallace continued,

> How do American actions since V-J Day appear to other nations? I mean by actions the concrete things like $13 billion [budgeted for] the War and Navy Departments, the Bikini tests of the atomic bomb and continued production of bombs, the plan to arm Latin America with our weapons, production of B-29s and planned production of B-36s, and the effort to secure air bases spread over half the globe from which the other half of the globe can be bombed. . . .
>
> These facts rather make it appear either 1) that we are preparing ourselves to win the war which we regard as inevitable or 2) that we are trying to build up a predominance of force to intimidate the rest of mankind. How would it look to us if Russia had the atomic bomb and we did not, if Russia had 10,000-mile bombers and air bases within a thousand miles of our coast lines and we did not?

Wallace especially attacked the U.S. proposal for international control of atomic energy. The United States had proposed to share atomic energy with the world at some unspecified time in the future. In exchange Russia would promise not to build any bombs and immediately give access to its own technical resources for purposes of verification. Meanwhile the United States could go on building its stockpile of atomic weapons. "Is it any wonder that the Russians did not show any great enthusiasm for our plan?" His letter closed with a call for rationality and understanding: "We should not act as if we too felt that we were threatened in today's world. We are by far the most powerful nation in the world, the only Allied nation which came out of the war without devastation and much stronger than before the war. Any talk on our part about the need for strengthening our defenses further is bound to appear hypocritical to other nations."[33]

Two years had passed since Wallace's rejection at the Democratic convention in Chicago. Roosevelt was dead. So were Harry Hopkins and Sidney Hillman. Perhaps the century of the common man was dead too. Wallace wasn't sure. Roosevelt's cabinet was gone except for Wallace. Time and his reduced position had not affected his popularity with many Democrats—the August 1946 Gallup poll showed him slightly ahead of Truman as the preferred standard-bearer in 1948—yet Wallace occupied a faintly ridiculous position, defending the very man who had defeated him.

In August, Wallace took a long break with his family at Farvue, tending chickens and plant-testing some radioactive fertilizer provided by his friend Boris Pregel. The house at Farvue slowly turned into a home. Wallace was especially pleased by the relocation of a wall, which reduced the size of the kitchen and expanded the library.

At the end of the month, he went on a long-planned return visit to Mexico, where he attended ceremonies marking the end of President Avila Camacho's six-year term. Ever since Camacho's inauguration in 1940, they had remained on warm terms, and the Mexican president personally asked the former vice president to make the visit.

Wallace stayed only eleven days. Too much time was filled with ceremonial functions to suit him, but he did inspect some farms with the Mexican agricultural minister Marte Gómez. The highlight of his trip, in Wallace's view, was a visit to the international experiment station founded at his suggestion by the Rockefeller Foundation. There he met Norman Borlaug and "was amazed to see corn that would go more than seventy bushels to the acre." He believed this foretold a stable foundation for Mexico's future.[34]

Wallace returned to Washington at eight in the morning on September 10, 1946. Three hours later he reviewed with Truman a speech meant for a liberal rally at Madison Square Garden in New York City.

His days in the Truman administration were numbered—ten.

CHAPTER TWENTY-TWO

"THE WAY TO PEACE"

The events of mid-September 1946 were the stuff of high drama played out as farce.

Franklin Roosevelt over the years had given little attention to Wallace's speech previews. Harry Truman, on the other hand, paid close heed, offering a running commentary while he read them. On the occasion of the Madison Square Garden speech, Wallace brought along duplicate texts. He and Truman could read in tandem. The speech, entitled "The Way to Peace," was mainly about foreign policy. Wallace knew it might be controversial. "We went over it, page by page, together—and again and again he said, 'That's right,' 'Yes, that is what I believe.' "[1]

One portion of the text drew an especially positive response. Wallace proposed to say, "In this connection I want one thing clearly understood, I am neither anti-British nor pro-British—neither anti-Russian nor pro-Russian." The president expressed empathic agreement.

"Do you want me to indicate that you are for this attitude?" Wallace asked. "Yes," Truman answered. Wallace penciled in a line and read it to the president: "And just two days ago, when President Truman read those words, he said they represented the policy of his Administration."[2]

It wasn't clear how Truman could square his support for Wallace's view with those of Secretary of State James Byrnes, then at the peace conference in Paris. Wallace could only assume that Truman understood what he was reading and, in his heart, approved.

"He gave every indication of adopting my complete attitude and was so eager that it be known as his complete attitude that he wanted a statement to that effect included in the speech," Wallace commented in his oral history. ". . . You wonder if Truman actually knew what Byrnes was doing."*3

Truman's expressed agreement with Wallace was not just for private consumption. On the day the speech was to be delivered, mimeographed copies of it were given to reporters and Truman was asked about it at his afternoon press conference. William Mylander of the *Des Moines Register* pointed out the sentence claiming "these words . . . represented the policy of this Administration."

"That is correct," Truman answered crisply.

"My question is, does that apply just for that paragraph or for the whole speech," Mylander asked.

"I approved the whole speech," Truman responded.4

Another reporter pressed further. "Mr. President, do you regard Wallace's speech as a departure from Byrnes' policy?"

"I do not," said Truman. "They are exactly in line."5

Truman may have seen no conflict, but reporters did. So did Undersecretary of State Will Clayton, who was running the State Department in Byrnes's absence. Clayton obtained a copy of the speech at about 6 P.M., only hours before its delivery time and frantically called White House Press Secretary Charles Ross, seeking to have it changed.

Undersecretary of the Navy John L. Sullivan also called Ross and warned the speech would force the president to choose between Byrnes and Wallace. But the president was due to play poker at Clark Clifford's home, and Ross would not disturb him. The speech would be delivered as it was.

But it wasn't. Wallace arrived at Madison Square Garden to find several of the rally's organizers in a state of alarm because the speech was altogether too evenhanded. Wallace intended to make some remarks critical of Russia, and it was feared the left-wing audience would react negatively. Wallace intended to say, for example, "We may not like what Russia is doing in Eastern Europe. Her type of land reform, industrial expropriation, and suppression of basic liberties offends the great majority of the people of the United States."6

Hannah Dorner, head of the Independent Citizens Committee of the Arts, Sciences, and Professions' office in New York City, insisted on changes. Wallace agreed to trim certain remarks critical of the Soviet Union. He later told reporters he had shortened the speech because of broadcast time constraints, but he privately admitted this was untrue.

*Four days earlier Byrnes had delivered a speech in Stuttgart, Germany, highly critical of Russia's actions in its zone of occupation—the area later known as East Germany—and calling for steps to allow "the German economy to function as an economic unit."

Wallace's changes were not enough to satisfy the crowd, however. Warmed to a fever pitch by a pro-Russia speech delivered by Senator Claude Pepper, the audience was in no mood to hear even mild criticism. Wallace was booed and hissed at several points, including his reference to Truman's name.

Wallace made several extemporaneous comments in response to the boo-ing. Of his off-the-cuff remarks, there is no exact record. But there was no doubt about the bulk of his speech, which followed the prepared text. He later published the full text in booklet form, including the excised portions critical of the Soviet Union. In substance it differed little from things he had been saying for several years. Among his remarks were these:

> During the past year or so, the significance of peace has been increased im-measurably by the atom bomb, guided missiles, and airplanes which soon will travel as fast as sound. Make no mistake about it—another war would hurt the United States many times as much as the last war. . . . He who trusts in the atom bomb will sooner or later perish by the atom bomb—or something worse.
>
> I say this as one who steadfastly backed preparedness throughout the thirties. We have no use for namby-pamby pacifism. But we must realize that modern inventions have now made peace the most enticing thing in the world—and we should be willing to pay a just price for peace. . . .
>
> The price of peace—for us and for every nation in the world—is the price of giving up prejudice, hatred, fear and ignorance. . . .
>
> Hatred breeds hatred. The doctrine of racial superiority produces a de-sire to get even on the part of its victims. If we are to work for peace in the rest of the world, we here in the United States must eliminate racism from our unions, our business organizations, our educational institutions, and our employment practices. Merit alone must be the measure of men.[7]

Economic nationalism and political isolationism were "as anachronistic as the dodo," he declared. A military alliance with the British was not the answer, ei-ther. "Make no mistake about it—the British imperialistic policy in the Near East alone, combined with Russian retaliation, would lead the United States straight to war unless we have a clearly defined and realistic policy of our own."

There followed a portion of the speech that Wallace soon regretted because he considered it open to misinterpretation:

> We most earnestly want peace with Russia—but we want to be met halfway. We want cooperation. . . .
>
> For her part, Russia can retain our respect by cooperating with the United Nations in a spirit of open-minded and flexible give-and-take.

The real peace treaty we need now is between the United States and Russia. On our part, we should recognize that we have no more business in the political affairs of Eastern Europe than Russia has in the political affairs of Latin America, Western Europe and the United States.[8]

Wallace thought the section reflected geopolitical reality. But it was interpreted by some as a repudiation of his own "one world" principles. Critics said he was endorsing old-fashioned "spheres of influence," which Wallace denied. What he had in mind, he said, was not spheres of influence but something like Franklin Roosevelt's "Good Neighbor Policy," which "built a workable system of regional internationalism that fully protected the sovereign rights of every nation—a system of multi-lateral action that immeasurable strengthened the whole world order."

Wallace closed by calling peace the "basic issue" facing voters in the coming midterm elections and in the presidential race two years distant. "How we meet this issue will determine whether we will live not in 'one world' or 'two worlds'—but whether we live at all."[9]

As he left the platform, the *New York Times* reporter James Haggerty asked whether he was surprised by the boos and hisses. "It was to be expected," Wallace replied. "I was following a straight American line."[10]

The speech got poor reviews. Publications ranging from the Communist Party's *Daily Worker* to the internationalist *New York Times* and the isolationist *Chicago Tribune* found something in it to criticize. Foreign correspondents, following the lead of *New York Times*'s James Reston, widely analyzed the speech as a shift in administration policy.

From Paris, Byrnes signaled his anger and dismay. Republican senator Arthur Vandenberg, with Byrnes at the peace conference along with Democratic senator Tom Connally, issued a statement saying Wallace had damaged "American unity" at the peace conference. "We [Republicans] can only cooperate with one Secretary of State at a time," declared the senator.[11]

Acting Secretary of State Will Clayton publicly said he did not understand how Truman could have authorized such a speech. Republican Robert Taft delivered a blistering attack on the floor of the Senate accusing Truman of caving in to his party's radical wing.

On Saturday, September 14, Truman sought refuge in a brief statement he read to reporters. There had been a "natural misunderstanding" concerning the remarks he had made at a press conference two days earlier, Truman admitted. His answer to the question concerning approval of the speech "did not convey the thought that I had intended it to convey," he said. "It was my intention to express the thought that I approved the right of the Secretary of Commerce to deliver the speech. I did not intend to indicate that I approved the speech as constituting a statement of the foreign policy of this country." Truman took no questions and left the room.[12]

That by no means put the matter to rest. Truman succeeded mainly in making himself look foolish. Newspapers pelted the White House with editorials questioning his competence and honesty. Wallace reached the same conclusion in his diffident way. "It was obvious from his statement he'd been lying, but I guess I got used to that kind of thing. Roosevelt had done that kind of thing, why shouldn't Truman?" Wallace asked in his oral history. ". . . There's a saying in the metrical version of the psalms, 'Put no trust in earthly princes,' a very profound and important piece of wisdom."[13]

Monday, September 16, began on a conciliatory note. Wallace called Truman and told him he "had done the only thing he could have done" in his disavowal two days earlier. Truman suggested they meet and see what they could do "without cutting the ground out from under Byrnes." He added, "I don't want to hurt anyone—either you or Byrnes."[14]

Shortly thereafter, however, Wallace issued a public statement that was anything but conciliatory. "I stand upon my New York speech," he said. ". . . I intend to continue my efforts for a just and lasting peace and I shall within the near future speak on this subject again."[15]

Wallace's statement threw Byrnes into a rage. From Paris he angrily cabled Truman, "If it is not possible for you, for any reason, to keep Mr. Wallace, as a member of your cabinet, from speaking on foreign affairs, it would be a grave mistake from every point of view for me to continue in office, even temporarily."[16]

Things sped downhill. On September 17 Press Secretary Charlie Ross learned that the columnist Drew Pearson had obtained a copy of Wallace's long private July 23 letter to Truman on Soviet-American relations and planned to begin printing portions of it the following day. Ross called Wallace to discuss the matter. Wallace tried to determine who leaked the letter and, after talking with Harold Young, concluded it had been given to Pearson by Joel Fisher, a Commerce Department aide who enjoyed currying favor with columnists.

Ross decided the best course was for Wallace to release the whole letter to the entire press corps so as to undercut the interpretation Pearson might put on it. Wallace put his aides to work on it. Later in the afternoon, having consulted with Truman, Ross called back and said the letter should not be given out.

It was too late. The Commerce Department had already released the letter. Truman, Pearson, and Byrnes were all livid. Wallace was none too happy himself.

While Washington swirled in confusion and recrimination, Wallace went to have tea with Supreme Court Justice Hugo Black. Nothing Black mentioned induced calm. "He said the only trouble with my speech was that it didn't go far enough," Wallace wrote in his diary. "He said I ought not to have put in any qualifications. . . . He said that of course my criticisms of Russia were well-founded but you couldn't confuse people by presenting both sides of the case. He said the one thing we had to keep in mind was that the Army and the State Department were carrying us into war with Russia just as fast as they could."[17]

Black had served in the Senate with Truman. What was he like? Wallace asked. Truman always voted right, said Black, and he was honest. "Then he went on and said the trouble with Truman was that he was a man with no background or understanding. He has no fundamental philosophy and very little knowledge of history. Because of his lack of background, Black thought it was a tragedy that Truman should be president."[18]

With Black's words still fresh in mind, Wallace met with Truman on September 18, armed with a tally of letters reacting to the Madison Square Garden speech. Of the 1,150 letters received at the Commerce Department, 950 were favorable. Wallace thought the ratio astounding, but Truman was in no mood to be impressed. The president was feeling a bit sorry for himself. He had spent more sleepless nights than at any time since the convention, Truman said, and Jimmie Byrnes had been "giving him hell" ever since Wallace spoke.

Wallace stood by the content of his speech. People were afraid the get-tough-with-Russia policy was leading to war, he said. "You yourself as Harry Truman really believed in my speech," he added, but people were beginning to doubt that the president was actually progressive. The crowd had booed the mention of Truman's name, Wallace noted. "But," Truman responded, "Jimmie Byrnes says I am pulling the rug out from under him. I must ask you not to make any more speeches touching on foreign policy. We must present a united front abroad."[19]

Truman flatly declared he did not have a get-tough policy. In a remarkable comment he said he liked Stalin personally and thought "he could do business face to face" with him. Unfortunately Stalin would not come to the United States. Equally remarkable, Truman promised he would ask for a loan for Russia as soon as the peace treaties were signed. Wallace was "dumbfounded." He replied to Truman, "Do you think for a moment that you can get a loan of this sort through Congress? I don't think you know your congress."[20]

As always, the atmosphere between them was "cordial and direct," Wallace observed. "We never had an unkind word." But Truman stuck by his foreign affairs embargo. Wallace argued the point. Elections were only six weeks away. Peace was an important issue. He needed to clear up the misunderstanding he had created about "spheres of influence" in his New York speech, he added. He could issue a disclaimer that he was speaking only for himself.[21]

"[I] made the point very strongly with Truman that I was gravely concerned with the probability that we were now taking actions which would lead to Russia taking reprisals against us twenty or thirty years hence, when Russia would be stronger than we," Wallace noted in his diary. The Russian population was increasing faster, and the country was more willing to endure hardships. Current U.S. tactics, he added, "may not lead to war now for the simple reason that the Russians are weak—but they will leave scars that can lead to war readily twenty or thirty years hence if the world situation is bad."

Wallace added bluntly, "I want to go on record now, for the sake of my children and grandchildren and great-grandchildren, as indicating if there is a war with Russia the criminals will be those who beat the tom-toms for war in 1946."

Truman "would have none of it," Wallace wrote in his diary. "I must quit talking about foreign affairs."[22]

At length, and very reluctantly, Wallace agreed. Press Secretary Charles Ross entered the discussion, and the three men hammered out a brief statement for reporters: "The President and the Secretary of Commerce had a detailed and friendly discussion after which the Secretary reached the conclusion that he would make no public statements or speeches until the Foreign Ministers Conference in Paris is concluded."

Ross asked, "What happens next October 15 or 20 when the conference is over? We are just postponing a decision."

"We can take that up later," Truman replied.

Outside the White House a reporter asked whether he was staying in the cabinet. "Yes, I am, Wallace replied.[23]

But not for long.

In his diary the following day, Truman summed up his reaction to the meeting:

Mr. Wallace spent two and one half hours talking to me yesterday. I am not sure he is as fundamentally sound intellectually as I had thought. He advised me that I should be far to the "left" when Congress is not in session and should move more to the "right" when Congress is on hand and in session. . . . He is a pacifist one hundred percent. He wants to disband our armed forces, give Russia our atomic secrets and trust a bunch of adventurers in the Kremlin Politboro. I do not understand a "dreamer" like that. The German-American Bund under Fritz Kuhn was not half so dangerous. The Reds, phonies and the "parlor pinks" seem to be banded together and are becoming a national danger.[24]

At 9:30 A.M. on Friday, September 20, 1946, Wallace was in his office reading a journal on new developments in chicken breeding when an aide brought
in a letter from President Truman. In harsh language the president demanded
Wallace's resignation. Cabell Phillips, a historian friendly to Truman, said the
letter was "intemperate and bitter." Wallace himself described it as being "of
a low level" but not profane.[25]

Wallace reached for the phone and called Truman directly. "You don't
want this thing out," he told Truman. The president agreed. "No, I'll send a
man over to pick it up," he said. Truman destroyed the letter, and no copy
of it remains; Wallace never said anything else about its contents. Truman
recognized that Wallace had made a genuinely magnanimous gesture. "He
was so nice about it I almost backed out," the president wrote his mother and
sister.[26]

There was no backing out, however. Wallace hung up the phone and
penned his letter, which read in its entirety,

Dear Harry:

As you requested, here is my resignation. I shall continue to fight for
peace. I am sure that you approve and will join me in that great endeavor.

Respectfully yours,
Henry A. Wallace[27]

Then he picked up the journal he had been reading and finished the article on chickens.

An hour after Truman received Wallace's resignation, he called a press conference and read a statement. It said in part,

The people of the United States may disagree freely and publicly on any
question, including that of foreign policy, but the Government of the
United States must stand as a unit in its relation with the rest of the world.

I have today asked Mr. Wallace to resign from the Cabinet. It had become clear that between his views on foreign policy and those of the
Administration—the latter being shared, I am confident, by the great body
of our citizens—there was a fundamental conflict. We could not permit
this conflict to jeopardize our position in relation to other countries. I
deeply regret the breaking of a long and pleasant official association, but I
am sure Mr. Wallace will be happier in the exercise of his right to present

his views as a private citizen. I am confirmed in this belief by a very friendly conversation I had with Mr. Wallace on the telephone this morning.[28]

Wallace responded that evening with a statement broadcast from his apartment at the Wardman Park. Flanked by Ilo, his daughter, Jean, and his poodle, Brutus, Wallace said,

> Winning the peace is more important than high public office. It is more important than any consideration of party politics.
> The success or failure of our foreign policy will mean the difference between life and death for our children and our grandchildren. It will mean the difference between the life and death of our civilization. It may mean the difference between the existence and the extinction of Man and of the world. It is therefore of supreme importance, and we should every one of us regard it as a holy duty to join the fight for winning the peace. I, for my part, firmly believe there is nothing more important that I can do than work in the cause of peace.[29]

He had no regrets about leaving government, or about the way in which it came about. "I always had in my mind that if I were going to get out of the cabinet I should get out on the peace issue," he later said. "Ever since Morgenthau and Ickes left, I figured it was only a question of months until I'd be getting out. I did want to get out on a basis which would help bring about an understanding between the United States and Russia. I wanted to dramatize peace."*[30]

In his oral history Wallace offered a detached analysis of Truman's decision to fire him:

> Truman may have been convinced politically that the cost of breaking with Byrnes was greater than the cost of breaking with me. I think that was probably the way it shaped up in his mind. I think he'd lost his personal

---

*There remained a contentious piece of unfinished business on Wallace's schedule. Bernard M. Baruch, who was serving as U.S. representative to the United Nations Atomic Energy Commission, felt Wallace had mischaracterized the U.S. position of international control of atomic energy. Baruch insisted they meet to discuss the matter. Partly at the urging of Eleanor Roosevelt, Wallace agreed to the meeting, which took place two days after he was fired.

Out of the meeting came an angry public exchange of denunciations and charges of bad faith between Wallace and Baruch. Wallace had the last word on October 3 in a lengthy statement published by the *New York Times* in which he accused Baruch of being "stubborn and inflexible" and "unable to distinguish the fundamental critical issues from their purely procedural aspects."

The two men never saw one another again, and, as Wallace predicted, the UN negotiations ended in stalemate, and the "frantic atomic armaments race" proceeded unfettered.

esteem for Byrnes at this time, but the combination of Vandenberg and Byrnes and Connally—two of them senators and one of them a former senator and all three of them known to Truman for many years—was just too much for him. So he swung over to their point of view. He didn't really want to do it but he was forced to do it.[31]

Wallace was correct on one point: Truman had lost confidence in Byrnes. Early in 1947 the president accepted Byrnes's resignation and replaced him with General George C. Marshall.

Whatever Truman's reasoning, many of Wallace's friends thought his response was remarkably restrained in light of his shabby treatment over the preceding ten days. But magnanimity was the order of the day. Wallace promised Bob Hannegan not to harm the Democratic Party's chances in the upcoming elections and even agreed to make campaign appearances.

Truman made his own show of generosity by sending his wife and daughter to attend the wedding of Wallace's daughter, Jean, a few days later. Truman himself did not attend, only because the wedding was held at a hotel where service workers were on strike, and he did not want to cross a picket line.

But gestures could not disguise reality. Wallace's firing exposed a rift in the Democratic Party, between politics and philosophy, deftly concealed for more than a decade by Franklin Roosevelt.

Wallace was deluged by some eight thousand letters and telegrams lamenting his dismissal. Messages came from world-famous artists and intellectuals and from ordinary citizens who simply admired a man of principle. The renowned deaf and blind humanitarian Hellen Keller wrote to Wallace in the rhetoric uniquely hers: "Rejoicing I watch you faring forth on a renewed pilgrimage looking not downward to ignoble acquiescence or around at fugitive expediency, but upward to mind-quickening statecraft and a life-saving peace for all lands." Albert Einstein was more direct: "Your courageous intervention deserves the gratitude of all of us who observe the present attitude of our government with grave concern."[32]

His old friend Donald Murphy, editor of *Wallaces' Farmer*, quoted from the Bible: "Who knows but thou art come into the kingdom for such a time as this." The writer Thomas Mann and his family wired Wallace, "Like millions of good Americans we not only share your views on foreign policy but are deeply impressed with your courage and consistency in defending them."[33]

The outpouring of admiration moved even the notoriously impersonal Wallace. He was convinced the sentiment conveyed by the letters was genuine and widespread. To many of those who wrote him, he responded along the lines of a paragraph he wrote to the columnist Max Lerner: "After recent events I am, in retrospect, very happy. The cause of peace has been strengthened. The chance of war has been lessened. I don't think I could have bought more with less no matter how hard I tried."[34]

Among the letters was a check for $10,000 from Anita McCormick Blaine, daughter of Cyrus McCormick, inventory of the mechanical reaper, and heiress to the International Harvester Company fortune. "You have put yourself upon the altar of the good of all mankind," she said. "You have become a symbol of all the Atlantic Charter contains and of more to come. You will lead us."[35]

Wallace was astonished. He asked Harold Young to put the money in trust and establish a system of accounts until its use could be determined.

Public response was heartening too. Editorialists had a field day with Truman's clumsy handling of the affair. "The New Deal as a driving force is dead within the Truman administration," said the *Chicago Sun*. One cartoon depicted a beat-up Wallace in the White House driveway, while Truman and his gang shook their fists at him and shouted "Peacemonger!" Claude Pepper attacked Truman so savagely that he was stricken from the Democratic Party's speakers list. And a conference of progressives, organized by the CIO, the NAACP, the National Farmers Union, and other liberal organizations, adopted a resolution urging Wallace, "Visit us at every crossroads in America [and] carry on with the confidence that you have the support of the millions upon millions who believe in the program of Franklin Roosevelt."[36]

Truman and his advisers closed ranks and admitted no error. "Well I had to fire Henry today," Truman wrote his mother and sister, adding, "The crackpots are having conniption fits." To underscore his intention to pursue a get-tough policy, he replaced Wallace as commerce secretary with Averell Harriman, the hard-line U.S. ambassador to Britain and former ambassador to Russia.[37]

Among Wallace's other sins, Truman wrote to a friend, he was not a political team player. "I don't know what Harriman's program will be but I hope it will reverse that situation." Simultaneously Truman issued an executive order forbidding any member of the executive branch from making public criticisms of U.S. foreign policy.[38]

Now came a whispered suggestion that would grow into a roar—about the "Americanism" of Wallace and his followers. Anonymous clean-cut men in gray suits, agents of J. Edgar Hoover's FBI, began to focus hard on Wallace and his movements, his mail and appointments, his associates and organizational ties. Almost everything was "Communist conspiracy" fodder.

In a note to the RFC head, George Allen, in late September, Hoover suggested Wallace had aided the Communists by getting himself fired. "I thought the President and you would be interested in knowing that national figures affiliated with the Communist Party and its front activities have expressed an opinion that the resignation of Mr. Wallace is a good move for them as it opens the issue of war with Byrnes and peace with Wallace."[39]

In the 1946 off-year elections, Americans delivered their verdict on Truman and his works. The vote was not about Wallace, although liberal disenchantment played a role, but about everything: labor union strife, inflation, price controls, housing shortages, cronyism, confusion, and communism. Even Truman's style, his penchant for playing poker and drinking bourbon and speaking rudely, took its toll. (Truman once referred to Wallace as a "cat bastard," although no one was certain what the term meant.) Truman's approval rating in the Gallup poll slid from 87 percent to 37 percent in one year.

Republicans seized the public mood with a masterly two-word slogan: "Had Enough?"

"Got enough meat?" asked one Republican orator. "Got enough houses? Got enough OPA? . . . Got enough strikes? . . . Got enough communism?" The last of these hit paydirt, especially in heavily Catholic areas. Senator Robert Taft of Ohio accused Truman of seeking a Congress "dominated by a policy of appeasing the Russians abroad and of fostering Communism at home."[40]

The archibishop of New York, Francis Cardinal Spellman, wrote in a magazine article shortly before the election that "only the bat-blind can fail to be aware of the Communist invasion of our country." The U.S. Chamber of Commerce weighed in with a widely distributed report entitled "Communist Infiltration in the United States." J. Edgar Hoover fanned the flames before the American Legion, charging that at least 100,000 Communists were loose in the nation's newspapers, movie studios, radio stations, "some churches, schools, colleges and even fraternal orders."[41]

The campaign wreaked disaster on the Democratic Party. Voters gave Republicans control of both houses of Congress for the first time since 1928. In New York, Governor Thomas E. Dewey rolled to reelection with a whopping 680,000-vote plurality. Two of the best-known anti-Communist crusaders, Richard M. Nixon and Joseph McCarthy, made their debut. Nixon, fresh out of wartime service in the navy, defeated the Democratic congressman Jerry Voorhis by linking him to the "Moscow-[CIO] PAC-Henry Wallace line."[42]

Probably no president could have stemmed the Republican tide, but the midterm elections of 1946 were nevertheless widely viewed as a repudiation of Harry Truman. Millions of Americans now saw him as a hapless accidental president soon to be turned out of office. J. William Fulbright, a young Democratic congressman from Arkansas, said he should appoint Republic senator Arthur Vandenberg secretary of state and resign from the presidency. The liberal *New York Post* said Truman was probably too incompetent to do even that right.

Wallace thought that Truman had to turn to the left if he hoped to survive. "As a result of this election the Democratic Party will either become more progressive or it will die. I do not expect it to die."[43]

❦

A short time after Wallace was fired from the cabinet, a handsome young man with a big idea came to see him at the Wardman Park. Michael Straight was thirty years old, a graduate of Cambridge University, and fresh out of wartime service as a flight instructor to French pilots. He was also publisher of the *New Republic*, thanks to his mother, who owned it.*

Founded in 1914 by a group of progressive thinkers—including Walter Lippmann, editor Herbert Croly, Professor Felix Frankfurter, the financier Willard Straight (Michael's father), and others—the *New Republic* was high-minded and influential. Contributions by some of the century's best-known intellectuals—John Maynard Keynes, Rebecca West, George Bernard Shaw, H. L. Mencken, Edmund Wilson, John Dos Passos, F. Scott Fitzgerald, Thomas Wolfe, Henry Miller, Langston Hughes—had appeared in its pages.

But the magazine was also small and unprofitable. Its paid circulation in the fall of 1946 was not much more than 36,000 a week. Michael Straight wanted to double that number, at least. His strategy was to broaden its coverage of issues, hire bright new writers, introduce artwork to its gray pages, and otherwise give the *New Republic* mass appeal. He envisioned its becoming a sort of "liberal *Time* magazine."[44]

The key to Straight's grand plan was to persuade Wallace to become the journal's editor. As Straight saw it, the former vice president was the nation's most famous liberal, he had an extensive journalistic background, and he was out of a job.

The young publisher was greeted by Ilo and Brutus and shown to a balcony overlooking Rock Creek Park, where Wallace and Harold Young were going over a huge stack of letters and telegrams. Among them were lucrative

---

*As a Cambridge undergraduate during the 1930s, Straight became part of a student Communist movement, which he believed was the most effective way of opposing Nazism. His associates included Kim Philby and Guy Burgess, who were later involved in a celebrated postwar Soviet spy ring. Straight returned to the United States in 1938 no longer a Communist, but he maintained silence about his past out of loyalty to his friends. During the Cold War, he disclosed his secret to the FBI in an effort to come to terms with his conscience. The subsequent investigation uncovered the activities of the secret Soviet agent Anthony Blunt and caused a major scandal in Britain.

Straight's activities as a student were still unknown during the time of Wallace's association with the *New Republic*.

job offers, book deals, speaking proposals, and a plea from the publisher of *Wallaces' Farmer* to return as editor.

Straight moved right into his case. Wallace, quiet and unkempt, stared at his shoes. Young, "a meaty Texan," in Straight's words, looked unhappy. "To Harold Young, *The New Republic* was a prospect about as inviting as exile in Siberia," Straight wrote in his memoirs.[45]

But Wallace was drawn to the idea. He observed that in "moments of personal crisis, his father and grandfather had turned to publishing," Straight recalled. Wallace savored the idea of having an office in New York City, close to his farm at South Salem. Moreover, the *New Republic* would offer a credible platform for his views on public issues.[46]

A few days later Wallace and Straight wrote out a nine-point agreement on a "grubby sheet of paper" making Wallace editor of the *New Republic* at a salary of $15,000 a year, equal to his salary as a cabinet officer, plus an expense account of $5,000. Money was not really an issue for Wallace. He and Ilo owned 40 percent of Pioneer Hi-Bred and earned dividends of more than $150,000 in 1946.

Wallace and Straight would share editorial responsibility and each have total freedom to express their views. Wallace could accept any speaking engagements he wished. He would take up his duties as of December 16, 1946. It was, he recalled, a "very loose arrangement."*

The *New Republic* announced Wallace's appointment in its October 21 issue with a front-page statement by Wallace himself. "I shall have the opportunity of saying exactly what I think at a time when a bi-partisan block mouthing the phrase 'One World' is really driving the world into two armed camps," he wrote. "As editor of *The New Republic* I shall do everything I can to rouse the American people, the British people, the French people, the Russian people and in fact the liberally-minded people of the whole world, to the need of stopping this dangerous armament race."[47]

Simultaneously Wallace opened an office at 2500 Q Street in Washington to look after his political affairs. The office, run by Harold Young and a small staff of paid and volunteer helpers, served as a clearinghouse for his speaking engagements and mail.

Anita McCormick Blaine's $10,000 gift was the nest egg for the political office. The money would be used for wide distribution of his July 23 letter to

---

*Wallace sent a friendly telegram to Dante M. Pierce, publisher of *Wallaces' Farmer*, notifying him of the decision to join the *New Republic*. "Knowing you as I do, I am sure you will wish me godspeed in the effort," Wallace said.

Pierce's responded grumpily. "He has made his choice," Pierce told the *Des Moines Register*. Pierce added that Wallace's name would be removed immediately from the masthead of *Wallaces' Farmer*, where he had been listed as "editor on leave" since 1933.

Truman on U.S.-Soviet relations, numerous speaking engagements, with special emphasis on university appearances, and a conference of "about one hundred sincere leaders . . . anxious to take concerted action for peace."[48]

Establishment of the Washington office raised a problem that would bedevil Michael Straight and the *New Republic* for the next year and a half. One way or another Wallace meant to make "peace" the central issue of the 1948 campaign. Straight agreed with Wallace's view, but he felt his journal's independence would be damaged if Wallace used it as a springboard for his own ambitions.

Those ambitions were anything but clear, as became apparent in his first editor's piece for the *New Republic*. "My job as editor of *The New Republic* is to help organize a progressive America," he began. "The American people have rejected, as they will always reject, a Democratic party that is not militantly progressive. . . . Of course, we need organization. The primary effort of progressives may be to rebuild the Democratic party as a liberal party. But we are the captives of no party. If the Democratic party is incapable of change, we shall strike out along other lines."[49]

Michael Straight took a deep breath and settled in for a bumpy ride.

Two weeks later Wallace spoke at a conference of liberals at the Hotel Commodore in New York. The meeting had been organized to meld two large, but debt-ridden, progressive organizations: the National Citizens Political Action Committee (NCPAC), an offshoot of the labor-affiliated CIO-PAC; and the Independent Citizens Committee of the Arts, Sciences, and Professions (ICCASP), a celebrity-packed group founded by the sculptor Jo Davidson.

The merger owed much to the death earlier in 1946 of Sidney Hillman, who dominated NCPAC, and the resignation in November of Harold Ickes as head of ICCASP. Ickes quit ostensibly over policy differences but really because he hadn't been paid his $25,000-a-year salary for months. With Hillman and Ickes out of the way, the two progressive organizations could join.

Wallace came out fighting. One could all but feel the earth shake underneath the Truman administration regulars. "We must make it clear to the administration that we, as progressives, would prefer the election of an out-and-out reactionary like Taft in 1948, to a luke-warm liberal. We want this to be a genuine two-party country and not a country operated by a fake one-party system under the guise of a bi-partisan bloc." He added, in words more brave than politic,

> We shall hold firmly to the American theme of peace, prosperity and freedom and shall repel all the attacks of the plutocrats and monopolists

who will try to brand us as reds. If it is traitorous to believe in peace, we are traitors. If it is communistic to believe in prosperity for all, we are communists. If it is red-baiting to fight for free speech and real freedom of the press, we are red-baiters. If it is un-American to believe in freedom from monopolistic dictation, we are un-American. I say that we are more American than the neo-Fascists who attack us. I say on with the fight![50]

A day later the two organizations joined to form the Progressive Citizens of American (PCA), open to anyone—"all progressive men and women in our nation, regardless of race, creed, color, national origin, or political affiliations"—who wanted to pay three dollars a year in dues. Roughly translated, this meant the PCA would admit Communists.[51]

Jo Davidson and radio commentator Dr. Frank Kingdon were elected co-chairmen. Labor leaders Phil Murray and A. F. Whitney agreed to serve as vice chairmen, although they did not attend the conference. C. B. "Beanie" Baldwin and Hannah Dorner became executive vice presidents until May 1947, when Dorner would resign and Baldwin assume day-to-day operations. Wallace himself did not join the PCA, because he felt that as editor of the *New Republic* he should not be affiliated with one particular group.

Wallace had spoken from the heart. He wrote the PCA speech himself and never regretted having given it. Later, when it was falsely charged that the PCA was covertly organized by pro-Russian Communists, Wallace would point to the speech as evidence to the contrary. "Those who put hatred of Russia first in all their feelings and actions do not believe in peace," he said. "We shall never be against anything simply because Russia is for it. Neither shall we ever be for anything simply because Russia is for it. We shall hold firmly to the American theme of peace, prosperity and freedom. . . ."[52]

It was a principled position but politically explosive.

Wallace couldn't see how widely he would be thought the PCA's true leader. And any organization that would admit Communists was bound to leave a mark on its leaders. To believe otherwise was naive. Nor did Wallace fully grasp the aims of the PCA's leaders. Wallace saw it as a tool to push Truman to the left; Baldwin and others saw it as a nascent political party, one ready to compete in the 1948 election with Henry Wallace as its candidate.

Most important, Wallace didn't see that, far from uniting progressives under a single effective banner, the formation of the PCA would lead to a left-wing fissure, with dire consequences for liberals generally and Wallace in particular.

The liberal crack-up began within days. On January 4, 1947, some 150 prominent liberals, many of them veterans of the New Deal, gathered in Washington under the sponsorship of the Union for Democratic Action to chart a separate course. It was an invitational affair that included such figures as theologian Reinhold Niebuhr; autoworkers leader Walter Reuther; NAACP head Walter White; Louisville mayor Wilson Wyatt; Minneapolis mayor Hubert Humphrey; former Office of Price Administration chief Leon Henderson; columnist Stewart Alsop; lawyer Paul Porter; and Harvard professors Arthur Schlesinger Jr. and John Kenneth Galbraith. Their patron saint, Eleanor Roosevelt, addressed the group at a testimonial dinner on the eve of the meetings.

Henry Wallace was not invited.

Out of this meeting was born the Americans for Democratic Action, which shared many PCA goals on economic policy and civil rights but parted company on the issue of communism. "We reject any association with Communism or sympathizers with communism in the United States as completely as we reject any association with Fascists or their sympathizers," said a statement issued at the close of the conference. A six-point declaration of principles supported Truman's foreign policy generally and the "Baruch Plan" for international control of atomic energy.[53]

Wallace was on the defensive. Communism or, more to the point, "anticommunism" had moved to the center of liberal debate. On January 10 Wallace appeared on *Meet the Press* and was peppered with questions about Communist participation in the PCA. "If you allow that little thing to dominate your mind, it means that you have become a red-baiter, a person who wants to sic the F.B.I. onto your neighbor; it interferes with everything you want to do," Wallace said.[54]

Liberal journals—except for the *New Republic*—began to portray the PCA-ADA split as a contest between Henry Wallace and Eleanor Roosevelt. Wallace tried to calm such talk. He did not belong to either organization, and neither did the former first lady. The latter publicly restated her support for the ADA, saying she had not joined it, only because she was a member of the U.S. delegation to the United Nations.

In February came another blow. Phil Murray withdrew his support of the PCA and recommended all leaders of CIO labor unions drop their affiliation with both organizations. The CIO's executive board followed with a formal ban in March.

Wallace still hoped for a consolidated liberal front. Perhaps even the Truman administration's foreign policy would improve. In a warm letter congratulating the new secretary of state, George C. Marshall, Wallace set out his vision for improved international relations in terms that presaged the Marshall Plan:

> In almost every nation that has suffered heavily in this war, men and women are desperately trying to alter the old order of things because the old order has brought them poverty, disaster and war. . . .

We have abandoned, almost by default, the sponsorship of these changes to Russia. We have permitted the Russians to parade themselves before all the colonial peoples of the world as the only enemy of "imperialism." Almost without a battle we have yielded to the Russians the loyalty of millions of workers and peasants because they believe the Russians and not ourselves are their only guarantors against hunger and war. We cannot permit this to go on or we shall find our only allies are the tired men who have lost the faith of their own people, the same men whom you characterized as "corrupt" and "reactionary" in China.[55]

Whatever hope Wallace held out for comity with his fellow liberals or other nations died on March 12, 1947. On that day Truman formally committed his administration to the "containment" policy advanced earlier by George Kennan, Averell Harriman, and Winston Churchill. Specifically, Truman called upon Congress to appropriate $400 million in aid to Greece and Turkey in order to block a Communist takeover.

"If Greece should fall under the control of an armed minority, the effect upon its neighbor, Turkey, would be immediate and serious," Truman declared. "Confusion and disorder might well spread throughout the entire Middle East. . . . Collapse of free institutions would be disastrous not only for them but for the world. . . . We must take immediate and resolute action."[56]

Then, in words that framed the Truman Doctrine, the president added, "I believe that it must be the policy of the United States to support free peoples who are resisting attempted subjugation by armed minorities or by outside pressures."

Wallace's response, swift and prophetic, came the next day in a long address on NBC radio. "Fellow Americans, it is not a Greek crisis that we face, it is an American crisis. It is a crisis of the American spirit," he said. "That which I feared when I wrote President Truman last July has come upon us."

> Yesterday President Truman, in the name of democracy and humanitarianism, proposed a military lend-lease program. He proposed a loan of $400 million to Greece and Turkey as a down payment on an unlimited expenditure aimed at opposing communist expansion. He proposed, in effect, that America police Russia's every border. There is no regime too reactionary for us provided it stands in Russia's expansionist path. There is no country too remote to serve as the scene of a contest which may widen until it becomes a world war.[57]

Humanitarian aid to Greece was warranted, Wallace said, as was aid to many other war-ravaged countries. But military assistance to repressive regimes, he added, was a "hopeless task" that had bankrupted Britain and would ruin the United States.

I say that this policy is utterly futile. No people can be bought. America cannot afford to spend billions and billions of dollars for unproductive purposes. The world is hungry and insecure, and peoples of all lands demand change. American loans for military purposes won't stop them. President Truman cannot stop change in the world any more than he can prevent the tide from coming in or the sun from setting. But once America stands for opposition to change, we are lost. America will become the most hated nation in the world. . . .

I certainly don't want to see communism spread. I predict that Truman's policy will spread communism in Europe and Asia. You can't fight something with nothing. When Truman offers unconditional aid to King George of Greece, he is acting as the best salesman communism ever had.

Financial preparations for war would lead quickly to a warlike mentality in America, Wallace predicted. "[Civil] liberties will be restricted; standards of living will be forced downward; families will be divided against each other; none of the values that we hold worth fighting for will be secure."[58]

The proper way to combat communism, Wallace concluded, was "by what William James called 'the replacing power of the higher affection.' In other words, we must give the common man all over the world something better than communism. I believe we have something better than communism here in America. But President Truman has not spoken for the American ideal."[59]

The first of Wallace's many predictions came true within days. On March 21 Truman issued an executive order establishing a "loyalty" program for all federal workers. Government loyalty boards, operating in secret, were given power to try and dismiss any worker who belonged to an organization deemed subversive by the attorney general.

The Progressive Citizens of America opposed the loyalty boards, as it had opposed military aid to Greece and Turkey. The Americans for Democratic Action supported Truman on both counts.

"On with the fight."[60]

CHAPTER TWENTY-THREE

"HAS AMERICA REALLY GONE CRAZY?"

❦

On the last day of March 1947, the Progressive Citizens of America rallied in Madison Square Garden to heap scorn on Truman's plan for military aid to Greece and Turkey. Featured speakers were Harvard astronomy professor Harlow Shapley, Elliott Roosevelt, sculptor Jo Davidson, and comedian Zero Mostel. The event sold out in three days.

Henry Wallace spoke last. "If the United Nations is untested, let us test it," he declared. "If the United Nations lacks support, let us support it. If the United Nations is weak, let us strengthen it."

He also attacked Truman's "loyalty board" program. Just as the Truman Doctrine would "turn the world against America," Wallace said, the loyalty program would "turn Americans against each other." Truman's program would "threaten everything in America that is worth fighting for," he added. "Intolerance is aroused. Suspicion is engendered. Men of the highest integrity in public life are besmirched. The president's executive order creates a master index of public servants. From the janitor in the village post office to the cabinet member, they are to be sifted and tested and watched and appraised. Their past and present, the tattle and prattle of their neighbors, are all to be recorded."

Intolerance, Wallace declared, "has an insatiable appetite. Whom will its inquisition condemn if this drive continues? Every American who reads the wrong books; every American who thinks the wrong thoughts; every American who means liberty when he says liberty; every American who stands up for civil rights; every American who speaks out for one world;

every American who believed in Willkie; every American who supported Roosevelt. Only they who say shibboleth shall pass by the gate."[1]

Wallace soon saw his prophecy fulfilled—at least the part about "men of the highest integrity in public life" being besmirched. Shortly after his Madison Square Garden appearance, he went on a two-week, five-nation speaking tour in Europe, which ended in his being called everything from a traitor to a lunatic.

Controversy over the tour began long before Wallace left American soil. In January, when the trip was announced, seventy Americans styling themselves as "liberals"—including Henry and Clare Booth Luce, Lawrence Spivak of the right-wing *American Mercury* magazine, former Brain Truster A. A. Berle, and broadcaster H. V. Kaltenborn—cabled Foreign Minister Ernest Bevin of Britain to warn that support for Wallace came only from "a small minority of Communists, fellow-travelers and what we call here totalitarian liberals."[2]

Wallace's supporters countered with a scroll bearing "Greeting and Friendship to the Progressives of Great Britain," signed by 132 notables, including Rexford Guy Tugwell, Carl Van Doren, Aaron Copland, Fredric March, Gene Kelly, Hellen Keller, Thomas Mann, Dashiell Hammett, and Arthur Miller. "The success of the United Nations depends on the continued cooperation of Great Britain, Russia and the United States," it said.[3]

Nothing could calm the fears of Wallace's critics. Four days before Wallace departed, Navy Secretary James Forrestal suggested in a cabinet meeting that Wallace's passport be revoked in order to prevent him from speaking overseas. Harry Truman rejected the idea as too controversial.

In fact, Truman extended a sort of olive branch to Wallace at his next press conference, saying he did not want to read anyone out of the Democratic Party and adding that he expected Wallace would support him in 1948. Wallace's response was not conciliatory. "I shall be campaigning in 1948 with all my power," he said, "but I will be campaigning for the ideals of the free world and the men who best express these ideals. I hope, but I cannot guarantee, that they will be on the Democratic ticket."[4]

Wallace came to England on April 8 carrying a large basket of hatching eggs, rousing amusement among members of the British press. A cartoonist portrayed him as a great chicken sitting atop a giant egg labeled "British-American-Soviet Understanding." The eggs, from one of Wallace's chicken-breeding experiments, were given to an agricultural experiment station.

Although he dined privately with the U.S. ambassador to Britain, Lewis Douglas, and the British prime minister, Clement Attlee, nothing else suggested Wallace was in England as anything other than a private citizen. Douglas boycotted Wallace's appearances and later criticized his remarks.

Wallace was there at the invitation of Kingsley Martin, editor of the *New Statesman*, a British journal with much the same editorial viewpoint as the

New Republic. "The strength and weakness of Wallace is that he has no place at all in the underworld of manoeuvre and intrigue," said a *New Statesman* editorial greeting Wallace's arrival. "Behind him there is nothing but the ideas that animate him, and the confidence his personality inspires by the mingled appeal of his kindliness and courage."[5]

In Europe, Wallace said no more about Truman's foreign policy than he had been saying at home. The tone was set in his first major address, at Central Hall in London. "The world is devastated and hungry," Wallace declared. "The world is crying out, not for American guns and tanks to spread more hunger, but for American plows and machines to fulfill the promise of peace." He proposed a ten-year, $50 billion assistance program administered by the United Nations to help war-torn countries, including Russia.[6]

Later, in a BBC radio address heard by some fifteen million people, Wallace said, "A great national awakening has occurred in Asia and in other parts of the world which we used to think of only as colonies. This new nationalism will turn to communism and look to the Soviet Union as their only ally, if the United States declares that this is the American century of power politics rather than the Century of the Common Man."[7]

Wallace's remarks drew quick denunciation in the U.S. Congress, then in the midst of debating the $400 million loan to Greece and Turkey. "No American citizen has the moral right to conspire with foreign peoples in order to undermine and to weaken the hand of his country," said Senator James Eastland of Mississippi.[8]

Wallace responded from abroad. "If it is a crime to work for peace in Britain, I stand convicted." For good measure he took another swipe at Red-baiting and loyalty boards. "I believe that this witch hunt is part of a larger drive to destroy the belief, which I share, that capitalism and communism can resolve their conflicts without resort to war."[9]

Even Michael Straight, traveling with Wallace and helping draft his speeches, counseled moderation. Wallace would have none of it. By April 12 Congress was in an uproar. Senator J. William Fulbright said his speeches sounded as if they had been drafted in the Kremlin. Senator Arthur Vandenberg accused Wallace of making "treasonable utterances." The *New York Times* described it as "probably the most vehement congressional reaction in years to the pronouncements of a public figure."[10]

Wallace would not bend. "There is only one circumstance under which phrases like 'treasonable utterances' could be used to describe my speeches," he declared. "That would be when we were at war. . . . The fact that such words as 'treason' have been used in describing my trip indicates that, in the minds of the men who use these phrases, we actually are at war."[11]

British reaction was fairly restrained, but in the United States the response neared hysteria. Representatives J. Parnell Thomas and John Rankin, the chairman and ranking member of the House Un-American Activities Committee (HUAC), called for Wallace's prosecution under the 1799 Logan Act, which prohibited private citizens from attempting to "influence the measures or conduct of any foreign government" in matters involving disputes with the United States. The act, which carried a $5,000 fine and three years imprisonment, "covers Wallace like a cloak," the congressmen declared.[12]

Walter Lippmann revived his portrait of Wallace as a man out of touch with reality, "a man trying earnestly to deal with a world which is too much for him, and like many another he is cracking under the strain." Truman maintained a discreet public silence, fearing any comment about "Henry's wild statements" would only give them more publicity. Privately he wrote a letter comparing Wallace to Aaron Burr, a vice president once tried for treason.[13]

But Truman readily unleashed conservative Attorney General Tom Clark to chastise Wallace at a political banquet. A man who "tells the people of Europe that the United States is committed to a ruthless imperialism and war with the Soviet Union tells a lie," Clark declared.[14]

Winston Churchill, out of office but hardly out of breath, jumped in near the end of Wallace's stay in England. Wallace, he said, was a "crypto-Communist," which he defined as "one who has not the moral courage to explain the destination for which he is making."[15]

Landing in Stockholm, Wallace fired back, "I refuse to be disturbed by name-calling or hatred, no matter how distinguished the source from which the name-calling comes. You cannot conquer hate by fighting it. Love creates a greater circle than hate." Churchill backed down and said he had been misquoted.[16]

In the United States, Eleanor Roosevelt watched in agony. "I have such confidence in Mr. Wallace's integrity," she wrote to Beanie Baldwin. "I am sure he has taken this course because he felt he had to, but with all my heart I wish for his own sake that he had not done so."[17]

She was not alone. Wallace's European tour had clearly harmed his cause. His congressional allies found themselves in a tough spot as they sought to block legislation giving military aid to Greece and Turkey. Significant initial opposition to the bill in the Senate withered rapidly. Only die-hard liberals such as Claude Pepper and Glen Taylor and a handful of southern isolationists continued to fight it.

Wallace, wrote the *New York Times* reporter Cabell Phillips, "should take to heart a brand new maxim" coined by his friends in the capital. "It is, 'He who throws boomerangs should learn to duck.' "[18]

By the time he reached Paris, the trip was in shambles. The broad coalition of French organizations and political figures that sponsored his visit crumbled, leaving Wallace primarily in the hands of Communist Party members eager to capitalize on his international fame.

Clearly uncomfortable, Wallace sought to balance his criticism of the United States with remarks aimed at Russia. "I believe that toughness breeds toughness and that both the United States and Russia, by their actions, have already undermined the solemn cause for which their young men died." At the Sorbonne an immense crowd heard him deliver a moderately worded call for international cooperation. Afterwards a group of French women presented him with a box containing their "most precious possessions"—the last letters they had received from husbands and boyfriends who were killed in the war.[19]

Even as Wallace spoke, the U.S. Senate passed the Greek-Turkish military aid bill by a vote of 67 to 23. Only seven Democrats voted against it.

Back in the United States on April 27, Wallace held a press conference in Harold Young's Georgetown apartment. The United States was "on the road to ruthless imperialism," but not yet there, he declared. He said nothing abroad that he hadn't said at home. He had "nothing but love" in his heart for the members of Congress who attacked him. As for his plans in 1948, Wallace said, "You can't tell what I will do next year."[20]

In one way Wallace counted the trip a success. The press had placed a "silken curtain" around him since his dismissal from the cabinet, he believed. The European tour had lifted it; he had spoken directly to some 160,000 people in three weeks, and millions heard him via radio.

"It is perhaps pardonable," wrote Frederick Kuh in the *Chicago Sun*, "that millions of Britons were pleased to learn that there are still prominent Americans who see Britain's destiny as something other than that of an atom absorber in a future U.S.-Soviet war."[21]

Otherwise the trip was a disaster. Congress, partly in reaction to him, had done the opposite of what Wallace wanted. Non-Communist French liberals were thrown into the arms of the Truman administration. The British Labour Party was left in turmoil. The party's leadership clearly wanted nothing to do with him, but 111 Labour members of Parliament signed a statement in support of his views.

Millions of Americans gained the impression Wallace had done something unseemly, if not unpatriotic. The Texas House of Representatives denounced the "activities and utterances" of "one Henry A. Wallace, an outcast from all political parties of American origin." The widely popular *Saturday Evening Post* greeted his return to the United States in mocking tones: "Now that the show is over, it looks as if Anglo-Saxon solidarity may have been cemented on at least one thing: heartfelt gratitude to the late FDR for giving Henry the business in the Democratic national convention of 1944."[22]

Wallace's very name now occasioned controversy. One congressman lambasted the Voice of America for broadcasting a review of *The Wallaces of Iowa*,

Russell Lord's biography of three generations of the Wallace family. The review was in German, and the congressman admitted he did not know what it said, but if it was about Henry Wallace it should not have been aired.

As the abuse mounted, Wallace's public standing sank precipitously. In December 1946 the Gallup poll showed 48 percent of Democratic voters favored Truman to be their party's nominee, as opposed to 24 percent who favored Wallace. In the wake of the European tour, the poll showed 79 percent favoring Truman compared with 9 percent for Wallace.

❧

"I've never seen such a swift change in a people toward intolerance and panic, and I'm a little panic-stricken," Michael Straight wrote to his mother in the early spring of 1947. ". . . The evil eats into the soul of everyone. Even Mrs. R. [Eleanor Roosevelt] freezes at Henry's name and wonders if there are communists on the staff of [the *New Republic*]. The P.C.A./A.D.A. split has finally divided progressives into 'safe' and 'unsafe' categories. . . . People who were friendly a month ago now say that Wallace should decide 'whether he loves America or Russia best.' . . . It's sad to see an individual or a nation lose self-confidence. A great part of the inquisition rises from a loss of nerve."[23]

But Henry Wallace did not want for nerve. Like the Old Testament prophets he so much admired, he would cry out the errors of his countrymen regardless of the cost.

In fact, Wallace went right out again on tour. Cleveland, Minneapolis, Chicago, Detroit, Austin, Los Angeles, Berkeley, San Francisco, Oakland, Vancouver, Portland, Denver, Bismarck, Raleigh, Montgomery, Newark, Washington, D.C.—everywhere his message was the same: Europe, including Eastern Europe and Russia, must be rehabilitated through a massive loan and aid program backed by the United States. Progressive economic and social programs must be enacted. The United Nations must be fully supported. The arms race must be brought under control.

"No one has yet explained what the Truman Doctrine is," he declared. "As nearly as we poor citizens can make out, it is a doctrine of unlimited aid to anti-Soviet governments. . . . Where it will all end is left to us to guess—and the guess is not pleasant to contemplate. The Doctrine was born in fear. It breeds hatred and hysteria. And hatred and hysteria are not going to help anyone in this troubled world. The Truman Doctrine may not lead to war. But it will never lead to peace."[24]

Wallace's cross-country marathon, an odd hybrid, looked like a political campaign, yet no election was at stake. The tour was jointly sponsored by the

Progressive Citizens of America, which wanted to advance its agenda, and by the *New Republic*, which wanted to boost its circulation.

Accordingly, Wallace traveled with three men of entirely separate motivations. Beanie Baldwin even then was angling to establish a new political party with Wallace as its leader. Michael Straight, in his heart an ADA liberal who didn't approve of the PCA, had nevertheless tied the fortunes of his magazine to the name of Henry Wallace. And Harold Young, Wallace's personal political adviser, still hoped his boss might challenge Harry Truman from within the Democratic Party.

For Wallace, the speaking tour was a campaign to bring salvation to a wayward nation. More than one reporter noted the quasi-religious fervor of Wallace and his crowds. Being with Wallace was "like traveling with a messiah and his disciples," wrote Howard M. Norton of the *Baltimore Sun*. "If fate and a fickle electorate combined to make Henry A. Wallace President of the United States (an honor he would be reluctant to reject), we would have a John the Baptist in the White House," reported Edwin A. Lahey in the *Chicago Daily News*.[*25]

Strange and unworldly though Wallace might be, however, thousands came to hear him, more than 100,000 people in May and tens of thousands more in June. Moreover, and astounding to reporters and political professionals, people paid for the privilege. Admission to the speeches ranged from 60 cents to $3.60. The average person paid $1.50 to get in, and usually donated more when the hat was passed during the rally. "I'm here, I've seen it, and I still don't believe it," Lahey wrote when 22,000 people piled into Chicago Stadium.[26]

As the speaking tour advanced, so did controversy. The *Chicago Daily News* editorially attacked Wallace under the headline "Reckless Demagogy." The *Chicago Herald-American* wrote off his appearance with the headline "Claque 'Nominates' Wallace President."[27]

University of Texas students taunted him with Soviet flags and a sound truck blaring The Internationale. In California, Wallace was denied use of the Hollywood Bowl, and officials at the University of California barred him from speaking on the Berkeley campus.

---

*Lahey, who accompanied the tour from Chicago to its stop in Denver, was fascinated by the complex blend of high intellect, religious conviction, plain habits, and personal awkwardness that made up Wallace's personality.

In Denver, as Lahey shared a meal with Wallace in a "Mexican saloon," they were approached by a friendly woman of low virtue. To Lahey's great amusement, Wallace was completely flustered. "Never in his years as a member of the Cabinet or as Vice-President had he encountered a crisis quite like the situation presented by Helen," Lahey wrote. Not wishing to appear rude, Wallace issued a mild rebuke in Spanish: "Maria Magdalena, adios." Helen was unfazed. Wallace said it again. Finally Lahey whispered something a little more stern in her ear and "she departed, still full of good will toward us."

It didn't matter. Wallace continued to draw enthusiastic crowds. At Gilmore Stadium in Los Angeles he drew thirty thousand raucous supporters. The actress Katharine Hepburn warmed up the crowd with a withering attack on the House Un-American Activities Committee, then focusing on Communist influence in the film industry. The collection plate yielded $31,625 from such notables as Charlie Chaplin and his wife, Oona O'Neill, Edward G. Robinson, John Garfield, and Hedy Lamarr.

Wallace gave the star-studded crowd what it wanted. "Today an ugly fear is spread across America—the fear of communism," he declared. "I say those who fear communism lack faith in democracy. I am not afraid of communism."

In blistering language Wallace threw open the door to a closet containing America's darkest moments:

> We burned an innocent woman on charge of witchcraft.
> We earned the scorn of the world for lynching negroes.
> We hounded labor leaders and socialists at the turn of the century.
> We drove 100,000 innocent men and women from their homes in California because they were of Japanese ancestry. . . .
> We branded ourselves forever in the eyes of the world for the murder by the state of two humble and glorious immigrants—Sacco and Vanzetti. . . .
> These acts today fill us with burning shame. Now other men seek to fasten new shame on America. . . . I mean the group of bigots first known as the Dies Committee, then the Rankin Committee, now the Thomas Committee—three names for fascists the world over to roll on their tongues with pride.[28]

The strident message, the crowds, his obvious dedication, the hint of a third-party candidacy, and the money he was raising got the attention of Democratic Party officials. Gael Sullivan, acting chairman of the Democratic National Committee, fired off an alarmed memo to the presidential aide Clark Clifford saying, "Wallace is a major consideration in 1948! Something should be done to combat him."[29]

The Department of State compiled a "Confidential" in-house document entitled "The Recent Foreign Policy Views of Henry A. Wallace," which concluded,

> The size of the audiences has amazed many commentators. Looking at the attendance records [the newspaper columnist] Doris Fleeson concluded that Wallace is "perhaps the only man in the U.S. with a genuine popular following as well as devoted disciples." And Roscoe Drummond, the *Christian Science Monitor*'s veteran political reporter, describing the Wallace tour

as "political barnstorming," said: "I have never seen a pre-convention campaign tour, even those of Wendell L. Willkie and Gov. Thomas E. Dewey, command even non-paying audiences of such size."[30]

For the FBI and HUAC Wallace's comings and goings became an obsession. Individuals who appeared with Wallace might be noted and investigated, their organizations linked together in a web of conspiracy. To merely attend his speeches was to court monitoring.

Wallace's last stop, a speech at the outdoor Watergate Amphitheater in Washington, D.C., brought a frontal assault from HUAC and other congressional conservatives. Representative Herbert A. Meyer, a Kansas Republican, denounced Wallace as "the evil tool of those who would destroy America" and called on the attorney general to "do his duty and indict this renegade." Congressman Alvin E. O'Konski, a Wisconsin Republican, sought an injunction in U.S. district court to prevent Wallace from speaking at the amphitheater, which was owned by the federal government.[31]

HUAC's chairman, J. Parnell Thomas, issued a "report" on the Southern Conference for Human Welfare, the organization sponsoring Wallace's appearance, calling it "a most deviously camouflaged Communist-front organization." Thomas also announced that HUAC would send "observers" to the rally.*[32]

Wallace responded sharply, saying the HUAC observers were intended "to scare government workers" from going to the meeting. "If the 'police state' has not yet arrived in the United States, the government workers will rebuke these tactics by turning out in force." They did. Some ten thousand people lined the banks of the Potomac River to hear the former vice president. They were met by FBI agents and HUAC investigators conspicuously taking pictures and jotting down license plate numbers of cars parked nearby. Clark Foreman opened the meeting with a greeting: "Friends, Americans, observers."[33]

Wallace was introduced by Senator Claude Pepper, his most stalwart congressional ally. "If an election could be held in the world today as to who was

---

*Dr. Clark Foreman, president of the Southern Conference for Human Welfare, fired back in a telegram to Thomas, charging the HUAC report was "one of lies and half truths" and asking to appear before the committee to defend his organization. Thomas ignored the request.

The situation reached a ludicrous low point on June 16, the day of Wallace's speech, when liberal Democratic congressman Chet Holifield read Foreman's telegram on the House floor. Mississippi congressman John Rankin, HUAC's ranking Democrat, immediately moved to expunge the telegram from the *Congressional Record* and was supported on a vote of 146 to 7. One of the seven members voting in opposition, California Democratic congresswoman Helen Gahagan Douglas, rose to say she planned to attend Wallace's speech and was roundly booed.

the world's formost private citizen . . . it would be the American citizen I now proudly present to you."[34]

Wallace issued his standard call for improved relations with the Soviet Union and once again dangled the possibility of forming a third party. "It will be important, if the Democratic party succumbs to Wall Street domination, to have a new party to let the people of the world know that those who believe in peace and understanding still have some means of expression. . . . It would provide the evidence that the United States has not gone completely imperialistic and psychopathic."[35]

Wallace returned to the *New Republic* in mid-June 1947 and gave no more public speeches until Labor Day.

"There is a reawakening in America," Michael Straight wrote to his mother in a hopeful moment near the end of the speaking tour. "The West is raging against the Republican Congress. The labor movement is feeling its way back to unity. There is strong opposition to the Truman Doctrine among thinking people. . . . We've proved wrong once more those clever critics who said that H.A.W. was the editor of a minor paper and no more. . . . No one is laughing any more."[36]

Straight had another cause for cheer. The magazine's circulation had more than doubled since Wallace signed on. A stable of talented young editors and writers had been assembled, including Theodore H. White, Penn Kimball, Joseph Lyford, and Tristram Coffin. The magazine had established itself at home and abroad as a beacon of liberalism. Hundreds of people came up to him during the speaking tour, Straight told his mother, and said, "It's all we have!"[37]

But there was a cloud on Straight's horizon: Henry. "In binding *The New Republic* to Wallace-the-Editor, I had bound myself to Wallace-the-Man," Straight wrote in his memoirs. ". . . I sensed, once again, that I was trapped. This time, the trap was of my own making."[38]

Straight had cut his ties with communism in 1938, and he saw trouble in the issue of Communist participation in the Progressive Citizens of America. As the speaking tour ended, Straight confronted Wallace directly, pointing out that the largest crowds had come in cities where the rallies were organized by "communist-led unions."

Straight asked, "What do you think of what I've told you about the Communists?" Wallace shrugged. "They get out the crowds."[39]

He simply wasn't interested in the mechanics of movement building. Nor was he engaged by ideological squabbling, so beloved by the left-wing New

York intelligentsia. He was not a Communist; he was a "progressive capitalist" who happened to believe in God. If Communists wanted to pay hard cash to hear a God-fearing capitalist speak, that was their business.

He wasn't even much interested in the magazine he supposedly edited. Usually Wallace spent three or four days a week in New York City, sleeping in a town house owned by Straight and walking the forty blocks to the *New Republic's* offices in a high-rise building at 40 East Forty-ninth Street. The rest of the week he spent at his farm growing his beloved tomatoes and strawberries.

Wallace's actual job was to write a weekly column. This he did personally, in pencil on a yellow pad, unless traveling, when the column was ghosted by a staff writer and given to Wallace for review. This schedule hardly occupied a man of Wallace's energy and intellect. He did sit in on editorial meetings, but by all accounts—including his own—he never was a hands-on editor.

That job was done by Bruce Bliven, and had been since the death in 1930 of Herbert Croly. Bliven enthusiastically accepted the title of "editorial director" when Wallace was named "editor," but his job remained the same.

Born in Iowa a year after Wallace, Bliven had met and admired the former vice president over the years. And he had a much deeper appreciation for Wallace's contribution to agriculture than most of the urban intellectuals who populated the *New Republic.* But Bliven was above all a professional journalist, trying to put out an interesting and respected magazine, and he disliked its being a vehicle for anyone's political ambitions. A thorough anti-Communist, Bliven also was distinctly uncomfortable with some of the people he saw around Wallace.

The marriage, then, was not altogether happy. Some magazine staff members found Wallace strange and distant. Theodore H. White called him a "bitter man, eccentric, ambitious, self-righteous," who cast a "grave and heavy presence" over the office. "Henry Wallace was a handsome man, his light-brown hair just turning silver, his clean, open face and muscled form instantly attractive to men and women alike, his personal kindliness well known," White wrote in his memoirs. "But underneath it all he was a self-intoxicated man with but two subjects of conversation—botanical genetics and himself, the latter subject complicated by an abnormal suspicion of others."[40]

Bliven considered lunchtime a particular "ordeal," since Wallace "was a fanatic on exercise, and got it by picking out a restaurant a mile or so away and walking to it at such a fast pace it could be described as running. . . . After lunch, if he paid the bill, one or the other of us would surreptitiously add to the tip he left." Both Bliven and Straight found Wallace's trait of closing his eyes while others talked in meetings to be perplexing and annoying.[41]

To Straight he seemed like a man suffering from chronic low-grade depression. More likely Wallace was simply bored. He often disappeared for hours in the company of a mysterious man named Max; Straight nervously suspected that Max was a political agent of some sort. Months later Straight discovered the mundane truth: Max was a retired East Side grocer fond of introducing the former vice president to his pals in one delicatessen after another. "Henry would return from these excursions with his overcoat pockets stuffed with tins of gefilte fish and bottles of borscht," wrote Straight.[42]

The happiest moments for the *New Republic* staff were the occasional visits to Farvue, where they could bask in Ilo's warm social grace and enjoy the fruit of Henry's labor. Wallace, dirt under his fingernails, would show off his latest patch of giant strawberries or introduce the city boys to a record-setting egg layer, then lead them to a dining table piled with tomatoes and melons and sweet corn.

Even on the farm, however, his unconventional genius stood out. Remarking on some delicious tomatoes, Bliven turned to Ilo and asked how Henry did it. "He fed them with radioactive fertilizer," Ilo replied calmly.*[43]

❧

While Henry Wallace grew his tomatoes and Michael Straight struggled to cope with the *New Republic*'s expanded staff and payroll, Beanie Baldwin was at work building a new political party.

With courtly southern manners and a soft-spoken voice that disguised his inner determination, Baldwin didn't seem like a man who could hammer together a "popular front" coalition of Communists, radicals, union organizers, intellectuals, artists, civil rights activists, and preening celebrities. But by mid-1947 he was well on his way.

After six months in operation the Progressive Citizens of America had 25,000 members and chapters in nineteen states. The debt inherited from two predecessor organizations was down and the PCA in the black. A campaign for national rent control drew wide attention. So, too, did its lobbying efforts on behalf of antilynching legislation.

A PCA "manifesto" demanding "effective measures to disarm Germany" was signed by such luminaries as Eugene O'Neill, Thornton Wilder, Edna Ferber, John P. Marquand, Katherine Anne Porter, and George S. Kaufman. The PCA's theater division, headed by José Ferrer and Lillian Hellman, worked to support the federal fine arts bill and to combat racial discrimination in theaters.

Its artists' division staged a protest of the State Department's cancellation of a traveling exhibit of American painting. (The show was dropped after Harry

---

*Stories of Wallace's experiments with radioactive fertilizer were a source of great amusement to the city folk. One day Wallace was walking down a New York City street with William Gailmor, a wisecracking radio personality heavily involved in the Progressive Party campaign. As they passed by a particularly fetching young woman, Gailmore muttered, "Radiated tomato." Wallace walked for two blocks in silence and then chuckled.

Truman viewed it and remarked, "If that's art, I'm a Hottentot.") The PCA sciences division, headed by Dr. Harlow Shapley, sought creation of the National Science Foundation and "complete freedom of scientific research and expression." The women's division held a month-long political workshop capped by a fashion show ("Fashion Is Politics") featuring six Broadway actresses.[44]

The PCA youth division, headed by Gene Kelly, led several hundred young people to Washington to lobby for federal aid to education, for the right to vote at age eighteen, and against peacetime military training. And the doctors' division provided free medical care to workers on strike.

Publicity was never a problem. If the press failed to notice, the House Un-American Activities Committee always called attention to the PCA. The committee's first hearing on the PCA was held July 21, when fourteen witnesses took turns exposing its nefarious plots. One Walter S. Steele, identified as chairman of the National Security Committee of the American Coalition of Patriotic, Civic, and Fraternal Societies, revealed that Communists and their allies were "pushing" for a third party through the PCA. Steel estimated there were five million Communists or members of Communist-front organizations in the United States, and he ominously reported that the *New Republic* was "financed almost exclusively by foreign capital."[45]

At the same time Baldwin and his main legal adviser, John Abt, a quiet man who had been the chief lawyer for the union leader Sidney Hillman, were actively researching voting laws in all forty-eight states to determine whether a new political party could get on the ballot.* By the summer of 1947 they had concluded it could in at least forty states. They needed only a candidate to head the ticket, and Baldwin had the man for the job.

*Lee Pressman, who served as chief counsel at the CIO under Philip Murray, later testified before HUAC that he and John Abt were members of a Communist cell when they worked at the Department of Agriculture in 1934. Abt pleaded the Fifth Amendment and declined to answer when questioned about his political affiliations by a one-man HUAC subcommittee run by Congressman Richard Nixon.

Both Pressman and Abt worked in the Agriculture Department's legal division under Jerome Frank. They left the department when Wallace fired Frank in the "liberal purge" of 1935. In his oral history Wallace said he had no recollection of meeting Abt while he was secretary of agriculture.

In early 1948 Baldwin asked Wallace to name Abt chief counsel to the Progressive Party. When Wallace met Abt to discuss the matter, the lawyer struck him as "a calm, level-headed person of very good intellect." Abt told Wallace he was not a Communist—he didn't say he never had been—but expressed concern that the party might be embarrassed because his wife, Jessica Smith, was publisher of a pro-Russia magazine called *American-Soviet Friendship.* Wallace replied, "In view of the fact that we stood for understanding with Russia, I didn't see why we should be against that," and Abt was given the job.

By odd coincidence, Jessica Smith had been married to Harold Ware, son of the notorious homegrown radical Mother Bloor. Ware organized a Communist cell in the Agriculture Department during the Hoover administration and died in a car accident shortly after Wallace became secretary.

Quietly, doggedly, by personal cajolery, and through the flattery of friends, Baldwin pushed Henry Wallace to lead the cause.

Wallace was half—but only half—convinced. His own frame of mind was a sort of "either/or" attitude: "Either Truman and the Democratic Party become liberal, or I will run for president on a third party ticket." It was a threat, Wallace commented, and it wasn't any more than a threat until late 1947, when he finally became convinced of Baldwin's ability to put together a genuine national party.[46]

But he may have been farther along the path to a presidential candidacy than he admitted even to himself.

In the summer of 1947 the Truman administration did offer his party's liberals some cause for hope. First came Secretary of State George Marshall's famous address at Harvard on June 5, calling for a massive program of "friendly aid" to assist European economic recovery. "Our policy is directed not against any country or doctrine but against hunger, poverty, desperation and chaos," Marshall declared. ". . . Any government that is willing to assist in the task of recovery will find full cooperation, I am sure, on the part of the United States Government. Any government which maneuvers to block the recovery of other countries cannot expect help from us."[47]

Announcement of the Marshall Plan was followed on June 20 by Truman's veto of the Taft-Hartley bill. The legislation made sweeping changes in federal labor laws, changes that unions regarded as odious. Among other things the bill gave the president authority to seek court injunctions to end strikes in cases of national emergency, required labor leaders to swear they were not Communists, and allowed states to pass "right to work" laws outlawing closed-shop agreements and union hiring halls.

Prominent liberals railed against the Taft-Hartley bill, and organized labor protested it on a massive scale. Truman's veto, as he anticipated, was immediately overridden by both houses of Congress, but his action did improve relations with a crucial element of the Democratic coalition.

Here, then, was at least a plausible "either" to Wallace's "or." Truman had given Wallace an attractive opportunity to declare victory and go home to his chickens.*

For a moment it seemed Wallace might do just that. He praised Truman's action on Taft-Hartley, and his first response to the Marshall Plan was cau-

*If Wallace had helped pass the bill giving military aid to Greece and Turkey, some observers thought he should get credit for bringing the Marshall Plan into reality. Dr. Rexford Guy Tugwell, in his book *A Chronicle of Jeopardy*, wrote, "Mr. Wallace had the right to claim that he, singlehandedly, at least changed the Truman Doctrine into the Marshall Plan. He did not exercise that right; but everyone knew that it was so. For in his speaking trips he had drawn enormous crowds, who had listened to his alternative with the hunger of a people frightened to the bone by the approach of what now seemed certain war."

tiously approving. The plan was not as sweeping as the $50 billion program Wallace had proposed, nor did it use the United Nations in the way he hoped, but it was a "great advance" over the Truman Doctrine.

"The Marshall Doctrine looks toward an overall program which is what I have been advocating all along," Wallace wrote in the *New Republic*. Most important, the Marshall Plan did not specifically exclude Russia or its satellites.[48]

The Progressive Citizens of America's board of directors, following Wallace's lead, expressed support for the Marshall Plan insofar as it was "consistent with the principles of the United Nations and the unity of the great powers."[49]

Such unity was not to be, however. In July, at a European Recovery Program conference, the Soviets signaled opposition to Marshall's plan. They feared it would lead to the restoration of German industrial power, the destruction of their sphere of influence in Eastern Europe, and their encirclement by hostile capitalist nations.

Wallace lamented Russia's decision. "I believe that the Soviet government should have accepted the opportunity," he wrote.[50] He called on the United States to try again by repudiating the Truman Doctrine and putting the European Recovery Program under the auspices of the United Nations. That would not happen, however, as long as Congress was under conservative control.

Slowly Wallace came to see the Marshall Plan as an instrument of the Cold War. In late July he told a reporter for the Yugoslavian news agency that he would oppose the Marshall Plan if its aim was "to revive Germany for the purpose of waging a struggle against Russia."[51]

As summer moved to fall, Wallace was pushed and pulled in all directions. Russia began pressuring its neighbors, especially Poland and Czechoslovakia, to stay out of the European Recovery Program. Formation of the Cominform, a worldwide propaganda unit tied to Soviet policy, further inflamed American fears of an international Communist conspiracy. William Z. Foster, head of the U.S. Communist Party, ended months of indecision by announcing his support of Wallace for president.* PCA activists, while remaining mostly silent about the Marshall Plan, ratcheted up the pressure for a third party.

---

*The endorsement of Wallace reversed Foster's position. He had led a movement to oust the long-time U.S. Communist Party chief Earl Browder precisely because of Browder's support for "popular front" politics.

Foster's endorsement of Wallace was entirely one-sided, however. When he dispatched the U.S. Communist party general secretary, Eugene Dennis, to meet Wallace, the encounter was not cordial. "All I said was that there were two things I wanted him to understand—that the Communist party does not believe in God, I do believe in God; the Communist party does not believe in progressive capitalism, I do believe in progressive capitalism," Wallace recalled. The whole meeting lasted five minutes.

Meanwhile, the Americans for Democratic Action went all out for the Marshall Plan. Polls showed that the American public overwhelmingly supported the ADA position. Old friends like the writer Paul de Kruif and Professor Irving Fisher warned Wallace: he was wandering into the political wilderness. "I should hate, for your own sake, to see you become a catspaw of those who are now applauding you," Fisher wrote.[52]

Respectable internationalists such as Henry Stimson, the former secretary of state and war, lectured Wallace in print. "The world's affairs cannot be simplified by eager words," Stimson wrote in *Foreign Affairs.* Longtime liberal allies, including Senator Claude Pepper and the labor leader A. F. Whitney, announced they had no intention of leaving the Democratic Party.[53]

The California attorney Robert Kenny, a national co-chairman of the PCA, announced the formation of a Democrats for Wallace group to challenge Truman from within the party. If progressive Democrats were faced with a choice between "Tweedledum and Tweedle Dewey," Kenny said, they would stay home. Even some Communists, including those affiliated with the American Labor Party, cautiously opposed the idea of a "popular front" third party.

Wallace watched and wavered. "Unless and until I am definitely proved wrong, I will stay within the Democratic party," he said in an interview on September 10.[54]

Confusion reigned. Baldwin went on trying to turn the PCA into a political movement. The PCA and Wallace came out against the Marshall Plan. The CIO came out for the Marshall Plan and against formation of a third party.

When it was announced in early fall that Wallace would again begin appearing at PCA rallies, Michael Straight reacted in despair. "I doubt if we have the strength to start a third party," Straight wrote to his mother. "Yet, it may be started anyway under auspices and with ambitions that will make it a hopeless adventure, a children's crusade. . . . The progressive movement is disintegrating under attack."[55]

Straight developed a desperate plan to rescue Wallace from the leftists. "It occurred to me that the best course would be to get Wallace out of the country," Straight wrote in his memoirs. "Palestine, I said to myself; they cannot stop him from going to Palestine." He planned to have a long talk with Wallace on the airplane, slow things down, wise him up, anything to block the momentum of a third-party candidacy. But it never happened. Immediately after the plane departed from New York, Straight became engaged in a chess match and never found the time, or the nerve, to speak his mind to Wallace.[56]

Wallace left for the Near East on October 17, 1947, a few days after the United States agreed to a UN plan to partition Palestine into independent

Jewish and Arab states. The trip was billed as a strictly journalistic enterprise under the auspices of the *New Republic*. Accompanying Wallace were Straight, Lewis Frank Jr., a Detroit labor activist hired by Straight as a speechwriter for the former vice president, and Gerold Frank (no relation), a writer and authority on Zionism.

Most of Wallace's time was spent visiting holy sites or advising farmers on kibbutzim regarding agricultural problems. It was a low-key journey. "When you see a former Vice President of the United States in battered tennis shoes and dusty gray slack suit sampling the soil of the Palestine desert, you've seen everything," noted one reporter. ". . . If he had been running for office in the Palestine desert he couldn't have looked more completely the country boy from Iowa or acted more completely the genuine role of world-famous agronomist and expert on Iowa corn and New Salem white leghorn pullets and hybrid strawberries."[57]

Wallace called for creation of a Jordan Valley authority, patterned after the TVA, and pleaded with Jews and Arabs to "abide faithfully by the ultimate decision of the United Nations." The dream of peace, he wrote later, was possible even in Palestine. "I saw evidence on the village level that the Jew and the Arab get along very well, provided hatred and discord are not incited from the outside."[58]

Wallace's only major public pronouncement during two weeks abroad was not about Palestine but about Red-baiting in the United States. On October 20 HUAC began a celebrated series of hearings on communism in Hollywood that eventually sent ten noted directors and screenwriters to jail. The PCA responded with a two-day Conference on Cultural Freedom and Civil Liberties. Wallace telegrammed his support:

> From here where Elijah fought the prophets of Baal and close to the mount where Jesus gave his famous sermon, people without fear ask, "Has America really gone crazy?" Is the un-American committee evidence that America is traveling the road to fascism? On behalf of millions everywhere you must answer no so loudly the people of the world can hear. You must destroy the un-American committee at the polls and in the courts, or it will destroy many of the foundations of democracy and Christianity.[59]

On the way home the Wallace party stopped in Rome, for dinner with U.S. Ambassador James Dunn and an audience with Pope Pius XII. The pope avoided answering when Wallace asked, "What are you going to do for Palestine?" But as a friendly gesture he offered Wallace his choice of a white or a black rosary. Wallace seemed uncertain, so the pope gave him both.[60]

Wallace returned to New York on November 4. The visit to Palestine had only increased his zeal for peace and the righteousness of his cause. He wrote,

> If the Anglo-Saxon peoples decline in importance during the last half of the twentieth century, it will be because they have failed to apply Christianity and democracy in their dealings with all the peoples of the world.
> . . .
>
> Isaiah, Christ, and Jefferson have not failed. Their principles of peace and justice between man and man are fundamental. We have failed because we have not applied their principles justly and fearlessly. . . .
>
> As long as every Foreign Office in the world is dominated by the doctrine of Machiavelli instead of the doctrines of Christ, we shall have war and the perpetuation of many kinds of dictatorship and falsehood as each of the nations prepares for the war.[61]

The course was set for the great crusade of 1948.

CHAPTER TWENTY-FOUR

"GIDEON'S ARMY"

AND THE LORD LOOKED UPON HIM, AND SAID, GO IN THIS THY
MIGHT, AND THOU SHALT SAVE ISRAEL FROM THE HAND OF THE
MIDIANITES: HAVE NOT I SENT THEE? BOOK OF JUDGES 6:14

Like everything about the Progressive Party campaign of
1948—from its Bible-quoting candidate to his folk-singing
followers, from its slickly packaged rallies to its stubborn
stand on civil rights—the announcement of Henry A. Wallace's presidential candidacy was unconventional and uncompromising.

It came on December 29, 1947, months before presidential
hopefuls customarily launched campaigns, and via radio at
10:30 P.M. with none of the usual political paraphernalia and
hoopla. Indeed, Wallace as yet had no party to run with. Instead, about forty friends and associates sat soberly in a Mutual Broadcasting System studio in Chicago to hear him speak.*

Wallace came out fighting. "Thousands of people all over
the United States have asked me to engage in this great fight,"
he declared. "The people are on the march." He added,

> We have assembled a Gideon's Army, small in number,
> powerful in conviction, ready for action. We have said

*Nobody else in Chicago heard Wallace. Mutual Broadcasting's Chicago out-
let, station WGN, refused to carry the speech on orders from its owner, arch-
conservative *Chicago Tribune* publisher Robert McCormick. He was a first
cousin of Anita McCormick Blaine, Wallace's chief financial backer, but in this
case politics easily outweighed family.

with Gideon, "Let those who are fearful and trembling depart." For every fearful one who leaves, there will be a thousand to take his place. A just cause is worth a hundred armies. We face the future unfettered, unfettered by any principle but the general welfare. We owe no allegiance to any group which does not serve that welfare. By God's grace, the people's peace will usher in the century of the common man.

Wallace dealt at length with arguments sure to be made against a third-party candidacy. He meant to put some steel in the spine of liberals who thought a vote for Wallace would be wasted because he could never win:

> When the old parties rot, the people have a right to be heard through a new party. They asserted that right when the Democratic party was founded under Jefferson in the struggle against the Federalist party of war and privilege of his day. They won it again when the Republican party was organized in Lincoln's time. The people must again have an opportunity to speak out with their vote in 1948. . . .
>
> The lukewarm liberals sitting on two chairs say, "Why throw away your vote?" I say a vote for a new party in 1948 will be the most valuable vote you have ever cast or ever will cast.
>
> The bigger the peace vote in 1948, the more definitely the world will know that the United States is not behind the bipartisan reactionary war policy which is dividing the world into two armed camps and making inevitable the day when American soldiers will be lying in their arctic suits in the Russian snow. . . .
>
> Let us stop saying, "I don't like it, but I am going to vote for the lesser of two evils."
>
> Rather than accept either evil, come out boldly, stand upright like men and say loudly so all the world can hear—"We are voting peace and security for ourselves and our children's children. We are fighting for old-fashioned Americanism at the polls in 1948. We are fighting for freedom of speech and freedom of assembly. We are fighting to end racial discrimination. We are fighting for lower prices. We are fighting for free labor unions, for jobs, and for homes in which we can decently live."

Wallace next addressed the Marshall Plan, then the ideological dividing line for liberals. Noting his steadfast support for humanitarian assistance to Europe, he added, "I have fought and shall continue to fight programs which give guns to people when they want plows." By acting outside the purview of the UN, the United States resembled "France and England after the last war and the end result will be the same—confusion, depression and war."

To those who called Wallace a pawn of "the communist line," he responded, "I am utterly against any kind of imperialism or expansionism whether sponsored by Britain, Russia or the United States, and I call upon Russia as well as the United States to look at all our differences objectively and free from that prejudice which hatemongers have engendered on both sides."[1]

The arguments Wallace made in his announcement speech would echo through his doomed campaign. Nothing was more apt, however, than his analogy to Gideon's Army, a fighting force made smaller, leaner, more dedicated before the fight began.* So, too, did Wallace's campaign seem always to grow smaller. "Our whole history was of people leaving," sighed an official of the Massachusetts Progressive Party.[2]

The departures began early, with Dr. Frank Kingdon, a well-known radio commentator and newspaper columnist who served as national co-chairman of the Progressive Citizens of America. Kingdon had early advocated a third party—he was the first person to urge the race—and was as late as November 1947 describing Wallace as "the people's candidate for president."[3]

Then Kingdon developed ambitions of his own. He decided to run for a U.S. Senate seat in New Jersey as a Democrat. So much had Kingdon's ardor for a third party cooled that he was not invited to the meeting on December 2 where Wallace met with his inner circle and agreed to run. A national PCA vice chairman, Bartley C. Crum, also resigned, and the radio commentator J. Raymond Walsh, head of the PCA's New York chapter, soon followed them out the door. A third-party campaign in 1948 would "kill the chance of progressive politics in America for a long time to come, possibly for the rest of your life," Walsh told his WMCA radio audience. Albert Deutsch, a writer for the liberal newspaper *PM*, and A. J. Liebling, the prominent press critic for the *New Yorker* magazine, also parted company with Wallace.[4]

No one made more noise in leaving than Kingdon, however. Two days after Wallace announced his candidacy, Kingdon viciously attacked him in the *New York Post*. "Who asked Henry Wallace to run? The answer is in the record. The Communist party through William Z. Foster and Eugene Dennis were the first. . . . The record is clear. The call to Wallace came from the Communist party and the only progressive organization admitting Communists to its membership."[5]

---

*The story of Gideon's Army is told in the chapters 6 through 8 of the Book of Judges. Gideon, a young farmer in Israel, was called by the Lord to lead a revolt against the Midianites in the twelfth century B.C. Some 32,000 men answered his call, but 22,000 left when he asked only the fearless to stay. The remaining force of 10,000 was pared to 300, when an angel of the Lord told Gideon to observe which of the men kept alert while drinking from a stream.

Gideon equipped his little army with trumpets and pitchers containing lamps. At night they surrounded the Midianites' camp and terrified them with the sound of the trumpets, the breaking of pitchers, and light from the lamps. The Midianites fled, and Gideon became Israel's ruler.

Kingdon's assertion was baseless—certainly Wallace gave no thought to Communist Party wishes in deciding to run—but it struck at his most vulnerable point.* The door was open for anyone who wanted to say "Wallace" and "Communist" in one breath. The Wallace movement, said the newspaper columnist Stewart Alsop, "has been indecently exposed for what it is: an instrument of Soviet foreign policy. . . . The bones revealed are communistic bones."[6]

Alex Rose, vice chairman of the American Labor Party, charged that Wallace had "been steadily absorbing the Communist line." The autoworker leader Walter Reuther called Wallace "a lost soul" and said, "It is tragic that he is being used by the Communists the way they have used so many other people."[7]

Harold Young, the hearty Texan who had devoted seven years of his life to looking after Henry Wallace's political interests, could only watch in dismay. He knew Wallace was a "front" for nobody, let alone for Communists. But Young could see where things were headed. In early January 1948 he packed his bags and said he was going back to Texas for a while. He never returned.

As for Young's feelings about Wallace and the 1948 campaign, he summed them up in two brief sentences: "Mr. Henry Wallace is one of the country's few great men. . . . The Progressive Party venture was a terrible mistake."[8]

In November 1948 Young cast his ballot for Harry Truman.

<hr>

"The Progressive Citizens of America have an internationally known candidate and are long on enthusiasm for him," the syndicated columnist Doris Fleeson wrote in mid-January 1948. "PCA is short of practically everything else it takes to run a Presidential campaign, including political talent, experience, money and organization."[9]

The challenge was formidable indeed. The PCA claimed to have about 100,000 members, with chapters in twenty-four states at the start of 1948. But no more than half its "members" were active dues payers. Only in New York, California, and Illinois did it have even a modicum of real strength.

<hr>

*The Americans for Democratic Action exploited Kingdon's break with Wallace, reprinting his column on the front page of *ADA World* and sending it by mail to thousands of liberals. The ADA's embrace of Kingdon was entirely cynical, as its director, James Loeb Jr., admitted in a letter to a friend: "I can assure you that [Kingdon] is purchaseable. He has double-crossed so many people that there is almost no one left for him to double cross."

Kingdon's split with the Wallace and the PCA turned out not to be of much help to his political aspirations. In March 1948, having failed to win the support of Frank Hague, the powerful and corrupt Democratic boss of Jersey City, Kingdon withdrew from the U.S. Senate race.

Financially the PCA was in the black, but it had not fully retired the debt left by its predecessors. It was not even close to having the $3 million deemed necessary to run a national campaign. Clearly the Wallace campaign could not rely on contributions from special-interest groups such as labor unions and businesses. Their financial loyalty was to the major parties. Donations would have to come from individual workers, homemakers, farmers, and professional people across the land, Wallace said. "I certainly don't know any other way. I don't think the corporations will finance it."*10

Most daunting of all was getting Wallace on the ballot. The progressives faced a bewildering thicket of state election laws and the entrenched power of major-party politicians and judges. Some states set very early deadlines for the formation of new parties. Others demanded nominating petitions signed by a large number of the state's residents. California required petitions signed by 10 percent of the number who voted in the last gubernatorial election, some 275,000 people.

And looming in the background was a proposal in Congress to bar from the ballot "un-American parties . . . directly or indirectly affiliated . . . with the Communist Party."

It was one thing to say "the people must have a choice." The practicalities of getting them that choice—of little interest to Wallace—was another thing altogether.

The job fell to Beanie Baldwin. Within a few weeks Baldwin engineered a formal declaration of PCA's intent to join with others in forming a new political party, accepted appointment as Wallace's campaign manager, established the Wallace for President Committee, set up headquarters in New York City with a paid staff of fifteen, and dispatched hundreds of eager volunteers to meet the petition and filing requirements in various states.†

In addition to Baldwin, the Wallace for President Committee consisted of the former Minnesota governor Elmer Benson, who served as chairman, and five co-chairman: financial angel Anita McCormick Blaine; former undersecretary of agriculture and governor of Puerto Rico, Dr. Rexford Guy Tugwell; prominent actor and singer Paul Robeson; sculptor Jo Davidson; and United

---

*One potential source of funds, everyone agreed, would never materialize: Henry A. Wallace's personal wealth. "Mr. Wallace is noted for his careful personal spending . . . [and] is not expected to contribute himself," the *New York Times* stated early in the campaign. The prediction proved largely accurate. Wallace donated only $1,000 to his campaign.

†Baldwin knew of the ballot-access problem, especially in California. This played a large role in his urging Wallace to formally announce his independent candidacy by the beginning of 1948. As it turned out, California was the site of one of Baldwin's early successes. Wallace workers (sometimes paid five or ten cents per name) were able to gather 482,781 signatures a full month before the mid-March deadline. Although the secretary of state determined that only 295,000 of the signatures were valid, they were more than enough to put Wallace on the ballot in California.

Electrical, Radio, and Machine Workers of America president, Albert J. Fitzgerald. Angus Cameron, editor in chief of the Little, Brown and Company publishing firm, served as treasurer.

The committee worked out of a four-story brownstone mansion at 39 Park Avenue in New York City, rented for $1,500 a month, an unlikely setting for a "people's campaign." Built in 1863 by the railroad baron Samuel Atterbury, its forty rooms featured high ceilings, crystal chandeliers, marble fireplaces, and elevators.

The tough left-wing New York congressman Vito Marcantonio later denounced the lavish building as "a big farce," but soon its bedrooms and sitting rooms hummed with fund-raisers, publicity agents, and mimeograph machines. The spacious main-floor ballroom served as a meeting room. The only quiet spot was a second-floor room where Wallace had an office. He was seldom there.

Small though it was, Gideon's Army aroused intense speculation about its impact. Liberals divided between those who believed it would force Truman to adopt a more accommodating foreign policy and those who thought it would doom the Democrats altogether. The liberal columnist Max Lerner called the Wallace campaign a "futile insurgent gesture" but nevertheless said "only a political miracle can stop Dewey now."[11]

The recently appointed Democratic national chairman, J. Howard McGrath, on the other hand, predicted Wallace's candidacy would help elect Democratic congressional candidates by bringing more liberals to the polls. Harry Truman let it be known that he did not "give a damn" about Wallace and fully expected to win.[12]

Estimates of "the Wallace vote" ranged from 500,000 (radio commentator J. Raymond Walsh) to five million (Socialist candidate Norman Thomas, columnist Frank Kingdon) to seven million (former Postmaster General James Farley) to ten or eleven million (Senator Wayne Morse, CIO general counsel Lee Pressman). Wallace himself thought he would draw between three and five million votes, a reasonable expectation. Virtually everyone expected Wallace's votes to come straight out of Truman's pocket.

Opinion polls still gave Truman a chance, especially if Dewey led the Republican ticket. An early Gallup poll asked voters to choose between Truman, Dewey, and Wallace. The result was Truman, 48 percent; Dewey, 41 percent; Wallace, 7 percent. (The same poll showed Truman falling to General Dwight D. Eisenhower.)

Seven percent would translate into about three million votes for Wallace. Even that, Republicans believed, would tip the balance in northern states and secure their victory in the electoral college. Already confident that victory was theirs in 1948, Republicans grew positively smug.

The *New Republic's* high-water mark under Michael Straight occurred the first week of January 1948. Circulation of that issue, published in the wake of Wallace's declaration of his candidacy, soared to almost 100,000. At the same time the magazine announced that Wallace would henceforth be only a "contributing editor," in light of his campaign burdens. Wallace's weekly column would continue. Even so, some of the magazine's staff members were uncomfortable. One editor promptly resigned.

Several weeks later the Progressive Party—still usually called the "New Party," for want of another name—reached a high point of its own. On a single day, February 18, Wallace basked in good news from three fronts: California progressives had collected more than enough signatures to put the new party on the ballot in the state's primary; a Wallace-backed candidate scored an unexpected victory in a special congressional election in New York; and U.S. Senator Glen H. Taylor, an Idaho Democrat, ended weeks of indecision and announced he would serve as Wallace's running mate.

The triumph of the American Labor Party candidate Leo Isacson in New York's Twenty-fourth Congressional District was especially sweet. That was Bronx boss Edward J. Flynn's home base. Flynn, who served as national party chairman in the early 1940s, had kept the district safely in Democratic hands for more than two decades. But in the 1948 special election Isacson tallied 22,697 votes to 12,578 for the Democrat Karl Propper. Wallace's support of Isacson dominated the race.

The *New York Herald Tribune*, strongly against Isacson, acknowledged the obvious. "Henry Wallace and the Left Wing have shown what they can do. . . . Mr. Wallace's man did it in such bone-crushing style that the third party has suddenly taken on a new importance." From Tampa, where he was campaigning, Wallace declared the vote a "repudiation of the get tough foreign policy" and a "real victory over bossism and machine politics."[13]

Glen Taylor's decision to accept the vice presidential nomination on Wallace's ticket was a victory of another sort—a victory of principle over personal ambition. The handsome forty-three-year-old Taylor never tired of telling people that being a U.S. senator was the best job he had ever had.

In truth it was almost the only job he had ever had. Taylor and his beloved wife, Dora, had survived the Depression years as troubadours—the Glendora Players—traveling from town to town performing a saucy song-and-dance show. They slept in a battered old Ford and lived off oatmeal cookies and canned peaches. Along the way "Cowboy Glen" crossed the line between entertainment and politics and began running for office in Idaho.

After unsuccessful runs for the U.S. Senate in 1940 and 1942—campaigning on horseback and wearing his trademark cowboy hat—Taylor pulled off a political miracle in 1944. He was, he liked to say, the first real actor ever elected to the Senate. In Washington he was an oddity, a cheerful and colorful maverick with an outgoing manner and total lack of guile. Here was a man who could, without a hint of self-consciousness, sing "Yes, We Have No Bananas" in Chinese.

And he understood publicity. The very day he arrived in Washington, Taylor made newsreels nationwide by gathering his wife and two young sons together and singing a little ditty he had written about not being able to find housing in the wartime capital. As Taylor played the banjo, they warbled (to the tune of "Home on the Range") "Oh give me a home / Near the Capitol Dome . . ."14

In late 1947 Taylor was back in the news. He set out to dramatize the cause of peace by riding a horse from Los Angeles to Washington, a modern-day Paul Revere calling out for international understanding. He made it 275 miles before President Truman called a special session of Congress. Taylor drove back in a car, took his horse out of its trailer, and rode it up the Capitol steps, grinning and waving to photographers.*

The progressive triumphs of mid-February 1948 were not without losses. Taylor's offbeat personality was widely caricatured as clownish and furthered the image of Wallace's party as a band of misfits. Leo Isacson's victory in the Bronx energized complacent Democratic Party regulars and redoubled the efforts of Philip Murray and other union leaders to halt pro-Wallace forces within organized labor. In the heartland, as Wallace should have foreseen, the New Party looked exotic and menacing and outside the mainstream of traditional politics.

And the successful petition drive in California ended once and for all the efforts of Wallace supporters operating within the Democratic Party. Liberal members of Congress such as Helen Gahagan Douglas and Chet Holifield were obliged to renounce the third party if they hoped to have Democratic backing. James Roosevelt, the state party chairman, was thrown into a high-profile power struggle with the former national party treasurer Ed Pauley, which ultimately resulted in Roosevelt's reluctant endorsement of Truman's policies.

*Taylor was the progressives' second choice. Everyone, including Wallace, preferred Senator Claude Pepper, a better-known and more experienced politician. Pepper had been saying for months that he did not intend to leave the Democratic Party, but a concerted effort was made to change his mind, including a final face-to-face meeting with Wallace at Farvue.

Pepper would not succumb, but he did feel bad about it. According to one account, Pepper listened to Taylor's speech announcing that he would be Wallace's running mate in a state of gloom. Sinking into a big chair with a drink in his hand, Pepper mumbled, "I wish I had the courage."

Throughout early 1948, as Baldwin and his cohorts labored to put muscle into their fledgling party, Henry Wallace crisscrossed the nation speaking to large and friendly crowds. But truly breaking through to the general public was no easy job. The substance of his remarks was all but smothered by "the communist issue."

Only the most rabid Red-baiters thought Wallace himself a Communist. But millions came to believe he was a "dupe" or a "fellow traveler" or a "pink" or the naive captive of leftist radicals. His party was portrayed constantly as a sort of Trojan horse housing evil men dedicated to overthrowing the American way of life.

Wallace tried a variety of responses, but none worked. Early in the campaign he remarked that he was not a Communist and added, "I'm not following their line. If they want to follow my line, I say God bless em." He appealed to the basic American concepts of liberty and fair play: "Our most precious freedoms are being underminded by the cry of 'Red! Red!' " The surest way of bringing communism to the United States was to let "reactionary capitalists drive the country into a depression."[15]

He attempted to distance himself from U.S. Communist Party members, saying the few he had met "sounded kind of pathetic, like poor lonesome souls." He tried to wrap himself in the mantle of Franklin Roosevelt, promising to do "exactly what he would have done" with respect to Communist support. This tack backfired when it was reported Roosevelt had said in 1944 that he did "not welcome the support of any person or group committed to communism or fascism."[16]

Trying to recover, Wallace proposed that all candidates for president sign a pledge reading, "I shall not knowingly accept the support of any individual or group advocating the limitation of democratic action for any other individual or group; nor the support of any individual or group which would restrict the civil liberties of others for reasons of race, color or creed; nor the support of any individual advocating the violent overthrow of the government of the United States."[17]

Other candidates ignored the challenge. The press denounced it as a ploy to divert attention. "The lot of a liberal is not always a happy one," Wallace muttered.[18]

Formulating an effective response to the Communist issue was complicated by politics within organized labor and the U.S. Communist Party. Philip Murray of the CIO and William Green of the AFL seized upon the Wallace campaign as a tool to maintain control of their unruly unions. "The Communist Party is directly responsible for the organization of a third party in the United States. There is no question about that," Murray told a gathering of textile workers.[19]

To dramatize the point, CIO leaders warned Harry Bridges, radical Australian-born leader of the longshoremen's union, that continued support for Wallace would result in a renewed attempt to deport him. Bridges stood his ground, and new deportation proceedings were begun. Inevitably Wallace's labor support withered.

The Communist Party leaders William Z. Foster and Eugene Dennis, to the contrary, were eager to advertise—indeed, exaggerate—their role in Wallace's party. "We Communists resolutely pioneered and used our political influence to help promote a new progressive political alignment," Dennis bragged. But such comments only fueled fear of the Wallace movement in the general populace.[20]

Most vexing of all were the dogged attacks on Wallace and his party by well-known liberals. The prominent newspaper columnist Dorothy Thompson led the way on national radio. "The Communist Party—let's tell the truth—initiated the movement for Wallace," she declared. "No other group called for it." A few days later reporter Alfred Friendly wrote a long article for the *Washington Post* headlined "Reds Picked Wallace to Run, May Quit Him." His thesis was that Communists decided to back Wallace "as a means of blocking the Marshall Plan."[21]

Friendly's story was followed by similar reports by Victor Riesel in the *New York Post* and Edwin Lahey in the *Chicago Daily News*. These and other accounts actually demonstrated that Wallace's criticism of U.S. foreign policy resembled those of foreign and domestic Communists. They proved nothing about the actual formation of the third party or Communist influence on Wallace's positions.

Nevertheless the articles formed the backbone of a widely distributed report by the ADA that sought to bond Wallace with communism. There all substantive debate ended. No need for ADA liberals to debate the merits of what he was saying.

A typical ADA statement, signed by Hubert H. Humphrey, Franklin D. Roosevelt Jr., Leon Henderson, and others, said, "Irrespective of Mr. Wallace's intentions, the goals of his sponsors are clear. They hope to divide progressives, create national confusion and insure the triumph of reactionary isolationism in 1948. They believe the achievement of these aims will serve the world interests of the international Communist movement."[22]

Even Eleanor Roosevelt found it "strange" that her longtime friend Henry Wallace and the Communists were "condemning with one voice the Marshall proposals."[23]

Norman Thomas, leader of the Socialist Party, weighed in frequently, chastising Wallace for refusing to dissociate himself from the Communists. Dwight Macdonald, editor of a small far-left journal called *Politics*, denounced

Wallace as an "apologist for Stalin" and "totalitarian" and "more and more a fellow traveller." For good measure Macdonald also called him an unprincipled "demagogue" and a "corn-fed mystic."[24]

Senator Robert F. Wagner, a New York Democrat, one of the Senate's great liberals, pronounced himself sadly disappointed by the former vice president and said the late Franklin Roosevelt was also. "We all want peace, but not peace at any price," Wagner declared. "Henry Wallace is asking for that when he asks for peace at the Soviet dictator's price. . . . Yes, the angels are weeping, and there is a great man and good friend of Henry Wallace who, I am sure, weeps with them."[25]

Many voices joined the chorus of criticism, but they had one thing in common: they were all liberals. This was no accident. Harry Truman and his aides were following the strategy laid out in a forty-three-page memorandum signed by the presidential counselor Clark Clifford in November 1947.

The Clifford memo advised Truman to stake out liberal election-year positions on key economic and social issues, ignore the left-wing assault on foreign policy issues, and let others do the dirty work in attacking Henry Wallace. Thus, when the Republican-controlled Congress gathered in January, Truman confronted it with a program calling for a forty-dollar tax cut for every taxpayer and dependent, an increase in corporation taxes, an increase in the minimum wage, legislation to protect civil rights, price and rent controls, and a national health insurance program.

Later Truman endorsed many of the recommendations made by his Committee on Civil Rights, including calls for a permanent civil rights commission, federal antilynching legislation, abolition of the poll tax, and establishment of a fair employment practices commission.

The goal was to undercut Wallace's strength among New Dealers without giving ground on foreign policy. But the key to the strategy's success, as Clifford understood, was to leave the tarring of Wallace to liberals outside the administration. In a section of his memo headed "The Insulation of Henry Wallace," Clifford wrote, "Every effort must be made *now* jointly and at one and the same time—although, of course, by different groups . . . to identify and isolate him in the public mind with the Communists. . . . [The] Administration must persuade prominent liberals and progressives—*and no one else*—to move publicly into the fray. They must point out that the core of the Wallace backing is made up of Communists and fellow-travellers . . . "(italics in the original).[26]

The shrewdness of Clifford's memo was not immediately apparent. Truman's civil rights initiative, for example, triggered talk of revolt among southern Democratic politicians. Many observers believed the loss of his southern base would seal his fate. Nor did ADA liberals suddenly flock to Truman's side. Many top

ADA members, including Franklin Roosevelt's sons, spent the spring of 1948 touting General Eisenhower as the savior of the Democratic Party.

And despite Clifford's urging, Truman attacked Wallace now and then. "I do not want and I will not accept the support of Henry Wallace and his Communists," Truman said at a Saint Patrick's Day dinner in New York City. "If joining them or permitting them to join me is the price of victory, I recommend defeat."[27]

Wallace responded in two radio appearances over the next forty-eight hours. "When he attempted to brand as 'Communists' those who support our fight for peace, Mr. Truman appealed to prejudice, because he could not answer us with reason."[28]

The vilification of Wallace and his followers soon yielded real-world consequences.

In April a mob of 2,500 surrounded a coliseum in Evansville, Indiana, where Wallace was to speak. Many held picket signs with messages such as "Dear Uncle Joe, How am I doing? Faithfully yours, Hank." Some in the crowd beat down the doors and swarmed through the lobby, preparing to enter the auditorium. Beanie Baldwin and several other Wallace aides were slugged. Club-swinging police managed to restore order but did not disperse the protesters. When Wallace finished speaking, he was escorted to a car but found himself trapped for an hour by his screaming detractors. An Evansville College religion professor was summarily fired for having appeared on the stage with Wallace.

In Indianapolis a hotel abruptly canceled arrangements for a luncheon to which three hundred Wallace supporters had been invited, and the head of the Indiana National Guard reneged on permission to use an armory building because the singer Paul Robeson, a black man, was to appear with Wallace.

Officials at the University of Iowa, in Wallace's home state, barred him from speaking on campus. When he moved to a public park, addressing some three thousand students, he was forced to dodge two eggs thrown from the audience. Moving on to Kansas, Wallace was greeted by a provocative headline in the *Wichita Beacon*: "Hot Reception Looms in K.C. for Wallace." In Missouri he was denied permission to speak on the campuses of both the University of Missouri and Stephens College. At an outdoor rally in Columbia, eggs were thrown again, his microphone was cut off twice, and a hundred determined hecklers managed to silence him for fifteen minutes.[29]

The liberal columnist Max Lerner, not a third-party supporter, decried the spirit of vigilantism at loose in West Virginia.[30]

In May, following a Wallace rally in Madison Square Garden, a full-scale riot broke out when members of the Catholic War Veterans attacked a group of progressive students picketing an anti-Russian motion picture showing at the nearby Roxy Theater. Mounted policemen swinging billy clubs cracked heads and herded scores of Wallace's followers into paddy wagons as they came to the students' assistance.

In Detroit, Police Commissioner Harry S. Toy, who said he thought Communists were entering the United States disguised as Canadian rabbis, said all radicals should be imprisoned. After the autoworker leader Walter Reuther was shot in his home by an unknown assailant, Toy rounded up Wallace supporters—almost all of them blacks or Jews—as suspects. When Wallace arrived in the city to speak, the acting mayor personally assigned a hundred uniformed officers to protect his safety.

So it went in city after city. At least Wallace had the protection of a famous face, the status of having been vice president, the buffer provided by a small traveling party. (His entourage included Jack Zuckerman, a New York City policeman, who served as a bodyguard.) Thousands of his followers had no such protection from violence or intimidation.

Scores of college professors and high school teachers lost their jobs. In Peoria, Illinois, the president of Bradley University flatly ordered his faculty not to associate with Wallace. The president of Western Reserve University, in Cleveland, warned faculty members "who go out on a limb" in supporting Wallace not to expect "assistance from the university." Ohio State University withdrew official recognition of a pro-Wallace student group, its board demanded that faculty take a loyalty oath, and its president launched an investigation into Communist activity by the campus YMCA.[31]

Pro-Wallace rallies at Duquesne University, the University of Pittsburgh, Harvard, Yale, the University of Colorado, and UCLA resulted in rowdy confrontations with protesters. At a Louisiana State University Wallace rally, the lights were cut off and a law professor who tried to speak in the darkness was pelted with vegetables. The president of Wilkes College, in New York, was obliged to explain his censorship of the student newspaper as a choice between freedom of speech and funding for a new gymnasium.

In Alabama a Wallace worker was arrested and sentenced to six months in jail for distributing pro-Wallace "Communist literature." In Chicago police raided a private apartment where fifteen young people, mostly University of Chicago students, were drinking Coca-Cola and talking about Wallace. "Those kids are a bunch of Communists," a police captain explained.[32]

Eleanor Roosevelt, while far from sympathetic to the Wallace campaign, decried the violence in her newspaper column as "fundamentally un-Christian and wrong." And, she added, "it is politically stupid."[33]

Newspapers happily piled on. Most notorious was the *Pittsburgh Press*, a Scripps-Howard newspaper, which throughout April published the names, addresses, and places of employment of more than one thousand people who signed Wallace nominating petitions in western Pennsylvania and suggested the FBI might want to check them out. Despite threats from employers only ten people retracted their signatures. When Wallace vigorously protested the newspaper's action, the *Press* replied editorially, "Gideon's Army, as Henry Wallace calls his followers, doesn't seem to like daylight." Newspapers in Tennessee, Ohio, Alabama, New Hampshire, and Massachusetts performed a similar service for their readers.[34]

Sometimes the efforts of Wallace's foes bordered on comedy. A judge in a New York child custody case announced he would take into account whether one of the parents supported Wallace. A local school board banned a book called *Twenty Modern Americans* because it contained a chapter on Wallace. When Wallace's chief poultry breeder from Farvue went to a New York airport to pick up some hatching eggs shipped from Europe, a U.S. Customs official deliberately threw one of the subversive eggs to the floor. "An enraged bureaucracy can be one of the nastiest manifestations of a police state . . . ," Wallace shrugged. "Undoubtedly he looked on my poultry expert as one of 'Henry Wallace's Communists' and began to see red."[35]

Other instances of the anti-Wallace hysteria were anything but comic. On May 7, 1948, Wallace supporter Robert W. New Jr., a twenty-eight-year-old maritime worker in Charleston, South Carolina, had his throat slit by a drunken fellow unionist who said New was a "nigger lover" and a Wallace supporter. The murderer, Rudolph Serreo, was defended in court by a former mayor of Charleston, Thomas P. Stoney, who virtually said the victim deserved to die for his political beliefs. "At the trial I will prosecute Bob New for raising unrest among the colored people in the South," said Stoney. "I will prosecute him also as the chairman of the Wallace committee and as [one of] the despicable, slick, slimy Communists prowling the waterfront."[36]

Serreo was allowed to plead guilty to voluntary manslaughter and given a three-year sentence.

Nor were public officials and New Party candidates immune. Most notable was the rough arrest of Glen Taylor in Birmingham on May 1. Taylor had gone to Alabama to address a meeting of the Southern Negro Youth Conference. There he ran afoul of a municipal ordinance forbidding integrated meetings and the city's police chief, Eugene "Bull" Connor, later to gain national notoriety for his treatment of civil rights workers. Even before Taylor arrived, Connor had made it clear he was unwelcome. "There's not enough room in town for Bull and the Commies," he said.

Asked for his reaction when he arrived in Birmingham, Taylor said, "Safety

Commissioner Connor can go to hell. I do what I think is right, let the chips fall where they may."

As Taylor prepared to enter the hall through an entrance marked "Colored," he was warned by police to use a rear entrance reserved for "Whites." Taylor was defiant. In his lively autobiography, Taylor recalled his thoughts: "I was a United States senator, and by God, I wasn't going to slink down a dark alley to get to a back door for Bull Connor or any other bigoted son of a bitch. I'd go in any goddamned door I pleased, and I pleased to go in that door right there."

In a flash he was shoved against the building by a burly policeman. Taylor came back swinging but several other policemen knocked him to the ground, tearing his suit on a strand of barbed wire and smashing his head on a concrete sidewalk. Soon the dazed senator found himself being driven slowly around town in a squad car while the police taunted him. "This is it—they're going to beat me to death," he said to himself.

Eventually Taylor was taken to the city jail and thrown into a stinking holding pen with the evening's catch of drunks, pimps, and pickpockets. One of his fellow prisoners approached and introduced himself. "They got me for pukin' on the sidewalk," he said. "What's your racket?" Taylor replied, "I am a United States senator, and they got me for trying to enter a meeting through a colored entrance." The man edged away in disbelief. "Obviously, he thought I was the craziest kook in the place," Taylor later wrote.

At length Taylor was photographed, fingerprinted, and released on bond. At a subsequent trial he was fined $50 and given a 180-day suspended sentence on charges of breach of peace, assault, and resisting arrest. The sentence was upheld by the Alabama supreme court; the U.S. Supreme Court declined to review the case. Taylor never paid the fine, and the matter ended quietly more than a year later when Governor James Folsom refused to ask for Taylor's extradition to Alabama.

After his release Taylor returned to the Capitol and recounted his astonishing experience in Birmingham on the Senate floor. "Not one senator opened his mouth," Taylor wrote. Not even Alabama's senators, Lister Hill (a former Wallace ally) and John Sparkman (later a Democratic vice-presidential candidate), said anything to apologize for their state's conduct.

The irony of the moment was neatly captured in a wire Taylor received from his running mate. "This dramatizes the hypocrisy of spending billions for arms in the name of defending freedom abroad, while freedom is trampled on here at home," Wallace said.[37]

CHAPTER TWENTY-FIVE

"TO MAKE THE DREAM COME TRUE"

On April 12, 1948, eighty-year-old May Brodhead Wallace, wife of one agriculture secretary and mother of another, died quietly, surrounded by members of her family. Henry A. Wallace's presidential campaign paused briefly while he attended her funeral in Des Moines.

"Her sense of reality, the all-wool-and-a-yard-wide type of integrity, the sensitive appreciation of human nature combined with hope and faith in the possibilities of life, are qualities which remain with me," former labor secretary Frances Perkins wrote to Wallace in a letter of condolence. Harry and Bess Truman also wired their sympathies. May Wallace was buried in Des Moines beside her beloved Harry.*[1]

Wallace returned quickly to his cause, struggling to make himself heard above the cacophony. He traveled widely, gave speeches, wrote columns, granted numerous interviews, issued pamphlets, wrote a short book, and kept up his active correspondence.

In addition, three times early in the year Wallace appeared before congressional committees. In February he testified against the European Recovery Program, opening with an 11,000-word

---

*The funeral brought together the far-flung children of Henry C. and May Wallace for the first time in many years. They were Henry A. Wallace of South Salem, New York; Mrs. Angus D. MacLay (Annabelle) of Birmingham, Michigan, wife of a Detroit utilities executive; Mrs. Charles Bruggemann (Mary) of Vevey, Switzerland, wife of a Swiss diplomat; John B. Wallace of St. Petersburg, Florida, an insurance and real estate man; James W. Wallace of Des Moines, an executive of the Pioneer Hi-Bred Corn Co.; and Mrs. Per Wijkman (Ruth) of Des Moines, wife of a Swedish diplomat.

statement arguing that it was not a plan for international understanding but a vehicle to dominate world markets. His reception was hostile, and Wallace at one point declined to answer an "irrelevant and futile" question.[2]

In March he appeared before the Senate Armed Forces Committee to oppose Truman's call for universal military training. His 5,500-word opening statement was later issued as a pamphlet called *The Wallace Plan or the Marshall Plan.* The country could get along without a draft, Wallace maintained, if the government adopted a less militaristic foreign policy, improved the pay and working conditions of enlisted men, and ended racial discrimination in the armed services.

And in May he delivered a blistering 3,000-word attack on the Mundt Nixon bill requiring registration of Communist Party members, disclosure of membership and contribution lists of "Communist Front" organizations as defined by the attorney general, and the immediate deportation of Communist aliens. Wallace called it "the most subversive legislation ever to be seriously sponsored in the United States Congress."[3]

But "Red fever" was engulfing America. Nothing Wallace could say was enough to bring him a respectful hearing. Nothing he could do would calm the nation's irrational fear.

Everything had turned on its head. The quiet son of Iowa soil had been transformed in the public mind into a wild-eyed fanatic bent on destroying the American way of life. The thoughtful scientist had become the impractical mystic. The ardent defender of World War II had become a Chamberlain-like appeaser. The deeply religious grandson of a Presbyterian minister had become an apostle of godless totalitarianism.

Events abroad only made things worse. News reports from Europe, Asia, and the Middle East continually reinforced the public impression that the world was in crisis, that diplomacy was impossible, that communism was the enemy. The Soviet Union, convinced that the United States and Britain were moving to partition Germany and reindustrialize the sectors under their control, moved tanks into Berlin. Land and canal access to the city was cut off. The United States began airlifting in relief supplies.

Food shortages plagued Europe, and the political climate boiled. The Greek government, propped up by President Truman's military assistance program, began executing hundreds of leftists. Britain teetered on the edge of bankruptcy. Italy was in turmoil. Yugoslavia made a show of independence from the Commintern. Britain, France, and the Benelux countries adopted a fifty-year mutual assistance pact. Finland signed a ten-year treaty with the Soviet Union. Senator Arthur Vandenberg declared that immediate passage of a bill providing $6.2 billion for the European Recovery Program was the only means of preventing World War III.

Nor did the rest of the world give cause for comfort. Chiang Kai-shek's hold on China grew increasingly tenuous. In Indochina nationalists operating under the Communist banner began their long battle to expel the French. India nearly dissolved in anarchy following the assassination of Gandhi. Korea began to divide into warring sectors. Iran declared martial law. The Middle East was awash in tension, punctuated by bomb blasts, as the deadline neared for the end of British control of Palestine. Only there did events redound in Wallace's favor, thanks to his steady support for creation of a Jewish state and the Truman administration's decision to withdraw its backing for the partition of Palestine.

Under pressure to offer a sort of running commentary on world affairs, Wallace sometimes made the worst of a bad situation. His most notable gaffe concerned Czechoslovakia, where a coalition government led by President Eduard Beneš collapsed in late February. Communists took complete control and moved to outlaw opposition parties. Wallace's first reaction was to call attention to the need for an understanding with Russia.

"The Czech crisis is evidence that a 'get tough' policy only provokes a 'get tougher' policy," Wallace said. ". . . The men in Moscow would, from their point of view, be utter morons if they failed to respond with acts of pro-Russian consolidation. . . . Only peace with Russia will stop the march toward war."[4]

Wallace had said much the same thing many times before, but this time his comments were clearly out of tune with the views of his countrymen. The very fact that he was talking about Czechoslovakia brought back memories of Munich and Neville Chamberlain and appeasement. Furthermore, President Beneš's government offered a textbook example of an arrangement that was supposed to give East European nations control over their domestic affairs while conceding foreign policy to the Soviet Union.

Then Wallace dug himself into an even deeper hole. On March 15, in the midst of an otherwise unremarkable news conference, he suddenly suggested the Communist coup in Czechoslovakia was in response to a right-wing plot to take over the government. And he asserted that U.S. Ambassador Laurence Steinhardt helped cause the crisis with a statement supportive of the rightists. As reporters clamored for details, Wallace glanced at a note handed to him by his aide Lew Frank and began to leave the room. (Much was made of the mysterious note; it was actually a reminder that he was late in leaving to catch a train.)

A reporter shouted a question about the death a few days earlier of Foreign Minister Jan Masaryk. The son of one of Czechoslovakia's founding fathers, Masaryk, although not a Communist, had been allowed to stay in power following the Communist takeover. He died after falling from a window of his third-floor apartment in the foreign ministry building. The Communists maintained it was suicide; almost everyone else thought it was murder.

Hurrying to leave, Wallace paused at the door to answer the question about Masaryk's death. "I live in the house that John G. Winant [the late U.S. ambassador to Britain] lived in and I've heard rumors why he committed suicide. Maybe Winant had cancer. Maybe Masaryk had cancer. Maybe Winant was unhappy about the fate of the world. Who knows?" With that he left the room.[5]

Wallace could offer little or no support for anything he had said. Press commentary denounced his comments as foolish and irresponsible. The *New York Times* editorialized, "We have a new standard for measuring just how valuable a contribution Mr. Wallace's Presidential candidacy is now making to the ideology of International Communism."[6] Steinhardt demanded an apology, which Wallace refused to give.

Four years passed before Wallace admitted, in a *This Week* magazine article entitled "Where I Was Wrong" that he had erred badly.

Increasingly beleaguered and frustrated, Wallace came up with a plan he hoped would dramatize the peace issue: an open letter to Joseph Stalin.

The letter flowed from an idea of Anita McCormick Blaine's. In her impetuous and idealistic way, Blaine suggested during a luncheon at her Chicago mansion that she and Wallace charter a plane and go meet with Stalin. Wallace did not immediately reject her idea but had reservations. He had been burned by the experience of his 1947 European tour, and no one could assure that Stalin would meet with them.

Evidence recently discovered in Soviet archives, however, indicates Wallace explored the Moscow trip more deeply than previously thought. He even prepared a list of topics he wished to discuss with Stalin. The list went to Stalin through Andrei Gromyko, Soviet ambassador to the United Nations, who received it via the Czechoslovakian ambassador, Dr. Vladimir Houdek. Stalin personally studied the document and made notations beside its points. For example, when Wallace suggested it would be necessary "to make a statement to the effect that stopping Cold War between USA and USSR would not mean sacrificing vital American principles or interests," Stalin noted, "We don't engage in any Cold War. It's being waged by the U.S."[7]

Wallace later claimed the trip idea fell victim to Anita Blaine's doctors, who opposed it on grounds of her age and health. Soviet archives suggest Stalin rejected it too.[8]

In any case he never went. But Wallace continued even so to seek a dialogue with Stalin. In April, without mentioning the idea to his political aides, he began toying with the idea of an open letter. Wallace discussed the idea with Blaine because "she always loved to be consulted and we'd talk things over."9

Once again Wallace secretly alerted Stalin, hoping to ensure a response. A message about the open letter, and some indication of its content, went from Ambassador Houdek to Gromyko to Stalin. Wallace said nothing about this even to his closest advisers.

Wallace decided at the beginning of May to release the open letter during a Madison Square Garden speech on the night of May 11, 1948.

A week before Wallace spoke, the U.S. ambassador to the Soviet Union, Walter Bedell Smith, called upon Foreign Minister V. M. Molotov to deliver a formal note regarding foreign policy and the U.S. election. Boiled down to its essentials, Smith's message was that Henry Wallace's candidacy would not influence Truman's foreign policy. The get-tough policy would stay tough. Smith's note ended with a diplomatic nicety: "As far as the United States is concerned, the door is always open for full discussion and the composing of our differences."10

Five days later the Soviet government seized upon that sentence to score a propaganda victory. It released an edited version of Smith's message and a response from Molotov, saying, "The Soviet government views favorably the desire of the government of the United States to improve these relations as expressed in said statement, and agrees to the proposal to proceed with this end in view, to a discussion and settlement of the differences existing between us."11

News of the Smith-Molotov exchange reached the United States on the eve of Wallace's speech. Immediately an embarrassed Truman administration had to explain that the door to full discussion was not open at all. Secretary of State George Marshall was reduced to saying that he and Smith were military men unfamiliar with the arcane ways of diplomats.

Wallace delivered his speech as planned on May 11, focusing on the letter to Stalin. Over objections raised by Beanie Baldwin, Wallace added a few lines to recognize the Smith-Molotov exchange. The Smith-Molotov messages suggested a "new and hopeful phase of international relations," Wallace said. Although both the U.S. and the Soviet notes were "characterized by the same self-righteousness which has led to the international crisis," he added, "they represent great hopes for those of us who have consistently maintained that peace is possible and they represent a severe blow to the propagandists on both sides who have insisted that the two nations cannot live at peace in the same world."12

In his open letter Wallace called for a series of "definite, decisive steps" to end the Cold War. These included arms reductions and the "outlawing of all methods of mass destruction"; a halt to the export of weaponry from one nation to another; the resumption of unrestricted trade between the United

States and the Soviet Union; lifting restrictions on the movement of citizens, journalists, and students "between and within" the United States and the USSR; the free exchange of scientific information between the two nations; and establishment of a new UN relief agency to coordinate international assistance.

"There is no misunderstanding or difficulty between the USA and USSR which can be settled by force," he concluded, "and there is no difference which cannot be settled by peaceful, hopeful negotiation. There is no American principle or public interest, and there is no Russian principle or public interest, which would have to be sacrificed to end the Cold War and open up the Century of Peace which the Century of the Common Man demands."[13]

For a moment it appeared Wallace had broken through the haze surrounding his candidacy. His proposals were arguably evenhanded and reasonable, especially in light of the Truman administration's blundering effort to explain away the content of Ambassador Smith's note. "It's always difficult to explain away a welch," the *New York Post* editorialized, "but Truman wins the grand prize, hands down, for not making sense. And, unfortunately for his re-election hopes, he chose to mumble the irresponsible nonsense at a time when Henry Wallace, speaking to a capacity crowd at Madison Square Garden, wasn't mumbling and made a great deal of sense."[14]

A week later Stalin replied to Wallace via a message over Moscow radio. He called the open letter a "most important document," which went well beyond the Smith-Molotov exchange by setting out "concrete proposals on all basic questions of differences between the U.S.S.R. and the United States." After summarizing these proposals, Stalin added, "It is possible to agree or disagree with the program of Mr. Wallace, but one thing is, nevertheless, beyond doubt: There is no statesman caring for peace and cooperation among the peoples who can ignore this program, since it reflects the hopes and strivings of the people toward consolidation of peace, and it doubtless will have the support of many millions of ordinary people."[15] Stalin said he did not know how the U.S. government felt about Wallace's proposals, but he noted that the Soviet Union considered them a "good and fruitful basis" for the settlement of international differences.

Campaigning in California, Wallace expressed surprise at Stalin's response. "If I have done anything that moves the world further toward peace, I feel that my campaign will have been a success," he told reporters. Whether or not he was really surprised, he certainly appeared so to reporters. In a speech that evening Wallace still glowed with optimism. "The significance of Premier Stalin's reply lies in the fact that the Russian government is truly prepared to discuss issues on their merit and is genuinely interested in finding a way for the two great powers to live at peace."[16]

His hopefulness was short-lived. Within twenty-four hours the Truman administration rejected Stalin's statement as a basis for bilateral negotiation. Secretary of State Marshall said Stalin's answer to Wallace was "meaningless," since the issues had already been discussed in the United Nations. Wallace shot back, "I might say that it is nice to have our State Department recognize the UN—even in this negative way. . . . But General Marshall's statement is hardly satisfying to people who need and want peace."[17]

Soon the open letter itself turned into ammunition against the man who wrote it. Once again Wallace was portrayed as having done something unpatriotic, if not illegal. Newspapermen and ADA liberals cited it as further proof of a candidacy hatched in the Kremlin or a candidate held prisoner by a leftist "palace guard." Vincent Sheean, writing in the *Saturday Evening Post*, said "there is only one possible conclusion: the whole business was simply a mechanism for giving Stalin's approval to an American Presidential candidate."[18]

State Department investigators, on George Kennan's request, launched an inquiry to determine whether Wallace and Stalin had collaborated. The FBI began its own investigation, prompted by Attorney General Tom Clark, who felt Wallace's message might violate the 1799 Logan Act, forbidding private citizens from engaging in diplomatic correspondence with a foreign power.

Both the State Department and the FBI explored a tip from the newspaper columnist Dorothy Thompson, who alleged collusion between Wallace and the Soviets. Thompson reasoned that since the twenty thousand copies of Wallace's speech distributed at Madison Square Garden alluded to the Smith-Molotov exchange, Wallace must have known about it well in advance. A printer could not have produced the speech in the twenty-two hours between publication of the Smith-Molotov exchange and the Madison Square Garden rally, Thompson asserted.

The State Department investigation was inconclusive, although it speculated gravely about the loyalties of the print shop. The FBI decided Thompson's suspicions were groundless, because a commercial printer could produce twenty thousand copies in three to four hours.

Not to be outdone, the House Un-American Activities Committee began compiling a list of people who commented favorably on the open letter to Stalin as evidence of their subversive tendencies.

Wallace came to view the open-letter episode as a kind of milestone—a symbolic moment when a window of opportunity was closed. Four years later, in giving his oral history to Columbia University, he commented, "When Russia was recovering from that extraordinary devastation which is beyond our imagination to comprehend back in 1945, 1946, 1947 and on into 1948, I'm convinced there was a great opportunity for us to take advantage of Russia's own self-interest to move in with a comprehensive program of one world along the line of the plan I have outlined again and again. . . . I don't know when that opportunity completely passed away. I think it was still open to a degree at the time of my letter to Stalin. Stalin's reply in May, 1948, indicates a willingness for conversation."[19]

❦

Buffeted by world events, bloodied by the campaign of violence and intimidation against them, Wallace and his Gideon's Army staggered toward their national convention. Six months of arduous effort had little to show for it. Wallace's standing in the Gallup poll had dropped from 7 percent in December to 5 percent in June. Wallace was hopelessly entangled in the "Communist issue" and was widely seen as a forlorn, if not pathetic, figure.* The New Party had utterly failed to break through the wall of opposition.

Some columnists said Wallace would quit before the election. They didn't know their man. He had been surprised by "the extent of the smear and the extent of the attitude of hate" directed toward him, but it didn't matter. Though he was bone tired from long days and constant travel, that didn't matter either. "My own slant," Wallace later commented, ". . . was conditioned by my biblical upbringing—even though I'm all alone I'll go ahead with what I think is right. That's what determined me. When it comes to a supreme issue like [peace], what if the whole world would be against me?"[20]

And, righteousness aside, Wallace continued to believe that his party held the balance of power in the election. Harry Truman must surely move leftward—or lose.

Virtually everything that happened at the Republican and Democratic national conventions that summer pointed to a president in deep political trouble. He is a "gone goose," Congresswoman Clare Boothe Luce crowed as Republicans gathered in Philadelphia on June 21.[21]

---

*Wallace was certainly not unaware of the political cost of his Communist support. On June 3 in Albuquerque he commented, "According to the newspapers I'm getting a lot of support from the Communists, and the Communist leaders seem to think they have to endorse me every day or so. There's no question that this sort of thing is a political liability. The Communists oppose my advocacy of progressive capitalism. They support me because I say that we can have peace with Russia. I will not repudiate any support which comes to me on the basis of interest in peace."

Three weeks later, speaking to twenty-five people in Center Sandwich, New Hampshire, Wallace virtually invited Communists to desert him. "I'm never going to say anything in the nature of red-baiting. But I must say this: if the Communists would run a ticket of their own this year, we might lose 100,000 votes but we would gain three million. I know if the Communists really wanted to help us, they would run their own ticket this year and let us get those extra votes."

He would go no further to distance himself from Communists, however. Frequently Wallace told his aides, "I must not say anything that would interfere with my ability to make peace in the world."

The Republican convention was a monument to smugness. The nomination of Governor Thomas E. Dewey of New York and Governor Earl Warren of California—popular and successful politicians from states with a combined seventy-two electoral votes—seemed a political triumph. Both men had moderate records on domestic issues and were seen as competent, honest executives. Both supported the bipartisan foreign policy and containment of communism.

A measure of the arrogance of the Republicans—one to cost them dearly on election day—was their vehement attack on Wallace. In a close election, almost all observers agreed, Wallace could spell the difference, but Republicans gave him no quarter. Congresswoman Luce called Wallace "Stalin's Mortimer Snerd," a reference to popular ventriloquist Edgar Bergen's dimwitted dummy, and said the New Party was composed of "economic spoonies and political bubbleheads . . . labor racketeers, native and imported Communists and foreign agents of the Kremlin."[22]

Keynote speaker Dwight Green, the governor of Illinois, called Wallace the last representative of the New Deal coalition "held together by bosses, boodle, buncombe and blarney." The New Deal party was never a "legitimate majority," Green said, as evidenced by the fact that without the "lunatic fringe" it cannot win. "Its dying hope is, win without Wallace. Our answer is, it couldn't win *with* Wallace."[23]

If the Republican convention unnerved Democrats, their own convention totally spooked them. The weeks prior to its opening were marked by a frantic liberal effort to dump Harry Truman and replace him with Dwight D. Eisenhower. When Eisenhower on July 5 said he would "not, at this time, identify myself with any political party," Senator Claude Pepper began an ill-formed movement to draft the general on a nonpartisan basis. Eisenhower responded with a telegram saying, "I will not accept even if nominated." Pepper promptly put himself forward as an alternative to Truman but withdrew his candidacy as the convention opened.*[24]

Struggling to quiet liberal discontent, Truman pleaded with Supreme Court Justice William O. Douglas to be his running mate. Douglas, not wanting to board a sinking ship, rebuffed him. Privately Douglas quipped that he could not be "a No. 2 man to a No. 2 man." Lacking a good alternative, Truman took Senator Alben Barkley of Kentucky as the vice presidential nominee.

---

*As of 1948 Eisenhower had never voted, because he believed professional military officers should stay out of partisan politics, and very little was known about his position on domestic issues. Among prominent liberals, Wallace was almost alone in taking note of the one concrete fact about Eisenhower's views. On April 2, 1948, Eisenhower testified before a congressional committee in favor of Truman's proposal for universal military training but denounced plans for desegregation of the armed forces. Wallace offered Eisenhower "a membership card in the New Party" if he would renounce his reactionary racial stance.

Well-liked by party regulars, Barkley was seventy years old and like Truman from a midsized border state, neither an advantage.[25]

Meanwhile, delegates warred over the platform, specifically its civil rights plank. To mollify southern segregationists, Truman wanted vague language patterned after the 1944 platform, which did little for black voters. Liberals wanted something more specific. Truman prevailed in committee, but liberals led by Hubert Humphrey carried their fight to the convention floor and won. The Democratic Party was at last on record opposing the poll tax, favoring federal antilynching legislation, and promising to desegregate the armed forces.

With that the Alabama delegate Handy Ellis grabbed a microphone and said, "We bid you good-bye." Out the door went thirteen Alabamans and all twenty-three members of the Mississippi delegation. A few days later politicians from across the South made the split official. Meeting in Birmingham, they formed the States' Rights Party, popularly known as the Dixiecrats, and adopted a platform dedicated to racial segregation. Governor J. Strom Thurmond of South Carolina and Governor Fielding Wright of Mississippi would run for president and vice president, respectively.

Truman's only good moment was his acceptance speech, a feisty address in which he vowed to win the election "and make these Republicans like it." In a brilliant stroke, he promised to call a special session of Congress on July 26 and give Republicans a chance to enact into law the airy generalities advanced in their platform. Unfortunately for Truman, the speech aired at 2 A.M. in a sweltering hall while a flock of white pigeons (supposed to be doves representing peace) flapped around.

Truman apparently ended the convention in worse shape than he had begun it. His party lay in three pieces, and he seemed destined to become a footnote to history. The Democratic Party, Beanie Baldwin quipped, had "nominated a Man Nobody Wanted and adopted a Program Nobody Meant."[26]

The Wallace campaign could draw no solace from Truman's troubles. As progressives gathered in Philadelphia on July 23, the New Party and its candidate were reeling.

For one embarrassing thing, Wallace had been dismissed from the *New Republic*. His departure, couched amicably as allowing him time to campaign, could not disguise the fact that the publisher Michael Straight clearly would not support Wallace's presidential bid. He saw no point in allowing Wallace to use the magazine's pages.

The New Party's 74-member platform committee added to its troubles, squabbling over everything from the wording of the preamble to a unified homeland for Macedonia. The result, a hefty 6,500-word document, pleased no one, including Henry Wallace and the platform committee chairman, Rexford Guy Tugwell. Some portrayed it as evidence that "party-line communists" controlled the proceedings.*

In fact, nobody controlled the platform committee. Its meetings were excruciatingly earnest and democratic. Even James Loeb, executive director of the Americans for Democratic Action, was allowed to appear and denounce the New Party to its face. Long arguments over proposed planks were settled by majority vote. Lee Pressman, the hard-charging labor lawyer who served as the committee's secretary, saw the debates as "a battle between the comma hounds." Tugwell so disliked a plank dealing with Puerto Rican independence that he threw up his hands and boycotted the committee's final two sessions.[27]

No matter how the party conducted itself, however, the fears of the American public only seemed to be confirmed. At convention time Gallup reported a whopping 51 percent of the public believed that the New Party was controlled by Communists; 21 percent did not believe it was, and 28 percent had no opinion.

Forty-eight hours before the convention, the New Party was hit again. A federal grand jury in New York indicted twelve members of the Communist Party's national board, including the party chairman, William Z. Foster, its general secretary, Eugene Dennis, and the *Daily Worker* editor John Gates. They were accused of violating the Smith Act of 1940, which proscribed teaching or advocating the violent overthrow of the U.S. government.

Virtually everyone in the Wallace campaign saw a deliberate attempt to cement the New Party to Communists. But there was uncertainty how—or whether—to respond. Wallace did not hesitate. He issued a lengthy statement

*Like the organizing documents of other American "third parties" the Progressive platform was far-reaching and prophetic. It called for the desegregation of public schools, an end to Jim Crow laws, open housing, national health insurance, equal rights for women, public day-care facilities, the minimum wage for farm workers, free trade, immigration reform, the direct election of presidents, home rule for the District of Columbia, indemnity for Japanese-Americans, collective bargaining for federal employees, new soil conservation programs, the vote for eighteen-year-olds, full taxation of capital gains, creation of a federal education department, and admission of Alaska and Hawaii to the Union. It also supported a minimum national pension of $100 a month at age sixty.

Wallace didn't like its call for public ownership of large banks, railroads, the merchant marine, electric power and gas utilities, and several industries dependent upon public funding such as the aircraft and synthetic-rubber sectors. Wallace, who consistently called himself a "progressive capitalist," probably could have imposed his will on the platform writers but did not wish to interfere. "I'm only your hired man, hoping someday to be given a 40-hour week," Wallace told the platform writers.

The chief advocate for Wallace's point of view on the committee was Williams College political scientist Frederick Schuman. The professor noted it would be highly ironic if Wallace, "the only businessman and capitalist currently running for President of the United States," were to be saddled with a socialist platform. Schuman was ignored.

saying, "Americans have far more to fear from those actions which are intended to suppress political freedom than from the teaching of ideas with which we are in disagreement." He noted that the indictments "make no charge of the commission of acts of force or violence" and predicted that the Smith Act would eventually be found unconstitutional as a violation of freedom of speech.*[28]

Then came the most damaging blow. At an afternoon news conference hours before the convention opened, packed with four hundred people, including the nation's premier journalists, Wallace was publicly confronted with the mysterious "guru letters." The result was a debacle.

Wallace's letters to the painter Nicholas Roerich and his associates had traveled a circuitous route since they were written. For several years they were in the hands of Frances Grant, a Roerich follower embittered by Wallace's break with the painter in 1935. During the 1940 campaign she sold the letters to the newspaper publisher Paul Block, whose attempt to publish them was forestalled by mutual blackmail between the Republican and Democratic parties. Cocktail party gossip had long held that the letters figured in Wallace's fall at the 1944 Democratic convention, but the rumors remained sub rosa.

Sometime during the mid-1940s the letters fell into the hands of Westbrook Pegler, a stridently reactionary columnist for the Hearst newspapers, who had no qualms about using them to destroy Wallace. Even in the bare-knuckled world of syndicated columnists, Pegler attracted controversy, but he could hardly be ignored. At the height of his career, he was among the most-read columnists in the nation, appearing in 120 newspapers with eight million readers.

"It can fairly be said that the two columnists who have the most influence in the country are [Walter] Lippman and Pegler," the liberal journalist George Seldes once wrote. "Lippmann influences all men of intelligence, Pegler is the monitor of the morons. Lippman has one of the best minds in America, Pegler is a mental hoodlum."[29]

Hoodlum or not, Pegler started printing portions of the guru letters in a series of lurid columns beginning in the summer of 1947. "The voters of this

---

*Wallace's prediction was slowly realized. Over time the government found Smith Act cases increasingly difficult to win, and in 1957 the law was effectively overturned by the Supreme Court. In the intervening years the government had brought 145 indictments under the Smith Act and had obtained 108 convictions.

Of the twelve men indicted in July 1948, eleven were tried and convicted after a nine-month trial in a lower Manhattan federal courthouse. William Z. Foster escaped trial because of his age and poor health. They were sentenced to prison terms ranging from three to five years and ordered to pay fines of $5,000. In addition, their five defense attorneys were held in contempt of court and imprisoned from one to six months.

The Supreme Court upheld the convictions in 1951 in the case of *Dennis* v. *United States*. Only Justices William O. Douglas and Hugo Black dissented. The Communist Party USA was "the least thriving of any fifth column in history," Douglas scoffed. "Only those held by fear or panic could think otherwise."

country are entitled to know whether or not those letters were written to a Russian whose followers regarded him as Almighty God and to members of this Russian's Oriental political and pseudo-religious cult by a man now running for President of the United States with a following composed mostly of Communist traitors," Pegler wrote in a typical column. In another burst of invective he declared, "The man who wrote those letters was, by American popular standards, as dizzy as a dervish. These letters are revolting in their idiotic, juvenile prattle of esoteric jargon."[30]

Month after month, as Pegler demanded he own up to authorship, Wallace simply ignored the matter. But at the tumultuous press conference on July 23, there was no place to hide. After some preliminary fencing over foreign affairs, Wallace was asked directly whether he repudiated the guru letters. "A tense, terrible silence seeped through the room," wrote Carle Hodge, a reporter for *Editor & Publisher*. ". . . Calmly, coolly, his face frozen now, Wallace replied: 'I never comment on Westbrook Pegler.' "

Two or three other reporters asked rephrased versions of the same question and received the same reply. Suddenly a tall, gray-haired man took the floor and said, "My name is Westbrook Pegler." He, too, demanded that Wallace say whether he wrote the letters. "I never engage in any discussions with Westbrook Pegler," Wallace said.

Smelling blood, reporters for the *Detroit News* and *Los Angeles Times* came to Pegler's defense. Wallace shot back, "I will not engage in any discussion with any stooge of Westbrook Pegler." A reporter for the *Washington Post*, struggling to control her emotions, said she was "not a stooge for anybody" but thought Wallace should answer the question. He refused.

At that point Wallace was confronted by H. L. Mencken, one of the century's most storied journalists. "Mr. Wallace, do you call me a stooge of Pegler," asked Mencken. The entire room, Wallace included, broke into laughter. Mencken continued, "If you won't answer the question as to whether you wrote those letters, tell us, at least, the reason you won't answer it."

"Because it is not important," Wallace said.[31]

In the larger sense Wallace may have been correct. The guru letters may have been, as the liberal Max Lerner wrote, "an idiot issue swollen into headlines by Pegler-Hearst venom." But that was cold comfort to Wallace and his aides. In a few disastrous minutes they had seen the focus of the national press corps turn from issues of foreign policy and the formation of a new political party to Wallace's long-ago interest in Roerich and his defiant refusal to explain himself. Beanie Baldwin and others stood ashen faced at the front of the room, stunned and immobilized, knowing they could now expect the worst.[32]

They were not disappointed. An editorial in the *Chicago Daily News* typified press response to Wallace's performance: "If only Wallace, the Master

Guru, becomes President, we shall get in tune with the Infinite, vibrate in the correct plane, outstare the Evil Eye, reform the witches, overcome all malicious spells and ascend the high road to health and happiness."[33]

❊

The men and women who planned the New Party convention wanted something different in American politics. Where the old parties adhered to hoary tradition, their convention would be fresh and dramatic. Where the old party gatherings were tightly controlled by bosses in smoke-filled rooms, theirs would be open and democratic, alive with music and spontaneity.

That was what they wanted, and to a large extent they got it. The New Party's organizers realized their aims completely—and their convention was judged a colossal failure.

What the New Party chieftains saw as democracy, the press viewed as no better than communism. Their genuine "people's convention"—open to a broad spectrum of young and old, black and white, working people and idealists—reporters portrayed as a callow mob of rabble. The centerpiece of the three-day convention, a theatrical open-air rally in which its candidates would take the stage, veteran newsmen saw as a fearful reminder of Nazi spectacles.

"The third party rally here over the weekend, carefully stage managed by a small group of pro-Communists, leaves a more unpleasant taste in the mouth than most such affairs," Joseph and Stewart Alsop wrote in their syndicated column. Another columnist, Peter Edson, declared, "There never was a political convention in which the program was so stage-managed, the candidates so handpicked, the platform so dictated by special interests . . . to promote what the American Communists are most interested in—the Russian foreign policy line."[34]

On only one point did New Party leaders and reporters agree: it was something different. As Edson put it, the convention was "the darndest thing that ever happened."

In all, 3,240 delegates and alternates, aged sixteen to eighty-eight, had come to Philadelphia.* That alone was different: triple the number of delegates at the Republican convention, double the attendance at the Democratic convention. Almost half of them—46 percent—belonged to trade unions; more than a quarter were military veterans.

---

*The party's organizers wished to hold the convention in Chicago, but they were able to cut costs significantly by meeting in Philadelphia, where the Republican and Democratic conventions were held in the preceding month. The major parties had jointly shared the $50,000 expense of equipping Convention Hall for their gatherings, and agreed to share the facility with the New Party for only $5,000.

The single East Coast location allowed television to extensively cover political conventions for the first time.

Among the delegates were two congressmen (Vito Marcantonio and Leo Isacson), a number of intellectuals and men of letters (Harvard historian F. O. Matthiesen, *New York Times* music critic Olin Downes), and two future U.S. senators (George McGovern and Quentin Burdick). Like McGovern three-quarters of the delegates had never before been in a political campaign. They arrived by train and on foot and in old jalopies. Many pitched tents or slept in their cars because they could not afford hotel rooms.

The first session, on the evening of Friday, July 23, set the tone. The meeting opened on time, delegates and spectators packed the hall and paid attention, speeches were short and to the point. There was no band. Instead, folk singers such as Pete Seeger and Michael Loring played banjos and led the crowd in rollicking versions of songs written or adapted for the occasion.* It reminded more than one reporter of a revival meeting.

*Among the adapted songs played at the convention were rewritten versions of "I've Got Sixpence," "The Battle Hymn of the Republic," and, of course, the "Iowa Corn Song." New songs included "We Are Building a New Party," with words and music by Pete Seeger and the folklorist Alan Lomax, "Friendly Henry Wallace," written by E. Y. "Yip" Harburg, who wrote *Finian's Rainbow*, and a bouncy crowd-pleasing ditty by Ray Glasser and Bill Wolff called "The Same Old Merry-Go-Round." Its words said in part:

> The donkey is tired and thin,
> The elephant thinks he'll move in,
> They fume and they fuss,
> But they ain't foolin' us
> Cause they're brothers right under the skin.
>
> It's the same, same, merry-go-round,
> Which one will you ride this year?
> The donkey and elephant bob up and down
> On the same merry-go-round.

Wallace's personal favorite was an old folk song entitled "Passing Through" with deep religious overtones:

> I saw Jesus on the cross
> On that hill called Calvary,
> "Do you hate mankind for what they done to you?"
> He said, "Talk of love, not hate,
> Things to do, it's getting late,
> I've so little time and I'm just passing through."

Wallace himself penned a new verse for the song:

> When the phony liberals leave,
> Let no Progressive grieve.
> One new party must be made of two.
> When the Marshall Plan is dead,
> And One World is just ahead,
> We'll all be brothers
> And no longer passing through.

Although distorted in the press, the party's rules were more democratic than those of either major party. The party committed itself to a one-man-one-vote principle, based on population (as opposed to voting structures weighted by states' political strength), and to hold a broad-based annual convention in the manner of the British Labour Party.

After a brief report from Beanie Baldwin, the party took a name with deep roots in American politics: the Progressive Party. Twice before in the twentieth century, third-party candidates had run under the Progressive banner. Henry Wallace would follow in the footsteps of the Republicans Theodore Roosevelt and Robert La Follette.

And unique in convention history, the keynote address was delivered by a black man. The first choice had been Dr. W. E. B. Du Bois, the famed sociologist, who turned it down because he thought of himself as more scholar than orator. Singer and actor Paul Robeson also declined.

So the keynote job fell to Charles P. Howard, an Iowa lawyer, publisher, and civil rights activist. Howard was a veteran of World War I, the father of three World War II servicemen, active in NAACP affairs, and a lifelong Republican.* He became interested in the Wallace campaign through his friendship with Viola Scott, Wallace's private secretary at the *New Republic*, who like Howard was active in black fraternal organizations.

Howard made the most of his moment in the sun, calling on the president to desegregate the armed forces immediately. "Mr. Truman, I ask you as Commander in Chief of the armed forces to sit down now and pick up your pen and write. Write the executive order which will abolish Jim Crow from the United States Army." He added, "The plain fact that I stand here before you

---

*As a defense lawyer Howard was said to have represented seventy-eight clients in death penalty cases, none of whom was hanged. His success was clouded, however, by a one-year suspension from legal practice in 1940 in a case involving $900 of a client's money. The money was returned, and the Iowa supreme court later reduced his suspension to six months.

The suspension only began Howard's troubles. Throughout the 1940s and 1950s he was a constant target of FBI surveillance and harassment, a campaign that J. Edgar Hoover personally instigated and directed. Hoover's interest in the Iowa attorney was triggered by a report that Howard was attempting to improve conditions among black recruits at the segregated Women's Army Corps training center at Fort Des Moines during World War II. In the late 1940s FBI agents attempted to build a sedition case against Howard, which finally was dropped for lack of evidence.

In 1950, following a well-publicized trip to the Soviet Union as Joseph Stalin's guest, Howard was subjected to disbarment proceedings by the Polk County Bar Association. He surrendered his license and moved to Chicago in 1951. In his later years Howard wrote a syndicated column covering UN affairs in New York City. He died in 1969 at age seventy-four. One of his sons, Joseph Howard, became a federal judge in Baltimore.

Repeated attempts by Howard's friends and the National Bar Association to restore his license posthumously, extending into the 1990s, were unsuccessful.

tonight defines our party. For the first time in my life, I am experiencing human dignity."[35]

Saturday, July 24, brought more of everything: speeches, singing, spirited debate, and bad press. In the afternoon delegates nominated and elected their presidential ticket, although everyone had known its identity for months. Wallace was nominated by Fred Stover, a feisty agrarian radical and president of the Iowa Farmers' Union. "Henry Wallace thinks big and sees far," Stover declared. "The pigmy men who lead the bipartisan coalition, however, think in thimble sizes and see as far as owls at high noon."[36]

Glen Taylor was nominated by Larkin Marshall, a black Georgian running on the Progressive Party's ticket for the U.S. Senate. Taylor's name was seconded by Wallace's sister Annabelle MacLay, vice chairman of the Progressive Party in Michigan, and Taylor's brother Paul, among others.

Wallace and Taylor had remained in their hotel rooms, in deference to tradition, but both men and their wives made a surprise appearance in Convention Hall shortly after they were nominated. Taylor carried his two-year-old son in his arms. Ilo Wallace, wearing a black suit and sprightly pink hat, stood at Henry's side. The crowd cheered itself hoarse for fifteen minutes, and the candidates left without saying a word.

Saturday night marked the Progressive's biggest break with custom.* That evening the entire convention moved from Convention Hall to Shibe Park, home of the Philadelphia Athletics baseball team, where the candidates would deliver their acceptance speeches at an outdoor rally. It was a risky venture. Shibe Park seated 32,000, and a half-filled stadium would have been embarrassing. Moreover, the convention organizers had set an admission fee ranging from 65 cents to $2.60.

---

*In another break with tradition the Progressive convention continued for a full day after the candidates accepted their nominations. On Sunday, July 25, the delegates returned to Convention Hall, where they debated and adopted the platform.

Reporters subsequently made much of an amendment to the platform called the Vermont Resolution, and cited its defeat as evidence of Communist control of the convention. The amendment would have stated, "Although we are critical of the present foreign policy of the United States, it is not our intention to give blanket endorsement to the foreign policy of any nation." Many delegates feared the amendment, bland though it was, smacked of appeasement to Red-baiters.

In fact, the Progressive convention organizers had barely noticed the Vermont Resolution and made no concerted effort to defeat it. Beanie Baldwin later said he would not have opposed it if it had come to his attention. The reason for their relaxed attitude was that they had already backed an amendment, drafted by Professor Frederick L. Schuman, which said, "Responsibility for ending the tragic prospect of war is a joint responsibility of the Soviet Union and the United States." The Schuman amendment, which Wallace had personally read and approved, was adopted by the convention with little debate.

To the amazement of reporters the stadium was filled to capacity. The $30,000 raised from ticket sales was more than enough to pay for the entire Progressive convention. "It will remain a thing of awe to professional politicians that people paid hard cash to see a man baptize his own party," wrote the Associated Press columnist Hal Boyle. "This was something new."[37]

Nor was that the end of it. Once inside, the crowd heard William Gailmor, the Progressives' entertaining pitch man, make his standard appeal for donations. In a routine repeated countless times at Progressive rallies, Gailmor would start by asking for someone to write a check for $1,000 and work his way downward to a "sea of green" one-dollar bills waved by everyone in the crowd. Then he would go for pocket change. By the time Gailmor finished, the crowd in Shibe Park had anted up an additional $50,000.

Before the candidates appeared, Paul Robeson spoke and sang and brought the crowd to a fever pitch. "What a mockery," Robeson exclaimed. "Our high standard of living for a minority in the richest country on earth! Absentee ownership still rules supreme. One percent of the population still owns as much wealth as one-third of the ill-housed, ill-fed, ill-clothed whom Roosevelt so feelingly described."[38]

Then came Taylor, the homespun cowboy, a showman with only an eighth-grade education who knew how to grab a crowd. Pulitzer Prize–winning writer Vardis Fisher once described him as "one of the greatest speakers of our time." The issue above all else, said Taylor, was "whether we shall live out our lives and the lives of our children in peace, or whether we shall perish. It is as simple and straightforward as that. It is life or death. It is peace or war."[39]

An entertainer to the end, Taylor accepted the nomination for vice president, gathered his wife, Dora, and their young sons, Arod (Dora spelled backward), P. J., and Gregory, on the stage, picked up his banjo, and led the crowd in singing "I Love You as I Never Loved Before."

Then the stadium darkened. A spotlight focused on a gate through which an open car appeared. In it was Henry A. Wallace, smiling and waving as he circled the baseball diamond. "It was a striking spectacle," wrote the *New York Times* columnist Anne O'Hare McCormick, "but there was something in the atmosphere, in the play of lights, in the dark mass of shouting people, that was too reminiscent for the comfort of observers who had witnessed similar scenes of acclaim for a potential 'savior' in Rome in the Twenties and in Berlin in the early Thirties."[40]

When he finally quieted the crowd, Wallace began as he had begun four years earlier at the Democratic convention. "The future belongs to those who go down the line unswervingly for all the liberal principles of political democracy regardless of race, color or religion. . . . Roosevelt can and will lead the United States in cooperation with the rest of the world toward that type of peace which will prevent World War III." Wallace continued,

> That was four years ago. . . . And what followed was the great betrayal. Instead of the dream we have inherited disillusion. Instead of the promised years of harvest, the years of the locust are upon us. In Hyde Park they buried our president—and in Washington they buried our dreams. One day after Roosevelt died, Harry Truman entered the White House. And 46 days later, Herbert Hoover was there. It was a time of comings and goings. Into the government came the ghosts of the Great Depression, the banking house boys and the oil-well diplomats.

By far the most controversial portion of his speech dealt with the Berlin blockade and the ongoing airlift of supplies to the divided city. "Berlin need not have happened," Wallace said. "Berlin did not happen. Berlin was caused. When we were set on the road of the 'get tough' policy, I warned that its end was inevitable. Berlin is becoming that end. . . . In all earnestness, I assure you that if I were president, there would be no crisis in Berlin today." He added,

> I say the peace of the world is far too fragile to be shuttled back and forth through a narrow air corridor in freighter planes. I say the lives of our children, and our children's parents, are far too precious to be left to the tempers of Second Lieutenants at road barriers where zone meets zone—or to the Generals who are quoted calmly as favoring a "show of strength." . . .
>
> There is not a single nation on the European continent prepared to put an army into the field to defend Anglo-Saxon, that is, British and American policies. We can buy generals with dollars, but we can't buy wartime armies. . . . We can buy governments, but we can't buy people. . . .
>
> Our prestige in Germany went sinking when we divided Germany and established the western sector as an American and British Puerto Rico—as a colony. When we did that we gave up Berlin politically, and we can't lose anything by giving it up militarily in a search for peace.

Wallace finished with a commitment to "renounce the support of those who practice hate and preach prejudice. . . . The support of all those who truly believe in democracy I accept."

A few moments of broadcast time remained, however, and Wallace continued to speak. Unbeknownst to his campaign aides and speechwriters, Wallace had written out two more paragraphs, rooted in the Book of Micah, which spoke from his dreamer's heart.

The American dream is the dream of the prophets of old, the dream of each man living in peace under his own vine and fig tree; then all the nations of the world shall flow up to the mountains of the Lord and man shall learn war no more. We are the generation blessed above all generations, because to us is given for the first time in all history the power to make the dream come true.

To make that dream come true, we shall rise above the pettiness of those who preach hate and factionalism, of those who think of themselves rather than the great cause they serve. All you who are within the sound of my voice tonight have been called to serve mightily in fulfilling the dream of the prophets and the founders of the American system.[41]

CHAPTER TWENTY-SIX

"AM I IN AMERICA?"

Came the Inquisition.

Five days after the Progressive convention concluded, Elizabeth Bentley, a frumpy round-faced woman in her forties appeared before a Senate investigating subcommittee. Her story: she had belonged to the Communist underground in the early 1940s, been the lover of a Soviet secret agent and, since 1945, a counterspy for the FBI. The government, she said, was riddled with Communists and "fellow travelers."

Bentley had told her story before, in front of a federal grand jury in New York—the same panel that had indicted the U.S. Communist Party's twelve top officials—and accused several Treasury and State Department employees of providing information to Communists. The grand jury returned no indictments and sent her home.

Enraged by the grand jury's inaction, FBI Director J. Edgar Hoover guided his spy to the Republican-controlled Congress, where he hoped for a better response. Congress, suffering through the special session forced upon it by President Truman, eagerly complied. Speaking before the Senate subcommittee, she cited only one current government employee, an obscure Commerce Department official named William Remington, as having passed information to the Communists.

Several days later Bentley was back on Capitol Hill, testifying before HUAC and generating bigger headlines. She identified the ringleader of Communist spies as Nathan Gregory Silvermaster. He had given her microfilmed classified information during the war, she said, adding that Communists had also gotten information from two New Deal figures—former assistant treasury secretary Harry Dexter White, whom Truman had appointed to head the International Monetary Fund, and Lauchlin Currie, a top economic adviser to Franklin Roosevelt.

Even John Rankin of Mississippi, the committee's ranking Democrat, doubted her testimony. Bentley had never met either White or Currie, and she was vague about the nature and value of their information.

Seeking to bolster Bentley's credibility, HUAC turned to another ex-Communist witness, Whittaker Chambers, a heavy, rumpled senior editor at *Time* magazine. Like Bentley, he had appeared before the grand jury in New York, naming some seventy-five government officials whom he had known as Communists until he quit the party in 1938. Chambers repeated many of the names to HUAC: John Abt, Lee Pressman, Victor Perlo, Nathan Witt, Charles Kramer, and Alger Hiss.

Now Washington was in an uproar. The press sensed a major espionage scandal, even though Chambers testified that none of the men he named, including Hiss, were spies. He said their purpose was to infiltrate the government and affect policy. Harry Dexter White demanded to appear before HUAC to clear his name. Silvermaster condemned Bentley as a "neurotic liar." Harry Truman denounced the hearings as a "red herring" intended to distract public attention from the "do-nothing" Republican Congress.[1]

On this, if on nothing else, Henry Wallace happily agreed with Truman. HUAC was using "the technique of political gangsterism and tyranny," Wallace said. The hearings were "the first step toward a reactionary police state."[2]

But Wallace had a particular problem not shared by Truman. Most of the people named by Bentley and Chambers had been associated with Wallace in some way. Hiss, Pressman, Abt, and others had worked in the legal department of the Agricultural Adjustment Administration. Silvermaster had served as an economist at the Board of Economic Warfare. White and Currie had been Wallace's friends and philosophical allies in the Roosevelt administration. Pressman, Abt, and Perlo were heavily involved with the Progressive Party.

Congressman Rankin demanded that Wallace be subpoenaed and brought before the committee to explain the "placing of communists" in key government positions. (No subpoena was issued.) Columnist Dorothy Thompson called him a "mask for communism." *Collier's* magazine editorially said, "Henry Wallace is the voice of Russia." Columnist Frank Kent called him a "biased, embittered, unbalanced man" who was leading the Communists and "every crackpot radical and opponent of the American way of life" to undermine the nation. Harold Ickes could not resist the opportunity to jab his old rival: "In effect, Wallace is a plant that has been forced under glass in a Communist hotbed."[3]

Amid the deluge there were ironies. Wallace actually had purged leftists from the Agriculture Department in 1935, among them Pressman and Abt.

Lauchlin Currie, the Roosevelt administration's leading exponent of Keynesian economics, had designed the World Bank and the International Monetary Fund, two pillars of postwar capitalism. Hiss owed his current position as president of the Carnegie Endowment for International Peace to John Foster Dulles, Dewey's foreign policy adviser.

But the summer of 1948 was no time for irony. Pressman, Abt, Kramer, and Perlo were hauled before HUAC, where they cited the Fifth Amendment and refused to answer questions. Harry Dexter White was granted his request to testify and gave a spirited defense of his career and principles. Three days later White died of a heart attack. "Harry D. White, my good friend and close associate on many New Deal committees, died Monday—a victim of the Un-American [J. Parnell] Thomas Committee," Wallace declared bitterly.[4]

Perhaps most ironic, the HUAC hearings, intended to bludgeon Harry Truman, hardly touched him. The brunt fell on Wallace and his fledgling party, an irony not lost on Thomas Dewey. After the election a county Republican chairman from New York State lamented to Dewey that if Wallace had not run, "all the extreme left wingers, screwballs, etc." would have been Truman's load to carry. "There is a lot to what you say about the Wallace candidacy," Dewey wrote back. "In many respects he helped the opposition more than he hurt them."[5]

In August, Henry Wallace began a tour of the South. "I don't think any person in American political life ever demonstrated the sheer personal courage that Wallace did in that trip through the South," Beanie Baldwin said later.[6]

No candidate for president had ever refused to speak before segregated audiences, to sleep in segregated hotels, to eat in segregated restaurants. Wallace's open defiance of Jim Crow focused on a national shame and marked a turn in the practice of politics. Henceforth, no candidate for president, especially a Democrat, would dare honor southern racial customs while courting black voters in northern cities.

For this Wallace received almost no credit and precious few votes. His small entourage was continually threatened and harassed. Signs with messages such as "Drop Dead" and "Peddle Your Junk in Moscow" greeted them. In Durham, North Carolina, a Wallace supporter was stabbed repeatedly during a melee before Wallace was escorted by an armed guard to the podium. At one point a mob surrounded the car carrying his secretary, Mabel Cooney, breaking the windshield and screaming racial epithets because she was seated next to a black woman. Wallace usually slept in the homes of black supporters and ate meals from a picnic basket. All hotels denied rooms to his party. In Dallas he was roused at 2 A.M. by a Western Union messenger with a telegram reading, "Get out of town!"

Often Wallace spoke in courthouse squares since public meeting halls barred integrated audiences. At least twice, in Alabama and again in Louisiana, he didn't speak at all, because the threat of violence was so palpable. Seldom could he utter more than a few sentences before being met by a chorus of boos and jeers, and eggs and tomatoes.* "You can call us black, or you can call us Red, but you can't call us yellow," said Clark Foreman, the veteran crusader for racial justice who accompanied Wallace on the tour.[7]

Some of the eggs and tomatoes hit home. Through it all Wallace remained composed for the most part. Only once, during an ugly demonstration in Burlington, North Carolina, did he briefly crack. Struck by several eggs thrown by a young boy sitting atop his father's shoulders, Wallace grabbed a bystander and shouted, "Are you an American? Am I in America?" The man responded with a shove.

"When Wallace grabbed the man, his face was livid and he was obviously angry," one of his aides recalled. "Then, as suddenly as that emotion had been aroused, something miraculous happened. His grip relaxed. The anger went out of his face, which took on the most gentle look I've ever seen." Wallace waved to the crowd and said, "Goodbye, my friends, I'll see you again."[8]

Otherwise his response to hostility was restrained. "I don't mind a little good natured throwing of eggs and tomatoes, but I'd much rather see that food being fed to children," he said after one attack. "The faces I've seen distorted by hatred are of people for whom I have in my heart profound compassion, because most of them have not had enough to eat."†[9]

Several times he preached to his Bible Belt audiences in terms they might understand. On a Birmingham radio station he asked listeners to join him in the Lord's Prayer, which he recited until he reached the line "Lead us not into temptation, but deliver us from evil." At that point Wallace added, "We believe in brotherhood. We believe in the brotherhood of man. The scriptures read: 'God hath made of one blood all the nations to dwell upon the face of the earth.' "[10]

---

*Use of the egg as an instrument of politics was deeply etched in Wallace's psyche. Later, in writing of his experience, Wallace recalled, "As a matter of fact to be assaulted by eggs is not a new thing in my family. My great grandfather, James Howell White, a Methodist minister in Ohio, was treated similarly. He took it with dignity I try to emulate."

The reverend was a abolitionist, and his home was assaulted with eggs by a proslavery mob, Wallace explained. "His wife, so our family story goes, wanted to wash the eggstains from the windows, but James White would not hear of it. Said he: 'Those stains can be washed away only by the rains of Heaven.' "

Wallace added, "I came back from the South with a deep conviction. It is this: So long as the brotherhood of Man is denied in any part of our land, all of our nation is in danger."

†Near the end of the southern tour, Wallace even tried to use some understated humor. Speaking in Tennessee, he said he was "expecting to see the day when every year chickens, bred by the new methods originated by my son [H. B.] and myself, will return to the south 10 million eggs for every one we have received. I hope they will be used exclusively for food, not politics." His prophecy, astounding as it must have seemed to his listeners, was more than fulfilled.

Even so, the trip was a searing experience. Wallace later commented in his oral history that seeing "human hate in the raw" was something he had "never been through before, and never care[d] to go through again."[11]

Immediately after leaving the South, Wallace spoke of his journey to 48,000 people in Yankee Stadium. "To me, fascism is no longer a second-hand experience. . . . No, fascism has become an ugly reality—a reality which I have tasted. I have tasted it neither so fully nor so bitterly as millions of others. But I have tasted it."[12]

Since it dramatized racial intolerance in the South, the trip struck the Progressive camp as a success. "As the direct result of Henry Wallace's trip through the South, millions of Americans who were not aware of the meaning of discrimination in the South have suddenly been jolted," Clark Foreman wrote in the *New York Star*. "Segregation is no work of fiction but a brutal fact. The conflict between American democracy and segregation hit home to millions."[13]

But it reaped no political benefit. Certainly Wallace won no new supporters, and southern newspapers roundly condemned his flouting of Jim Crow laws as a provocation to violence.* Typical was the comment of Jonathan Daniels, a sometime aide to Truman and son of Wallace's old friend Josephus Daniels, in the *Raleigh News and Observer*: "Henry Wallace came into the South not wishing to understand it but to irritate it. He has left the South not wishing to understand it but to use his unfortunate experience in it as propaganda in the North and in the world."[14]

If the southern tour really meant to win support from liberal blacks and whites, the ploy failed. ADA publications called it hypocritical and Wallace a Johnny-come-lately to civil rights.† NAACP leaders, who once saw Wallace as a close ally, would not rally to his side. As one put it, "The black minority cannot afford the luxury of futile protest."[15]

---

*In one respect, at least, Wallace agreed that he had gone too far in defying local custom. By sleeping in the homes of black residents, he was "really slapping the southern tradition. . . . You can't change the customs of people that fast." Two years later he learned that Foreman also felt that the policy was a mistake. "It made us carpet-baggers," Foreman said.

The policy of refusing to sleep in segregated hotels apparently was set by the campaign manager, Beanie Baldwin, and never discussed with the candidate.

†Among the weaknesses in Wallace's civil rights record cited by the ADA and others were his neglect of southern sharecroppers while agriculture secretary, his failure to desegregate employee cafeterias at the Agriculture and Commerce departments, his refusal to meet with prominent black leaders seeking clemency for a convicted murderer while vice president, and his inaction at the Commerce Department in desegregating the Census Bureau and the restaurant at National Airport.

There was truth as well as exaggeration in the charges. In any case, his civil rights record as a government official was good enough for the African Academy of Arts and Research to honor him in 1945 with its first annual Wendell Willkie Memorial Award as "the person deemed to have contributed most to international leadership and international associations based upon the principles of equal justice for all."

Prominent black Progressives sought vainly to appeal to rank-and-file black voters. Paul Robeson called Wallace "the most improved white man" he ever knew. Here, too, Harry Truman was a lucky man. The president's record on civil rights, although better than Franklin Roosevelt's, was far from perfect. But black voters could see that Truman's record was strong enough to upset the Dixiecrats. "You may not believe Truman," one elderly black minister told Charles Howard, "but the Dixiecrats believe him, and that's enough for me."[16]

For Ilo Wallace the 1948 campaign was agony. Seeing her Henry splattered with eggs, hearing him taunted as a "nigger lover" who should "go back to Russia," and watching as his reputation was dragged through the mud tortured her. Only six years earlier her husband had been vice president of the United States and heir apparent to Franklin Roosevelt. Now the likes of Westbrook Pegler were calling him "Old Bubblehead" and a "drooling mystic" little short of a traitor.

Mostly she kept to herself at Farvue except on occasions demanding her presence with her husband, and then she appeared silently at his side. Only Elinor Gimbel, the impeccably correct head of the Progressive Party's women's division, could lure her off the farm to attend some luncheons, but even there she offered little beyond small talk.

Privately, however, Ilo had a good deal to say. "She has always been very violently anti-communist and I suppose she picks up gossip from her lady friends who are usually quite conservative," Wallace remarked in his oral history. She suspected her husband was being ill used by the people running his campaign. She didn't trust Beanie Baldwin, and she loathed John Abt. She disliked the fiery rhetoric of Wallace's speeches because it "didn't sound like Henry." (His speechwriter Lew Frank once asked her if she could identify which portions of a speech he had written and which were penned by Wallace himself; Ilo guessed almost entirely wrong.)[17]

Her small-town midwestern upbringing left her uncomfortable around blacks and Jews. And she had no use for the sharp-edged, ill-mannered urban radicals traipsing through her home, leaving ashes on the floor and rings on her furniture. "They may not be Communists, but they surely don't know how to behave in a living room," she grumbled.[18]

The feeling seems to have been mutual on the part of "Beanie's boys" at party headquarters. There she was regarded as a small-minded annoyance. Speechwriters seeking to tailor remarks to a mass audience would sarcastically ask whether "Ilo would understand it." Her attempts to meddle with her husband's activities and utterances, chiefly through her friendship with Mabel Cooney, Wallace's secretary, were keenly resented.[19]

Wallace simply stayed out of it. He didn't discuss politics with his wife—he never even talked to her about the southern debacle—and he didn't discuss Ilo with his political associates. Once, in a moment of irritation, he was said to have remarked, "The only thing she admires is respectability." If he did say such a thing, it was an anomaly. He simply expected his wife to support him as she always had, and she did. "I would say she went along with my idealism in the campaign and was a good sport," he commented in his oral history.[20]

Ilo Wallace's relations with the Progressive campaign was hardly its biggest worry. The stately Park Avenue brownstone boiled in crisis. One minute Wallace was being thrown off the ballot in Ohio. The next minute six top Progressive officials in western states had quit. Two minutes later the Progressive candidate for the U.S. Senate in Illinois was being stoned while police stood by and did nothing.

"Everything was a fire alarm," said one party worker. "We were trying to do so much, in such a short time, that we were always racing to meet some deadline; as soon as we finished one hurry-up job, they were breathing down our necks regarding another one."[21]

Beneath the appearance of disarray, however, lay grit and determination. The Progressives worked hard and were often inventive. Some 25 million copies of 140 separate Progressive publications—fliers, pamphlets, songbooks, organizational how-to booklets—poured out of the party's headquarters. Published in seventeen different languages, ranging from Spanish to Croatian, the material aimed at a wide array of ethnic groups.

Prominent artists contributed to the propaganda, including Ben Shahn, who designed a widely reproduced campaign poster and a satiric sketch later displayed in New York's Museum of Modern Art. "Wallace Seals," in imitation of the popular Christmas Seals, were affixed to thousands of letters. Recordings featuring Paul Robeson and Pete Seeger singing Progressive songs were released. The campaign even founded its own weekly newspaper, the *National Guardian*, with the help of novelist Norman Mailer and the prominent journalists Cedric Belfrage, John T. McManus, James Aronson, and Jess Gitt.*

A staff of speechwriters, planners, schedulers, and advance men struggled to keep Wallace and Taylor on the road almost constantly. Wallace traveled

---

*The Progressives hoped their paper could break through the wall of hostility and silence erected by the mainstream press, but its founding came too late to have any impact. By the end of the campaign, only two newspapers in the nation had endorsed Wallace: the Communist *Daily Worker* in New York, and the *York Gazette*, whose publisher, Jess Gitt, was chairman of the Progressive Party in Pennsylvania.

The *Guardian* long outlived the Progressive Party itself, although Belfrage, a British national who served as its original editor, was hounded out of the country in the mid-1950s. Former *New York Times* reporter James Aronson continued as its editor and maintained its hard-edged independent radical tone.

some 25,000 miles during the fall campaign, appearing in almost every state, often speaking several times a day. Taylor, laboring in virtual anonymity, went almost as far, usually with his wife and small children in tow.

The party's biggest headaches, of course, were getting on the ballot and raising enough money. Through a combination of hard work, legal acumen, and blind luck, the Progressives succeeded beyond their own expectations. By election day they were on the ballot in one form or another in all but three of the forty-eight states. The exceptions were Oklahoma, Nebraska, and Illinois.*

In addition, Ohio made it next to impossible to vote for Wallace. The Republican secretary of state, declaring that some of Wallace's followers were Communists, barred his name from the ballot under a law prohibiting "un-American" candidates from seeking office. Wallace supporters had to vote instead for his electors, who were not identified by party on the ballot.

The Progressives fared better in the South, where the late-starting Thurmond campaign motivated several state legislatures to rewrite election laws. Since it was impossible to ease laws for one party but not another, the Progressives were able to appear on the ballot in every southern state.†

In raising money the Progressives had similar success. Defying political tradition, they raised tens of thousands of dollars by charging admission to their political rallies and thousands more by pleading for change from those who had already paid to attend. The party knocked on doors, held a hat at factory gates, sold literature and posters.

---

*The Progressives gave up Oklahoma without a fight, but John Abt and his legal team struggled mightily in Illinois. The obstacle was a complicated state election law that gave outsized influence to rural areas. Chicago area Republicans saw the advantage of having Wallace on the ballot, since he would draw votes from the Democrats, but downstate Republicans were unconvinced. The downstate Republicans prevailed.

Abt challenged the Illinois law all the way to the U.S. Supreme Court, which on October 21 upheld its constitutionality by a 6-to-3 vote. Chief Justice Fred Vinson, writing for the majority, said, "To assume that political power is a function exclusively of numbers is to disregard the practicalities of government." Dissenting were Justices Hugo Black, William O. Douglas, and Frank Murphy. "The notion that one group can be granted greater voting strength than another is hostile to our standards for popular representative government," Douglas wrote.

The obtuseness of the rural Republicans would cost them dearly. On election day Harry Truman carried Illinois by a margin of 33,612 votes out of almost four million cast. Virtually all observers concluded Dewey would have carried the state if Wallace had been on the ballot.

†In Alabama the Dixiecrats simply took over the existing Democratic Party and listed Strom Thurmond as their candidate. Thus, ironically, Wallace appeared on the ballot in Alabama and Truman did not.

The Progressives made a similar effort of their own in Minnesota. Under the direction of former governor and senator Elmer Benson, national chairman of the Wallace campaign committee, the Progressives came close to seizing control of the Democratic-Farmer-Labor Party. A determined effort by Mayor Hubert Humphrey of Minneapolis, then running for a U.S. Senate seat, managed to avert the plan. The Progressives did qualify for the Minnesota ballot as a third party, however.

But their biggest source of cash continued to be the unwavering Anita McCormick Blaine. Federal election laws of the era placed no limit on individual contributions to a presidential campaign, and Blaine gave the Wallace campaign, the national Progressive Party, and its state affiliates more than $745,000 in 1948 alone, plus thousands more before and after.

Red hunters were forever searching for evidence that the Kremlin lay behind left-wing causes in the United States; as Wallace observed slyly, they should have been looking at the International Harvester Company of Chicago, Illinois, the source of Anita Blaine's fortune.

These fund-raising techniques and Anita Blaine's deep pockets allowed the Progressives to exceed their $3 million goal. The Wallace campaign spent liberally on chartered planes and paid broadcasts and a headquarters staff of well over one hundred. Even so, it ended the campaign with a modest surplus of about $20,000.

So much money was raised and spent that Progressives earned the dubious distinction of having waged, on a per-vote basis, the most costly campaign in American history—about $3 for every vote Wallace received.

No amount of money or energy or legal talent could salvage the situation. By fall most Americans had simply stopped listening to Henry Wallace and his party. His views, when reported at all, were usually near the back of the newspaper. Progressives were page-one news only when Red hunters took another swipe at them. In early October, speaking at a rally in Los Angeles, Wallace issued an ambitious fourteen-point plan for lasting peace. "Peace is a million times more attractive than that dangerous dream of the American Century."[*22]

*The plan suggested by Wallace included prohibiting anyone from making policy who had a personal financial stake in the decisions, taking private profit out of war production, banning the export of weapons by any nation to any other nation, reestablishing the UN relief agency, and removing occupation forces from Germany, Japan, Greece, and Korea.

"I don't think we are going to have an actual shooting war right away," Wallace said. "But irresponsible men are playing around with the idea of war. . . . These men must be stopped."

Wallace's speech at Gilmore Stadium occurred nine days after President Truman spoke at the same location. Even though Wallace charged admission and Truman did not, Wallace attracted 6,000 more people than the president.

In their speeches Truman and Wallace conducted a sort of long-distance debate about the third party. Said Truman, "There are . . . some people with true liberal convictions whose worry over the state of the world has caused them to lean toward a third party. To these liberals I would say in all sincerity—think again. The fact that the Communists are guiding and using the third party shows that the party does not represent American ideals. . . . A vote for the third party will not promote the cause of American liberalism, but will injure it. . . . Don't waste your vote."

Wallace responded, "Mr. Truman has warned you against wasting your votes. I give you the same warning. Don't waste your vote on a candidate who defeated himself when he drove the New Dealers from his administration. A vote for Truman is a vote without meaning. I am against wasting votes."

His plan drew no response from public, politicians, or press. Wallace had been tuned out. The Gallup poll had shown Wallace at 7 percent in early 1948; ten months later it had him down to 4 percent.

Surrounded by a "paper curtain"—Wallace's term for the newspaper blackout—the Progressives increasingly took to radio. A dozen times during the final three weeks of the campaign, Wallace addressed voters over one or another network.

"Three years ago we demonstrated that a highly militarized state—the German Nazi state—could not win when it faced the resistance of freedom-loving peoples everywhere," Wallace said over the Mutual Broadcasting System. "Yet today, in Washington, the men who make policy have based the future of our country on military might. . . . It didn't work for Hitler, and it won't work for us."[23]

In predicting that Truman would be "the worst defeated candidate in history," Wallace for once accepted the conventional wisdom.[*24] Everybody concluded the president was a political dead man. In fact, Harry Truman, all feistiness and folksiness, was not only alive and kicking but rapidly reassembling his Democratic base, and doing so with the very plan Wallace had long advocated: he was running as a liberal.

Truman's platform called for a higher minimum wage and lower inflation, for decent housing and universal health care, for the rights of working people and the regulation of business. He was campaigning as the Roosevelt of old—against the "economic royalists" and the "Republican gang" in the "good-for-nothing Congress" and even against Herbert Hoover. Truman was the scrappy outsider, running against "a man with a calculating machine where his heart ought to be."[25]

Truman's performance may have been, as Wallace claimed, an "obvious fraud." But it was working.[26]

Truman also benefited from the mathematics of America's winner-take-all, two-party tradition. Wallace could argue that a vote for the Progressives would force the two major parties to recognize and accommodate a sizable bloc of Americans. Rank-and-file liberals, however, feared Dewey and the Republican Congress and moved back to Truman in droves. The pollster George Gallup later concluded that "as many as one-third of the people who said in

---

*Wallace may have believed what he was saying, but he had reason to know better. Several months earlier the statistician Louis Bean, Wallace's longtime friend and colleague, had published a slender volume entitled *How to Predict Elections*, which correctly forecast that 1948 would be a Democratic year. Wallace had great faith in Bean's methods and several times had forwarded his electoral predictions to Franklin Roosevelt.

late October that they were going to vote for Mr. Wallace shifted to Mr. Truman" during the final ten days of the campaign.*27

On election morning Henry and Ilo Wallace voted at the South Salem library. Then Wallace spent the day with his flowers and chickens, and in the evening drove to New York City, where he joined Paul Robeson and party workers singing Progressive songs. "Wallace seemed to be in very good spirits," Beanie Baldwin recalled, "and I don't think I detected how hurt he was."28

The rout of Gideon's Army was complete and overwhelming. Truman polled more than 24 million popular votes and 303 electoral votes to Dewey's 22 million popular votes and 189 electoral votes. The Dixiecrat Strom Thurmond ran third, with 1,169,032 popular and 39 electoral votes, and Wallace last. He received 1,157,063 popular votes and no electoral votes.

Nor did he come close to carrying a state. New York was his best state, accounting for almost half of his national total, but even there he topped out at 8 percent. Nationally, he got only 2.38 percent of the total.

In the entire United States, Wallace carried only thirty precincts. With the exception of seven precincts in the Tampa area, where Wallace was popular with Spanish-speaking cigar crafters, his success was entirely in black and Jewish districts in New York and California. His home state of Iowa gave Wallace 12,125 votes, about 1 percent of the total. In only three states—New York, Michigan, and Maryland—did Wallace win enough votes to make a difference in the outcome. Dewey carried all three states.†

Only one congressional candidate running under the Progressive banner, Vito Marcantonio, survived. All of the party's U.S. Senate candidates were crushed. None won enough votes to make a difference between a Democratic or a Republican victory.

That evening Wallace made three rather bitter statements by radio, vowing to fight on. "Unless this bi-partisan foreign policy of high prices and war is promptly reversed, I predict that the Progressive Party will rapidly grow

---

*The Progressives were plagued throughout the fall campaign by the charge that their real purpose was to destroy the Democratic Party and elect a reactionary president and Congress, so as to enhance their own chances in 1952. To counter the accusation, C. B. Baldwin announced the withdrawal of Progressive congressional candidates in thirteen districts so as to boost Democratic chances.

This gave rise to a semipublic dispute between Baldwin and Wallace. "Some day we will have to build a party, Beanie," Wallace said. After press reports of a split between Wallace and his campaign manager appeared, Wallace issued a statement saying, "I have had complete confidence in Beanie for years. I still have. . . . He's running the campaign just the way it should be run."

†If Wallace had been able to deny Truman just 29,294 votes in three other states—Illinois, California, and Ohio—the shift in electoral votes would have been enough to elect Dewey. A shift of only 12,487 votes from Truman to Wallace in California and Ohio would have thrown the election into the House of Representatives, where Dixiecrats held the balance of power.

into the dominant party as the cup of iniquity of the old parties overflows. To save the peace of the world the Progressive Party is more needed than ever before."[29]

It was hardly a typical concession speech. The word "defeat" was never mentioned. Nor did Wallace congratulate the winner. But Ilo Wallace knew defeat when she saw it. As the results poured in, burying her husband and his party, she wept loudly and said, "I told him so all the time. He should never have done it."[30]

In the wake of the election, Progressives put a good face on it. "We come here not as people who lost—but as people who won," Wallace told a meeting of the Progressive Party's national committee two weeks after the election. ". . . So far as words go, the Democrats—as a result of our pressure—campaigned on a more forward-looking program than ever before in the history of the Democratic Party."[31]

At the opposite end of the political spectrum, some observers agreed the Progressives had made their mark. "It is said by political commentators that Mr. Wallace made a bad showing because he got few votes," the *Wall Street Journal* editorialized. "What they neglect is that Mr. Wallace succeeded in having his ideas adopted, except in the field of foreign affairs. From the time that Mr. Wallace announced he would run for President, Mr. Truman began to suck the wind from Mr. Wallace's sails by coming out for more and more of the Wallace domestic program."[32]

To except "the field of foreign affairs" was to make a large exception, however. Wallace could only hope that Truman's victory would free him to move leftward on foreign policy, as he had on domestic issues. A couple of days after the election, Wallace wrote Truman, "Now that you have been elected in your own right on the basis of your own campaign with a good majority in the Senate and House, it is possible for you to stand firmly and squarely on your own feet in service to the American people and the world. . . . You cannot give them what they expect unless you promptly end the Cold War."[33]

Wallace now dedicated himself to that end. "The Democrats have promised to examine every avenue of approach to peace and a settlement with Russia," Wallace told the Progressives. "Let's hold them to it. They have promised civil liberties legislation. Let's hold them to it. . . . If we retreat now, civilization is lost. I have just begun to fight."[34]

Wallace aimed to keep the Progressive Party going, to make it viable in American politics, perhaps even to run again for president. His goal was strongly shared by Baldwin, Abt, and others at the core of the Wallace campaign. They moved the party into more modest quarters and settled in for the long haul.

But stout talk and brave intentions could not change reality. The election had all but destroyed Henry Wallace's credibility as a political figure and removed the Progressive Party to the fringe of public life. Harry Truman could count votes, and there were precious few in Wallace's pocket.

Each new chapter in the Red scare only further isolated Wallace and his party.

In December 1948, while the House Un-American Activities Committee was publishing a report linking Communists to the Progressive campaign, Congressman Richard M. Nixon, the youngest and shrewdest member of the committee, was making spectacular revelations. From a pumpkin patch on Whittaker Chambers's Maryland farm, Nixon produced microfilm of secret government documents supposedly stolen by Alger Hiss for transmittal to the Russians.

A few days later Hiss was indicted on perjury charges in connection with the slander suit he had brought against Chambers. Five days after Hiss's indictment another accused former State Department official, Laurence Duggan, died after falling from a window in his New York City office. Duggan had accompanied Vice President Wallace on his 1943 tour South America and was said by Senator Karl Mundt to have been a member of a six-man espionage team in the State Department. Reporters asked when the other five spies would be identified, and Mundt replied lightly, "We'll name them as they jump out of windows."[35]

President Truman, contrary to Wallace's hopes, was moving the Cold War to the center of U.S. foreign policy. In January 1949 he proposed the Point Four program and plans to sign the North Atlantic Treaty. He named Dean Acheson, an ardent advocate of containment, as secretary of state to replace the ailing George Marshall.

The most benign of these developments was Point Four, a low-cost program intended to offer U.S. technical assistance to underdeveloped countries. Wallace said he "couldn't help smiling," because the humanitarian impulse behind Point Four was what he had been advocating for years. "Eventually they will have to come completely around to my way of thinking or they are going to get into some real trouble," he remarked. Still, Wallace disliked the fact that the United Nations had once again been disregarded.[36]

Far more troubling to Wallace was the North Atlantic Treaty Organization (NATO), which placed the United States in permanent military alliance with Canada and the nations of Western Europe. Under the treaty's terms an armed attack against any member nation would be regarded as an attack against all of them. In Wallace's view, NATO was a "most flagrant" violation of the UN Charter, which "irrevocably splits the world in two," and condemned Americans to a costly and dangerous arms race with the Soviet Union.[37]

Nothing better illustrated Wallace's fall than his appearances on Capitol Hill. Congressmen who had listened to his views with respect were now openly hostile, if not derisive, toward him. At a February hearing of the House Foreign Affairs Committee, where Wallace spoke against continued funding for the European Economic Program, representatives questioned his patriotism and motives. "Would you prefer living under capitalism or communism," one asked. "I am living in the United States," Wallace said with a laugh. "I like it here. I am not trying to overthrow the government."*[38]

Things got worse when Wallace went before the Senate Foreign Relations Committee in May to testify against the North Atlantic Treaty. There Wallace was peppered for more than four hours with questions implying that he was little more than an agent of Soviet propaganda. Virtually no attention was paid to Wallace's prepared testimony. "Are we threatened by the Soviet Union?" Wallace asked. He answered his question:

> That nation lost 10,000,000 lives in the war. The most productive sectors of its economy were destroyed. After two-and-one-half years of reconstruction its production has just regained the prewar level. . . .
>
> Does anyone seriously believe that the Soviet Union wants another war? The most ardent advocates of the unsuccessful two year-old, get-tough-with-Russia policy admit that the Soviet Union does not want war. They even concede that the Soviet Union fears war. The single fact is that the Soviet Union cannot attack the United States. As the *Wall Street Journal* cynically said, if the Russians wanted to attack us, "they would have to swim to get here.". . .[39]

The senators ignored the message. They were there to attack the messenger. Senator Brien McMahon, a Connecticut Democrat, said Wallace was conjuring up a "gigantic conspiracy," which virtually accused the White House and State Department of treason. Senator J. William Fulbright, an Arkansas Democrat, hinted Wallace might be motivated by bigotry after he said that "certain elements in the hierarchy of the Catholic Church" were involved in the war hysteria. Chairman Tom Connally, a Texas Democrat, treated the witness as a joke. When Wallace said NATO might make Russia behave as a "wild, desperate cornered beast," Connally asked, "Did you say corned beef?"[40]

---

*The congressmen's doubts about Wallace's loyalties apparently inspired similar thoughts by newspaper reporters. A *New York Times* account of the hearing, written by C. P. Trussell, reported that Wallace was asked by a photographer to "give the closed-fist salute of the Soviets. Mr. Wallace obliged." Two weeks passed before the *Times* admitted the incident did not take place and apologized.

The committee approved the North Atlantic Treaty unanimously, and the full Senate ratified it by a vote of 83 to 13.

The Progressives tried taking their case to the people. They organized a nationwide "peace tour" featuring Wallace and two left-wing European politicians, H. Lester Hutchinson of the British Labour Party and the Italian Socialist Michele Giua. Over a three-week period the trio spoke in fifteen cities before 100,000 people—raising an additional $150,000 for the Progressive Party—with no impact on public opinion.

Wallace trudged on—he gave more than thirty speeches in the first seven months of 1949—but his pronouncements shifted in tone. At first barely noticeable, then with increasing force, his views on U.S. foreign policy were paired with criticism of the Soviet Union.

Soviet suppression of civil liberties in the satellite nations must stop; it was "high time both [communism and capitalism] abandon their extreme positions."[41] Before a church group he said the Soviet Union had no greater claim to moral superiority than did the United States; both countries should put their faith in the United Nations.

This change in thinking moved through Wallace's private comments and his relations with the Progressive Party. It was obvious, even to one so oblivious to political mechanics, that he headed a party with scant popular support. In a special election following the death of the New York congressman Sol Bloom, the Progressive candidate ran a miserable fourth in a four-way race won by Franklin D. Roosevelt Jr. As the party's base of support withered, its control by Communists and hard-line ideologues increased. By fall he was warning Lew Frank, his former speechwriter, that the Progressives must separate themselves from Communists "in every possible way but without red baiting."[42]

Wallace truly disliked the confrontational tactics, sometimes leading to violence, employed by some Progressives. On one occasion several veterans groups disrupted an open-air concert featuring Paul Robeson in the town of Peekskill, New York. A riot ensued, and the event was canceled. Robeson defiantly vowed to return the following week and called upon progressive-minded citizens to rally behind him. Cool to the idea, Wallace refused to attend the concert, which ended in a rock- and bottle-throwing melee and numerous arrests. Wallace did attempt to reach Governor Thomas Dewey by phone to urge proper police protection.

"I thought [Robeson's supporters] were deliberately courting violence and they would get what they asked for," Wallace remarked in his oral history.[43]

Life on the farm was looking more and more attractive. "The more I see of humanity both east and west right now," Wallace wrote to a friend, "the better I am impressed with gladioli, strawberries and chickens." In September, Wallace rejected Congressman Vito Marcantonio's pleas that he run for the U.S. Senate in New York as a candidate of the American Labor and Progressive parties. This decision drew reports that Wallace intended to withdraw from politics altogether. But Wallace was not yet inclined to abandon the public stage. "Hell no," he said when asked whether he was about to become a full-time farmer.[44]

The growing estrangement between Wallace and his party deepened in early 1950. In January, Wallace appeared before HUAC to answer accusations made by the radio commentator Fulton Lewis Jr. that he was responsible for the wartime shipment of uranium to Russia. Wallace flatly denied the charge and added, "I state unhesitatingly that I am proud of my participation as vice-president . . . when the war situation was most critical."[45]

As Progressives neared the first of the "annual" conventions promised in their party rules, Wallace set a price for his continued support—that the party demonstrate concretely its independence from Communist control. Specifically it should adopt some version of the "Vermont Resolution," a statement saying the party gave no blanket endorsement to the foreign policy of any nation, and pledge its support for "progressive capitalism" in the United States. Beanie Baldwin, knowing that the Progressive Party without Wallace was doomed, promised to give him what he wanted.

The three-day convention, held in Chicago's Lakeland Auditorium, began on February 26, 1950. Henry Wallace delivered the keynote address before some twelve hundred delegates and spectators. "Wallace looks well," wrote Murray Kempton. "His complexion is ruddy; the weary, slightly puzzled look is gone from his eyes, and the hair, whose cowlick was once his trademark, is now smoothly combed." But he also looked to Kempton and others like a man who would prefer to be elsewhere. The public "still thinks of this as Henry Wallace's Progressive Party," said Kempton, but "he seemed oddly detached from its destinies."[46]

Wallace made it clear the party must broaden its base of support and "stand before the American people as being Americans, first, last and always." The party's principles "are vastly different from those of the Communist Party," he declared, adding, "Our philosophy is not based upon the principles of Marxism or Leninism. Our program is based upon reform by constitutional and democratic processes. We believe in progressive capitalism, not socialism."[47]

His hour-long speech was interrupted thirty-one times by applause, but total silence greeted him when he said, "The United States and Russia stand out today as the two big brutes of the world. Each in its own eyes rests on high moral principles, but each in the eyes of other nations is guided by force and force alone."[48]

The audience "was respectful but uninspired," Kempton wrote. ". . . For this was not a Wallaceite audience. Its members were ready to concede him the right to distribute blame equally between Stalin and Truman, but their hearts weren't in it." Nor had Wallace set out to win their hearts. Shortly after the speech he left Chicago for four days in Des Moines and took no further hand in the convention's deliberations.[49]

Wallace's abrupt departure exactly indicated the problem, wrote the journalist I. F. Stone. "Wallace is a big man: the heir to Roosevelt, a giant in the pygmy world of the Left, a man with international prestige. Whether he likes it or not, he is the leader of the Progressive Party. It does no good to proclaim that it is 'an independent indigenous American party' and to disown the Reds. Independence is proved by day-to-day action, not by frantic, intermittent verbal efforts at disentanglement. If Wallace had done the hard work of hammering out party policy, the policy would be independent."*[50]

For the time being, however, an uneasy relationship between Wallace and the party continued. Baldwin forced through resolutions adequate to Wallace's demands. A statement adopted by the delegates recognized that the United States and Russia "have both made mistakes in foreign policy" but should work together for "international peace and cooperation." In Des Moines, Wallace faintly praised the platform as "generally satisfactory"; he would remain the party's titular leader.[51]

The truce lasted four months.

On June 24, 1950, North Korean troops in Russian-made tanks crossed the thirty-eighth parallel, the artificial line separating Korea's northern and southern sectors. Immediately the United States went before the UN Security Council, challenging North Korea's troop movement as an act of unprovoked Communist aggression. By a vote of 9 to 0, the Security Council agreed. The Soviet Union, then in the midst of a Security Council boycott protesting the UN's refusal to recognize China's new Communist government, was not present to cast a veto.

Korea's situation threw the Progressive Party leadership into a moral and political crisis.

On July 6 the executive committee met in emergency session to formulate a response to developments in Korea. Most of the party's leadership lined up against

---

*Beanie Baldwin would have agreed with Stone. "I heard him say many times quite candidly that although he had respect for the people in the Progressive Party and the kind of fight they were making, he was not interested in political parties as such," Baldwin said in his oral history.

U.S. intervention: C. B. Baldwin, Vito Marcantonio, Lillian Hellman, Paul Robeson, Leo Isacson, John Abt, and others. On the other side was Henry Wallace.

After two days of argument Wallace received a call from Ilo; he should return quickly to Farvue. There he was put in contact with UN Secretary-General Trygve Lie, who pleaded for Wallace's support, stressing that his "importance in world political opinion was very great." At a subsequent secret meeting Lie showed Wallace a memorandum entitled "Legal Aspects of Security Council Action in Korea," which convinced him the UN's position was both legal and moral.[52]

In New York City the Progressive executive committee differed. To its members the UN action was unjustified as long as China was excluded from membership. Debate rambled on until July 10, when amendments offered by Wallace to strengthen the party's position on Communist aggression were defeated on a motion by Paul Robeson.

The following day Wallace called Baldwin, saying he would not endorse the executive committee's statement. Wallace then proposed several more amendments, which were rejected unanimously. Four days later, after informing key Progressive Party supporters of his position, Wallace issued a personal "statement of conscience" on Korea.

"I want to make it clear that when Russia, the United States and the United Nations appeal to force, I am on the side of the United States and the United Nations," he said. "Undoubtedly the Russians could have prevented the attack by the North Koreans and undoubtedly they could stop the attack any time they wish. I hold no brief for the past actions of either the United States or Russia but when my country is at war and the United Nations sanctions that war, I am on the side of my country and the United Nations."[53]

It was hardly an unqualified endorsement of U.S. policy. He added prophetically,

> The United States will fight a losing battle in Asia as long as she stands behind feudal regimes based on exorbitant charges of land lords and money lords. Russia is using a mightier power than the atom bomb as long as she helps the people get out from under their ancient aggressors. But we in the United States have a still mightier power if we will only use it for the people.[54]

Wallace's statement on Korea split the Progressive Party forever, but he remained with it for three weeks, waiting to hear the opinions of rank-and-file Progressives. He received numerous expressions of support—Rexford Tugwell was among those who cheered him—but none from the party's executive committee. On August 8, 1950, Wallace resigned from the party with a curt, two-paragraph letter to Beanie Baldwin:

> In view of the actions recently taken by the national committee of the Progressive Party and the various state committees, I am convinced I can more effectively serve the cause of peace by resigning from the national committee and the executive committee of the Progressive Party.
> You will, therefore, take this letter as my formal resignation from the party.*[55]

He was sixty-one years of age. During his life he had been a Republican, a Democrat, and a Progressive. Each political journey had ended in his disillusionment and departure. Henry A. Wallace was now alone.

---

*"I think there were a lot of factors in his decision to leave the Progressive Party," Baldwin later commented, "and I think that Mrs. Wallace was one of the major factors."

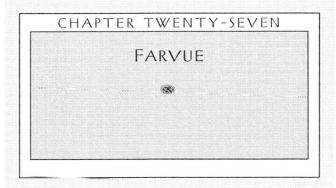

CHAPTER TWENTY-SEVEN

FARVUE

Henry Wallace returned to his farm. To some he appeared bitter and withdrawn. Dr. Samuel Rosen, a physician friend, said Wallace seemed "an undemonstrative, very ungraceful, profoundly lonely man." To others he seemed relaxed and fit, not at all the "restless, unsettled, distracted" man of recent years.[1]

The difference rested on the conversation at hand. If discussing politics, Wallace was abrupt and seldom forthcoming; when talking of agriculture and science, he could be almost serene.

Richard Wilson, the *Des Moines Register* reporter who had covered Wallace since they arrived together in Washington at the start of the New Deal, visited Wallace in South Salem and found him as comfortable and energetic as he had been in earlier years. Wilson even wondered whether the former vice president might make some sort of public comeback.

Clearly Wallace—"by far the most widely known and controversial Iowan of the first half of the twentieth century"—had been overwhelmingly repudiated by his countrymen, Wilson wrote. But so had Herbert Hoover been repudiated, only to claw his way back into public acceptance over a period of years. "Could it be that in the next 10 to 15 years of his life [Wallace] will be restored to that fickle mistress, the general public esteem?"[2]

The answer was mostly no. Wallace would live another fifteen years, but for several reasons he never returned to the good graces of the broad American public. Unlike Hoover,

who clung loyally to the Republican Party, Wallace was a pariah to all political parties, including the one he started. He returned the enmity. In his 1951
oral history he remarked, "I don't think I'll be hooked up with any party. I've
seen enough of the undesirable elements of all three of them so that I'm very
glad to leave all three of them alone."[3]

And Hoover devoted great energy to restoring his reputation by writing
books and keeping himself in the public eye; Wallace shunned the limelight
and did little to explain his career. He wrote no memoirs—Ilo Wallace, in
particular, thought no good would come from an autobiography—and ordered both his wartime diaries and his 5,197-page oral history sealed for ten
years after his death.

The result was a long, slow decline into obscurity marked by a certain acceptance of his outcast status. "I have done what I could," he remarked at the
close of his oral history. "I see no chance for further service now or for a long
time to come. At any rate for the moment I shall do my best to enhance my
appreciation of those forms of life which have not been contaminated by low-
grade politics. Enhancement of the quality of the soil and the quality of life
of all kinds is one of the chief ends of man—one of the best ways of glorify-
ing God and enjoying him forever."[4]

Privately Wallace reflected at length about his hard ride through public life
and the steep fall he took at the end. His grandfather and mentor, Uncle
Henry Wallace, would not have been surprised. "My grandfather knew better than to get directly into political life," Wallace remarked in his oral history. "He chose the course of educating by writing and speaking. As a result
he was universally beloved. If he had been in politics he would have been
hated by many people. Against the background of his time he preached the
same doctrine which I have preached, but he resolutely stayed out of politics
because he thought politics would destroy his usefulness. He was a wise man."[5]

But Henry A. did not regret his path. "I did try to apply [my grandfather's]
ideas in politics with results he would have anticipated. The experience has been
worthwhile, and I do not regret anything except the great trouble which is coming to the United States of America and the world in the troublous years ahead."[6]

Inevitably he had suffered the fate of a prophet, Wallace believed.

Any political figure who sees certain ancient forces passing out of the picture and certain new forces arising and who attempts to lead his people in
a way to understand and use the new forces constructively will be maligned.

In my case the forces which moved against me strongly through specific individuals were Tory Britain, the Roman Catholic Church, Reactionary Capitalism, the Nationalist Chinese (and certain other foreign groups which base their hopes for a return to power and their ancient landholdings on a war between the USA and the USSR). These groups have operated through our press and radio and through certain reactionaries in both the Democratic and the Republican parties. En masse these groups represent a dying past, but the mere consciousness of dying gives them a desperate determination and an eager willingness to use any means whatsoever to obtain their purpose.[7]

All in all, he decided, it was good he had fallen short of the presidency in 1945. No figure as divisive and controversial as he could have led a nation like the United States.

Nor would opposing forces let Wallace retire gracefully from public life and adopt the role of a respected country squire. Throughout the early 1950s, as long as any political mileage could be gained from it, his opponents continued their campaign of vilification. Wallace struck back as best he could, disputing the specifics of accusations made against him, brooking no slur upon his patriotism or slander about his governmental career. Here and there he won a battle, but the war was hopeless.

The celebrated "Who lost China?" debate illustrated his dilemma. In the fall of 1951 Louis Budenz, one of several ex-Communists then making a career out of testifying about subversion before congressional committees, charged that Wallace had written a secret report to President Roosevelt in 1944 recommending that Chiang Kai-shek be forced into a coalition with the Chinese Communists. Wallace made this recommendation, Budenz claimed, at the urging of John Carter Vincent and Owen Lattimore, who he said were assigned by the Communist Party to "guide" the vice president during his trip to China.

Budenz's accusations, based entirely on hearsay, were patently false in all respects, and Wallace set out immediately to refute them. He wrote a detailed letter to President Truman noting that his report to Roosevelt, which had never been made public, did not contain the recommendation Budenz ascribed to it and was not written with the help of Vincent or Lattimore. He sent similar letters, including copies of his report to Roosevelt, to the Senate Internal Security Subcommittee chairman, Pat McCarran, a Nevada Democrat.

McCarran responded by issuing a subpoena to Wallace on October 3, 1951, ordering him to appear for questioning the very next day. Since Wallace had never shown the slightest unwillingness to appear before congressional committees, the subpoena's only purpose was humiliation.

Wallace appeared before the full subcommittee on October 17, 1951, accompanied by attorney George Ball, to "indignantly deny" Budenz's charges.* "It would be beneath my dignity to compare my record in 1944 with that of the professional ex-communist whose elastic conscience is apparently equal to any emergency," Wallace said. "The documents and history are on my side." After the hearing Wallace released the complete text of his 1944 report on China, which the *New York Times* published in full.[8]

The subcommittee ignored him. Wallace's testimony and the documentary evidence he offered were not mentioned in the subcommittee's final report. As the China debate raged, enveloping not only Wallace and the State Department experts but even former Secretary of State George Marshall, Wallace made another appeal for fairness to the subcommittee member Homer Ferguson, a Michigan Republican.

In a letter hand-carried to Ferguson's home by Wallace's daughter, Jean, Wallace wrote, "It is a humiliating experience when a man who has served his country to the best of his ability in high public office for 12 years, is dragged before a Senate Committee . . . and then to have no attention paid to his sworn, public testimony in the final report. May God grant that you may never have to undergo such an experience."[9] Ferguson responded politely, and they continued a futile exchange of letters.

By that time, March 1953, McCarthyism raged. Wallace was battling smears on multiple fronts. A book by Harvard historian William Henry Chamberlain, *America's Second Crusade*, quoted General Leslie R. Groves, military director of the Manhattan Project, to the effect that he considered Wallace a security risk and had stopped providing the vice president with information about the bomb.

Another book, *Mr. President*, contained excerpts of Harry Truman's personal diaries and private letters, in which Truman accused a member of his cabinet, identified as Mr. X, of being "a pacifist 100 per cent" who wanted to "give Russia our atomic secrets."[10]

There was the posthumous publication of Navy Secretary James Forrestal's diaries, which claimed that Wallace (not Henry Stimson) was "completely, everlastingly and wholeheartedly in favor of giving [the atomic bomb] to the Russians." And there was Whittaker Chambers's accusation in his book *Wit-*

---

*Wallace did not particularly want legal representation, but Joseph Alsop vehemently insisted on the presence of counsel. Alsop knew Budenz's charges were false but felt Wallace "would be slaughtered" if he tried to defend himself. Alsop personally arranged for Ball's services after several other lawyers had turned him down.

Ball, who later served as undersecretary of state in the Kennedy administration, liked Wallace but considered him a somewhat difficult client. "I found him modest, compassionate and gentle, but the obstinacy of his idealism [made him] quite incapable of comprehending his own predicament."

ness that a Communist cell led by Harold Ware existed in the Agriculture Department when Wallace was secretary in the 1930s.[11]

To each of these accusations Wallace gave forceful and detailed replies. To General Groves he wrote, "I was not in your chain of command and it was not within your power to either submit or withhold reports from me." To Harry Truman he sent a furious telegram. "After reading this incredible diary entry in your own handwriting I could not believe my eyes. Therefore I ask you to confirm or deny that Mr. X is I." (Press Secretary Joseph Short replied that Truman "does not wish to comment" on the book.) To editors at Viking Press, publishers of the Forrestal diaries, Wallace demanded that his denial be carried in future editions.[12]

Particularly difficult to quash were the statements of Whittaker Chambers regarding Communist influence in the Agricultural Adjustment Administration. The accusations appeared not only in his widely read book but in excerpts published by the *Saturday Evening Post* and in numerous other accounts of Communist activity in government that appeared in newspapers and magazines. To each of these Wallace replied along the lines of a letter he sent to the *New York Times:*

> First, the Harold Ware referred to never was in the U.S. Department of Agriculture while I was Secretary. This man was on the U.S. Department of Agriculture roll while the Agriculture Secretaries chosen by Coolidge and Hoover were in control. . . .
>
> Second, a very short time after the cell was organized in the AAA of the U.S. Department of Agriculture, I fired some of the members and most of the rest left as a result of the celebrated purge which took place in 1935. No one knew they were communists until [Lee] Pressman so testified more than 10 years later. I fired them because I disagreed with the policies they advocated and felt there could not be a satisfactory relationship between the Department and the Congress until they left.[13]

But the accusations and innuendos continued unabated; as quickly a Wallace put down the false report about the "Ware cell" in one publication, it popped up again somewhere else. The cumulative effect was to make it possible for almost anyone to say almost anything about Henry A. Wallace. Former Vice President Alben Barkley in his memoirs, *That Reminds Me*, wrote that after 1940 Wallace was troubled by symptoms of "increasing mysticism which later made it possible for the left-wing groups to exploit him." Westbrook Pegler reported that "Bubblehead" was trying to crossbreed a leghorn chicken with a french fry.[14]

Harvey Matusow, a forelorn figure who specialized in telling Senator Joseph McCarthy what he wanted to hear—and later recanted all of it in a book entitled *False Witness*—testified he had "seen and sold" a pamphlet by Wallace published by the left-wing Institute of Pacific Relations, without quite explaining what crime had been committed.[15]

Wallace replied to every slight, rising before sunrise, banging out scores of letters on a manual typewriter atop a metal desk in his office at Farvue.

To the radio commentator Fulton Lewis Jr.: "Last week, Thursday if I remember correctly, while in the process of attacking Phillip Young, you stated that among his other drawbacks he had worked in FEA under me. . . . I have no recollection of Young myself, and I was never head of FEA."[16]

To the *New York Daily News* gossip columnist and television personality Ed Sullivan: "[In reference to] your column of June 11, 1953 in the *Daily News* in which you say, 'Henry Wallace cautioned by medics about his health.' Actually I don't have a doctor and have not had for a number of years. My last complete physical examination a couple of years or so ago indicated 115 degrees blood pressure, heart in perfect condition, kidneys likewise and all the rest. I have been in bed on account of health only about half a day in the last 20 years and that half day was on account of the flu."[17]

Much lay beyond response, of course, because it remained out of sight in the files of the FBI. For many years, dating back to his service as agriculture secretary and beginning in earnest when he was vice president, the FBI had kept a careful eye on Henry A. Wallace.

Tips from the agency's network of informants and from anonymous "100 percent Americans," alleging suspicious activities, were patiently investigated. Agents attended his political rallies, carefully noting everything from what was said to the skin color of the audience. His mail was opened and photocopied—although FBI files indicate the agency understood this was illegal and took steps to eliminate references to this activity from its records—and the phones of political colleagues were tapped. There is some indication wiretaps were placed on his phones at the Department of Commerce. Over time the FBI's Wallace files bulged to thousands of pages, including hundreds of investigative memos and copies of speeches, newspaper clippings, and letters of inquiry.*

The FBI's interest in Wallace never flagged. As late as 1962, a dozen years after Wallace withdrew from active politics, the FBI was still adding material

---

*In 1983 the *Des Moines Register* obtained 539 pages of FBI documents relating to Wallace under a Freedom of Information Act request. Many of the documents were heavily censored. More than a thousand additional documents were withheld as too sensitive to release. In 1998 the FBI released additional material from its Wallace file in response to a renewed Freedom of Information Act request filed by the authors. This material ran to 1,089 pages and included the documents originally released in 1983. The FBI cited the privacy concerns of persons mentioned in the files in again extensively censoring the material.

to his file. In 1958, when the seventy-year-old former vice president applied for a passport to visit with plant breeders and his sister Mary in Europe, the FBI duly made note of it in its files.

By far the most serious FBI investigation of Wallace concerned allegations that he leaked atomic secrets or arranged for the shipment of uranium to the Soviet Union. The source of the allegations remains unclear, but they may have had their origins in ten cartons of material turned over to the FBI by General Groves.

The general apparently took an intense dislike to Wallace after he was kept waiting for an appointment with the vice president in 1944. (When Wallace heard about Groves's complaint, he wrote the general a sharp note saying, "If I kept you waiting it was because I had something better to do.")[18]

That a small amount of uranium—insufficient for purposes of weaponry or even research—was shipped to the Soviet Union during the war was clear. That Wallace had nothing to do with the shipment was equally certain.

Suspicions about Wallace were kept alive by his friendship with Boris Pregel, a Russian-born Jew who controlled most of the uranium reserves in Canada and the Belgium Congo. Pregel, who provided small amounts of diluted radioactive materials for Wallace's agricultural research at Farvue, remained an object of distrust to the FBI. In 1951 the FBI received a tip from Senator Pat McCarran's office, based on a source it refused to identify, that Wallace had had a conversation about the atomic bomb with "a subversive agent" in Philadelphia in 1943 or 1944. An FBI memo on the matter said the unnamed agent asked for additional information on the bomb and "Wallace is reported to have said to the subversive agent that he had gotten the U-235 for the agent and that that should be enough."[19]

The FBI seized upon the idea that the "subversive agent" was Pregel and explored the tip extensively. "Keep after this. We must nail it down," FBI Director J. Edgar Hoover noted at the bottom of one report. At the bottom of another report, Hoover wrote, "Get after this at once. I want no evasion. Try & find out what it is."[20]

But the FBI's investigation of the supposed 1940s meeting, like its other investigations of Wallace, eventually evaporated. Wallace could hardly have passed along secrets he didn't possess.

The extensive FBI file on Henry Wallace—aside from its odious whiff of racism and antisemitism—proved not much more than Wallace himself noted in his diary on December 19, 1944: "Hoover specializes in building up a file against various public figures. . . . Hoover is apparently on his way to become an American Himmler."[21]

Halfway through the 1950s, professional ex-Communist witnesses and FBI counterspies were still smearing Wallace before receptive congressional committees. On October 19, 1954, Matthew Cvetic, an omnipresent figure at Red-scare hearings, told a Senate committee that Henry Wallace and Glen Taylor knew from the outset that the Progressive Party was "controlled" by Communists. A few days later FBI secret agent Herbert A. Philbrick—author of *I Led Three Lives* and fictionalized hero of a television series similarly named—told congressmen that Communists had written Wallace's 1948 acceptance speech.

Over time, however, the headlines generated by such "revelations" grew smaller. Slowly the grip of postwar anti-Communist hysteria relaxed its hold on the nation's attention. Bit by bit the public pillorying of Henry Wallace receded. Gradually he was, if not redeemed, at least forgotten. How did he feel about living in "comparative obscurity," a reporter asked when he arrived virtually unnoticed in Des Moines. "I like it," said Wallace.[22]

Occasionally a reporter who had covered his tumultuous public career—an Ed Lahey or a Cabell Phillips—would seek him out for a where-are-they-now story about the erstwhile firebrand. Usually Wallace would agree reluctantly to the interview.

The stories followed a pattern. Ilo Wallace, gracious and grandmotherly, would treat the reporter to a meal piled high with chops, baked potatoes, beet greens, homemade biscuits, and apple butter, followed by scrumptious strawberry shortcake.

After lunch would come a visit to Wallace's comfortable library, lined floor to ceiling with books on three walls, where he would make a few restrained remarks about current affairs. "The cold war is not going to end while either the United States or the Soviet Union has anything to gain from it," he told Lahey. "The Russians need it to keep their people in check, and I think we are finding it necessary to stay on a war economy to maintain full employment."[23]

Then Wallace would plop on his battered brown hat and lead the reporter on a tour of his wondrous farm. Gone in an instant was the caution, the sometimes hollow laugh and moody defensiveness, with which he answered political questions. Now Wallace moved with the "big, loping gait of a man who is impatient to get on with whatever he has to do next," Phillips wrote.[24]

Excitedly he would lead his guests past the seedbeds and through the barns of his carefully managed experimental farm, showing off delicious golfball-sized strawberries, mammoth hydroponic tomatoes grown in gravel-filled tanks, mysterious Chinese cabbage ultra-rich in vitamin C, rows of experimental corn specially tailored to prosper in the cool New York spring, eye-popping gladioli bombarded with gamma rays to produce shades of crimson and garnet.

And the chickens.

Reporters were always awed by the sheer number of chickens—as many as five thousand pullets and roosters, up to fifteen thousand chicks—their infinite variety, the enormous complexity of the whole operation. Wallace was working toward development of the perfect chicken, which would lay the perfect egg, Lahey wrote, and do it in less time and at lower cost than other varieties. The search involved a constant process of inbreeding and crossbreeding chickens, weeding out undesirable strains, and promulgating desirable characteristics.

"Every chicken is banded from birth, and every egg laid is carefully marked and noted in a big ledger," Lahey added. "The big book in the Wallace barn shows the egg laying and the hatching record for every hen. The weight of a hen's eggs, their shape, color, and viscosity are all recorded meticulously. Infants born in our best hospitals do not have such elaborate charts as the chicks born in the batteries of incubators in the Wallace chicken houses."[25]

Newspapermen could only pretend to understand all that was happening at Farvue, but they could see it was serious business and that Henry Wallace could not have been happier. "As a misfit politician in the first place, he has no nostalgic hankering for the gilded prominence, the hysterical cheers, the strident oratory or the competitive intrigues of the political arena," Phillips wrote.[26]

Here was no defeated man living his twilight years in bitterness and sorrow. Here was a man at play in the field of his special genius. "The highest joy of life," he remarked in his oral history, "is complete dedication to something outside of yourself."[27] The same combination of qualities that made Wallace difficult to understand among politicians and urban intellectuals brought him success and respect on the farm: his love of physical labor, his orderly scientific mind, his outsized curiosity and willingness to question conventional wisdom, his touch of mysticism.

The element of mysticism, his sense of oneness with all living things, baffled city folk. Once, when he was vice president, a group of New York City writers and artists had invited Wallace to an evening of conversation and asked what the key to successful plant breeding was. They had expected a long, scholarly dissertation on genetics, but Wallace unhesitatingly gave a four-word reply that dumbfounded his audience: "Sympathy for the plant."[28]

In 1956 Henry A. Wallace collaborated with William L. Brown, chief of scientific research and later president of Pioneer Hi-Bred, on a delightful history of corn titled *Corn and Its Early Fathers*. Before they wrote anything about the corn plant, Wallace and Brown quoted from *Gulliver's Travels:* "And he gave it for his opinion, that whoever could make two ears of corn, or two blades of grass, to grow upon a spot of ground where only one grew before, would deserve better of mankind, and do more essential service to his country, than the whole race of politicians put together."[29] Or as Wallace himself put it near the end of his oral history, "Jesus took on himself the highest of all missions when he said that he came to give a more abundant life to humanity. The improved quality and increased abundance of life is a progressive matter and has to do not only with human life but with all plants and animals as well."[30]

Thus measured, Wallace's latter years were rewarding and productive. He produced a variety of short-stemmed gladioli that would unfold after being cut and placed in a vase, greatly increasing its commercial viability. He searched endlessly for a strawberry combining the intense flavor of European varieties with the large American size so easy to pick and ship. (His quest was hampered by a decreasing sense of taste, hastened by allergies aggravated by the constant presence of chickens. In his final years Wallace called upon his daughter, Jean Douglas, to describe the taste of his berries.)

His chickens came to dominate the world. Hy-Line chickens, a subsidiary of Pioneer Hi-Bred, at one point accounted for about three-quarters of all egg-laying poultry sold commercially worldwide. Even a quarter century after Wallace's death, descendants of his chickens were laying one of every three eggs eaten by Americans, according to Bob Arvidson, chief of Hy-Line's research division. Worldwide the figure approached 50 percent.

Corn, of course, remained a great passion. He was in frequent touch with Raymond Baker and other Pioneer Hi-Bred scientists and was intimately familiar with their efforts to develop new types of high-yielding, disease-resistant corn. He established a small research station in Jamaica and helped start research programs in Cuba and Guatemala, striving to improve tropical corn.

He wrote and lectured on corn breeding, germ plasm, genetics and disease resistance, nutrition, and other aspects of scientific agriculture.

He traveled widely but without fanfare, usually on agricultural matters. Once or twice a year he would disappear into Pioneer's cornfields or conference with his son H. B., who headed the company's poultry division. (His other son, Bob, ran the Hy-Line hatchery in Doylestown, Pennsylvania.) Occasionally he would show up in Central America to discuss ways of improving agricultural production with scientists there. In 1958 he drove 2,900 miles through Europe, meeting with plant breeders in several countries, without being recognized by a single reporter.

To the company's business operation he gave little attention. As Pioneer Hi-Bred flourished financially, reporting an unbroken string of profits throughout the 1950s and 1960s, Wallace continued to live a comfortably frugal life. He still drove an unpretentious Plymouth or Volkswagon, sometimes turning off the motor while going downhill to save gas, and served mainly as his own secretary and bookkeeper. On the farm he employed four men to help with the experimental work, but his calloused hands and ruddy complexion attested to the fact that he did much manual labor himself.

Only on research did he spend liberally, any amount necessary, and he advised the men who ran Pioneer to do likewise. He never attempted to patent anything. His philosophy of business, as of agriculture and politics, was always to stay ahead of his time.

❈

What is a liberal? Henry Wallace asked in a May 1, 1953, address to a Harvard Law School forum.

He answered, "To me a liberal is one who believes in using in a nonviolent, tolerant and democratic way the forces of education, publicity, politics, economics, business, law and religion to direct the ever-changing and increasing power of science into channels which will bring peace and the maximum of well-being both spiritual and economic to the greatest number of human beings. A liberal knows that the only certainty in this life is change but believes that the change can be directed toward a constructive end."[31]

As he spoke, liberalism in America was at a low ebb. Republicans controlled the White House and both houses of Congress. Joseph McCarthy rode high in the Senate. The celebrated Rosenberg atomic espionage case was reaching its climax. U.S. troops fought a grim and bloody war in Korea. Even if President Eisenhower wanted to do anything liberal—and there was no evidence he did—Wallace doubted he could. "War and the tensions leading to war are the great destroyers of the liberal spirit," Wallace declared.[32]

Under these circumstances what were liberals to do? First, he said, liberals must be ready with a program for full employment not dependent upon the military-industrial complex. "In 1910 William James wrote an article on 'The Moral Equivalent of War.' What I ask the liberal of 1953 to do is find the 'Economic Equivalent of War' in a world whose normal trading economy has been continually shattered for 39 years." Liberals must push for a stronger and more efficient United Nations, free trade, and economic development assistance to Third World countries.[33]

True liberals, he said, cannot "look on Russia and communism as the only cause of the present state of world tensions. The real cause, which the Russians skillfully utilize for their own ends, is that the farmers and workers in countries like India and Iran produce only two or three percent as much as they do in countries like the USA and Canada. . . . [The] poverty-stricken men of the world who usually have a yellow, brown or black skin are more and more aching to pay back the white man for his airs of superiority."[34]

But finally, Wallace added, liberals must examine themselves. "The great peril of liberalism is its tendency to become materialistic," he said. "Because liberalism is tolerant it also tends to be without faith in anything which is outside the realm of physical perception. . . . Liberals must look on religion as the hope of the future rather than the dead hand of the past. Democracy and science are not enough. Full employment and efficiency are not enough. Full respect for other races and religions is not enough."[35]

It would later be said of Wallace that he lurched erratically to the right after breaking with the Progressive Party in 1950 and returned over time to the Republican Party he had once abandoned. Certainly he criticized the Soviet Union as never before. And, as always, critics found reason to quarrel with him.

But no fair reading of his public statements would support the charge that Wallace retreated into isolationism, nationalism, or bitter conservatism. He no more returned to the Republican Party than he did to the Democratic Party, and his fundamental philosophy never changed. He remained to the end a champion of world government, nuclear disarmament, expanded world trade, and international development programs.

In a long biographical essay describing his "political odyssey," published by *Life* magazine in 1956, Wallace addressed the question of whether he had undergone a change of heart. "I have of course changed my attitude toward Russia several times, as have most Americans over the past 25 years. But I have not changed my basic views, and I have clung resolutely to my ultimate ideal that America's security can be preserved by means of an international organization strong enough to enforce peace."[36]

Like his father and grandfather before him, Wallace was attracted to causes rather than to men, to philosophy rather than to parties. In 1952, having come to regard the Progressive Party as little more than a Stalinist sect, he publicly endorsed no presidential candidate. Privately he voted for the Democratic candidate, Adlai Stevenson, who once had worked for him at the Department of Agriculture.

Before the 1956 election Wallace said he would support President Eisenhower if he ran again and Adlai Stevenson if the president chose not to seek reelection. When Eisenhower announced he would run, Wallace kept his promise. In a letter to Stevenson explaining his stance, Wallace said he believed that Eisenhower was "utterly sincere" in his desire to serve the cause of peace. Privately he thought Eisenhower was in a better position to control the U.S. military than Stevenson.*[37]

*Unknown to the public, Wallace had begun corresponding with Eisenhower and his influential brother, Dr. Milton Eisenhower, who was the first person Wallace hired at the Agriculture Department. In a 1953 exchange with the president, Wallace warned that the new leader of the Soviet Union, Georgi Malenkov, was "abysmally ignorant" about "the actual facts of our physical world." He noted that Malenkov was the man chiefly responsible for the prominence of the Soviet plant breeder Trofim Lysenko, whom Wallace considered an "energetic, fanatic, ruthless, ambitious" scientific fraud.

Eisenhower wrote back a warm letter of thanks, saying he had studied Wallace's letter "carefully" and planned to share it with his brother.

Wallace stuck with Eisenhower even after the Republican national chairman Leonard Hall gratuitously attacked him in an article on the vice presidency published by *This Week* magazine. Hall asserted that Franklin Roosevelt "stuffed Henry Wallace down the throat" of the Democratic Party in 1940 and, by dumping Wallace four years later, admitted "what a colossal mistake he had made." Wallace offered a heated reply to the magazine and privately wrote to Hall that he had responded in an "undeservedly mild way."*38

Wallace continued to correspond with President Eisenhower through his second term, on subjects like China, India, a forthcoming U.S. visit by the Soviet leader Nikita Khrushchev, and general Third World economic development. Clearly Wallace thought Eisenhower more liberal than his party, stealthily pushing for peace in a country geared for war. Always Eisenhower wrote back in friendly, personal terms.

Slowly Wallace's admiration for Eisenhower began to affect even his attitude toward Vice President Richard Nixon, the ardent anti-Communist who remained anathema to most liberals. After a late-1956 Gridiron dinner in Washington, at which Wallace spoke and praised Nixon's dignified manner in office, the two chatted cordially. Subsequently they corresponded about foreign policy matters.

Then, as Nixon prepared to run for the presidency in 1960, Wallace was invited by Nixon to meet with him in Washington. The forty-minute meeting, on March 11, 1960, was "completely secret," Wallace said. The former vice president slipped in and out of Nixon's hideaway office in the Capitol unnoticed by reporters or senators. No public mention of the meeting was made during Wallace's lifetime. The only account of it was a twelve-page, handwritten memo Wallace wrote to himself. It was discovered by the authors at Farvue many years after Wallace's death.

"Nixon had written me a year or so earlier asking me to call on him when I was in Washington," Wallace said. "Nixon makes a much stronger impres-

---

*Wallace's letter to Hall was indeed mild compared with the one he wrote to former President Truman on March 10, 1956. Wallace had earlier demanded that Truman repudiate the "Mr. X" statement in the book *Mr. President*, which said a member of his cabinet was twice as dangerous "as the German American bund under Fritz Kuhn." In response to Wallace's letter, Truman sent an autographed copy of volume 1 of his *Memoirs*, which did nothing to repair the damage done to Wallace's reputation. Wallace was livid.

"I know how deeply you love your daughter and how you wish to avoid doing anything which will hurt her," Wallace wrote back. "Well, I have three children and eleven grandchildren and I feel that . . . you have left a time bomb which will blow up and hurt my children and grandchildren. . . . I had hoped your Christian conscience and your belief in God would cause you to right the wrong which some base, uninformed person caused you to commit. When a President calls a former Vice President something worse than a traitor we have before us something without precedent. I cannot believe that you wish this dirty, unacknowledged smear to stand. . . ."

sion face to face than over the air or in photos. He was exceedingly cordial and sat on the couch beside me." The discussion centered largely on foreign policy and on the farm program as it affected international relations. Wallace began by warning Nixon there was trouble head:

> I told him that Eisenhower had furnished the country a period of needed rest, that the next President might be facing a period as critical as that from 1861–65. I said no man in his right senses would want to be President with the situation as it will be in the 1960s, that it would require a very high sense of service. . . . I spoke at some length on the extraordinary force of the na-tionalistic trend in the newer nations. . . . I said the aspirations of the Com-mon Man destructively led might be far more dangerous than the atom bomb.

Nixon asked for his views on disarmament, and Wallace proposed an in-novative ten-year plan in which half the savings would be put into a UN fund for development in Third World nations. If Russia would not join in that ap-proach, Wallace suggested, "we should spell out the projects country by coun-try which could be started if it were not for Russian recalcitrance."

After twenty-five minutes of talk Nixon asked Wallace to stay another quar-ter hour, and they began to discuss politics. Wallace mentioned his "high es-teem" for Adlai Stevenson and explained that he had supported Eisenhower in 1956 because he "thought Eisenhower would be in a better position than Stevenson to hold the extreme right wing in check." Nixon said he believed his opponent in the 1960 presidential race would be John F. Kennedy.

> He asked what I thought of Kennedy. I countered by saying that if you elected Kennedy you were also electing his father. Nixon said he under-stood Joe [Kennedy] was quite a rough character. To this I agreed but also said Joe, as ambassador to the Court of St. James, was exceedingly helpful to me in putting over the cotton-rubber trade just before the war broke out. Nixon said if Kennedy and [Senator Hubert H.] Humphrey were to debate face to face he thought Humphrey would get the best of it. He seemed really fond of Humphrey.[39]

They never met again. Wallace did not specifically endorse anyone in the 1960 race, but near the end of the campaign he gave Nixon a de facto boost with a much noted blast at Kennedy's farm program. The Democrat proposed to raise farm income to total parity with city dwellers through a program of "supply management," a plan Wallace considered wildly unrealistic.[40]

Kennedy brushed the matter aside. The new president arranged for Henry and Ilo Wallace to attend his inauguration ceremony and luncheon in the

Capitol. It was the first inaugural Wallace had attended since 1944, and he was touched by Kennedy's gesture. "At no time in our history have so many tens of millions of people been so completely enthusiastic about an Inaugural Address as about yours," Wallace wrote Kennedy afterwards. Wallace was especially pleased that Kennedy had invited his "old friend" Robert Frost to deliver a poem at the ceremony.[41]

In his speech accepting the Democratic nomination, Kennedy had spoken of a "New Frontier," a catchphrase that came to identify his administration. Wallace, perhaps from pride of authorship, believed the phrase was taken from his 1934 book, *New Frontiers*. Whatever its origin, he said it appealed to him "more than the slogans 'New Deal' or 'Square Deal' or 'New Freedom.' The New Frontier suggests aspiration, adventure, mutual striving toward the unknown."[42]

Although he warmed to the young administration, he was not an unabashed admirer. Kennedy's adventuristic foreign policies, especially the Bay of Pigs fiasco, made Wallace shiver. But he liked the Alliance for Progress initiative to foster economic development in Latin America and, somewhat surprisingly, found Kennedy's farm program a sensible and progressive attempt to deal with the thorny problem of huge surpluses in basic commodities.

Within a matter of months Wallace was saying kind words in public about Secretary of Agriculture Orville Freeman. The secretary responded with a series of letters to Wallace that were friendly to the point of effusiveness. "[I] know if the present Secretary of Agriculture is able to muster only part the insight and demonstrate a bit of the leadership of Secretary of Agriculture Henry Wallace that the record will indeed be a memorable one," Freeman wrote in February 1962. A few months later Wallace wrote to Kennedy, "As an ex-Secretary of Agriculture I wish to express my opinion that it would be impossible for you to get as good a Secretary of Agriculture as you have right now in the Hon. Orville Freeman."[43]

In May 1962 Freeman brought Wallace back to the Agriculture Department to deliver an address marking its centennial as a government agency. Hundreds of employees lined the halls to applaud the legendary former secretary as he toured the department he had once steered.

His address reviewed the breathtaking changes that had occurred in agriculture during his lifetime. The Iowa farm on which he was born in 1888, he pointed out, wasn't too different from the farm of his grandfather's boyhood, a place where men and horses labored for an hour to produce a bushel of corn. Seventy-four years later the American farm had been revolutionized by machines and pesticides and hybrid seed. A competent farmer could produce a bushel of corn with less than six minutes of labor.

As always, Wallace embraced change. He hungered to know more and do more to improve life on Earth. "Scientific understanding is our joy. Economic and political understanding is our duty. Our objective is the understanding of life at all its varied levels. . . . Continually I crossbreed strawberries and grow them from seed," Wallace told the Agriculture Department employees. "Each year I wait to see what they look like the next year. I recommend to all of you that you become gardeners. Then you will never die, because you have to live to see what happens next year."[44]

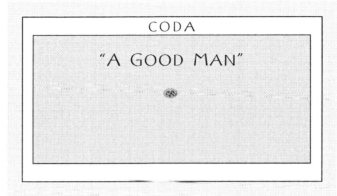

CODA

"A GOOD MAN"

As he approached the age of seventy-five, it seemed Henry A. Wallace might go on gardening forever. Now heavier, his hair a snowy white, and suffering from sinus problems, he otherwise seemed in prime condition. He ran half a mile every day and could still do twenty-two push-ups. His blood pressure was 130 over 75, and his heart and lungs were normal. When he turned seventy-five, on October 8, 1963, Wallace told friends he fully expected to be around for his one-hundredth birthday.

He thrived on long days, still sleeping only four or five hours a night, and enjoyed a vigorous game of tennis on weekends. Bob Arvidson, Pioneer's chief poultry breeder, regularly visited Farvue and recalled the routine: long hours of work in the barns, followed by an evening of discussion in the library. After Arvidson collapsed into bed around midnight, he could hear Wallace in his office banging out notes on his typewriter to guide the next day's activity.

Wallace had taught himself Italian and was learning Portuguese. He enjoyed lecturing on such topics as "Genetics of Disease Resistance" and "Development of Improved Crops." He was collaborating with University of Maryland research scientist George Darrow on a book about strawberries. Occasionally in later years he would read a mystery novel or watch a television program with his grandson David, but the books in his well-used library overwhelmingly reflected the serious nature of his intellectual pursuits. To the town librarian he was the man who knew everything; when she was stumped by a reference question, she simply called Wallace for the answer.

In December 1963 Wallace traveled to Central America, where he delivered the commencement address at the Pan-American School of Agriculture in Zamorano, Honduras, an institution he had been associated with for two decades. Do not fear hard work, he told the students. "Muscular illiteracy must end. Many a religious order has found that work enriches the soil, strengthens the body, and sanctifies the soul."[1]

He came back to Central America in April 1964 to check on corn-breeding experiments in the region. It was there, in a part of the world he treasured, that mortality began to catch up with him.

First came a peculiar experience in El Salvador. Wallace spotted an unusual-looking nut and impulsively tasted it. The nut was bitter, and he spit it out. Later he was told it was poisonous and had killed a cow that had eaten one. A short time later, while "very rapidly" climbing a pyramid at Huehuetenango, in Guatemala, his left foot began to drag. He assumed the dragging would go away. It didn't.[2]

By June 1964 the problem with his foot was severe enough to interfere with his tennis. He played his last game in July. In August he checked himself into a hospital in Danbury, Connecticut, about twenty miles from Farvue, for tests. Dr. Joseph Belsky, the attending physician, surmised the nature of the problem but temporarily elected not to "reveal to Mr. Wallace such a dire diagnosis that he was completely unprepared to receive."[3]

A month passed with no improvement. In October, Wallace made a trip to Iowa, where he delivered a rambling, low-key talk in Harlan, Iowa, touching on topics ranging from corn production to foreign affairs.

"We lost Cuba in 1959 not only because of Castro but also because we failed to understand the needs of the farmer in the back country of Cuba from 1920 onward," he declared. ". . . The common man is on the march, but it is up to the uncommon men of education and insight to lead that march constructively. The century of the common man can be a century of bloodshed and confusion—Viet Nam multiplied one hundred fold."[4]

Three days later in Des Moines, Wallace made his last public appearance. Speaking to a reunion of West High School graduates, Wallace paid tribute to his long-shuttered alma mater and, typically, said the school could have been better. "Our adolescence in its sentimental vagueness coincided with a simple, adolescent U.S.A., a nation without world responsibilities," Wallace declared. "We were taught in a fragmentary, incomplete way. Our grandchildren are being taught more completely. May they outdistance us as completely as the auto outdistances the horse. But in so doing may they never lose humility in facing the ultimate unknowns. And may the Divine Spark live in their souls forever."[5]

Many in the audience noticed his unusually husky voice and awkward movements. Wallace offered no explanation. He did not know the reason himself.

In November, Wallace went to the Mayo Clinic in Rochester, Minnesota, for further tests. There Dr. Belsky's early diagnosis was confirmed. Wallace had amyotrophic lateral sclerosis (ALS), a rare neuromuscular degenerative disease. Often called Lou Gehrig's disease after the famous "Iron Man" of baseball who died of it in 1941, ALS is one of modern medicine's most intractable mysteries. Its cause and cure were unknown in Gehrig's day, and remained so a half century later. Only one thing is certain: ALS is always fatal.

On the average, ALS patients lived about two years after contracting the disease. Wallace calculated, therefore, that he could expect to die in July 1966, when he would be seventy-seven years and nine months old—and he was utterly determined to beat the odds. If he could not defeat the disease entirely, he said, at least he intended to reach his eightieth birthday and see the progress of his beloved plants.

Wallace approached his death with the tools characteristic of his uncommon life: keen scientific intellect and respect for fact, voracious curiosity and willingness to experiment with the unconventional, prodigious physical endurance, courage, and strong spiritual faith. He intently absorbed the medical literature. He speculated freely in letters to doctors and friends.

Could the disease have something to do with the clouds of DDT in which he had worked for years? With the nut he had tasted in El Salvador? Why did natives on Guam have a higher incidence of ALS than anyone else? Could the human body be genetically reprogrammed?

He consulted with leading authorities in the U.S. medical establishment. He sought help from those on the unorthodox fringes of European research. He kept copious notes on the progress of the disease—measuring his strength by his ability to do push-ups or the amount of time it took to climb the steps to his doctor's office—and the effect of various treatments on his body.

He tried everything. He received the standard physical therapy recommended by leading doctors, and he learned the "autohypnosis" technique suggested by a "doctor of last resort." He took lyophilized cells, procaine mixed with caffeine, something called Bogomolets serum, shark liver extract, methyl testosterone, high doses of vitamins B and C (taken intramuscularly), calcium gluconate (taken intravenously), and a protein-dissolving enzyme called Wobe-Mugos (taken either as "candy" or as a suppository). The Wobe medicine, which Wallace believed for a time to be helpful, was supplied surreptitiously by Dr. Max Wolf, an eighty-year-old New York physician, because it had not been approved by the Food and Drug Administration.[6]

"I look on myself as an ALS guinea-pig, willing to try out almost anything," Wallace wrote.[7]

In March 1965 Wallace flew to Europe and, using his sister Mary's home in Vevey, Switzerland, as a base, began consulting specialists in nerve diseases and "cell therapy." While there he underwent a sinus operation and a tonsil-lectomy, which doctors thought might stop his chronic low-grade infections. Later, in the United States, he voluntarily underwent biopsies in the hope doctors could learn more about ALS from the body of a living patient. Wallace, one of his doctors wrote, "is ruled by a great will to live and it is astonishing how he can take pain."[8]

But despite all, Wallace was losing the fight. Inch by inch, muscle by muscle, his body was ceasing to function. First his left foot, then his left arm, became unusable. He continued to write letters, typing with his right hand. His lower back muscles shut down. He could move laboriously with the aid of a foot brace and a walker, but he was terrified of falling. At times he could not pull himself off the toilet. "You try to be independent, but you just cannot." Coughing was difficult, swallowing food even more so. The labor of eating was equal to running half a mile, he said. By mid-1965 he had lost thirty-five pounds.[9]

"Truly ALS is a unique experience," he wrote. "There is no pain. Apparently your eyes and brain are not affected. Therefore, you can calmly watch the rest of your body slowly disintegrate. . . . ALS gives you a ringside seat at your own dissolution." He described it as "a little like a disembodied spirit in purgatory."[10]

He never stopped trying. He never lost interest in life, in his strawberries and chickens and the latest corn research news from Iowa. When he could no longer work in the fields, he drove his car to the end of the rows and watched others work. "I had a lot of psychic input, but no physical input," he wrote.[11]

Even public policy occupied him. Wallace began a remarkable exchange of letters with President Lyndon Johnson concerning his ideas for stemming the ongoing flight of farmers from the land, a plight that had concerned the Wallaces for three generations. Wallace suggested an innovative program to decentralize industry, perhaps using the "War on Poverty" program as a mechanism, so farm families could find enough part-time work in nearby towns to sustain themselves on the land.

Johnson expressed interest, and Wallace was heartened. He was greatly alarmed, however, by Johnson's Vietnam policies, which were bringing Wallace's Cold War nightmares to life. Unable to speak, he scrawled on a tablet to a visiting friend, "The policies of Truman and Byrnes will yet make this country bleed from every pore."[12]

By the fall of 1965 Wallace could see the end approaching. "No matter how joyous my spirits, I cannot help realizing month by month the gradual retreat of muscle control," he wrote. He updated his will, made sure his taxes were in order, and in late September entered the National Institutes of Health in Bethesda, Maryland, for experimental treatment and research. At NIH doctors put an opening in his neck to the esophagus for the intake of food and medicines, conducted a biopsy, and provided suction machines and drugs to prevent the flow of mucus and saliva to his lungs.[13]

At NIH Wallace began a moving diary, actually a collection of undated notes, entitled "Reflections of an ALSer." He recalled his sorrow at not being able to work in the soil during the last season of his life. "It was a terrible disappointment not to get into the strawberry and gladiolus fields to see what my children were doing. It seemed like I had become psychically bankrupt. Nevertheless, I arranged for strawberry and gladiolus hybridization as usual. I just have to see what my plant children will look like in 1966 and 1967."[14]

He would go on fighting as long as he could take breath, he wrote. "If you cannot contribute as much as you take, what good are you?" He was overwhelmed by the kindness shown to him by the NIH staff, and by books and flowers from friends and well-wishers. First Lady Lady Bird Johnson sent a "most impressive" bouquet and a beautiful longhand note.[15]

On October 28 Wallace was returned to Farvue by ambulance. There his family had transformed the dining room into a comfortable downstairs bedroom, equipped with a hospital bed and newly installed spacious bathroom. He rested comfortably for several days, attended by nurses around the clock, sometimes adding a few words to his "Reflections."

"Here as I write I look to the east through my New York farm window and see the ridge which is Ridgefield, Connecticut. Everyone has been so utterly good and kind to me, both here and at NIH. After listening to the radio and reading the newspapers and looking at TV, the mind becomes oppressed by the viciousness of man. But there is another aspect of man—kindliness to those in great need. This ALSer has had a rich experience with the goodness of man as exhibited toward those who are unfortunate."[16]

Shortly after writing those words the disease silently spreading through his body reached the last vital muscles, those bringing air to his lungs. On the morning of Thursday, November 18, 1965, breathing became so difficult that his family returned him to Danbury Hospital. There, at 11:15 A.M., with Ilo and his sister Mary by his side, Henry Agard Wallace ended his long and eventful journey on Earth.

A funeral service was held two days later at the Wallace's church, St. Stephens Episcopal, in Ridgefield, Connecticut. Three hundred people attended the simple twenty-minute service and heard the rector read from the 46th and 121st Psalms. ("I will lift up mine eyes unto the hills.") At his request there was no eulogy, no sermon, no hymn. Wallace's body lay in a plain gray coffin covered by a pall of crimson and purple brocade. The only flowers were sprays of his white gladioli and a red-white-and-blue wreath from President Johnson.

A few of the old New Dealers came. Former Postmaster General James A. Farley was there. So were the statistician Louis Bean and Beanie Baldwin. Secretary of Health, Education, and Welfare John W. Gardner represented the president. A clump of teenagers watched the long black limousines pull beside the church and wondered what could have drawn them to Ridgefield. "Who was he?" one of them asked.

The body was cremated in Bridgeport and the ashes flown to Des Moines. There another memorial service was held on November 21, and a burial in the family plot at Glendale Cemetery.

Many a verbal brick had been thrown at Henry A. Wallace during his robustly unquiet life. But in death the words were kind. Lyndon Johnson called him "an original American voice" whose views were "not always popular, but they were sincere." Harry Truman called him "an asset to the country," and Thomas E. Dewey praised Wallace's "unique contribution to the world's standard of living."[17]

Glen Taylor, who sacrificed his public career to run with Wallace, reminded the nation that a prophet had fallen: "Practically everything Wallace advocated then has been acted on since—that's the way it is with people who are in the vanguard." Dr. Paul Mangelsdorf, head of the Harvard University Botanical Museum, commented, "It was Wallace's fate to be often regarded as a 'dreamer' when actually he was only seeing in his own pragmatic realistic way some of the shapes of things to come, and more often than not he was right."[18]

"History cannot ignore him and we shall not forget him," said Secretary of Agriculture Orville Freeman. "No single individual has contributed more to the abundance we enjoy today than Henry Wallace."[19]

Vice President Hubert H. Humphrey, a sometime admirer and sometime adversary, offered a tribute Wallace himself would have treasured: "Henry Wallace was a scientist and a statesman, a politician and a philosopher who was devoted and dedicated to peace—but above all he was a good man."[20]

NOTES

ABBREVIATIONS

CUOH	"The Reminiscences of Henry Agard Wallace," Columbia University Oral History
Diary	Diary of Henry Agard Wallace, Special Collections, University of Iowa Library
DMR	*Des Moines Register*
DMT	*Des Moines Tribune*
Family	Uncataloged papers in possession of Wallace family members
FDR	Franklin Delano Roosevelt
FDRL	Franklin D. Roosevelt Library
HAW	Henry Agard Wallace
HST	Harry S. Truman
HSTL	Harry S. Truman Library
Interview	Personal interviews conducted by the authors
ISU	Iowa State University Library, Special Collections
LOC	Library of Congress
NA	National Archives
NYT	*New York Times*
TNR	*New Republic*
UI	University of Iowa Library, Henry A. Wallace Papers, Special Collections
USDA	U.S. Department of Agriculture
WF	*Wallaces' Farmer* and its successor publication, *Wallaces' Farmer and Iowa Homestead*

CHAPTER 1: "GOOD FARMING, CLEAR THINKING, RIGHT LIVING"

1. Edward L. Schapsmeier and Frederick H. Schapsmeier, *Henry A. Wallace of Iowa: The Agrarian Years, 1910–1940* (Ames: Iowa State Univ. Press, 1968), p. 18; CUOH, p. 35.
2. Henry Wallace, *Uncle Henry's Own Story*, 3 vols. (Des Moines: Wallace Publishing, 1917–19), 1:90.
3. Ibid., p. 126.
4. Ibid., 2:18.
5. Ibid., p. 21.
6. Ibid., p 48.
7. Russell Lord, *The Wallaces of Iowa* (Boston: Houghton Mifflin, 1947), p. 105.
8. Ibid., p. 106.
9. Dan Wallace, "Just a Little History," UI.
10. CUOH, p. 6.
11. Ibid., p. 4.
12. Ibid., p. 7.
13. Ibid., pp. 15–16.
14. Lord, *Wallaces*, p. 107.
15. CUOH, pp. 2–3.
16. HAW, "The Uniqueness of George Washington Carver," Sept. 12, 1954, UI speech file.
17. Wallace, *Uncle Henry's Own Story*, 2:67.
18. Lord, *Wallaces*, p. 130.
19. Cited in Joel Timm, "Shameful Venality: The Pierce-Wallace Controversy and the Election of 1896," *Palimpsest* 71 (Spring 1990): 4.
20. *WF*, Sept. 18, 1896.
21. Wallace, *Uncle Henry's Own Story*, 2:75.
22. CUOH, p. 4.
23. Ibid., p. 18.
24. Wallace, *Uncle Henry's Own Story*, 2:77.
25. *Traer (Iowa) Clipper*, April 14, 1933.
26. Henry Wallace, *Uncle Henry's Letters to the Farm Boy*, 4th ed. (New York: Macmillan, 1918), p. 167.
27. Wallace, *Uncle Henry's Own Story*, 2:92.
28. Lord, *Wallaces*, p. 141.
29. Ibid., p. 138.

CHAPTER 2: "WHAT'S LOOKS TO A HOG?"

1. CUOH, p. 20.
2. Ibid., p. 27.
3. Ibid., p. 29.
4. Ibid., p. 27.
5. HAW and William L. Brown, *Corn and Its Early Fathers* (Lansing: Michigan State Univ. Press, 1956), p. 94.
6. Lord, *Wallaces*, p. 150.
7. Paul de Kruif, *Hunger Fighters* (New York: Harcourt, Brace, 1928), p. 190.
8. HAW and Brown, *Corn*, pp. 97–98.
9. HAW, "The West High That Was," Oct. 17, 1964, Family.
10. CUOH, p. 41.
11. Ibid.
12. Ibid., p. 42.

13. Ibid.
14. CUOH, p. 40.
15. Ibid., pp. 40–41.
16. HAW, "West High."
17. Ibid., p. 47.
18. Ralph Waldo Trine, *In Tune with the Infinite* (Indianapolis: Bobbs-Merrill, 1908), p. 25.
19. CUOH, p. 49.
20. "Recollections of Henry A. Wallace at Iowa State" file, ISU.
21. CUOH, p. 64.
22. "Recollections," ISU.
23. Ibid.
24. CUOH, p. 52.
25. Ibid., p. 57.
26. Ibid., p. 56.
27. Richard Lowitt and Judith Fabry, eds., *Henry A. Wallace's Irrigation Frontier* (Norman: Univ. of Oklahoma Press, 1991), p. 223.
28. "Recollections," ISU.
29. Henry Wallace to HAW, Oct. 7, 1909, UI.
30. Schapsmeier, *Agrarian Years*, p. 23.
31. CUOH, p. 54
32. Interview, Dorothy Stackpole, South Salem, N.Y., 1990.
33. *Kansas City Star*, Aug. 1, 1948.
34. Lord, *Wallaces*, p. 165.
35. Schapsmeier, *Agrarian Years*, pp. 14–15.
36. Lord, *Wallaces*, p. 166.
37. Ibid.
38. *DMR*, Feb. 23, 1916.
39. *Tributes to Henry Wallace* (Des Moines: Wallace Publishing, 1919), p. 206.
40. Des Moines Capital, Feb. 26, 1916.
41. Lord, *Wallaces*, p. 167.
42. "Wallace Family Covenant," UI.

CHAPTER 3: "THE FIGHT . . . WILL GO ON."

1. Lord, *Wallaces*, pp. 190–91.
2. *WF*, Dec. 1, 1916.
3. Ibid., Dec. 29, 1916.
4. Ibid., Nov. 24, 1916.
5. Lord, *Wallaces*, p. 170.
6. *WF*, March 31, 1917.
7. Ibid., April 6, 1917.
8. Ibid., May 11, 1917.
9. Ibid., May 4, 1917.
10. Ibid., June 9, 1917.
11. A dispassionate account of the Wallaces' dispute with Hoover over hog prices can be found in HAW's *Agricultural Prices* (Des Moines: Wallace Publishing, 1920), pp. 30–35.
12. Schapsmeier, *Agrarian Years*, p. 42.
13. Lord, *Wallaces*, pp. 167–68.
14. Schapsmeier, *Agrarian Years*, p. 44.
15. *WF*, Feb. 12, 1920.
16. Lord, *Wallaces*, p. 169.

17. Ibid., p. 214.
18. HAW, *Democracy Reborn*, ed. Russell Lord (New York: Reynal & Hitchcock, 1944), p. 97.
19. HAW, *Agricultural Prices*, p. 16.
20. Ibid., p. 20.
21. CUOH, p. 99.
22. Ibid.
23. Donald L. Winters, *Henry Cantwell Wallace as Secretary of Agriculture, 1921–1924* (Urbana: Univ. of Illinois Press, 1970), p. 45.
24. Ibid., p. 58.
25. Ibid.
26. Ibid., p. 58
27. Lord, *Wallaces*, p. 216.
28. Ibid., p. 217.
29. Edward L. Schapsmeier and Frederick H. Schapsmeier, "Disharmony in the Harding Cabinet: Hoover-Wallace Controversy," *Ohio History* 75 (Summer 1966): 135.
30. Lord, *Wallaces*, p. 234.
31. *WF*, June 24, 1921.
32. HAW, Democracy Reborn, p. 117.
33. Cited in Derk Bodde, "Henry A. Wallace and the Ever-Normal Granary," *Journal of Asian Studies* 5 (Aug. 1946): 413.
34. Ibid., p. 415.
35. Lord, *Wallaces*, p. 231.
36. CUOH, p. 119.
37. HAW, *New Frontiers* (New York: Reynal & Hitchcock, 1934), p. 145.
38. Lord, *Wallaces*, p. 237.
39. HAW, *New Frontiers*, p. 145.
40. Schapsmeier, *Agrarian Years*, p. 62.
41. HAW, *New Frontiers*, p. 146.
42. Cited in Francis Russell, *The Shadow of Blooming Grove: Warren G. Harding and His Times* (New York: McGraw-Hill, 1968), p. 582.
43. H. C. Wallace to family members, Aug. 4, 1923, UI.
44. Ibid.
45. Ibid.
46. Cited in David Burner, *Herbert Hoover: A Public Life* (New York: Knopf, 1979), p. 169.
47. Schapsmeier, *Agrarian Years*, p. 75.
48. Henry C. Wallace, *Our Debt and Duty to the Farmer* (New York: Century, 1925), p. 8.
49. Ibid., p. 192.
50. H. C. Wallace to HAW, Oct. 10, 1924, family papers.
51. *Washington Star*, Oct. 25, 1924.
52. *Washington Sunday Star*, Oct. 26, 1924.
53. Lord, *Wallaces*, p. 257.
54. *WF*, Nov. 4, 1925.

CHAPTER 4: "A REVOLUTION . . . IS COMING."

1. HAW, "Corn Breeding Experience and Its Probable Eventual Effect on the Technique of Livestock Breeding," April 21, 1938, UI speech file.
2. HAW, "Corn and People," Oct. 14, 1964, UI speech file.
3. HAW, "Corn Breeding Experience."
4. Ibid.
5. James Wallace, "Henry A. Really Knew His Corn," *DMR*, Oct. 31, 1976.

6. HAW, "Corn Breeding Experience."

7. HAW, "Corn and People."

8. HAW, "Corn Breeding Experience."

9. A. Richard Crabb, *The Hybrid-Corn Makers* (New Brunswick: Rutgers Univ. Press, 1947), p. 148.

10. HAW and Earl N. Bressman, *Corn and Corn Growing* (New York: John Wiley, 1949), book jacket.

11. CUOH, p. 96.

12. "Recollections," ISU.

13. "Henry Agard Wallace: 'Editor and Plant Breeder,' " *Corn* (Corn Industries Research Foundation), Nov.–Dec. 1965, p. 3.

14. H. C. Wallace, *Our Debt and Duty*, p. 214.

15. Ibid., p. xiv.

16. Ibid., p. 231.

17. HAW, *New Frontiers*, p. 151.

18. "The Reminiscences of James D. LeCron," Columbia University Oral History, p. 24.

19. Ibid., p. 21.

20. Interview, Jean Wallace Douglas, Washington, D.C., 1989.

21. Interview, Henry B. Wallace, Colorado Springs, Colo., 1989.

22. Interview, Robert Wallace, Washington, D.C., 1989.

23. Interview, H. B. Wallace, 1989.

24. Interview, Simon Casady, Jr., Des Moines, Iowa, 1990.

25. HAW, *Statesmanship and Religion* (New York: Round Table Press, 1934), p. 116; HAW, "Religion of the Whole Man and of the Whole Society," Feb. 24, 1938, UI.

26. Ibid., p. 46.

27. Ibid., pp. 46–47.

28. HAW, "Church and School in Democratic Capitalism," Feb. 23, 1938, UI.

29. Ibid., p. 45.

30. Ibid., p. 88.

31. CUOH, pp. 48–49.

32. "The Reminiscences of Paul H. Appleby," Columbia University Oral History, p. 12.

33. Lord, *Wallaces*, p. 432.

34. See Charles Samuel Braden, *These Also Believe: A Study of Modern American Cults and Minority Religious Movements* (New York: Macmillan, 1949), pp. 221–55.

35. Ibid., p. 242.

36. Ibid. pp. 310–11.

37. HAW to Church of St. Francis, Aug. 30, 1925, UI.

38. I. S. Cooper to HAW, Oct. 16, 1926, UI.

39. Interview, H. B. Wallace.

40. HAW to L. E. Johndro, Oct. 24, 1931, UI.

41. J. W. Wallace, "Henry A. Really Knew His Corn."

42. *WF*, Aug. 30, 1926.

43. Schapsmeier, *Agrarian Years*, p. 104.

44. Ibid., p. 106.

45. Lord, *Wallaces*, p. 273.

46. Schapsmeier, *Agrarian Years*, p. 108.

47. Ibid.

CHAPTER 5: "A COMPLETE BREAK WITH ALL THAT I HAD BEEN"

1. Lord, *Wallaces*, p. 276.

2. CUOH, p. 140.

3. Ibid., p. 138.
4. Ibid., p. 152.
5. Ibid., p. 117.
6. Ibid., pp. 101–2.
7. Lord, *Wallaces*, p. 289.
8. CUOH, p. 158, Lord, *Wallaces*, p. 290.
9. CUOH, p. 160.
10. *WF*, Oct. 26, 1929.
11. Ibid , Nov. 16, 1929.
12. Ibid., Feb. 22, 1930.
13. Harold Lee, *Roswell Garst* (Ames: Iowa State Univ. Press, 1984), pp. 39–40.
14. Ibid., p. 40.
15. CUOH, p. 162.
16. Lord, *Wallaces*, p. 285.
17. HAW to Roy N. Harrop, July 21, 1930, UI.
18. HAW, *Causes of the World Wide Depression of 1930* (Des Moines: Wallace Publishing, 1930), p. 16, UI.
19. CUOH, p. 163.
20. HAW to Ellsworth Huntington, Oct. 13, 1930, UI.
21. HAW to Frank Robey, Feb. 8, 1931, UI.
22. HAW to J. M. Bixler, Jan. 8, 1931, UI.
23. HAW to J. N Hughes, May 28, 1931, UI.
24. HAW to Paul Walter, June 18, 1931, UI
25. HAW to Mark Hyde, May 28, 1931, UI.
26. HAW to J. A. Record, Jan. 7, 1931, UI.
27. Interview, H. B. Wallace, Colorado Springs, Colo.
28. HAW to Mark Hyde, July 14, 1930, UI.
29. Charles Roos to HAW, undated 1931, UI.
30. Ibid.
31. Ibid.
32. Chas. Roos to HAW, Sept. 30, 1931; Roos to HAW, Dec. 16, 1931, UI.
33. HAW to Chas. Roos, undated, 1932, UI.
34. Interview, H. B. Wallace.
35. HAW to L. E. Johndro, Jan. 5, 1932, UI.
36. HAW to W. H. Dower, returned on letter dated Oct. 14, 1931, UI.
37. HAW to L. E. Johndro, Oct. 24, 1931, UI.
38. HAW to L. E. Johndro, Jan. 19, 1932; Johndro to HAW, Feb. 4, 1932, UI.
39. HAW to L. E. Johndro, Feb. 24, 1932; Johndro to HAW, undated, UI.
40. Chas. Roos to HAW, Jan. 15, 1932; HAW to Roos, Feb. 4, 1932, UI.
41. L. E. Johndro to HAW, Sept. 19, 1932, UI.
42. CUOH, p. 5184.
43. Schapsmeier, *Agrarian Years*, pp. 135–36.
44. CUOH, pp. 165–66.
45. Ibid., p. 166.
46. Ibid.
47. Cited in Lord, *Wallaces*, p. 316.
48. CUOH, p. 148.
49. HAW to R. M. Bronson and H. R. Cloud, July 18, 1932, UI.
50. W. H. Dower to HAW, Sept. 9, 1932, UI.
51. Chas. Roos to HAW, July 14, 1932, UI.
52. HAW to B. M. Eckert, Oct. 5, 1932, UI.

53. Schapsmeier, *Agrarian Years*, p. 154.
54. CUOH, p. 177.
55. HAW to FDR, Sept. 22, 1932, UI.
56. HAW to Henry Morgenthau, Oct. 24, 1932, UI.
57. *WF*, Oct. 15, 1932.
58. HAW to Bernard Baruch, Nov. 9, 1932, UI.
59. Chas. Roos to HAW, Nov. 10, 1932, UI.
60. HAW to F. P. Finn, Dec. 14, 1932; HAW to R. E. Malloy, Nov. 11, 1932, UI.
61. "Tape recorded interview with Henry Wallace by R. G. Tugwell," June 23, 1957, FDRL.
62. Ibid.
63. CUOH, p. 182.
64. Ibid., p. 183.
65. Wallace-Tugwell interview, FDRL.
66. Ibid.
67. Ibid.
68. CUOH, pp. 188–89.
69. Raymond Moley, *27 Masters of Politics* (New York: Funk & Wagnalls, 1949), p. 80.
70. CUOH, pp. 190–91.

CHAPTER 6: "A QUARTER TURN OF THE HEART"

1. LeCron CUOH, pp. 18–19.
2. *DMR*, Feb. 27, 1933.
3. *DMR*, March 14, 1933.
4. Unpublished background paper on HAW in *DMR* files.
5. Lord, *Wallaces*, pp. 324–25.
6. Richard Lowitt, ed., *Journal of a Tamed Bureaucrat: Nils Olsen and the BAE, 1925–1935* (Ames: Iowa State Univ. Press, 1980), p. 155.
7. *New York Post*, Oct. 19, 1948.
8. George Martin, *Madam Secretary: Frances Perkins* (Boston: Houghton Mifflin, 1976), p. 8.
9. Ibid., p. 9.
10. CUOH, p. 207.
11. Ibid.
12. Milton S. Eisenhower, *The President Is Calling* (Garden City, N.Y.: Doubleday, 1974), p. 71.
13. CUOH, p. 213.
14. Rexford G. Tugwell, *Roosevelt's Revolution* (New York: Macmillan, 1977), p. 53.
15. Ibid., p. 68.
16. HAW, *New Frontiers*, p. 167.
17. Radio address, *National Farm and Home Hour*, March 10, 1933, UI.
18. *DMR*, March 11, 1933.
19. HAW, *New Frontiers*, p. 164.
20. Ibid.
21. Theodore Saloutos, *The American Farmer and the New Deal* (Ames: Iowa State Univ. Press, 1982), p. 46.
22. Cited in Arthur M. Schlesinger Jr., *The Coming of the New Deal*, (Boston: Houghton Mifflin, 1958), p. 40.
23. *DMR*, May 2, 1933.
24. Leland L. Sage, *A History of Iowa* (Ames: Iowa State Univ. Press, 1974), pp. 297–98.
25. HAW, *New Frontiers*, p. 190.
26. Ibid., p. 161.
27. CUOH, p. 210.

28. Cited in Schlesinger, *Coming of the New Deal*, p. 44.

29. Ferner Nahn, quoted on book jacket of 1st ed. of *New Frontiers*.

30. Ibid., p. 188.

31. Richard Wilson, "Wallace: A Man Who Left Little But Good," *DMR*, Nov. 24, 1965.

32. Sherwood Anderson, "No Swank," *Today*, Nov. 11, 1933.

33. Quoted on the book jacket of *New Frontiers*, 1st ed.

34. HAW, *New Frontiers*, pp. 169–70.

35. Lord, *Wallaces*, p. 353.

36. Saloutos, *American Farmer*, p. 88.

37. John Franklin Carter (the "Unofficial Observer"), *The New Dealers* (New York: Simon and Schuster, 1934), p. 148.

38. George N. Peek with Samuel Crowther, *Why Quit Our Own* (New York: Van Nostrand, 1936), p. 99.

39. Saloutos, *American Farmer*, p. 55.

40 Cited in Lord, *Wallaces*, p. 358.

41. HAW, *New Frontiers*, p. 171.

42. Ibid., pp. 174–75.

43. Ibid., p. 193.

44. Ibid., p. 178.

45. Ibid., p. 180.

46. Ibid., pp. 183–84.

47. Ibid., p. 196

48. Ibid., p. 200.

49. Peek, *Why Quit Our Own*, p. 144.

50. *DMR*, Oct. 9, 1933.

51. Lord, *Wallaces*, p. 361.

52. Tugwell, *Roosevelt's Revolution*, p. 189.

53. Saloutos, *American Farmer*, p. 96.

54. Ibid.

55. Tugwell, *Roosevelt's Revolution*, p. 193.

56. Ibid., p. 198.

57. Carter, *New Dealers*, p. 84.

58. Tugwell, *Roosevelt's Revolution*, p. 109; *DMR*, Dec. 17, 1933.

59. Tugwell, *Roosevelt's Revolution*, p. 192.

60. Ibid., p. 210.

61. Lord, *Wallaces*, p. 338.

62. Ibid.

63. Ibid., p. 337.

64. HAW, *New Frontiers*, p. 11.

65. HAW, "Lecture to World Fellowship of Faiths Conference," Sept. 11, 1933, UI.

66. HAW, "Statesmanship and Religion," Dec. 7, 1933.

67. Lord, *Wallaces*, p. 363.

CHAPTER 7: "FRAGRANCE FROM THAT OTHER WORLD"

1. Jacqueline Decter, *Nicholas Roerich: The Life and Art of a Russian Master* (Rochester, Vt.: Park Street Press, 1989), p. 121.

2. Robert C. Williams, *Russian Art and American Money, 1900–1940* (Cambridge: Harvard University Press, 1980), p. 133.

3. Ibid., p. 125.
4. F. Grant to HAW, Oct. 25, 1929, UI.
5. HAW to the Roerich Museum, July 6, 1931, UI.
6. HAW to F. Grant, Feb. 22, 1932, UI.
7. HAW to "M," Rosenman file, undated, FDRL.
8. HAW to N. Roerich, Rosenman file, March 22, 1933, FDRL.
9. CUOH, p. 5107.
10. HAW to N. Roerich, undated but probably April 1934, Rosenman file, FDRL.
11. HAW to N. Roerich, June 17, 1933, UI.
12. A key to the code words accompanies the letters in the Rosenman file at the FDRL.
13. HAW to unknown addressee, Dec. 21, 1933; HAW to unknown addressee, undated; HAW to unknown addressee, Dec. 14, 1933, Rosenman file, FDRL.
14. Helena de Roerich to FFDR, Oct. 10, 1934, FDRL.
15. HAW to FDR, Oct. 28, 1933, UI.
16. CUOH, pp. 5102–3.
17. "Reminiscences of Knowles Ryerson," special collections, Univ. of California at Davis, p. 233.
18. Ibid.
19. Ibid.
20. Ibid., p. 234.
21. Ibid., p. 236.
22. Ibid.
23. Ibid., p. 237.
24. H. MacMillian to K. Ryerson, June 1, 1934, NA.
25. H. MacMillian to K. Ryerson, June 10, 1934, NA.
26. H. MacMillian to K. Ryerson, June 24, 1934, NA.
27. H. MacMillian to Arthur Garrels, July 20, 1934; communiqué, Georges de Roerich to HAW, NA.
28. Ryerson, "Reminiscences," pp. 245–46.
29. Ibid., p. 246.
30. Ibid.
31. Ibid., p. 248.
32. HAW to N. Roerich, Sept. 20, 1934, NA.
33. "The Roerich Pact," *Bulletin of the Pan American Union* 59 (May 1935): 362.
34. Decter, *Roerich*, p. 135.
35. HAW to L. Horch, July 3, 1935, NA.
36. HAW to N. Roerich, July 3, 1935; E. Bressman to N. Roerich, July 9, 1935, NA.
37. E. Bressman to G. Roerich, July 20, 1935; G. F. Allen to N. Roerich, Aug. 21, 1935, NA.
38. R. W. Moore to HAW, Aug. 24, 1935; HAW to G. Roerich, Sept. 4, 1935, NA.
39. HAW to N. Roerich, Sept. 21, 1935, NA.
40. LeCron CUOH, p. 40.
41. HAW to W. E. Howell Jr., Sept. 24, 1935, NA.
42. HAW to H. Roerich, Sept. 24, 1935.
43. HAW to J. Grew, Oct. 24, 1935, UI.
44. HAW to G. Helvering, Oct. 1, 1935, NA.
45. HAW to H. Morgenthau Jr., Jan. 23, 1936, UI.
46. HAW to Dodd Mead & Co., undated draft, UI.
47. See, e.g., HAW to H. H. Lehman, Jan. 18, 1936, UI.
48. Ibid.
49. HAW to K. Ryerson, Oct. 11, 1935; K. Ryerson to HAW, Oct. 23, 1935, UI.
50. HAW to H. G. MacMillan, Nov. 6, 1935, and Dec. 12, 1936, UI.

CHAPTER 8: "WHOSE CONSTITUTION?"

1. Roswell Garst to Garst & Thomas Salesmen, Nov. 20, 1965, Family.
2. Interview, Raymond Baker, Johnston, Iowa.
3. Donald N. Duvick, "The Genesis and Evolution of Plant Breeding in the Hi-Bred Corn Company" (draft manuscript), p. 15, Family.
4. HAW and William L. Brown, *Corn and Its Early Fathers*, rev. ed. (Ames: Iowa State Univ. Press, 1988), p. 118.
5. Ibid.
6. W. Lippmann to HAW, May 7, 1934, UI.
7. *Washington Star*, June 16, 1934, LOC.
8. *DMR*, April 15, 1934.
9. *Collier's*, April 2, 1934; *Time*, May 15, 1934.
10. *Collier's*, April 2, 1934.
11. *DMR*, Sept. 5, 1934.
12. Cited in Lord, *Wallaces*, pp. 430–44.
13. Ibid., p. 440.
14. *Baltimore Sun*, Aug. 27, 1937; *Washington Post*, May 11, 1935.
15. Paul Ward, "Wallace the Great Hesitator," *Nation*, May 8, 1935, p. 535.
16. Carter, *New Dealers*, p. 84.
17. Tugwell, *Roosevelt's Revolution*, p. 44.
18. CUOH, p. 387.
19. Ibid., p. 386.
20. Cited in Lawrence J. Nelson, "The Art of the Possible: Another Look at the 'Purge' of the AAA Liberals in 1935," *Agricultural History* 57 (July 1979): 418.
21. Ibid.
22. Ibid., pp. 422–23.
23. Sidney Baldwin, *Poverty and Politics: The Rise and Decline of the Farm Security Administration* (Chapel Hill: Univ. of North Carolina Press, 1968), pp. 81–82.
24. CUOH, p. 375.
25. Lord, *Wallaces*, p. 405.
26. Baldwin, *Poverty and Politics*, p. 93.
27. Ibid., p. 95; CUOH, p. 379.
28. Lord, *Wallaces*, pp. 406–7.
29. Tugwell, *Roosevelt's Revolution*, p. 260; LeCron CUOH, p. 73.
30. Raymond Gram Swing, "The Purge," *Nation*, Feb. 13, 1935, p. 180.
31. CUOH, p. 380.
32. HAW, *New Frontiers*, p. 160.
33. HAW, "Confusion, Choice and Unified Action," June 20, 1935, UI.
34. *DMR*, April 28, 1935.
35. Kenneth S. Davis, *FDR: The New Deal Years, 1933–1937* (New York: Random House, 1986), p. 610.
36. Ibid., p. 611.
37. *Washington Star*, Jan. 6, 1936, LOC.
38. HAW, "Remarks on the Supreme Court Decision," Jan. 7, 1936, UI.
39. HAW, *Whose Constitution: An Inquiry into the General Welfare* (New York: Reynal & Hitchcock, 1936), pp. 87, 93.
40. *DMT*, Jan. 21, 1936.
41. Ibid.
42. HAW, "The New Farm Legislation," March 3, 1936, UI.
43. HAW, *Democracy Reborn*, p. 117.

44. Schapsmeier, *Agrarian Years*, p. 221.
45. HAW, *Whose Constitution*, p. 239.
46. Ibid., p. 106.
47. Ibid., p. 113.
48. CUOH, p. 470.
49. *Washington Post*, June 4, 1936.
50. CUOH, p. 408.
51. *National Party Platforms, 1840–1972*, 5th ed., ed. Donald Bruce Johnson and Kirk H. Porter (Urbana: Univ. of Illinois Press, 1973), p. 362.
52. Ibid.
53. *DMR*, June 24, 1936.
54. CUOH, p. 425.
55. Schapsmeier, *Agrarian Years*, p. 229.
56. CUOH, p. 426.
57. HAW to FDR, Sept. 11, 1936, UI.
58. Herb Plambeck, "The National Drought Conference in Des Moines: When FDR and Alf Landon Met," *Palimpsest* 68 (Spring 1987): 196.
59. *DMR*, Sept. 4, 1936.
60. HAW, "Forward with Roosevelt," Oct. 29, 1936, UI.
61. Schapsmeier, *Agrarian Years*, p. 232.
62. *DMR*, Oct. 8, 1936.
63. Davis, *New Deal Years*, p. 648.

CHAPTER 9: "UP IN SMOKE"

1. Cited in Lord, *Wallaces*, p. 460.
2. Ibid., pp. 460–61.
3. HAW, *New York Times Magazine*, Jan. 3, 1937.
4. HAW, "The Rural Resettlement Administration of the Department of Agriculture," Jan. 12, 1937, UI.
5. CUOH, p. 465.
6. Kenneth S. Davis, *FDR: Into the Storm, 1937–1940* (New York: Random House, 1993), p. 85.
7. Ibid., p. 74.
8. *DMR*, March 23, 1937.
9. HAW, "The Impact of Technology," April 1, 1937, UI.
10. Joseph Alsop and Turner Catledge, *The 168 Days* (Garden City, N.Y.: Doubleday, Doran, 1938), p. 122.
11. Davis, *Into the Storm*, p. 91.
12. CUOH, p. 453.
13. Davis, *Into the Storm*, p. 95.
14. HAW to FDR, July 22, 1937, noted in CUOH, pp. 469–70.
15. CUOH, p. 464.
16. Ibid.
17. Davis, *Into the Storm*, p. 139.
18. William E. Leuchtenburg, *Franklin D. Roosevelt and the New Deal* (New York: Harper Torchbooks, 1963), p. 245.
19. Ibid.
20. Quoted in CUOH, p. 480.
21. CUOH, pp. 486–89.
22. Ibid., p. 482.
23. Quoted in CUOH, p. 508.

24. HAW, "The New Farm Act," March 7, 1938, UI.
25. Ibid.
26. CUOH, p. 5166.
27. Rexford G. Tugwell, *The Democratic Roosevelt* (Garden City, N.Y.: Doubleday, 1957), p. 462.
28. Appleby CUOH, p. 171.
29. *DMR*, Jan. 9, 1938.
30. Ibid., Jan. 10, 1938.
31. Ibid., Feb. 20, 1938.
32. Ibid.
33. CUOH, p. 501.
34. Harold L. Ickes, *The Secret Diary of Harold Ickes*, vol. 2 *The Inside Struggle* (New York: Simon and Schuster, 1954), p. 394.
35. Bernard F. Donahoe, *Private Plans and Public Dangers: The Story of FDR's Third Nomination* (Notre Dame, Ind.: Univ. of Notre Dame Press, 1965), p. 44.
36. Ibid., p. 52.
37. CUOH, p. 531.
38. Ibid., p. 533; Ickes, *Inside Struggle*, p. 412.
39. CUOH, pp. 529–30.
40. Ibid., p. 529.
41. Ibid., p. 533.
42. *DMR*, May 25, 1938.
43. Ibid., June 7, 1938.
44. Davis, *Into the Storm*, p. 279.
45. HAW, "Progressive Democracy and What It Means to Vermont," Sept. 20, 1938, UI.
46. HAW, "Address at Council Bluffs," Oct. 17, 1938, UI.
47. *DMR*, Oct. 23, 1938.
48. CUOH, pp. 5191–92.
49. Interview, Jean Wallace Douglas.
50. LeCron CUOH, p. 51.
51. Ibid., pp. 58–59.
52. Ibid., p. 26.
53. Appleby CUOH, pp. 168–69.
54. Interview, Jean Wallace Douglas.
55. LeCron CUOH, p. 66.
56. Ibid., pp. 52–53.
57. Interview, William L. Brown, Johnston, Iowa.
58. Gove Hambidge, *The Prime of Life* (Garden City, N.Y.: Doubleday, Doran, 1942), pp. 191–92.
59. Ibid., pp. 191–95.

CHAPTER 10: "DEMOCRACY IS ON TRIAL TODAY."

1. *NYT*, Aug. 19, 1934.
2. HAW, "Capitalism, Religion and Democracy," Feb. 24, 1938, UI.
3. Davis, *Into the Storm*, p. 457.
4. Ibid.
5. CUOH, p. 552.
6. HAW, "Reconciliation of Conflict," Sept. 17, 1937, UI.
7. Ibid.
8. HAW, *The Price of Freedom* (1939 pamphlet), UI.
9. HAW, "An Approach to Eugenics," April 21, 1938, UI.

10. Ibid.
11. HAW, "Racial Theories and the Genetic Basis for Democracy," Feb. 12, 1939.
12. Ibid.
13. Ibid.
14. Ibid.
15. *Washington Post*, Feb. 19, 1934; *Washington Star*, Nov. 3, 1935; *DMR*, Nov. 15, 1936.
16. *DMR*, Jan. 24, 1937.
17. *Saturday Evening Post*, July 3, 1937.
18. *Look*, March 15, 1938; *Time*, Dec. 19, 1938.
19. Cited in Lord, *Wallaces*, pp. 431–42.
20. *DMR*, April 8, 1939.
21. Donahoe, *Private Plans*, p. 101.
22. Ibid., p. 88.
23. *DMR*, July 30, 1939.
24. Quoted in CUOH, p. 558.
25. Davis, *Into the Storm*, p. 461.
26. Ibid., p. 517.
27. HAW, "Farmers, Consumers and Middlemen and Their Food Supplies in Time of War," Sept. 8, 1939, UI.
28. Donahoe, *Private Plans*, p. 79.
29. James A. Farley, *Jim Farley's Story* (New York: McGraw-Hill, 1948), p. 184.
30. *DMR*, Oct. 26, 1939.
31. CUOH, p. 609.
32. Ibid.
33. *NYT*, Oct. 26, 1939.
34. Ibid., Oct. 27, 1939.
35. CUOH, p. 609.
36. HW to Ruth Wijkmam, Oct. 9, 1939.
37. M. Nelson McGeary, *Gifford Pinchot: Forester-Politician* (Princeton: Princeton Univ. Press, 1960), p. 253.
38. CUOH, p. 769.
39. CUOH, p. 886.
40. HAW, "The Strength and Quietness of Grass," June 21, 1940, UI.
41. CUOH, p. 630.
42. Ibid.
43. Ibid.
44. Quoted ibid., p. 1018.
45. Quoted ibid., p. 1102.
46. Ibid.
47. HAW, "Memorial Day," May 29, 1940, UI.
48. Davis, *Into the Storm*, p. 484.
49. CUOH, pp. 1199–1200.
50. Ibid., p. 1200.
51. Ibid., p. 1114.
52. Ibid., p. 1080.
53. Ibid., p. 1188.
54. *Farley's Story*, p. 254.
55. Ibid., pp. 254–55.
56. Ibid., p. 255.
57. CUOH, p. 1184.
58. Appleby CUOH, p. 174.

59. CUOH, p. 1214.
60. Davis, *Into the Storm*, p. 556.

CHAPTER 11: "THAT ONE MAN WAS ROOSEVELT."

1. Diary, June 28, 1940.
2. Donahoe, *Private Plans*, pp. 166–67; Frances Perkins, *The Roosevelt I Knew* (New York: Viking Press, 1946), pp. 132–33.
3. Appleby CUOH, p. 213.
4. R. Craig Sautter and Edward M. Burke, *Inside the Wigwam: Chicago Presidential Conventions, 1860–1996* (Chicago: Wild Onion Books, 1996), p 182.
5. Donahoe, *Private Plans*, p. 171.
6. Appleby CUOH, p. 219.
7. Samuel Rosenman, *Working with Roosevelt* (New York: Da Capo Press, 1952), p. 207.
8. Ibid.
9. Appleby CUOH, p. 220.
10. *Farley's Story*, p. 293.
11. Donahoe, *Private Plans*, pp. 174–75.
12. Ibid., p. 175.
13. CUOH, p. 1231.
14. *Farley's Story*, p. 302.
15. Grace Tully, *FDR, My Boss* (New York: Scribners, 1949), p. 239.
16. *Farley's Story*, p. 300.
17. Ibid.
18. *Official Report of the Proceedings of the Democratic National Convention of 1940* (Washington, D.C.: Democratic National Committee, 1940, p. 199.
19. Ibid., p. 212.
20. Ibid., p. 216; *DMR*, July 19, 1940.
21. Donahoe, *Private Plans*, p. 176.
22. *Official Report*, p. 224.
23. Martin, *Madam Secretary*, p. 434. Eleanor Roosevelt, *This I Remember* (New York: Harper, 1949), p. 218.
24. Martin, *Madam Secretary*, p. 434.
25. Rosenman, *Working*, p. 219.
26. Ibid.
27. *Official Report*, pp. 238–39.
28. Donahoe, *Private Plans*, p. 177.
29. Quoted in CUOH, pp. 1232–33.
30. *Official Report*, pp. 252–55.
31. George Allen, *Presidents Who Have Known Me* (New York: Simon and Schuster, 1950), pp. 130–31.
32. *Washington Times-Herald*, July 24, 1940, LOC.
33. *Washington Daily News*, July 20, 1940; *Washington Evening Star*, July 19, 1940, LOC.
34. *Washington Evening Star*, July 19, 1940, LOC.
35. *Washington Times-Herald*, July 24, 1940, LOC.
36. *Washington Post*, July 28, 1940.
37. Ibid., July 19, 1940.
38. Ibid.; *DMR*, July 26, 1940.
39. "Private Lives" by Edwin Cox, undated, LOC.
40. *NYT*, July 23, 1940.
41. *Washington Daily News*, July 19, 1940, LOC.
42. *Washington Times-Herald*, July 20, 1940, LOC.

43. Associated Press, July 20, 1940.
44. *Washington Post,* July 22, 1940.
45. *DMT,* July 26, 1940.
46. *Washington Post,* July 28, 1940; *Washington Daily News,* July 27, 1940, LOC.
47. Dean Albertson, *Roosevelt's Farmer: Claude R. Wickard in the New Deal* (New York: Columbia Univ. Press, 1961), p. 160.
48. Ibid.
49. HAW, *Democracy Reborn,* p. 48.
50. Dillon Myer to L. H. Bean, Aug. 23, 1940; E. N. Bressman to L. H. Bean, Aug. 16, 1940, UI.
51. M. Ezekiel to L. H. Bean, Aug. 15, 1940; G. Hambidge to L. H. Bean, Sept., 1940, UI.
52. CUOH, pp. 1110–11.
53. USDA press release, Aug. 19, 1940, LOC.
54. *NYT,* Aug. 16, 1940.
55. *DMR,* Aug. 20, 1940.

CHAPTER 12: "A FUNNY WAY TO LIVE"

1. *DMR,* April 4, 1948, published by arrangement with *Newsweek.*
2. Rosenman, *Working,* p. 248.
3. Jonathan Daniels, *White House Witness, 1942–1945* (Garden City, N.Y.: Doubleday, 1975), p. 184.
4. *DMR,* April 4, 1948.
5. Ibid.
6. Ibid.
7. Ted Morgan, *FDR: A Biography* (New York: Simon and Schuster, 1985), p. 533.
8. R. J. C. Butow, "The FDR Tapes," *American Heritage,* Feb.–March 1982, p. 21.
9. Ibid.
10. *DMR,* Aug. 29, 1940.
11. HAW, "Acceptance Address," Aug. 29, 1940, UI.
12. Ibid.
13. *DMR,* Aug. 29, 1940; *Chicago Tribune,* Aug. 29, 1940.
14. FDR to HAW, Aug. 29, 1940, UI.
15. CUOH, p. 1259.
16. Associated Press, Sept. 6, 1940.
17. *DMR,* Sept. 7, 1940.
18. *Illinois State Register,* Sept. 6, 1940.
19. *DMR,* Sept. 13, 1940; Harold L. Ickes, *The Secret Diary of Harold L. Ickes,* vol. 5, *The Lowering Clouds* (New York: Simon and Schuster, 1954), p. 324.
20. Davis, *Into the Storm,* p. 583.
21. Ibid., p. 613.
22. Steve Neal, *Dark Horse: A Biography of Wendell Willkie* (Lawrence: Univ. Press of Kansas, 1989), p. 214.
23. Rosenman, *Working,* p. 235.
24. *Time,* Sept. 21, 1940.
25. HAW, "War Prosperity," Sept. 24, 1940, UI.
26. HAW, "Judaism and Americanism," *Menorah Journal,* July–Sept. 1940, p. 127.
27. CUOH, p. 1250.
28. *DMR,* April 4, 1948.
29. Joe Martin, *My First Fifty Years in Politics* (New York: McGraw-Hill, 1960), p. 117.
30. CUOH, p. 5107.
31. Rosenman, *Working,* p. 238.
32. Ibid., p. 239.

33. Ibid., p. 242.
34. HAW, "Address at Madison Square Garden," Oct. 31, 1940, UI.
35. HAW, "Keeping out of War," Nov. 1, 1940, UI.

CHAPTER 13: "CAN THE VICE PRESIDENT BE USEFUL?"

1. May Wallace to HAW, Nov. 6, 1940; HAW to May Wallace, Nov. 12, 1940, UI.
2. CUOH, p. 1286.
3. *Christian Science Monitor*, Dec. 2, 1940.
4. Ibid.
5. CUOH, p. 1291.
6. Eric Sevareid, *Not So Wild a Dream* (Columbia: Univ. of Missouri Press, 1995), p. 146.
7. *Life*, Dec. 16, 1940.
8. Josephus Daniels, *Shirt-Sleeve Diplomat* (Chapel Hill: Univ. of North Carolina Press, 1947), p. 349.
9. Ibid.
10. Ibid.
11. LeCron CUOH, p. 142.
12. *WF*, Feb. 22, 1941.
13. Ibid.
14. CUOH, p. 1291–92.
15. Paul Mangelsdorf, "Henry Agard Wallace (1888–1965)," *Year Book of the American Philosophical Society*, 1966, p. 195.
16. Ibid.
17. Cited in *Franklin D. Roosevelt: His Life and Times: An Encyclopedic View*, ed. Otis L. Graham, Jr., and Meghan R. Wander (Boston: G. K. Hall, 1985), p. 153.
18. *DMR*, Jan. 21, 1941.
19. Ibid.
20. CUOH, p. 1400.
21. *DMR*, Jan. 22, 1941.
22. CUOH, p. 1400.
23. HAW, "Remarks to Electoral College," Jan. 22, 1941, UI.
24. HAW, "Democracy's Road Ahead in the World Crisis," Feb. 22, 1941, UI.
25. CUOH, p. 1302.
26. Ibid., p. 1302–3.
27. Ibid., p. 1305.
28. Ibid., p. 1301.
29. Ibid., p. 1297.
30. *DMR*, March 18, 1941; *NYT*, March 16, 1941.
31. *NYT*, March 16, 1941.
32. Edward L. Schapsmeier and Frederick H. Schapsmeier, *Prophet in Politics: Henry A. Wallace and the War Years, 1940–1965* (Ames: Iowa State Univ. Press, 1970), p. 8.
33. *DMR*, Aug. 1, 1941.
34. HAW, "America's Second Chance," April 8, 1941, UI.
35. *Washington Evening Star*, Aug. 2, 1941.
36. Donald M. Nelson, *Arsenal of Democracy: The Story of American War Production* (New York: Harcourt, Brace, 1946), p. 116.
37. Ibid., p. 139.
38. *Current Biography*, 1942, p. 658.
39. Ibid., p. 659.
40. *Nelson*, Arsenal, p. 156.

41. CUOH, p. 1308.
42. Ibid.
43. Ibid., p. 1310.
44. Nelson, *Arsenal*, p. 160.
45. CUOH, pp. 1379–80.
46. Ibid., p. 1379.
47. Bruce Catton, *The War Lords of Washington* (New York: Harcourt, Brace, 1948), pp. 47–48.
48. Ibid., p. 49; Edward L. Schapsmeier, *War Years*, p. 11.
49. Nelson, *Arsenal*, p. 169.
50. CUOH, p. 1374.
51. Quoted Robert Sherwood, *Roosevelt and Hopkins: An Intimate History* (New York: Harper, 1948), p. 357.
52. *New York Herald Tribune*, Sept. 17, 1941.
53. HAW to FDR, Nov. 8, 1941, FDRL.
54. HAW, "Foundations of the Peace," *Atlantic Monthly*, Dec. 1941.
55. CUOH, p. 1423.
56. Nelson, *Arsenal*, p. 184.

CHAPTER 14: "THE CENTURY OF THE COMMON MAN"

1. Richard Rhodes, *The Making of the Atomic Bomb* (New York: Simon and Shuster, 1986), p. 379.
2. Schapsmeier, *War Years*, p. 16.
3. Rhodes, *Atomic Bomb*, p. 398.
4. Diary, Aug. 8, 1945.
5. *NYT*, Oct. 12, 1941.
6. Nelson, *Arsenal*, p. 16.
7. Ibid., p. 20.
8. *DMR*, March 29, 1942.
9. CUOH, pp. 407–8.
10. Ibid., p. 408.
11. Schapsmeier, *War Years*, p. 29.
12. Quoted in CUOH, p. 1450.
13. Ibid., p. 1452.
14. Ibid.
15. Quoted ibid., p. 1458.
16. *St. Louis Post-Dispatch*, April 14, 1942.
17. Diary, May 28, 1942.
18. Ibid., May 19, 1942.
19. *DMR*, Dec. 17, 1942.
20. Ibid., March 29, 1942.
21. Ibid.
22. Ibid.
23. CUOH, p. 1467.
24. Bascom N. Timmons, *Jesse H. Jones: The Man and the Statesman* (New York: Holt, 1956), p. 339.
25. Ibid., pp. 341–42.
26. Schapsmeier, *War Years*, p. 60.
27. HAW, "The Price of Free World Victory," May 8, 1942, UI.
28. *Life*, Feb. 17, 1941.
29. HAW, "Price of Free World Victory."
30. Addison Parker to HAW, May 9, 1942, UI; D. R. Murphy to HAW, May 11, 1942, UI; CUOH, p. 1549.

31. CUOH, p. 1550.
32. Ibid., p. 1553.
33. HAW to H. R. Luce, May 16, 1942, UI; CUOH, p. 1551.
34. Scott Hart, *Washington at War, 1941–1945* (Englewood Cliffs, N.J.: Prentice-Hall, 1970), pp. 78–79.
35. Juan Ramón Jiménez, "Henry A. Wallace, El Major," published in Spanish in *Cuadros Americanos* in 1944; translated excerpts were published in *DMR*, May 30, 1965.
36. Jo Davidson, *Between Sittings* (New York: Dial Press, 1951), p. 336.
37. Ibid., p. 337.

CHAPTER 15: "GEORGE"

1. *DMR*, April 11, 1941.
2. *NYT*, June 5, 1956.
3. Timmons, *Jones*, p. 312.
4. Lord, *Wallaces*, p. 497.
5. Ibid., p. 498.
6. Torbjorn Sirevag, *The Eclipse of the New Deal and the Fall of Vice President Wallace* (New York: Garland, 1985), p. 120; Jesse H. Jones with Edward Angly, *Fifty Billion Dollars: My Thirteen Years with the RFC, 1932–1945* (New York: Macmillan, 1951), p. 422.
7. Ibid., p. 45.
8. CUOH, p. 1360.
9. Schapsmeier, *War Years*, p. 45.
10. Timmons, *Jones*, p. 323.
11. Ibid.
12. *NYT*, July 12, 1942.
13. Ibid.
14. CUOH, p. 1447.
15. Ibid., pp. 1443–44.
16. Diary, May 26, 1942.
17. Schapsmeier, *War Years*, p. 59.
18. Diary, Nov. 26, 1942.
19. Ibid.
20. I. F. Stone, *The War Years, 1939–1945* (Boston: Little, Brown, 1988), p. 138.
21. Ibid., pp. 138–41.
22. CUOH, p. 2542.
23. HAW, "Why Did God Make America?" June 11, 1942, UI.
24. Schapsmeier, *War Years*, p. 55.
25. Ibid., p. 54.
26. Diary, June 15, 1942.
27. HAW, "A Tribute to Russia," Nov. 8, 1942, UI.
28. Ibid.
29. Diary, Dec. 11, 1942.
30. Ibid., Dec. 19, 1942.
31. CUOH, p. 1842.
32. Ibid., pp. 2101–5.
33. Diary, Dec. 28, 1942.
34. HAW, "World Organization," Dec. 28, 1942, UI.
35. *Current Biography*, 1942, p. 659.
36. Ibid.
37. Ibid.
38. Sirevag, *Eclipse*, p. 125.

39. Ibid.
40. Ibid., p. 126.
41. HAW, "The New Isolationism," March 8, 1943, UI.
42. HAW, "Three Philosophies," March 8, 1943, UI.
43. Ibid.
44. *New York Sun*, March 11, 1943; *Washington Times-Herald*, March 9, 1943, LOC.
45. *NYT*, March 19, 1943.
46. HAW, *Democracy Reborn*, p. 227.
47. "Henry A. Wallace in Chile," source and date unknown, LOC.
48. Ibid.
49. HAW, *Democracy Reborn*, p. 228.
50. C. G. Bowers to Cordell Hull, March 29, 1943, LOC.
51. Cited in *DMR* report on the FBI's Wallace file, Sept. 4, 1983.
52. Lord, *Wallaces*, p. 505.
53. *Baltimore Sun*, April 26.
54. Diary, May 22, 1943.
55. Ibid.
56. CUOH, p. 2480.
57. Lord, *Wallaces*, p. 510.
58. Schapsmeier, *War Years*, pp. 62–63.
59. Sirevag, *Eclipse*, p. 542; Schapsmeier, *War Years*, p. 63.
60. Schapsmeier, *War Years*, p. 63.
61. HAW, "George," June 6, 1943, UI.

CHAPTER 16: "THOUGH HE SLAY ME"

1. Schapsmeier, *War Years*, p. 64.
2. "Statement by Vice President Wallace, Chairman, Board of Economic Warfare," June 29, 1943, UI.
3. Ibid.
4. Stone, *War Years*, p. 169.
5. "Statement by Vice President Wallace," UI.
6. "Statement of Jesse Jones, Secretary of Commerce, in Reply to Charges Made by Vice President Wallace," June 29, 1943, UI.
7. Sherwood, *Roosevelt and Hopkins*, p. 740.
8. CUOH, p. 2550.
9. Ibid., p. 2551.
10. James F. Byrnes, *All in One Lifetime* (New York: Harper, 1958), p. 192.
11. CUOH, p. 2553
12. Ibid.
13. Ibid., p. 2554.
14. Diary, July 1, 1943.
15. William D. Hassett, *Off the Record with F.D.R., 1942–1945* (New Brunswick: Rutgers Univ. Press, 1958), p. 183.
16. Stone, *War Years*, p. 167.
17. Schapsmeier, *War Years*, pp. 67–70.
18. Diary, July 6, 1943.
19. John Morton Blum, ed., *The Price of Vision: The Diary of Henry A. Wallace, 1942–1946* (Boston: Houghton Mifflin, 1973), p. 223.
20. Sirevag, *Eclipse*, p. 129.
21. *Washington Times-Herald*, July 16, 1943, LOC.

22. Schapsmeier, *War Years*, p. 70.
23. Sirevag, *Eclipse*, p. 543.
24. Jones, *Fifty Billion Dollars*, pp. 503–6.
25. CUOH, p. 2583.
26. Stone, *War Years*, p. 172.
27. *DMR*, July 16, 1943.
28. Quoted in CUOH, p. 2593.
29. HAW, "Our Choice," July 23, 1943, UI.
30. Ibid.
31. CUOH, p. 2679.
32. Ibid., p. 2594.
33. Ibid., pp. 2613, 2674.
34. W. A. White to HAW, Aug. 10, 1943; HAW to W. A. White, Aug. 19, 1943, UI.
35. CUOH, p. 2747.
36. Ibid., p. 2698.
37. Diary, July 20, 1943.
38. CUOH, p. 2678.
39. Ibid., p. 2836.
40. Ibid., p. 2709.
41. HAW, "What We Fight For," Sept. 11, 1943, UI.
42. HAW, "Transportation," Oct. 20, 1943, UI.
43. HAW, "We Must Save Free Enterprise," *Saturday Evening Post*, Oct. 23, 1943.
44. Ibid.
45. Editorial, *Christian Century*, Oct. 1943, quoted in CUOH, p. 2719.
46. *Washington Evening Star*, Oct. 26, 1943.
47. Diary, Oct. 17, 1943; CUOH, p. 2835.
48. CUOH, p. 2785.
49. *Washington Evening Star*, Nov. 21, 1943, LOC.
50. Morgan, *FDR*, p. 691.
51. James MacGregor Burns, *Roosevelt: The Soldier of Freedom, 1940–1945* (New York: Harcourt Brace Jovanovich, 1970), p. 409.
52. Diary, Dec. 17, 1943.
53. Quoted in CUOH, pp. 3011–12.
54. Quoted ibid., p. 3007.
55. Quoted ibid., p. 3012.
56. HAW, "Jackson Day," Jan. 22, 1944, UI.
57. CUOH, p. 3040.
58. *Washington Post*, Jan. 23, 1944.
59. HAW, "What America Can Have," Feb. 7, 1944, UI.
60. HAW, "America Can Get It," Feb. 9, 1944, UI.
61. HAW, "Men and Dollars," Feb. 12, 1944, UI.
62. HAW, "Address of Vice President Henry A. Wallace at the Dinner of the American Palestine Committee," March 9, 1944, UI.
63. *NYT*, April 9, 1944.
64. Allen Drury, *A Senate Journal, 1943–1945* (New York: McGraw-Hill, 1963), p. 137.

CHAPTER 17: "THE DREAMER"

1. Diary, March 10, 1944.
2. CUOH, p. 3200.

3. Ibid., p. 2915.

4. Edward B. MacMahon and Leonard Curry, *Medical Cover-ups in the White House* (Washington, D.C.: Farragut, 1987), p. 95.

5. Ibid., p. 97.

6. Diary, April 7, 1944.

7. Ibid.

8. *Atlanta Constitution*, April 2, 1943; *Grand Rapids Herald*, Jan. 4, 1943, LOC.

9. Walter Lippman, *Public Persons* (New York: Liveright, 1976), p. 154.

10. *Atlanta Constitution*, April 2, 1943.

11. J. T. Salter, ed., *Public Men in and out of Office* (Chapel Hill: Univ. of North Carolina Press, 1946), pp. 101, 104.

12. CUOH, p. 5184.

13. John Boyle O'Reilly, "The Dreamer," quoted in letter from Addison Parker to HAW, March 16, 1944, UI.

14. Addison Parker to HAW, March 16, 1944, UI.

15. Ibid.

16. HAW, "Remarks on Asia," April 17, 1944, UI.

17. Ibid.

18. CUOH, p. 3356.

19. HAW with Andrew Steiger, *Soviet Asia Mission* (New York: Reynal & Hitchcock, 1945), p. 21.

20. John N. Hazard, *Recollections of a Pioneering Sovietologist* (New York: Oceana Publications, 1984), p. 70.

21. Diary, June 17, 1944.

22. "Transcript of remarks by Ambassador Harriman to reporters," June 18, 1944, FDRL.

23. Barbara Tuchman, *Stilwell and the American Experience in China*, 1911–45, (New York: Macmillan, 1970), p. 320.

24. Diary, June 22, 1944.

25. CUOH, p. 3359.

26. Diary, June 24, 1944.

27. *DMR*, June 21, 1944.

28. John Paton Davies Jr., *Dragon by the Tail: American, British, Japanese, and Russian Encounters with China and One Another* (New York: Norton, 1972), pp. 305–8; Joseph W. Alsop with Adam Platt, *I've Seen the Best of It: Memoirs* (New York: Norton, 1992), p. 298; Robert P. Newman, *Owen Lattimore and the "Loss" of China* (Berkeley: Univ. of California Press, 1992) p. 113.

29. HAW, *Soviet Asia Mission*, p. 22.

30. Schapsmeier, *War Years*, pp. 95–96.

31. Davies, *Dragon*, p. 309.

32. David Caute, *The Great Fear: The Anti-Communist Purge under Truman and Eisenhower* (New York: Simon and Schuster, 1978), p. 312.

33. HAW to Harry S. Truman, Sept. 19, 1951.

34. Ibid.

35. HAW, *Soviet Asia Mission*, p. 33.

36. HAW, "Where I Was Wrong," *This Week Magazine*, Sept. 7, 1952.

37. Quoted in HAW, *Soviet Asia Mission*, p. 194.

38. Allen, Presidents, p. 118.

39. Ibid., p. 122.

40. CUOH, p. 1443.

41. Ibid., pp. 430–31.

42. Ed Pauley, "Memorandum to Jonathan Daniels," undated, p. 2, FDRL.

43. Ibid., p. 3.

44. John T. Flynn, *You're the Boss* (Westport: Greenwood Press, 1947), p. 195; *FDR's Quiet Confidant: The Autobiography of Frank C. Walker*, ed. Robert H. Ferrell (Niwot, Univ. Press of Colorado, 1997), p. 147.

45. Allen, *Presidents*, p. 119.

46. Drury, *Journal*, p. 214.

47. Morgan, *FDR*, p. 726.

48. Anthony Cave Brown, *"C": The Secret Life of Sir Stewart Graham Menzies, Spymaster to Winston Churchill* (New York: Macmillan, 1987), p. 483.

49. Ibid., p. 484.

50. Ibid., p. 483.

51. Ibid., p. 484

52. Flynn, *Boss*, p. 197.

53. James Roosevelt and Sidney Shalett, *Affectionately, F.D.R.: A Son's Story of a Lonely Man* (New York: Harcourt, Brace 1959), p. 351.

CHAPTER 18: "THE SAME OLD TEAM"

1. CUOH, p. 3363.

2. Ibid.

3. Harold L. Ickes, Diaries, July 9, 1944, LOC.

4. Ibid.

5. CUOH, pp. 3364–65.

6. Jim Bishop, *FDR's Last Year, April 1944–April 1945* (New York: Morrow, 1974), pp. 96–97.

7. CUOH, p. 3366.

8. Ibid., pp. 3366–67.

9. Pauley, "Memorandum," p. 7.

10. Thomas F. Eagleton and Diane L. Duffin, "Bob Hannegan and Harry Truman's Vice Presidential Nomination," *Missouri Historical Review* 90 (April 1996): 272.

11. Walker, *Quiet Confidant*, p. 154.

12. Ibid.

13. CUOH, p. 3368.

14. Ibid., pp. 3368–69; Norman M. Littell, *My Roosevelt Years*, ed. Jonathan Dembo. (Seattle: Univ. of Washington Press), p. 256.

15. Drury, *Journal*, p. 218.

16. CUOH, pp. 3370–73.

17. Drury, *Journal*, p. 218.

18. Quoted in CUOH, p. 3374.

19. Drury, *Journal*, p. 219.

20. CUOH, p. 3409.

21. Ibid., p. 3411.

22. Eagleton and Duffin, "Hannegan," p. 276.

23. Walker, *Quiet Confidant*, p. 162.

24. Littell, *Roosevelt Years*, p. 257.

25. David McCullough, *Truman* (New York: Simon and Schuster, 1992), p. 310.

26. *DMR*, July 18, 1944.

27. Walker, *Quiet Confidant*, p. 170.

28. CUOH, p. 3404.

29. Cabell Phillips, *The Truman Presidency: The History of a Triumphant Succession* (New York: Macmillan, 1966), p. 45.

30. CUOH, p. 3405.

31. Phillips, *Truman Presidency*, p. 46.

32. CUOH, p. 3334; *DMR*, July 19, 1944.
33. Littell, *Roosevelt Years*, p. 255.
34. *DMR*, July 19, 1944.
35. Jake More to HAW, July 18, 1944, UI.
36. *DMR*, July 20, 1944.
37. Littell, *Roosevelt Years*, pp. 265–66.
38. McCullough, *Truman*, p. 314.
39. HAW, "Address . . . Seconding the Nomination of President Roosevelt," July 20, 1944, UI.
40. CUOH, p. 3432.
41. Quoted in CUOH, p. 3430.
42. George Norris to HAW, July 22, 1944, UI.
43. Bishop, *FDR's Last Year*, p. 108.
44. James McGregor Burns, *Roosevelt: The Soldier of Freedom*, 1940–1945 (New York: Harcourt Brace Jovanovich, 1970), p. 507.
45. *DMR*, July 21, 1944.
46. Ibid.; McCullough, *Truman*, p. 316.
47. Claude D. Pepper with Hays Gorey, *Pepper: Eyewitness to a Century* (New York: Harcourt Brace Jovanovich, 1987), p. 135.
48. Drew Pearson quoted in CUOH, p. 3434.
49. Sautter and Burke, *Wigwam*, p. 202.
50. C. B. Baldwin, "Report on the Democratic National Convention, 1944," Feb. 27, 1951, quoted in CUOH, pp. 3383–88.
51. Littell, *Roosevelt Years*, p. 279; *DMR*, July 22, 1944.
52. CUOH, p. 3449.
53. Ibid., p. 3387.
54. Littell, *Roosevelt Years*, pp. 281–82.
55. Eagleton and Duffin, "Hannegan," p. 283.
56. Littell, *Roosevelt Years*, p. 283.
57. Ibid., p. 284.

CHAPTER 19: "POETIC JUSTICE"

1. CUOH, p. 3376.
2. Ibid., p. 3390.
3. Ibid., p. 3415.
4. Ibid., p. 3390.
5. *DMR*, July 23, 1944.
6. CUOH, pp. 3424, 3420.
7. Ibid., p. 3420.
8. Ibid., p. 3417.
9. Quoted ibid., p. 3429.
10. H. L. Ickes to HAW, July 24, 1944, UI, quoted in CUOH, p. 3399.
11. Quoted in CUOH, p. 3432.
12. Eleanor Roosevelt, *My Day* (New York: Pharos Books, 1989), p. 217.
13. CUOH, p. 3473.
14. Ibid., p. 3470.
15. *Washington Post*, Aug. 13, 1944.
16. Diary, Aug. 3, 1944.
17. CUOH, p. 3426.
18. Ibid., p. 3443.
19. Ibid., p. 3458; quoted in CUOH, p. 3469.

20. H. L. Ickes to HAW, July 24, 1944, UI.
21. Diary, Aug. 29, 1944.
22. *DMR,* Oct. 18, 1944.
23. HAW, "The New Liberalism," Sept. 21, 1944, UI.
24. HAW, "New York Speech," Oct. 31, 1944, UI.
25. HAW, "Broadcast . . . in Harlem," Oct. 1, 1944, UI.
26. Quoted in CUOH, p. 3508.
27. Ibid.
28. Quoted ibid., p. 3512.
29. Quoted ibid., p. 3514.
30. Diary, Nov. 10, 1944.
31. Quoted in CUOH, p. 3579.
32. Diary, Dec. 20, 1944.
33. Ibid.
34. Ibid.
35. Diary, Jan. 13, 1945.
36. Ibid., Jan. 19, 1945.
37. Ibid.
38. *NYT,* Jan. 21, 1945.
39. Diary, Jan. 20, 1945.
40. Quoted in Timmons, *Jones,* p. 354.
41. Ibid., p. 357.
42. Ibid., p. 358.
43. Drury, *Journal,* p. 345.
44. Quoted in Timmons, *Jones,* p. 360.
45. Quoted in Lord, *Wallaces,* p. 546.
46. Drury, *Journal,* p. 348.
47. *NYT,* Jan. 25, 1945.
48. Quoted in Lord, *Wallaces,* p. 548.
49. Drury, *Journal,* p. 349.
50. Lord, *Wallaces,* p. 549.
51. Drury, *Journal,* p. 549.
52. Ibid., p. 354.
53. HAW, "Statement . . . before the Senate Committee on Commerce," Jan. 25, 1945, UI.
54. CUOH, p. 3643.
55. Drury, *Journal,* pp. 349–50.
56. *DMR,* Feb. 4, 1945.
57. HAW, *Sixty Million Jobs* (New York: Reynal & Hitchcock and Simon and Schuster, 1945), p. 4.
58. Bishop, *FDR's Last Year,* p. 473.
59. CUOH, p. 3643.

CHAPTER 20: "THIS MUST NOT BE."

1. Drury, *Journal,* p. 389.
2. H. H. Humphrey to HAW, April 12, 1945, UI.
3. Donald R. McCoy, *The Presidency of Harry S. Truman* (Lawrence: Univ. Press of Kansas, 1984), p. 25.
4. CUOH, p. 3692.
5. Diary, April 27, 1945.
6. Ibid.
7. Ibid.

8. CUOH, p. 3704.
9. HAW to Vincent Swan, April 19, 1945, UI.
10. McCoy, *Presidency*, p. 29.
11. Quoted in CUOH, p. 3708.
12. Ibid., p. 3713.
13. Ibid., p. 3715.
14. Diary, May 3, 1945.
15. Quoted in CUOH, p. 3741.
16. Diary, May 6, 1945.
17. Ibid., May 4, 1945.
18. Ibid., May 15, 1945.
19. Ibid., May 18, 1945.
20. Ibid., May 29, 1940.
21. HAW, "In Memoriam of Franklin D. Roosevelt," June 4, 1945, UI.
22. Diary, May 29, 1945.
23. Lord, *Wallaces*, p. 556.
24. Schapsmeier, *War Years*, p. 134.
25. HAW, *Sixty Million Jobs*, p. 91.
26. Quoted in James Waterman Wise, *Meet Henry Wallace: An Illustrated Biography* (Boni and Gaer, 1948), pp. 50–51.
27. Schapsmeier, *War Years*, p. 130.
28. CUOH, p. 3978.
29. Ibid., p. 3977.
30. HAW, "Remarks before the National Citizens Political Action Committee," Sept. 13, 1945, UI.
31. Diary, Aug. 10, 1945.
32. Ibid., Aug. 17, 1945.
33. Ibid., Sept. 5, 1945.
34. Quoted in Richard Walton, *Henry Wallace, Harry Truman and the Cold War* (New York: Viking, 1976), pp. 53–54.
35. Diary, Sept. 21, 1945; HAW, "Observations by HAW on Cabinet Meeting of Friday, Sept. 21, 1945," quoted in CUOH, pp. 4100–103.
36. *NYT*, Sept. 22, 1945.
37. CUOH, p. 4105.
38. Ibid., pp. 4105–8.

CHAPTER 21: "ONE WORLD OR NO WORLD"

1. Quoted in CUOH, pp. 4140–44.
2. Ibid.
3. Diary, Oct. 15, 1945.
4. Ibid., Dec. 11, Oct. 27, 1945.
5. Quoted ibid., Nov. 9, 1945.
6. CUOH, pp. 4174–75.
7. Statement by HAW before the Special Committee on Atomic Energy, Jan. 31, 1946, HSTL.
8. CUOH, p. 4176.
9. Ibid., p. 4254.
10. Diary, Nov. 16, 1945.
11. Ibid., Dec. 4, 1945.
12. CUOH, p. 4338.
13. Diary, Dec. 14, 1945.
14. Ibid.

15. Ibid., Nov. 28, 1945.
16. CUOH, p. 4057.
17. McCoy, *Presidency*, p. 77.
18. Diary, Jan. 2, 1946.
19. T. H. Watkins, *Righteous Pilgrim: The Life and Times of Harold L. Ickes, 1874-1952* (New York: Henry Holt, 1990), p. 831.
20. Ibid., p. 832.
21. CUOH, p. 4513.
22. Diary, Feb. 15, 1946.
23. Quoted in Robert J Donovan, *Crisis and Conflict: The Presidency of Harry S Truman, 1945–1948* (New York: Norton, 1977), p. 188.
24. McCoy, *Presidency*, p. 80.
25. Donovan, *Crisis*, p. 191.
26. Diary, March 5, 1946.
27. Ibid.
28. HAW, "An Address . . . at Dinner in Honor of W. Averell Harriman," March 19, 1946, UI.
29. Diary, March 15, 1946.
30. Quoted in CUOH, pp. 4668–70.
31. *Life*, May 20, 1946; *Washington Times-Herald*, May 16, 1946.
32. Curtis D. MacDougall, *Gideon's Army*, 3 vols. (New York: Marzani & Munsell, 1965), 1:59.
33. HAW to HST, July 23, 1946, UI.
34. CUOH, p. 4941.

CHAPTER 22: "THE WAY TO PEACE"

1. Diary, Sept. 10, 1946.
2. Ibid.
3. CUOH, p. 4953.
4. Walton, Cold War, p. 99.
5. Ibid.
6. Both John Morton Blum, in *Price of Vision*, pp. 661–69, and Richard J. Walton, in *Cold War*, pp. 100–108, offer extensive accounts of the speech and its various deletions and additions, although, as Walton states, "there is no entirely satisfactory text" of the speech as it was actually delivered.
7. HAW, "The Way to Peace," Sept. 12, 1946, UI.
8. Ibid.
9. Ibid.
10. *NYT*, Sept. 13, 1946.
11. *Newsweek*, Sept. 23, 1946.
12. Walton, *Cold War*, p. 110.
13. CUOH, p. 4984.
14. Diary, Sept. 16, 1946.
15. *NYT*, Sept. 17, 1946.
16. Walton, *Cold War*, p. 112.
17. Diary, Sept. 16, 1946.
18. Ibid.
19. Ibid., Sept. 18, 1946.
20. Ibid.
21. Ibid.
22. Ibid.
23. Ibid.

24. Quoted in Donovan, *Crisis*, p. 227.

25. Phillips, *Truman Presidency*, p. 153; UCOH, p. 5028.

26. CUOH, p. 5028; Donovan, *Crisis*, p. 228.

27. HAW to HST, Sept. 20, 1946.

28. Quoted in CUOH, p. 5026.

29. Ibid., p. 5033.

30. Ibid., p. 4985.

31. Ibid., pp. 4985–86.

32. Helen Keller to HAW, Oct. 11, 1946; Albert Einstein to HAW, Sept. 18, 1946, UI.

33. D. R. Murphy to HAW, Sept. 18, 1946; Thomas Mann to HAW, Sept. 21, 1946, UI.

34. HAW to Max Lerner, Sept. 28, 1946, UI.

35. A. M. Blaine to HAW, Sept. 22, 1946, UI.

36. Quoted in Donovan, *Crisis*, p. 229; Frank McKenna cartoon, source and date not given, UI; Walton, *Cold War*, p. 119.

37. Quoted in Phillips, *Truman Presidency*, p. 154.

38. Donovan, *Crisis*, p. 228.

39. Ibid.

40. Ibid., p. 231.

41. Ibid., p. 234.

42. Caute, *Great Fear*, p. 27.

43. MacDougall, *Gideon's Army*, 1:101.

44. Interview, Bethesda, Md.

45. Michael Straight, *After Long Silence* (New York: Norton, 1983), p. 204.

46. Ibid.

47. *TNR*, Oct. 21, 1946.

48. HAW to A. M. Blaine, Nov. 29, 1946, UI

49. TNR, Dec. 16, 1946.

50. HAW, "Unity for Progress," Dec. 29, 1946, UI.

51. MacDougall, *Gideon's Army*, 1:119.

52. HAW, "Unity for Prognosis."

53. MacDougall, *Gideon's Army*, 1:121.

54. Walton, *Cold War*, p. 135.

55. HAW to G. C. Marshall, Jan. 13, 1946, UI.

56. Walton, *Cold War*, p. 144.

57. HAW, "Text of Address . . . Over NBC," March 13, 1947, UI.

58. Ibid.

59. Ibid.

60. HAW, "Unity for Progress."

CHAPTER 23: "HAS AMERICA REALLY GONE CRAZY?"

1. HAW, "Back to the United Nations," March 31, 1947, UI.

2. MacDougall, *Gideon's Army*, 1:133.

3. Ibid., p. 132.

4. Ibid., p. 134.

5. *New Statesman and Nation*, April 12, 1947.

6. HAW, " . . . Speech Delivered at Central Hall, Westminster," April 11, 1947, UI.

7. MacDougall, *Gideon's Army*, 1:136.

8. Ibid., p. 135.

9. Ibid.

10. *NYT*, April 13, 1947.

11. MacDougall, *Gideon's Army*, 1:136.
12. Ibid.
13. *Washington Post*, April 15, 1947; Schapsmeier, *War Years*, p. 173.
14. MacDougall, *Gideon's Army*, 1:138.
15. Ibid.
16. Ibid., p. 139.
17. Walton, *Cold War*, p. 153.
18. *NYT*, April 22, 1947.
19. MacDougall, *Gideon's Army*, 1:142.
20. *DMR*, April 28, 1947.
21. Quoted in Straight, *Silence*, p. 210.
22. MacDougall, *Gideon's Army*, 1:137; *Saturday Evening Post*, May 1, 1947, p. 160.
23. Michael Straight to Dorothy Elmhirst, March 10, 1947. Excerpts of Straight's letters to his mother were provided by him to the authors.
24. HAW, "Address . . . at Chicago," May 14, 1947, UI.
25. Quoted in Walton, *Cold War*, p. 156; *Chicago Daily News*, May 28, 1947.
26. MacDougall, *Gideon's Army*, 1:155.
27. Ibid., p. 156.
28. HAW, Text of Los Angeles speech, May 19, 1947, UI.
29. Gael Sullivan to Clark Clifford, June 6, 1947, HSTL.
30. Dept. of State, internal memorandum, June 6, 1947, HSTL.
31. MacDougall, *Gideon's Army*, 1:167.
32. Walter Goodman, *The Committee* (New York: Farrar, Straus and Giroux, 1964), p. 200.
33. Walton, *Cold War*, pp. 158–59.
34. MacDougall, *Gideon's Army*, 1:168.
35. HAW, "Speech . . . at the Water Gate," June 16, 1947, UI.
36. Michael Straight to Dorothy Elmhirst, June 1, 1947.
37. Ibid.
38. Straight, *Silence*, p. 215.
39. Ibid.
40. Theodore H. White, *In Search of History* (New York: Harper & Row, 1978), pp. 256–57.
41. Bruce Bliven, *Five Million Words Later: An Autobiography* (New York: John Day, 1970), pp. 268–69.
42. Straight, *Silence*, p. 205.
43. Ibid., p. 204.
44. MacDougall, *Gideon's Army*, 1:152.
45. *Boston Post*, July 22, 1947, LOC.
46. CUOH, p. 5079.
47. Phillips, *Presidency*, p. 183.
48. MacDougall, *Gideon's Army*, 1:170.
49. Ibid.
50. *TNR*, July 14, 1947.
51. MacDougall, *Gideon's Army*, 1:185.
52. Quoted in Schapsmeier, *War Years*, p. 176.
53. Ibid., p. 174.
54. MacDougall, *Gideon's Army*, 1:199.
55. Michael Straight to Dorothy Elmhirst, Aug. 4 and Sept. 20, 1947.
56. Straight, *Silence*, p. 217.
57. *Chicago Sun*, Oct. 30, 1947, LOC.
58. MacDougal, *Gideon's Army*, pp. 211–12.
59. Ibid., p. 212.

60. Ibid.
61. *TNR*, Dec. 22, 1947.

CHAPTER 24: "GIDEON'S ARMY"

1. HAW, "Announcement Address," Dec. 29, 1947, UI.
2. MacDougall, *Gideon's Army*, 3:628.
3. Ibid., 1:231.
4. Ibid., p. 243.
5. Ibid.
6. Ibid., pp. 248–49.
7. Ibid., p. 249.
8. Ibid., p. 235.
9. *Washington Star*, Jan. 16, 1948, LOC.
10. Karl M. Schmidt, *Henry A. Wallace: Quixotic Crusade 1948* (Syracuse: Syracuse Univ. Press, 1960), p. 156.
11. *PM*, Dec. 30, 1947, NA.
12. MacDougall, *Gideon's Army*, 2:337.
13. *New York Herald Tribune*, Feb. 19, 1948; MacDougall, *Gideon's Army*, 2:325.
14. F. Ross Peterson, *Prophet without Honor: Glen H. Taylor and the Fight for American Liberalism* (Lexington: Univ. of Kentucky Press, 1974), p. 34.
15. *PM*, Feb. 2, 1948, NA; HAW, "Address," April 19, 1948, UI.
16. *Milwaukee Sentinal*, Dec. 31, 1947, NA; MacDougall, *Gideon's Army*, 1:304.
17. *PM*, Feb. 2, 1948, NA.
18. MacDougall, *Gideon's Army*, 1:305.
19. Walton, *Cold War*, p. 285.
20. Ibid., p. 258.
21. MacDougall, *Gideon's Army*, 1:249–50; *Washington Post*, May 2, 1948.
22. Walton, *Cold War*, p. 305.
23. Ibid., p. 298.
24. Ibid., p. 311.
25. Allen Yarnell, *Democrats and Progressives: The 1948 Presidential Election as a Test of Postwar Liberalism* (Berkeley: Univ. of California Press, 1974), pp. 49–50.
26. Papers of Clark M. Clifford, HSTL.
27. Yarnell, *Progressives*, pp. 57–58.
28. Ibid., p. 59.
29. MacDougall, *Gideon's Army*, 2:368.
30. Ibid., p. 395.
31. Ibid., p. 400.
32. Ibid., p. 396.
33. Ibid., p. 392.
34. *Pittsburgh Press*, April 13, 1948, NA.
35. HAW, "Address," April 19, 1948, UI.
36. MacDougall, *Gideon's Army*, 2:407.
37. Glen H. Taylor, *The Way It Was with Me* (New York: Lyle Stuart, 1979), pp. 341–56; MacDougall, *Gideon's Army*, 2:391.

CHAPTER 25: "TO MAKE THE DREAM COME TRUE"

1. Frances Perkins to HAW, April 16, 1948, UI.
2. *DMR*, Feb. 25, 1948.

3. HAW, "Prepared Statement on the Mundt-Nixon Bill," May 29, 1948, UI.

4. Walton, *Cold War*, p. 202.

5. *NYT*, March 16, 1948.

6. Ibid., March 19, 1948.

7. Notes on Soviet archival materials relating to Wallace were made available to the authors by Russian scholars. They wish not to be identified.

8. See CUOH, pp. 5056–57, for Wallace's account of the "open letter."

9. Ibid., p. 5057.

10. Walton, *Cold War*, p. 216.

11. Ibid.

12. HAW, "Address," May 11, 1948, UI.

13. Ibid.

14. *New York Post*, May 13, 1948, NA.

15. MacDougall, *Gideon's Army*, 2:355.

16. Ibid., p. 356.

17. Ibid.

18. *Saturday Evening Post*, Sept. 18, 1948, p. 23.

19. CUOH, pp. 5137–38.

20. Ibid., p. 5118.

21. MacDougall, *Gideon's Army*, 2:463.

22. Ibid.

23. Ibid., p. 464.

24. Ibid., p. 475.

25. Robert H. Ferrell, ed., *Off the Record: The Private Papers of Harry S. Truman* (New York: Harper & Row, 1980), pp. 141–42.

26. *DMR*, July 16, 1948.

27. MacDougall, *Gideon's Army*, 2:542.

28. HAW, "Statement on Smith Act Indictments," July 20, 1948, UI.

29. George Seldes, *Facts and Fascism* (New York: Ballentine Books, 1943), p. 244.

30. *Washington Times Herald*, March 9, 1948.

31. MacDougall, *Gideon's Army*, 2:496–98.

32. Ibid., p. 499.

33. *Chicago Daily News*, July 27, 1948, NA.

34. *Washington Post*, July 26, 1948; MacDougall, *Gideon's Army*, 2:488.

35. C. P. Howard, "Keynote Address," July 23, 1948, Progressive Party papers, UI.

36. F. W. Stover, "Address Nominating Henry A. Wallace for President," July 24, 1948, Progressive Party papers, UI.

37. Associated Press, July 25, 1948, NA.

38. Paul Robeson, "Address," July 24, 1948, Progressive Party papers, UI.

39. Taylor, *Way It Was*, p. 255; G. H. Taylor, "Address," July 24, 1948, Progressive Party papers, UI.

40. *NYT*, July 26, 1948.

41. HAW, "Address," July 24, 1948, UI.

CHAPTER 26: "AM I IN AMERICA?"

1. Goodman, *Committee*, p. 249; Phillips, *Presidency*, p. 228.

2. HAW, "Address on NBC," Aug. 12, 1948.

3. Walton, *Cold War*, p. 242; *Collier's*, Oct. 30, 1948; MacDougall, *Gideon's Army*, 3:692–93.

4. MacDougall, *Gideon's Army*, 3:687.

5. Donovan, *Crisis*, p. 415.

6. Columbia University Oral History, "Reminiscences of C. B. Baldwin," p. 20.

7. *Raleigh News and Observer*, Sept. 1, 1948, NA.
8. MacDougall, *Gideon's Army*, 3:712.
9. Ibid., p. 713.
10. Ibid., p. 722.
11. CUOH, p. 5123.
12. HAW, "Speech," Sept. 9, 1948, UI.
13. *New York Star*, Sept. 7, 1948, NA.
14. *Raleigh News and Observer*, Sept. 17, 1948, NA.
15. MacDougall, *Gideon's Army*, 3:654.
16. Ibid., p. 680.
17. CUOH, p. 5142.
18. MacDougall, *Gideon's Army*, 3:600.
19. Ibid., p. 602.
20. Ibid., p. 600; CUOH, p. 5142.
21. Schmidt, *Crusade*, p. 122.
22. HAW, "A 14 Point Program," Oct. 2, 1948, UI.
23. HAW, "Broadcast . . . over WNBC," Oct. 22, 1948, UI.
24. HAW, "Speech," Oct. 25, 1948, UI.
25. Phillips, *Presidency*, p. 232.
26. HAW, "Speech," Oct. 25, 1948, UI.
27. Quoted in MacDougall, *Gideon's Army*, 3:855.
28. Baldwin CUOH, p. 36.
29. HAW, "Broadcast," Nov. 2, 1948, UI.
30. MacDougall, *Gideon's Army*, 3:883.
31. HAW, "Speech," Nov. 13, 1948, UI.
32. *Wall Street Journal*, Nov. 8, 1948.
33. HAW to HST, Nov. 5, 1948, UI.
34. HAW, "Speech," Nov. 13, 1948.
35. Goodman, *Committee*, p. 267. For information on the relationship of Harry Dexter White, Laurence Duggan, and Lauchlin Currie with Soviet intelligence, see *The Haunted Wood* by Allen Weinstein and Alexander Vassiliev, *Many are the Crimes: McCarthyism in America* by Ellen Schrecker, *Verona: Decoding Soviet Espionage in America* by John Earl Haynes and Harvey Klehr, and *The Sword and the Shield* by Christopher Andrew and Vasili Mitrokhin. These works also contain various references to Wallace. In *The Sword and the Shield* (p. 109) it is stated that if FDR had died while Wallace was vice president and he had become president, "it had been his intention to make Duggan his Secretary of State and White his Secretary of Treasury." The author's source: "We are indebted for information of Henry Wallace's plans for Duggan and White to Professor Harvey Klehr." In *Verona* (p. 139) John Earl Haynes and Harvey Klehr write: "[Wallace] told the press that White was his first choice for Secretary of Treasury." For this statement Haynes and Klehr cite Malcolm Hobbs: "Confident Wallace *aides* come up with startling cabinet notions (Overseas News Service Dispatch, 22 April 1948)" (emphasis added). No similar reference to Duggan is provided. Although Wallace knew both White and Duggan and thought highly of them, the authors found no evidence of such Wallace intention.
36. CUOH, p. 5099.
37. HAW to members of the U.S. Senate, July 5, 1949, UI.
38. *NYT*, Feb. 24, 1949.
39. HAW, "Prepared Statement before the Senate Foreign Relations Committee," May 5, 1949, UI.
40. *NYT*, May 6, 1949; Tom Connally, as told to Alfred Steinberg, *My Name Is Tom Connally* (New York: Crowell, 1954), p. 336.
41. HAW. "Address," Sept. 12, 1949, UI.
42. HAW to L. C. Frank, Oct. 15, 1949, UI.

43. CUOH, p. 5127.
44. HAW to L.C. Frank, Oct. 15; *[New York] Daily Compass*, Sept. 15, 1949, NA.
45. *DMT*, Jan. 26, 1950.
46. *New York Post*, Feb. 27, 1950.
47. HAW, "Address," Feb. 24, 1950, UI.
48. Ibid.
49. *New York Post*, Feb. 27, 1950.
50. I. F. Stone, *The Truman Era, 1945–1952* (Boston: Little, Brown, 1953), p. 161.
51. *DMR*, Feb. 27, 1950.
52. Schapsmeier, *War Years*, p. 204.
53. HAW, "Personal Statement . . . on the Korean Situation," July 15, 1950, UI.
54. Ibid.
55. HAW to C. B. Baldwin, Aug. 8, 1950, UI.

CHAPTER 27: FARVUE

1. Samuel Rosen and Daniel D. Gillmor, *The Autobiography of Dr. Samuel Rosen* (New York: Knopf, 1973), p. 126; *DMR*, Jan. 2, 1950.
2. *DMR*, Jan. 2, 1950.
3. CUOH, p. 5158.
4. Ibid., p. 5197.
5. Ibid., pp. 5193–94.
6. Ibid., p. 5194.
7. Ibid., p. 5191.
8. *NYT*, Oct. 18, 1951.
9. HAW to Homer Ferguson, March 12, 1953, UI.
10. Quoted in Schapsmeier, *War Years*, p. 220.
11. Ibid., p. 219.
12. HAW to L. R. Groves, March 7, 1951; HAW to HST, March 12, 1952, HSTL, UI.
13. HAW to *NYT*, Aug. 25, 1953, UI.
14. Quoted in Schapsmeier, *War Years*, p. 219.
15. Ibid., p. 217.
16. HAW to Fulton Lewis Jr., Nov. 17, 1953, UI.
17. HAW to Ed Sullivan, June 12, 1953, UI.
18. HAW to L. R. Groves, March 7, 1951, UI.
19. *DMR*, Sept. 4, 1983.
20. Ibid.
21. Diary, Dec. 19, 1944.
22. *DMR*, Feb. 6, 1954.
23. Reprinted in *DMR*, April 3, 1951.
24. *NYT*, Oct. 6, 1963.
25. *DMR*, April 3, 1951.
26. *NYT*, Oct. 6, 1963.
27. CUOH, p. 5179.
28. HAW, *Democracy Reborn*, p. 52.
29. Henry A. Wallace and William L. Brown, *Corn and Its Early Fathers* (Lansing: Michigan State Univ. Press, 1956), p. v.
30. CUOH, p. 5179.
31. HAW, "Liberalism Re-appraised," May 1, 1953, UI.
32. Ibid.
33. Ibid.

34. Ibid.
35. Ibid.
36. *Life*, May 14, 1956.
37. HAW to A. E. Stevenson, Aug. 18, 1956, UI.
38. *This Week*, Feb. 26, 1956; HAW to Leonard Hall, March 3, 1956, UI.
39. Family.
40. *NYT*, Oct. 27, 1960.
41. HAW to J. F. Kennedy, Jan. 22, 1961, Family.
42. HAW, "A New Dealer Looks at the New Frontier," Dec. 28, 1961, UI.
43. O. L. Freeman to HAW, Feb. 16, 1962, Family; HAW to J. F. Kennedy, May 20, 1962, Family.
44. HAW, "The Evolution of United States Agriculture as Related to Changes in Economic and Institutional Patterns," May 15, 1962, UI.

CODA: "A GOOD MAN"

1. HAW, "Commencement Address," Dec. 7, 1963, UI.
2. HAW, "Reflections of an ALSer," Nov. 1965, Family.
3. J. L. Belsky to Mrs. H. A. Wallace, May 1, 1968, Family.
4. HAW, "Corn and People," Oct. 14, 1964, UI.
5. HAW, "The West High That Was," Oct. 17, 1964, Family.
6. Patrick M. McGrady Jr., *The Youth Doctors* (New York: Coward-McCann, 1968), p. 143.
7. HAW, "ALSer."
8. McGrady, *Youth Doctors*, p. 149.
9. HAW, "ALSer."
10. Ibid.
11. Ibid.
12. Uncataloged notes, Family.
13. HAW, "ALSer."
14. Ibid.
15. Ibid.
16. Ibid.
17. *DMR*, Nov. 19, 1965.
18. *NYT*, Nov. 19, 1965.
19. *DMR*, Nov. 19, 1965.
20. Ibid.

BIBLIOGRAPHY

BOOKS

Abels, Jules. *Out of the Jaws of Victory.* New York: Henry Holt, 1959.

Acheson, Dean. *Present at the Creation: The State Department Years.* New York: Norton, 1969.

Adams, Henry H. *Harry Hopkins.* New York: Putnam, 1977.

Albertson, Dean. *Roosevelt's Farmer: Claude R. Wickard in the New Deal.* New York: Columbia Univ. Press, 1961.

Allen, George. *Presidents Who Have Known Me.* New York: Simon and Schuster, 1950.

Alperovitz, Gar. *Atomic Diplomacy: Hiroshima and Potsdam.* New York: Simon and Schuster, 1965.

Alsop, Joseph, and Turner Catledge. *The 168 Days.* Garden City, N.Y.: Doubleday, Doran, 1938.

Andrew, Christopher and Vasili Mitrokhin. *The Sword and the Shield: The Mitrokhin Archive and the Secret History of the KGB.* New York: Basic Books, 1999.

Andrews, Clarence A., ed. *Growing Up in Iowa: Reminiscences of 14 Iowa Authors.* Ames: Iowa State Univ. Press, 1978.

Aronson, James. *The Press and the Cold War.* Indianapolis: Bobbs-Merrill, 1970.

Ashby, Newton B. *The Ashbys in Iowa: A Family History.* Tuscon: self-published, 1925.

Atkinson, Carroll. *The New Deal: Will It Survive the War?* Boston: Meador Press, 1942.

Bailey, Stephen Kemp. *Congress Makes a Law: The Story Behind the Employment Act of 1946.* New York: Columbia University Press, 1950.

Baldwin, Sidney. *Poverty and Politics: The Rise and Decline of the Farm Security Administration.* Chapel Hill: Univ. of North Carolina Press, 1968.

Ball, George. *The Past Has Another Pattern.* New York: Norton, 1982.

Bancroft, T. A., ed. *Statistical Papers in Honor of George W. Snedecor.* Ames: Iowa State Univ. Press, 1972.

Barkley, Alben. *That Reminds Me.* Garden City, N.Y.: Doubleday, 1954.

Barros, James. *Trygve Lie and the Cold War: The UN Secretary-General Pursues Peace, 1946–1953.* DeKalb: Northern Illinois Univ. Press, 1989.

Baruch, Bernard M. *Baruch.* 2 vols. New York: Holt, Rinehart and Winston, 1957–60.

Barzman, Sol. *Madmen and Geniuses: The Vice Presidents of the United States.* Chicago: Tollet, 1974.

Bean, Louis H. *How to Predict Elections.* New York: Knopf, 1948.

Beard, Charles A. *President Roosevelt and the Coming of War, 1941.* Hamden, Conn.: Archon Books, 1968.

Belfrage, Cedric. *The American Inquisition, 1945–1960.* Indianapolis: Bobbs-Merrill, 1973.

Benedict, Murray R. *Farm Policies of the United States, 1790–1950.* New York: Twentieth Century Fund, 1953.

Bentley, Eric, ed. *Thirty Years of Treason: Exerpts from Hearings before the House Un-American Activities Committee, 1938–1968.* New York: Viking, 1971.

Berchloss, Michael R. *Kennedy and Roosevelt.* New York: Norton, 1980.

Berger, Jason. *A New Deal for the World: Eleanor Roosevelt and American Foreign Policy.* New York: Social Science Monographs, 1981.

Berle, A. A. *Navigating the Rapids, 1918–1971.* New York: Harcourt Brace Jovanovich, 1973.

Berlin, Sir Isaiah. *Washington Dispatches, 1941–1945.* Edited by H. G. Nicholas. Chicago: Univ. of Chicago Press, 1981.

Bernstein, Barton, ed. *Politics and Policies of the Truman Administration.* Chicago: Quadrangle, 1970.

Biddle, Francis. *The Fear of Freedom.* Garden City, N.Y.: Doubleday, 1951.

Binkley, Wilfred N. *American Political Parties: Their Natural History.* New York: Knopf, 1959.

Bishop, Jim. *FDR's Last Year, April 1944–April 1945.* New York: Morrow, 1974.

Bliven, Bruce. *Five Million Words Later: An Autobiography.* New York: John Day, 1970.

Blum, John Morton, ed. From the Morganthau Diaries. 3 vols. Boston: Houghton Mifflin, 1959–67.

———. *The Price of Vision: The Diary of Henry A. Wallace, 1942–1946.* Boston: Houghton Mifflin, 1973.

———. *V Was for Victory: Politics and American Culture during World War II.* New York: Harcourt Brace Jovanovich, 1976.

Bothwell, Robert. *Eldorado: Canada's National Uranium Company.* Toronto: Univ. of Toronto Press, 1984.

Bowles, Chester. *Promises to Keep.* New York: Harper & Row, 1971.

Boylan, James R. *The New Deal Coalition and the Election of 1946.* New York: Garland, 1981.

Braden, Charles Samuel. *These Also Believe: A Study of Modern American Cults and Minority Religious Movements.* New York: Macmillan, 1949.

Brinkley, David. *Washington Goes to War.* New York: Knopf, 1988.

Brown, Anthony Cave. *"C": The Secret Life of Sir Stewart Graham Menzies, Spymaster to Winston Churchill.* New York: Macmillan, 1987.

Brown, Anthony Cave, and Charles B. MacDonal. *On a Field of Red.* New York: Putnam, 1980.

Brownlow, Louis. *A Passion for Anonymity.* Chicago: Univ. of Chicago Press, 1958.

Bundy, McGeorge. *Danger and Survival.* New York: Random House, 1988.

Burns, James MacGregor. *Roosevelt: The Lion and the Fox.* New York: Harcourt, Brace, 1956.

———. *Roosevelt: The Soldier of Freedom, 1940–1945.* New York: Harcourt Brace Jovanovich, 1970.

Byrnes, James. *All in One Lifetime.* New York: Harper, 1958.

———. *Speaking Frankly.* New York: Harper, 1947.

Cantril, Hadley, and Mildred Strunk. *Public Opinion, 1935–1946.* Princeton: Princeton Univ. Press, 1951.

Caro, Robert. *The Years of Lyndon Johnson: The Path to Power.* New York: Knopf, 1982.

Carr, Robert K. *The House Committee on Un-American Activities, 1945–1950.* Ithaca: Cornell Univ. Press, 1952.

Carter, John Franklin (as the "Unofficial Observer"). *The New Dealers.* New York: Simon and Schuster, 1934.

Casdorph, Paul D. *Let the Good Times Roll: Life at Home in America during World War II.* New York: Paragon House, 1989.

Catton, Bruce. *The War Lords of Washington*. New York: Harcourt, Brace, 1948.

Caute, David. *Fellow Travellers: A Postscript to the Enlightenment*. London: Weidenfeld and Nicolson, 1973.

———. *The Great Fear: The Anti-Communist Purge under Truman and Eisenhower*. New York: Simon and Schuster, 1978.

Chambers, Whittaker. *Witness*. New York: Random House, 1952.

Chapple, Joe Mitchell. *Life and Times of Warren G. Harding*. Boston: Chapple, 1924.

Clayton, Will. *Selected Papers of Will Clayton*. Edited by Frederick Dobney. Baltimore: Johns Hopkins Press, 1971.

Cochran, Bert. *Labor and Communism: The Conflict That Shaped American Unions*. Princeton: Princeton Univ. Press, 1978.

Cochran, Thomas C. *The Great Depression and World War II, 1929–45*. New York: Scott Foresman, 1968.

Coit, Margaret L. *Mr. Baruch*. Boston: Houghton Mifflin, 1957.

Cole, Cyrenus. *Iowa through the Years*. Iowa City: Iowa State Historical Society, 1940.

———. *History of the People of Iowa*. Cedar Rapids: Torch Press, 1921.

Cole, Wayne S. *Roosevelt and the Isolationists, 1932–45*. Lincoln: Univ. of Nebraska Press, 1983.

Connally, Tom (as told to Alfred Steinberg). *My Name Is Tom Connally*. New York: Crowell, 1954.

Connery, Robert Howe. *Rockefeller of New York*. Ithaca: Cornell Univ. Press, 1979.

Conquest, Robert. *Kolyma: The Arctic Death Camps*. New York: Viking, 1978.

Coolidge, Calvin. *The Autobiography of Calvin Coolidge*. New York: Cosmopolitan, 1929.

Crabb, Richard A. *The Hybrid Corn Makers*. New Brunswick: Rutgers Univ. Press, 1947.

Cranston, Sylvia. *HPB: The Extraordinary Life and Influence of Helena Blavatsky—Founder of the Modern Theosophical Movement*. Tarcher/Putnam Books, 1933.

Dallek, Robert. *Franklin Roosevelt and American Foreign Policy, 1932–1945*. New York: Oxford Univ. Press, 1979.

Daniels, Jonathan. *Frontier on the Potomac*. New York: Macmillan, 1946.

———. *The Time between the Wars*. Garden City, N.Y.: Doubleday, 1966.

———. *Washington Quadrille: The Dance beside the Documents*. Garden City, N.Y.: Doubleday, 1968.

———. *White House Witness, 1942–45*. Garden City, N.Y.: Doubleday, 1975.

Daniels, Josephus. *Shirt-Sleeve Diplomat*. Chapel Hill: Univ. of North Carolina Press, 1947.

Darrow, George W. *The Strawberry: History, Breeding and Physiology*. New York: Holt, Rinehart and Winston, 1966.

Davis, Kenneth S. *Experience of War: The United States in World War II*. Garden City, N.Y.: Doubleday, 1965.

———. *FDR: Into the Storm, 1937–1940*. New York: Random House, 1993.

———. *FDR: The New Deal Years, 1933–1937*. New York: Random House, 1986.

Decter, Jacqueline. *Nicholas Roerich: The Life and Art of a Russian Master*. Rochester, Vt.: Park Street Press, 1989.

De Kruif, Paul. *The Hunger Fighters*. New York: Harcourt, Brace, 1928.

———. *The Sweeping Wind*. New York: Harcourt, Brace & World, 1962.

Denisoff, R. George. *Great Day Coming: Folk Music and the American Left*. Urbana: Univ. of Illinois Press, 1971.

Divine, Robert A. *The Age of Insecurity: America, 1920–1945*. Reading, Mass.: Addison-Wesley, 1968.

———. *Foreign Policy and U.S. Presidential Elections, 1940–48*. New York: New Viewpoints, 1974.

———. *Roosevelt and World War II*. Baltimore: Johns Hopkins Press, 1969.

———. *Second Chance: The Triumph of Internationalism in America during World War II*. New York: Atheneum, 1967.

Donahoe, Bernard F. *Private Plans and Public Dangers: The Story of FDR's Third Nomination*. Notre Dame, Ind.: Univ. of Notre Dame Press, 1965.

Donovan, Robert J. *Conflict and Crisis: The Presidency of Harry S. Truman, 1945–1948*. New York: Norton, 1977.

Dorfman, Joseph. *Thorstein Veblen and His America*. New York: Viking, 1931.

Dorsett, Lyle. *Franklin D. Roosevelt and the City Bosses*. Port Washington, N.Y.: Kennikat Press, 1977.

Douglas, Roy. *From War to Cold War*. New York: St. Martin's Press, 1981.

Douglas, William O. *Go East Young Man*. New York: Random House, 1974.

Drury, Allen. *A Senate Journal, 1943–1945*. New York: McGraw-Hill, 1963.

Duberman, Martin B. *Paul Robeson*. New York: Knopf, 1988.

Dugger, Ronnie. *The Politician*. New York: Nation, 1982.

Dunlap, Leslie W. *Our Vice Presidents and Second Ladies*. Metuchen, N.J.: Scarecrow Press, 1988.

Durr, Virginia Foster. *Outside the Magic Circle: The Autobiography of Virginia Foster Durr*. University: Univ. of Alabama Press, 1985.

Eames, Charles. *A Computer Perspective*. Cambridge: Harvard Univ. Press, 1973.

Eccles, Marriner. *Beckoning Frontiers*. New York: Knopf, 1951.

Farago, Ladislas. *The Game of the Foxes: The Untold Story of German Espionage in the United States and Great Britain during World War II*. New York: McKay, 1971.

Farley, James A. *Jim Farley's Story: The Roosevelt Years*. New York: McGraw-Hill, 1948.

Fehrenbach, T. R. *F.D.R.'s Undeclared War, 1939 to 1941*. New York: McKay, 1967.

Feis, Herbert. *The China Tangle, the American Effort in China from Pearl Harbor to the Marshall Mission*. New York: Atheneum, 1967.

———. *Churchill, Roosevelt, Stalin*. Princeton: Princeton Univ. Press, 1957.

———. *From Trust to Terror: The Onset of the Cold War, 1945–1950*. New York: Norton, 1970.

———. *1933: Characters in a Crisis*. Boston: Little, Brown, 1966.

Ferrell, Robert. *George C. Marshall*. New York: Cooper Square Publishers, 1966.

———. *Off the Record: The Private Papers of Harry S. Truman*. New York: Harper & Row, 1980.

Fite, Gilbert C. *George N. Peek and the Fight for Farm Parity*. Norman: Univ. of Oklahoma Press, 1954.

Flynn, Edward J. *You're the Boss*. Westport: Greenwood, 1947.

Flynn, John T. *The Roosevelt Myth*. New York: Devin-Adair, 1948.

Freeland, Richard M. *The Truman Doctrine and the Origins of McCarthyism, 1946–48*. New York: Knopf, 1972.

Freidel, Frank. *Franklin D. Roosevelt: Launching the New Deal*. New York: Little, Brown, 1973.

Friedrich, Carl J. *The New Belief in the Common Man*. Boston: Little, Brown, 1942.

Funigiello, Philip J. *Toward a National Power Policy: The New Deal and the Electric Utility Industry, 1933–41*. Pittsburgh: Univ. of Pittsburgh Press, 1973.

Fussell, Betty. *The Story of Corn*. New York: Knopf, 1992.

Gaddis, John Lewis. *The Long Peace: Inquiries into the History of the Cold War*. New York: Oxford Univ. Press, 1967.

———. *The United States and the Origins of the Cold War, 1941–1947*. New York: Columbia Univ. Press, 1972.

Gardner, Lloyd C. *Architects of Illusion: Men and Ideas in American Foreign Policy, 1941–49*. Chicago: Quadrangle, 1974.

———. *The New Deal: New Frontiers and the Cold War: A Reexamination of American Expansion, 1933–45*. New York: Monthly Review Books, 1969.

Garraty, John A. *The Great Depression*. Garden City, N.Y.: Anchor Press, 1987.

Garson, Robert A. *The Democratic Party and the Politics of Sectionalism, 1941–48*. Baton Rouge: Louisiana State Univ. Press, 1974.

Garwood, Ellen Clayton. *Will Clayton: A Short Biography*. Austin: Univ. of Texas Press, 1958.

Gellman, Irwin F. *Good Neighbor Diplomacy: United States Policies in Latin America, 1933–1945*. Baltimore: Johns Hopkins Univ. Press, 1979.

Gilliam, Dorothy. *Paul Robeson: All-American*. Washington, D.C.: New Republic, 1976.

Goldman, Eric. *The Crucial Decade: America, 1945–1955.* New York: Knopf, 1956.

———. *Rendezvous with Destiny: A History of Modern American Reform.* New York: Knopf, 1970.

Goldstein, Joel K. *The Modern American Vice-Presidency: Transformation of a Political Institution.* Princeton: Princeton Univ. Press, 1982.

Goodman, Walter. *The Committee.* New York: Farrar, Straus and Giroux, 1964.

Graham, Otis L., Jr., and Meghan R. Wander, eds. *Franklin D. Roosevelt: His Life and Times: An Encyclopedic View.* Boston: G. K. Hall, 1985.

Hachey, Thomas E., ed. *Confidential Dispatches: Analyses of America by the British Ambassador, 1939–1945.* Evanston: New Univ. Press, 1974.

Hambidge, Gove. *The Prime of Life.* Garden City, N.Y.: Doubleday, Doran, 1942.

Hamby, Alonzo L. *Beyond the New Deal: Harry S. Truman and American Liberalism.* New York: Columbia Univ. Press, 1973.

Hamilton, Carl. *In No Time at All.* Ames: Iowa State Univ. Press, 1974.

Hammond, Paul. *The Cold War Years: American Foreign Policy since 1945.* New York: Harcourt, Brace and World, 1969.

Harnack, Curtis. *We Have All Gone Away.* Ames: Iowa State Univ. Press, 1981.

Harper, Alan D. *The Politics of Loyalty: The White House and the Communist Issue, 1946–52.* Westport: Greenwood, 1969.

Harriman, Averell. *Peace with Russia.* New York: Simon and Schuster, 1959.

Harriman, W. Averell, and Elie Abel. *Special Envoy to Churchill and Stalin, 1941–46,* New York: Random House, 1975.

Harrison, Gilbert. *A Timeless Affair: The Life of Anita McCormick Blaine.* Chicago: Univ. of Chicago Press, 1979.

Hart, Jeffrey. *From This Moment On: America in 1940.* New York: Crown, 1987.

Hassett, William D. *Off the Record with F.D.R., 1942–1945.* New Brunswick: Rutgers Univ. Press, 1958.

Haynes, John Earl. *Communism and Anti-communism in the United States: An Annotated Guide to Historical Writings.* New York: Garland, 1987.

Haynes, John Earl, and Harvey Klehr. *Verona: Decoding Soviet Espionage in America.* New Haven: Yale University Press, 1999.

Hazard, John N. *Recollections of a Pioneering Sovietologist.* New York: Oceana Publications, 1984.

Hechler, Ken. *Working with Truman: A Personal Memoir of the White House Years.* New York: Putnam, 1982.

Hellman, Lillian. *Scoundrel Time.* Boston: Little, Brown, 1976.

Herring, George C., Jr. *Aid to Russia, 1941–46: Strategy, Diplomacy, the Origins of the Cold War.* New York: Columbia Univ. Press, 1973.

Hesseltine, William B. *The Rise and Fall of Third Parties: From Anti-Masonry to Wallace.* Washington, D.C.: Public Affairs Press, 1948.

Hewlett, Richard G., and Oscar E. Anderson. *The New World, 1939–1946: A History of the U.S. Atomic Energy Commission.* University Park: Pennsylvania State Univ. Press, 1962.

Hillman, William. *Mr. President.* London: Farrar, Straus & Young, 1952.

Hine, Robert V. *California's Utopian Colonies.* San Marino: Huntington Library, 1953.

Hiss, Alger. *Recollections of a Life.* New York: Henry Holt, 1988.

Hitchinson, William J. *Lowdon of Illinois: The Life of Frank O. Lowdon.* Chicago: Univ. of Chicago Press, 1957.

Hollingsworth, Harold M., and William F. Holmes, eds. *Essays on the New Deal.* Austin: Univ. of Texas Press, 1969.

Holt, Rackham. *George Washington Carver: An American Biography.* Garden City, N.Y.: Doubleday, Doran, 1943.

Hoopes, Townsend. *The Devil and John Foster Dulles.* London: Andre Deutsch, 1974.

Hoover, Herbert. *American Ideals versus the New Deal.* New York: Scribners, 1936.

———. *The Memoirs of Herbert Hoover, 1929–1933.* New York: Macmillan, 1952.

Hull, Cordell. *The Memoirs of Cordell Hull.* 2 vols. New York: Macmillan, 1948.

Hurd, Charles. *When the New Deal Was Young and Gay.* New York: Hawthorn, 1965.

Ickes, Harold. *Autobiography of a Curmudgeon.* New York: Reynal & Hitchcock, 1943.

———. *The Secret Diary of Harold L. Ickes.* 3 vols. New York: Simon and Schuster, 1953–54.

Isaacson, Walter, and Evan Thomas. *The Wise Men: Six Friends and the World They Made.* New York: Simon and Schuster, 1986.

Jacobs, Leonard J. *Cornhuskers' Battle of the Bangboards.* Des Moines: Wallace-Homestead, 1975.

Jayakar, Pupul. *Krishnamurti: A Biography.* San Francisco: Harper & Row, 1986.

Jones, Jesse H., with Edward Angly. *Fifty Billion Dollars: My Thirteen Years with the RFC, 1932–1945.* New York: Macmillan, 1951.

Josephson, Matthew. *Sidney Hillman: Statesman of American Labor.* Garden City, N.Y.: Doubleday, 1952.

Kagan, Paul. *New World Utopians.* New York: Penguin, 1975.

Kahn, Albert E. *Matusow Affair.* Mount Kisco, N.Y.: Moyer Bell, 1987.

Kahn, Gordon. *Hollywood on Trial: The Story of Ten Who Were Indicted.* New York: Boni and Gaer, 1948.

Kempton, Murray. *Part of Our Time: Some Ruins and Monuments of the Thirties.* New York: Simon and Schuster, 1955.

Kennan, George F. *Memoirs.* 2 vols. Boston: Little, Brown, 1967–72.

Kimball, Penn. *The File.* New York: Harcourt Brace Jovanovich, 1983.

Kingdon, Frank. *An Uncommon Man: Henry Wallace and 60 Million Jobs.* New York: Readers Press, 1945.

Kirkendall, Richard S. *The New Deal: The Historical Debate.* New York: John Wiley, 1973.

———. *Social Scientists and Farm Policy in the Age of Roosevelt.* Columbia: Univ. of Missouri Press, 1966.

———. *The United States, 1929–45: Years of Crisis and Change.* New York: McGraw-Hill, 1974.

Kloppenburg, Jack, Jr. *First the Seed: The Political Economy of Plant Biotechnology, 1492–2000.* New York: Cambridge Univ. Press, 1988.

Krock, Arthur. *Memoirs: Sixty Years on the Firing Line.* New York: Funk and Wagnalls, 1968.

Lader, Lawrence. *Power on the Left: American Radical Movements since 1946.* New York: Norton, 1979.

LaFeber, Walter. *America, Russia and the Cold War, 1945–1966.* New York: John Wiley, 1967.

Lash, Joseph P. *Dealers and Dreamers: A New Look at the New Deal.* New York: Doubleday, 1988.

———. *Eleanor and Franklin.* New York: Norton, 1971.

———. *A World of Love: Eleanor Roosevelt and Her Friends, 1943–62.* Garden City, N.Y.: Doubleday, 1984.

Latham, Earl. *The Communist Controversy in Washington.* Cambridge: Harvard Univ. Press, 1966.

Leahy, William D. *I Was There.* New York: McGraw-Hill, 1950.

Leaming, Barbara. *Orson Welles.* New York: Penguin, 1983.

Lee, Harold. *Roswell Garst: A Biography.* Ames: Iowa State Univ. Press, 1984.

Leuchtenburg, William E. *Franklin D. Roosevelt and the New Deal, 1932–1940.* New York: Harper Torchbooks, 1963.

———. *In the Shadow of FDR.* Ithaca: Cornell Univ. Press, 1989.

Lieberman, Joseph J. *The Scorpion and the Tarantula: The Struggle to Control Atomic Weapons, 1945–49.* Boston: Houghton Mifflin, 1970.

Lilienthal, David E. *The Journals of David E. Lilienthal.* 7 vols. New York: Harper & Row, 1964–83.

Lindley, Ernest K. *Half Way with Roosevelt.* New York: Viking, 1936.

Lipset, Seymour Martin, and Earl Raab. *The Politics of Unreason: Right-Wing Extremism in America, 1790–1970.* New York: Harper & Row, 1970.

Littell, Norman M. *My Roosevelt Years.* Edited by Jonathan Dembo. Seattle: Univ. of Washington Press, 1987.

Long, Huey P. *Every Man a King.* New Orleans: National Book, 1933.

Lord, Russell. *The Wallaces of Iowa.* Boston: Houghton Mifflin, 1947.

Louchheim, Katie, ed. *The Making of the New Deal: The Insiders Speak.* Cambridge: Harvard Univ. Press, 1983.

Lowitt, Richard, and Judith Fabry, eds. *Henry A. Wallace's Irrigation Frontier.* Norman: Univ. of Oklahoma Press, 1991.

McAuliffe, Mary Sperling. *Crisis on the Left: Cold War Politics and American Liberals, 1947–54.* Amherst: Univ. of Massachusetts Press, 1978.

McCarthy, James Remington. *The New Pioneers.* Indianapolis: Bobbs-Merrill, 1934.

McCoy, Donald R. *Angry Voices: Left-of-Center Politics in the New Deal Era.* Lawrence: Univ. of Kansas Press, 1958.

———. *The Presidency of Harry S. Truman,* Lawrence: Univ. Press of Kansas, 1984.

McCullough, David. *Truman.* New York: Simon and Schuster, 1992.

Macdonald, Dwight. *Henry Wallace: The Man and the Myth.* New York: Vanguard, 1947.

MacDougall, Curtis D. *Gideon's Army.* 3 vols. New York: Marzani & Munsell, 1965.

McElvaine, Robert S. *The Great Depression.* New York: Times Books, 1984.

McGeary, M. Nelson. *Gifford Pinchot: Forester-Politician.* Princeton: Princeton Univ. Press, 1960.

McJimsey, George. *Harry Hopkins: Ally of the Poor and Defender of Democracy.* Cambridge: Harvard Univ. Press, 1987.

MacMahon, Edward B., and Leonard Curry. *Medical Cover-ups in the White House.* Washington: Farragut, 1987.

Madison, James H. *Heartland: Comparative Histories of the Midwestern States.* Bloomington: Indiana Univ. Press, 1988.

Markowitz, Norman D. *The Rise and Fall of the People's Century: Henry A. Wallace and American Liberalism, 1941–1948.* New York: Free Press, 1973.

Martin, George W. *Madam Secretary: Frances Perkins.* Boston: Houghton Mifflin, 1976.

Martin, Joe (as told to Robert J. Donovan). *My First Fifty Years in Politics.* New York: McGraw-Hill, 1960.

Matusow, Allen J. *Farm Policies and Politics in the Truman Years.* Cambridge: Harvard Univ. Press, 1967.

May, Gary. *China Scapegoat: The Diplomatic Ordeal of John Carter Vincent.* Washington, D.C.: New Republic Books, 1979.

Mazuzan, George T., and J. Samuel Walker. *Controlling the Atom: The Beginnings of Nuclear Regulation, 1946–1962.* Berkeley: Univ. of California Press, 1985.

Meade, Marion. *Madame Blavatsky: The Woman behind the Myth.* New York: Putnam, 1980.

Melton, J. Gordon. *Biographical Dictionary of American Cult and Sect Leaders.* New York: Garland, 1986.

Messer, Robert L. *The End of an Alliance: James F. Byrnes, Roosevelt, Truman and the Origins of the Cold War.* Chapel Hill: Univ. of North Carolina Press, 1982.

Michelson, Charles. *The Ghost Talks.* New York: Putnam, 1944.

Miller, Nathan. *F.D.R.: An Intimate History.* Garden City, N.Y.: Doubleday, 1983.

Millis, Walter, ed. *The Forrestal Diaries.* New York: Viking, 1951.

Mills, George. *Rogues and Heroes from Iowa's Amazing Past.* Ames: Iowa State Univ. Press, 1972.

Moley, Raymond. *The First New Deal.* New York: Harcourt, Brace & World, 1966.

———. *27 Masters of Politics.* New York: Funk & Wagnalls, 1949.

Morgan, Ted. *FDR: A Biography.* New York: Simon and Schuster, 1985.

Morison, Elting E. *Turmoil and Tradition: A Study of the Life and Times of Henry L. Stimson.* New York: Atheneum, 1964.

Morrison, Joseph L. *Josephus Daniels: The Small-d Democrat.* Chapel Hill: Univ. of North Carolina Press, 1966.

Mosher, Martin L. *Early Iowa Corn Yield Tests and Related Later Programs.* Ames: Iowa State Univ. Press, 1962. [Introduction by Henry A. Wallace]

Moskow, Warren. *Roosevelt and Willkie.* Englewood Cliffs, N.J.: Prentice-Hall, 1968.

Namorato, Michael V. *Rexford G. Tugwell: A Biography.* New York: Praeger, 1988.

Nash, Gerald D. *The American West Transformed: The Impact of the Second World War.* Bloomington: Indiana Univ. Press, 1985.

Navasky, Victor S. *Naming Names.* New York: Penguin, 1980.

Nelson, Donald. *Arsenal of Democracy: The Story of American War Production.* New York: Harcourt, Brace, 1946.

Norris, George. *Fighting Liberal: The Autobiography of George W. Norris.* New York: Macmillan, 1954.

Nourse, E. G. *Economics in Public Service.* New York: Harcourt, Brace, 1953.

————. *Three Years at the Agricultural Adjustment Administration.* New York: Da Capo Press, 1971.

Ogilvie, William Edward. *Pioneer Agricultural Journalists.* Chicago: A. G. Leonard, 1927.

Olsen, Nils A. *Journal of a Tamed Bureaucrat: Nils Olsen and the BAE, 1925–1935.* Edited by Richard Lowitt. Ames: Iowa State Univ. Press, 1980.

Paarlberg, Don. *Towards a Well-Fed World.* Ames: Iowa State Univ. Press, 1988.

Paelian, Garabed. *Nicholas Roerich.* Agoura, Calif.: Aquarian Educational Group, 1974.

Parrish, Thomas. *Roosevelt and Marshall.* New York: Morrow, 1989.

Paterson, Thomas G. *Cold War Critics.* Chicago: Quadrangle, 1971.

————. *On Every Front: The Making of the Cold War.* New York: Norton, 1979.

Patterson, Richard S., and Richardson Dougall. *The Eagle and the Shield: A History of the Great Deal of the United States.* Washington, D.C.: Department of State Publication No. 8900, 1978.

Pearson, Drew. *Diaries, 1949–59.* New York: Holt, Rinehart & Winston, 1974.

Pepper, Claude, with Hays Gorey. *Pepper: Eyewitness to a Century.* New York: Harcourt Brace Jovanovich, 1987.

Perkins, Frances. *The Roosevelt I Knew.* New York: Viking, 1946.

Perkins, Van L. *Crisis in Agriculture: The Agricultural Adjustment Administration and the New Deal, 1933.* Berkeley: Univ. of California Press, 1969.

Perrett, Geoffrey. *America in the Twenties: A History.* New York: Simon and Schuster, 1982.

Peterson, F. Ross. *Glen Taylor: Idaho's Liberal Maverick.* Boise: Idaho State Univ. Press, 1974.

————. *Prophet without Honor: Glen H. Taylor and the Fight for American Liberalism.* Lexington: Univ. Press of Kentucky, 1974.

Philbrick, Herbert A. *I Led Three Lives.* New York: McGraw-Hill, 1952.

Phillips, Cabell. *From the Crash to the Blitz, 1929–39.* New York: Macmillan, 1975.

————. *The Truman Presidency: The History of a Triumphant Succession.* New York: Macmillan, 1966.

Powers, Richard. *Secrecy and Power: The Life of J. Edgar Hoover.* New York: Free Press, 1987.

Pratt, Julius William. *Cordell Hull, 1933–44.* New York: Cooper Square Publishers, 1964.

Rasmussen, Wayne, ed. *Readings in the History of American Agriculture.* Urbana: Univ. of Illinois Press, 1960.

Rasmussen, Wayne, and Gladys Baker. *The Department of Agriculture.* New York: Praeger, 1972.

Rhodes, Richard. *The Making of the Atomic Bomb.* New York: Simon and Schuster, 1986.

Robeson, Paul. *Here I Stand.* Boston: Beacon, 1958.

Rogow, Arnold. *James Forrestal: A Study of Personality, Politics and Policy.* New York: Macmillan, 1963.

Roosevelt, Eleanor. *This I Remember.* New York: Harper, 1949.

————. *Autobiography of Eleanor Roosevelt.* New York: Harper, 1961.

————. *My Day.* New York: Pharos Books, 1989.

Roosevelt, Elliott. *As He Saw It.* New York: Duell, Sloan and Pearce, 1946.

————, ed. *F.D.R.: His Personal Letters.* New York: Duell, Sloan and Pearce, 1950.

Roosevelt, James, and Sidney Shalett. *Affectionately, F.D.R.: A Son's Story of a Lonely Man.* New York: Harcourt, Brace, 1959.

Rosen, Samuel, and Daniel D. Gillmor. *The Autobiography of Dr. Samuel Rosen.* New York: Knopf, 1973.

Rosenman, Samuel. *Working with Roosevelt*. New York: Da Capo Press, 1952.

Ross, Irwin. *The Loneliest Campaign*. New York: New American Library, 1968.

Rowley, William D. *M. L. Wilson and the Campaign for the Domestic Allotment*. Lincoln: Univ. of Nebraska Press, 1970.

Sage, Leland L. *A History of Iowa*. Ames: Iowa State Univ. Press, 1974.

Saloutos, Theodore. *The American Farmer and the New Deal*. Ames: Iowa State Univ. Press, 1982.

Saloutos, Theodore, and John D. Hicks. *Agricultural Discontent in the Middle West, 1900–1939*. Madison: Univ. of Wisconsin Press, 1951.

Salter, J. A., ed. *Public Men in and out of Office*. Chapel Hill: Univ. of North Carolina Press, 1946.

Sargent, James E. *Roosevelt and the Hundred Days*. New York: Garland, 1981.

Sawyer, Gordon. *The Agribusiness Poultry Industry: A History of Its Development*. New York: Exposition Press, 1971.

Schacht, John W., ed. *Three Progressives from Iowa: Gilbert Haugen, Herbert Hoover, Henry A. Wallace*. Iowa City: Center for the Study of Recent Iowa History, 1980.

Schapsmeier, Edward L., and Frederick H. *Henry A. Wallace of Iowa: The Agrarian Years, 1910–1940*. Ames: Iowa State Univ. Press, 1968.

———. *Prophet in Politics: Henry A. Wallace and the War Years, 1940–1965*. Ames: Iowa State Univ. Press, 1970.

Schlesinger, Arthur, Jr. *The Age of Roosevelt*. Boston: Houghton Mifflin, 1957.

———. *The Coming of the New Deal*. Boston: Houghton Mifflin, 1958.

———. *The Politics of Upheaval*. Boston: Houghton Mifflin, 1988.

———. *The Vital Center*. New York: Da Capo Press, 1949.

Schmidt, Karl M. *Henry A. Wallace: Quixotic Crusade 1948*. Syracuse: Syracuse Univ. Press, 1960.

Schrecker, Ellen. *Many Are the Crimes: McCarthyism in America*. New York: Little, Brown, 1998.

Schweider, Dorothy, ed. *Patterns and Perspectives in Iowa History*. Ames: Iowa State Univ. Press, 1973.

Seldes, George. *Witness to a Century*. New York: Ballantine Books, 1987.

Sheed, Wilfrid. *Clare Boothe Luce*. New York: Dutton, 1982.

Sherwood, Robert E. *Roosevelt and Hopkins: An Intimate History*. New York: Harper, 1948.

Shidler, James H. *Farm Crisis, 1919–1923*. Berkeley: Univ. of California Press, 1957.

Shover, John L. *Cornbelt Rebellion: The Farmers' Holiday Association*. Urbana: Univ. of Illinois Press, 1965.

Sirevag, Torbjorn. *The Eclipse of the New Deal and the Fall of Vice President Wallace*. New York: Garland, 1985.

Smith, Richard Norton. *Thomas E. Dewey and His Times*. New York: Simon and Schuster, 1982.

———. *An Uncommon Man: The Triumph of Herbert Hoover*. New York: Simon and Schuster, 1984.

Solberg, Carl. *Hubert Humphrey: A Biography*. New York: Norton, 1984.

Steel, Ronald. *Walter Lippmann and the American Century*. Boston: Little, Brown, 1980.

Steinberg, Alfred. *The Bosses*. New York: Macmillan, 1972.

Stimson, Henry L., and McGeorge Bundy. *On Active Service in Peace and War*. New York: Octagon, 1948.

Stone, I. F. *The Truman Era, 1945–1952*. Boston: Little, Brown, 1953.

———. *The War Years, 1938–1945*. Boston: Little, Brown, 1988.

Straight, Michael. *After Long Silence*. New York: Norton, 1983.

Sullivan, Patricia. *Days of Hope: Race and Democracy in The New Deal Era*. Chapel Hill: University of North Carolina Press, 1996.

Sulzberger, Cyrus L. *A Long Row of Candles: Memoirs and Diaries, 1934–1954*. Toronto: Macmillan, 1969.

Swanberg, W. A. *Luce and His Empire: A Personal Adventure*. New York: Scribners, 1972.

———. *Norman Thomas: The Last Idealist*. New York: Scribners, 1976.

Taylor, Glen H. *The Way It Was with Me*. New York: Lyle Stuart, 1979.

Theoharis, Athan G. *Beyond the Hiss Case: The FBI, Congress and the Cold War*. Philadelphia: Temple Univ. Press, 1982.
———. *Seeds of Repression: Harry S Truman and the Origins of McCarthyism*. Chicago: Quadrangle, 1971.
Timmons, Bascom N. *Garner of Texas: A Personal History*. New York: Harper, 1948.
———. *Jesse H. Jones: The Man and the Statesman*. New York: Holt, 1956.
Truman, Harry S. *Memoirs*. 2 vols. Garden City, N.Y.: Doubleday, 1955–56.
———. *Off the Record: Private Papers of Harry S. Truman*. New York: Harper & Row, 1980.
Truman, Margaret. *Harry S Truman*. New York: William Morrow, 1973.
Tuchman, Barbara. *Stilwell and the American Experience in China* (1911–45). New York: Macmillan, 1970.
Tugwell, Rexford Guy. *The Brains Trust*. New York: Viking, 1968.
———. *The Democratic Roosevelt*. Garden City, N.Y.: Doubleday, 1957.
———. *Roosevelt's Revolution*. New York: Macmillan, 1977.
———. *In Search of Roosevelt*. Cambridge: Harvard Univ. Press, 1972.
Tully, Grace. *FDR, My Boss*. New York: Scribners, 1949.
Walker, Frank C. *FDR's Quiet Confidant: The Autobiography of Frank C. Walker*. Edited by Robert H. Faerrell. Niwot: Univ. Press of Colorado, 1997.
Walker, J. Samuel. *Henry A. Wallace and American Foreign Policy*. Westport: Greenwood, 1976.
Wallace, Henry. *Trusts and How to Deal with Them*. Des Moines: Wallace Publishing, 1899.
———. *Uncle Henry's Own Life Story*. 3 vols. Des Moines: Wallace Publishing, 1917–19.
Wallace, Henry A. *Agricultural Prices*. Des Moines: Wallace Publishing, 1920.
———. *America Must Choose*. New York: Foreign Policy Association, 1934.
———. *The American Choice*. New York: Reynal & Hitchcock, 1940.
———. *The Century of the Common Man*. New York: Reynal & Hitchcock, 1943.
———. *Christian Bases of World Order*. Freeport, N.Y.: Abingdon-Cokesbury, 1943.
———. *Democracy Reborn*. Edited by Russell Lord. New York: Reynal & Hitchcock, 1944.
———. *Henry Wallace Says*. New York: New Republic Books, 1948.
———. *New Frontiers*. New York: Reynal & Hitchcock, 1934.
———. *Our Job in the Pacific*. San Francisco: Institute of Pacific Relations, 1944.
———. *Paths to Plenty*. Washington, D.C.: National Home Library Foundations, 1938.
———. *The Price of Freedom*. Washington, D.C.: National Home Library Foundation, 1940.
———. *Sixty Million Jobs*. New York: Reynal & Hitchcock, Simon and Schuster, 1945.
———. *Statesmanship and Religion*. New York: Round Table Press, 1934.
———. *Technology, Corporations and the General Welfare*. Chapel Hill: Univ. of North Carolina Press, 1937.
———. *Toward World Peace*. New York: Reynal & Hitchcock, 1948.
———. *Whose Constitution: An Inquiry into the General Welfare*. New York: Reynal & Hitchcock, 1936.
Wallace, Henry A., and E. Bressman. *Corn and Corn Growing*. Des Moines: Wallace Publishing, 1923.
Wallace, Henry A., and William Brown. *Corn and Its Early Fathers*. Lansing: Michigan State Univ. Press, 1956.
Wallace, Henry A., and George W. Snedecor. *Correlation and Machine Calculation*. Ames: Iowa State College, 1925.
Wallace, Henry A., and Andrew Steiger. *Soviet Asia Mission*. New York: Reynal & Hitchcock, 1945.
Wallace, Henry A., et al. *Prefaces to Peace*. New York: Reynal & Hitchcock, 1943.
Wallace, Henry C. *Our Debt and Duty to the Farmer*. New York: Century, 1925.
———. *Education for the Iowa Farm Boy*. Des Moines: Wallace Publishing, 1912.
———. *Theodore Roosevelt, Preacher of Righteousness*. Des Moines: Wallace Publishing, 1919.
Walton, Richard J. *Henry Wallace, Harry Truman and the Cold War*. New York: Viking, 1976.

Weinstein, Allen, and Alexander Vassiliev. *The Haunted Wood: Soviet Espionage in America—The Stalin Era.* New York: Random House, 1999.

White, Graham, and John Maze. *Harold Ickes of the New Deal.* Cambridge: Harvard Univ. Press, 1985.

———. *Henry A. Wallace: His Search for the New World Order.* Chapel Hill: Univ. of North Carolina Press, 1995.

White, Theodore H. *In Search of History.* New York: Harper & Row, 1978.

Whitfield, Stephen J. *A Critical American: The Politics of Dwight Macdonald.* Hamden, Conn.: Archon Books, 1984.

Wilcox, Earley Vernon, and Flora H. Wilson. *Tama Jim.* Boston: Stratford, 1930.

Williams, Irving G. *The Rise of the Vice-Presidency.* Washington, D.C.: Public Affairs Press, 1956.

Williams, Robert C. *Russian Art and American Money, 1900–1940.* Cambridge: Harvard Univ. Press, 1980.

Winters, Donald L. *Henry Cantwell Wallace as Secretary of Agriculture, 1921–1924.* Urbana: Univ. of Illinois Press, 1970.

Wise, James Waterman. *Meet Henry Wallace: An Illustrated Biography.* New York: Boni and Gaer, 1948.

Wolfskill, George, and John A. Hudson. *All But the People: Franklin D. Roosevelt and His Critics, 1933–39.* London: Macmillan. 1969.

Yarnell, Allen. *Democrats and Progressives: The 1948 Presidential Election as a Test of Postwar Liberalism.* Berkeley: Univ. of California Press, 1974.

Young, Donald. *American Roulette: The History and Dilemma of the Vice Presidency.* New York: Holt, Rinehart & Winston, 1965.

THESES AND DISSERTATIONS

Adcock, Cynthia L. "Popular Front Politics in America, 1948–54: A Study of the Left Progressives." M.A. thesis, Columbia Univ., 1963.

Anderson, James Marcus. "The Attitude of Henry A. Wallace on Soviet Society and Soviet-American Relations." M.A. thesis, Univ. of South Dakota, 1975.

Bailey, Percival R. "Progressive Lawyers: A History of the National Lawyers Guild, 1936–1958." Ph.D. diss., Rutgers Univ., 1979.

Bernham, R. Leon. "The Purge in the AAA." Ph.D. diss., Emory Univ., 1987.

Bladholm, Helen Ann. "Glen Hearst Taylor: Principles, Politics and the Cold War." M.A. thesis, Northeastern Illinois Univ., 1972.

Brown, John Cotton. "The 1948 Progressive Campaign: A Scientific Approach." Ph.D. diss., Univ. of Chicago, 1949.

Capalbo, Joseph P. "Looking Backward: The Policies and Positions of Henry A. Wallace." Ph.D. diss., Rutgers Univ., 1974.

Chin, Laura. "The Wallace Mission: Prelude to Failure." M.A. thesis, George Washington Univ., 1971.

Clarksson, Linda E. "Henry A. Wallace and China." M.A. thesis, Univ. of Northern Iowa, 1978.

Errico, Charles Joseph, Jr. "Foreign Affairs and the Presidential Election of 1940." Ph.D. diss., Univ. of Maryland, 1973.

Fitz-Simons, Daniel W. "Henry A. Wallace: Diplomat, Ideologue and Administrator, 1940–45." Ph.D. diss., St. Johns Univ., Jamaica, N.Y., 1977.

Hamby, Alonzo Lee. "Harry S Truman and American Liberalism, 1945–48." Ph.D. diss., Univ. of Missouri, 1965.

Hamilton, Mary Allienne. "A Progressive Publisher and the Cold War: J. W. Gitt and the *Gazette and Daily,* York, Pennsylvania, 1946–1956." Ph.D. diss., Michigan State Univ., 1980.

Laurence, Erwin. "*The New Republic* Magazine's Policies towards Russia." M.A. thesis, Stanford Univ., 1952.

Lavin, Thomas. "*The New Republic* and American Diplomacy, 1933–47." M.A. thesis, Illinois State Univ., 1975.

Mulqueen, Robert E. "The View from Eleventh and Walnut: Farm Prices, the McNary-Haugen Bill and the Political Formation of Henry A. Wallace," Unpublished paper, Iowa State Univ., 1984.

Radosh, Ronald. "The Economic and Political Thought of Henry A. Wallace." M.A. thesis, Univ. of Iowa, 1960.

Sullivan, Patricia Ann. "Gideon's Southern Soldiers: New Deal Politics and Civil Rights Reform, 1933–1948." Ph.D. diss., Emory Univ., 1983.

Wallace, Henry A. "Mathematical Inquiry into the Effect of Weather on Corn Yield." M.Agr. thesis, Iowa State Univ., 1920.

Webster, Lindsley E. "Thirteen Ventures in Political Guidance: The Books of Henry A. Wallace, 1934–46." M.A. thesis, Clark Univ., 1955.

Weiler, Richard M. "Statesmanship, Religion and the General Welfare: The Rhetoric of Henry A. Wallace." Ph.D. diss., Univ. of Pittsburgh, 1980.

ARTICLES

Alexander, Jack. "Henry A. Wallace: Cornfield Prophet." *Life*, Sept. 2, 1940, pp. 80–87.

Anderson, Clifford. "The Metamorphosis of American Agrarian Idealism in the 1920's and 1930's." *Agricultural History* 35 (Oct. 1961): 182–88.

Appleby, Paul. "Roosevelt's Third Term Decision." *American Political Science Review* 46 (Sept. 1952): 754–65.

Bancroft, T. A. "Roots of the Iowa State University Statistical Center, 1914–1950." *Iowa State University Journal* 57, no. 1 (Aug. 1982): 3–10.

Bernstein, Barton J. "Roosevelt, Truman and the Atomic Bomb: A Reinterpretation." *Political Science Quarterly* 90 (Spring 1975): 23–69.

Bliven, Bruce. "An Iowan in New York." *Palimpsest* (Oct. 1971): 494–544.

Bodde, Derek. "Henry A. Wallace and the Ever-Normal Granary." *Far Eastern Quarterly* (later called *Journal of Asian Studies*), 5 (Aug. 1946): 411–26.

Bogue Allan G. "Changes in Mechanical and Plant Technology: The Corn Belt, 1910–1940." *Journal of Economic History* 43 (March 1983): 1–25.

Burns, Richard Dean, and Charyl L. Smith. "Nicholas Roerich, Henry A. Wallace and the 'Peace Banner': A Study in Idealism, Egocentrism and Anguish." *Peace & Change: A Journal of Peace Research* 2 (Spring 1973): 40–49.

Divine, Robert A. "The Cold War and the Election of 1948." *Journal of American History* 59 (June 1972): 90–110.

Errico, Charles J. and J. Samuel Walker. "The New Deal and the Guru." *American Heritage* 40, no. 2 (March 1989): 92–95.

Ezekiel, Mordacai. "Henry Wallace, Agricultural Economist." *Journal of Farm Economics* 48 (Nov. 1966): 789–802.

Finlay, Mark R. "Dashed Expectations: The Iowa Progressive Party and the 1948 Election." *Annals of Iowa* 49 (Summer 1988) 329–48.

Fox, Karl A. "Agricultural Economists as World Leaders in Applied Econometrics, 1917–1933." *American Journal of Agricultural Economics* 68 (May 1986): 381–86.

Hale, William Harlan. "What Makes Wallace Run?" *Harper's*, March 1948, pp. 241–48.

Hamby, Alonzo L. "Henry A. Wallace, the Liberals and Soviet-American Relations." *Review of Politics* 30 (April 1968): 153–69.

———. "Sixty Million Jobs and the People's Revolution: The Liberals, the New Deal and World War II." *Historian* 30 (Aug. 1968): 578–98.

Heaster, Brenda L. "Who's on Second: The 1944 Democratic Vice Presidential Nomination." *Missouri Historical Review* 80: (Jan. 1986): 156–75.

"Henry A. Wallace and Iowa Agriculture." *Annals of Iowa* 47 (Fall 1983): 85–234.

Herring, Hubert. "Henry III of Iowa." *Harper's*, Feb. 1943, pp. 282–91.

High, Stanley. "Whose Party Is It?" *Saturday Evening Post*, Feb. 6, 1937, p. 10.

———. "Will It Be Wallace?" *Saturday Evening Post*, July 3, 1937, p. 3.

Hochmuth, Marie. "Henry A. Wallace." *Quarterly Journal of Speech* 34 (Oct. 1948): 322–26.

Ickes, Harold. "My Twelve Years with FDR." *Saturday Evening Post*, June 5 to July 24, 1948.

Isern, Thomas D. "The Erosion Expeditions." *Agricultural History* 59 (April 1985): 181–91.

Jarnigan, Robert A. "The Men Who Made Pioneer." *Iowan* 28 (Fall 1979): 16–23.

Kelly, John L. "An Insurgent in the Truman Cabinet: Henry A. Wallace's Effort to Redirect Foreign Policy." *Missouri Historical Review* 77 (Oct. 1982): 64–93.

Kempton, Murray. "The Progressives' Long Winter." *Nation*, March 11, 1950, pp. 219–21.

Kirkendall, Richard S. "Commentary on the Thought of Henry A. Wallace." *Agricultural History* 41 (April 1967): 139–42.

———. "Corn Huskers and Master Farmers: Henry A. Wallace and the Merchandizing of Iowa Agriculture." *Palimpsest* 65 (May–June 1984): 82–93.

———. "Henry A. Wallace's Turn toward the New Deal, 1921–24." *Annals of Iowa*, 3d ser., 49 (Winter–Spring 1988): 221–39.

Kirschner, Don S. "Henry A. Wallace as Farm Editor." *American Quarterly* 17 (Summer 1965): 187–202.

Lader, Lawrence. "The Wallace Campaign of 1948." *American Heritage* 28, no. 1 (Dec. 1976): 42–51.

Lambert, C. Roger. "Want and Plenty: The Federal Surplus Relief Corporation and the AAA." *Agricultural History* 46 (July 1972): 390–400.

Leslie, Kenneth. "Wallace on War." *Protestant*, Jan.–Feb. 1948, pp. 1–17.

Levering, Ralph B. "The Overselling of Henry Wallace." *Reviews in American History* 5 (Dec. 1977): 554–59.

Lord, Russell. "M. L. Wilson—A Contemporary Memoir." *Land* (Summer 1941): 242–52.

Lowitt, Richard. "Henry A. Wallace and the 1935 Purge in the Department of Agriculture." *Agricultural History* 53 (July 1979): 607–21.

MacNeil, Neil. "How to Rig a Convention." *Saturday Evening Post*, Oct. 26, 1940, pp. 29ff.

McManus, Robert Cruise. "The Red Mole." *Freeman*, Oct. 16, 1950, pp. 54–56.

Murphy, Donald R. "The Centennial of a Farm Paper." *Palimpsest* 37 (Sept. 1956): 449–80.

Nelson, Lawrence J. "The Art of the Possible: Another Look at the 'Purge' of the AAA Liberals in 1935." *Agricultural History* 57 (Oct. 1983): 416–35.

Nuhn, Ferner. "Wallace of Iowa." *New Republic* 74 (March 15, 1933): 125–27.

Partin, John W. "Roosevelt, Byrnes and the 1944 Vice-Presidential Nomination." *Historian* 42 (Nov. 1979): 85–100.

Paterson, Thomas G. "The Abortive American Loan to Russia and the Origins of the Cold War, 1943–46." *Journal of American History* 56 (June 1969): 70–92.

Peterson, F. Ross. "Tightening the Dive toward War: Glen Taylor, the 1948 Progressives and the Draft." *Pacific Northwest Quarterly* 61 (Jan. 1970): 41–45.

Phillips, Cabell. "That Baffling Personality, Mr. Wallace." *New York Times Magazine*, Feb. 8, 1944.

Polenberg, Richard. "Henry A. Wallace and American Liberalism." *Reviews in American History* 1 (Dec. 1973): 579–83.

Riley, Glenda, and Richard S. Kirkendall. "Henry A. Wallace and the Mystique of the Farm Male, 1921–33." *Annals of Iowa* 48 (Summer–Fall 1985): 32–55.

Rosen, Jerold A. "Henry A. Wallace and American Liberal Politics, 1945–48." *Annals of Iowa* 44 (Fall 1978): 462–74.

Rosenof, Theodore. "The Economic Ideas of Henry A. Wallace, 1933–48." *Agricultural History* 41 (April 1967): 143–53.

Ross, Hugh. "Roosevelt's Third Term Nomination." *Mid-America* 44 (April 1962): 80–95.

Schapsmeier, Edward, and Frederick Schapsmeier. "Disharmony in the Harding Cabinet: Hoover-Wallace Conflict." *Ohio History* 75 (Summer 1966): 126–36.

———. "Henry A. Wallace: Agrarian Idealist or Agricultural Realist?" *Agricultural History* 51 (April 1967): 127–37.

———. "Henry A. Wallace: New Deal Philosopher," *Historian* 32 (Feb. 1970): 177–90.

———. "Religion and Reform: A Case Study of Henry A. Wallace and Ezra Taft Benson." *Journal of Church and State* 21 (Fall 1979): 525–35.

Schuyler, Michael W. "The Hair Splitters: Reno and Wallace, 1932–33." *Annals of Iowa* 43 (Fall 1976): 403–29.

Shrifgiesser, Karl, "A Portrait of That Mystic Farmer, Secretary Wallace." *North American Review* 127 (Spring 1939). 100–108.

Sillars, Malcolm O. "Henry A. Wallace's Editorials on Agricultural Discontent." *Agricultural History* 26 (Oct. 1952): 132–40.

Sirevag, Torbjorn. "The Dilemma of the American Left in the Cold War Years: The Case of Henry A. Wallace." *Americana Norvegica* 4 (1973):   .

Stone, I. F. "The Anti-Wallace Plot." Nation, Dec. 19, 1942, pp. 671–72.

Straight, Michael. "Days with Henry Wallace." *New Republic*, Dec. 4, 1965, pp. 9–11.

Swain, Bruce M. "Henry A. Wallace and the Guru Letters: A Case of Successful Stonewalling." *Mid-American Review* 69 (Jan. 1987): 5–19.

Szilard, Leo. "Reminiscences." *Perspectives in American History* 2 (1968) 94–151.

Tugwell, Rexford G. "Progressives and the Presidency." *Progressive* 13 (April 1949): 5–7.

Walker, J. Samuel. "Henry A. Wallace as Agrarian Isolationist, 1921–1930." *Agricultural History* 49 (July 1975): 532–42.

——— . "No More Cold War: American Foreign Policy and the 1948 Soviet Peace Offensive." *Diplomatic History* 5 (Winter 1981): 75–91.

Wallace, Henry A. "AE: A Portrait Out of an Ancient Age." *Colby Library Quarterly*, May 1955, pp. 28–31.

———. "America—Recluse or Trader?" *Collier's*, Feb. 2, 1935, pp. 7–8, 50–51.

———. "Corn That Made Iowa." *Wallaces' Farmer* Aug. 20, 1955, p. 16.

———. "Henry Wallace Tells of His Political Odyssey." *Life*, May 14, 1956, p. 174.

———. "Toward an Inter-American Culture." *New York Times Magazine*, July 9, 1939, pp. 3, 20.

———. "Veblen's *Imperial Germany and the Industrial Revolution*." *Political Science Quarterly* 55 (Sept. 1940): 435–45.

———. "Why a Third Party in 1948?" *Annals of the American Academy of Political and Social Science* 259 (Sept. 1948): 10–16.

Wallace, Henry A., and Alonzo Taylor. "Review of *The Corn and Hog Surplus of the corn Belt*." *Journal of Farm Economics* 14 (July 1932): 506–11.

Wallace, Kevin. "Henry Agard Wallace." *New Yorker*, Aug. 13, 1960, pp. 65–75.

Ward, Paul. "Wallace the Great Hesitator." *Nation*, May 8, 1935, pp. 535–38.

Warren, Wilson J. "The 'People's Century' in Iowa: Coalition-Building among Farm and Labor Organizations, 1945–50." *Annals of Iowa* 49 (Summer 1988): 371–93.

Wechsler, James A. "My Ten Months with Wallace." *Progressive*, Nov. 1948, pp. 4–8.

Yarnell, Alan. "The Democratic Party's Response to the American Progressive Party in 1948." *Washington State University Research Studies* 39 (March 1971): 20–32.

———. "Liberals in Action: The ADA, Henry Wallace and the 1948 Election." *Washington State University Research Studies* 40 (Dec. 1972): 260–73.

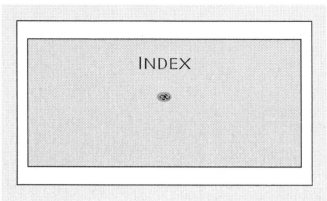

INDEX

Cvetic, Matthew, 517
Czechoslovakia, 88, 192, 452
  HAW's gaffe concerning, 473

Dahl, Roald, 342–43, 373n
Daily Worker, 422, 481, 497n
Daniels, Jonathan, 495
Daniels, Josephus, 249, 358, 365, 495
Darling, J. H. "Ding," 110, 112
Darrow, Clarence, 118, 189
Darrow, George, 526
Darwin, Charles, 67
Davidson, Jo, 281–82, 374, 433, 434, 438, 460
Davies, John Paton, Jr., 337, 338
Davis, Chester, 85, 116, 153–57, 161, 163
Davis, Elmer, 244, 278
Davis, John W., 71
Davis, Kenneth S., 199
Dawson, William L., 374
De Haro, Rafael, 255
de Kruif, Paul, 369, 453
Delano, Franklin, 57n
Democratic-Farmer-Labor Party, U.S., 498n
Democratic National Convention of 1944,
      353–66, 418, 442
  aftermath of, 367–72
  Byrnes and, 353–56
  "clear it with Sidney" catchphrase in, 354–55
  FDR-Hannegan letter and, 358–59, 361
  FDR's acceptance speech at, 361–62
  first session of, 357–58
  guru letters and, 482
  HAW's organization at, 357
  HAW's speech at, 359–61
  Ickes on, 369
  Truman nominated in, 364–67
  "We want Wallace" demonstration in, 362–63
Democratic National Conventions:
  of 1932, 102
  of 1936, 165
  of 1940, 204n, 208, 213–23, 225
  of 1948, 478, 479–80, 484
Democratic Party, U.S., 10, 18, 54, 84, 86, 94,
      100, 101, 180, 293, 309, 359, 360, 374,
      378, 382, 384, 395, 408, 417, 433, 439,
      444, 447, 451, 453, 457, 482, 501n, 502,
      512, 521, 522
  anti-Wallace movement in, 339–41

Court-packing plan and, 172, 175–76
Dixiecrats' split from, 480
guru letters and, 231–34
HAW's firing and, 428–29
and HAW's ouster from BEW, 313
HAW's perception of, 368–69
HAW's registration with, 164–65
oil industry and, 287
see also specific elections
Democrats for Wallace, 453
Denmark, 205
Dennis, Eugene, 452n, 458, 465, 481
Dennis v. United States, 482n
"Deserts Shall Bloom Again, The" (Roerich), 141
Des Moines Register, 54, 78, 110, 112, 127, 138,
      151, 167, 179–80, 184, 195, 196, 224,
      235, 236, 242, 252, 256, 257, 270, 313,
      356, 420, 432n, 510, 515n
Despotic Democracy, 145
destroyers-for-bases deal, 237
Detroit News, 483
Deutsch, Albert, 458
Dewey, Thomas E., 208, 212, 213, 331, 348,
      370, 374, 375, 430, 446, 461, 479, 493,
      498n, 500, 501, 531
Dies, Martin, 273–74, 275
Dies Committee, 445
domestic allotment plan, 101–2, 104, 122, 123,
      154
  Agricultural Adjustment Act and, 115–17, 119
Donovan, William J. "Wild Bill," 320
Dorner, Hannah, 420, 434
Dos Passos, John, 431
Doubleday, Abner, 79
Douglas, Helen Gahagan, 463
Douglas, Jean Wallace (daughter), 49n, 75, 186,
      188, 224, 427, 428, 513, 519
Douglas, Lewis, 137, 439
Douglas, William O., 209, 216, 317, 341, 348,
      349, 350, 352–53, 355, 361, 367, 479,
      482n, 498n
Dower, William H., 97–99, 103
Downes, Olin, 485
"Dreamer, The" (O'Reilly), 329
"Dreamer's Peace, The" (Grand Rapids Herald
      editorial), 328
Drummond, Roscoe, 445–46
Drury, Allen, 324, 342, 351–52, 380, 381, 382